Lecture Notes in Computer Science 5287

Commenced Publication in 1973
Founding and Former Series Editors:
Gerhard Goos, Juris Hartmanis, and Jan van Leeuwen

Uwe Brinkschulte   Tony Givargis
Stefano Russo (Eds.)

Software Technologies for Embedded and Ubiquitous Systems

6th IFIP WG 10.2 International Workshop, SEUS 2008
Anacarpi, Capri Island, Italy, October 1-3, 2008
Proceedings

Volume Editors

Uwe Brinkschulte
University of Frankfurt
Faculty of Computer Science and Mathematics
Chair for Embedded Systems
Frankfurt am Main, Germany
E-mail: brinks@es.cs.uni-frankfurt.de

Tony Givargis
University of California, Irvine
Department of Computer Science
Center for Embedded Computer Systems
Irvine, CA, USA
E-mail: givargis@uci.edu

Stefano Russo
Università di Napoli Federico II
Dipartimento di Informatica e Sistemistica
Naples, Italy
E-mail: stefano.russo@unina.it

Library of Congress Control Number: 2008935377

CR Subject Classification (1998): C.3, C.2, D.4.7, E.1, H.3.4, I.2.11

LNCS Sublibrary: SL 3 – Information Systems and Application, incl. Internet/Web and HCI

ISSN 0302-9743

ISBN 978-3-540-87784-4 Springer Berlin Heidelberg New York

Springer is a part of Springer Science+Business Media

springer.com

© IFIP International Federation for Information Processing 2008

Typesetting: Camera-ready by author, data conversion by Scientific Publishing Services, Chennai, India
Printed on acid-free paper   SPIN: 12530472   06/3180   5 4 3 2 1 0

Preface

Embedded and ubiquitous computing systems have considerably increased their scope of application over the past few years, and they now also include mission- and business-critical scenarios. The advances call for a variety of compelling issues, including dependability, real-time, quality-of-service, autonomy, resource constraints, seamless interaction, middleware support, modeling, verification, validation, etc.

The International Workshop on Software Technologies for Future Embedded and Ubiquitous Systems (SEUS) brings together experts in the field of embedded and ubiquitous computing systems with the aim of exchanging ideas and advancing the state of the art about the above-mentioned issues. I was honored to chair the sixth edition of the workshop, which continued the tradition of past editions with high-quality research results. I was particularly pleased to host the workshop in the wonderful scenario of Capri, with its stunning views and traditions.

The workshop started in 2003 as an IEEE event, and then in 2007 it became a flagship event of the IFIP Working Group 10.2 on embedded systems. The last few editions, held in Hakodate (Japan), Vienna (Austria), Seattle (USA), Gyeongju (Korea), and Santorini (Greece), were co-located with the IEEE International Symposium on Object/Component/Service-Oriented Real-Time Distributed Computing (ISORC).

This year, SEUS was held as a stand-alone event for the first time, and, despite the additional organizational difficulties, it resulted in a high-quality event, with papers from four continents (from USA, Europe, East Asia and Australia), (co-) authored and presented from senior scientists coming from academia or leading industrial research centers.

SEUS 2008 would not have been possible without the effort of many people, first of all, the authors, who contributed with their invaluable advances in the field. I am particularly thankful to the Program Co-chairs, Uwe Brinkshulte and Tony Givargis, and to the Program Committee members for their great work in selecting the best papers and making up the technical program that is contained this book. I would also like to thank Local Arrangements Chairs Marcello Cinque, Domenico Cotroneo, and Isabella Scarpa, for their effort in organizational issues. I am greatly thankful to Kane Kim and Franz Rammig for their continuous support and advice. Finally, thanks are due to Springer and to the following supporting institutions: IFIP WG 10.2; the Federico II University of Naples, that hosted the workshop in its congress center in Anacapri; and the Italian Inter-universities Consortium for Informatics (CINI) for organizational support.

October 2008   Stefano Russo

Message from the Program Co-chairs

It was a great pleasure for us to welcome attendees to Capri and to announce the technical program of the 6th IFIP Workshop on Software Technologies for Future Embedded and Ubiquitous Systems (SEUS 2008). Following the success of SEUS 2007, the first workshop edition sponsored by IFIP, the current edition continued with its focus on topics like emerging applications, software architecture and programming models, model-driven development, quality-of-service and performance, middleware and operating systems, synthesis, verification and protection, pervasive and mobile systems, organic computing, real-time, and wireless embedded systems. In contrast to previous editions, SEUS 2008 was held as a stand-alone event for the first time.

SEUS 2008 was a forum where researchers and practitioners with substantial experience and serious interests in advancing the state of the art and the state of practice in the field of future embedded and ubiquitous computing systems gather and engage in a review of the areas, exchange of significant developments, and brain-storm on promising directions for future research. The program was composed of invited and submitted contributions, both undergoing a strict review process by the international and well-reputed Program Committee. We selected 38 high-quality papers, contributions that present advances in integrating the fields of embedded computing and ubiquitous systems.

Many people worked hard to make SEUS 2008 a success. We would like to thank the Program Committee members and the reviewers for their hard work and for their input in the selection of papers. We would also like to thank all those who submitted papers for their efforts and for the quality of their submissions. Furthermore, this conference would not have been possible without the great work of the General Chair, Stefano Russo, and the local arrangements provided by Marcello Cinque, Domenico Cotroneo and Isabella Scarpa. Finally, special thanks to Kane Kim for his invaluable support and advice.

October 2008

Uwe Brinkshulte
Tony Givargis

Organization

General Chair

Stefano Russo   Federico II University of Naples, Italy

Program Co-chairs

Uwe Brinkschulte   University of Karlsruhe, Germany
Tony Givargis   University of California-Irvine, USA

Program Committee

Gabriella Carrozza	Federico II University of Naples, Italy
Tharam Dillon	Curtin University of Technology, Australia
Stephen A. Edwards	Columbia University, USA
Sebastian N. Fischmeister	University of Waterloo, Canada
Kaori Fujinami	Tokyo University of Agriculture and Technology, Japan
Chris Gill	Washington University, St. Louis, USA
Jan Gustafsson	Malardalen University, Sweden
Doo-Hyun Kim	Konkuk University, Korea
Tei-Wei Kuo	National Taiwan University, Taiwan
Sunggu Lee	POSTECH, Korea
Yunmook Nah	Dankook University, Korea
Yukikazu Nakamoto	University of Hyogo and Nagoya University, Japan
Roman Obermaisser	Vienna University of Technology, Austria
Michael Paulitsch	Honeywell AES Centers of Excellence, USA
Peter Puschner	Vienna University of Techonology, Austria
Franz J.Rammig	University of Paderborn, Germany
Theo Ungerer	University of Augsburg, Germany
Frank Vahid	University of California, Riverside, USA
Allan Wong	Hong Kong Polytech, China

Publication and Local Arrangements Co-chairs

Marcello Cinque	Federico II University of Naples, Italy
Domenico Cotroneo	Federico II University of Naples, Italy
Isabella Scarpa	Consorzio Interuniversitario Nazionale per l'Informatica, Italy

Supporting Institutions

IFIP Working Group 10.2 "Embedded Systems"
Dipartimento di Informatica e Sistemistica, Federico II University of Naples,
 Italy
Consorzio Interuniversitario Nazionale per l'Informatica, Italy

Table of Contents

Model-Driven Development

Middleware

Real Time

Quality of Service and Performance

Applications

Pervasive and Mobile Systems

Wireless Embedded Systems

Synthesis, Verification and Protection

Using UML 2.1 to Model Multi-agent Systems

Darshan S. Dillon, Tharam S. Dillon, and Elizabeth Chang

Digital Ecosystems and Business Intelligence Institute,
Curtin University of Technology Perth, Australia
{Darshan.Dillon,Tharam.Dillon,
Elizabeth.Chang}@cbs.curtin.edu.au

Abstract. The use of UML 2.1 to model a broad range of systems is evident from the variety of UML diagrams in academia and in the marketplace. One class of systems currently gaining popularity are Multi-Agent Systems. There are efforts underway to use UML to model these systems and these efforts are both productive and form the basis for both a methodology and a notation for systems of this type.

1 Introduction

In this paper we first introduce what an Agent is, the key characteristics of an Agent, the scope of this paper in terms of what we model in Multi-Agent Systems, and finally future directions.

2 What Is an Agent ?

In order to define what an agent is we should first consider a definition from the literature.

An agent is a computer system that is situated in some environment, and that is capable of autonomous action in this environment in order to meet its design objectives.[1]

From this definition a number of points are clear. Firstly, the location of the computer program is important. This is so because the program can migrate from one machine to another. This is not the usual pattern of behaviour for computer programs. They usually are installed, configured and run on a particular machine. They do not *travel*, as such. Secondly, the computer program is capable of acting automously, which means it is not dependant on any other program. This goes together with the fact that agents are mobile. They can be launched by a user on a particular machine, and travel, severing their connection with the user and concentrating their state related information within themselves. Thirdly, the computer program is goal-driven and can choose to act in a way that satisfies it's design objectives. Most computer programs are data-driven, reacting to inputs.

Finally, agents play an important role in embedded and ubiqitious computer systems. They are particularly important in goal-oriented or mission-oriented environments. The modeling and design of agents is an important first step for the building of agent- based systems.

U. Brinkschulte, T. Givargis, and S. Russo (Eds.): SEUS 2008, LNCS 5287, pp. 1–8, 2008.
© IFIP International Federation for Information Processing 2008

3 Characteristics of an Agent[2]

There are six key characteristics of an agent. They are as follows.

1. Autonomous – That is, an agent can perform independently from other agents by making decisions based on it's internal state and information from it's environment.
2. Sociable – That is, an agent can co-operate and collaborate with other agents by using a common language to communicate with each other.
3. Service Discovery – Agents are able to identify desired services.
4. Reactive – That is, an agent is pro-active. It can perform tasks that may be beneficial to the user even though it has not been explicitly asked to perform those tasks.
5. Mobility – Agents can move across networks from any location. They can be assigned a task and sent over the web after which their connection to the user can be severed. Their state can be centralized within themselves.
6. Goal-Driven Execution – Each Agent has a goal that is it constantly trying to meet.

4 Scope

As with any paper, we need to define the scope we will work within. In the case of this paper, we will seek to illustrate how sociable and goal-driven nature of agents can be expressed using UML 2.1.

5 Agent Characteristics Modelled

5.1 Sociable

In modeling Agents, one of their key characteristics is that they are sociable. This means that they are able to interact with each other in order to co-operate, collaborate and negotiate with respect to information, knowledge and services. Very often each agent will have only part of the full picture needed to solve the problem at hand. The ability to subdivide the tasks in order to reduce the complexity of the problem, have individual agents work only on their aspect of the problem, and then combine sub-solutions into a final solution is extremely helpful and productive.

In AgentUML, previous researchers have been modeling Agent protocols[5,6] using a non-standard version of sequence diagrams where each rectangle represents an agent playing a different role. We say non-standard because the rectangles at the head of lifelines are meant to represent classes, not agents. Having multiple rectangles each representing the same Agent is also non-standard, where each rectangle represents the Agent playing a particular role.

Each agent is defined by specifying a specific set of roles that it plays. Each role could be associated with a distinct interface. These interfaces could be specified by a technique called method lifting outlined below. Method lifting defines a composite class. What are composite classes ? If we first consider a hierarchy of component classes, each of which has an interface. If we relate these component classes to a composite class that also has an interface, and which is formed by taking a selection of methods from the interfaces of the component classes. This process of relating the interface of component classes to the interface of a composite class is known as method lifting. In the example below, the methods A, B & C are individually chosen from different component classes and combined in the composite class at the head of the hierarchy. This is shown below.

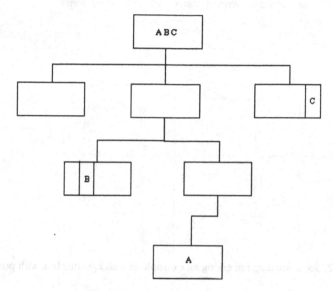

Fig. 1. An example of Method Lifting [3]

Secondly, a particular class may have more than one lifeline. For example, a particular class may have many ports, each one with it's own lifeline. This is invaluable in the case of modeling Agents since we need the facility to be able to represent an Agent in a sequence diagram, where it plays more than one role concurrently. You can see figure 2 for an example of this. The agent may be represented by a rectangle, and have many ports, each with it's own lifeline. In the case of the method lifting paradiagm above the composite class may have many interfaces, each of which chooses a selection of methods from a hierarchy of component classes used as the source for method lifting. A sequence diagram where a composite classes that have more than one port is shown below in figure 2.

Generally, communication between objects is done in UML in a sequence diagram, or a communication diagram (used to be called a collaboration diagram in UML 1.x). They are semantically similar although a sequence diagram can generally be made to contain additional information. A sequence diagram is generally defined across the page by a series of rectangles, each of which represents a class. Each of these rectangles has a dotted line running vertically down the page. These dotted lines are known as lifelines. As you go down the page, time passes as messages flow between objects.

A sequence diagram where composite classes have more than one port is shown below in figure 2.

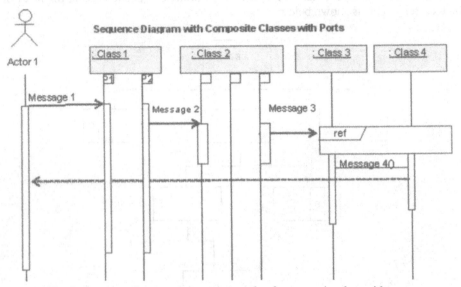

Fig. 2. Sequence diagram giving an example of a composite class with ports

In terms of previous work done using ports to represent an Agent/Class playing different roles Hanish & Dillon[8] have previously used a similar and related approach.

We now proceed to an illustrative example involving a set of Agents, one of which (Agreement Agent) plays two roles concurrently represented by P1 and P2. Depending on which role the agent is acting in when it sends/receives messages will the sequence diagram show arrows to/from a particular lifeline for the agent. The corresponding sequence diagram of a rental car being returned to a depot (for a car rental system) and payment being done by the customer is shown below.

If we follow the sequence across and down the page, we note a number of points. Firstly, P1 (or port 1) represents the :Agreement agent in it's role to establish status. P2 represents the :Agreement agent in it's role to perform transactions. Note that each port has it's own lifeline. If there are two ports, this signifies two roles that are played by the agent from which the ports come. Initially, the request is made to return a car. Secondly, the Agreement agent checks that the car is fine, and receives a message back that this is so. The same agent then performs a transaction to request the money owing on the car and the customer agent pays the money. Note that the Agreement agent plays two different roles here. Firstly, the role to check the status of the car, and secondly to perform the transaction. Then, the Agreement agent sets the status of the car to "free", and receives a message back from the Vehicle agent that the car status is "free". Again, the Agreement agent is acting in its role to compute status of the car. The Agreement agent makes a request to the Customer agent to set it to free. The Customer agent sets the status to free and returns the message to the

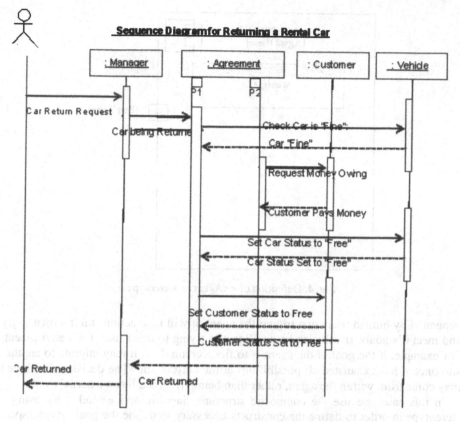

Fig. 3. Sequence Diagram illustrating Sociability of Agents

Agreement agent that the Customer is free. Finally, the Agreement agent sends a message to the Manager agent that the car is returned, and the Manager agent sends a message that the car is returned to the Employee.

All the interaction between different Agents is shown on this sequence diagram. Importantly, an agent (Agreement) is shown playing two different roles on the same sequence diagram (Status and Transaction) in the same timeframe.

5.2 Goal-Driven

Being goal driven is a feature of many different agents. In order to consider what this means we can reexamine the concept of search space. Forward-chaining begins with data which drives the reasoning toward goals. Backward-chaining goes backwards decomposing goals into subgoals and then checking to see if any of them is true. If so, the ultimate goal is considered to be true. If not, then the process of decomposition is continued.

Most traditional software is not goal driven as such, but is a black box. That is, specific combinations of inputs lead to specific outputs. The fact that an agent has an overriding goal, regardless of the specifics of it's processing, endows it with many other features. Specifically, it will be pro-active. ie. even if there are no events

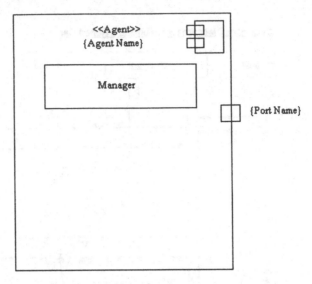

Fig. 4. Definition of <<Agent>> stereotype

generated by human users that trigger the agent, it will take actions on it's own to try and meet it's goals. It will also be intelligent in trying to make use of it's enviroment. For example, if the goal of the agent is to find certain data, it may migrate to another site once it has exhausted all possibilities at the current site. The decision to migrate may come from within the agent, rather than being triggered by an external event.

In this case, we use the composite structure diagram, and extend it by using a stereotype in order to define the constructs necessary to define the goal-driven aspect of an Agent.

The basic definition for a composite structure diagram in UML 2.1 is as follows.[4]

"A composite structure diagram is a diagram that shows the internal structure of a classifier, including its interaction points to other parts of the system. It shows the configuration and relationship of parts, that together, perform the behavior of the containing classifier.

Class elements have been described in great detail in the section on class diagrams. This section describes the way classes can be displayed as composite elements exposing interfaces and containing ports and parts."

Below (in figure 4) is contained the definition of the <<Agent>> stereotype based on the composite structure . diagram. From the definition it must have a name, at least a Manager part which controls the efforts of the Agent to achieve a goal, and at least one port, which relates to it's playing a role.

Having seen the definition of an <<Agent>> stereotype we can proceed to an example to realize it's usage. In the case of the Agreement agent in the Car Rental system, we can model the goal driven aspect of the agent by a Composite Structure Diagram with Parts, and Ports. Each part represents a distinct area of processing within the agent. Each port represents a different role played by the agent. The diagram encapsulating this information is shown in figure 5.

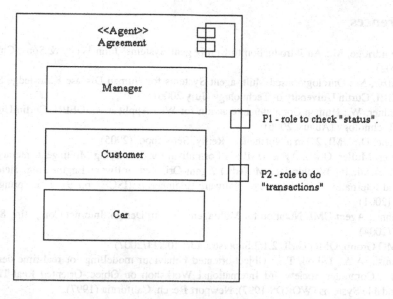

Fig. 5. Composite Structure Diagram representing Goal Driven characteristic of Agent

Note that the same two ports that were present in the sequence diagram are also present here. Each of the ports is a construct which enables the Agent to interact with the environment and with other Agents. For example, if the goal of the Agent is to close out processing with respect to a specific Rental Agreement, then the Agent will have to consult the Goal Driven part of the Agent to decide to check the car and the customer processing part of the Agent to finalize return and payment, and the goal driven part itself to see that the necessary checklist of items have been finalized for the return of the car.

6 Conclusion

This paper has examined the use of UML 2.1 to model Multi-Agent Systems. In particular, we have examined and illustrated the Agent characteristics of being Sociable and also Goal-Driven. Specifically, in order to illustrate the fact that Agents are sociable we used a sequence diagram with ports. In order to illustrate the fact that Agents are goal-driven we used a composite structure diagram where the Agent is modeled with ports, which is new in UML 2. The use of ports is central where each port represents the Agent playing a different role.

Future work may include the modeling of Agents to illustrate other characteristics of an Agent discussed in section 3.

Acknowledgement. The authors would like to acknowledge the invaluable assistance and suggestions of Maja Hadzic as we authored this paper.

References

1. Wooldridge, M.: An Introduction to MultiAgent Systems. John Wiley & Sons, Chichester (2002)
2. Hadzic, M.: Ontology-based Multi-agent Systems for Human Disease Knowledge Sharing. DEBII, Curtin University of Technology (July 2006)
3. Gardner, W.: Human Computer Interaction for Web Application. DEBII, Curtin University of Technology (August 2006)
4. PIlone, D.: UML 2.0 in a Nutshell. O'Reilly, Sebastopol (2005)
5. Bauer, Muller, Odell: Agent UML: A Formalism for Specifying Multiagent Interaction. In: Ciancarini, P., Wooldridge, M. (eds.) Agent-Oriented Software Engineering. Held at the 22nd International Conference on Software Engineering (ISCE), pp. 91–103. Springer, Berlin (2001)
6. Huhns,: Agent UML Notation for Multiagent System Design. Internet Computing 8(4), 63–71 (2004)
7. OMG Group, OMG UML 2.1.2 Superstructure (02/11/2007)
8. Hanish, A.A., Dillon, T.S.: Object-oriented behaviour modelling for real-time design. In: IEEE Computer Society 3rd International Workshop on Object-Oriented Real-Time Dependable Systems (WORDS 1997), Newport Beach, California (1997)

Designing Fault-Tolerant Component Based Applications with a Model Driven Approach

Brahim Hamid, Ansgar Radermacher, Agnes Lanusse, Christophe Jouvray,
Sébastien Gérard, and François Terrier

CEA, LIST
Laboratoire d'Ingénierie dirigée par les modèles pour les Systèmes Embarqués
Boite 65, Gif sur Yvette, F-91191 France
{brahim.hamid,ansgar.radermacher,agnes.lanusse,
christophe.jouvray,sebastien.gerard,francois.terrier}@cea.fr

Abstract. The requirement for higher reliability and availability of systems is continuously increasing even in domains not traditionally strongly involved in such issues. Solutions are expected to be efficient, flexible, reusable on rapidly evolving hardware and of course at low cost. Model driven approaches can be very helpful for this purpose. In this paper, we propose a study associating model-driven technology and component-based development. This work is illustrated by the realization of a use case from aerospace industry that has fault-tolerance requirements: a launch vehicle.

UML based modeling is used to capture application structure and related non-functional requirements thanks to the profiles CCM (CORBA Component Model) and QoS&FT (Quality of Service and Fault Tolerance). The application model is enriched with infrastructure component dedicated to fault-tolerance. From this model we generate CCM descriptor files which in turns are used to build boot-code (static deployment) which instantiates, configures and connects components. Within this process, component replication and FT properties are declaratively specified at model level and are transparent for the component implementation.

Keywords: Connector, CORBA Component Model, Distributed applications, Model-driven approach, Profile QoS+FT, Replication.

1 Introduction

A distributed system is a system which involves several computers, processors or processes which cooperate in some way to do some task. However, such systems require a specific treatment of faults. Faults may be hardware defects (link failures, crashes) or software faults which prevent a system to continue functioning in a correct manner.

In such systems, solutions are expected to be efficient, flexible, reusable on rapidly evolving hardware and of course at low cost. Model-driven engineering [19] provides a very useful contribution for the design of fault-tolerant systems, since it bridges the gap between design issues and implementation preoccupation. It helps the designer to concentrate on application structure and required behavior and permits to specify in a separate way non-functional requirements such as Quality of Service and/or fault-tolerance

U. Brinkschulte, T. Givargis, and S. Russo (Eds.): SEUS 2008, LNCS 5287, pp. 9–20, 2008.

issues that are very important to guide the implementation process. The model(s) can be analyzed at a very early stage in order to detect potential misconceptions; and then, exploited by specific tools through several steps of model transformation and/or interleaving with platform models in order to produce the application components and configuration files.

In this paper, we propose a study associating model-driven approach and component-based development to design distributed applications that has fault-tolerance requirements. We focus on the run-time support offered by the component framework, notably the replication-aware interaction mechanism and additional system components for fault-detection and reference management. To illustrate the power of our approach we examine a test case from aerospace industry that has fault-tolerance requirements: a launch vehicle.

UML based modeling is used to capture application structure and related non-functional requirements thanks to two specialized extensions CCM (CORBA Component Model) [13] and QoS&FT (Quality of Service and Fault Tolerance) OMG profiles [15]. From this model we generate descriptor files (according to Deployment and Configuration standard (DnC) [14]). These descriptors are in turn used to configure a devoted infrastructure consisting of a container/component based architecture and to load configured components. Within this process, component replication and FT properties are declaratively specified at model level and are transparent for the component implementation.

The work is conducted in the context of a national project called *"Usine Logicielle"*[1]. This project is three-folded : modeling, validation and infrastructure/middleware support along with configuration support.

The rest of the paper is organized as follows. In the next section we present the model including the distributed computing systems, component model and the connector extension. In Section 3, we present briefly the proposed framework to implement fault-tolerance mechanisms. Section 4 describes the proposed methodology to design fault-tolerant distributed applications for component systems. We outline the profiles used on model level and describe the code generation and platform configuration process. In section 5 we review some related works. The last section summarizes and gives an outlook of future work.

2   Background

In this section, we outline two different aspects: the assumptions about the underlying computing system (mainly its network) and the component platform, namely the CORBA Component Model extended with the connector paradigm.

2.1   Distributed Computing System Model

A distributed system is a set of processes (or processors) and communication links. Processes communicate and synchronize by sending and receiving messages through

---

[1] This work has been performed in the context of the Usine Logicielle project of the System@tic Paris Région Cluster (http://www.usine-logicielle.org).

the links. The network topology is unspecified and each node communicates only with its neighbors. Two processes are considered as neighbors if and only if there is a link (channel) between them. We deal exclusively with connected topologies. A process can fail by crashing, i.e. by permanently halting. A process can also produce wrong computation results (e.g. due to spontaneous bit failures). Communication links are assumed to be reliable. The system is improved by failure detector modules. After a node fails, a dedicated protocol involving these modules notifies all neighbors of this node about the failure.

Networks are asynchronous in the sense that processes operate at arbitrary rates and messages transfer delay are unbounded, unpredictable but finite. We assume that message order is preserved. To implement failure detection, the dedicated protocol use a weak form of synchrony such as [1,6].

2.2   Fault-Tolerance Mechanisms

Fault-tolerance can be achieved by multiple mechanisms, for instance parity checking on memory on a hardware level. In the scope of this paper, furthermore to use fault detection functionality, we consider replication management. Obviously, replication relates to hardware as well as to software. With respect to hardware, it means that processing resources (nodes) and network links are replicated. With respect to software it denotes that the same component instance is deployed on multiple nodes. There are different well known variants of how redundant components may work, they fall in three main categories: all replicas can execute the same request and results are voted ("hot" or active with vote), only a single replica is active ("cold") or mixed policies where replicas are active but only one, the master sends its result. Indeed, the actual redundancy policy chosen for an application results from a compromise between powerful redundancy mechanisms offering better reliability at a high cost in terms of price, communication, size and weaker mechanisms in terms of recovery time but at lower costs. These considerations are particularly important in the domain of embedded systems and have driven our will to promote flexible design and implementation of such mechanisms.

In this experiment, the faults handled relate to hardware fault (node not responding) detected by the Fault Detector component through liveliness control as described below, and software error (no answer or wrong result from a replica detected by the voting mechanism). If a software error is detected on the result coming from a replica, the node on which this replica resides is desactivated and considered as faulty.

2.3   Connector Extension of the CORBA Component Model(CCM)

Our work is based on the CORBA Component Model (CCM) extended with the connector paradigm. A main advantage of this model is its separation of business code located in the component from the non-functional or service code located within a container.

The CCM standard supports three different communication paradigms (port types): synchronous method calls based on CORBA (provided/required interface), event publishing and reception and the recently added streaming. One drawback is that the implementation of such communication mechanisms is generally fixed, i.e. a CCM implementation provides a single realization of the interactions between port types. This is quite restrictive, in particular for embedded systems requiring:

1. *Flexible interaction implementations*
2. *Additional communication models or variations of existing communication models*

There is no way to model this in a suitable way within the standard CCM model.

The limitations of this standard have driven us to propose an extension named the *eC3M* which introduces the concept of *Connector* in the context of *Component/Container* paradigm. This permits the definition of specific interaction semantics and to associate multiple implementations of a particular one when defining the deployment configuration. The connector extension to CCM has first been published in [18]. Here, we'll have a short look at it with a focus on specific connectors supporting the interaction with replicated components.

A connector has certain similarities with a component. It has a type definition consisting of ports providing or requiring interfaces and an implementation chosen at deployment time. The main difference is (1) its genericity – its interfaces are adapted to the component using it and (2) it is a *fragmented* entity: since the connection between a component and its connector is always a direct local call, each port of the connector is co-located with the component it is connected with.

3   Our Infrastructure

We propose a simple infrastructure based on a set of non functional components. It has similar elements as in FT-CORBA [11], but since these are realized as CCM components they are independent of an ORB, in particular the connector extensions allows for choosing different interaction implementations. The separation between components and containers in CCM allows to keep fault-tolerance aspects out of the business code. Only the container and the associated connector fragments (which can be seen as part of the container) manage FT aspects.

3.1   Fault-Tolerance Framework

Here we show the set of non-functional (control) components used to support fault-tolerance and the run-time support, notably the replication-aware interaction mechanisms. To handle faults, we use the following control components:

1. *A fault detector (FD):* Each node is equipped with a fault detector to detect other faulty nodes. These components communicate with each other to build the list of faulty nodes. This component implements a fault detection protocol such as heartbeat or interrogation. In our framework, we use the following: at periodic rate, each fault detector (source node) performs broadcasting of aliveness requests to all other nodes (destination nodes). A requested destination node answers (or not) the source node. Thus, each fault detector node maintains the list of nodes and their states (alive, not alive).

2. *A fault tolerance manager (FTM):* The fault tolerance manager component performs reconfiguration to deal with detected faults [7]. It keeps tracks of ongoing status of replicas and defines fault processing. Reconfiguration is defined as the operation of transition from a source mode to a target mode when an event (faulty node) occurs. This is to keep the number of valid replicas, i.e after each failure occurrence, it checks that the number of valid replicas is higher than the minimum number of replicas. That is, the FTM changes the configuration of the system to satisfy the dependability requirements specified by the designer of the application at the design level.

3. *A replica manager (RM):* The role of this component is to store references of all replicated components (replicas) on a certain node. This component is not replicated, but deployed on each node. It handles a list of references to replicated components deployed in this node. It enables the creation /deletion replicas and their deployment in the case of dynamic reconfiguration.

Instances of these control components are activated on each node. However, the fault tolerance manager instance is in a leader mode on only one node, which may change dynamically when a faulty node event occurs.

3.2 Replication at a Connector Level

In the context of fault tolerance, a connection with a replicated component should perform group communication, i.e. the transparent communication with a set of replicas. Whereas this could be done with standard CCM and a specific CORBA implementation supporting group communication, it would be impossible to configure and control it (in case for instance of node failures) from standard CCM. As shown in the Section 2.3, the communication system is abstracted at a connector level. Since it is responsible for incoming and outgoing messages, it is an ideal place for the integration of replication protocol. Therefore, the user code interacts transparently with a group of replicas. Along with a replicated instance, the fragments of a connector are replicated as well.

Currently, we implemented an active replication ("hot") with vote mechanism as a proof of concept. In this variant, all replicas of a component instance are active at a given time and synchronize entries (optional) and results by a vote. We can separate the realization of a connector supporting this replication style into two phases. In the first, a unique request has to be distilled and sent to all replicas. In the second, the message is received by all replicas of the destination component and these (optionally) have to check that all got the same message.

Replicated components have a voter object in their container and a reference to this object is automatically passed to the connector fragment. The voter object is part of the run-time required for fault-tolerance. The code validates (*acknowledgeRequests*) the parameters with the other replicas by means of the voter object, before it sends a message to all replicas to the target object. The call of method *acknowledgeRequest* blocks until the result has been confirmed. If the current replica is leader, it sends the request to all replicas of the *server* fragment thanks to the *replica manager* instance in that node. Moreover, the *fault detector* instance is invoked to avoid sending request to the crashed node.

4 Designing Fault-Tolerant Distributed Applications (MDE Approach)

As described above, a simple redundancy management system can be implemented thanks to specific middleware components devoted to generic mechanisms such as fault-detectors, voters and so on...and specialized services implemented into connectors.

Here we describe how a MDE approach can help developers design their application and take full benefits of this infra-structure to build flexible efficient fault-tolerant component based applications. We present the approach chosen and the tools developed to support it.

Our laboratory *LISE* [2] has developed a tool that supports UML modeling (Papyrus UML [3]) based on the Eclipse environment. This tool suite provides a graphic UML modeling editor and code generation components (Java, C, C++). The tool supports also advanced UML profile management. We have developed additional plug-ins which generate CCM descriptor files from a model containing component instances with fault-tolerance requirements.

Our methodology is illustrated by means of a test case from aerospace industry that has fault-tolerance requirements: a launch vehicle. For simplicity, many functions of this test case have been omitted. Two components are identified:

- Calculation component $(Calc)$: this component makes some computations and then invokes the *display* method provided by the interface of the $(Display)$: component.
- Display component $(Display)$: it is responsible of displaying the result of the computations done by the $Calc$ components. It provides *display* method through its interfaces to be used by the $Calc$ components.

The sample application is described as follows: a calculation component is periodically activated by a timer; the result of the calculation is passed to a display component. Here, component $Calc$ is replicated three times and we use an active with voting replication style. For this application, dependability requirement is that it must tolerate one node crash.

4.1 Application Modeling

Application modeling when dealing with component based approaches consists of describing components, their required and offered services and then define component instances and finally how these instances are connected to form the final system.

The modeling basis is UML on which a variant of the profile for CORBA Component Model (eC3M) is applied. The application is described in terms of components and provided and required interfaces; profile properties permit to complete the description so that complete IDL can be generated from the description. Assembly characteristics

---

[2] Laboratory of Model Driven Engineering for Embedded Systems, which is part of the CEA LIST.
[3] http://papyrusuml.org

and deployment information are also provided through the eC3M profile with stereo-types close to DnC concepts. From this information deployment plans can be generated for regular applications.

To handle fault-tolerant requirements we apply a complementary profile named *FT profile* which is composed of a subset of QoS&FT [15] and uses NFP (Non Functional Properties) sub-profile of MARTE [16] (standard UML profile for Modeling and Analysis of Real-Time Embedded systems). Stereotypes dedicated to fault-tolerance specify the fault-detection policy, replication management style, replica group management style etc.. Fig.1 shows the structure of this profile. Black ended arrows denote concept extension (stereotype *FTInitialReplicationStyle* is an extension of UML Class). White ended arrows are standard UML generalization relations.

Once application components and interfaces have been defined, the system software architecture is described thanks to the UML composite diagram used to specify an assembly and hierarchical components. This diagram permits to determine what are the constitutive *parts* of the system and how they are inter-connected. Fig.2 shows the composite diagram corresponding to our sample application. The diagram indicates that the application consists of one component *calc*, one component *display* and one component *timer*. Connectors are defined between *timer* and *calc*, and *calc* and *display*. This is the description of the system without infrastructure components.

Since we want to specify that redundancy is required we stereotype component *calc* with *FTActiveWithVotingReplicationStyle* stereotype and we indicate that membership policy is controlled by infrastructure and that initial number of replicas will be 3. In the same manner we indicate that connectorType of the connector between *calc* and *display* is *ConnFTCORBA* which means that a connector support for fault tolerance based on CORBA should be used (see next section).

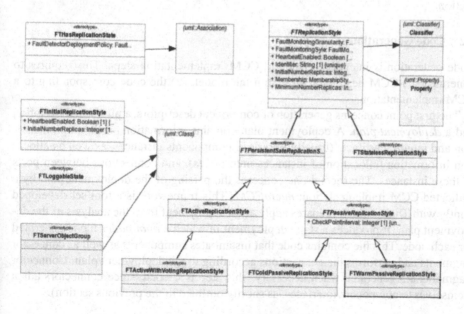

Fig. 1. The structure of the FT-Profile

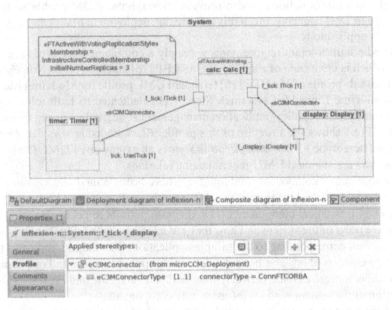

Fig. 2. Applying fault-tolerance stereotypes

From this model we can configure the final application, install binary files, generate appropriate connectors and configure specialized infrastructure services. This process follows several steps and uses different transformation tools described in the next section.

4.2 Code Generation

Code generation is intended to support CCM implementation steps. This requires to generate : (1) CCM descriptor files from the model, (2) the code corresponding to a CCM implementation.

The first point concerns generation of component descriptors, a platform description and a *deployment plan*. A deployment plan contains information on the implementation and required artifacts (usually libraries), components instances, as well as allocation information (allocation of instances onto nodes), and connections between ports of these instances. The second one concerns the parsing of the deployment plan by a dedicated CCM implementation: *microCCM*. This framework is a tool set developed jointly with Thales which prepares application deployment from the analysis of the deployment plan. It produces a static deployment in which a *bootloader* file is generated for each node. This file contains code that instantiates components as well as connector fragments and performs the connections according to the deployment plan. Connector fragments are generated when necessary (this step is needed, since connectors adapt themselves to component interfaces, as shortly outlined in the previous section).

```
void FTCORBA_IDisplay_client::display (CORBA::Float value)
{
    if (m_voter != NULL) {
        // calculate hash of request (used to simplify comparisons).
        Hash hash;
        hash.add (m_voter->getRequestNr ());
        hash.add (value);
        m_voter->acknowledgeRequest (hash.get ());
    }
    if (amILeader ()) {
        for (int i = 0; i<MAX_NR_OF_NODES; i++) {
            if (myRM->isOnNode ("DISPLAY",i) && !myFD->is_faulty_node(i))
                myRM->getObj ("DISPLAY",i)->display (value);
        }
    }
}
```

Fig. 3. Code of connector fragment associated with the node in which *Calc* component is deployed

The following code (see Fig.3) gives a rough idea of the generated code contained within a connector fragment. In this case, fragment that is responsible for sending a result from the calculation component towards the display component.

4.3 Discussion

Overhead of connector fragments code : The following table provides an idea about the overhead of the connector fragments at some node. The figures are obtained for a prototype on a Linux PC. As said before, the bootloader file performs the instantiations and configuration of components and connector fragments and the connections between these. The connector fragments use a naming scheme that correspond to their name followed by the interface to which they adapt to and followed finally by the port name within the connector type. The overhead of a connector supporting fault-tolerance is relatively small, in general it depends on the number of operations and their parameters. The voter run-time adds about 11 Kb.

Efficiency, evolutivity, reusability : In order to use another replication style it suffices to (1) adapt our infrastructure to deal with such a replication style, i.e. provide a connector and (2) specify the use of this connector by means of a stereotype attribute of a connection on model level (as shown in Fig.2). A re-generation of the descriptor files and the connector generation will take this change automatically into account.

Thus, multiple deployment variants can be easily produced and tested (benchmarked) and optimized to find a suitable solution.

5   Related Work

Some CORBA implementations provided proprietary fault tolerance mechanisms such as OmniORB, Orbix and Orbacus. They are based on an embedded set of "contact

text	data	bss	dec	filename
13788	12	828	14628	gcc_linux_mico/obj/bootloader.o
372	4	1	377	gcc_linux_mico/obj/CCM_hooks.o
2936	4	1	2941	gcc_linux_mico/obj/CORBA_IFault_Detector_client.o
2339	4	1	2344	gcc_linux_mico/obj/CORBA_IFault_Detector_server.o
3245	4	1	3250	gcc_linux_mico/obj/FT_CORBA_IDisplay_client.o
1271	4	1	1276	runtime/FT/gcc_linux_mico/obj/ReferenceSet.o
11458	5	1	11464	runtime/FT/gcc_linux_mico/obj/Voter_impl.o

Fig. 4. Overhead of the connector fragments corresponding to the proposed implementation for a prototype on a Linux PC

details" within an interoperable object reference (IOR). These solutions are vendor specific and not interoperable. Therefore, the OMG standardizes fault-tolerant mechanisms (short FT-CORBA) [12] within the CORBA specification. The replication manager interface is the core of the FT-CORBA infrastructure, inheriting from three interfaces that deal with object groups, a generic factory and the fault-tolerance properties. The latter is also referred to by the FT-profile outlined in this paper. A full implementation of the FT-CORBA specification tends to be "big", therefore it is not implemented by many ORBs, in particular not by ORBs that are tailored for small and medium embedded systems.

AQuA (Adaptive Quality of service Availability, see[17] and [9]) is incompatible with FTCORBA. Fault-tolerance is obtained by active or passive replication and requires reliable group communication. It allows developers to specify the desired level of dependability, through the configuration of the system according to the availability of resources and the faults occurred. This system uses QoS contract as in Quality Objects [20]. The group communication service is based on Ensemble [8].

The AFT-CCM (Adaptive Fault-Tolerance) model [5] is based on CCM and treats fault-tolerance as a specific QoS requirement. For each component with fault-tolerance requirements, an AFT manager is created. This seems to be quite costly, but enables the modification of QoS parameters at run-time such as the replication coordinator implementing the replication technique (one component for each replica). A prototype of this system was built using OpenCCM (http://openccm.objectweb.org) running under ORBacus. Only passive replication style was implemented since active replication style requires group communication mechanisms that are not supported in the used ORB. Another approach for CORBA components replication is studied in [10]. This approach uses interceptor objects that accomplish replication management: each replicated component is associated with an interceptor object. In the AFT-CCM, a generic connector is used to avoid the implementation of a new interceptor object for each new component.

The MEAD (Middleware for Embedded Adaptive Dependability) group has proposed a fault-tolerant CCM in cooperation with Raytheon. This extension uses additional descriptor files containing deployment rules and container descriptions that specify the fault-tolerance properties of the application. The link between components and

FT services (including fault monitoring, checkpoint (log) components) is done at the container level. There is a separation between logical and physical assembly in CCM process: for example, the number of replicas is logical and the placement is a physical concern. This deployment is achieved using an assembly manager/deployer that is installed at each host. Both active and passive replication styles are supported by the proposed extension using the extended virtual synchrony model [2]. This model guarantees that events are delivered in the same order at each node.

Different modeling approaches can be followed, several specialized description languages have been defined and are well adapted to describe system implementation (AADL and its error annex [3,4]), EAST ADL which focuses particularly on the specification of allocation constraints, or some dedicated languages devoted to the development of critical systems based on formal techniques and synchronous calculus (as in the SCADE tool). But none of these approaches are well suited to the Container/Component paradigm.

The main difference between the fault-tolerant CCM approaches above and our approach is the focus on a specification based on UML and a standardized profile (QoS+FT). Another difference is that we integrated the fault-tolerance mechanism into a generic CCM extension. Note that our connectors replace interaction tailoring via interceptors that are used by other approaches to enable transparent replication.

6   Summary and Future Work

We have shown that fault-tolerant applications can be generated directly from a specification of the architecture (component assembly & deployment) in UML and component descriptions as well as their implementation. The whole approach is largely based on standards: UML with CCM as well as a fault-tolerance profile and the execution middleware based on CCM. The extension of the middleware renders it more flexible and enables the transparent support for group communication. Unlike other approaches, the connector extension of the middleware is not a specific extension for fault-tolerance – fault tolerance is merely a good example of the enhanced flexibility that can be achieved within this component approach. It is then possible to implement distributed applications onto heterogeneous platforms running under different operating systems and communication stacks at low cost and with high implementation efficiency. The application are currently runs on a PC using Linux and on a GR-XC3S-1500 LEON development board using RTEMS OS (a Posix compliant). The latter is used to show that our approach may be used easily to design embedded systems.

The next steps are primarily a support for an automatic re-configuration of the application, for instance the transition between a nominal and a reduced-functionality mode. Re-configuration mechanisms in a non-FT context are already implemented by the project partner Thales; and recently we propose a model driven approach to help specify reconfigurability issues [7]. The challenges of the integration include for instance the replication of the component performing the reconfiguration steps. Another objective for the near future is to implement other replication styles than the active with vote and to examine footprint and performance overheads in detail.

References

1. Chandra, T.D., Toueg, S.: Unreliable failure detectors for reliable distributed system. Journal of the ACM 43(2), 225–267 (1996)
2. Dumitras, T., Srivastava, D., Narasimhan, P.: Architecting and implementing versatile dependability. In: de Lemos, R., Gacek, C., Romanovsky, A. (eds.) Architecting Dependable Systems III. LNCS, vol. 3549, pp. 212–231. Springer, Heidelberg (2005)
3. Feiler, P., Rugina, A.: Dependability Modeling with the Architecture Analysis & Design Language (AADL). Technical report, CMU/SEI-2007-TN-043 (2007)
4. Feiler, P.H., Gluch, D.P., Hudak, J.J.: The Architecture Analysis & Design Language (AADL): An Introduction. Technical report, CMU/SEI-2006-TN-011 (2006)
5. Fraga, J., Siqueira, F., Favarim, F.: Adaptive Fault-Tolerant Component Model. In: Ninth IEEE international workshop on Object-Oriented Real-Time Dependable Systems (2003)
6. Hamid, B.: Distributed fault-tolerance techniques for local computations. Ph.D thesis, University of Bordeaux 1 (2007)
7. Hamid, B., Lanusse, A., Radermacher, A., Gérard, S.: Designing Reconfigurable Component Systems with a Model Based Approach. In: Workshop on Adaptive and Reconfigurable Embedded Systems, APRES (to appear, 2008)
8. Hayden, M.G.: The Ensemble System. Ph.D thesis, Cornell University (1998)
9. Kobusinska, A., Kobusinski, J., Szychowiak, M.: An Analysis of distributed platforms applying replication mechanisms. Technical Report Report RA-014, Poznan University of Technology (2001)
10. Lung, L.C., Favarim, F., Santos, G.T., Correia, M.: An Infrastructure for Adaptive Fault Tolerance on FT-CORBA. In: ISORC 2006: Proceedings of the Ninth IEEE International Symposium on Object and Component-Oriented Real-Time Distributed Computing (ISORC 2006), Washington, DC, USA, 2006, pp. 504–511. IEEE Computer Society Press, Los Alamitos (2006)
11. OMG. CORBA Core specification, Version 3.0.3. OMG Document formal/2004-03-12 (2004)
12. OMG. CORBA Core specification, Version 3.0.3. OMG Document formal/2004-03-12 (2004)
13. OMG. CORBA Component Model Specification, Version 4.0, 4. OMG Document formal/2006-04-01 (2006)
14. OMG. Deployment and Configuration of Component Based Distributed Applications, v4.0. OMG document ptc/2006-04-02 (2006)
15. OMG. UML Profile for Modeling Quality of Service and Fault Tolerance Characteristics and Mechanisms, 5. OMG Document formal/2006-05-02 (2006)
16. OMG. UML Profile for MARTE. OMG document ptc/07-08-04 (2007)
17. Ren, Y., Cukier, M., Sanders, W.H.: An adaptive algorithm for tolerating value faults and crash failures. IEEE transaction on parallel an distributed systems 2, 173–192 (2001)
18. Robert, S., Radermacher, A., Seignole, V., Gérard, S., Watine, V., Terrier, F.: Enhancing interaction support in the corba component model. In: From Specification to Embedded Systems Application
19. Schmidt, D.: Model-driven engineering. IEEE computer 39(2), 41–47 (2006)
20. Zinky, J.A., Bakken, D.E., Schantz, R.E.: Architectural support for quality of service for CORBA objects. Theory and Practice of Object Systems 3(1) (1997)

Model Based Synthesis of Embedded Software

Daniel D. Gajski, Samar Abdi, and Ines Viskic

Center for Embedded Computer Systems
University of California, Irvine, CA 92617
{gajski,sabdi,iviskic}@uci.edu

Abstract. This paper presents SW synthesis using Embedded System Environment (ESE), a tool set for design of multi-core embedded systems. We follow a design process that starts with an application model consisting of C processes communicating via abstract message passing channels. The application model is mapped to a platform net-list of SW and HW cores, buses and buffers. A high speed transaction level model (TLM) is generated to validate abstract communication between processes mapped to different cores. The TLM is further refined into a Pin-Cycle Accurate Model (PCAM) for board implementation. The PCAM includes C code for all the communication layers including routing, packeting, synchronization and bus transfer. The generated embedded SW provides a library of application level services to the C processes on individual SW cores. Therefore, the application developer does not need to write low level SW for board implementation. Synthesis results for an multi-core MP3 decoder design, using ESE, show that the embedded SW is generated in order of seconds, compared to hours of manual coding. The quality of synthesized code is comparable to manually written code in terms of performance and code size.

1 Introduction

Multi-core embedded systems are being increasingly used to meet the complexity and performance requirements of modern applications. Embedded application developers need a library of communication services to validate and debug their multi-threaded code. On the other hand, system designers need to provide board prototypes and system SW for application development. Model based design is widely seen as an enabler for early application development before the prototype is ready. Software simulation models for multi-core embedded systems may be created at various levels of abstraction for different purposes. Models at higher abstraction levels, such as TLM, execute faster and are therefore better for application development. However, with higher abstraction, there are fewer design details to allow realistic estimation of design metrics. Pin-cycle accurate models (PCAMs) provide accurate performance estimates and are required for prototyping. However, they are too slow to use for application development. Furthermore, PCAMs require an implementation of **core, platform and application-specific** system SW services on top of the SW core's instruction set. Some of these services are available directly in an RTOS for the SW core. Others, such as external communication methods, must be manually written or may require RTOS configuration.

Integrated design environments, such as ESE [3], are needed to transform application level models into platform specific TLMs for exploration and PCAMs for implementation. In this paper we will discuss the model based design methodology of ESE, with

U. Brinkschulte, T. Givargis, and S. Russo (Eds.): SEUS 2008, LNCS 5287, pp. 21–33, 2008.
© IFIP International Federation for Information Processing 2008

focus on embedded SW synthesis. Our methodology and synthesis technique allows automatic transformation of application level models with abstract message passing communication into PCAMs with an embedded SW stack of communication services. The automation not only cuts design time, but results in modular embedded SW that is consistent with the application level model.

2 Related Work

There has been significant research in model based design for embedded systems in the recent years. Standardization approaches such as AUTOSAR [2] and OSEK [4] provide common API and middleware for automotive SW development. On the other hand, system level design languages such as SystemC [5] and SpecC [9] allow multi-core system modeling with simulation speeds suitable for SW development. Such efforts have provided the groundwork for developing and deploying model automation tools such as the one presented in this paper.

There has also been much work in embedded system modeling frameworks and SW code generation from specific input languages. POLIS [7] (Co-Design Finite State Machine), DESCARTES [19] (ADF and an extended SDF), Cortadella [8] (petri nets) and SCE [10] (SpecC) provide limited automation for SW generation from certain models of computation. In contrast, our approach provides a C based input with multi-core support and has been demonstrated with actual board implementation.

Modular communication modeling has been proposed for application domains such as real-time systems and platforms such as heterogeneous multi-core systems. Kopetz [13] proposes component model for dependable automotive systems. Sangiovanni-vincentelli [21] has proposed a three phase simulation model for platform based design. These approaches tackle security, dependability and heterogeneity at the system level, but require underlying SW services and tools to implement the models. Communication optimization techniques [18,20,17] on the other hand have dealt primarily with platform and application transformations using simulation models. In contrast, our communication SW synthesis focuses on code generation for accurate optimization feedback and is fast and flexible enough to incorporate application and platform modifications on the fly.

Hardware dependent SW [15] has been a topic of active research lately and our work contributes to it. Commercial vendors provide a board support package (BSP) [6,1] with their board IDEs, but such software is customized for the limited set of IP cores available or synthesizable on the board. Most academic approaches so far have dealt with porting of simulation models on RTOS, discounting external communication. Herrara [12] proposes overloading SystemC library elements to reuse the same model for specification and target execution, but partly replicates the simulation engine on the host and thereby imposes strict input requirements. Krause [14] proposes generation of source code from SystemC mapped onto an RTOS, while Gauthier's method [11] provides generation of application-specific RTOS and the corresponding application SW. Both techniques cannot be extended to muti-core platforms with inter-core communication synthesis. Yu [23] shows generation of application C code from concurrent SpecC, which requires the initial system modeling to be done in SpecC. The Phantom Serializing Compiler [16] translates multi-tasking POSIX C code input into sequential

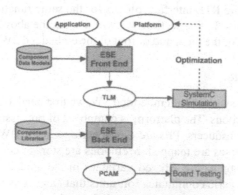

Fig. 1. ESE Design Flow

C code by custom scheduling, but is a purely SW core-specific optimization. Schirner [22] also proposes hardware dependent synthesis from SpecC models but only considers platforms with single core connected to several peripherals. In contrast to all the above techniques, ESE provides generation of core, platform and application-specific embedded SW for multi-core systems, starting from an abstract C based application model.

3   Model Based Design with ESE

Our model based design methodology is shown in Figure 1. We start with an application model that consists of C processes communicating via synchronized point-to-point handshake channels and shared variables. The platform definition is a graphical net list of processing elements (PEs), buses and transducers. Processes and variables in the application model are mapped to the PEs in the platform. Channels are mapped to routes in the platform. If the route includes a buffer, then the communicated data may need to be broken up into smaller packets according to the buffer size limitations. The above design decisions and data models of PEs, buses and RTOSes are used by the *ESE Front-End* to generate a TLM. The TLM models the PEs as SystemC modules connected to the communication architecture model consisting of bus channels and buffer modules. The original application processes are encapsulated as SystemC threads instantiated inside the PE modules. The point-to-point channel accesses of the application model are mapped into equivalent packet transactions routed over the communication model.

The step of refining the TLM into a PCAM is performed by the *ESE Back-End*. The component data models in TLM are replaced with respective implementation libraries in the PCAM. Synchronization is modeled in the TLM via abstract SystemC flags and events. The flag and event accesses must be transformed into interrupts or polling in the PCAM. Similarly, the packet transactions over the bus channels in the TLM must be transformed into equivalent arbitration and data transfer cycles on the system buses. The transformations applied to the model result in various C functions per SW core. These functions form the embedded SW library for that core. If there are HW IPs in the platform, they will require RTL interface blocks for the same functions, with platform specific timing constraints. In this section, we will discuss the above models in greater detail to provide an idea of the input and output of the embedded SW synthesis process.

3.1 Platform Template

In order to automate the synthesis of embedded SW, we first need to define the platform components and connections. The platform is composed of processing elements (PEs), memories, buses and transducers. PEs are our generic term for HW and SW cores on which application processes are mapped. Memories are storage cores that do not have any active thread of computation. Shared variables in the application are mapped to memories. Buses are generic communication units that can act as point-to-point links or shared buses with arbitration. Buses have well defined protocols and may connect to compatible ports on a given core.

Transducers are generic interface cores that provide functionality of (1) protocol conversion and (2) store-and-forward static routing. Transducers consist of internal buffers and may connect to incompatible buses via different ports. For each bus connection, they have an IO interface and a *Request Buffer*. This request buffer stores all send/receive requests made to the transducer for storing and forwarding data on a channel. Thus, they allow sending data from one PE to another if the two PEs are not connected to a common bus. A route in the platform is a sequence of buses and transducers with the following regular expression:

$$PE_{sender} \rightarrow Bus_0 \rightarrow [\ Transducer_i \rightarrow Bus_i \rightarrow\ ]^* PE_{receiver}$$

Channels in the application are mapped to routes in the platform. As a result, each transducer in the platform may have several channels routed through it. For each such channel, the transducer defines (1) a unique buffer partition to be used by data on that channel, (2) a unique bus address for a send request, and (3) a unique bus address for a receive request. Since transactions on a channel are sequential, the partitioning of transducer buffers guarantees safety and liveness of implementation, provided the application model is safe and live.

3.2 Application Model

Figure 2. shows the application model of an MP3 Decoder. The decoding algorithm is captured with a set of eight concurrent processes, each executing sequential C code. Process *Huffman Decoder* inputs MP3 stream organized in frames, performs Huffman decoding, re-quantization and frame reordering. The frames are then classified into either left or right stereo stream and processed separately. *Left* and *Right Alias Reduction* processes reduce the aliasing effects in frames, while the *Left and Right IMDCTs* convert the frequency domain samples to frequency sub-band samples. The two *DCT* processes transform the individual frequency sub-bands into PCM samples and send them to the PCM process for correction verification.

Communication in application model is enabled with calls to (a) *send/recv* methods for direct process communication, and (b) *read/write* methods for accessing variables shared between processes. The *send/recv* methods are encapsulated in

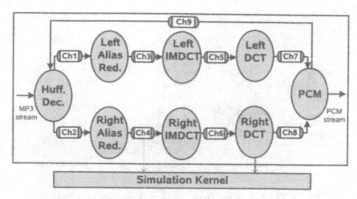

Fig. 2. Application model

process-to-process channels with no message buffering. Instead, process-to-process channels follow handshake synchronization semantics, where the receiver process blocks until the sender has sent the communicated data. All communication in MP3 Decoder is modeled using process-to-process channels *Ch1* through *Ch9*.

On the other hand, the communication with *read/write* methods is unblocking. The shared variables are in the global scope and are accessed with unsynchronized *access channels*. The two communication mechanisms are sufficient to model more complex communication services such as FIFOs, mutexes, mailboxes or events. Therefore, the synthesis of the basic communication models of handshake channels and shared variable access channels is necessary and sufficient for implementing any inter-process communication service at this level of abstraction.

The set of processes, variables and channels are built on top of the SystemC simulation kernel, as shown on Figure 2. The processes execute as concurrent threads on the simulation kernel. The process to process channels use the notify-wait semantics of the kernel events to implement handshake synchronization. The shared variables are modeled as passive SystemC modules that export read and write interfaces, which are used to connect them to the access channels. Interfaces are also defined for processes to allow connection to channels. A well defined interface template provides a communication API with the following functions, where $< i >$ is the name of used interface:

- $< i >$_Send(void *data, int size)_ Synchronized send
- $< i >$_Recv(void *data, int size)_ Synchronized receive
- $< i >$_Write(void *data, int size)_ Non-blocking write
- $< i >$_Read(void *data, int size)_ Non-blocking read

By separating the communication interface from the rest of the computation code, we are able to successively refine only the interface implementation code. The API provided to the application developer stays the same throughout SW synthesis.

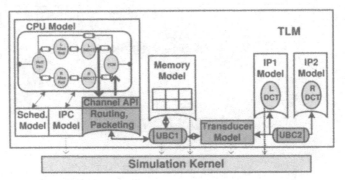

Fig. 3. TLM resulting from application to platform mapping

3.3 Transaction Level Model

The TLM is derived by mapping the application model in Section 3.2 to an embedded platform. The platform components are modeled with a well defined SystemC code template. PEs are modeled as SystemC modules that instantiate application processes. The system buses are modeled with a *universal bus channel* (UBC), that provides methods for synchronized send/receive, non-blocking read/write and memory service. Memories are modeled as SystemC modules with a local array. Transducers are modeled as SystemC modules with local buffer and controller threads for each bus interface.

Figure 3 shows the TLM of the MP3 Decoder. Processes *Left* and *Right DCT* are mapped to the HW units ($IP1$ and $IP2$), while all other processes reside in a SW core (*CPU*) model. The route between the core and the HW units includes two UBCs and a *Transducer*. Access to units from the SW core is modeled with *Channel API* that encapsulate routing and packeting methods. These methods in turn are implemented with the UBC functions. Routing includes programming the *Transducer* with encoded route using UBC *write* method. Packeting divides the message into data packets of selected size. Since multiple processes are mapped to the SW core, a dynamic scheduler model that exports a threading API emulates processor multitasking.

Channels between processes in the SW core are implemented with an inter-process communication (IPC) model. The IPC and scheduler model are only core dependent and can be included into the TLM from a library. However, the external communication code is application, platform and core dependent. Therefore, its has to be generated for every communication change in the design.

3.4 Pin-Cycle Accurate Model

The TLM is refined into a PCA model that is used for board implementation. Board design tools such those from Xilinx and Altera can be used to convert PCAMs into bitstreams for board implementation. Board debugging tools can then be used to run and debug the design in real time.

Figure 4. shows the PCAM of the MP3 Decoder. The platform consisting of one SW core and two IP units connected with two buses and a transducer is now modeled in

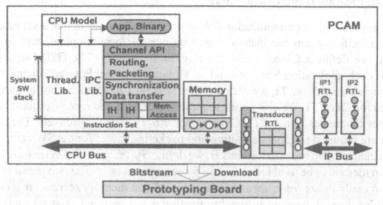

Fig. 4. PCAM refined from TLM for board prototyping

synthesizable RTL. The six MP3 Decoder processes mapped to a SW core are compiled with the appropriate C compiler (e.g. Xilinx compiler for Microblaze core) and linked with the system SW libraries for download. The processes mapped to hardware can be either synthesized using C-to-RTL tools or replaced with the respective RTL IP. The system SW stack includes the threading and IPC libraries of the RTOS, and the external communication library generated by our synthesis tool. The RTOS itself may consist of several other services such as file handling, memory management, standard C library, networking and so on.

The communication SW library consists of four layers as shown in Figure 4. The lowest layer consists of a set of interrupt handlers (IHs) and memory access functions. Each application level handshake channel requires synchronization that may be implemented as interrupt or polling. For interrupt based synchronization an IH is implemented per handshake channel. For polling implementation, a memory mapped flag is implemented in the slave device that is periodically checked by the master SW core. The memory access functions also provide basic IO to the peripherals. The synchronization and data transfer layer consists of C methods that use the IHs and memory access methods to manage packet level synchronization and bus word transfers. The higher level layers for routing and packeting and the channel API are imported directly from the TLM. In summary, the communication in PCAM is implemented with core specific C methods as opposed to SystemC kernel methods in TLM.

4 Embedded SW Generation

In this section we describe the embedded SW synthesis and code generation from a set of design parameters. The design parameters are determined from the application and platform decisions as well as core properties and are treated as constants for SW code generation. Two layers of communication functions are generated, namely for routing/packeting and synchronization/transfer. These functions are specific to the interface of the application process. An example shows a typical code synthesized for a *Send* interface.

4.1   Communication Design Parameters

In order to automate the communication SW code generation, we define a set of communication specific system parameters. Based on our platform template, explained in Section 3.1, we define a *Global Static Routing Table (GSRT)*. The GSRT stores the mapping of each application level channel to a platform route. For each channel *Ch*, routed through a transducer *Tx*, we define *BufferSize(Tx, Ch)* to be the buffer partition size in bytes for *Ch* on *Tx*. We also define the transducer send and receive request buffer addresses per channel as *SendRB(Tx, Ch)* and *RecvRB(Tx, Ch)*, respectively. The above parameters are required to generate routing and packeting layers for the SW core.

For each channel Ch, routed over a bus B, we define $SyncType(B, Ch)$ to be the synchronization method to be used for *ch* for the route segment at B. The two possible synchronization methods are *Interrupt* and *Polling*. For direct memory accesses that do not require routing through transducer, synchronization is not required. A synchronization flag table is maintained for each core. Each channel *Ch* gets a unique entry *SyncFlag_Ch* in this table. For interrupt based synchronization, we also define a binding from the interrupt source to the flag and the handler instance. For polling, the flag is bound to an address in the slave PE. Finally, for the data transfer implementation, we define the bus word size and the low to high address range for each channel Ch on bus B as $AR(B, Ch)$. For each SW core we also define *WordSize* as the number of bytes per word.

4.2   Routing and Packeting

The communication functions are synthesized for each interface *i* that is bound to a channel *Ch*. Since we allow only static routing, a route object *Rt* is stored in the *GSRT* corresponding to each channel. Note that the GSRT does not need to be part of the communication library, since the routing per channel is static. The route for *Ch* determines the channel packet size as follows:

$$PktSz = Min\ (\ \forall Tx \in Rt,\ BufferSize(Tx, Ch)\ )$$

Hence, packet size is the largest data size that can fit into any transducer buffer allocation for Ch. Again, note that $PktSz$ is a constant per channel, due to static routing.

The code generated for the interface communication method is a do-while loop, with a temporary variable to keep track of already sent/received data. A lower level method *i_SyncTr* is called by the routing/packeting layer to synchronize with the corresponding process and send or receive each packet.

4.3   Synchronization and Transfer

The routing of channel *Ch* determines the synchronization code generated inside the *i_SyncTr* method. Given the route object *Rt*, as obtained from the GSRT, we determine the first bus *B* in *Rt*. We also determine if *Rt* contains any transducers. If so, we assign *Tx* to be the first transducer in *Rt*. The first step of packet synchronization is top make a transducer request for the transaction. This is done by generating code to write the packet size (in bytes) into the request buffer at the address given by the parameter $SendRB(Tx, Ch)$ or $RecvRB(Tx, Ch)$, depending on the transaction type. Once the

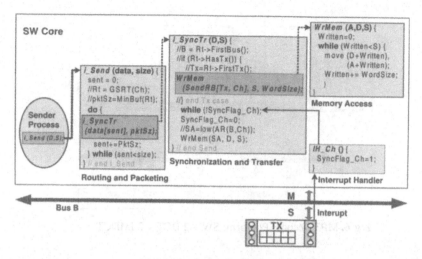

Fig. 5. Embedded SW code example

request is written, the transducer initiates lower level synchronization via interrupt or polling, just like any other slave core.

Lower level synchronization is implemented by generating code for busy waiting over flag *SyncFlag_Ch* in the *i_SyncTr* method. The flag is either set by the interrupt handler for *Ch* or by the corresponding slave core, in case of polling. The busy-wait code is followed by *resetting* the synchronization flag. Finally, data transfer is performed by generating a call to the core-specific *WrMem* or *RdMem* functions. These functions write or read data of given bytes using bus transactions of size *WordSize*. The starting address of the transfer is obtained from the address range *AR(B,Ch)*.

Figure 5 shows an example for the embedded SW code generated for send method of interface *i*. The sender process is mapped to a SW core, and its interface *i* is connected to bus *B*. Interface *i* is bound to channel *Ch* that is routed over *B* and transducer *Tx* and onto the destination core. Interrupt signal (*Interrupt*) from the transducer to the SW core is used for synchronization, and is bound to handler *IH_Ch* and flag *SyncFlag_Ch*.

5   Experimental Results

Figure 6 shows a multi-core design with an MP3 decoder application mapped to a platform consisting of one SW core (*Microblaze*) and four HW cores (*Left/Right DCT and IMDCT*) used as accelerators. The HW cores use a *DoubleHandshake (DH) Bus* interface, while the SW core is connected to the *Open Peripheral Bus (OPB)*. Since the two bus protocols are incompatible, a transducer is used to interface between the cores. The block diagram of the stereo MP3 application with left and right channel decoding blocks is shown inside *Microblaze*.

We created four mappings of the application, that we refer to as *SW+1DCT, SW+2D CT, SW+2IMDCT* and *SW+2DCT+2IMDCT*, with parts of the application mapped to the hardware accelerators, as indicated by the mapping name. As the DCT and IMDCT

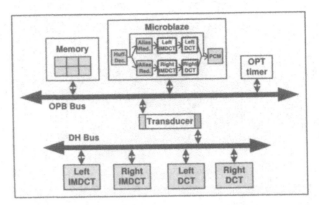

Fig. 6. MP3 Decoder Platform: SW + 2 DCT + 2 IMDCT

processes are moved from SW core to the HW cores, the inter-core bidirectional channels are routed over the OPB, DH buses and transducer Tx. The communication SW on *Microblaze* for PCAMs of the different designs are generated using our SW synthesis tool. Xilinx EDK [6] is used to convert our generated PCAMs into bitstream for implementation on the FF896 Virtex-II device. The decoding performance for all the synthesized designs is measured with an OPB timer on the board, using a common MP3 input file.

Table 1 shows a comparison between manually implemented and automatically synthesized PCAMs using quality metrics of SW code size and communication delay. It can be seen that the synthesized SW binary is only marginally larger than manual implementation (between 1-4%). However, the performance of the synthesized code, as measured by the on-chip timer, is 6-9% better than manual implementation. The code quality difference was because the manual implementation shared the synchronization function for different application channels, while the synthesized code had unique synchronization function for each channel. Therefore, the manual code had fewer total instructions, but incurred more instruction fetches for each communication call at run-time.

Table 1. Comparison of manual vs. synthesized PCAMs of the MP3 Decoder

	Design	Code size(in bytes) (% diff.)	Total comm. delay (in cycles) (% diff.)	Total comm. delay (in ms)
Manually implemented PCAM	SW+1DCT	171,362	957,060	35.45
	SW+2DCT	160,640	1,914,120	70.89
	SW+2IMDCT	163,492	1,875,588	69.46
	SW+2DCT+2IMDCT	153,420	3,789,708	140.36
Automatically generated PCAM	SW+1DCT	172,072 (+4.14%)	949,932 (-7.44%)	35.18
	SW+2DCT	161,280 (+3.98%)	1,899,864 (-7.44%)	70.04
	SW+2IMDCT	164,132 (+3.91%)	1,863,972 (-6.19%)	69.04
	SW+2DCT+2IMDCT	153,624 (+1.33%)	3,763,836 (-6.83%)	139.40

Table 2. Comparison of manual vs. synthesized communication SW

	Design	Code size (in lines) (% diff.)	Development Time (% diff.)
Manual communication library	SW+1DCT	162	5 h + 2 h
	SW+2DCT	192	5 h + 2.5 h
	SW+2IMDCT	192	5 h + 2.5 h
	SW+2DCT+2IMDCT	252	5 h + 3.5 h
Synthesized communication library	SW+1DCT	168 (+3.70%)	5 h + 0.14 s (-28%)
	SW+2DCT	208 (+8.33%)	5 h + 0.14 s (-33%)
	SW+2IMDCT	208 (+8.33%)	5 h + 0.14 s (-33%)
	SW+2DCT+2IMDCT	288 (+13.83%)	5 h + 0.14 s (-37%)

Table 2 shows a comparison of lines of code between manual and synthesized embedded SW. Due to difference in synchronization implementation, as mentioned above, we can see that synthesized source code is marginally larger than manual code. The development time includes the 5 hours that it took to define the application level channels and the design parameters. It took 2-4 hours to implement and test the manual communication code. In contrast, with the given parameters, our synthesis tool generated the embedded SW library in fraction of a second. This resulted in an overall development time savings of 33% on average.

6 Conclusions

We presented a model based technique and methodology for synthesis of embedded SW for heterogeneous multi-core systems. The novelty of our work lies in defining embedded system models at different abstraction level with clear synthesis semantics. Application level models were defined as a set of processes communicating via message passing channels and shared variables. A well defined, yet highly flexible, platform template and associated design parameters were presented. We also presented a synthesis procedure to generate core, application and platform specific embedded SW for the design. Synthesis results for an MP3 decoder example demonstrated the applicability of our technique for large industrial size embedded systems. Our automatic embedded SW synthesis reduces overall design time, while consistently providing better performance and negligible increase in code size over manual implementation. For future work, we are investigating SW synthesis from dependability and security oriented application models. We are also working extending our model based design framework with application and platform templates for real-time architectures such as time triggered network.

Acknowledgments. This work builds on several years of system level design research at Center for Embedded Computer Systems, UC Irvine. We wish to thank Hansu Cho for providing the Verilog implementation of transducers, Pramod Chandraiah for the C reference of the MP3 Decoder, and Gunar Schirner for discussions on hardware dependent software.

References

1. Altera SOPC Builder, http://www.altera.com/
2. Automotive Open System Architecture, http://www.autosar.org/
3. Embedded System Environment, http://www.cecs.uci.edu/~ese/
4. OSEK, http://www.osek-vdx.org/
5. SystemC, OSCI, http://www.systemc.org/
6. Xilinx Embedded Development Kit, http://www.xilinx.com/
7. Balarin, F., et al.: Hardware-Software Co-Design of Embedded Systems: The POLIS Approach. Kluwer, Dordrecht (1997)
8. Cortadella, J., et al.: Task generation and compile time scheduling for mixed data-control embedded software. In: Proceedings of the Design Automation Conference (June 2000)
9. Gajski, D., Zhu, J., Domer, R., Gerstlauer, A., Zhao, S.: SpecC: Specification Language and Methodology. Kluwer Academic Publishers, Dordrecht (January 2000)
10. Gerstlauer, A., Shin, D., Peng, J., Domer, R., Gajski, D.D.: Automatic, layer-based generation of system-on-chip bus communication models. IEEE Transactions on Computer-Aided Design of Integrated Circuits and Systems 26(9) (September 2007)
11. Guthier, L., Yoo, S., Jerraya, A.: Automatic generation and targeting of application specific operating systems and embedded systems software. In: Proceedings of the Design Automation and Test Conference in Europe, pp. 679–685 (2001)
12. Herrera, F., Posadas, H., Snchez, P., Villar, E.: Systematic embedded software generation from systemc. In: Proceedings of the Design Automation and Test Conference in Europe (2003)
13. Kopetz, H., Obermaisser, R., Salloum, C.E., Huber, B.: Automotive software development for a multi-core system-on-a-chip. In: SEAS 2007: Proceedings of the 4th International Workshop on Software Engineering for Automotive Systems, Washington, DC, USA, p. 2. IEEE Computer Society, Los Alamitos (2007)
14. Krause, M., Bringmann, O., Rosenstiel, W.: Target software generation: an approach for automatic mapping of systemc specifications onto real-time operating systems. Design Automation for Embedded Systems 10(4) (December 2005)
15. Makkelainen, T.: Hds from system-house perspective. In: Hardware dependent Software Workshop at DAC (2007)
16. Nacul, A.C., Givargis, T.: Lightweight multitasking support for embedded systems using the phantom serializing compiler. In: Proceedings of the Design Automation and Test Conference in Europe, pp. 742–747 (2005)
17. Pasricha, S., Park, Y.-H., Kurdahi, F.J., Dutt, N.: System-level power-performance trade-offs in bus matrix communication architecture synthesis. In: CODES+ISSS 2006: Proceedings of the 4th international conference on Hardware/software codesign and system synthesis, pp. 300–305. ACM, New York (2006)
18. Pinto, A., Carloni, L.P., Sangiovanni-Vincentelli, A.L.: Constraint-driven communication synthesis. In: Proceedings of the Design Automation Conference, pp. 783–788 (2002)
19. Ritz, S., et al.: High-level software synthesis for the design of communication systems. IEEE Journal on Selected Areas in Communications (April 1993)
20. Ryu, K.K., Mooney, V.: Automated bus generation for multiprocessor soc design. In: Proceedings of the Design Automation and Test Conference in Europe, p. 10282 (2003)
21. Sangiovanni-Vincentelli, A., et al.: A next-generation design framework for platform-based design. In: Conference on Using Hardware Design and Verification Languages (DVCon) (February 2007)

22. Schirner, G., Gerstlauer, A., Dömer, R.: Automatic generation of hardware dependent software for mpsocs from abstract system specifications. In: Proceedings of the Asia-Pacific Design Automation Conference, pp. 271–276 (2008)
23. Yu, H., Dömer, R., Gajski, D.: Embedded software generation from system level design languages. In: Proceedings of the Asia-Pacific Design Automation Conference, pp. 463–468 (2004)

Formal Specification of Gateways in Integrated Architectures

R. Obermaisser

Vienna University of Technology, Austria

Abstract. Complex embedded computer systems can encompass multiple application subsystems, such as a multimedia, a powertrain, a comfort and a safety subsystem in the in-vehicle electronic system of a typical premium car. Information exchanges between these application subsystems are essential to realize composite services that involve more than one application subsystem and to reduce redundant computations and sensors. A major challenge is to resolve the property mismatches at the interfaces between application subsystems, such as incoherent naming, divergent syntax, or different communication protocols. Also, fault isolation capabilities are required to prevent common mode failures induced by the propagation of faults between application subsystems. The contribution of this paper is a formal specification of gateways that contain structured collections of time-sensitive variables associated with timing information (called real-time databases) in order to separate the application subsystems. The formal specification can serve as a basis for automatic code generation or formal verification.

1 Introduction

Large distributed embedded systems (e. g., complete on-board electronic system of a car) consist of numerous application subsystems, each providing a part of the overall application functionality. Designers follow a divide-and-conquer strategy in order to manage the system's complexity by structuring the overall functionality into nearly-independent subsystems [1, chap. 8]. For example, in-vehicle electronics are usually grouped into several domains, including the safety-related powertrain and chassis domains, as well as the non-safety critical comfort and multimedia domains [2]. Each domain comprises a set of Electronic Control Units (ECUs) interconnected by a network (e. g., Controller Area Network (CAN) [3], FlexRay [4]).

However, the subdivision of the overall system usually does not lead to fully independent application subsystems. Interactions between application subsystems are required for improved quality-of-service, for implementing application services that span more than one application subsystem, and for exploiting redundancy [5].

The requirement of sharing information between application subsystems becomes a challenge, if the overall system encompasses heterogeneous application subsystems, which exchange messages using different communication protocols, incoherent naming, and divergent syntax or semantics. In this case, property mismatches at the interfaces between application subsystems need to be resolved.

U. Brinkschulte, T. Givargis, and S. Russo (Eds.): SEUS 2008, LNCS 5287, pp. 34–45, 2008.

In previous work [5], we have introduced a framework for the realization of gateways between application subsystems as part of the Dependable Embedded Components and Systems (DECOS) architecture [6]. The gateways proposed in this framework support selective redirection of information between networks in conjunction with the necessary property transformations. Central to this framework is a *real-time database* [7, p. 289], which is contained in the gateway and stores real-time images for the information exchange between the interconnected networks.

This paper describes the formal specification of these gateways. The formal gateway specification is expressed using state machines with timing constraints and gateway-specific operations (e. g., operations for accessing the real-time database). Existing solutions for the specification of real-time systems, such as timed automata [8], calendar automata [9] and time-triggered automata [10], were considered for developing this formal gateway specification. The formal gateway specification serves as the input for an automatic code generation tool, which yields data structures and code that serve as a parameterization of a generic architectural gateway service. Furthermore, the formal gateway specification is a baseline for the formal verification of systems using the proposed gateways.

The paper is structured as follows. Section 2 explains the gateway framework. The formal specification of the gateways is the focus of Section 3. The gateway specification formally captures the information to control the behavior of the gateway (i. e., selective redirection and property transformations). Section 4 gives an overview of the model-based generation of the gateways using the gateway specification as a starting point. The paper concludes with a discussion in Section 5.

2   Gateways Based on a Real-Time Database

A real-time system can be modeled using a set of *real-time entities* [11], which are significant state variables that are located in the computer system or the environment. The current value of such a real-time entity is called a *real-time image* and can be sent within a message on network. Redirection of information through a gateway occurs when a real-time image contained in a message is required by another Distributed Application Subsystem (DAS) connected to the gateway. We denote such a real-time image that is relevant at the gateway as a *convertible element*.

The presented gateways recombine convertible elements acquired from one network into messages for another network, while converting between different temporal and syntactic specifications and resolving naming incoherences. For this purpose, the gateway maintains a real-time database with convertible elements called the *gateway repository*. The gateway repository decouples the different networks accessed by the gateway and allows the convertible elements that are necessary for constructing a particular message to arrive at different points in time.

In addition, the gateway contains for each accessed DAS a so-called *network-adapter*, which implements the communication protocol of the network of the DAS and performs information exchanges between the network and the gateway repository (see Figure 1).

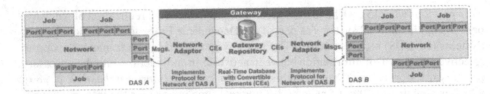

Fig. 1. Gateway

2.1 Network Adaptors

A network adaptor can acquire convertible elements from a network and write them into the gateway repository. Depending on the protocol, the acquisition of a message with convertible elements can involve the exchange of several messages at input and output ports, e. g., the transmission of a request message before a response message carrying the convertible elements arrives. Secondly, a network adaptor can read convertible elements from the gateway repository, construct messages and disseminate them on a network. Thereby, information can be redirected between networks, if the read convertible elements have been placed in the gateway repository by another network adaptor.

The specification of the network adaptors occurs using state machines with timing constraints and will be explained in Section 3.

2.2 Gateway Repository

For the storage of convertible elements, the gateway repository takes into account the information semantics of convertible elements. Due to the respective characteristics of state and event semantics, the gateway repository distinguishes two types of storage elements in analogy to state and event ports. For convertible elements with state semantics, the repository contains state variables that are overwritten whenever a new version of the convertible element arrives (update-in-place). Convertible elements with event semantics, on the other hand, are stored in queues.

In addition to the data of the convertible elements, the gateway repository also stores meta-information about convertible elements. The meta-information maintained in the gateway repository includes three dynamic attributes (most recent update instant, update request indication, number of queued instances) and a static attribute (temporal accuracy offset).

- **Most Recent Update Instant.** The point in time of the most recent update t_{update} is a dynamic attribute associated with each convertible element with state semantics. t_{update} is set to the current time t_{now}, whenever a network adaptor overwrites the convertible element in the gateway repository.
- **Temporal Accuracy Interval and Offset.** Due to the dynamics of real-time entities, the validity of convertible elements is time-dependent. For this reason, the gateway repository maintains for each convertible element with state semantics a dynamic attribute called the *temporal accuracy interval* d_{acc}. At any given instant, d_{acc} denotes how long the convertible element will still remain a valid image of the respective real-time entity in case no update of the convertible elements occurs in the meantime.

The *temporal accuracy offset* d_{offset} is a static attribute that determines the temporal accuracy interval immediately after an update of the convertible element. In conjunction with the instant of the most recent update, the temporal accuracy offset allows to compute the temporal accuracy interval of a convertible element: $d_{acc} = d_{offset} - (t_{now} - t_{update})$. Hence, only the temporal accuracy offset needs to be stored in the gateway repository, because the temporal accuracy interval can be computed on-the-fly.

- **Update Request Indication.** In order to support on-demand communication activities, the gateway repository contains boolean *update request indications*. For a convertible element with state or event semantics, the respective update request indication b_{req} denotes whether a new convertible element needs to be transferred into the gateway repository. By setting the update request indication, a network adaptor can demand convertible elements from the other network adaptors. A network adaptor receiving messages from a network can initiate receptions conditionally, based on the value of the update request indication.
- **Number of Queued Instances.** Every convertible element with event semantics possesses this dynamic attribute. It denotes the number of instances of the convertible element that are currently queued in the gateway repository.

Using the introduced attributes, we can control the behavior of a network adaptor. For example, the meta-information provides the network adaptors with information for the decision whether to actively engage in the acquisition of convertible elements for the update of the gateway repository. A network adaptor can react to the imminent invalidation of temporal accuracy, e. g., by starting a protocol to perform an update of the convertible element in the gateway repository.

3   Formal Specification of Gateways

This section formally defines a gateway with multiple network adaptors and a real-time database. Based on the notion of the gateway state, we also describe the execution of a gateway over time.

3.1   Definition of Network Adaptor

A network adaptor is a state machine with local variables, clock variables, locations, and edges. An edge interconnects two locations of the network adaptor and can be associated with a guard, assignments to variables and communication actions. The guard expresses a boolean condition, which defines whether the edge can be taken. Communication actions are used to express interactions with the gateway repository and the ports. Variables are used to capture the internal state of the network adaptor. In particular, variables can store messages and convertible elements. In a communication action, variables can serve as the source for the transfer of a convertible element into the gateway repository or the transfer of a message to a port for being transmitted. In analogy, variables can serve as the destination when executing a communication action to read a convertible element from the gateway repository or to receive a message from a port.

Formally, a network adaptor is a tuple $\langle L, l, X, R, E \rangle$, where

L is a finite set of symbols denoting locations,

$l \in L$ is the initial location,

X is a finite set of clocks $X = \{X_1, X_2, ...\}$,

R is a set of local variables: $R \subset \{(a,b)|a \in \mathbb{N} \wedge b \in \mathfrak{P}(\mathbb{N})\}$ Each local variable is associated with a name $a \in \mathbb{N}$. We call the set of all variable names $\eta(R) := \{z|\exists(z,b) \in R\}$. In addition, each variable possesses a corresponding domain described by a subset of $\mathbb{N}$. We use the function $domain(x)$ to determine the domain of a variable with name x: $domain(x) := b$ where $(a,b) \in R \wedge x = a$

E is a set of edges: $E \subseteq L \times L \times \Phi(\bar{Z}) \times \alpha(\bar{Z}) \times \chi(\bar{Z})$, where

  $\bar{Z}$ is the state of the gateway (cf. Section 3.3)

  Φ is the guard defined by the function $\bar{Z} \mapsto \{\mathbb{T}, \mathbb{F}\}$

  α is the assignment action defined by the function $\bar{Z} \mapsto \bar{R}$, where $\bar{R}$ denotes the local variables state (cf. Section 3.3), i.e., the values of the local variables at a certain point in time

  χ is the communication action defined by a function $\chi : \bar{Z} \mapsto \mathfrak{P}(\mathbb{N}) \times \mathfrak{P}(\mathbb{N}) \times \mathfrak{P}(\mathbb{N}) \times \mathfrak{P}(\mathbb{N})$, controlling in each state $\bar{Z}$ the effect of the network adaptor on the port and repository state. $\chi(\bar{Z}) = (C_{out}, C_{in}, M_{in}, M_{out})$, where C_{out} is the set of convertible elements, which are pushed into the gateway repository. The set of messages pulled out of the gateway repository is captured by C_{in}. M_{in} is the set of messages, which are received by the gateway, i.e., transferred from a port to variables. M_{out} is the set of messages, which are sent by the gateway, i.e., transferred from variables to a port.

3.2 Definition of a Gateway

A gateway consists of one or more network adaptors, ports with messages, and the gateway repository with convertible elements. Formally, a gateway is a tuple $Z = \langle A, V, M, C, Y \rangle$, where

A is a finite set of network adaptors: $A = < A_0, A_1, ..., A_z >$,

  $A_0 = < L_0, l_0, X_0, R_0, E_0 >, ..., A_z = < L_z, l_z, X_z, R_z, E_z >$

V is the global set of variables (i.e., local variables of all network adaptors extended with network adaptor names): $V = \{(c,b)|c = (i,a) \wedge (a,b) \in R_i \wedge 0 \leqslant i \leqslant z\}$

M is a finite set of messages: $M \subset \{(u,v,p,n,d,\tau)|u \in \mathbb{N}, v \subset \eta(V), p \in \{ET,TT\},$ $n \in \mathbb{N}, d \in \mathbb{N}, \tau : domain(v) \mapsto domain(v)\}$, where each message possesses a message name u, a set of associated variables v, a control paradigm p, a queue length n (only relevant for event information), and a temporal accuracy offset d (only relevant for state information). A transfer syntax can be specified using the function $\tau : domain(v) \mapsto domain(v)$ The associated variables are defined with respect to the set of all variable names $\eta(V) := \{z|\exists(z,b) \in V\}$.

C is a finite set of convertible elements: $C \subset \{ (u,v,p,n,d)|u \in \mathbb{N}, v \subset \eta(V), p \in \{ET,TT\}, n \in \mathbb{N}, d \in \mathbb{N}\}$, where each convertible elements possesses a name u, a set of associated variables v, a control paradigm p, a queue length n (only relevant for event information), and a temporal accuracy offset d (only relevant for state information).

Y is the global set of clocks (i.e., local clock variables of all network adaptors extended with network adaptor names): $Y = \{((z,a),b)|b \in \mathbb{N}, a \in X_i \wedge 0 \leqslant i \leqslant z\}$

3.3   Gateway State

The capturing of the gateway state serves the definition of the execution semantics of a gateway. The gateway state embodies all past history of the gateway. Thus, at any specific time the future outputs of the gateway depend only on the current state of the gateway and the future inputs (i. e., messages at ports).

Formally, the state of a gateway $\bar{Z} = \langle t, \bar{V}, \bar{M}, \bar{C}, \bar{Y} \rangle$ at time t consists of the global time t ($t \in \mathbb{N}$), the variables state $\bar{V}$, the message state $\bar{M}$, the repository state $\bar{C}$, and the clocks state $\bar{Y}$. These constituting elements of the gateway state will be explained in the following.

State of Variables. At a certain time t, the variables state $\bar{V}$ of the gateway encompasses the values of the local variables of all network adaptors:

$$\bar{V} \subset \{(x,y) | \exists (a,b) \in V \text{ with } a = x \wedge y \in b\} \quad \text{where} \quad \underbrace{\forall_{x \in \eta(V)} |(x,y) \in \bar{V}| = 1}_{\text{exactly one value for each variable}}$$

The name of each variable is a 2-tuple ($x \in \mathbb{N} \times \mathbb{N}$) identifying the network adaptor and the local variable. The value y of the variable is an element of the variable domain.

In addition, we can also define the local variables state $\bar{R}$ of a single network adaptor, where each variable name is a natural number ($x \in \mathbb{N}$).

$$\bar{R} \subset \{(x,y) | \exists (a,b) \in R \text{ with } a = x \wedge y \in b\} \quad \text{where} \quad \underbrace{\forall_{x \in \eta(R)} |(x,y) \in \bar{R}| = 1}_{\text{exactly one value for each variable}}$$

Port State. The port state consists of the state of the state ports ($\bar{M}^{(tt)}$) and the state of the event ports ($\bar{M}^{(et)}$). Each element of the port state ($\bar{M}^{(tt)}$ and $\bar{M}^{(et)}$) is a 5-tuple $< x, y, z, l, t >$, where x is a message name, y is a variable name, z is a value, l is the number of queued elements, and t is the global point in time of the last update.

Formally, we can define the state of event and state ports as follows:

$$\bar{M}^{(tt)} \subset \{(x,y,z,1,t) | \exists (u,v,p,n,d,\tau) \in M, \exists (a,b) \in V \text{ with } x = u \wedge y \in v \wedge y = a \wedge z \in b \wedge p = \text{TT}, t \in \mathbb{N}\}$$
$$\bar{M}^{(et)} \subset \{(x,y,z,l,0) | \exists (u,v,p,n,d,\tau) \in M, \exists (a,b) \in V \text{ with } x = u \wedge y \in v \wedge y = a \wedge z \in b^n \wedge p = \text{ET} \wedge l \in \{0, 1, ..., n\}\}$$

For state ports, the queue length in the 5-tuple is always 1, because state ports provide no message queues. The value z of a constituting variable v of a message u is an element of the variable's domain b. For event ports, l is the actual number of messages and must be smaller or equal to the maximum queue length. The value z is an element of the Cartesian power b^n of the domain b over the maximum queue length n. We model the queue at an event port as a vector of dimension n, where the first vector element represents the most recently enqueued message.

The port state needs to assign exactly one value to each constituting variable of a message. In order to express this property, we demand that the following constraint holds:

$$\bigvee_{(x,y)\in S_{msg}} \left|(x_1, y_1, z_1, l_1, t_1)\in \bar{M}^{(tt)} \text{ with } x_1 = x \wedge y_1 = y\right| + \left|(x_2, y_2, z_2, l_2, t_2)\in \bar{M}^{(et)} \text{ with } x_2 = x \wedge y_2 = y\right| = 1$$

$$S_{msg} = \{(x,y)|(u,v,p,n,d,\tau)\in M \wedge u = x \wedge v = y\}$$

Repository State. The repository state encompasses the state of convertible elements with state information ($\bar{C}^{(tt)}$) and the state of convertible elements with event information ($\bar{C}^{(et)}$). For each convertible element the repository state ($\bar{C}^{(tt)}$ and $\bar{C}^{(et)}$) contains a 6-tuple $< x, y, z, l, t, r >$, where x is a convertible element name, y is a variable name, z is a value, l is the number of queued elements, t is the global point in time of the last update, and r is the number of update request indications.

Formally, we can define the repository state as follows:

$$\bar{C}^{(tt)} \subset \{(x,y,z,1,t,0)|\exists(u,v,p,n,d)\in C, \exists(a,b)\in V \text{ with } x = u \wedge y \in v \wedge y = a \wedge z \in b \wedge p = \text{TT}, t \in \mathbb{N}\}$$

$$\bar{C}^{(et)} \subset \{(x,y,z,l,0,r)|\exists(u,v,p,n,d)\in C, \exists(a,b)\in V \text{ with } x = u \wedge y \in v \wedge y = a \wedge z \in b^n \wedge p = \text{ET} \wedge l \in \{0,1,...,n\}, r \in \mathbb{N}\}$$

For the convertible element with event information, l is the actual number of convertible elements in the queue, b^n is the Cartesian power of the domain b over the maximum queue length n, and r is the number of requested convertible elements.

The repository state needs to assign exactly one value to each combination of convertible element name and variable name. In order to express this property, we demand that the following constraint holds:

$$\bigvee_{(x,y)\in S_{msg}} \left|(x_1, y_1, z_1, l_1, t_1)\in \bar{M}^{(tt)} \text{ with } x_1 = x \wedge y_1 = y\right| + \left|(x_2, y_2, z_2, l_2, t_2)\in \bar{M}^{(et)} \text{ with } x_2 = x \wedge y_2 = y\right| = 1$$

$$S_{msg} = \{(x,y)|(u,v,p,n,d,\tau)\in M \wedge u = x \wedge v = y\}$$

Clock State. At any specific time, the clock state consists of the values of all clock variables.

$$\bar{Y} \subset \{(x,y)|x \in Y, y \in \mathbb{N}\} \quad \text{where} \quad \underbrace{\bigvee_{x\in Y} |(x,y)\in \bar{Y}| = 1}_{\text{exactly one value for each clock}}$$

3.4 Formal Definition of Gateway Execution

In the execution of a gateway, we can distinguish two types of transitions, namely *timed transitions* and *untimed transitions*. In the following these two types of transitions and the sequence of their execution will be explained.

Timed Transitions. During the execution of a timed transition, a tick of the global time base elapses. The time progress of one tick is reflected by incrementing the clock variables by a value of one, while the variables state, port state, and repository state remain unchanged. Formally, a *timed transition* $\bar{Z}_i \xrightarrow{T} \bar{Z}_{i+1}$ is defined as follows:

$$\bar{Z}_i = \left\langle t_i, \bar{V}_i, \bar{M}_i^{(tt)}, \bar{M}_i^{(et)}, \bar{C}_i^{(tt)}, \bar{C}_i^{(et)}, \bar{Y}_i \right\rangle,$$

$$\bar{Z}_{i+1} = \left\langle t_{i+1}, \bar{V}_{i+1}, \bar{M}_{i+1}^{(tt)}, \bar{M}_{i+1}^{(et)}, \bar{C}_{i+1}^{(tt)}, \bar{C}_{i+1}^{(et)}, \bar{Y}_{i+1} \right\rangle$$

$$t_{i+1} = t_i + 1, \bar{V}_{i+1} = \bar{V}_i, \bar{M}_{i+1}^{(tt)} = \bar{M}_i^{(tt)}, \bar{M}_{i+1}^{(et)} = \bar{M}_i^{(tt)}, \bar{C}_{i+1}^{(tt)} = \bar{C}_i^{(tt)}, \bar{C}_{i+1}^{(et)} = \bar{C}_i^{(tt)}$$

$$\bar{Y}_i = \{\{x_1, y_1\}, \{x_2, y_2\}, ...\}, \bar{Y}_{i+1} = \{\{x_1, y_1 + 1\}, \{x_2, y_2 + 1\}, ...\}$$

Untimed Transitions. The execution of untimed transitions is instantaneous. During an untimed transition $\bar{Z}_i \xrightarrow[A]{I,O} \bar{Z}_{i+1}$ a network adaptor A processes input (i. e., incoming messages I and outgoing messages O at ports) and executes assignment and communication actions. Like a timed transition, an *untimed transition* $\bar{Z}_i \xrightarrow[A]{I,O} \bar{Z}_{i+1}$ links a source state $\bar{Z}_i$ with a target state $\bar{Z}_{i+1}$:

$$\bar{Z}_i = \left\langle t_i, \bar{V}_i, \bar{M}_i^{(tt)}, \bar{M}_i^{(et)}, \bar{C}_i^{(tt)}, \bar{C}_i^{(et)}, \bar{Y}_i \right\rangle,$$

$$\bar{Z}_{i+1} = \left\langle t_{i+1}, \bar{V}_{i+1}, \bar{M}_{i+1}^{(tt)}, \bar{M}_{i+1}^{(et)}, \bar{C}_{i+1}^{(tt)}, \bar{C}_{i+1}^{(et)}, \bar{Y}_{i+1} \right\rangle$$

As described in Section 2, ports are the interface between the gateway and the networks. Consequently, both the gateway and the networks can cause changes to the port state. The effects on the port state due to networks are captured by the sets I and O:

$$I = \{(u_1, v_1, z_1), (u_2, v_2, z_2), \ldots \mid \underset{j=1,2,\ldots}{\forall} \; : \; u_j \in \eta(M) \wedge \exists(a,b) \in V \text{ with } a = v_j \wedge z_j \in b\}$$

$$O = \{(u_1, v_1), (u_2, v_2), \ldots \mid \underset{j=1,2,\ldots}{\forall} \; : \; u_j \in \eta(M) \wedge v_j \in \eta(V)\}$$

$$\eta(M) = \{u | \exists(u, v, p, n, d, \tau) \in M\}$$

The set I contains tuples each with a message name, a variable name and a value of the respective value domain. The value is used to perform an update-in-place of the message at a state port or to enqueue a message at an event port. The set O contains only message and variable names, which are used to dequeue messages at event ports. $\eta(M)$ is the set of all message names.

The update of the port state is defined below. The new state of a state port is the union of the unmodified ports (i. e., no update by the gateway or a network) and the ports with updated messages (i. e., either through the network or through the communication action of a network adaptor). In case of an update-in-place of the port, the most recent update instant is equal to the current global time t.

$$\bar{M}_{i+1}^{(tt)} = \underbrace{\{(x,y,z,l,t') \in \bar{M}_i^{(tt)} \mid x \notin M_{out} \wedge \not\exists(u,v,b) \in I \text{ with } u = x\}}_{\text{neither send operation nor update of port through communication system}} \cup$$

$$\underbrace{\{(x,y,z,l,t'') \mid t'' = t \wedge (x,y,z',l,t') \in \bar{M}_i^{(tt)} \wedge \exists(u,v,b) \in I \text{ with } u = x \wedge y = v \wedge z = b\}}_{\text{communication system delivers msg. to port}} \cup$$

$$\underbrace{\{(x,y,z,l,t'') \mid t'' = t \wedge (x,y,z',l,t') \in \bar{M}_i^{(tt)} \wedge x \in M_{out} \wedge \exists(i,j) \in \bar{V}_{i+1} \wedge i = y \wedge z = j\}}_{\text{value of a variable is copied as part of a send operation of a state message}}$$

In analogy, the new state of an event port is the union of the unmodified ports and the ports with enqueued or dequeued messages.

$$\bar{M}_{i+1}^{(et)} = \underbrace{\{(x,y,z,l,0) \mid ((x,y,z',l',0) \in \bar{M}_i^{(et)} \wedge \exists(u,v,b) \in I \text{ with } u = x \wedge v = y \wedge (x,y,z,l,0) = enqueue(x,y,z',l',0,b))\}}_{\text{communication system delivers event message to port}} \cup$$

$$\underbrace{\{(x,y,z,l,0) \mid (x,y,z',l',0) \in \bar{M}_i^{(et)} \wedge (u,v) \in O \wedge u = x \wedge v = y \wedge l = l'-1\}}_{\text{communication system retrieves event message from port}} \cup$$

$$\underbrace{\{(x,y,z,l,0) \mid (x,y,z',l',0) \in \bar{M}_i^{(et)} \wedge x \in M_{out} \wedge \exists(i,j) \in \bar{V}_{i+1} \wedge i = y \wedge (x,y,z,l,0) = enqueue(x,y,z',l',0,j)\}}_{\text{send operation of an event message}} \cup$$

$$\underbrace{\{(x,y,z,l,0) \mid (x,y,z',l',0) \in \bar{M}_i^{(et)} \wedge x \in M_{in} \wedge l = l'-1\}}_{\text{receive operation of an event message}} \cup$$

$$\underbrace{\{(x,y,z,l,0) \in \bar{M}_i^{(et)} \mid x \notin M_{out} \wedge x \notin M_{in} \wedge (x,y) \notin O \wedge \not\exists(u,v,b) \in I \text{ with } u = x \wedge v = y\}}_{\text{neither send operation, receive operation, nor update of port through communication system}}$$

Networks can deliver messages to a port, thereby adding another queue element (first line in the definition of $\bar{M}_{i+1}^{(et)}$). Also, networks can retrieve a message from a port, thus leading to the removal of a message from the queue (second line in the definition). Furthermore, the addition or removal of messages can occur through the send and receive operations within the communication action (lines 3 and 4 in the definition).

In the definition of the port state update, we use a supporting function $enqueue$, which inserts an additional message at the queue of an event port. The message queue of an event port with a maximum length of n is represented as a vector of size n. $enqueue$ rotates all messages in this queue using a matrix multiplication of the vector. Subsequently, the new message is inserted at position 1 of the vector.

$$enqueue(x, y, z, l, n, d) = (x, y, z', l', d) \text{ where } l' = l+1 \wedge z' = z \cdot \begin{pmatrix} 0 & 0 & \cdots & 0 & 0 \\ 1 & 0 & \cdots & 0 & 0 \\ 0 & 1 & & \vdots & \vdots \\ & & & & \\ 0 & 0 & \ddots & 0 & 0 \\ 0 & 0 & \cdots & 1 & 0 \end{pmatrix} + \begin{pmatrix} n \\ 0 \\ 0 \\ \vdots \\ 0 \end{pmatrix}$$

The update of the gateway repository state is similar to the update of the port state. However, the union contains only the unmodified convertible elements and the convertible elements altered by the communication actions. Unlike the ports, the gateway repository is only accessed by the gateway (and not by the networks). In case of an update-in-place, the most recent update instant t'' of the convertible element is set to the current global time t.

$$\bar{C}_{i+1}^{(tt)} = \underbrace{\{(x,y,z,l,t') \in \bar{C}_i^{(tt)} \mid x \notin C_{out}\}}_{\text{no push operation (state information)}} \cup \underbrace{\{(x,y,z,l,t'') \mid t'' = t \wedge (x,y,z',l,t') \in \bar{C}_i^{(tt)} \wedge x \in C_{out} \wedge \exists (i,j) \in \bar{V}_{i+1} \wedge i = y \wedge j = z\}}_{\text{variable is copied as part of a push operation of a convertible element with state information}}$$

$$\bar{C}_{i+1}^{(et)} = \underbrace{\{(x,y,z,l,0) \mid (x,y,z',l',0) \in \bar{C}_i^{(et)} \wedge x \in C_{out} \wedge \exists (i,j) \in \bar{V}_{i+1} \wedge i = y \wedge (x,y,z,l,0) = enqueue(x,y,z',l',0,j)\}}_{\text{push operation of a convertible element with event information}} \cup$$

$$\underbrace{\{(x,y,z,l,0) \in \bar{C}_i^{(et)} \mid x \notin C_{in}\} \cup \{(x,y,z,l,0) \mid (x,y,z',l',0) \in \bar{C}_i^{(et)} \wedge x \in C_{in} \wedge l = l'-1\}}_{\text{pull operation of a convertible element with event information}} \cup$$

$$\underbrace{\{(x,y,z,l,0) \in \bar{C}_i^{(et)} \mid x \in C_{out} \wedge x \notin C_{in}\}}_{\text{neither push nor pull (event information)}}$$

The new variables state is the union of the variables which remain unchanged by communication actions, the variables which are assigned a new value through a pull operation (i. e., new value from the gateway repository), and the variables which are assigned a new value through a receive operation (i. e., new value from a port). In the definition of the variables state, we use a supporting function $front$, which yields the first element in the queue of a port or a convertible element in the gateway repository.

$$front(z, l, n) = z \cdot e_l \text{ where } e_l \text{ is the canonical unit vector of dimension } n$$

$$e_1 = \begin{pmatrix} 1 & 0 & 0 & \cdots & 0 \end{pmatrix}^T, \; e_2 = \begin{pmatrix} 0 & 1 & 0 & \cdots & 0 \end{pmatrix}^T, \; e_n = \begin{pmatrix} 0 & 0 & 0 & \cdots & 1 \end{pmatrix}^T$$

Finally, the global time and the clock state of an untimed transition remain unchanged (i. e., $\bar{Y}_{i+1} = \bar{Y}_i$, $t_{i+1} = t_i$).

Sequence of Timed and Untimed Transitions. A gateway contains an ordered set of network adaptors. The execution of the network adaptors occurs in cycles. Starting with the first network adaptor, untimed transitions are taken as long as guards Φ of the first network adaptor are fulfilled. When no guard is satisfied any more, the execution proceeds with the second network adaptor. A cycle terminates with the last network adaptor when no more untimed transitions of the last network adaptor can be executed, because no guard is satisfied. At this point, a timed transition is taken advancing the value of all clock variables by 1. Subsequently, the next cycle starts with the execution of untimed transitions of the first network adaptor.

$$\bar{V}_{i+1} = \{(i,j) \mid (i,j) \in \underbrace{\alpha(\bar{Z}_i)}_{\substack{\text{variables after}\\\text{assignment}}} \wedge \underbrace{\not\exists (u,v,p,n,d) \in C \text{ with } (i \in v \wedge u \in C_{in})}_{\text{no pull operation operation affecting this variable}} \wedge \underbrace{\not\exists (u,v,p,n,d,\tau) \in M \text{ with } (i \in v \wedge u \in M_{in})}_{\text{no receive operation operation affecting this variable}} \} \cup$$

$$(i,j) \mid (i,j') \in \underbrace{\alpha(\bar{Z}_i)}_{\substack{\text{variables after}\\\text{assignment}}} \wedge \underbrace{\exists (u,v,p,n,d) \in C \text{ with } (i \in v \wedge u \in C_{in})}_{\text{pull operation affecting this variable}} \wedge \underbrace{(x,y,z,l,t,r) \in \bar{C}_i^{(st)} \wedge x = u \wedge y = i \wedge j = z}_{\substack{\text{value } z \text{ of state-conv.elem. read from the gateway repository}\\\text{and used as new value } j \text{ of the variable } i}} \cup$$

$$(i,j) \mid (i,j') \in \underbrace{\alpha(\bar{Z}_i)}_{\substack{\text{variables after}\\\text{assignment}}} \wedge \underbrace{\exists (u,v,p,n,d) \in C \text{ with } (i \in v \wedge u \in C_{in})}_{\text{pull operation affecting this variable}} \wedge \underbrace{(x,y,z,l,t,r) \in \bar{C}_i^{(et)} \wedge x = u \wedge y = i \wedge j = front(z,l,n)}_{\substack{\text{value } z \text{ of event-conv.elem. read from the gateway repository}\\\text{and used as new value } j \text{ of the variable } i}} \} \cup$$

$$(i,j) \mid (i,j') \in \underbrace{\alpha(\bar{Z}_i)}_{\substack{\text{variables after}\\\text{assignment}}} \wedge \underbrace{\exists (u,v,p,n,d,\tau) \in M \text{ with } (i \in v \wedge u \in M_{in})}_{\text{receive operation affecting this variable}} \wedge \underbrace{(x,y,z,l,t) \in \bar{M}_i^{(st)} \wedge x = u \wedge y = i \wedge j = \tau(z)}_{\substack{\text{value } z \text{ of state msg. read from the port}\\\text{and used as new value } j \text{ of the variable } i}} \} \cup$$

$$(i,j) \mid (i,j') \in \underbrace{\alpha(\bar{Z}_i)}_{\substack{\text{variables after}\\\text{assignment}}} \wedge \underbrace{\exists (u,v,p,n,d,\tau) \in M \text{ with } (i \in v \wedge u \in M_{in})}_{\text{receive operation affecting this variable}} \wedge \underbrace{(x,y,z,l,t) \in \bar{M}_i^{(et)} \wedge x = u \wedge y = i \wedge j = \tau(front(z,l,n))}_{\substack{\text{value } z \text{ of event msg. read from the port}\\\text{and used as new value } j \text{ of the variable } i}} \}$$

$$\bar{Z}_k \xrightarrow[A_0]{I_k,O_k} \bar{Z}_{k+1} \xrightarrow[A_0]{I_{k+1},O_{k+1}} \cdots \xrightarrow[A_0]{I_{l-1},O_{l-1}} \bar{Z}_l \xrightarrow[A_1]{I_l,O_l} \bar{Z}_{l+1} \xrightarrow[A_1]{I_{l+1},O_{l+1}} \cdots \xrightarrow[A_1]{I_{m-1},O_{m-1}} \bar{Z}_m \xrightarrow[A_2]{I_m,O_m} \cdots \bar{Z}_n \xrightarrow[A_x]{I_n,O_n} \bar{Z}_{n+1} \xrightarrow[A_x]{I_{n+1},O_{n+1}} \cdots \xrightarrow[A_x]{I_{o-1},O_{o-1}} \bar{Z}_o \xrightarrow{T} \bar{Z}_{o+1} \xrightarrow[A_0]{I_o,O_o} \bar{Z}_{o+1} \xrightarrow[A_0]{I_{o+1},O_{o+1}} \xrightarrow[A_0]{I_p,O_p} \cdots$$

guard of network adaptor A_0 is enabled · guard of network adaptor A_1 is enabled · guard of network adaptor A_x is enabled · timed transition · guard of network adaptor A_0 is enabled

transitions of all network adaptors $A_0...A_x$ of the gateway

4 Model-Based Generation of Gateways

Based on the introduced formal specification of the gateway, we have realized a tool for automatic code generation of gateways in a prototype implementation of the DE-COS architecture [12,13]. The protoype implementation consists of five nodes interconnected by the Time-Triggered Protocol (TTP) [14], a cluster with three nodes interconnected by the Controller Area Network (CAN), and a cluster with three nodes interconnected by the Local Interconnect Network (LIN). The gateways execute within the TTP nodes, each of which is a multiprocessor node consisting of a connector unit and two application computers.

The purpose of the connector unit is the implementation of the time-triggered communication protocol for the physical network. The connector unit provides the application computers with a global time base and supports the periodic exchange of state messages at a priori specified global points in time. The connector unit contains a TTP communication controller and is realized using a single board computer equipped with a MPC855 PowerPC from Freescale.

The application computers host the application software (i. e., jobs belonging to one or more DASs) in conjunction with the gateways. Each application computer is implemented on a Soekris net4521 embedded computer from Soekris Engineering[1], which

---

[1] www.soekris.com

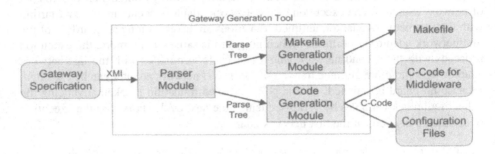

Fig. 2. Overview of Gateway Generation Tool

is based on a 133 MHz 486 class ElanSC520 processor from AMD. We deploy on all application computers the real-time Linux variant LXRT/RTAI [15] extended by a time-triggered scheduler [12] as the operating system. Time-triggered LXRT/RTAI tasks are used both for executing the jobs containing the application code, as well as for the middleware implementing the gateways.

As an input, the code generation tool uses an instance of a UML meta-model that has been derived from the formal definition of a gateway in Section 3. UML was selected for the code generator due to the availability of code libraries (e. g., for parsing and checking compliance to the meta-model) that have eased the implementation of the code generation tool. In addition, a wide range of supporting tools (e. g., editors for creating UML models) can be used for creating gateway specification models.

Both the code for the network adaptors and configuration data structures are automatically generated from the gateway specification model using a *gateway generation tool*. The tool is based on the XML C parser toolkit developed for the Gnome project. It takes as input an XML Metadata Interchange (XMI) representation of the gateway specification UML model. The output of the code generation tool are C source files with code for the network adaptors and configuration data structures.

Figure 2 depicts the structure of the gateway generation tool. The parser module processes the XMI input and builds a parse tree in memory. The parse tree is used for producing code for the gateway middleware, as well as for constructing a makefile.

5   Discussion

The use of gateways for the interconnection of networks with different communication protocols is an important problem that has received much attention in previous work. Many authors have focused on formal specifications based on communicating finite state machines. This paper describes a novel solution for the specification of gateways based on a real-time database in-between the interconnected networks. The real-time database stores temporally accurate real-time images in conjunction with meta information (e. g., instant of most recent update, information w.r.t. to update requests). The major benefit of the real-time database is the ability for a constructive realization of gateways in distributed real-time systems. Large, complex gateways can be divided into smaller modules, which are not only simpler but facilitate reuse and localize changes. For each network, developers can independently specify which messages update the real-time database and which messages are sent with the information from the real-time database. The introduced state machines with timing constraints provide a powerful and intuitive formalism for this task. They enable developers to specify the protocols for accessing specific networks along with the corresponding syntax and naming transformations.

Acknowledgments

This work has been supported in part by the European IST project ARTIST2 under project No. IST-004527.

References

1. Simon, H.A.: The Sciences of the Artificial. MIT Press, Cambridge (1996)
2. Leen, G., Heffernan, D.: Expanding automotive electronic systems. Computer 35(1), 88–93 (2002)
3. Gmbh, R.B.: Stuttgart, Germany. CAN Specification, Version 2.0 (1991)
4. FlexRay Consortium. BMW AG, DaimlerChrysler AG, General Motors Corporation, Freescale GmbH, Philips GmbH, Robert Bosch GmbH, and Volkswagen AG. FlexRay Communications System Protocol Specification Version 2.0 (July 2004)
5. Obermaisser, R.: A model-driven framework for the generation of gateways in distributed real-time systems. In: Proc. of the 28th IEEE Real-Time Systems Symposium, Tucson, Arizona, USA (September 2007)
6. Obermaisser, R., Peti, P., Huber, B., El Salloum, C.: DECOS: An integrated time-triggered architecture. e&i journal (journal of the Austrian professional institution for electrical and information engineering) 3, 83–95 (2006), http://www.springerlink.com
7. Kopetz, H.: Real-Time Systems, Design Principles for Distributed Embedded Applications. Kluwer Academic Publishers, Dordrecht (1997)
8. Alur, R.: Timed automata. In: Halbwachs, N., Peled, D.A. (eds.) CAV 1999. LNCS, vol. 1633, pp. 8–22. Springer, Heidelberg (1999)
9. Dutertre, B., Sorea, M.: Modeling and verification of a fault-tolerant real-time startup protocol using calendar automata. In: Lakhnech, Y., Yovine, S. (eds.) FORMATS 2004 and FTRTFT 2004. LNCS, vol. 3253, pp. 199–214. Springer, Heidelberg (2004)
10. Krcal, P., Mokrushin, L., Thiagarajan, P.S., Yi, W.: Timed vs time-triggered automata. In: Proc. of the 15th International Conference on Concurrency Theory (September 2004)
11. Kopetz, H., Kim, K.H.: Temporal uncertainties in interactions among real-time objects. In: Proc. of Ninth Symposium on Reliable Distributed Systems, Huntsville, AL,USA, October 1990, pp. 165–174 (1990)
12. Huber, B., Peti, P., Obermaisser, R., El Salloum, C.: Using RTAI/LXRT for partitioning in a prototype implementation of the DECOS architecture. In: Proc. of the Third Int. Workshop on Intelligent Solutions in Embedded Systems (May 2005)
13. Obermaisser, R., Peti, P.: Realization of virtual networks in the decos integrated architecture. In: Proc. of the 14th Int. Workshop on Parallel and Distributed Real-Time Systems (April 2006)
14. Time-Triggered Protocol TTP/C – High Level Specification Document (July 2002)
15. Beal, D., et al.: RTAI: Real-Time Application Interface. Linux Journal (April 2000)

Model-Integrated Development of Cyber-Physical Systems

Gabor Karsai and Janos Sztipanovits

Institute for Software-Integrated Systems
Vanderbilt University
Nashville, TN 37205, USA
gabor.karsai@vanderbilt.edu, janos.sztipanovits@vanderbilt.edu

Abstract. Cyber-physical systems represent a new class of systems that integrate physics with computation. Their correct design is frequently of great importance as they are applied in safety- or business-critical contexts. This paper introduces a model-integrated development approach that addresses the development needs of such systems through the pervasive use of models. A complete model-based view is proposed that covers all aspects of the hardware and software components, as well as their interactions. Early experiments and work in progress are also reported.

Keywords: model-driven development, model-integrated computing, cyber-physical systems, executable models, system integration.

1 Introduction

Cyber-physical systems (CPS) are systems that combine a physical system with an embedded information processing system such that the resulting system has novel capabilities that could not be achieved by either the physical or the computational entity alone[1]. To give examples for a cyber-physical system consider an unmanned aerial vehicle with active (fixed) wings. In such a UAV, an embedded controller monitors the airflow over the wing surface and modulates it through electromechanical actuators to ensure laminar flow such that the vehicle is capable of extreme maneuvers. Another example is a structural beam whose deflection is active monitored and modified through a piezoelectric actuator, resulting in a lighter, thinner structure whose resulting physical properties ('strength') is greater than that of the original beam without the embedded controller.

It is easy to see that the design of such systems cannot be accomplished following the classical strictly disciplinary approach – the design of the physical and computational aspects is an integrated activity. Design decisions made in one aspect (e.g. selecting the scheduling technique used in the embedded software) interacts with the physical component and has profound consequences on the dynamic properties of the entire system. We argue that the design of such systems could only be accomplished by taking an integrated view and co-designing the physical with the computational.

---

[1] This definition of cyber-physical systems is due to Janos Sztipanovits.

U. Brinkschulte, T. Givargis, and S. Russo (Eds.): SEUS 2008, LNCS 5287, pp. 46–54, 2008.
© IFIP International Federation for Information Processing 2008

Model-driven development of embedded software systems [1] has gained acceptance during the past decade, and it is the de-facto approach used in systems industries (automotive and aerospace), and is well-supported by industrial-strength commercial tools, like Simulink/Stateflow [2] and Matrix-X [3]. Benefits of the model-driven approach are obvious, and the industry has built up a significant amount of knowledge and well-tested solutions.

The question naturally arises: are cyber-physical systems fundamentally different such that they need a different development approach, or the current approach is sufficient and no new research is necessary? In this paper we propose an answer to this question that is based on experience with the existing tools and practices, and the proposed answer is: we need new techniques, and a new view.

Our argument is as follows. The engineering of non-software artifacts is often based on models that typically have a computational manifestation (i.e. an executable form in some computational sense). The engineering of software using model-based techniques is an active area of research and it started to find its way into the overall software engineering practice. However, very little is being done with regard to an *integrated* approach, where both the 'physical artifacts' and the software would be engineered based on a set of coupled models. The closest practice comes to this ideal is the approach followed in Simulink/Stateflow and Matrix-X: 'plant models' and executable controller models are (co-)simulated in a shared simulation environment, under the control of a simulation engine. The approach increases the productivity of domain (in this case, control) engineers, because they don't have to deal with the accidental complexities of software engineering, and the tools (and the hardware platforms) are powerful enough such that code automatically generated could be immediately used in the application.

However, we believe this is not sufficient for the next generation of CPS-s. First, the approach does not consider the properties of the execution platforms (i.e. the properties and performance of processing units, the operating systems, the middleware, the QoS machinery, etc.). Although new tools like TrueTime [4] make progress in this direction, it is unclear how arbitrary platforms should be modeled and analyzed. Second, the Model of Computation (MoC) [5] used by the tools is rather limited: it is almost always some variant of the approach followed in the synchronous languages. Other approaches, like CDMA-style communication, or publish-subscribe approaches, or even priority based scheduling with potential priority inversion are rarely considered. Third, it is unclear how algorithms that apply search, do not have a guaranteed termination time, or are of the anytime variety could be considered in the systems. We simply don't have good models of the dynamics for such algorithms, and thus the analysis of the end-to-end system is very difficult to do.

In an engineering process for CPS-s we need to address the above and other issues related to para-functional properties like security, reliability, fault tolerance, etc. Modern development techniques, like extreme programming, test-based development, and continuous integration also need to be considered, as these represent the best practices in the industry today – and their track record is well-documented. In the paper we propose a fully model-integrated approach that allows the combined use of such techniques.

2 Models and Cyber-Physical Systems

If one needs to consider a full spectrum modeling for CPS-s, a scheme shown on the figure below could be used as a starting point. On the left we show the 'model elements', on the right their 'real world' counterparts are shown that exists in the implementation.

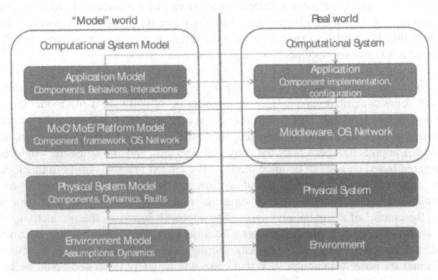

Fig. 1. Models and the real world in Cyber-Physical Systems

Note that the 'real world' includes the 'application software' as implemented on some computation platform (that includes the component middleware, operating system, compute engines, network), that is layered upon and interacts with a physical system (the 'hardware' of the CPS), which then interacts with the physical environment. What is envisioned here is a complete model-integrated approach across all levels of the hierarchy. In short, one needs models for the environment (that is outside of the CPS), for the physical system (that is part of the CPS but is not computational), for the computational platform (that includes all hardware and software elements that are reusable across different CPS-s), and for the application (i.e. the software that implements all the functions of the CPS).

As we assume model-driven development, orthogonal to the models we find the tools that support modeling (i.e. model creation and editing), model analysis (i.e. verification, validation, etc.) and synthesis (i.e. implementation generation). There are various tools in existence today that address some of the problems here (e.g. dedicated modeling environments, code generators, code verification tools), but they are often difficult to use together, in an integrated manner. For CPS-s better tool integration is needed that is based on the semantic integration of the models used across the layers. After all, we need to model a physical system's dynamics, and study how it interacts with the dynamics of the implementation of a particular MoC on a specific hardware and software platform.

2.1 Challenges in CPS

Developers of CPSs face several challenges, many of which are well-known from the work on embedded systems. Here we would like to highlight a few challenging aspects that arguably have received less attention in the past.

First, CPSs imply a major *integration problem*. Both the system that is being built, as well as the process used to build it are highly heterogeneous and unforeseen interactions often arise. There are two major perspectives on integration: model integration and system integration.

Model integration problems arise when we want to simulate, for instance, the entire CPS, including all implementation layers. One needs simulators that (1) either follow the same, shared execution semantics (which seems to be the approach used in Simulink where all simulations are executed in continuous time), or (2) they are federated and can run under the control of a coordinating authority (which is the approach followed in the HLA model). The situation is further complicated by the fact that models are often on different levels of abstraction, and one needs different models of the same system for different work (e.g. transaction level models vs. register transfer level models for hardware). Another problem in model integration is the decoupling between models used in design, the model verification tools, and the final executable system. When subjecting design models to analysis (e.g. model checking), we need to carry over the results to the final system, i.e. the system as implemented by executable code running on a real, physical software and hardware platform. Often design languages (e.g. UML activity diagrams) and analysis languages (e.g. SMV model checker's language) are different, and we need to use translators. However these translators must be correct for the analysis results be valid. We need this triangle of design models / analysis models / executable models 'verified' such that analysis results are provably true for the executable system.

System integration is perhaps the most challenging aspect of CPS engineering, but arguably, this is the area where models are extremely beneficial. The physical and the computational parts of the CPS have to be designed together, and should be modeled and analyzed together. Note that this is notably different from hardware-software codesign, where functions are designed in a common framework, and where the partitioning is decided late in the process. In CPSs the 'hardware' is not computational and thus it is fixed early on, such that the computational part has to be designed accordingly. Naturally, codesign techniques are highly applicable to the design of the 'cyber' part. As discussed in more detail below, for the system integration we envision an incremental, simulation-based development and integration approach. The concept is that initially the entire system is executed in a simulated environment, and later simulated parts are incrementally replaced by real implementations and real hardware.

The second major challenge is the *support for certification* of CPSs that are used in critical environments (e.g. vehicles, medical systems, etc.). Note that we need end-to-end certification, according to current practices followed in the aerospace industry ('we certify the airplane, not the software'). However, this approach becomes very hard to sustain, and a modular approach is more desirable. One can consider three methods for providing arguments for certification: simulation-based, verification-based, and hardware-based testing. In the first, a high-fidelity simulation of the physical system and environment is created, that is independently validated. Next, the computational 'stack' is subjected to exhaustive testing in the 'context' provided by the simulation. Here, the simulation must be 'interface-compatible' with the real physical system, i.e. the interfaces that the computational system interacts with must be the same as in the real implementation. For the second, verification-based approach we build assurances via checking the models of computational system and/or the code itself. Obviously, this necessitates robust and verified translations on the models, as discussed above. For the third, the computational system is tested in the context of a hardware test setup, and arguments for certification are collected through exhaustive testing again. In summary, when certification is needed for CPSs the development process and tools should incorporate various elements to produce the arguments to be used in the certification process. These steps and tools need to become part of the toolchain.

The third group of challenges includes *mode changes* and *fault management*. CPSs often have a large number of operational modes, where their dynamics and behavior are radically different. For instance an aircraft flies very differently when landing than in cruising mode. The CPS should be prepared to handle and manage these different modes and changes between modes. Often we cannot simply reinitialize software components upon mode changes as this would lead to intolerable transients.

The ultimate test for modal systems is the management of faults. Faults can happen in the physical system, in the platform, as well as in the application software, and the application needs to be prepared for handling them. Obviously, fault needs to be detected, their primary cause isolated, and then a corrective action needs to be taken. This process is traditionally known under the name 'Fault Detection, Isolation, and Recovery', FDIR. A good CPS design is not only a functional design, but it also anticipates faults and has provisions for managing them, through the steps described above. Whenever the CPS is in a critical application, such fault management is unavoidable, and it has to be 'designed in' to the system from the beginning. Fault management may include simply redundancy management (which involves complex mode changes), but could also be as complex that a full FDIR approach is needed. In complex physical systems, continuous on-line testing and verification is often used for FDIR. For CPSs these techniques need to be applied to the software ingredients as well.

2.2 An Approach to Development and Integration

As it was emphasized in the previous section, integration is of utmost importance in CPSs: in fact the definition of this category refers to it. Hence, the integration of the physical and the computational should be *the* key design activity; in fact, it should possibly drive the entire design process.

Here we propose a continuous integration process that establishes the interfaces between the physical and computational from the beginning, and the integration of the system is performed continuously. This approach is not new for software developers: the concept of nightly build and continuous integration is a well-known practice today. Here, we extend this idea in the context of CPSs.

The approach requires some assumptions about the CPS design as follows. We assume that the system is constructed in layers (as shown on the figure below), and for each layer we have models that are executable (perhaps with the help of simulation engine).

The general layers of a CPS include the environment, the physical systems, the coputational platform, and the application. The computational platform interacts with the physical system via sensors and actuators, and the application interacts with the platform via APIs. Note that this is the same organization discussed earlier.

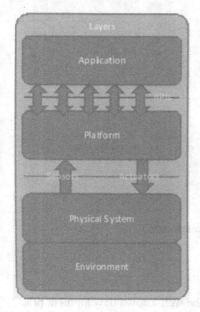

Fig. 2. Layers of CPS design

In the proposed continuous integration approach we assume that models are available for each layer, and these models could be used in an executable form. Initially, these could be low-fidelity, approximate models, that are incrementally replaced by high-fidelity models, and finally with implementations.

The key observation about this approach is that interface and architecture design are primary activities. In fact, architecture modeling and analysis is done early in the design process. Furthermore, interfaces are designed early. As the basic tenet of systems engineering, interfaces are designed first, well-before the system is implemented. In the scheme above this involves at least two essential interfaces: the one between the computational and physical world, and the other one between the application and the platform. Architecture is a primary driver, and it needs to be designed and refined, before the component implementation happens. Architecture models should be preserved and used throughout the development process.

We envision that eventually high-fidelity models of the platform and the physical system are available. While for physical devices this is a well-established practice, for software systems (platforms) this is not always possible, as it could be too expensive to develop. In this situation, the (software) models could be low-fidelity, and they need to be replaced with real implementations as soon as feasible.

The key process element in the above approach is the continuous existence of an executable system, with a concrete architecture, well-defined interfaces, and an executable form. This can give the designers an early feedback about their work, and for the customers the opportunity for early evaluation. The design and implementation evolves from a fully simulated version to a fully implemented version as shown on the figure below.

The development starts with a fully simulated system, then the real computational platform is introduced (as this is the hardest to model and simulate). Note that the real platform should have timing-accurate interfaces towards a (real-time) simulation engine, and functional interfaces towards the simulated application. This step is followed by a step where the real application is run on the real platform, with a simulated physical system and environment, and the final step is the full realization of the real system.

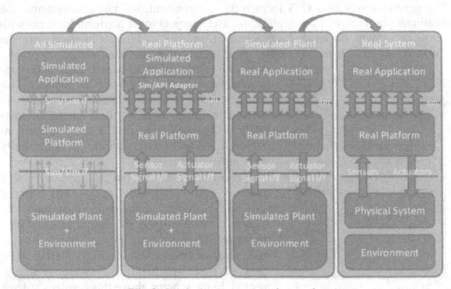

Fig. 3. Continuous concurrent integration

3 Related Work

The approach described above has grown out from the well-known development practices of model-driven development [6,7]. In the various MDD approaches the use of models is pervasive, models are used for 'higher-order', domain-specific programming, for code generation, and for analysis and verification. Our approach uses these techniques and concepts, but it also considers the effects of and the integration with the physical system and the environment.

The use of simulation in developing complex embedded systems is a well-known practice as well [8]. The use of simulations to approximate the behavior of software systems has been proposed in [9]. A key concept for carrying over results from simulations to implementations is 'model continuity' has been proposed in [12]. These techniques provide valuable insights into the simulation-based integration of systems, and technology (e.g. the DEVS-based approach for simulation) for actually time-synchronization and coordination. The proposed approach builds on these foundations, but extends and integrates them with the model-based development framework.

4 Status

We have started work on an integrated toolchain [10][13] that supports the development paradigm outlined above. The toolchain uses Simulink/Stateflow as the primary simulation environment (for fully simulated implementations). The platform modeling aspect is handled with a modified version of the TrueTime package, which allows the co-simulation of controller models, platform models, and physical plant models. The controller models are then imported into our modeling tool that supports a modeling language called EsMoL, which is then used to specify (1) hardware platform models, (2) software component models (whose implementation comes from the Simulink controller models), and (3) deployment models that connect the two. A set of integrated code generator tools produces executable code from the models that could be run either in the Simulink environment, or on a target platform. If the code is run in Simulink, physical plant models and TrueTime platform models could be used to study how the 'real code' runs against a simulated platform and plant. We have two target platforms: one is a TTP/C cluster from TTTech Inc.: a time-triggered platform of four controllers connected via a TTP/C bus running periodically scheduled components; the other one is a software emulation of the TTP/C cluster using Linux nodes connected via an isolated TCP/UDP network. For the latter, we have built a scheduler tool to compute time-triggered scheduled. The code generators produce all the 'wrapping code' needed to run controller code on the platform. The toolsuite also includes interfaces towards verification tools: the code generators produce the code executable code first in an abstract form that could be used to 'print' imperative code. This way the executable code could be subjected to analysis via using a tool like the Java Path Finder (JPF) [14]. Currently we are testing the toolchain on various applications following the development paradigm described.

5 Conclusions

In this paper we have introduced a framework for the design of cyber-physical system that is model-based and places great emphasis on early integration, based on the models. Some elements of the framework are already available (e.g. modeling languages and generators for embedded systems), and technology is available [11] for constructing the rest. Currently we are working on realizing and trying out a toolchain that implements the concepts and architecture described above, and which also integrates code verification tools.

Acknowledgements

This work was sponsored (in part) by the Air Force Office of Scientific Research, USAF, under grant/contract number FA9550-06-0312. The views and conclusions contained herein are those of the authors and should not be interpreted as necessarily representing the official policies or endorsements, either expressed or implied, of the Air Force Office of Scientific Research or the U.S. Government.

References

1. Karsai, G., Sztipanovits, J., Ledeczi, A., Bapty, T.: Model-integrated development of embedded software. Proceedings of the IEEE 91(1), 145–164 (2003)
2. Mathworks, Inc., http://www.mathworks.com
3. National Instruments, http://www.ni.com
4. Cervin, A., Henriksson, D., Lincoln, B., Eker, J., Årzén, K.-E.: How Does Control Timing Affect Performance? IEEE Control Systems Magazine 23(3), 16–30 (2003)

5. Lee, E.A., Sangiovanni-Vincentelli, A.L.: A denotational framework for comparing models of computation. Technical Report UCB/ERL M97/11, EECS Department, University of California, Berkeley (1997)
6. Model-Driven Architecture, http://www.omg.org/mda
7. Model-Integrated Computing,
   http://www.isis.vanderbilt.edu/research/MIC
8. Papp, Z., Dorrepaal, M., Verburg, D.J.: Distributed Hardware-in-the-Loop Simulator for Autonomous Continuous Dynamical Systems with Spatially Constrained Interactions. In: Proceedings of the 17th international Symposium on Parallel and Distributed Processing. IPDPS, April 22 - 26, 2003, vol. 119, p. 1. IEEE Computer Society, Washington (2003)
9. Huang, D., Sarjoughian, H.S.: Software and Simulation Modeling for Real-time Software-intensive System. In: The 8th IEEE International Symposium on Distributed Simulation and Real Time Applications, Budapest, Hungary, October, pp. 196–203.
10. Sztipanovits, J., Karsai, G., Neema, S., Nine, H., Porter, J., Thibodeaux, R., Volgyesi, P.: Towards a Model-based Toolchain for the High-Confidence Design of Embedded Systems. In: Work-in-Progress Workshop at the Real-Time Application Systems conference (2008)
11. Karsai, G., Ledeczi, A., Neema, S., Sztipanovits, J.: The Model-Integrated Computing Toolsuite: Metaprogrammable Tools for Embedded Control System Design. In: IEEE Joint Conference CCA, ISIC and CACSD, Munich, Germany (2006)
12. Hu, X., Zeigler, B.P.: Model continuity in the design of dynamic distributed real-time systems. IEEE Transactions on Systems, Man, and Cybernetics, Part A 35(6), 867–878 (2005)
13. Porter, J., Karsai, G., Volgyesi, P., Nine, H., Humke, P., Hemingway, G., Thibodeaux, R., Sztipanovits, J.: Towards Model-Based Integration of Tools and Techniques for Embedded Control System Design, Verification, and Implementation. In: The Models 2008 workshop on Model Based Architecting and Construction of Embedded Systems (submitted, 2008)
14. Visser, W., Havelund, K., Brat, G., Park, S., Lerda, F.: Model Checking Programs. Automated Software Engineering Journal 10(2) (April 2003)

Towards a Middleware Approach for a Self-configurable Automotive Embedded System

Isabell Jahnich[1], Ina Podolski[1], and Achim Rettberg[2]

[1] University of Paderborn/C-LAB, Germany,
[2] Carl von Ossietzky University Oldenburg, Germany
isabell.jahnich@c-lab.de, ina.podolski@c-lab.de,
achim.rettberg@informatik.uni-oldenburg.de

Abstract. In this paper a middleware architecture for distributed automotive systems that supports self-configuration by dynamic load balancing of tasks is presented. The inclusion of self-configurability is able to offer reliability within the multimedia network of the vehicle (Infotainment). Load balancing of tasks could be applied if an error occurred within the network. The error detection in the network and the load balancing should run automatically. Therefore, the middleware architecture has to deal on one hand with the error detection and on the other hand with the migration of tasks. Additionally, to enable the migration it is important to identify the requirements of all electronic control units (ECU) and tasks within the network.

1 Introduction

Future application scenarios for vehicle electronic systems include on one side the access to mobile devices that build ad-hoc networks with the built-in devices of the vehicle and on the other side the support of robustness, redundancy and dependability within the vehicle network. Modern electronic vehicle networks have to be as flexible as possible to cope the actual requirements. The idea to build up a self-configurable system could help to overcome these requirements. A mobile device could automatically be attached and integrated in the existing system if the system supports self-configurability. If an ECU has a failure all task could be migrated to other ECUs inside the vehicle network by a self-configurable system middleware. Self-configuration could be applied to distributed networks. In modern vehicles three types of networks are built in. That is namely the *Powertrain*, *Body* or *Chasis* and *Infotainment* network. Within the *Powertrain* safety critical tasks like the anti-blocking system and the motor management are located. The *Body* or *Chasis* network contains also critical tasks, but the vehicle will run if a failure occurs. The window opener is a typical task of this network. The *Infotainment* network consists of more or less media based tasks, like the radio or navigation system. Due to safety critical reasons our approach will focus on the *Infotainment* network.

To increase the quality of the vehicle it is important to built in fault-tolerant systems in the network. In a distributed system fault-tolerance can be include in three ways: Replication, redundancy, and diversity. While the former provides multiple

U. Brinkschulte, T. Givargis, and S. Russo (Eds.): SEUS 2008, LNCS 5287, pp. 55–65, 2008.
© IFIP International Federation for Information Processing 2008

identical instances of a system, the tasks and requests are directed to all of them in parallel, and the choosing of the correct result is based on a quorum, redundancy is characterized by multiple identical instances and a switching to one of the remaining instances in case of failure. Diversity provides different implementations of a system that are used like replicated systems.

A self-configurable system is able to provide redundancy, diversity and replication of tasks, therefore, it helps to make the system more stable.

In the context of self-configuration of automotive systems redundancy of data, applications, and tasks can be used to get an increased fault-tolerance in case of ECU failures. Crucial data, applications or tasks are distributed as backup components on the ECUs of the vehicle system that they can be used of or executed by other ECU if their originally ECUs failed.

The way of distribution and the number of replicas and the decision which components are replicated depends on an adequate algorithm. At this costs of replication and migration and load of other ECUs will be considered.

In the following a vehicle middleware architecture is presented that supports self-configuration by load balancing strategies for non-critical tasks within the *Infotainment* network. In our case we enable a dynamic reconfigurable system by load balancing. In existing approaches self-configuration is enabled, by including redundancy and replication of tasks during design time. This is a static system reconfiguration. Furthermore, our middleware offers services to realize a load balancing based on different strategies for the *Infotainment* network. This work is part of the DySCAS project (ref.). The main objective of the DySCAS project is the elaboration of fundamental concepts and architectural guidelines, as well as methods and tools for the development of self-configurable systems in the context of embedded vehicle electronic systems. The reason is the increasing demand on configurational flexibility and scalability of the systems imposed by future applications which will include simultaneous access to a number of mobile devices and ad-hoc networking with the built-in devices.

The rest of the paper is organized as follows: Section 2 will describe the related work in the field of research where our architectural approach is located. As a motivation for this paper Section 3 motivates and describes a use case scenario. Afterwards our middleware architecture is presented, see Section 4. In Section 5 we describe the load balancing strategy we use within the middleware. A short description of the simulation and some early results are discussed in Section 6. We conclude the paper with a summary and give an outlook for future work.

2 Related Work

In this section we will give a short overview of existing load balancing approaches to support self-configuration and on middleware approaches in automotive systems.

There are several publications regarding load balancing and extensive research has been done on static and dynamic strategies and algorithms [6].

On the one hand, load balancing is a topic in the area of parallel and grid computing, where dynamic and static algorithms are used for optimization of the simultaneous task execution on multiple processors. Cybenko addresses the dynamic load balancing for distributed memory multiprocessors [3]. In [5] Hu et. al. regard an optimal dynamic algorithm and Azar discusses on-line load balancing. Moreover Diekmann et. al. differentiate between dynamic and static strategies for distributed memory machines [4]. Heiss and Schmitz introduce the Particle Approach that deals with the problem of mapping tasks to processor nodes at run-time in multiprogrammed multicomputer systems solved by considering tasks as particles acted upon by forces.

All these approaches have the goal of optimizing the load balancing in the area of parallel and grid computing by migrating tasks between different processors, while our approach focuses the direct migration of selected tasks to a newly added resource. Furthermore we regard load balancing that is located on the middleware-layer.

Moreover there are static approaches, like [11], that address a finite set of jobs, operations and machines, while our approach deals with a dynamic set of tasks and processors within the vehicle system.

Balasubramanian, Schmidt, Dowdy, and Othman consider in [7], [9], and [8] middleware load balancing strategies and adaptive load balancing services. They introduce the Cygnus, an adaptive load balancing/monitoring service based on CORBA middleware standard. Their concept is primarily described on the basis of a single centralized server, while decentralized servers that collectively form a single logical *Load Balancer* is not explained in detail.

Moreover the topic of dynamic reconfigurable automotive systems is regarded in [2], [1], [13] and [14]. In the following paragraphs we discuss several middleware approaches for automotive systems.

The Autosar consortium [19] suggested a middleware approach based on a run-time environment (RTE). The RTE is developed to support a common infrastructure for automotive systems. The self-configurability developed in our approach will enrich the Autosar RTE especially by dynamic reconfiguration management through load balancing.

In [15] a formal specification for developing distributed, embedded, real-time control systems is described. The middleware supports dependable, adaptive dynamic resource management based on replicated services.

An additional approach according fault-tolerance and dynamic reconfiguration is discussed in [16]. Again replicated services are used in this model. In [17] a middleware architecture for telematics software based on OSGi and AMI-C specification is presented. An application manager is introduced for telematic applications. The architecture enable in-vehicle terminal to provide various telematics services to increase driver's safety.

The authors of [18] describe trends for automotive systems. They give an overview of requirements for middleware systems in this area. Especially what industry demands for such middleware services. Hiding the distribution and the heterogeneity of such platforms is demanded as well as providing high-level services (e.g. mode and redundancy management) and ensuring QoS.

3 Motivation

In this section we give a motivation for our approach. We identify three use cases:

- Task fails on an ECU and have to migrate to another one
- ECU has a defect - all task will be migrated
- New device is attached to the network

As an example we will use the second use case. If an ECU of the vehicle *Infotainment* system failed, a migration to another ECU within the vehicle that is able to execute the applications or tasks should be possible. Thus it is possible to migrate for example tasks of the ECU with the radio system to the ECU running the navigation system.

After the failure occurred within the vehicle the system starts a self-reconfiguration without avoiding overloading ECUs. The self-reconfiguration is surely based on specific characteristics from the tasks and the ECUs. That means, it has to be ensured that a task could only run on an ECU that is able to execute it.

In consideration of all running processes and the resources situation within the vehicle network appropriate services decide on a possible load balancing according to different strategies and initiate the task migration where required. Thus in our example where an error occurred inside the radio system the appropriate tasks migrate from the radio to the navigation system. Let us assume that the navigation system respectively the ECU is able to run the tasks from the radio system.

4 Proposed Middleware Architecture

To realize the use case scenario (failure in the radio system) described above and other possible services for example device detection a middleware architecture is required that fulfills several requirements. We introduce four sub-modules to handle self-configuration in the middleware. The *Event Management* detects failures in the vehicle network and it is responsible for detection and removal of additional ECUs. Detailed information and capabilities of existing ECUs as well as the registration of newly added devices is realized within the *Device Registration* module. All status information and the resource load of each ECU within the vehicle are stored by the *Resource Management*. Finally, the Load Balancing initiates the task migration based on specific characteristics and requirements of the tasks and ECUs. In the following we give a more detailed view of the middleware.

The operating system builds the interface between the hardware and the middleware (see Figure 1). Additionally, device drivers are necessary for specific hardware parts. The tasks run on top of the middleware. Middleware is a software layer that connects and manages application components running on distributed hosts. It exists between network operating systems and application components. The middleware hides and abstracts many of the complex details of distributed programming from application developers. Specifically, it deals with network communication, coordination, reliability, scalability, and heterogeneity. By virtue of middleware, application developers can be freed from these complexities and can focus on the application's own functional requirements.

Before explaining the design of our automotive middleware and the specific services, we enumerate the five requirements of automotive middleware. These requirements are resource management, fault-tolerance, and specialized communication model for automotive networks, global time base, and resource frugality. These requirements are derived from the distributed, real-time, and mission-critical nature of automotive systems and differentiate automotive middleware from conventional enterprise middleware products.

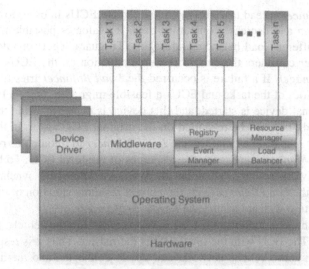

Fig. 1. Self-configurable architecture

A vehicle has a real-time nature. It is a system in which its correctness depends not only on the correctness of the logical result, but also on the result delivery time. Since a vehicle is subject to various timing constraints, every component in a vehicle should be designed in a way that its timing constraints are guaranteed a-priori. At the same time, the timing constraints of a vehicle should be guaranteed in an end-to-end manner since an automobile is a distributed system and its timing constraints are usually specified across several nodes. For example, let us consider a typical timing constraint of an automobile. If pressing a brake pedal is detected at the sensor node, then the brake actuator node must respond to it within 1 ms. To meet this constraint, there must be a global *Resource Manager* that calculates the required amount of resources on each node and actually makes resource reservations to network interface controllers and operating systems on distributed nodes. Automotive middleware is responsible for such resource management.

The middleware in our approach includes four components that offer specific services: *Registry*, *Event Manager*, *Resource Manager* and *Load Balancer*.

The *Event Manager* is responsible for the failure detection and the device discovery. If a failure occurred the Event Manger triggers the *Load Balancer* to initiate a feasible migration of tasks. Additionally, if a new device is added to the automotive system via technologies like Bluetooth or WLAN for example, it is recognized by the *Event Manager* component. Vice versa the *Event Manager* also notices the detaching of the device. In both cases it will inform the *Registry* of the middleware about the availability or the detaching of the additional device.

Existing and new devices are registered and detached devices are unsubscribed within the *Registry* service. During the registration the specific characteristics of the device (like memory, CPU, etc.) are stored within the *Registry*. Due to the distributed system the Registries of each vehicle ECU (Electronic Control Unit) communicate with each other to guarantee that each *Registry* of an ECU knows the actual status of all devices within the network inclusive of the newly added devices.

The *Load Balancer* spread tasks between the vehicle ECUs in order to get optimal resource utilization and decrease computing time. It evaluates possible migration of tasks based on different load balancing strategies. To guarantee a suitable migration the *Load Balancer* considers the current resource situation on the ECUs with aid of the *Resource Manager*. If a failure is occurred the *Load Balancer* tries to find based on the characteristics of the tasks and ECUs a feasible migration. Once a load balancing on an additional device is started, and this device is detached while the migrated tasks are executed, they will be re-started on the original ECU again. In this case the *Event Manager* is responsible to inform the *Load Balancer* to initiate this re-start.

The *Resource Manager* supervises the resources of the local ECU. To be aware of the complete network resource situation all *Resource Manager*s synchronize with each other. Thus the *Load Balancer* gets the current resource situation of the complete vehicle infrastructure with aid of its local *Resource Manager*.

In our approach, the middleware is located on each ECU in the vehicle. Every ECU has a unique ID. The ECU with the lowest ID is the master. Thus it is responsible for the control of the entire vehicle network, and newly connected and the detaching of additional devices are discovered by its *Event Manager*, device information is registered by its *Registry*, and its *Load Balancer* is responsible for the evaluation of the possible migration with the aid of the local *Resource Manager*. If the master ECU fails a new master will be chosen with the aid of the Bully-Algorithm [10].

The failure detection if a node fails will be handled by a hardware interrupt. It initiates an error correction in our middleware. That means, to correct the error, tasks of the omitted node are migrated to other ones, which are able to execute them. In this paper we will not focus on the failure detection but on error correction. Therefore, our middleware must be able to migrate tasks. A detailed knowledge of the task characteristics is needed. It is important to know if it is a real-time task or not.

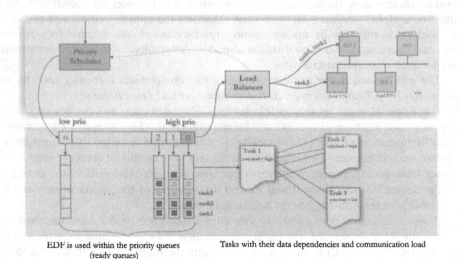

EDF is used within the priority queues   Tasks with their data dependencies and communication load
(ready queues)

Fig. 2. Failure correction handling - the task migration mechanism

Figure 2 presents our approach for task migration. We assume that each task has a priority and we have a detailed knowledge about their hardware requirements. Additionally, the data dependencies between the tasks are known. As we can see from figure 2 we start with a priority scheduler. He will schedule the tasks according their priority in priority queues. That means, we have for each priority an own task queue. Within the queues the tasks are scheduled by a simple earliest deadline first (EDF) scheduler to ensure a flexible schedule [12]. Real-time (RT) tasks have a high priority. The *Load Balancer* works on the priority queues beginning from the queue with the highest up to the lowest priority. For each selected task a possible set of ECUs who are able to execute the task is evaluated. After that a data dependency check will be done. That means, we look at those tasks that interact with the inspected one. In that case the interaction is weak the *Load Balancer* selects an ECU from the previously evaluated set of ECU and finally migrate the task to that one and delete the task in the priority queue. In case of a strong interaction the *Load Balancer* will try to avoid unnecessary busload, by selecting an ECU from the ECU set that is able to execute both tasks. Afterwards both tasks will be deleted in the priority queue. If the *Load Balancer* could not find a possible ECU for migration the task will be deleted from the queue with the outcome that a migration is not possible.

The previous paragraph give an overview of the migration, but there are still some open issues we will discuss in the following. If an ECU with more than one task running on it fails we will migrate the tasks to one or more ECUs according the classification of the tasks (see Figure 2). That means tasks with high-priority will migrated first followed by the other ones. During the migration phase the timing of the tasks are taken into account. After a task migration we have to decide to start the task new or from that state before the ECU fails, but how to recognize this state? Therefore, we need the context of the task. Our solution is the following, if we have a context available (e.g. store in an external flash memory of the ECU and still available) we will invoke the task with the context, otherwise not. This gives a brief overview how our middleware migrate tasks. Finally the decision which tasks are migrated is done by the *Load Balancer*, see section 6.

Figure 3 shows a sequence diagram where a failure occurred in the radio system. We assume the tasks from the radio system can migrated to the navigation system.

As we can see in Figure 3 the *Event Manager* detects the failure of the radio system, this is done by the function failure_detection(error_code). Afterwards the *Event Manager* triggers the *Load Balancer* with the initialize() function. The *Load Balancer* ask for all device information from the *Registry* (req_loads(*device[0..n])). Then the *Resource Manager* runs the schedule() function to calculate all possible schedules. The *Load Balancer* will get the device information back from the *Resource Manager* with ack_loads(*device[0..n]). Finally the *Load Balancer* will calculate (initiate_load_balancer()) which tasks could be move from device with the failure to another one based on the information of the schedules, the load of each processing element in the car-network, the communication costs and regarding the feasibility. In our case he will decide to move tasks from the radio to the navigation system.

In the last paragraph we describe the interactions between the four tasks, which are necessary to support load balancing. Now we will discuss the internal data structure of our middleware. The *Event Manager* triggers the *Registry* and initialize the *Load Balancer*. The *Registry* itself interacts with the *Resource Manager* and the *Load Balancer*. The *Resource Manager* hands over the actual status of the entire system to the *Load Balancer*.

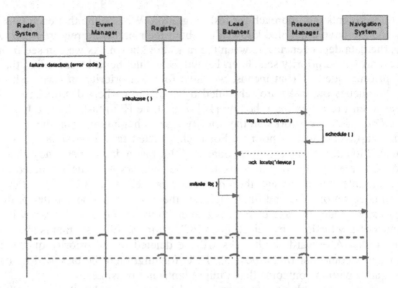

Fig. 3. Failure detection of the radio system

To perform the scheduling in the *Resource Manager* we can select between different scheduling strategies. They are instantiated within the scheduling mechanism class of the internal data structure.

The *Registry* as well as the scheduling mechanism needs information's of all tasks and devices. This is handled by the so called list class. It contains linked lists of devices and tasks and offers functions to manage the lists. As described before list offers all functions to manage the task list, but additionally functions to set the status of the tasks are needed. The status of the task is running, waiting or sleeping. Besides this the task manager is able to create a new task. The information of a task is stored in the data structured provided by the task control block. The parameters of the generated structure are set by the task manager with functions from the list class. The list class uses the functions from the task control block to get information's from tasks.

For the devices we have the same functions available as for the tasks. This is realized in the device control block. Each device has a list containing the task-id's that are running on the device. By setting the global variables of our middleware we can initialize the system and can set it in running mode.

5 Load Balancing Strategy

There are several possibilities to balance the load after an error happened inside the vehicle *Infotainment* network. Initiated by the *Load Balancer* component the new resources can be used and applications or tasks can be migrated to the additional device.

In the following the cost-based load balancing strategy is briefly described. Within the cost based strategy the *Load Balancer* evaluates possible migration of tasks from one ECU to another. He evaluates a set of ECUs where the task could be migrated. Hence that the migration is only a useful option if

- the cost of migrating is lower than the cost of keeping tasks with their original device and
- it is feasible to migrate a task or a set of tasks from one ECU to another one (*feasibility*).

The cost benefit ratio for tasks of busy devices is computed which helps the *Load Balancer* to form the decision of whether to migrate or not. The calculation of migration costs of task is realized according to the priority list of the Most Loaded strategy. Most Loaded generates a priority list which ranks the tasks from the busiest processor. In that way the tasks with the highest priority will be migrated to the resources of the additional device.

Let us assume we have tasks t_i with $i = 1$ *to* n, and the utilization of the task running on an ECU is u_i. Additionally, let U_j the maximum utilization of ECU e_j with $j = 1$ *to* m. Then the upper bound for the *utilization* of an ECU e_j is:

$$\sum_{i=1}^{n} u_i \leq U_j$$

For the communication we can make the following assumptions. Let c_k with $k = 1$ *to* r the communication channels in the vehicle and C_k the maximum costs a channel c_k has. Furthermore, let $m_{i,k}$ the cost task t_i produce on channel c_k. Then we can define the following bound for the *communication cost* a channel c_k:

$$\sum_{i=1}^{n} m_{i,k} \leq C_k$$

Now our *Load Balancer* has to find an optimal balancing for all tasks within in the vehicle network regarding the utilization, communication cost and the feasibility. This can be done with integer linear programming (ILP) or other optimization methods. This is ongoing work right now and in the final version of the paper we will show some simulation results.

6 Simulation and Results

In this section we will describe the implementation status of our middleware w.r.t. simulation and results. Our middleware was implemented in C code. We choose C, because it is more or less the language used for ECUs. Therefore, the code transfer from a PC based simulation to a real target platform doesn't need too much effort.

The implementation follows the class diagram structure presented in the previous section, see Figure 5. Within the PC based simulation we are able to parameterize our virtual software tasks and virtual ECUs with real values to achieve a software simulation of the entire system. The simulation is due to the fact that we use real values, near to the real system behavior.

As we figured out from the simulation that the migration time, to start a task on an ECU needs more time as our implemented scheduling and load balancing approach. Therefore, the time our middleware needs is dominated by the task migration of the underlying hardware (ECUs).

7 Conclusion and Outlook

We presented a middleware architecture for automotive systems that enables dynamic load balancing within the *Infotainment* network. The integration of load balancing is a step towards a self-reconfiguration within the vehicle and to integrate redundancy by task migration. We focus on a specific use case scenario whereby an error occurred within the vehicle network. Tasks running on the ECU with an error are migrates to another ECU by regarding the so-called feasibility, utilization and communication costs. With the help of the requirements, we described the middleware architecture and their enrichment with new services to support the distribution and exchange of tasks. Furthermore, we present briefly a cost-based load balancing strategy we will use for our approach.

Future work will be a detailed evaluation of the already existing load balancing strategies in the context of automotive systems. Additionally, the extension of existing or the development of new load balancing strategies will be done together with the implementation of the proposed architecture.

Acknowledgements

This project was funded by the EU Commission within the project DySCAS (Dynamically Self-Configuring Automotive Systems).

References

[1] Athony, R., Ekelin, C., Chen, D., Törngren, M., de Boer, G., Jahnich, I., et al.: A future dynamically reconfigurable automotive software system. In: Proceedings of the Elektronik im Kraftfahrzeug, Dresden, Germany. LNCS. Springer, Heidelberg (2006)

[2] Athony, R., Rettberg, A., Jahnich, I., Ekelin, C., et al.: Towards a dynamically reconfigurable automotive control system architecture. In: Rettberg, A., Dömer, R., Zanella, M., Gerstlauer, A., Rammig, F. (eds.) Proceedings of the IESS 2007, Irvine, California, USA. Springer, Heidelberg (2007)

[3] Cybenko, G.: Dynamic load balancing for distributed memory multiprocessors. J. Parallel Distrib. Comput. (1989)

[4] Diekmann, R., Monien, B., Preis, R.: Load balancing strategies for distributed memory machines. In: Satz, H., Karsch, F., Monien, B. (eds.) Multiscale Phenomena and Their Simulation, pp. 255–266. World Scientific, Singapore (1997)

[5] Hu, Y.F., Blake, R.J.: An optimal dynamic load balancing algorithm, vol. DL-P-95-011 (1995), http://citeseer.ist.psu.edu/hu95optimal.htm

[6] Hui, C.-C., Chanson, S.T.: Improved strategies for dynamic load balancing. In: IEEE Concurrency (1999)

[7] Jaiganesh, B., Douglas,: Evaluating the performance of middleware load balancing strategies (2004), http://citeseer.ist.psu.edu/635250.html

[8] Othman, O., Schmidt, D.: Optimizing distributed system performance via adaptive middleware load balancing. In: Othman, O., Schmidt, D.C. (eds.) ACM SIGPLAN Workshop on Optimization of Middleware and Distributed Systems (OM 2001), Snowbird, Utah, June 18, 2001 (2001)

[9] Othman, O., Schmidt, D.C.: Issues in the design of adaptive middleware load balancing. In: LCTES 2001: Proceedings of the ACM SIGPLAN workshop on Languages, compilers and tools for embedded systems, pp. 205–213. ACM Press, New York (2001)

[10] Stoller, S.: Leader election in distributed systems with crash failures. Technical report, Indiana University, April 1997, p. 169 (1997)

[11] van der Zwaan, S., Marques, C.: Ant Colony Optimisation for Job Shop Scheduling. In: Proceedings of the Third Workshop on Genetic Algorithms and Artificial Life (GAAL 1999) (1999)

[12] Buttazzo, G.C.: Hard real time computing systems. Kluwer Academic Publishers, Dordrecht (2000)

[13] Jahnich, I., Rettberg, A.: Towards Dynamic Load Balancing for Distributed Embedded Automotive Systems. In: Rettberg, A., Dömer, R., Zanella, M., Gerstlauer, A., Rammig, F. (eds.) Proceedings of the IESS 2007, Irvine, California, USA. Springer, Heidelberg (2007)

[14] Jahnich, I., Podolski, I., Rettberg, A.: Integrating Dynamic Load Balancing into the Car-Network. In: 4th Proc. of the Electronic Design, Test and Application (DELTA 2008), Hong Kong, January 23–25 (2008)

[15] Ravindran, B., Welch, L.R., Kelling, C.: Building Distributed Scalable Dependable Real-Time Systems. In: Proceedings of the IEEE Conference on Engineering of Computer-Based Systems, March 24-28 (1997)

[16] Chaaban, K., Shawky, M., Crubillé, P.: A Distributed Framework For Real-Time In-Vehicle Applications. In: Proceedings of the 8th International IEEE Conference on Intelligent Transportation Systems, Vienna, Austria, September 13–16 (2005)

[17] Kim, M., Choi, Y., Moon, Y., Kim, S., Kwon, O.: Design and Implementation of Status based Application Manager for Telematics. In: The 8th International Conference on Advanced Communication Technology (CACT), February 20-22 (2006)

[18] Navet, N., Song, Y., Simonot-Lion, F., Wilwert, C.: Trends in Automotive Communication Systems. In: Proceedings of the IEEE (June 2005)

[19] http://www.autosar.org

Context-Aware Middleware for
Reliable Multi-hop Multi-path Connectivity

Paolo Bellavista, Antonio Corradi, and Carlo Giannelli

Dip. Elettronica, Informatica e Sistemistica - Università di Bologna
Viale Risorgimento, 2 - 40136 Bologna - Italy
Tel.: +39-051-2093001; Fax: +39-051-2093073
{paolo.bellavista,antonio.corradi,carlo.giannelli}@unibo.it

Abstract. The widespread diffusion of portable devices with multiple wireless interfaces, e.g., UMTS/GPRS, IEEE 802.11, and/or Bluetooth, is enabling multi-homing and multi-channel scenarios, possibly made up by multi-hop cooperative paths towards the traditional Internet infrastructure. There is the need for novel middleware supports, aware of innovative context information, to select and dynamically re-configure the most suitable interfaces and connectivity providers for each client application. In particular, novel middlewares should effectively exploit concise and lightweight context indicators about expected node mobility, path throughput, and energy availability to take proper connectivity management decisions at session startup and to promptly re-configure them with limited overhead at runtime. Here, we present how our MMHC middleware originally uses mobility/throughput/energy context to manage connectivity opportunities effectively, i) by filtering out connectivity opportunities that are considered insufficiently reliable, and ii) by carefully evaluating the residual candidates in two distinguished local/global management phases to achieve the most suitable tradeoff between promptness and management costs.

1 Introduction

Nowadays mobile devices, usually equipped with multiple wireless interfaces, can get connectivity to the traditional wired Internet by taking advantage of multiple connectivity opportunities provided by many infrastructure-based components, which tend to be ubiquitously available, e.g., IEEE 802.11 Access Points (APs) or UMTS Base Stations (BSs). In the following, we will call these connectivity components as *infrastructure connectors*. In addition, the increasing and increasing resources of mobile terminals potentially enable novel and more complex scenarios where client nodes can also help other clients to achieve Internet connectivity in a peer-to-peer fashion, e.g., via Bluetooth Personal Area Network (PAN) or IEEE 802.11 Independent Basic Service Set (IBSS) connections, by acting as intermediate entities in a multi-hop (possibly heterogeneous) path towards the Internet. We use the term *peer connectors* to indicate these novel connectivity opportunities. Peer connectors are in charge of creating and properly managing a simple and small Mobile Ad-hoc NETwork (MANET) with the peers in proximity and of correctly routing packets between their MANET and the Internet by exploiting the near infrastructure connectors.

U. Brinkschulte, T. Givargis, and S. Russo (Eds.): SEUS 2008, LNCS 5287, pp. 66–78, 2008.

The increased complexity of this scenario enabled by the concurrent exploitation of infrastructure/peer connectors is widely counterbalanced by the potential benefits of exploiting a significantly wider set of heterogeneous connectivity opportunities, among which to dynamically choose based on system/user/node/application-specific requirements, e.g., load balancing available connectors, always exploiting connectivity opportunities that are for free, preserving node battery, or respecting bandwidth requirements, as exemplified in Section 2. Of course, it is inappropriate to leave to client application designers the whole burden of properly managing the wide set of Multi-hop Multi-path Heterogeneous Connectivity (MMHC) opportunities that are dynamically available. Therefore, we claim the crucial role of client-side middleware solutions for effective MMHC management.

These middlewares should have effective visibility of different kinds of innovative context data to take proper MMHC decisions, especially to ensure usability of enabled MMHC opportunities by selecting the ones expected to be more reliable during the service session that will be established. In particular, lightweight estimations about client mobility (with regards to both fixed infrastructure and mobile peer connectors) could allow to exclude the connectors that are probably going out of the coverage area of the considered client soon, thus reducing the space of connectivity opportunities to take into account. Similarly, context data about the estimated throughput achievable by a single wireless hop and by the multi-hop path composed by that hop can help filtering out connectivity opportunities that do not comply with session quality requirements. Finally, context data about the residual energy of involved connectors could help in balancing energy consumption among connectors and in taking proactive re-configuration operations of currently exploited paths if some composing hops are expected to fail soon due to power exhaustion.

According to these context awareness needs, we have designed and implemented our innovative middleware for multi-hop multi-path connectivity management, called MMHC [1]. MMHC properly handles different kinds of context data, from user preference profiles to application requirements, from Received Signal Strength Indications (RSSI) for mobility estimations to battery power indicators, to select and dynamically re-configure the most suitable MMHC opportunity for each running application. In particular, in this paper, we originally focus on how MMHC portably gathers mobility/throughput/energy context data and exploits them to perform lightweight connectivity management. The primary ideas are i) of exploiting context data to reduce the space of potential candidates for selected connectivity opportunities and ii) of splitting management operations into a local phase (where mainly local context is exploited to achieve rapid, effective, but sub-optimal MMHC decisions) and a global phase (where lightweight distributed context guides proactive path re-configuration and procedures for role switch to counteract node failures/exits). Given the extreme dynamicity of the addressed deployment scenarios, the main goal is the selection of connectivity opportunities with an expectation of reasonable reliability for the served applications. The first results obtained by deploying the MMHC middleware prototype* over real testbeds demonstrate the feasibility of the approach, with limited overhead and MMHC selection/re-configuration times compatible with most applications.

---

* The code of the MMHC prototype is available for download, together with additional implementation insights and experimental results, at http://lia.deis.unibo.it/research/ MMHC/

2 Deployment Scenario and Problem Statement

The MMHC scenario relevantly improves the traditional networking capabilities of wireless environments. First of all, it extends connectivity opportunities via multi-hop ad-hoc paths, thus allowing the Internet access of nodes not directly in the coverage area of infrastructure connectors. Second, it enables the exploitation of multiple paths simultaneously, e.g., to improve the overall throughput available at a client node. Third, it permits to increase connectivity availability, e.g., by enabling the rapid re-routing of traffic flows to other paths when the exploited one becomes unavailable.

To better and practically point out these advantages, let us rapidly sketch an example of a possible MMHC deployment scenario. Consider the realistic case of a group of tourists moving together and sharing pictures via Wi-Fi/Bluetooth single-hop links. Due to their limited coverage range, there could be the need for multi-hop paths to reach target friends who are currently lingering in a shop; that is enabled by collaborating tourist devices that, for instance, can transparently exploit IEEE 802.11 in ad-hoc mode to receive packets and Bluetooth to forward them along the right direction, e.g., node C in Figure 1. In addition, some tourists may be willing to periodically publish their pictures on their Web blogs even if they have no direct UMTS connectivity, e.g., they do not want to subscribe to a local UMTS provider while visiting Italy. These tourists can benefit from Bluetooth multi-hop ad-hoc connectivity toward the devices of friends with flat-rate UMTS subscription, who offer them free Internet connectivity, e.g., node A. Note that tourists' mobility may reduce the reliability of MMHC opportunities; usually there is the need to favor the selection of MMHC opportunities with compatible reliability (especially in terms of expected durability).

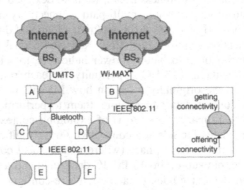

Fig. 1. An example of MMHC scenario

Similarly, when moving from city to city by train, tourists should be able to exploit MMHC opportunities offered by other passengers, possibly in other wagons, reachable via multi-hop heterogeneous paths, and connected to the Internet via Wi-Fi/WiMAX APs, such as node B. In this case the nodes tend to move together (joint mobility) and MMHC opportunities have similar expected durability. Therefore, MMHC selection should not only be mobility-aware, but also consider application-specific quality requirements, e.g., expected throughput. Moreover, if node A leaves the network, e.g., to limit its battery consumption, node D can reroute its active connections from node A to

B, thus minimizing user-perceived service disruption. However, in that case, node C would have no access to the Internet anymore, since A was its only connector. It could be useful that nodes in that simple MANET self-organize themselves to provide new Internet access opportunities, for instance with node F starting to play the role of connector, thus providing C with connectivity towards BS_2.

We claim that, to support the effective self-organization of MMHC networks, there is the need of proper, effective, and concise context data describing capabilities and characteristics of available connectivity opportunities. Novel context indicators about expected node mobility, path throughput, and energy availability are needed to take proper MMHC management decisions at session startup and to promptly re-configure them at runtime, with limited overhead and impact on on-going service sessions.

3 Context Data for MMHC Management

We claim that MMHC management decisions should primarily take into account enhanced forms of context data, such as expected *node mobility* and *path throughput*, which are specific representatives, respectively, of the general properties of reliability and quality. On the one hand, given that clients and peer connectors are all mobile and may join/leave their networks abruptly, MMHC reliability is far more "fragile" than in traditional AP/BS single-hop connectivity. On the other hand, once reliability is potentially ensured as the primary goal, it is reasonable to perform MMHC management depending on coarse-grained estimated throughput. Let us note that, as better detailed in the following, it is possible to obtain these context data with reasonable accuracy by means of localized and lightweight exchange of monitoring information. In addition, MMHC management should consider the *energy availability* of the whole network. Based on coarse-grained and lightweight information about the battery of peer connectors, it is possible: i) to fairly exploit node energy capabilities; and ii) to proactively reconfigure the network when the battery level of a peer connector goes under a threshold, thus avoiding abrupt path disruptions due to battery exhaustion.

3.1 MMHC Node Mobility

We claim that mobility awareness is the most important context information needed to take proper MMHC management decisions, especially with the aim of choosing reliable connectivity opportunities based on durability expectations. Even if the literature is starting to recognize that claim, there are currently no practical, lightweight, decentralized, and client-side ways for coarse-grained estimation of node mobility. In our previous work [1], we have experimentally shown how to obtain mobility indicators by exploiting only lightweight local monitoring.

In particular, we claim that, in first approximation, single-hop connection durability depends on mutual mobility of involved nodes and coverage range of the employed wireless technology. These two simple parameters concisely summarize two main properties affecting reliability in wireless environments: user mobility, as the inclination to either stay close to or move away from nodes offering connectivity, and wireless technology characteristics, e.g., higher durability of medium-range IEEE 802.11 links if compared with short-range Bluetooth ones.

By delving into finer details, we define mutual mobility as the mobility relationship between a given participating node X and a fixed/mobile device offering connectivity to X, such as an AP or a collaborating peer connector. We introduce two indicators: i) *CMob* to measure X's mobility with regard to a fixed AP/BS device; ii) *Joint* to evaluate X's tendency to move together with another mobile peer (relative stillness). Both indicators have a value in the [0, 1] range and are inferred via a simplified technique based on RSSI measurement at X and on RSSI variation in a recent timeframe; additional details about how to effectively obtain these indicators are in [1, 2].

For each single-hop path opportunity, we propose to quantitatively evaluate its Endurance Estimation (EE), i.e.:

$$EE = (1 - CMob) \bullet CR \qquad \text{for APs/BSs} \qquad (1)$$
$$EE = Joint \bullet CR \qquad \text{for mobile peers} \qquad (2)$$

where Coverage Range (CR) is in [0, 1] and, in first approximation, only depends on the exploited wireless technology.

While EE provides single-hop context information about expected durability, obtained locally without any access to distributed monitoring data, we introduce Path Mobility (PM) for coarse-grained evaluation of multi-hop path durability:

- PM is equal to EE in the case of a single-hop path;
- the PM of a k-hop path is equal to the EE of the kth hop multiplied by the PM of the remaining sub-path starting from the $(k-1)^{th}$ node.

Let us observe that PM quickly degrades while increasing the number of path hops, to model the desired effect of strongly favoring the selection of short durable paths. In fact, the MMHC goal is not of supporting the complex realization of any kind of MANET, but only to enable short reliable ad-hoc paths towards infrastructure connectors, even by abruptly filtering out connectivity opportunities that are estimated too unreliable because of excessive mobility.

3.2 MMHC Path Throughput

Similarly to context data about mobility for coarse-grained estimations of connector reliability (to infer MMHC opportunity durability), we have worked to properly model the expected throughput of potentially available multi-hop heterogeneous paths depending on lightweight monitoring data. In particular, based on our large campaign of measurements on heterogeneous wireless networks, we have observed that three elements are crucial, in first approximation, for throughput: i) the wireless technology of each single-hop sub-path, ii) the number of hops in the path, and iii) the number of clients/peer connectors simultaneously served by each connector in the path. Other factors, which have partial influence on the overall path performance, are not so relevant for a coarse-grained throughput estimation. For instance, about iii), we have experimentally verified that in the challenging case of simultaneous transmit/receive operations by all clients over the same single-hop link up to throughput saturation, competing devices tend to fairly share the total bandwidth. We adopt the conservative simplifying assumption that in any case a node can achieve a maximum throughput inversely proportional to the number of active nodes on that single-hop (see Figure 2). Given the above considerations, we propose a simplified lightweight model to evaluate Estimated Throughput (ET):

$$ET = NB \qquad \text{for APs/BSs} \qquad (3)$$
$$ET = (1 - HD) \bullet MT\,/\,\#clients \qquad \text{for mobile peers} \qquad (4)$$

where Nominal Bandwidth (NB) depends on the exploited wireless technology, Hop Degradation (HD) models per-hop throughput degradation (experimentally measured and set to 20% in first approximation), which is almost independent of the number of local clients, and Maximum Throughput (MT) is the expected maximum throughput toward the wired Internet, i.e., min {ET of previous single-hop sub-path, NB of the considered single-hop sub-path}. Note that the number of clients is not considered in the case of direct connections to APs/BSs, also given the practical impossibility to portably obtain this information when working with currently deployed AP/BS network equipment. Let us finally stress again that this procedure for ET estimation is only a rough calculation of actual runtime throughput, but is very simple and lightweight, thus enabling scarcely intrusive comparison of multi-hop paths.

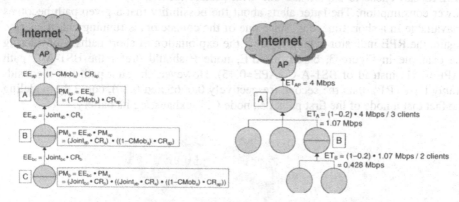

Fig. 2. Our coarse-grained PM (left) and ET (right) estimation

3.3 MMHC Energy Availability

While PM and ET are useful to provide estimations about mobility-related durability and throughput, they do not provide any information about expected path durability due to energy consumption. Analogously to what presented before, MMHC adopts a simplifying approach for coarse-grained and lightweight energy considerations. The primary ideas are of simply avoiding the paths composed by nodes with low battery levels and of not overloading a small set of connectors with a large amount of traversing traffic to avoid to quickly consume their batteries due to traffic routing. The goal is twofold: i) preserving the battery level of each node, by focusing on those nodes whose battery level is running out, and ii) trying to increase path durability. Let us rapidly point out that the MMHC approach does not replace but is additional to other more sophisticated and effective techniques for power consumption reduction, e.g., IEEE 802.11 awake/doze periodic state switch or Bluetooth Sniff/Park states.

By going into finer details, MMHC distributes context information related to Node Battery Level (NBL) and thus permits to take informed decision sufficiently in advance for reconfiguring the network prior to path disruption. In particular, we define the Average Path Energy (APE) indicator of the kth hop of the path as:

$$APE_k = \frac{(APE_{k-1}) \cdot (K-1) + NBL_k}{k} \tag{5}$$

i.e., the average battery level of nodes in the path to the Internet. In addition, we define the Residual Path Energy (RPE) indicator as:

NBL_1 for the 1st hop of the path   (6)
$NBL_k \cdot RPE_{k-1}$ for the kth hop of the path   (7)

Note that APE and RPE convey different context information. The former gives a fairness estimation about the distribution of power consumption, useful to quantitatively compare available paths. For instance, given two paths with good ET values, MMHC can chose to exploit the one with greater APE to optimize peer connector power consumption. The latter alerts about the possibility that a given path becomes unavailable in a short time, e.g., since one of the connectors is running out of energy. Again, the RPE indicator is built to favor the exploitation of short paths. Considering the example in Figure 3, based on APE, node F should prefer the BS1-A-C path (APE=0.51) instead of BS1-A-C (APE=0.45). However, the first path has a considerably lower RPE than the second (respectively 0.0665 and 0.20), correctly modeling the fact that a node of the first path, i.e., node C, is exhausting its battery.

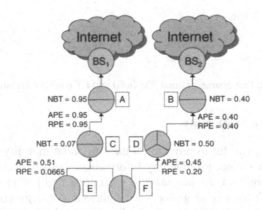

Fig. 3. APE and RPE estimation for two different paths

4 Local and Global Management for Reliable Paths in MMHC

We envision the self-organization of MMHC networks as a two-phase procedure: a local phase where nodes aim to quickly achieve a form of Internet connectivity at session startup and a global phase where nodes coordinate themselves to incrementally improve their network exploitation in terms of availability and quality.

The local phase performs connector evaluation rapidly and efficiently to ensure prompt but sub-optimal response; it is based on context data that is either locally available (EE) or gathered at single-hop connection establishment time (PM and ET), thus providing coarse-grained estimation of path reliability and quality. In particular, the local phase is reactively activated only when an active single-hop connection fails, e.g., because one in-use connector becomes unavailable. In this phase, nodes:

1) gather RSSI sequences of their visible peer connectors to compute CMob/Joint;
2) perform a single-hop connection with the most reliable connector from the point of view of mobility, i.e., with greatest EE;
3) estimate PM and ET of the whole path, by gathering and exploiting PM and ET of previous hops in case of peer connectivity.

Nodes connected to multiple connectors exploit PM and ET values to estimate which is the most suitable path. Due to the volatility of MMHC networks, the main purpose of these evaluations is to ensure path durability, while throughput is considered only as a secondary objective. In fact, MMHC allows users to specify the Required Reliability (RR) for each of their applications (RR ranges in the [0,1] interval, with 1 for maximally privileging reliability at the expense of throughput). By delving into finer details, MMHC nodes:

1) as a first try, select the path with greatest ET among the only paths with PM >= 80% RR. If at least one compliant path is found, the algorithm stops;
2) otherwise, they also examine paths with PM >= 50% RR. If at least one compliant path is found, the algorithm stops;
3) otherwise, they take into account any potentially available path, with no more limitations on the space of connectivity opportunities.

Let us point out that the local management phase leads to the establishment of a tree-network topology: connections can only follow bottom-up paths because they are built up from clients towards the Internet access points. For instance, in Figure 1 clients can achieve Internet connectivity by establishing 1-to-many tree-like connector/client relationships; clients connected to multiple connectors can access multiple tree-networks simultaneously; instead, connectors cannot exploit connectivity offered by their clients at the same time.

The global phase is in charge of enhancing the connectivity paths established in the local phase, by ensuring long-term availability. It exploits a wider set of context data and connectivity opportunities. On the one hand, APE and RPE data are spread to proactively modify network topology to avoid nodes with scarce battery. On the other hand, the already established connectivity allows clients with simultaneous connection to multiple connectors to periodically notify their single-hop connectors that they can potentially work as bridges among different tree-networks. In this phase, nodes:

1) periodically collect up-to-date context data about PM, ET, APE, and RPE of available paths from peer connectors/clients;
2) change routing rules when the currently exploited path becomes unavailable or its RPE value goes below 0.1;
3) select new paths, as the local phase does, by privileging paths with APE in the [0.5, 1.0] range (preferred exploitation of nodes with high battery resources):

a. if the new path exploits a new connector, the involved nodes simply have to change their local routing rules;
b. if the new path uses a client connected to other tree-networks, a role-switch procedure is triggered (see below).

This metric is conservative, by proactively triggering a network reconfiguration only based on APE: However, it is easy to change MMHC behavior to adopt more aggressive approaches that take into account also ET and other parameters, at the cost of additional monitoring overhead.

It is worth noting that the local phase is rather static, letting nodes establish new connections only when already available ones disappear. Instead, the global phase provides dynamic network management not only by changing the exploited connector via routing rule updates, but also by switching the role between connectors and clients (role-switch procedure). In fact, role-switch relevantly improves topology dynamicity and widens networking opportunities: for instance, a connector can select, as next-hop to the Internet, one of its current clients such as node F in Figure 4. Then, MMHC starts its role-switch procedure as follows:

1) the connector notifies its client that there is the need for role-switch;
2) the client enables forwarding capabilities and update routing rules;
3) the connector starts forwarding packets to the selected client.

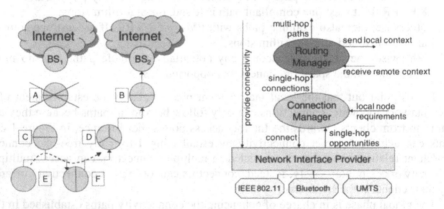

Fig. 4. Nodes C/F role-switch procedure after node A failure   **Fig. 5.** MMHC middleware architecture

The role-switch procedure affects only the pair of nodes directly involved in it (localized management operation). After the switch, the original connector is still the node contributing to the existence of the physical network, e.g., working as Bluetooth master and DHCP server; the novel element is that the old client starts playing the role of gateway. In this way, the role-switch procedure imposes limited overhead, e.g., not requiring the time consuming establishment creation of new single-hop links (see Section 5) and permits the decoupling of the roles of connection establisher and gateway. In addition, other possible clients of a connector are not affected by role-switch: they keep on sending packets to their old connector, thus possibly delving into sub-optimal node configurations but limiting reconfiguration actions to minimize manager overhead. Figure 4 shows how C and F reconfigure their network after A failure; note that E continues to exploit C as peer connector, which forwards packets to F.

5 Architecture and Implementation Insights

Figure 5 gives a high-level overview of our middleware architecture, which is layered to properly separate connection/routing level local/global management operations and to limit the unnecessary visibility of implementation details, thus increasing usability. *Network Interface Provider* (NIP) provides homogeneous access to heterogeneous interfaces and local context sources; it provides a common API by hiding low-level peculiarities of underlying drivers and operating systems. *Connection Manager* performs single-hop connections; it gathers RSSI sequences to evaluate CMob/Joint and EE for any single-hop MMHC opportunity; on this basis, it takes local decisions on the subset of single-hop paths to activate. *Routing Manager* works to perform multi-hop paths; it manages routing rules and triggers role-switch procedures when needed.

For the sake of briefness, to give a practical idea of some MMHC implementation issues, here we focus on how (lower layer) MMHC achieves portability over different platforms. Additional details are available on the MMHC Web site. The current MMHC prototype supports IEEE 802.11 and Bluetooth interfaces, by including wrappers for both Linux and Windows XP/Vista. Wi-Fi interfaces are accessed via Linux Wireless Extensions on Linux client nodes and via the Microsoft Network Driver Interface Specification User-mode I/O (NDISUIO) on Windows XP/Vista (NDISUIO is platform-dependent but portable among different wireless interface implementations). For instance, NIP exploits the NDISUIO function `DeviceIOControl()` to query the `OID_802_11_BSSID_LIST_SCAN` object to retrieve the complete list of currently reachable connectors, either IEEE 802.11 APs or peer nodes in ad-hoc configuration. Bluetooth interfaces are accessed via the standard API provided by the BlueZ protocol stack on Linux client nodes, while via the API provided by the Windows Driver Kit and the Software Development Kit on Windows XP/Vista. For example, NIP achieves visibility of the set of Bluetooth devices in proximity by invoking `BluetoothFindFirstDevice` and `BluetoothFindNextDevice` functions.

In addition, NIP can gather battery-related context information on both Linux and Windows XP. In the former case, it exploits `status` and `info` files in the `/proc/acpi/battery/BAT0` directory; it estimates the NBL parameter comparing the `remaining capacity` and the `last full capacity` values. In the latter case, the System Event Notification Service (SENS) `BatteryLevel` property is exploited to access the battery status and directly get the NBL parameter.

We have worked and are working on the extensive experimental validation of the MMHC prototype. Due to space limitations, here we rapidly present some performance measurements about MMHC overhead, by referring to the MMHC Web site for additional experimental results. MMHC has demonstrated to add a limited overhead, negligible if compared with the long delays imposed by several wireless technologies to handle handovers and establish new connections, e.g., the Bluetooth inquiry [3]. In particular, we have tested Connection and Routing Manager performance when creating new single-hop connections and managing routing rules for multi-hop paths. In the case of a new Wi-Fi/Bluetooth connector joining the managed network, Connection Manager spends 3.102/17.916s to configure the new single-hop connection, e.g., due to 3.041/14.370s to discover the connector (almost all deriving from long Wi-Fi/Bluetooth standard operations), only 0.039/0.116s to evaluate the connector suitability (under MMHC responsibility), and 0.022/3.430s to connect to it via association/PAN connection. Routing Manager is much faster, requiring only 273ms on average to establish a new path: 60ms to select the best path and consequently update routing rules, the remaining time to distribute context data.

The main performance differences between the two interface types have been exhibited for connector discovery and connection establishment: the longer IEEE 802.11 discovery phase is mainly due to the time for setting up the ad-hoc mode, which is of infrequent usage and not optimized in several Wi-Fi cards; Bluetooth inquiries and PAN connections are slower than IEEE 802.11 scans and associations [3]. In addition to interface types, the reported indicators have demonstrated to significantly depend on card model and driver implementations. For instance, Orinoco Gold interfaces have exhibited larger IEEE 802.11 ad-hoc throughput than PROWireless cards (about 6 times) because the latter only support ad hoc transmission at 1MB/s. Similarly, MMHC can halve the Bluetooth inquiry period over MS operating systems at the expense of risking not to sense a small fraction of connectors, as proposed first in [13]; that optimization is impossible with Linux-based BlueZ drivers.

Let us stress that the greater delay for network setup than for network reconfiguration justifies the MMHC approach, with a local management phase reactively activated only when a single-hop connection is lost and a global phase that periodically updates routing rules to optimize performance once the network is working (to shorten the long and expensive startup phase of first connection establishment).

6 Related Work

Several proposals have recently investigated some specific partial aspects of the MMHC scenario. For instance, [4] points out the primary technical aspects of WLAN-based multi-hop networks, while [5] aims to extend cellular network capabilities via relay stations, with the main goal of increasing cellular coverage. [6] and [7], instead, specifically address the issue of managing client mobility among heterogeneous multi-hop networks. Other proposals focus on the effective allocation of the shared wireless medium frequencies and the scheduling of time slots to minimize interferences and packet collisions [8, 9]. These contributions were crucial for the full understanding of both the theory and the main characteristics of multi-hop networks. However, they did not concentrate on realistic, feasible, and practical solutions to guide the design and implementation of prototypes for seamless and mobility-aware MMHC. Also [10] and [11] provide some relevant contribution by identifying major drawbacks and weaknesses of theoretical work in the literature; however, they do not propose practical solutions to address these weaknesses.

In a wider perspective, it is possible to note that most work in the literature proposes elegant but complex models for MMHC, without considering concise context indicators to simplify MMHC management (reduced overhead at the expense of limited distance from decision optimality). In particular, only recent contributions start to recognize the importance of providing lightweight mechanisms to maximize reliability.

To the best of our knowledge, [12] is the only notable proposal that practically addresses the issue of improving network reliability by spreading context data about path robustness; however, it does not estimate availability based on mobility/energy considerations and does not consider path quality as our MMHC prototype does.

7 Conclusions

Recent research activities are starting to recognize the suitability of novel middlewares to leverage the adoption of MMHC scenarios, thus fully exploiting the frequent, ubiquitous, and heterogeneous networking opportunities available nowadays. Our research work points out how innovative context data are crucial to inform management solutions that effectively answer to the reliability, throughput, and availability requirements of running applications. In particular, our MMHC prototype demonstrates the feasibility of our approach, with prompt sub-optimal connectivity decisions and limited costs, thanks to the proper adoption of a reactive local management phase for connectivity establishment at session startup and a proactive global management phase for connection re-configuration.

The promising results already achieved are stimulating our further work. In particular, we are investigating effective models to dynamically evaluate and evolve the trust degree that clients, in a completely decentralized way, associate to their peer connectors, in order to affect connectivity offerings via incentives. In addition, we are extending the MMHC prototype to transparently handle also the splitting of the traffic flow of a single application at a client along different multi-hop heterogeneous paths.

References

1. Bellavista, P., Corradi, A., Giannelli, C.: A Layered Infrastructure for Mobility-Aware Best Connectivity in the Heterogeneous Wireless Internet. In: First Int. Conf. MOBILe Wireless MiddleWARE, Operating Systems, and Applications (Mobilware), Austria (February 2008)
2. Bellavista, P., Corradi, A., Giannelli, C.: Evaluating Filtering Strategies for Decentralized Handover Prediction in the Wireless Internet. In: 11th IEEE Symp. Computers and Communications (ISCC), Italy (June 2006)
3. Ferro, E., Potorti, F.: Bluetooth and Wi-Fi Wireless Protocols: a Survey and a Comparison. IEEE Wireless Communications 12(1), 12–26 (2005)
4. Faccin, S.M., Wijting, C., Kenckt, J., Damle, A.: Mesh WLAN Networks: Concept and System Design. IEEE Wireless Communications 13(2), 10–17 (2006)
5. Le, L., Hossain, E.: Multihop Cellular Networks: Potential Gains, Research Challenges, and a Resource Allocation Framework. IEEE Communications Magazine 45(9), 66–73 (2007)
6. Pack, S., Shen, X., Mark, J.W., Pan, J.: Mobility Management in Mobile Hotspots with Heterogeneous Multihop Wireless Links. IEEE Communications Magazine 45(9), 106–112 (2007)
7. Lam, P.P., Liew, S.C.: Nested Network Mobility on the Multihop Cellular Network. IEEE Communications Magazine 45(9), 100–104 (2007)

8. Badia, L., Erta, A., Lenzini, L., Zorzi, M.: A General Interference-Aware Framework for Joint Routing and Link Scheduling in Wireless Mesh Networks. IEEE Network 22(1), 32–38 (2008)
9. Cheng, H.T., Zhuang, W.: Joint Power-Frequency-Time Resource Allocation in Clustered Wireless Mesh Networks. IEEE Network 22(1), 45–51 (2008)
10. Conti, M., Giordano, S.: Multihop Ad Hoc Networking: the Theory. IEEE Communications Magazine 45(4), 78–86 (2007)
11. Conti, M., Giordano, S.: Multihop Ad Hoc Networking: the Reality. IEEE Communications Magazine 45(4), 88–95 (2007)
12. Baumann, R., Heimlicher, S., Plattner, B.: Routing in Large-Scale Wireless Mesh Networks Using Temperature Fields. IEEE Network 22(1), 25–31 (2008)
13. Peterson, B.S., Baldwin, R.O., Kharoufeh, J.P.: Bluetooth Inquiry Time Characterization and Selection. IEEE Trans. on Mobile Computing 5(9), 1173–1187 (2006)

Service Orchestration Using the Chemical Metaphor

Jean-Pierre Banâtre[1], Thierry Priol[1], and Yann Radenac[2],*

[1] INRIA/IRISA
Campus de Beaulieu, F-35042 Rennes Cedex, France
jean-pierre.banatre@irisa.fr, thierry.priol@irisa.fr
[2] Research Center for Grid and Service Computing
Institute of Computing Technology, Academy of Sciences
Beijing 100080, P.R. China
yann.radenac@software.ict.ac.cn

Abstract. Service-oriented architectures (SOA) provide sets of operations through a network. A program built mainly upon calling services is called an orchestration of services. Different programming languages can be used to be the "glue" between services in an orchestration. This article shows how a programming language inspired by a chemical metaphor can be used to program service orchestration.

1 Introduction

Service-based infrastructures are shaping tomorrow's distributed computing systems. It is rather difficult to come up with a strict definition, widely accepted, of what is a service. In the scope of this paper, a service can be seen as a set of operations that are available on a machine or through a network. After several attempts to design distributed programming paradigms, such as remote-procedure call [1], distributed objects [2] or distributed components [3], the service paradigm seems to solve one of the main issue when dealing with distributed systems: how to design loosely-coupled distributed applications based on the composition of a set of independent software modules called services that are spread over a set of resources available on a network such as the Internet. The loosely-coupled aspect is important when dealing with a distributed system. It allows an application to adopt a late binding to software modules. Services are discovered and brokered at runtime and bound when needed. This provides a lot of flexibility enabling the selection of the best services, in terms of Qualities of Service (QoS) such as performance and cost, but also to cope with failures since a given service can be replaced at runtime. It is foreseen in the near future that the programming of distributed applications will be just the expression of the composition of services available on the Internet. In fact, the Internet will be considered as

---

* This work was partially carried out for the EchoGRID IST project n°045520, funded by the European Commission.

U. Brinkschulte, T. Givargis, and S. Russo (Eds.): SEUS 2008, LNCS 5287, pp. 79–89, 2008.

a large scale computing system that shares some similarities with the microprocessors we have in our desktop or laptop computers but of course with a larger computing granularity. Internet will provide access, acting as a bus, to a large number of processing and storage units under the form of utility computing systems such as Grids [4] or Cloud computers like the Google [5] and Amazon [6] ones. To conclude with this analogy, services could be considered as the instruction set of such distributed computing infrastructures. With such analogy, the issue that is immediately emerging is how to express the instruction and data flows? Another issue that prevents us to go further in the analogy between a microprocessor and a service-based computing infrastructure is that failures can occur at any time and it is considered as a basic property of any distributed system.

Expressing the control and data flows, or simply workflows, in such large scale distributed computing infrastructures is thus challenging in many aspects. We think that existing approaches to express workflows need to be rethought to take into account the large scale dimension of these infrastructures allowing massively parallel coarse-grain computations and the dynamicity due to frequent failures. This paper investigates the use of an unconventional approach which is chemical programming that possesses two nice properties: it is implicitly parallel and autonomic. It gets its inspiration from the chemical metaphor, formally represented here by a chemical language called HOCL which stands for Higher-Order Chemical Language [7]. In HOCL, computation is seen as reactions between molecules in a chemical solution. HOCL is higher-order: reaction rules are molecules that can be manipulated like any other molecules, i.e., HOCL programs can manipulate other HOCL programs. Reactions only occur locally between few molecules that are chosen non-deterministically. The execution is implicitly parallel since several reactions can occur simultaneously and it can also be be seen as chaotic and possesses nice autonomic properties as shown in [8]. This model has already been applied in the contexts of Grid workflow enactment [9,10] and of Desktop Grids [11] and shown its suitability to express coordination of computations.

The objective of this paper is to show, through an example, that chemical programming can be a good candidate for service programming, such as the composition and coordination of services. On one side, applications are programmed in an abstract manner describing essentially the chemical coordination between (not necessarily chemical) abstract services. On the other side, chemical programs are specifically provided to the service run-time system in order to obtain the expected qualities of service in terms of efficiency, reliability, security, etc. These programs can be seen as special coordination programs providing guidelines to the runtime system allowing a better use of resources in order to obtain the expected Quality of Service.

Section 2 introduces chemical programming through the HOCL language. Section 3 shows how to orchestrate services using HOCL. In section 4, we present briefly some of the main existing approaches to express workflow of services in the Web Services framework. Finally, we conclude in Section 5.

2 Chemical Programming Model

A chemical program can be seen as a (symbolic) chemical solution where data is represented by floating molecules and computation by chemical reactions between them. When some molecules match and fulfill a reaction condition, they are replaced by the result of the reaction. That process goes on until an inert solution is reached: the solution is said to be inert when no reaction can occur anymore. Formally, a chemical solution is represented by a multiset and reaction rules specify multiset rewritings.

We use a higher-order chemical programming language called HOCL [7]. HOCL is based on the γ-calculus [12], a higher-order chemical computation model which can be seen as an higher-order extension of the Gamma language [13]. In HOCL, every entity is a molecule, including reaction rules.

A program is a molecule, that is to say, a multiset of atoms $(A_1, \ldots, A_n)$ which can be constants (integers, booleans, etc.), sub-solutions $(\langle M \rangle)$ or reaction rules. Compound molecules (M_1, M_2) are built using the associative and commutative (AC) operator ",". The corresponding AC laws formalize the Brownian motion and can always be used to reorganize molecules.

The execution of a chemical program consists in triggering reactions until the solution becomes inert.

A reaction involves a reaction rule **one** P **by** M **if** V and a molecule N that satisfies the pattern P and the reaction condition V. The reaction consumes the rule and the molecule N, and produces M. Formally:

$$(\text{one } P \text{ by } M \text{ if } V), \ N \longrightarrow \phi M$$
$$\text{if } P \text{ match } N = \phi \text{ and } \phi V$$

where ϕ is the substitution obtained by matching N with P. It maps every variable defined in P to a sub-molecule from N. For example, the rule in the following solution

$$\langle 0, \ 10, \ 8, \ \text{one } x{::}\text{Int by } 9 \text{ if } x > 9 \rangle$$

can react with 10 (the variable x is mapped to 10). They are replaced by 9. The solution becomes the inert solution $\langle 0, \ 8, \ 9 \rangle$.

A molecule inside a solution cannot react with a molecule outside the solution (the construct $\langle . \rangle$ can be seen as a membrane). A HOCL program is a solution which can contain reaction rules that manipulate other molecules (reaction rules, sub-solutions, etc.) of the solution.

In the remaining of the paper, we use some syntactic sugar such as declarations **let** $x = M_1$ **in** M_2 which is equivalent to M_2 where all the free occurrences of x are replaced by M_1. The reaction rules **one** P **by** M **if** C are one-shot: they are consumed when they react. Their variant denoted by **replace** P **by** M **if** C are n-shot, i.e., they do not disappear when they react (like in Gamma).

There are usually many possible reactions making the execution of chemical programs highly parallel and non-deterministic. Since reactions involve only a few molecules and react independently of the context, many distinct reactions can occur at the same time. For example, consider the following program that computes the prime numbers lower than 10 using a chemical version of the Eratosthenes' sieve:

$$\text{let sieve} = \textbf{replace}\, x, y \,\textbf{by}\, x \,\textbf{if}\, x \,\text{div}\, y \,\textbf{in}$$
$$\langle \text{sieve}, 2, 3, 4, 5, 6, 7, 8, 9, 10 \rangle$$

The rule sieve reacts with two integers x and y such that x divides y, and replaces them by x (i.e., removes y). Initially several reactions are possible, for example sieve, $2, 8$ (replaced by sieve, 2) or sieve, $3, 9$ (replaced by sieve, 3) or sieve, $2, 10$ or etc. The solution becomes inert when the rule sieve cannot react with any couple of integers in the solution, that is to say, when the solution contains only prime numbers. The result of the computation in our example is $\langle \text{sieve}, 2, 3, 5, 7 \rangle$.

To access within a sub-solution (e.g., to get the result of a sub-program), a reaction rule has to wait for its inertia. That means that a reaction rule matches only inert sub-solutions. For example, if we want to compute the largest prime number lower than 10, we can use the previous program as a sub-program, i.e., a sub-solution, and then compute the maximum of its result:

$$\text{let sieve} = \textbf{replace}\, x, y \,\textbf{by}\, x \,\textbf{if}\, x \,\text{div}\, y \,\textbf{in}$$
$$\text{let max}\ = \textbf{replace}\, x, y \,\textbf{by}\, x \,\textbf{if}\, x \geq y \,\textbf{in}$$
$$\langle\langle \text{sieve}, 2, 3, 4, 5, 6, 7, 8, 9, 10 \rangle,\ \textbf{one}\langle \text{sieve} = s,\ \omega \rangle\, \textbf{by}\, \omega,\ \text{max} \rangle$$

Initially, the one-shot rule cannot react with the non-inert sub-solution, and only reactions inside the sub-solution can occur. When the sub-solution becomes inert, the one-shot rule matches the sub-solution: the variable s matches the rule named sieve and the variable ω matches all the remaining atoms of the solution (the prime numbers). In the reaction, the one-shot rule and the sub-solution are replaced by the prime numbers (ω) and the rule max which, in turn, triggers new reactions until one element remains. More formally, the execution steps occur as follows:

$$\langle\langle \text{sieve}, 2, 3, 4, 5, 6, 7, 8, 9, 10 \rangle,\ \textbf{one}\langle \text{sieve} = s,\ \omega \rangle\, \textbf{by}\, \omega,\ \text{max} \rangle$$
$$\downarrow *$$
$$\langle\langle \text{sieve}, 2, 3, 5, 7 \rangle,\ \textbf{one}\langle \text{sieve} = s,\ \omega \rangle\, \textbf{by}\, \omega,\ \text{max} \rangle$$
$$\downarrow$$
$$\langle 2, 3, 5, 7, \text{max} \rangle$$
$$\downarrow *$$
$$\langle 7, \text{max} \rangle$$

This example shows the higher-order property of HOCL: the one-shot rule removes and adds other (named) rules. This property allows to express coordination of chemical programs within the language.

The examples provided here are simple and fine grain in order to illustrate the mechanisms of chemical programming through HOCL. But HOCL can also be used as a coordination language of services (coarse grain).

3   Service Orchestration Using HOCL

A service orchestration is a program that describes a coordination of services. HOCL can be used as a data-driven coordination language according a chemical metaphor. For example, the previous HOCL examples can be viewed as data-driven coordination of integers and of functions on integers (div, $\geq$).

3.1   Coordination with HOCL

In [9], workflows are expressed as chemical program. It shows that all coordination mechanism of workflow can be translated into a chemical setting. The enactment of workflows can also be described by a chemical program. In fact, many classical coordination mechanism can be expressed as a chemical coordination [14]: sequential execution, parallel execution, mutual exclusion, atomicity, message passing, shared memory, rendez-vous, Kahn networks, etc.

HOCL programs are self-organizing systems [8]. When a HOCL program reaches an inert state (i.e., a stable state), and if then some new molecules are added (i.e., perturbation of the system), then some new reactions happen with the new molecule until a new inert state is reached (i.e., a new stable state). A simple mail system has been developed as an example of programming self-organization with HOCL. It features self-healing, self-optimizing, self-protection and self-configuration.

HOCL as a coordination language has also been applied to program Desktop Grids. A Desktop Grid is made of non dedicated resources (e.g., any personal computer connected on the Internet). Such a grid can be highly volatile and non reliable. In [11], HOCL is used as a coordination language to specify the execution of a simple ray-tracer in a Desktop Grid. The HOCL program contains rules that adapt the on-going executions of programs according to the availability of resources in the Desktop Grid.

3.2   Orchestrating Services with HOCL

Principle. A chemical service architecture consists of a solution of services, i.e., a solution of sub-solutions, each representing one service (cf Figure 1).

A service is represented by a solution that contains molecules performing the operations that this service proposes. To call a service, one adds a molecule of the form Call:s:n:p in the solution representing the called service, where s is the calling service, n is the identifier of the call for the calling service, and p are the parameters for the operation to be performed.

When a service makes a call to another service it generates a molecule of the form ExtCall:s:n:p where s is the called service, n is the identifier of the call for the current (calling) service, and p are the parameters for the operation to be performed.

At a given time, a service may be running different computations related to different simultaneous call. That's why, to prevent a service to mix the computation and the result of different and independent calls, each call has a unique identifier n

```
let  withdrawServiceCall =
        replace  serv1 : ⟨ ExtCall : serv2 : n : param ,  w⟩
              by  serv1 : ⟨w⟩ ,   Call : serv1 : serv2 : n : param
in
let  depositServiceCall =
        replace  Call : serv1 : serv2 : n : param ,   serv2 : ⟨w⟩
              by  serv2 : ⟨ Call : serv1 : n : param ,  w⟩
in
⟨withdrawServiceCall ,  depositServiceCall ,
  Service1 : ⟨ ... ⟩ ,  ... ,  ServiceN : ⟨ ... ⟩
⟩
```

Fig. 1. Generic chemical service architecture

A call is performed in two steps by two rules. The rule withdrawServiceCall extracts an ExtCall molecule from a service sub-solution and puts it in the main solution. The rule depositServiceCall takes a call in the main solution and forwards it into one corresponding service sub-solution.

Two remarks:

- A call to a service to perform an action, and a call to a service to provide a result are just two ordinary calls: there is no distinction between the two calls. In fact, a call message and its result message are not explicitly coupled like in a RPC for example.
- According to the semantics of HOCL, a rule may react only with an *inert* solution. So the rules withdrawServiceCall and depositServiceCall could only react with inert sub-solutions, i.e., with services that do not do any computation, i.e., with services that only perform communication (input or output of calls). In fact, that inertia constraint may be released for these two rules. These two rules manage molecules that represent messages. So these molecules are independent of computations happening inside the solutions representing the services. Adding or removing a call from these solutions do not depend on the internal state of these solutions. So adding a call to or removing a call from a solution that represents a service can happen even if the solution is not inert.

A travel organizer example. Let's take the example of a travel organizer (cf Figure 2). This travel organizer makes the reservations of a flight and a hotel according some parameters provided by a user.

The service is a solution named TravelOrgService. It contains an integer used as a counter to provide unique identifiers to separate different molecules related to different calls. For each call to the travel organizer service, the rule find-FlightHotel generates two calls: one call to a flight service and one call to a hotel service. It also updates the counter, and stores the reference to that call as a molecule $s{:}m{:}n$ where $s{:}m$ identifies the calling service, and n is the identifier to

---

```
let findFlightHotel =
      replace Call : s : m : p,  n
            by ExtCall : FlightService : n : param,
               ExtCall : HotelService : n : param,
               s : m : n,  (n+1)
in
let resultFlightHotel =
      replace Call : FlightService : n : f,
              Call : HotelService : n : h,
              s : m : n
            by ExtCall : s : m : ( f : h )
in
TravelOrgService : ⟨0, findFlightHotel, resultFlightHotel⟩
```

Fig. 2. A travel organizer service in HOCL

---

this call to the travel organizer service. The rule resultFlightHotel reacts when the results are available. The results appear as two calls: one from a flight service, and one from a hotel service. They both concern the same initial call identified by the counter n. Then the rule generates a call back to the calling service s with its identifier m, and the flight and hotel results $f{:}h$.

Execution example. We describe here a possible execution of the travel organizer example (cf Figure 3). The system is represented by a solution that contains the rules withdrawServiceCall and depositServiceCall that perform the calls, the sub-solutions representing the services (the travel organizer service, the flight services and the hotel services), and two calls to the travel organizer by two different users.

```
⟨withdrawServiceCall, depositServiceCall,
  TravelOrgService : ⟨findFlightHotel⟩,
  FlightService : ⟨Name : AirFrance , ... ⟩,
  FlightService : ⟨Name : BritishAirways , ... ⟩,
  HotelService : ⟨Name : Accor , ... ⟩,
  ... ,
  Call : UIService1 : TravelOrgService : ( Dates1 : Places1 : Pref1 ),
  Call : UIService2 : TravelOrgService : ( Dates2 : Places2 : Pref2 )
⟩
```

Fig. 3. Running the travel organizer service in HOCL

Two users have queried a search for their travel and the system has added the respective calls of the form Call:UIServiceX:TravelOrgService:... into the main solution, where UIServiceX is the identifier of the user interface service that has emitted the call to the travel organizer service TravelOrgService, where DatesX, PlacesX are the dates and places constraints for the required travels, and PrefX some additional preferences. Initially, the rule depositServiceCall can forward the two calls to the travel organizer service. Then the travel organizer will generate the calls to the flight services and the hotel services using the rule findFlightHotel. Then the rule withdrawServiceCall will extract the calls to the main solution, and the rule depositServiceCall will forward these calls to a corresponding service. After, some reactions these services will generate their result inside their solution as an ExtCall molecule addressed to the travel organizer. The rules withdrawServiceCall and depositServiceCall will then bring these messages to the travel organizer. When both result from the flight service and the hotel service are available inside the TravelOrgService for the same initial call, the rule resultFlightHotel will generate an external call to the service that invoked the travel organizer service. Finally, the rule withdrawServiceCall will extract that result from the travel organizer service solution and put it in the main solution, so that it is available to the external world (outside the main solution).

At any time, at execution time in particular, some new services may be added inside the main solution, and some services may be removed from the main solution. This is not a problem, since a coupling between a call and a corresponding service is dynamic and non deterministic. The service type of the called service must be satisfied: for example, several services provide a flight service, and a call to a service flight may react with any of them.

4   Related Work

Coordination and composition of services have attracted a lot of attention of both the industry and the academia. Several approaches have been proposed following either the orchestration or the choreography paradigms. These two paradigms differ from their execution scenario which is mainly centralized for the first one and distributed for the later.

Starting from industry-led initiatives, the standard approach to compose Web Services is the Business Process Execution Language, WS-BPEL [15]. WS-BPEL is a language that provides several powerful control flow structures such as condition, loops, switches and activities, such as Web Service invocation, can be executed either sequentially or concurrently. In addition, WS-BPEL provides variables to store temporary data and fault compensation. WS-BPEL is very verbose largely due to XML root and it shares some similarities with programming languages. Its level of abstraction is rather very low forcing programmers to "think parallel" and to anticipate all possible failures during the workflow execution. Finally, since WS-BPEL is about orchestration, workflow execution is centralized thanks to a WS-BPEL engine. Regarding choreography, the main standard today is the Web Service Choreography Description Language, WS-CDL [16]. Choreography models the interactions and dependencies between a set of services by describing their exchanges of messages. As for

WS-BPEL, WS-CDL provides control structures such as sequence, parallel and choice. Loops are allowed thanks to the WorkUnit activity that provides a way to repeat the execution of an activity depending on a guard condition. As for WS-BPEL, WS-CDL is based on XML and thus is verbose with a low level of abstraction.

On the research side, there is a vast amount of work dealing with Web Service composition. One of the main drawback of WS-BPEL is its lack of formal semantics. In [17,18], a formal semantics of some of the WS-BPEL features, such as the specification of events, fault and compensation handler behaviors or transactions, are introduced. As chemical programming takes its root from rewriting systems, we can mention the work presented in [19] that describes a dynamic service customization and composition framework for Web services based on a rule-based service integration language with concepts borrowed from rewriting systems. Composition of services using an Event-Condition-Action rule based approach, that is even closer to chemical programming, is described in [20]. Self-coordination of Web Services using a Linda-like tuple space, similar to a multiset in our approach, is introduced in [21].

5   Conclusion and Future Work

Originally, the Gamma formalism was invented as a basic paradigm for parallel programming [13]. It was proposed to capture the intuition of a computation as the global evolution of a collection of atomic values evolving freely. Gamma appears as a very high level language which allows programmers to describe programs in a very abstract way, with minimal constraints and no articial sequentiality. Later, it became clear that a necessary extension to this simple formalism was to allow elements of a multiset to be Gamma programs themselves, thus introducing higher-order. This lead to the HOCL language used in this paper.

Basically, the chemical paradigm (as introduced in HOCL) offers four basic properties: mutual exclusion, atomic capture, parallelization and serialization. These properties have been exploited in [14] in order to give a chemical expression of well known coordination schemes.

Along the same lines, this paper investigates the utilization of the Chemical Programming Model, in order to describe Service Coordination. We develop this idea with a simple, yet practical, example dealing with travel organization. The example developed throughout section 3 shows that our approach provides a very abstract and generic way of programming service orchestration. This is made possible due to the higher order property of HOCL. Programs (services) can be handled naturally by appropriate synchronization rules. Here, we have limited our investigations to service orchestration, it is clear that we could have tackled more elaborated synchronization schemes dealing with service choreography.

References

1. Birrell, A.D., Nelson, B.J.: Implementing remote procedure calls. ACM Trans. Comput. Syst. 2(1), 39–59 (1984)
2. OMG: The Common Object Request Broker: Architecture and Specification V3.0. Technical Report OMG Document formal/02-06-33 (June 2002)
3. Open Management Group (OMG): CORBA components, version 3. Document formal/02-06-65 (June 2002)
4. Foster, I., Kesselman, C. (eds.): The Grid 2: Blueprint for a New Computing Infrastructure, 2nd edn. Morgan Kaufmann Publishers, San Francisco (2003)
5. Google app engine, http://code.google.com/appengine
6. Amazon services, http://aws.amazon.com
7. Banâtre, J.P., Fradet, P., Radenac, Y.: Generalised multisets for chemical programming. Mathematical Structures in Computer Science 16(4), 557–580 (2006)
8. Banâtre, J.P., Fradet, P., Radenac, Y.: Chemical specification of autonomic systems. In: Proc. of the 13th Int. Conf. on Intelligent and Adaptive Systems and Software Engineering (IASSE 2004) (2004)
9. Németh, Z., Pérez, C., Priol, T.: Workflow enactment based on a chemical metaphor. In: The 3rd IEEE International Conference on Software Engineering and Formal Methods (September 2005)
10. Németh, Z., Pérez, C., Priol, T.: Distributed workflow coordination: Molecules and reactions. In: The 9th International Workshop on Nature Inspired Distributed Computing, p. 241. IEEE, Los Alamitos (2006)
11. Banâtre, J.P., Le Scouarnec, N., Priol, T., Radenac, Y.: Towards "chemical" desktop grids. In: Proceedings of the 3rd IEEE International Conference on e-Science and Grid Computing (e-Science 2007). IEEE Computer Society Press, Los Alamitos (2007)
12. Banâtre, J.P., Fradet, P., Radenac, Y.: Principles of chemical programming. In: Abdennadher, S., Ringeissen, C. (eds.) Proceedings of the 5th International Workshop on Rule-Based Programming (RULE 2004). ENTCS, vol. 124, pp. 133–147. Elsevier, Amsterdam (2005)
13. Banâtre, J.P., Le Métayer, D.: Programming by multiset transformation. Communications of the ACM (CACM) 36(1), 98–111 (1993)
14. Banâtre, J.P., Fradet, P., Radenac, Y.: Classical coordination mechanisms in the chemical model. In: From semantics to computer science: essays in honor of Gilles Kahn. Cambridge University Press, Cambridge (2008)
15. Barreto, C., Bullard, V., Erl, T., Evdemon, J., Jordan, D., Kand, K., Knig, D., Moser, S., Stout, R., Ten-Hove, R., Trickovic, I., van der Rijn, D., Yiu, A.: Web services business process execution language version 2.0 (May 2007), http://www.oasis-open.org/committees/wsbpel
16. Ross-Talbot, S., Fletcher, T.: Web services choreography description language: Primer (June 2006)
17. Mazzara, M., Govoni, S.: A case study of web services orchestration. In: Jacquet, J.-M., Picco, G.P. (eds.) COORDINATION 2005. LNCS, vol. 3454, pp. 1–16. Springer, Heidelberg (2005)
18. Lucchi, R., Mazzara, M.: A pi-calculus based semantics for ws-bpel. Journal of Logic and Algebraic Programming (January 2007)
19. Chen, J.: Rewrite rules as service integrators. In: Antoniou, G., Boley, H. (eds.) RuleML 2004. LNCS, vol. 3323, pp. 182–187. Springer, Heidelberg (2004)

20. Chen, L., Li, M., Cao, J.: A rule-based workfow approach for service composition. In: Pan, Y., Chen, D.-x., Guo, M., Cao, J., Dongarra, J. (eds.) ISPA 2005. LNCS, vol. 3758, pp. 1036–1046. Springer, Heidelberg (2005)
21. Maamar, Z., Benslimane, D., Ghedira, C., Mahmoud, Q.H., Yahyaoui, H.: Tuple spaces for self-coordination of web services. In: SAC 2005: Proceedings of the 2005 ACM symposium on Applied computing, pp. 1656–1660. ACM, New York (2005)

Guiding Organic Management in a Service-Oriented Real-Time Middleware Architecture

Manuel Nickschas and Uwe Brinkschulte

Institute for Computer Science
University of Frankfurt, Germany
{nickschas,brinks}@es.cs.uni-frankfurt.de

Abstract. To cope with the ever increasing complexity of today's computing systems, the concepts of organic and autonomic computing have been devised. Organic or autonomic systems are characterized by so-called self-X properties such as self-configuration and self-optimization. This approach is particularly interesting in the domain of distributed, embedded, real-time systems. We have already proposed a service-oriented middleware architecture for such systems that uses multi-agent principles for implementing the organic management. However, organic management needs some guidance in order to take dependencies between services into account as well as the current hardware configuration and other application-specific knowledge. It is important to allow the application developer or system designer to specify such information without having to modify the middleware. In this paper, we propose a generic mechanism based on capabilities that allows describing such dependencies and domain knowledge, which can be combined with an agent-based approach to organic management in order to realize self-X properties. We also describe how to make use of this approach for integrating the middleware's organic management with node-local organic management.

1 Introduction

Distributed, embedded systems are rapidly advancing in all areas of our lives, forming increasingly complex networks that are increasingly hard to handle for both system developers and maintainers. In order to cope with this *explosion of complexity*, also commonly referred to as the *Software Crisis* [1], the concepts of *Autonomic* [2,3] and *Organic* [4,5,6] Computing have been devised. While Autonomic Computing is inspired by the autonomic nervous system (which controls key functions without conscious awareness), Organic Computing is inspired by information processing in biological systems. However, both notions boil down to the same idea of having systems with *self-X properties*, most importantly *self-configuration*, *self-optimization* and *self-healing*. More specifically,

U. Brinkschulte, T. Givargis, and S. Russo (Eds.): SEUS 2008, LNCS 5287, pp. 90–101, 2008.

- *self-configuration* means the system's ability to detect and adapt to its environment. An example for this property would be the plug-and-play found in modern computers, which is used to automatically detect and configure certain attached devices;
- *self-optimization* allows the system to autonomously make best use of the available resources, and deliver an optimal performance;
- *self-healing* describes the detection of and automatic recovery from run-time failures, for example by using heartbeat signals and restarting services that are not responding in time.

To present to the applications a homogeneous view on a distributed system of heterogeneous components, there usually is a layer called *middleware* on top of the components' individual operating systems, making the distributed nature of the system mostly transparent to the application developer. Within an organic computing system, we expect the middleware layer to autonomously achieve a high degree of transparency. This includes self-configuration even within a dynamic environment (such as found in ad-hoc networks), self-optimization at run-time, and self-healing in case of failures, thus providing a robust, efficient and uniform platform for the applications without human maintenance or intervention.

Another increasingly important requirement for today's distributed embedded systems is *real-time capability*. A real-time system must produce results and react to events in a timely, predictable manner, guaranteeing temporal restraints that are imposed by the applications.

In [7], we have proposed a service-oriented organic real-time middleware architecture that achieves self-X properties through a multi-agent-based approach. Services act as intelligent agents that use an auction mechanism to coordinate. These agents may move around within the system, finding optimal nodes to run on, and tasks are allocated to agents that are most appropriate. This approach handles self-organization and self-optimization. However, a mechanism needs to be devised that describes and defines dependencies between services, between resources and between tasks in order to provide guidance for task and resource allocation. This mechanism must also be able to describe properties of the hardware (such as attached sensors or actors or available resources). Since that kind of information is often domain specific, it is essential that the application or system designer be able to specify these properties without modifying the middleware, therefore a generic mechanism is needed. In this paper, we propose an approach for such a mechanism.

In Sect. 2 we mention related work. Section 3 gives an overview about our own architecture and motivates the need for guiding organic management in more detail. In Sect. 4 we describe our mechanism and analyze its properties. Sect. 5 shows how to combine that approach with our agent-based middleware architecture in order to achieve a sensible organic management, and Sect. 6 how to integrate it with the node-local organic management. Finally, in Sect. 7 we provide an example that demonstrates our ideas.

2   Related Work

In autonomic and organic computing, much research has been done in recent years (e.g. [8] for an overview). There are different approaches for implementing organic middlewares. The DoDOrg project [9] develops a digital organism consisting of a large number of rather simple, reconfigurable processor cells, which coordinate through an artificial hormone system. The $OC\mu$ middleware [10] features an observer-controller architecture with centralized organic managers. It targets smart office buildings with powerful, connected networks rather than embedded real-time systems. The service-oriented real-time middleware OSA+ [11] has a low footprint and is very scalable, thus it is particularly suitable for embedded distributed real-time systems. However, it does not feature self-X properties. The general architecture for an organic, service-oriented middleware inspired by the OSA+ approach has been developed in [12]. For this architecture, we described an agent-based approach for implementing self-X properties in [7], which uses concepts from multi-agent systems for coordination and task allocation. A short summary of our approach is given in Sect. 3. We are currently implementing and evaluating the proposed mechanism within the CAR-SoC project [13,14].

Other agent-based approaches for organic middlewares, such as [15,16,17], do not feature real-time capabilities. To our knowledge, a flexible, generic mechanism for describing service and resource dependencies in a service-oriented middleware has not yet been developed. Services in OSA+ are fixed on the resources they manage, and tasks are dispatched globally. Other approaches use central planning or do not consider dependencies at all.

3   Overview and Motivation

For an organic middleware, a *service-oriented* architecture proves to be a good choice. For implementing self-configuration, self-optimization and self-healing, a modular concept is vital. In such an architecture, tasks are processed by *services*, which in most cases are not part of the middleware core, but run as independent, loosely coupled entities, leading to a *microkernel design*. We have proposed and explained in detail such a design in [7]; here, we will only give a short overview. We have chosen a microkernel-based approach primarily for *scalability, flexibility, reliability, recovery* and *extensibility*. In our proposed system, services are *intelligent agents* as defined in [18]. Task allocation is done using an auction mechanism based on *ContractNet* [19,20]. This mechanism uses cost/benefit calculations in order to determine the most suitable service agent for processing a given task. This approach is distributed (i.e. does not require central control, thus avoiding a single point of failure) and real-time capable.

In addition to influencing the task allocation mechanism by computing sensible cost/benefit functions, service agents can perform self-optimization by negotiating with other agents (potentially swapping or delegating already allocated tasks if this proves to be more optimal) or by migrating to another node of the distributed system that is more suitable. Sandholm [21] has shown that an optimal task allocation can achieved in a *ContractNet* that allows re-allocation of tasks in certain ways. By periodically re-evaluating the current task allocation and agent distribution, and appropriate reactions, the system will also adapt to a changing environment. In addition, the middleware core can start or shut down service agents on particular system nodes as needed in order to improve scalability and optimize work load.

All this should happen autonomously, without human intervention or configuration. However, dependencies between tasks or between agents, the need for particular resources and hardware limitations on particular nodes restrict the configuration space for an agent. For example, if a task needs a certain resource locally, an agent can only offer to process it if it sits on a node that has that resource available. Or, a particular agent can only run on a node that has a certain hardware sensor attached. Or an agent might require another service running on the same node in order to perform certain functions or run at all. In order to define such restraints and dependencies, a mechanism is needed that guides the system's self-configuration in a way that does not require manual intervention after initial setup. In particular, the following properties are desirable:

- Many dependencies and restraints are application-specific. Thus we need a generic mechanism that is separated from the middleware implementation such that the application developer (or even the user) can define them as needed.
- The same is true for describing the hardware configuration. A node's operating system must be able to communicate its hardware setup (such as attached sensors and actors) to the middleware in a way that is flexible and extensible. It must not be necessary to recompile or reconfigure the middleware if e.g. a new type of hardware device is available; an application service that supports this device should be able to recognize its existence and to make use of it without explicit support by the middleware.
- The mechanism needs to be real-time capable.
- The mechanism should be transparent to the application. In particular, it should not matter for the application *where* (on which node and by which service agent) a task is executed, as long as it is executed at all. Of course, the application needs to be able to specify the requirements for processing a task.

In the following sections we propose and describe a mechanism that has these properties.

4   A Capability-Based Mechanism for Guiding Organic Management

The proposed mechanism is based on so-called *capabilities*. Roughly speaking, a capability c is a globally unique, possibly application-specific identifier representing a particular feature, ability or resource. More formally, we have a set C

containing all known capabilities, hence $c \in C$. Most of the time we will consider *sets of capabilities*, taken from the power set $\mathcal{P}(C)$. Furthermore, on a given node, we have a set R of hardware resources (such as sensors or actors) and a set A of service agents. The subset $A^0 \subset A$ shall denote agents currently not running on the node, whereas $A^1 \subset A$ is the set of currently executing agents.

A hardware resource $r \in R$ provides a set $S_r^{prov} \in \mathcal{P}(C)$ of supported capabilities. A service agent $a \in A$, on the other hand, usually requires a certain set of capabilities $S_a^{req} \in \mathcal{P}(C)$ to run. Moreover, a running service agent might provide additional capabilities $S_a^{prov} \in \mathcal{P}(C)$ to the node it is executed on.

This allows the specification of dependencies between services, such that a service will only be started on a node if another service is already running on that node, or formally, an agent $b \in A^0$ can be started on the node if and only if

$$S_b^{req} \subset \left(\bigcup_{a \in A^1} S_a^{prov} \cup \bigcup_{r \in R} S_r^{prov} \right).$$

The management of capabilities of a node's resources and agents then boils down to performing set operations, and since we are targetting the real-time domain, we need to consider if those can be implemented efficiently. In particular, the middleware core needs to *join* sets and it needs to test if one set is a *subset* of another. For removing capabilities from sets, *subtraction* is needed.

A very time-efficient implementation represents capability sets by *bitstrings*, with each bit representing a given capability that is either present or not. In this case, the afforementioned set operations boil down to bit-wise logical operations that can be done efficiently in constant time. Let S and $T \in \mathcal{P}(C)$ be capability sets, and s and t the corresponding bitstrings. Then the following are equivalent:

Set operation	Logical operation
$S \cup T$	s OR t
$S - T$	s AND NOT t
$T \subset S$?	$(s$ AND t$) = $ t ?

If the core maintains a capability set containing all offered capabilities (by joining S^{prov} for all resources as well as started services), it can check if a given service agent can be started in constant time. Removing a service, however, can only be done in constant time if we can assume that a capability cannot be provided by more than one resource or agent; only then can we use set substraction to remove the provided capabilities from the global set. Otherwise, the core needs to check all remaining providers for that capability, so this operation needs linear time (in the number of resources and running agents).

One drawback of this mechanism is the fact that the global number of capabilities must be known beforehand (at compile time) in order to guarantee constant time operations; otherwise, one needs to provide for dynamically growing capability sets. Another drawback is that the representation of a capability set is not the most space efficient. If we have n capabilities in the system, we need a bitstring of length n to represent a capability set regardless of the number of elements contained. A single capability, however, can be represented as an integer number and mapped to its corresponding bit using a list of bitmasks for set operations.

If the real-time constraints and hardware resources allow for a more complex implementation, one can also use a more dynamic approach, for example using a hierachical tree structure containing named capabilities, where each node acts as a namespace for its children. A capability is then described by its path starting from the root of the tree. The most prominent advantage of such an approach is that it is dynamically extensible; the number of known capabilities needs not to be known beforehand, and the use of namespaces allow for arbitrarily (application-specific) named capabilities without the risk of collisions. However, this data structure does not allow for constant-time processing of sets.

5   Combining the Capabilities-Based Approach with Service Agents

As summarized in Sect. 3, we have proposed a middleware architecture that realizes self-X properties using service agents that coordinate using an auction mechanism. Essentially, for a given task, an announcement is sent out to suitable agents within the system – where the suitability of an agent can be checked by comparing its set of provided capabilities to the task's set of required capabilities. Every suitable agent determines the cost processing the task would incur and sends this information to the core. The agent with the best offer gets awarded the task.

For this auction mechanism, it is vital that a service agent be able to compute a sensible cost/benefit function for processing the task. Such a function should consider the cost of using needed resources, and also capture quality-of-service parameters (such that the price for processing a task depends on the quality of the result). Thus, it makes sense to attach cost information directly to the capabilities. This means, that using a resource is mapped to "using" a capability, and the provider of that capability (e.g. the node operating system or another service agent) determines an appropriate cost value. Of course, the same is true for delegating subtasks to other agents, which also would be mapped to using the corresponding set of capabilities. Quality-of-service parameters can be attached to the cost inquiry. Thus, the total cost for processing a given task is composed of the cost of the needed resources and subtask processing, represented by the corresponding capabilities.

6   Integrating Capabilities with Node-Local Organic Management

Within the *CAR-SoC* project, we are currently implementing our proposed approach in a middleware we call *CARISMA*[1]. CAR-SoC aims to build a

---

[1] Connected Autonomous Real-time Intelligent Service-based Middleware Architecture.

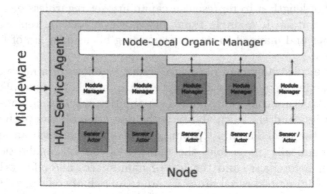

Fig. 1. Integration of node-local and global organic management. The shaded parts are components of the HAL Service agents, while white boxes belong to local organic management.

distributed embedded real-time system, with organic properties being employed throughout the whole stack. The individual nodes within the network run an operating system (called *CAROS* [22]) that features node-local organic management as described in [23]. We will not go into this concept in detail here, but only summarize the basic principles in a very concise and simplified manner as far as it concerns the interaction of the middleware layer's organic manager with the individual nodes (Fig. 1).

CAROS employs a two-staged organic management approach. On the lower level, small management units, so-called *Module Managers*, each manage a small set of system parameters, usually tied to a specific hardware or software module. Module managers receive raw monitoring data and can directly change the system parameters they manage. If a decision cannot be made on this lowest level, pre-interpreted monitoring data in a generic format is forwarded to the upper level, the node-local organic manager, which can make decisions based on node-wide status information.

As it turns out, this approach integrates very well with the capability-based approach for global organic management we propose here. A special middleware service agent (called HAL Agent, for Hardware Abstraction Layer) manages the interaction between the middleware core and the underlying node operating system. Its main task is to translate the specific hardware features into capabilities, and to attach a sensible cost/benefit function to using a given capability in order to influence the global organic management by way of the afforementioned auctioning mechanism. To accomplish that, the HAL agent registers itself as a module manager for the system parameters that can be monitored and/or influenced by the middleware layer.

On the middleware level, using a capability will generally require the usage of node resources. The module manager for a given resource attaches a *cost scale* to using that resource. In addition, system parameters might need to be adjusted. For example, using a capability might require a certain amount of processing power, which in turn might require to increase the node's processor frequency. On the node level, any actor that changes system parameters also has a cost scale attached. Changing a parameter, or a combination of parameters, will improve or worsen the node's state; for example, increasing the processor frequency in order to offer required computing power also increases energy consumption and system temperature and therefore the overall cost value of the action. In order to influence the global organic management, the node's cost scales are integrated by the HAL Agent and attached to the capabilities to be used by the global auctioning mechanism. Summarizing this, the cost/benefit function for using a given capability is derived from both the cost scales for the needed resources and for changing the node's state.

On the other hand, the HAL Agent can also register its own actors on the node level, thus allowing the node's organic manager to actively influence global organic management. For example, one actor might be "move this service from this node to another". The attached cost scale would reflect the possible alternative locations for running the given service (obtained as the result of an auctioning round). Another possibility might be to change quality-of-service (QoS) parameters of a running service in order to improve the node's state; the cost scale the HAL agent provides for this actor would reflect the incurring quality degradation on a global level.

This shows that within the architecture proposed in the CAR-SoC project, both global and local organic management can interact in various ways. Capabilities as suggested here allow mapping global properties to local resources and system parameters and vice versa. This diversity in implementation of organic features will be very interesting to explore; in particular, how to fine-tune the balance between the global and local organic managers, since both levels can influence the other's decisions passively (by modifying cost values) or actively (by performing actions).

7   Example

For a better understanding, we will in this section discuss a simple example that demonstrates auction-based task allocation using capabilities in order to provide self-X properties. For the sake of brevity and simplicity, we will only describe the global level of organic management and not consider the interaction with the node-local organic management as described in Sect. 6.

Consider the front lighting control of a car. We assume that this car has a left and a right headlight, a left and a right turn signal and a left and a right front fog light. These lights are controlled by two microcontrollers running our agent-based middleware (Fig. 7). As example scenario for self-X properties, consider that one of the turn signals breaks and can no longer be used. The system shall detect this failure and then autonomously decide to let the corresponding fog light blink in the future, since this behavior (signaling a turn with a fog light) is still safer than not signaling a turn at all. In addition, if the fog light also stops working, the system shall decide to use the headlight instead (which is

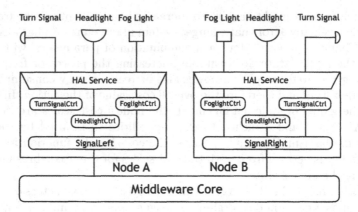

Fig. 2. Example scenario. Two controllers (Node A and B) each control three lights. Hardware is accessed through the HAL service providing appropriate capabilities. Control services make these available to higher-level, more complex services such as *SignalLeft* and *SignalRight*.

the worst method, but still better than nothing). This is an example for *self-healing*.

The system nodes provide capabilities (possibly through a hardware abstraction layer service HAL) that describe the hardware configuration. Each node has the capabilities HEADLIGHT, TURNSIGNAL and FOGLIGHT. In addition, the physical location of these lights needs to be defined, so the nodes have the capabilities RIGHT resp. LEFT. Each light is controlled by a service that allows to toggle its state and that monitors the function of the corresponding light. Thus, these services need the corresponding capability to run, and they provide the capabilities ON and OFF for their lamp. In addition, information about the nature of the light is provided. All lights can ILLUMINATE the road, and all lights can SIGNAL a turn. However, they are not equally suited for these tasks, so these capabilities carry a cost value[2] with them that describes how appropriate a job is for the given light. Here, application-specific knowledge is used in order to influence the organic management appropriately. Since a headlight can illumante the road quite well, the cost is 0; on the other hand, using it as a turn signal is only desired if it is the only working light left, so we associate a cost of 100 with that. A fog light can illuminate the road somewhat, but not very good. We give it a cost of 50. It also can signal a turn if necessary, and is preferred to the headlight for that task, so the cost for signaling should not be 0, but also less than 100. We give it a 50. The turn signal can hardly illuminate the road, but we still want to turn it on if the other lights are all broken; so the cost for illumination is 500. Of course, it signals a turn for free because it is the preferred device for that task. The services, capabilities and cost are summarized in Tab. 1.

---

[2] Note that the absolute number does not matter; it is the relation between different cost values that guides task allocation.

Table 1. System services in the example scenario, provided capabilities and associated cost. The left table shows the capabilities provided by the hardware configuration of the two nodes; the right table shows the services for controlling the lighting.

Service	Capability	Cost
Node A HAL	HEADLIGHT	0
	FOGLIGHT	0
	TURNSIGNAL	0
	LEFT	0
Node B HAL	HEADLIGHT	0
	FOGLIGHT	0
	TURNSIGNAL	0
	RIGHT	0

Service	Capability	Cost
HeadlightCtrl	ON	0
	OFF	0
	ILLUMINATE	0
	SIGNAL	100
FoglightCtrl	ON	0
	OFF	0
	ILLUMINATE	100
	SIGNAL	50
TurnSignalCtrl	ON	0
	OFF	0
	ILLUMINATE	500
	SIGNAL	0

7.1 Capabilities in Action

Now, services for signaling a right or left turn shall be started. To run, these services (named *SignalLeft* and *SignalRight*) need the capabilities SIGNAL and LEFT or RIGHT, respectively. Consider the service *SignalLeft*. The middleware core can only start this on Node A, which provides the necessary capabilities. If all lights are working, *SignalLeft* will use the SIGNAL capability provided by the *TurnSignalCtrl* service, since it is the cheapest. It can then offer the capability SIGNAL_LEFT with an attached cost of 0 to the application. Now assume that the blinker lamp breaks. *TurnSignalCtrl* will notice this and notify the system that it can no longer provide its capabilities. This information is forwarded to *SignalLeft*. It now tries to find another service that provides the SIGNAL capability; *FoglightCtrl* can do this for 50. This means that SIGNAL_LEFT is still being provided to the application, but for a cost of 50 now. Only if the fog light also breaks will *SignalLeft* resort to the headlight, since it is even more expensive to use. Should all lights on the left side be disabled, *SignalLeft* could no longer find the SIGNAL capability and would need to shut down. A similar scenario can be imagined for road illumination, causing the system to resort to the fog light if the headlight breaks, and still using the turn signal if all else is gone.

7.2 Summary

This example demonstrates how capabilities can be used to describe the hardware configuration of a system, and how an auction-based task allocation mechanism can make use of appropriately defined capabilities for realizing self-configuration and self-healing.

8 Conclusion

In this paper, we have presented a method for describing dependencies between services and resources in a service-oriented organic middleware. In such a middleware, self-X properties are realized by allocating tasks to the most suitable service, and executing services on the most suitable node. This information is often application-specific and cannot be hard-coded within the middleware. We have shown a generic mechanism based on capabilities that allows guiding the organic management. It is possible to specify both dependencies between services and dependencies on resources. By combining the capability mechanism with an auction-based task allocation mechanism as described in [7], self-optimization, self-configuration and self-healing can be achieved.

We are currently implementing the proposed mechanism in our middleware CARISMA, which is part of the CAR-SoC project [13]. This project extends the focus of organic computing to the hardware by developing an embedded hard-real-time system supporting autonomic computing principles. CARISMA closely interacts with the local (per-node) organic management to create a robust self-configuring, self-optimizing and self-healing distributed system. We have described how we plan to integrate both the global and node-local organic management by mapping capabilities and attached cost functions to local monitors and actors.

References

1. Gibbs, W.W.: Software's chronic crisis. Scientific American, 72–81 (September 1994)
2. Kephart, J.O., Chess, D.M.: The vision of autonomic computing. IEEE Computer, 41–50 (January 2003)
3. Horn, P.: Autonomic Computing: IBM's Perspective on the State of Information Technology. IBM Research, Armonk (October 2001)
4. Müller-Schloer, C., v.d. Malsburg, C., Würtz, R.P.: Organic computing. Aktuelles Schlagwort in Informatik Spektrum, 332–336 (2004)
5. Schmeck, H.: Organic computing – a new vision for distributed embedded systems. In: Proc. of the Eighth IEEE International Symposium on Object-Oriented Real-Time Distributed Computing (ISORC 2005), pp. 201–203. IEEE Computer Society, Los Alamitos (2005)
6. VDE/ITG/GI: Positionspapier Organic Computing: Computer und Systemarchitektur im Jahr 2010 (2003)
7. Nickschas, M., Brinkschulte, U.: Using multi-agent principles for implementing an organic real-time middleware. In: Proc. 10th IEEE International Symposium on Object and Component-Oriented Real-Time Distributed Computing (ISORC 2007), Santorini, Greece, pp. 189–195. IEEE Computer Society, Los Alamitos (2007)
8. Deutsche Forschungsgemeinschaft: DFG SPP 1183 Organic Computing
9. Becker, J., Brändle, K., Brinkschulte, U., Henkel, J., Karl, W., Köster, T., Wenz, M., Wörn, H.: Digital on-demand computing organism for real-time systems. In: ARCS Workshops, GI. LNI, vol. 81, pp. 230–245 (2006)

10. Trumler, W.: Organic Ubiquitous Middleware. Ph.D thesis, Universität Augsburg (2006)
11. Picioroagǎ, F.: Scalable and Efficient Middleware for Real-Time Embedded Systems. A Uniform Open Service Oriented, Microkernel Based Architecture. Ph.D thesis, Université Louis Pasteur, Strasbourg (December 2004)
12. Nickschas, M.: Konzeption einer Anwendungsschnittstelle für eine echtzeitfähige Middleware mit Selbst-X-Eigenschaften. Master's thesis, Universität Karlsruhe (TH) (September 2006)
13. Uhrig, S., Maier, S., Ungerer, T.: Toward a Processor Core for Real-time Capable Autonomic Systems. In: Proceedings of the 5th IEEE International Symposium on Signal Processing and Information Technology, December 2005, pp. 19–22 (2005)
14. Kluge, F., Mische, J., Uhrig, S., Ungerer, T.: Car-SoC – towards an autonomic SoC node. In: ACACES 2006, L'Aquila, Italy, July 2006, Academia Press, Ghent, Belgium (2006) (Poster Abstracts)
15. Kasinger, H., Bauer, B.: Combining multi-agent-system methodologies for organic computing systems. In: Proceedings of the 16th International Workshop on Database and Expert Systems Applications (DEXA 2005). IEEE Computer Society, Los Alamitos (2005)
16. Mamei, M., Zambonelli, F.: Self-organization in multi agent systems: A middleware approach. In: Engineering Self-Organising Systems, pp. 233–248 (2003)
17. Serugendo, G.D.M., Gleizes, M.P., Karageorgos, A.: Self-organization in multi-agent systems. Knowl. Eng. Rev. 20(2), 165–189 (2005)
18. Weiss, G. (ed.): Multiagent Systems. A Modern Approach to Distributed Artificial Intelligence. The MIT Press, Cambridge (1999)
19. Smith, R.G.: The contract net protocol: High-level communication and control in a distributed problem solver. IEEE Transactions on Computers C-29(12), 1104–1113 (1980)
20. Sandholm, T.W.: An implementation of the contract net protocol based on marginal cost calculations. In: Proceedings of the 12th International Workshop on Distributed Artificial Intelligence, Hidden Valley, Pennsylvania, pp. 295–308 (1993)
21. Sandholm, T.W.: Contract types for satisficing task allocation: I Theoretical results. In: AAAI Spring Symposium Series: Satisficing Models, Stanford University, CA, March 1998, pp. 68–75 (1998)
22. Kluge, F., Mische, J., Uhrig, S., Ungerer, T.: An Operating System Architecture for Organic Computing in Embedded Real-Time Systems. In: Rong, C., Jaatun, M.G., Sandnes, F.E., Yang, L.T., Ma, J. (eds.) ATC 2008. LNCS, vol. 5060. Springer, Heidelberg (2008)
23. Kluge, F., Uhrig, S., Mische, J., Ungerer, T.: A two-layered management architecture for building adaptive real-time systems. In: Proceedings of the 6th IFIP Workshop on Software Technologies for Future Embedded & Ubiquitous Systems (SEUS 2008) (2008)

Self-describing and Data Propagation Model for Data Distribution Service

Chungwoo Lee[1], Jaeil Hwang[1], Joonwoo Lee[1], Chulbum Ahn[1], Bowon Suh[1],
Dong-Hoon Shin[1], Yunmook Nah[1], and Doo-Hyun Kim[2]

[1] Department of Computer Science and Engineering, Dankook University,
126 Jukjeon-dong, Suji-gu, Yongin-si, Gyeonggi-do, 448-701, Korea
{cman,jihwang,jwlee,ahn555,bwsuh,dhshin,ymnah}@dblab.
dankook.ac kr
[2] Department of Internet and Multimedia Engineering, Konkuk University,
1 Hwayang-dong, Gwangjin-gu, Seoul 143-701, Korea
doohyun@konkuk.ac.kr

Abstract. To realize real-time information sharing in generic platforms, it is especially important to support dynamic message structure changes. For the case of IDL, it is necessary to rewrite applications to change data sample structures. In this paper, we propose a dynamic reconfiguration scheme of data sample structures for DDS. Instead of using IDL, which is the static data sample structure model of DDS, we use a self describing model using data sample schema, as a dynamic data sample structure model to support dynamic reconfiguration of data sample structures. We also propose a data propagation model to provide data persistency in distributed environments. We guarantee persistency by transferring data samples through relay nodes to the receiving nodes, which have not participated in the data distribution network at the data sample distribution time. The proposed schemes can be utilized to support data sample structure changes during operation time and to provide data persistency in various environments, such as real-time enterprise environments and connection-less internet environments.

Keywords: data distribution service, dynamic message reconfiguration, persistency, real-time information sharing.

1 Introduction

Recently, real-time distributed data processing requirements are ever increasing in many real-world applications, such as weapon systems, sensor-based embedded systems [1,2], airplane software, flight simulator [3,4], and normal business systems [5]. In the past, such real-time processing techniques were primary concern in the military applications, which have to develop embedded systems for weapon systems. Nowadays, it becomes essential to share and utilize various information and knowledge in real-time, even in the normal business environments. For example, the OLTP data need to be transferred in real-time to enterprise data warehouse for more

U. Brinkschulte, T. Givargis, and S. Russo (Eds.): SEUS 2008, LNCS 5287, pp. 102–113, 2008.

correct decision making. To realize such real-time information sharing in more generic platforms, it is especially important to support dynamic message structure changes. To realize such real-time distributed environments, real-time distributed middleware technologies are required. RT-CORBA, which was evolved from CORBA, TMO, which was developed at UCI, and DDS (Data Distribution Service), which is announced as a standard specification by OMG, are representative middleware technologies for such environments. RT-CORBA is a standard proposed by RT-SIG of OMG to allow QoS specification, real-time service and performance optimization, which have not been well supported in CORBA [6,7]. TMO is a natural and syntactically minor but semantically powerful extension of the conventional objects [8,9]. DDS is a publish-subscribe model for real-time environments and was adopted as a middleware standard to develop data distribution services by OMG [10,11,12]. These middleware technologies have some problems to be used in the real-time business environments, because they often require dynamic changes of message structures, as compared to the embedded environments, which seldom require data structure changes. Such changes are required because of database schema changes or XML document structure changes. For the case of IDL (Interface Definition Language), it is necessary to rewrite applications to change data sample structures.

In this paper, we propose a dynamic reconfiguration scheme of data sample structures for DDS and explain the APIs to support such dynamic restructuring of data sample structures in distributed real-time applications. We also describe how to support persistency, which is one of important QoS (Quality of Service) elements of DDS. Instead of using IDL, which is the static data sample structure model of DDS, we use a self describing model using data sample schema, as a dynamic data sample structure model to support dynamic reconfiguration of data sample structures. In our case, we can dynamically support data sample structure changes, because data sample schema can be determined in run-time. We explain how to create and change data sample structures and how to send and receive data samples using data sample schema. We also propose a data propagation model to provide data persistency in distributed environments. We guarantee persistency by transferring data samples through relay nodes to the receiving nodes, which have not participated in the data distribution network at the data sample distribution time. Finally, to show the usefulness and efficiency of our schemes, some experimental results are shortly provided. The proposed schemes can be utilized to support data sample structure changes during operation time and to provide data persistency in various environments. The remainder of this paper is organized as follows. Section 2 describes overview of data distribution service. A dynamic reconfiguration scheme of data sample structures for DDS are proposed in Section 3. Section 4 explains how to support persistency and section 5 provides some experimental results. Finally, section 6 concludes the paper.

2 Overview of Data Distribution Service

DDS is networking middleware that simplifies complex network programming. It implements a publish/subscribe model for sending and receiving data, events, and commands among the nodes. Nodes that are producing information (publishers) create *topics* (e.g., temperature, location, pressure) and publish *samples* (data values of topics). DDS takes care of delivering the sample to all subscribers that declare an interest in that topic. DDS handles all the transfer chores: message addressing, data marshaling and de-marshalling (so subscribers can be on different platforms than the publisher), delivery, flow control, retries, etc. Any node can be a publisher, subscriber, or both simultaneously. The DDS publish-subscribe model virtually eliminates complex network programming for distributed applications.

The DDS specification describes two levels of interfaces. A lower DCPS (Data-Centric Publish-Subscribe) level is targeted towards the efficient delivery of the proper information to the proper recipients. According to the conceptual model of DCPS [13], 'Publisher,' 'Subscriber,' 'DataReader,' 'DataWriter,' and 'Topic' are 'DomainEntity.' Also, 'DomainEntity' and 'DomainParticipant' are 'Entity.' 'Entity' has a relationship with 'QosPolicy.' Each 'Publisher' can have multiple 'DataWriters' and each 'Subscriber' can have multiple 'DataReaders.' An optional higher DLRL (Data Local Reconstruction Layer) level allows for a simple integration of DDS into the application layer.

In the network-centric model usually used in previous middleware technologies, the position of receiving node must be specified, like 'Node 1 sends data to Node 2.' Therefore, special treatments were required for sending nodes when positions of receiving nodes are changed or new receiving nodes are inserted. As compared to this, the DCPS of DDS does not specify the position of receiving nodes. Sending nodes just specify topic of data and receiving nodes receive data when they are interested in the topic of current data. For example, node 1 sends data to the DDS network specifying that the topic of that data is 'A.' At node 2, if the topic of the data that the node wants to receive is 'A,' it waits for that topic from the DDS network and receives the data having that topic. As such, the DDS network is extendable and flexible, because position changes of receiving nodes and insertions of new receiving nodes do not affect the network.

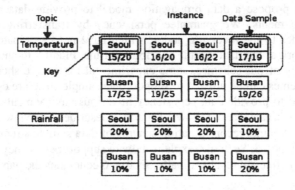

Fig. 1. Instance examples

Figure 1 shows example instances of two topics 'Temperature' and 'Rainfall.' The field values, such as 'Seoul' and 'Busan,' which identify instances, are called *keys*. A group of data having the same key is called an *instance*. Each instance shows the history of data samples having the same key. Each individual data within an instance is called a *data sample*, which is the unit of data transmission in DDS networks. The DDS provide QoS elements, such as USER_DATA, TOPIC_DATA, GROUP_DATA, DURABILITY, PRESENTATION, DEADLINE, OWNERSHIP, LIVELINESS, PARTITION, RELIABILITY, HISTORY, etc.

3 Self-describing Model to Support Dynamic Reconfiguration

In this section, we describe a self-describing model and data sample schema to support dynamic reconfiguration of data samples.

3.1 Self-describing Model

The IDL is used to define data structures of data samples in the DDS standard specification. Therefore, data structures of data samples are fixed and application programs have to be rebuilt to change data structures during system operation. To allow dynamic definition of sample structures, there must exist ways to define data structures and transmit such structures dynamically.

Fig. 2. Schema model

Figure 2 shows the proposed schema model. In our self-describing model of DDS, data schema is first broadcasted as a built-in topic and then data samples, with data structure identifiers attached, are transmitted.

3.2 Data Sample Schema

An entity to define a data structure of data samples is called a *data sample schema*, which is an enumerated list of data types of corresponding data fields in a data sample. This structure must exist in the DomainParticipant before the corresponding data samples are created or interpreted. The structure of internal topic DCPSSchema to transmit schema information is shown in Table 1.

The 'key' is used to manage schema changes. The 'participant_key' is the DCPS key which make registration of the given data sample schema. Therefore, only data samples created by this participant can reference this schema. In the 'topic_name,' the topic of data sample referencing this schema is specified. The sequence number given to this schema is recored in the 'schema_seq.'

Figure 3 shows an example using data sample schema. The schema S with key value 1 and sequence number 1, created by the participant 1 to send topic T, is

Table 1. The structure of DCPSSchema

Field name	Type	Meaning
key	BuiltinTopicKey_t	DCPS key to identify registration
participant_key	BuiltinTopicKey_t	DCPS key of the participant which make registration of data sample schema
topic_name	string	topic name associated with data sample schema
schema_seq	integer	sequence number of data sample schema
field_count	integer	number of fields of data sample schema
field_types	TypeArray_t	array of field data types

broadcasted to the DCPSSchema. The schema S consists of 3 fields, with data types {INTEGER, STRING, FLOAT}. For data transmission, the Publisher writes a sample D1 with the sample schema S. It first writes the key value 1 and sequence number 1 for the sample schema S in the header of the data sample. Then, the values of each fields, 1234(the value of 0th field), 3(the length of the first field), "DKU"(the value of the first field), 0.5678(the value of the second field) are written. The Subscriber receiving this data sample D1 uses the key value 1 and sequence number 1 to identify the data sample schema S and interprets the data sample using this schema.

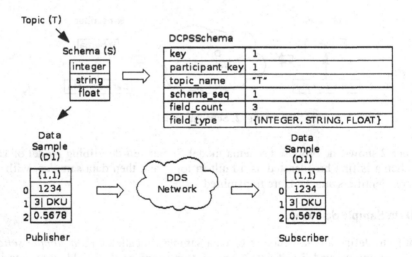

Fig. 3. Example of schema usage

Now, let's see how data sample structures can be dynamically reconfigured, as shown in Figure 4. Suppose we have data samples D1 and D2, all following the schema S. The key value and schema sequence number in the header information of D1 and D2 is (1,1). Also suppose that the data sample schema S is changed dynamically to S', having field data types {INTEGER, STRING} and such change is updated into the DCPSSchema. Data samples, such as D3 and D4, which are created after this schema change, will have new header information (1,2), which means the key value is

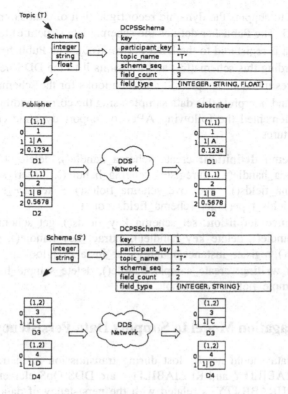

Fig. 4. Example of schema change

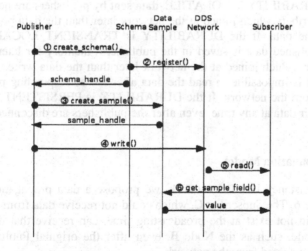

Fig. 5. Schema handling sequence

the same but the sequence number is incremented(changed). The Subscriber can now interpret new data samples by new schema S', because the sequence number in the header of data samples is now 2.

The workflow to support the dynamic reconfiguration of data sample structures is shown in Figure 5. The Publisher defines the schema(data structure) to send data(①). Then, this schema is registered to the DDS network(②). The Publisher then creates a data sample regarding this schema(③) and transmits it to the DDS network(④). The Subscriber receives this data sample(⑤) and then looks for the schema referenced by this data sample and interprets this data sample using the corresponding schema(⑥).

We have implemented the following APIs to support dynamic configuration of data sample structures.

- **APIs for schema definition:** create_schema_handle(), delete_schema_handle(), register_schema_handle(), unregister_schema_handle(), insert_schema_fields(), append_schema_fields(), remove_schema_fields(), replace_schema_fields(), get_schema_fields_type(), get_schema_fields_count
- **APIs for instance definition:** set_schema_key_fields(), get_schema_key_fields(), create_key_handle(), delete_key_handle(), extract_key_handle(), set_key_field(), get_key_field(), register_instance(), unregister_instance(), lookup_instance()
- **APIs for data writing:** create_sample_handle(), delete_sample_handle(), write(), read(), set_sample_field(), get_sample_field()

4 Data Propagation Model to Support Data Persistency

The enterprise data should not be lost during transmission in distributed environments. The DURABILITY and RELIABILITY are DDS QoS elements related with data loss. The DURABILITY is related with the persistency of data transmitted by publishers and the RELIABILITY is related with the reliability of communication lines. If the DURABILITY is VOLATILE, data sent by publishers are not saved at all and those subscribers which joined at the network later than the data publishing time can not read the data. If the DURABILITY is TRANSIENT_LOCAL or TRANSIENT, the published data is saved in the publishers' memory for later request and those subscribers which joined at the network later than the data write time can read the data. But, it is impossible to read the data after the corresponding publishers are disconnected from the network. If the DURABILITY is PERSISTENT, all subscribers can read their data at any time, even after the publishers are disconnected from the network.

4.1 Data Propagation Model

To support persistency in DDS network, we propose a data propagation model, as shown in Figure 6. The Subscriber C, which could not receive data from the Publisher A because it did not exist at the broadcasting time, can receive that data from the intermediary node, such as the Node B, even after the original Publisher, such as Node A, is disconnected from the network.

To realize this propagation model, we need intermediary nodes, also called relay nodes, that can propagate data instead of the publishing node. In our method, every participant whose DURABILITY is PERSISTENT can take role of intermediary nodes. Each intermediary node is required to have a persistent repository for data

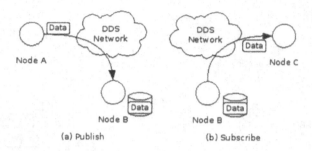

Fig. 6. Data propagation model

propagation. Each intermediary node stores its received data in its persistent repository and forwards received data if required. The structure of persistent repository for an intermediary node is shown in Table 2.

Table 2. The structure of persistent repository

Field name	Type	Meaning
participant_key	BuiltinTopicKey_t	DCPS key of the publisher which sent data sample
instance_key	KeyValue_t	instance key of data sample
sample_count	integer	number of stored data samples
samples	Integer	array of {sample_seq, sample}

When a data sample is received by an intermediary node, it is stored in the entry of persistent repository with the matching 'participant_key' and 'instance_key.' The corresponding 'sample_count' is incremented, while the sample itself is stored in the 'samples' array. Because the resources for persistent repositories are limited, we can not allow every data sample to be stored. We have to manage only recent history by limiting the number of history according to the system configuration. We can decide the detail limitation by using the QoS element DURABILITY_SERVICE, as shown in Table 3.

Table 3. The QoS element DURABILITY_SERVICE

attribute	Meaning
service_cleanup_delay	interval to delete all samples in persistent repository
history_kind	store every sample(KEEP_ALL) or recent sample(KEEP_LAST)
history_depth	number of recent samples to be kept, when history_kind is KEEP_LAST
max_samples	maximum number of samples to be stored in the repository
max_instances	maximum number of instances to be stored in the repository
max_samples_per_instance	maximum number of samples to be stored per instance

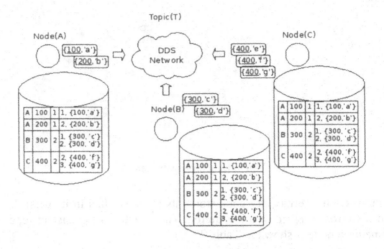

Fig. 7. Example using persistent repositories

Figure 7 is an example showing the use of persistent repositories. Suppose the DURABILITY of all nodes A, B and C are specified as PERSISTENT. Also, assume the 'history_kind' is KEEP_LAST and the 'history_depth' is 2 for all nodes, meaning that all three nodes keep last 2 data samples.

Figure 7 shows the status of persistent repositories after the Node A send data samples {100, 'a'}, {200, 'b'}, the Node B send data samples {300, 'c'}, {300, 'd'}, and the Node C send data samples {400, 'e'}, {400, 'f'}, {400, 'g'}. Here, the values, such as 100 and 200, are key values.

4.2 Data Propagation Protocol

The protocol to receive data which can not be received at the broadcasting time is shown in Figure 8.

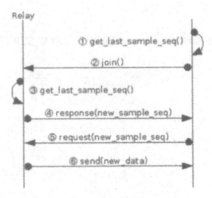

Fig. 8. Data propagation protocol

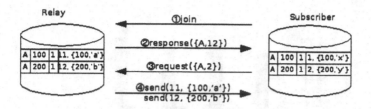

Fig. 9. Case of new subscriber with lower sample number

The newly joined subscriber checks the last sample number from its own persistent repository(①). The new subscriber then sends 'join' message to the DDS network(②). Each intermediary node gets its last data sample number(③) and responds this last number to the subscriber(④). The new subscriber compares sample numbers and send transmission request, if the sample number of itself is less than one of the sample numbers of intermediary nodes(⑤). The intermediary node which receives transmission request sends the required data to the new subscriber(⑥).

Figure 9 shows an example case where newly joined subscriber has a last sample number(2) less than one of the last sample number(12) of the intermediary nodes. The relay node send two samples {100, 'a'} and {200, 'b'} whose sample numbers are greater than 2.

5 Experiments

For our experiments, we used the API of the open source project ORTE (Ocera Real-Time Ethernet) 0.3.1[14] which implements the RTPS (Real-Time Publish-Subscribe) protocol [15], the low level communication protocol of DDS. In a distributed environments consisting of 1 publisher and 3 subscribers, we compared turnaround delays of DDS/IDL with DDS/Schema(the proposed method). We also compared such delay for the case implemented by Sun Java System Message Queue 3.7[16], which is a kind of message queue middleware for ESB(Enterprise Service Bus) service.

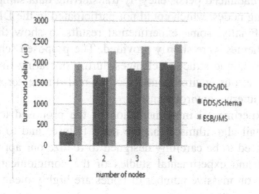

Fig. 10. Turnaround delay time in distributed environments

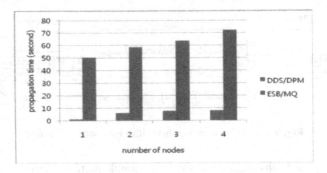

Fig. 11. The initial sample propagation time of subscribers

Figure10 shows the turnaround delay in distributed environments. The turnaround delay for DDS/IDL was 2,012µs, DDS/Schema was 1,956µs and ESB/JMS was 2,448µs. This result shows us that the performance of DDS/IDL and DDS/Schema is almost the same, but the proposed method has better ability allowing dynamic reconfiguration of data sample structures without re-programming overhead.

We also compared the data propagation time in the test system consisting of 4 participants. Figure 11 shows the initial data sample propagation time of subscribers. The propagation time for DDS/DPM(the proposed method) was 8 seconds, while ESB/MQ was 72.1 seconds, which shows us that our persistency mechanism is faster than ESB/MQ.

6 Conclusion

In this paper, we proposed a dynamic reconfiguration scheme of data sample structures for DDS. We also described how to support persistency, which is one of important QoS elements of DDS. Instead of using IDL, which is the static data sample structure model of DDS, we used a self describing model using data sample schema. We also proposed a data propagation model to provide data persistency in distributed environments. We guaranteed persistency by transferring data samples through relay nodes to the receiving nodes, which could not participated in the DDS network at the broadcasting time. Finally, some experimental results to show the usefulness and efficiency of our schemes were shortly provided. The proposed schemes can be utilized to support data sample structure changes during operating time and to provide data persistency in various environments, such as real-time enterprise environments and connection-less internet environments.

Our effort for experimental implementation of the proposed techniques is at an early stage. The detail algorithms to handle node failures and to optimize message passing overheads need to be carefully designed to realize our approach. We believe that both analytical and experimental studies of the communication overhead and performance aspects on massive number of nodes are highly meaningful subjects for future research.

Acknowledgments. This research was supported by the Ministry of Knowledge Economy, Korea, under the Information Technology Research Center support program supervised by the Institute of Information Technology Advancement (grant number IITA-2008-C1090-0801-0031). This work was also supported by the Korea Science and Engineering Foundation (KOSEF) grant number R01-2007-000-20958-0 funded by the Korea government (MOST).

References

1. Pardo-Castellote, G., Schneider, S.: The Network Data Delivery Service: Real-Time Data Connectivity for Distributed Control Applications. In: Proc. IEEE International Conference on Robotics and Automation, pp. 2870–2876. IEEE Press, Los Alamitos (1994)
2. Schneider, S.A., Ullman, M.A., Chen, V.W.: ControlShell: A Real-Time Software Framework. In: Proc. IEEE International Conference on Systems Engineering, pp. 129–134. IEEE Press, Los Alamitos (1991)
3. Kuhl, F., Weatherly, R., Dahmann, J.: Creating Computer Simulation Systems. Prentice Hall, Englewood Cliffs (1999)
4. Dahmann, J.S., Morse, K.L.: High Level Architecture for Simulation: An Update. In: Proc. 2nd International Workshop on Distributed Interactive Simulation and Real Time Applications, pp. 32–40 (1998)
5. Khosla, V., Pal, M.: Real Time Enterprises: A Continuous Migration Approach. Information, Knowledge, Systems Management 3(1), 53–79 (2002)
6. Schmidt, D.C., Kuhns, F.: An Overview of the Real-Time CORBA Specification. Computer 33(6), 56–63 (2000)
7. Cooper, G., DiPippo, L., Esibov, L., Ginis, R., Johnston, R., Kortman, P., Krupp, P., Mauer, J., Squadrito, M., Thuraisingham, B., Wohlever, S., Wolfe, V.: Real-Time CORBA Development at MITRE, NRaD, Tri-Pacific and URI. In: Proc. IEEE Workshop on Middleware for Distributed Real-Time Systems and Services, pp. 69–74. IEEE Press, Los Alamitos (1997)
8. Kim, K.H.: A TMO Based Approach to Structuring Real-Time Agents. In: Proc. 14th IEEE International Conference on Tools with Artificial Intelligence, pp. 165–172. IEEE Press, Los Alamitos (2002)
9. Kim, K.H.: APIs for Real-Time Distributed Object Programming. IEEE Computer, 72–80 (2000)
10. Zieba, B., Sinderen, M.: Preservation of Correctness During System Reconfiguration in Data Distribution Service for Real-Time Systems(DDS). In: Proc. 26th IEEE International Conference on Distributed Computing Systems Workshops, pp. 30–35. IEEE Press, Los Alamitos (2006)
11. Pardo-Castellote, G.: OMG Data-Distribution Service: Architectural Overview. In: Proc. 23rd International Conference on Distributed Computing Systems Workshops, pp. 200–206 (2003)
12. Hugues, J., Pautet, L.: A Framework for DRE middleware, an Application to DDS. In: Proc. 9th IEEE International Symposium on Object and Component-Oriented Real-Time Distributed Computing, pp. 224–231. IEEE Press, Los Alamitos (2006)
13. Data Distribution Service for Real-time Systems, V1.2. OMG (2007)
14. Smolik, P., Sebek, Z., Hanzalek, Z.: ORTE-Open Source Implementation of Real-Time Publish-Subscribe protocol. In: Proc. 2nd International Workshop on Real-Time LANs in the Internet Age, pp. 68–72. Universidade de Porto, Porto (2003)
15. Real-Time Publish-Subscribe (RTPS) Wire Protocol Specification, V.1.0. ICE (2004)
16. Schmidt, M.T., Hutchison, B., Lambros, P., Phippen, R.: The Enterprise Service Bus: Making Service-Oriented Architecture Real. IBM Systems Journal 44(4), 781–797 (2005)

Improving Real-Time Performance of a Virtual Machine Monitor Based System

Megumi Ito* and Shuichi Oikawa

Department of Computer Science, University of Tsukuba
1-1-1 Tennodai, Tsukuba, Ibaraki 305-8573, Japan

Abstract. This paper describes our approach to enable Gandalf VMM (Virtual Machine Monitor) to be interruptible. Although Gandalf is shown to be a lightweight VMM, the detailed performance analysis using PMC (Performance Monitoring Counters) showed Gandalf executes with interrupts disabled for a rather long duration of time. By making Gandalf interruptible, we are able to make VMM based systems more suitable for embedded and ubiquitous systems. We analyzed the requirements to make Gandalf interruptible, designed and implemented the mechanisms to realize it. The experimental results shows that making Gandalf interruptible significantly reduces a duration of execution time with interrupts disabled while it does not impact the performance.

1 Introduction

As embedded and ubiquitous systems are rapidly moving towards having multi-core CPUs in order to balance performance and power consumption, there is more need for virtualized execution environments to be used in those systems. Such virtualized execution environments are realized upon virtual machine monitors (VMMs) [4]. VMM based systems enable the provision of secure and reliable, yet efficient execution environments.

A major barrier of employing VMMs on embedded and ubiquitous systems is their limited resources. In order to overcome such a barrier, we have been developing a lightweight VMM, called Gandalf, that targets those resource constrained systems [7,8]. It currently operates on IA-32 CPUs, and two independent Linux operating systems (OSes) concurrently run on it as its guest OSes. The code size and memory footprint of Gandalf is much smaller than that of full virtualization. The number of the modified parts and lines is significantly fewer than paravirtualization, so that the cost to bring up a guest OS on Gandalf is extremely cheap. Guest Linux on Gandalf performs better than XenLinux. Therefore, Gandalf is an efficient and lightweight VMM that suits resource constrained embedded and ubiquitous systems.

The detailed performance analysis, which was performed by using CPU's performance monitoring counters (PMC), also revealed Gandalf executes with interrupts disabled for a rather long duration of time [8]. This is because Gandalf handles events that

---

* She is currently with IBM Research, Tokyo Research Laboratory. Work conducted when she was with University of Tsukuba.

U. Brinkschulte, T. Givargis, and S. Russo (Eds.): SEUS 2008, LNCS 5287, pp. 114–125, 2008.

are reported as faults, and such handling of faults is usually done with interrupts disabled. There paper describes our effort to improve Gandalf's real-time performance. We analyzed the requirements to make Gandalf interruptible, designed and implemented the mechanisms to realize it. The experimental results show that making Gandalf interruptible significantly reduces a duration of execution time with interrupts disabled while it does not impact the performance.

The rest of this paper is organized as follows. Section 2 describes the overview of Gandalf VMM. In Section 3 we describe how we made Gandalf interruptible. Section 4 shows the performance of interruptible Gandalf and Section 5 describes the related work. Finally, Section 6 concludes the paper.

2   Overview of Gandalf

This section describes the overall architecture of Gandalf, a multi-core CPU oriented lightweight VMM. It targets the IA-32 architecture [6] as a CPU and Linux as a guest OS. Fig. 1 shows the structure of a Gandalf VMM based system. Gandalf is a

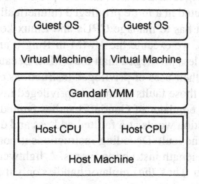

Fig. 1. Structure of Gandalf based system

Type-I VMM, which executes directly upon a host physical machine and creates multiple virtual machines for guest OSes. The virtual machines are isolated from each other, so that a guest OS can execute independently on each virtual machine. Gandalf keeps the management of physical hardware resources as simple as possible in order to implement a lightweight VMM for embedded systems. Therefore, Gandalf tries to manage resource spatially rather than temporarily whenever possible. For example, Gandalf maps one physical CPU to one virtual CPU while many other VMMs multiplex multiple virtual CPUs on one physical CPU to be shared among multiple virtual machines. Gandalf's spatial resource management scheme enables a simpler and smaller implementation and then leads to a lightweight VMM, while the multiplexing model tends to impose higher overheads for the management of virtual CPUs and virtual machines. In this paper, we use the term VMM interchangeably to mean Gandalf if not otherwise specified.

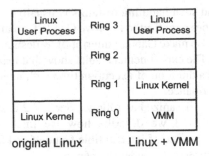

Fig. 2. Privilege level usage

The IA-32 architecture provides 4 privilege levels (rings) from 0 to 3. A numerically less privilege level is more privileged; thus, Ring 0 is the most privileged. Some important instructions, which operate on the machine state, are called privileged instructions, and can be executed only in Ring 0. As the left part of Fig. 2 shows, Linux normally executes its kernel in Ring 0 and its user processes in Ring 3. Thus, the kernel can manage CPUs using privileged instructions and can protect itself from user processes. A VMM needs to be executed in a more privileged (numerically less) level than Linux kernels because the VMM has to manage CPUs and Linux kernels. Therefore, as the right part of Fig. 2 shows, we execute the VMM in Ring 0 and the Linux kernels in Ring 1, which is one level less privileged than the VMM. Because we moved the Linux kernels from Ring 0 to 1, their uses of privileged instructions cause general protection faults. The VMM handles those faults to emulate privileged instructions appropriately. The privileged instruction emulator of Gandalf handles faulted instructions. The emulator first reads the instruction words at a faulted address and decodes them to find out which instruction caused the fault. Decoding instructions is complicated especially for IA-32 because of variable length instruction words. A lightweight emulator requires a simpler instruction decoder. Thus, the emulator handles only the privileged instructions that the Linux kernels execute.

Native Linux kernels normally use all the physical memories in the system. However, when executing multiple Linux kernels on a VMM at the same time, they need to divide up the physical memory. We allocate the upper area of the physical address space for the VMM, divide the remaining area, and allocate a divided part for each Linux. The left most part of Fig. 3 shows the physical memory map. Shadow paging is used to enforce Linux kernels to use only the allocated physical memories [8]. Shadow paging lets Linux kernels manage their own page tables (guest page tables) and separates them from the shadow page table that is referenced by a physical CPU. The VMM manages the shadow page table in order to keep its consistency with guest page tables and also to observe improper uses of physical memories. Concerning a virtual address space, there needs to be an area where a VMM resides. Linux kernels, however, normally use all the virtual address space, which overlaps the virtual memory area for the VMM. To avoid Linux kernels accessing the VMM, we exclude the virtual memory area for the VMM from the available virtual memory for

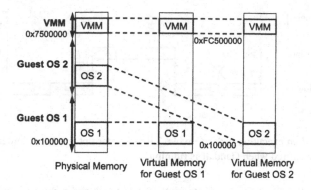

Fig. 3. Memory map

Linux kernels by modifying the source code.[1] We also use the segment mechanism to limit the accessible virtual memory space. For simplicity, we allocate the upper area of the virtual address space for the VMM.

3 Interruptible Gandalf

We have shown that Gandalf is a lightweight VMM from intensive performance evaluations using CPU's performance monitoring counters (PMC) [8]. The evaluations using PMC also revealed Gandalf executes with interrupts disabled for a rather long duration of time. This is because Gandalf handles events that are reported as faults, such as general protection faults and page faults. A guest Linux's execution of a privileged instruction causes a general protection fault, and Gandalf handles the fault to emulate the instruction. When a page fault occurs, Gandalf handles the fault to maintain the shadow page table. It is natural for those faults to be handled with interrupts disabled because the causes of those faults are themselves indivisible.

Embedded systems require quick and timely responses to interrupts. An interrupt can be an event that processes have been waiting for; thus, in that case, it unblocks those processes. For example, a timer interrupt unblocks a process that has been sleeping for a certain time. Gandalf enables the quick and timely handling of an interrupt by a guest OS when it is not running. An interrupt invokes the guest Linux's corresponding interrupt handler directly without Gandalf's intervention. This is possible because Gandalf's spatial resource management scheme maps one physical CPU to one virtual CPU and it is guaranteed that all interrupts go to the same guest Linux.

If a lower priority process caused a fault and invoked a VMM before the timer interrupt occurred, however, the delivery and handling of the interrupt is delayed because the VMM executes with interrupts disabled. Such a delay of handling an interrupt causes the priority inversion problem. Therefore, it is important for a VMM to be interruptible, so that it can handle an interrupt that occurs even while the VMM are handling a fault.

---

[1] Only one line of a modification is needed for this change.

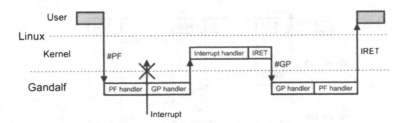

Fig. 4. Example of an execution path to invoke Linux's interrupt handler in order to respond to an interrupt that occurred when Gandalf is running

We successfully made Gandalf interruptible and reduced a duration where Gandalf executes with interrupts disabled. The rest of this section describes in detail the design and implementation of interruptible Gandalf.

3.1 Rationale

We first investigate the mechanisms to make Gandalf interruptible. Supposing Gandalf is interruptible, Fig. 4 depicts an example execution path that Gandalf responds to an interrupt, which occurred when Gandalf is handling a page fault of a user process. When Linux's user process causes a page fault, Gandalf's page fault handler is invoked. An interrupt occurs while the page fault handler is still running. Since the corresponding interrupt handler is in the Linux kernel and a CPU does not allow a handler in a lower privilege ring to be invoked, an attempt to invoke the handler in Ring 1, which is for the Linux kernel, causes a general protection fault. Gandalf's general protection fault handler finds that the interrupt caused the fault; thus, it manually invokes the Linux's corresponding interrupt handler. When Linux finishes the interrupt handling, it executes the IRET instruction to return from the handler. Such an execution of IRET again causes a general protection fault because IRET cannot be used to return to the higher privilege ring. Gandalf's general protection fault handler takes this chance to resume the execution of the page fault handler.

This example suggests that, in order to handle interrupts occurred during Gandalf's execution, Gandalf needs to support the nest of traps because the appropriate handling of general protection faults is required during the original trap handling. Specifically, interruptible Gandalf needs to be able to invoke Linux's interrupt handler during Gandalf's execution and to have the handler return to Gandalf to resume its execution. In this scheme, during the execution of Linux's kernel or user process, an interrupt still can directly invoke Linux's interrupt handler without Gandalf's intervention. Since the execution is in the Linux for the most of time, it is advantageous to keep the lightweight interrupt handling implemented in Gandalf.

3.2 Invoking Linux's Interrupt Handler

If an interrupt occurs during the execution of Gandalf with interrupts enabled, the invocation of Linux's interrupt handler causes a general protection fault because of the IA-32's protection architecture as described above. Gandalf's general protection fault

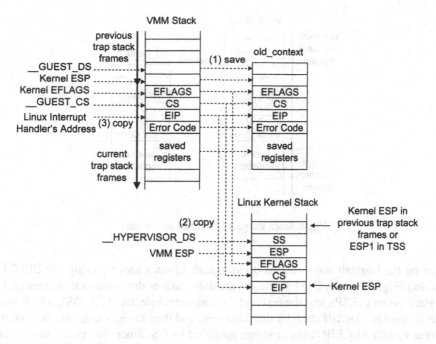

Fig. 5. Manipulation of Gandalf and the Linux kernel stacks for the preparation to invoke Linux's interrupt handler from Gandalf

handler is invoked by two reasons, Linux's execution of privileged instructions and interrupts; thus, it has to be able to differentiate between them and to identify the exact cause of the fault. The handler can distinguish interrupts from the execution of privileged instructions by looking at the error code of a fault. A general protection fault pushed an error code onto the VMM stack, and its value is different for each reason. If it finds the fault was caused by an interrupt, it reads the ISR (In-Service Register) in APIC (Advanced Programmable Interrupt Controller) to obtain the interrupt number; therefore, all information needed to invoke Linux's interrupt handler can be obtained.

Once Gandalf's general protection fault handler obtains the necessary information to invoke Linux's interrupt handler, Gandalf sets up the stacks of Gandalf and the Linux kernel to prepare for the invocation. Both of the stacks need to be manipulated because they carry different information. The preparation takes the following three steps. First, Gandalf saves the current context by copying the current stack frame on the Gandalf stack to the old context save area, which was allocated in advance at the boot time (Fig. 5 (1) save). It also need to save some additional bytes above the current frame because they are corrupted by the third step, which will be described below. Only one save area is needed because the following interrupts are handled directly in Linux and can avoid general protection faults. Second, Gandalf pushes the interrupted context information onto the Linux kernel stack and creates the structure as if the interrupt directly invoked the Linux's interrupt handler (Fig. 5 (2) copy). The pushed data is used to return to Gandalf after Linux's interrupt handler finished handling the interrupt. The next section describes the returning to Gandalf in detail. Finally, Gandalf sets up the stack

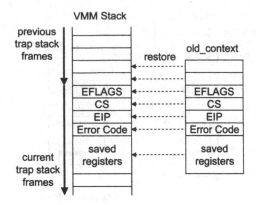

Fig. 6. Stack usage when return to Gandalf

frame on the Gandalf stack so that it can upcall Linux's handler using the IRET instruction (Fig. 5 (3) copy). IRET restores the data, such as the instruction pointer (EIP), the stack pointer (ESP), and the text and data segment selectors (CS, DS), which were pushed onto the Gandalf stack by the third step, and then the execution starts from the address specified by EIP at the privilege specified by CS. Since the current implementation pushes the DS and ESP values onto the previous trap stack frame and corrupts 8 bytes, they are also saved in the first step described above.

3.3   Returning to Gandalf

After Linux's interrupt handler finished handling an interrupt, Linux executes the IRET instruction to resume the interrupted execution. When Gandalf invokes Linux's interrupt handler as described above, the execution of IRET with the stack frame created by Gandalf causes a general protection fault. The CS in the stack frame to be used by IRET points to Gandalf's text segment, of which privilege is higher than Linux's segment. Since IRET does not allow the execution to return to the higher privilege, Gandalf receives a general protection fault handler and finds that Linux's interrupt handler finished its execution.

When Gandalf's general protection fault handler finds that the cause of a fault is Linux's execution of IRET and also that there is valid information saved in the old context save area, it determines that is needs to resume the interrupted execution. The information to be restored was saved at the first step to invoke Linux's interrupt handler (Fig. 5 (1) save). Gandalf restores the interrupted context by copying data from the old context save area back to the Gandalf stack (Fig. 6) and makes the stack the same as the point when interrupt just occurred. Gandalf then executes IRET to return to the interrupted point and resume the execution.

3.4   Implementation

We implemented the mechanisms to make Gandalf interruptible described in the previous sections, and enabled interrupts at the following sections in Gandalf:

- handle_set_pte() hypercall,
- flush_shadow_pgd() hypercall,
- a part of the page fault handler where the shadow page table is updated,
- INVLPG emulator in the general protection handler.

These sections manipulate shadow page tables and the number of executing instructions are large; thus, making these sections interruptible are considered to be effective in order to decrease the total number of interrupt masked cycles in Gandalf.

4 Performance

We experimented with a single guest OS to evaluate the costs to make Gandalf interruptible and its improvement in the total number of interrupt masked cycles in Gandalf. We used the Dell Precision 490 equipped with the Intel Xeon 5130 2.0 GHz processor. We used Linux 2.6.18 with few changes required for the guest OS to run on Gandalf VMM. We employed PMC (Performance Monitoring Counter) to measure the total number of interrupt masked cycles. The experiment to measure the interrupt latency was also performed. We performed the same experiments with the native Linux 2.6.18 and paravirtualized XenLinux[2] on Xen 3.1 [1], and compared their results with those of Gandalf.

4.1 Evaluation with LMbench Microbenchmark

First, we show the results from the LMbench benchmark programs [11] in Fig. 7. The LMbench consists of a number of benchmark programs that measure the basic operation costs of an OS. We chose three programs, pipe latency, process fork-and-exit and process fork-and-exec, to make the baseline of the performance. From the results, we can compare the performance of interruptible Gandalf with the non-interruptible version of Gandalf, the original Linux, and Xen.

The results show that Linux on Gandalf performs slightly slower than the original Linux for those benchmark programs, but much faster than Xen. Although Xen applies paravirtualization to XenLinux for better performance, Gandalf outperforms Xen by its simple and lightweight design and implementation.

The differences between the interruptible and non-interruptible versions of Gandalf are negligible. Interruptible Gandalf slows down only 5% at most for process fork-and-exit, but it performs almost the same (less than 1%) for the rest of the benchmark programs.

4.2 Interrupt Masked Cycles

We further analyze the differences between the interruptible and non-interruptible versions of Gandalf by using PMC (Performance Monitoring Counter) provided by the target CPU. PMC counts the number of occurrences of the selected events. PMC can also be configured to count an event that occurred only when the execution is in Ring 0.

---

[2] This version of XenLinux is also based on Linux 2.6.18. Therefore, we used the same version 2.6.18 of the original Linux, XenLinux, and Linux on Gandalf for fair comparisons.

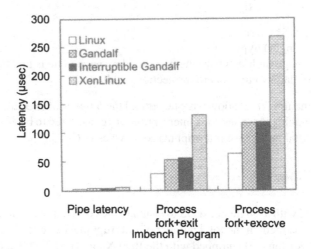

Fig. 7. Basic performance evaluation performed by using the LMbench benchmark programs

By this feature, we can see what portion of the number of events occurred in a VMM, which executes in Ring 0. There are many kinds of events PMC can count, such as L1 and L2 cache misses, TLB misses, and so on. We used PMC to investigate why Gandalf outperforms Xen and found that the memory footprint is the major source of overheads in Xen [8].

This paper focuses on the CYCLES_INT_MASKED event, by which PMC counts the cycles when interrupts are disabled (masked). We used the three programs that are not from the LMbench benchmark but function the same as them. Fig. 8 shows the results of the measurements that were performed on the both versions of Gandalf and the original Linux. For the both versions of Gandalf, the measurements were performed to count events occurred in all protection rings and only in Ring 0. The events in Ring 0 means that they occurred during the execution of Gandalf only.

The results show that the interrupt masked cycles are significantly reduced on interruptible Gandalf for the process fork-and-exit and process fork-and-exec programs. The results from the pipe latency program are almost the same. As described in Section 3.4, Gandalf currently enables interrupts only during certain sections, which are considered large enough, so that the costs of upcalling Linux's interrupt handler pays. Those sections are mostly related to the manipulation of shadow page tables. The process fork-and-exit and process fork-and-exec programs exercises those sections that are made interruptible. Therefore, we see the significant difference. On the other hand, the execution of the pipe latency program does not involve the manipulation of shadow page tables; thus, we do not see any improvement.

4.3 Interrupt Latency

Finally, we show the measurement results of the interrupt latency on the both versions of Gandalf, the original Linux, and Xen, in Fig. 1. We measured the latency from the time the interrupt handler in the Linux kernel starts to handle the interrupt until the

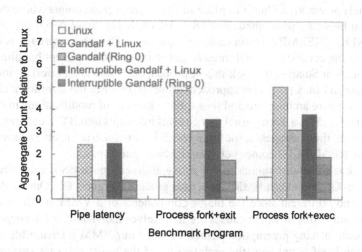

Fig. 8. Comparison of CYCLES_INT_MASKED counts

Table 1. Results of interrupt latency

	Native Linux	Gandalf	Interruptible Gandalf	Xen
TSC counts	21868	22908	22977	23902
latency (μsec)	10.96	11.48	11.52	11.98

time the process waiting for the interrupt resumes its work, using the RTC (Real-Time Clock) device.

Comparing with the native Linux, interruptible Gandalf is 5.1% slower while the non-interruptible version of Gandalf is 4.8% slower. The differences between the interruptible and non-interruptible versions of Gandalf are very small and negligible. Although Gandalf is slower than the native Linux, it can respond to the interrupt faster than Xen.

The evaluation results described in Section 4 have shown that the effort of making Gandalf interruptible significantly reduced the sections where interrupts are disabled while it does not impact the performance. We, however, need to investigate where we can further reduce the sections where interrupts are still disabled.

5 Related Work

There have been lots of efforts to make OS kernels preemptive in order to improve the real-timeliness of systems. Preemptive kernels can dispatch a higher priority process, which was made runnable by an event, such as an interrupt or a message, while another process is executing in the kernel. Non-preemptive kernels allow another process to be dispatched only at the certain point where the current process finished its execution in the kernel and is returning to the user level. There are mainly two approaches to make kernels preemptive. One is to place multiple preemption points where the current process can be safely preempted. The DEC ULTRIX [2], Sun OS 5.0 [9], and Linux 2.6's CONFIG_PREEMPT option took this approach. The other approach is to handle interrupts in the context of kernel threads and to make such interrupt handling threads schedulable. Sun Solaris [10] took this approach, and there is an effort to incorporate such changes in Linux [13]. This approach, however, requires the significant changes to the kernel software architecture and thus quite a number of modifications in the kernel source code. L4 [5] is a microkernel that convert interrupts into IPC messages, and then threads handle the messages at the user level. L4 microkernel itself is, however, not preemptive. REAL/IX [3] comes between the two approaches.

Our work is somewhat similar to the above efforts to make OS kernels preemptive, supposing an OS kernel is a VMM and a user process is a guest OS. Our work is, however, inherently different since the major components of a VMM are the handlers of exceptions and faults, of which causes are themselves indivisible. We incorporated the first approach, placing preemption points, to make our VMM interruptible. Although the approach itself is not new, the architecture of the target software system is completely different; thus, this work is a step to make VMMs more suitable for embedded systems.

6 Conclusion

We described our approach to enable Gandalf VMM to be interruptible. Although Gandalf was shown to be a lightweight VMM, the detailed performance analysis using PMC showed that Gandalf executes with interrupts disabled for a rather long duration of time. By making Gandalf interruptible, we are able to make VMM based systems more suitable for embedded and ubiquitous systems. We analyzed the requirements to make Gandalf interruptible, designed and implemented the mechanisms to realize it. The experimental results showed that making Gandalf interruptible significantly reduced a duration of execution time with interrupts disabled while it did not impact the performance. We will further investigate where we can reduce the sections where interrupts are currently disabled.

References

1. Barham, P., Dragovic, B., Fraser, K., Hand, S., Harris, T., Ho, A., Neugebauer, R., Pratt, I., Warfield, A.: Xen and the Art of Virtualization. In: Proceedings of the 19th ACM Symposium on Operating System Principles, October 2003, pp. 164–177 (2003)
2. Fisher, T.: Real-Time Scheduling Support in Ultrix-4.2 for Multimedia Communication. In: Rangan, P.V. (ed.) NOSSDAV 1992. LNCS, vol. 712, pp. 321–327. Springer, Heidelberg (1993)
3. Furht, B., Parker, J., Grostick, D.: Performance of REAL/IX-Fully Preemptive Real Time UNIX. ACM SIGOPS Operating Systems Review 23(4), 45–52 (1989)
4. Goldberg, R.P.: Survey of Virtual Machine Research. IEEE Computer (June 1974)
5. Hartig, H., Hohmuth, M., Liedtke, J., Schonberg, S., Wolter, J.: The Performance of μ-Kernel-Based Systems. In: Proceedings of the 16th ACM Symposium on Operating System Principles (October 1997)

6. Intel Corporation. IA-32 Intel Architecture Software Developer's Manual
7. Ito, M., Oikawa, S.: Meso virtualization: Lightweight Virtualization Technique for Embedded Systems. In: Obermaisser, R., Nah, Y., Puschner, P., Rammig, F.J. (eds.) SEUS 2007. LNCS, vol. 4761, pp. 496–505. Springer, Heidelberg (2007)
8. Ito, M., Oikawa, S.: Lightweight Shadow Paging for Efficient Memory Isolation in Gandalf VMM. In: Proceedings of the 11th IEEE International Symposium on Object and Component-Oriented Real-Time Distributed Computing (ISORC 2008) (May 2008) (to appear)
9. Khanna, S., Serbree, M., Zolnowsky, J.: Realtime Scheduling in SunOS 5.0. In: Proceedings of the Winter 1992 Usenix Conference, pp. 375–390 (1992)
10. Kleiman, S., Eykholt, J.: Interrupts as Threads. ACM SIGOPS Operating Systems Review 29(2), 21–26 (1995)
11. McVoy, L., Staelin, C.: LMbench: Portable Tools for Performance Analysis. In: Proceedings of the USENIX Annual Technical Conference, January 1996, pp. 279–294 (1996)
12. Meyer, R., Seawright, L.: A Virtual Machine Time Sharing System. IBM Systems Journal 9(3), 199–218 (1970)
13. Real-Time Linux Wiki, http://rt.wiki.kernel.org/
14. Rosenblum, M., Garfinkel, T.: Virtual Machine Monitors: Current Technology and Future Trends. IEEE Computer, 39–47 (May 2005)

A Two-Layered Management Architecture for Building Adaptive Real-Time Systems

Florian Kluge, Sascha Uhrig, Jörg Mische, and Theo Ungerer

Department of Computer Science - University of Augsburg
86159 Augsburg, Germany
{kluge,uhrig,mische,ungerer}@informatik.uni-augsburg.de

Abstract. The concepts of Autonomic and Organic Computing (AC/OC) promise to make modern computer systems more secure and easier to manage. In this paper, we extend the observer/controller architecture typically used in AC/OC systems towards a new target area – embedded real-time systems. As a result we present a two-layered management architecture. We discuss aspects of internal communication and design a communication model. Finally, we present a generic classification system for the upper layer of the management architecture.

1 Introduction

Academic and industrial research investigate concepts to master the growing complexity of today's computer systems. In 2001, IBM introduced the concept of *Autonomic Computing* (AC) [1] for the management of growing IT infrastructures with focus on the so-called *Self-X properties* of *Self-Configuring*, *Self-Healing*, *Self-Optimising*, and *Self-Protecting*. In 2003, Kephart and Chess presented an architecture for the design of such self-X systems [2]. A productive system is embedded into a loop of *Monitor, Analyse, Plan,* and *Execute*. The different stages of this *MAPE cycle* have access to a common *knowledge* base. The MAPE cycle optimises the operations of the underlying productive system with respect to the self-X properties.

Müller-Schloer introduced the concept of *Organic Computing* (OC) in 2004 [3] to convey the ideas of Autonomic Computing into the field of embedded computing devices. Richter et al. developed a generic observer/controller architecture for the design of OC systems [4]. Here, similar to the MAPE architecture, the production system is embedded into the control loop of observation and control which aims to improve the system's operation. Both the MAPE cycle as well as the observer/controller architecture can be equipped with functionalities for the learning resp. prediction of behaviour.

Both concepts have the following features in common: Based on monitoring of relevant system parameters, the management unit (called Autonomic or Organic Manager) models in its observer part (Monitor, Analyse; MA- -) the current system state. The monitored data is aggregated with previous state information and analysed. Future trends may be predicted. The controller part (Plan,

U. Brinkschulte, T. Givargis, and S. Russo (Eds.): SEUS 2008, LNCS 5287, pp. 126–137, 2008.

Execute; - -PE) plans new actions and triggers their execution on the System under Observation/Control (SuOC), i.e. the productive system. These architecure models are designed very generic and do not take the particular requirements of embedded hard real-time systems into account.

Within the German Science Foundation (DFG) priority program *Organic Computing*, there are some projects dealing with real-time or embedded systems. The project DoDOrg [5] investigates a digital organism for real-time applications. It aims at the use of reconfigurable hardware to implement virtual organs that can handle specific tasks. In the EPOC project [6], methods of performance analysis and optimisation are developed. The ASoC project aims at the development of an architecure and design methodology to embed autonomic and organic computing principles into a System-on-Chip [7]. However, neither of these projects does address the fundamental concepts of software architectures for embedded real-time systems in depth. Solomon et al. presented a reference architecture for autonomic real-time systems [8], but did not incorporate the resource constraints of embedded systems.

The contribution of this paper is an analysis of applying the concepts of Autonomic and Organic Computing to embedded real-time systems. It is based on the observation that the extensive analysis and the planning part are not feasible for real-time applications. Therefore a new two-layered reaction system inspired by the natural reflex system is proposed. An extensive analysis of communication concepts leads to a detailed communication model between the two layers. On base of this communication model and on further requirements from real-time systems we developed a classification system for the derivation of reactions responding to harmful states of the managed system.

In section 2 we present the two-layered management architecture. Section 3 gives a detailed discussion of communication between the two layers, and in section 4 we present DCERT, a concept for *Dynamic Classification in Embedded Real-Time systems*. Section 5 concludes this paper.

2   The Two-Layered Management Architecture

In the targeted environment of embedded systems we have to heed several constraints originating in hardware restrictions and application requirements. Hard real-time applications must never miss a deadline. So it is necessary to guarantee that an AC/OC management does not influence the timing behaviour of such an application in any unpredictable way. The microcontrollers and the software usually are built to fit, so that no money is wasted on unused performance. Simultaneously, the AC/OC management should support the real-time operation of such systems and therefore provide fast reactions with a fixed timing overhead that has a low upper bound in terms of execution cycles.

An embedded system usually comprises a vast range of parameters relevant for system monitoring. Also, there are many points where decisions of the management can be applied to. However, the interpretation of all monitored parameters

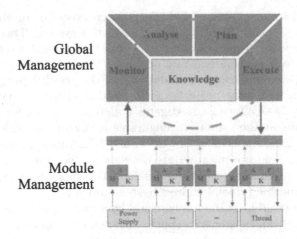

Global
Management

Module
Management

Fig. 1. The two-layered management architecture

would be very expensive. Also, in most cases it is possible to find a reasonable solution when regarding only a small subset of all parameters. There might be better solutions, when taking a larger set of parameters into account, however due to planning or learning algorithms this would happen at the cost of a higher reaction time possibly without any upper timing bound.

The following example will clarify this idea. As initial situation, a observer service monitors the progress of a real-time application thread. If the application impends to miss its deadline, several countermeasures are possible. The easiest solution would be to increase the processing time of the application, if possible. This solution only needs to monitor two parameters: the knowledge of the application's progress and the possibility to increase the processing time. Also there is just one parameter affected, the processing time of the thread. A further solution is to increase the clock frequency, which however affects the power consumption. Finally, the monitoring information of several embedded control units (*ECUs*) can be brought together. Then it can be decided to move the application to a higher-performance ECU or one with more free processing time. However, the latter two solutions, especially the last one, need to evaluate much more data.

Therefore, we introduce two levels of decision making (see fig. 1). On the lower level, small management units (*Module Managers*) are attached to distinct hardware or software modules. These module managers only work on a very small parameter set and hence, they comprise just a small and static rule set. Thus, they can reach a decision very fast within an upper bounded timing budget. These module managers correspond to the reflexes in nature.

If a module manager has performed its reaction or cannot find a solution for a specific state, it conducts a pre-interpretation of the monitored data. This abstracted information is forwarded to the *Global Manager*. The pre-interpretation transforms the monitored data into a domain common to all module managers.

Thus, the global manager and the algorithms it comprises can be designed in a generic way. Furthermore, the module managers place their actions to the global manager's disposal.

The global manager merges the abstract monitoring information of all module managers. It takes over, if a global view of all modules is required to react to some failure state. For decision making, several techniques are possible. This could be some kind of classifier system or generic rules, but also a planner to deduce complex operation sequences. Using these techniques, the global manager infers necessary actions from the current monitoring data. These actions are executed within the module managers that provided them.

The module managers need not implement the complete MAPE cycle. As figure 1 shows, several parts can be left out. If only the Planning part is missing (MA-E), the the monitoring information is always forwarded to the global manager for decision making. Sometimes, it may be also sensible to build pure monitors, although these must always be accompanied by an analysis component for the data abstraction (MA- -). An example for such a module would be the monitoring of a battery. Apparently, there are no actions that can be executed directly on the battery. It is even possible to define a pure actor module (- - -E). However, the developer has to be very careful in this case, as most action have some kind of preconditions in their related module that must be met for their execution.

The partition of the AC/OC Management into two layers has several advantages. Another approach would be to develop application-specific AC/OC Managers, which are based on a broad parameter set. However, this would decrease their reusability and increase development costs, because for each new application with a different parameter set a new set of managers would have to be developed. The proposed small module managers are bound to a distinct hard- or software module, instead to a specific application. They can be reused in several similar applications, thus saving development costs.

Using complex managers based on a broad parameter set inevitably leads to complex decision processes in the manager. This aggravates the timing analysis of an application using such managers. Small managers will bring less overhead into the application, so the timing behaviour will not be influenced that much and will be easier to analyse.

The solution of complex problems in the global manager is done by a generic rule system. Specificity for an application results from the combination of module managers and from the developer-defined system strategies. The derivation process itself is not influenced by the nature of its application.

3 Communication between the Two Management Layers

3.1 Information Flows

Within the two-layered management architecture, we have to regard two information flows. On the one hand, the module managers provide status messages to the global management **within a single node**. These status messages represent the current parameter values monitored by the module managers. The values are mapped to a common domain, to keep the communication interface between the two layers lean. Also, the global manager is able to compare the status messages regardless of their origin.

On the other hand, the global management notifies the module managers about its decisions. Thus, the execution of appropriate reactions is triggered.

Synchrony. Synchrony in the communication between the two management layers concerns the question how far the appearance of status messages triggers the derivation of reactions. There is no point in triggering a decision for each single status message that is received by the global management. This would only lift the work of the module managers up to the global level. Instead, the global management must accumulate the status messages of several module managers for some time before devising a reaction. Only this way the reaction would be based on a real global view. Hence, the process of decision making should run rather asynchronously to the module-global communication.

3.2 Types of Monitors and Actors

For the design of a communication model it is necessary to take a look at the ways monitors and actors can be implemented.

Monitors. Runtime information, i.e. status messages, can be generated in the following ways:

- **Instrumentation:** The monitored application's code is instrumented with small code blocks that generate status messages. Thus, the module manager is integrated directly into the application code.
- **Monitoring Service:** The module manager runs as a service independently of the real applications. If at one point it cannot cope with the parameter values it is responsible for, it raises an event.
- **Explicitly:** The module manager generates the status message on explicit enquiry of the global manager.

Each of these approaches has its own problem domain, where it fits best. Application instrumentation could be used to monitor and evaluate the application's runtime behaviour at predefined points. To monitor a battery continuously, it is possible to use a observer service running independently, e.g. at a low priority or as a timer-driven interrupt service routine. Simple status requests for a processor's current clock frequency would be done directly by explicit requests from the global manager.

As these examples show, in a final system most likely all three of these monitoring concepts will be used. Thus, they must all be taken into account by the design of the global management and the communication interface.

Actors. System design must also distinguish at what place the derived reactions are executed. Clearly, the execution is the duty of the module managers' actors, however following the above concepts there are several ways to implement an actor:

- **Within the Application**: This approach raises two problems. First, there needs to be some way of synchronisation between the application and the global management. Second, the reaction will influence the timing behaviour of the application and thus must be developed very carefully.
- **Separate Service**: The influences on the timing behaviour of the application as well as the global management are minimal in this case. However, there is again the problem of synchronisation between the global management and the reaction service.
- **Part of the Global Management**: Here, no synchronisation problems occur, but the actor may delay the global management in its operation in an unpredictable way.

Like the generation of status messages, all of these ways have their own domain where they perform best. So the design decisions for the actor should be based mostly on the complexity of the actor's task.

3.3   Communication Model

Based on the preceding discussion of communication parameters, we are now able to propose a basic model for the communication between the module managers and the global management.

Collection of Status Messages. Basically two concepts exist that can be applied to the communication between the two layers, the *Observer Pattern* and *Polling*. Both have their dis-/advantages for use in system monitoring. Through the observer pattern, communication is minimised. However, it stays unclear, when the global management should derive a reaction. As mentioned it is not sensible to trigger a decision for each single status message. On the other hand, using periodic polling, the decision process would start just after all messages are collected. But also in this case there are problems. The communication between the two layers is very high, as each module is questioned regularly. The whole process of message collection and possible decision making is gone through even if there is no real necessity due to a sound system state.

On this account, we propose a hybrid solution consisting of two modes.

GM async. Only the global manager's monitoring service is active. The module managers notify the global manager about critical states. These status messages are accumulated. If a predefined critical limit is reached, the whole management is switched into mode *GM sync*.

GM sync. Now the global management starts actively collecting status messages from all modules. Based on these data, it goes through the decision process. After the execution of the derived reactions, the system falls back into mode *GM async*.

Using this model, the global management is only executed if it is really necessary. Simultaneously we ensure that it works on a complete global view of the system without the overhead of *periodic* polling. The definition of the critical limit for the activation of the the global management presents a degree of freedom to the developer. It is not necessary that each module manager can publish messages to the communication layer in mode *GM async*.

Reaction. Reactions always should be executed synchronously to the decision process. Apparently, the global manager should play the active part and notify the affected actors about its decision. Thus, most of the reactions will be executed through the global manager. Actors that run as separate services or integrated into an application have to provide a broker actor that is notified in their place. This broker will activate the reaction service, or set a flag for the application-integrated actor.

4   Decision-Making of the Global Management

This section describes a concept for *Dynamic Classification in Embedded Real-Time systems* (DCERT). Its basic ideas relate to the fields of Learning Classifier Systems (LCS) [9] and automated planning [10,11]. Both concepts have in common that their algorithmic implementation is independent of the problem domain they are applied to, i.e. they present generic concepts.

In LCS, for an input state a reaction is derived using a dynamic rule set. A learning function, usually coupled with a genetic algorithm, modifies and improves the rule set over time. The rules are usually based on a combination of *true/false/don't care*-values. This allows an easy choice of rules matching the input state. Each classification cycle usually brings the system one step further towards its target state. However, during the advancement of the rule set by the genetic algorithm it is possible for disadvantageous rules to arise. Although these might be removed later by the learning function, in our problem domain they must not occur at all.

The basic target of automated planning is to derive a series of actions that will bring the system from a given start state into a predefined end state. Bad states are completely avoided. Although, the planning process itself is very complex and can consume lots of processing time. This is not applicable in the domain of real-time systems, which are usually embedded computers with limited performance.

In the design of the DCERT system, we unite the advantages of these two concepts, but simultaneously avoid their worst disadvantages.

4.1   Monitors - Status Messages

The module managers respectively their monitoring parts have access to the raw values of their associated parameters. For communication with the global management, these raw values are mapped into an abstract threefold metric.

Definition 1 (Status Parameters and Messages). σ *denotes a monitored system parameter. Its raw value is mapped into the characteristics* σ^+, σ^- *(extreme states),* σ^0, *and in special cases* $\sigma^\pm$. *The set of all monitored parameter is denoted as* $\Sigma = \{\sigma_1, \sigma_2, \ldots, \sigma_n\}$.

σ itself represents a monitored systems parameter. Its characteristics σ^+, σ^- can represent extreme states like "energy level high/low" or the possibilities for actions, like "clock frequency can be in-/decreased". In the latter case, also the $\sigma^\pm$ characteristic can be used to denote the possibility for increment **and** decrement. The σ^0 characteristic represents a balanced state.

The state messages can be furnished with a semantic meaning denoting preferred and undesired states.

Definition 2 (Status Semantics). Σ_+ *resp.* Σ_- *denote the sets of preferred resp. undesired states. If* $\sigma_k^+ \in \Sigma_+$, *then* $\sigma_k^- \in \Sigma_-$. *A semantic rating is not required for every* $\sigma_k \in \Sigma$.

States contained in the semantic set usually represent states that have important influence on the operation of the whole system. States not contained in the semantic set only have marginal influence on the operation, or none at all. However, they may be preconditions for some reactions and thus are necessary to be monitored. An order extends the semantic set:

Definition 3 (State Order). *The state order is a total order* $\leq$ *on the semantic sets with the following properties:*

- $\sigma_k^- \leq 0 \; \forall \sigma_k^- \in \Sigma_-; \; 0 \leq \sigma_k^+ \; \forall \sigma_k^+ \in \Sigma_+$
- $\sigma_i^x \leq \sigma_k^z \Leftrightarrow \sigma_i^{-x} \geq \sigma_k^{-z}, (x \neq 0, z \neq 0, i \neq k)$

The latter status semantics and state order are user-defined. They provide a way for the developer to influence the behaviour of the system and can be altered at runtime. The choice of Σ and the relation of the σ_k to specific system parameters depends on the application. The semantic set of states provides a canonical trigger for mode change of the Global Manager from **GM async** to **GM sync** (cf. 3.3), because these states have *per definitionem* heavy influence on the proper operation of the system. However, the user may define another boundary state as trigger.

The basic design of the state messages allows an efficient implementation by means of bit sets. The order of the states can be represented by a state's position in a bit string.

For the selection of actors, we need to equip the states from the semantic set with weights. Therefore, we state the following requirements:

Definition 4 (State Weights). *A weight* w_{σ^+} *for a semantic state* $\sigma_+ \in \Sigma_+$ *has the following properties:*

- $w_{\sigma^-} = -w_{\sigma^+}$, *and*
- $\sigma, \tau : \sigma^+ \leq \tau^+ \Leftrightarrow w_{\sigma^+} \leq w_{\tau^+}$

Which values are assigned to these weights again lies in the responsibility of the developer.

Example 1. Monitored Parameters

States	Description
$E^+/E^0/E^-$	energy consumption high/normal/low
$B^+/B^0/B^-$	battery power high/acceptable/low
$T^+/T^0/T^-$	timing behaviour of an application thread (soft real-time) frequently free time until deadline/timing behaviour ok/frequently deadline misses
$F^+/F^0/F^-$	clock frequency can be increased / in-/decreased
order	$0 \leq \mathbf{E^+} \leq \mathbf{B^+} \leq \mathbf{T^+}$ (desired states), $\Sigma_+ = \{E^+, T^+, B^+\}$

4.2 Actors

In the reaction path, the main elements are actors:

Definition 5 (Actor). *An actor is a 5-tuple $A = (a, V, N, E, s)$ with syntactic elements a, V, N and semantic elements E, s:*

- *performed action a,*
- *precondition $V \subset \Sigma$, which must be met by the current system state,*
- *postcondition $N \subset \Sigma$, which are guaranteed for the subsequent system state,*
- *optional preconditional states $E \subset \Sigma$, these can be used to decrease the costs s of the action a; the actor guarantees to balance/remove these states, if they are prevailing,*
- *cost scale value s denoting the complexity and costs k of action a.*

The syntactic and semantic elements of an actor constitute the base for decision making.

Example 2. Actors

	incfreq	decfreq
a	increase of clock frequency f by x MHz	decrease of clock frequency f by x MHz
V	$\{F^{+/0}, B^{+/0}\}$ f can be increased **and** there is sufficient energy left	$\{F^{-/0}\}$ f can be decreased
N	$\{F^-\}$ f can be decreased	$\{F^+\}$ f can be increased
E	$\{T^-, E^+\}$ application's timing behaviour will be increased, energy consumption will increase	$\{T^+, E^-\}$ no more surplus processing time, energy consumption will decrease
s	s_{inc} cheap	s_{dec} cheap

4.3 Decisions

The aim of the decision logic is to select such actors that balance prevalent undesired states as far as possible.

Definition 6 (World State and Basic Candidates). *The world state* $S \subset \Sigma$ *contains the current state messages of all registered monitors. Based on this set the basic candidate actors* A_{basic} *can be chosen as*

$$A_{basic} = \{A \mid A \; Actor \; and \; V_A \subseteq S\}$$

Filtering. A further and finer selection of actors shall avoid that prevailing states are treated multiple times or even aggravated. At this point also the complexity of an action will be regarded.

1. An evaluation of the actors' postcondition N_A removes such actors that would aggravate a prevailing state $(N_A \cap S = \emptyset)$.
2. The costs of a reaction should be as low as possible. In the first place, this would exclude complex actors with a high cost scale value c_A and a possibly high benefit from the reaction. However, their optional pre-conditional states that are met by the current systems state, i.e. $E_A \cap S$ can be used to decrease their costs. Thus, also complex reactions can be chosen, if only they promise to have a good influence on the general system state. The directive for the decreasing of costs can be chosen freely by the developer. We will propose an example in sect. 4.4.
3. Finally, DCERT should avoid that prevailing system states are treated repeatedly in one reaction. Therefore, only actors are chosen whose optional preconditions are pairwise disjoint in respect to the current state, i.e. $(E_A \cap S) \cap (E_B \cap S) = \emptyset$ for actors A, B. Actors that have a higher influence on the system state are preferred. This influence is measured as the weight of $E_A \cap S$ using the weight metric of definition 4.

The decision process is designed in a way that makes it possible to exchange monitors and actors online.

4.4   Implementation Remarks

The definition of DCERT gives the developer some freedom in the choice of metrics and weights. In the following section we will describe the baseline of our approach to implement a DCERT-based autonomic management.

Status messages can occur in four characteristics at most $(\sigma^+, \sigma^-, \sigma^0, \sigma^{\pm}$, see def. 1). Thus, each monitored parameter can be represented by two bits in a bit string. The position of a parameter in this bit string simultaneously relates to its weight. The weights of parameters (def. 4) increase exponentially with increasing importance and thus also determine the weights order (def. 3). Accordingly, the *cost scale* value s of an actor (def. 5) should be chosen proportional to the cost's logarithm, i.e. $s \sim \log_2 c$.

In these baselines we see several advantages for the implementation of DCERT in embedded real-time systems. Through the use of bit strings, a whole set of monitored parameters can be represented by one or more integer variables. Only the maximum number of monitored parameters must be limited. The set operations on such an integer are performed using bitwise logic operators, which are usually supported natively by the processor.

The cost reduction of an action can be done using the integer logarithm of the weight of the fulfilled optional preconditions, i.e. $\log_2 w(E_A \cap S)$. Hence, the most important fulfilled state defines the cost reduction.

5   Conclusion and Future Work

We presented an architecture which will ease the introduction of the AC/OC concepts into the domain of embedded real-time systems. The small module managers allow a fast and cheap reaction. On the higher level of the global management, more complex and more sophisticated reactions will be deduced. Although we used the MAPE cycle throughout this paper for our illustrations, our architecture concept is not refined to it.

A discussion of communication aspects led to the design of a communication model between the module managers and the global management. The global monitoring is performed using a hybrid solution of the observer pattern and polling. The execution of reactions follows a similar model.

The presented DCERT system is used in the global management to devise reactions, if the capabilities of the module managers do not suffice. It is based on Learning Classifier Systems and Automated Planners, bringing together the advantages of both concepts for the use in real-time systems.

The global manager may also exchange status messages with the global managers of other nodes in a distributed system. A middleware managing a distributed system of several nodes can be integrated using a pseudo-module.

Although throughout this paper we regarded only a single node, our concepts are also applicable in distributed systems. A middleware connecting the single nodes can be integrated by providing another module manager to the global management on each node. This module is able to introduce monitoring information from other nodes and to initiate distributed reactions. In the future we will integrate the presented architecture into the CAR-SoC project [12]. It will be built on top of our operating system CAROS [13], which is designed to support the concepts of Organic Computing inherently. By an integration with the CARISMA middleware [14] we will also prove its applicability for distributed embedded real-time systems.

References

1. Horn, P.: Autonomic Computing: IBM's Perspective on the State of Information Technology. IBM Manifesto, IBM Corporation (2001)
2. Kephart, J.O., Chess, D.M.: The Vision of Autonomic Computing. IEEE Computer 36(1), 41–50 (2003)
3. Müller-Schloer, C.: Organic computing: on the feasibility of controlled emergence. In: CODES+ISSS 2004: Proceedings of the 2nd IEEE/ACM/IFIP international conference on Hardware/software codesign and system synthesis, pp. 2–5. ACM Press, New York (2004)

4. Richter, U., Mnif, M., Branke, J., Müller-Schloer, C., Schmeck, H.: Towards a Generic Observer/Controller Architecture for Organic Computing. In: Informatik 2006 - Informatik für Menschen, Band 1, Beiträge der 36, Jahrestagung der Gesellschaft für Informatik e.V (GI), October 2-6, 2006, pp. 112–119 (2006)
5. Becker, J., Brändle, K., Brinkschulte, U., Henkel, J., Karl, W., Köster, T., Wenz, M., Wörn, H.: Digital On-Demand Computing Organism for Real-Time Systems. In: ARCS Workshops, GI. LNI, vol. 81, pp. 230–245 (2006)
6. Stein, S., Hamann, A., Ernst, R.: Real-time Management in Emergent Systems. In: Hochberger, C., Liskowsky, R. (eds.) Emergent Systems, GI. LNI, vol. 93, pp. 104–111 (2006)
7. Herkersdorf, A., Rosenstiel, W.: Towards a framework and a design methodology for autonomic integrated system. In: INFORMATIK - GI Workshop on Organic Computing, Ulm, Germany, pp. 610–615 (2004)
8. Solomon, B., Ionescu, D., Litoiu, M., Mihaescu, M.: Towards a Real-Time Reference Architecture for Autonomic Systems. In: SEAMS 2007: Proceedings of the 2007 International Workshop on Software Engineering for Adaptive and Self-Managing Systems, Washington, DC, USA, p. 10. IEEE Computer Society, Los Alamitos (2007)
9. Holland, J.H.: Processing and processors for schemata. In: Jacks, E.L. (ed.) Associative Information Processing, pp. 127–146. American Elsevier, New York (1971)
10. Russell, S., Norvig, P.: Artificial Intelligence: A Modern Approach. Prentice Hall, Englewood Cliffs (1995)
11. Ghallab, M., Nau, D., Traverso, P.: Automated Planning: Theory and Practice. Morgan Kaufman, San Francisco (2004)
12. Uhrig, S., Maier, S., Ungerer, T.: Toward a Processor Core for Real-time Capable Autonomic Systems. In: Proceedings of the 5th IEEE International Symposium on Signal Processing and Information Technology, pp. 19–22 (2005)
13. Kluge, F., Mische, J., Uhrig, S., Ungerer, T.: An Operating System Architecture for Organic Computing in Embedded Real-Time Systems. In: Rong, C., Jaatun, M.G., Sandnes, F.E., Yang, L.T., Ma, J. (eds.) ATC 2008. LNCS, vol. 5060, pp. 343–357. Springer, Heidelberg (2008)
14. Nickschas, M., Brinkschulte, U.: Guiding Organic Management in a Service-Oriented Real-Time Middleware Architecture. In: Proceedings of The 6th IFIP Workshop on Software Technologies for Future Embedded & Ubiquitous Systems (SEUS 2008), Capri Island, Italy. Springer, Heidelberg (2008)

Real-Time Access Guarantees for NAND Flash Using Partial Block Cleaning

Siddharth Choudhuri and Tony Givargis

Center for Embedded Computer Systems,
School of Information and Computer Sciences,
University of California, Irvine CA, USA
{sid,givargis}@uci.edu

Abstract. Increasing use of NAND flash in newer application domains has been possible due to lowering cost per GB, consumer demands for storage and advantages of NAND flash over traditional disks. However, NAND flash has its idiosyncrasies resulting in asymmetric read/write times due to garbage collection and wear leveling requirements. Such asymmetric (non-deterministic) read/write times poses a challenge for the adoption of NAND flash in real-time systems.

We present the implementation details of a flash translation layer called *GFTL* that guarantees strict upper bounds on read/write times that are comparable to a theoretical ideal case. Such guarantees are made possible by dividing the source of non-determinism into deterministic intervals using our proposed approach called partial block cleaning. Using partial block cleaning, the process of garbage collection is divided into several smaller, deterministic steps. Partial block cleaning comes with an overhead of additional space requirements. We provide a proof on the limit of the additional space requirements.

Keywords: NAND flash, real-time, file system, embedded systems.

1 Introduction

The use of NAND flash as a storage subsystem is on the rise. NAND flash manifests itself in a wide variety of embedded systems such as mp3 players, digital camera cards, USB based flash drives, set-top boxes, routers to name a few. The driving forces behind the widespread adoption of NAND have been − *(i)* The advantages of NAND flash over hard disk drives such as small form factor, shock resistance and fast access times; *(ii)* The falling cost per GB of NAND flash [1] [2]; and *(iii)* The push from end users for increased storage in consumer electronics. With lowering cost per GB, NAND flash is poised to be used in newer application domains that impose timing guarantees on storage accesses. For example, the One Laptop Per Child (OLPC) project, Canon's HD camcoder use NAND flash as the only non-volatile storage medium [3][4]. While the economics of price has been favorable, the use of NAND flash in mission critical and real-time applications that demand determinism, has been a challenge due to NAND flash idiosyncrasies.

U. Brinkschulte, T. Givargis, and S. Russo (Eds.): SEUS 2008, LNCS 5287, pp. 138–149, 2008.

NAND flash has certain unique characteristics that are atypical of either RAM or hard disk drives. Specifically, NAND flash does not support in-place updates, i.e., an update (re-write) to a *page* (the minimum of write) is not possible, unless a larger region containing the page (known as a *block*) is first erased. Erase operation on a block is an order of magnitude slower, making it undesirable. Further, a block has a limited erase lifetime (typically 100,000) after which a block becomes unusable. Such characteristics require special handling of NAND flash using either a dedicated file system or wrapping the NAND flash with a layer of hardware/software known as the *flash translation layer* (FTL). The FTL performs three important functions *(i)* Exports a view of NAND flash that resembles a disk drive, thereby hiding the peculiarities of NAND flash. Thus, an FTL translates a read/write request from the file system (*sector*) into a specific ⟨*block, page*⟩ of the NAND flash; *(ii)* Reclaims space by erasing obsoleted blocks (due to out of place updates), also known as *garbage collection*; *(iii)* Performs *wear leveling* to make sure that blocks across a flash get evenly erased.

NAND flash management (wear leveling and garbage collection) is workload dependent resulting in asymmetric read/write times. Therefore, typically FTLs do not provide service guarantees. Such asymmetric read/write latency might be tolerable for single-threaded or dedicated applications. However, as we move towards newer application domains, a deterministic service guarantee becomes desirable to design and run applications.

In this paper, we present implementation details of an FTL called as *GFTL* (for Guarantee Flash Translation Layer) based on the concept of "partial block cleaning". An FTL based on partial block cleaning is capable of providing strict service guarantees for file system accesses (reads/writes) independent of the state or utilization of the flash. Partial block cleaning comes at a cost of additional flash storage. It is our opinion that with rising capacities and lowering cost per GB, additional NAND flash overhead (less than 20% across benchmarks) to provide deterministic guarantee is tolerable. The following are the contributions of this paper:

- GFTL algorithms for read/write access to a NAND flash which provides strict service guarantees due to partial block cleaning.
- Proof for determining the limit on additional space requirements for GFTL.

The rest of the paper is organized as follows: Section 2 briefly describes the NAND flash characteristics. Section 3 presents our problem formulation followed by Section 4 which describes the read/write algorithms for GFTL and presents a proof on the space overhead of GFTL. Section 5 describes the benchmarks used followed by results. Section 7 summarizes related work followed by conclusion.

2   Preliminaries

A NAND flash consists of multiple *erase blocks*. Each such erase block is further divided into multiple *pages*, a page being the minimum unit of data transfer (read/write). Associated with each page is a spare area known as the *Out Of*

Band (OOB) area, primarily meant to store the Error Correction Code (ECC) of the corresponding page (also used to store meta-data such as inverse page table). A page is 512 bytes for older, small block NAND flash and 2 KB for newer large block NAND flash. Three basic operations can be performed on a NAND flash. An *erase* operation "wipes" an entire erase block turning every byte into all 1s i.e., `0xff`. A *write* operation works on either a page or an OOB area, selectively turning desired 1s into 0s. A *read* operation reads an entire page or an OOB area. Updates (re-writes) are out-of-place i.e., directed to a different page unless the entire block is erased. Table 1 depicts NAND flash specifications for the basic operations. There are two possible mappings between a sector and

Table 1. NAND flash specifications

Characteristics	Samsung 16MB Small Block	Samsung 128MB Large Block
Block size	16384 (bytes)	65536 (bytes)
Page size	512 (bytes)	2048 (bytes)
OOB size	16 (bytes)	64 (bytes)
Read Page	36 (usec)	25 (usec)
Read OOB	10 (usec)	25 (usec)
Write Page	200 (usec)	300 (usec)
Write OOB	200 (usec)	300 (usec)
Erase	2000 (usec)	2000 (usec)

a ⟨block, page⟩. A page based mapping where a translation table maps each sector to a ⟨block, page⟩ pair. However, the size of translation table can become a limiting factor as flash size increases. In order to deal with such a problem, a block based translation layer is widely used. For instance, in one of the popular block based translation layers known as NFTL [5], a sector is divided into a virtual block and an offset. The virtual block maps to a physical block (known as the primary block) on the NAND flash. In case of a rewrite (or if the primary block is full), a new physical block called a secondary block is chosen to perform the writes. When the two blocks become full, an operation known as fold merges the primary and the replacement blocks into a new primary block and freeing the old primary and replacement block. Garbage collection is invoked either when the NAND flash runs out of space (which does a fold across several blocks) or using a heuristic. Interested reader can find more details on mapping and garbage collection heuristics in [6] [7]. For the rest of the paper, the term flash refers to NAND flash. Table 2 denotes the terminology used throughout the paper (to be described in later sections)

3   Problem Formulation

We model I/O request (incoming from file system to the FTL) as a real-time task $\tau = \{p, e, d\}$ where p is the periodicity, e is the execution time and d is the

Table 2. Terminology

Symbol	Definition
T_{wrpg}	Time to write a page and OOB area
T_{rdpg}	Time to read a page
T_{rdoob}	Time to read an OOB area
T_{er}	Time to erase a block
π	Pages per block
N	Number of blocks
L	Length of the write pending queue

deadline. Without loss of generality, we assume that p is equal to d. We have two kinds of tasks: a read request task $\tau_r = \{p_r, e_r\}$, and a write request task $\tau_w = \{p_w, e_w\}$. p_r and p_w denote "how often" a read or write request arrives from the file system. e_r is the time taken to search for a given sector, read the corresponding $\langle block, page \rangle$ of the flash, and return a success/failure to the file system. Similarly, e_w is the time taken to write a sector to a given $\langle block, page \rangle$. The bounds on p and e are determined by the FTL. Specifically, a *lower bound* on p (denoted by $\mathcal{L}(p)$) determines the maximum request arrival rate that an FTL can handle. The worst case execution time, i.e., an *upper bound* on e (denoted by $\mathcal{U}(e)$), determines the worst case rate at which requests are serviced by the FTL. For a file system, $\mathcal{U}(e)$ represents the *average memory access time* (AMAT) for read/write and $\mathcal{L}(p)$ represents the maximum rate at which requests are issued to the flash.

A flash needs to perform flash management (wear leveling and garbage collection) which involves erasing atleast one or more blocks. T_{er} is the longest *atomic* operation on a flash, i.e., when a block is being erased, the flash is locked and hence non-interruptible. Therefore, T_{er} is the limiting factor which decides the inter-arrival time (periodicity) of requests. Therefore, in an ideal case, $\mathcal{L}(p)$ is at least T_{er}. The latency due to T_{er} could be hidden by having buffers in the RAM. However, while this solution works in an average case, in a worst case scenario (i.e., when every access results in a block erase), one would require an infinitely large buffer in RAM as the arrival rate would exceed the service rate. Table 3 depicts the bounds guaranteed by GFTL (details in the next section).

Table 3. Service guarantee bounds

Bounds	Ideal	GFTL
$\mathcal{U}(e_w)$	T_{wrpg}	T_{wrpg}
$\mathcal{U}(e_r)$	$T_{rdpg} + T_{rdoob}$	$\pi T_{rdoob} + T_{rdpg}$
$\mathcal{L}(p_r)\ \mathcal{L}(p_w)$	T_{er}	$T_{er} + \max\{\mathcal{U}(e_w), \mathcal{U}(e_r)\}$

GFTL guarantees (Table 3) a worst case execution time for writes that is as good as an ideal case and a worst case execution time for reads that is marginally $((\pi - 1)T_{rdoob})$ larger than an idea case. Further, GFTL provides service guarantees for requests that have an inter-arrival time $[\mathcal{L}(p)]$ that is only slightly larger than an ideal case while still performing garbage collection.

4   Technical Approach

GFTL is a block based approach. A sector is treated as a *logical address* and a *logical block* is derived from the most significant bits of the logical address (Figure 1). A *block mapping table* is used to map a logical block to a physical block of flash. For a given flash with N blocks, there is a 1 : 1 mapping between the logical blocks and the physical blocks, resulting in N entries in the block mapping table. Further, GFTL requires an additional Q blocks for a *write queue*.

4.1   GFTL Writes

The first write to a given virtual block is written to a free physical block. Due to a 1 : 1 mapping, a free physical block is guaranteed to be available. Once a physical block is found, pages are written sequentially starting from page 0. The sector number is written in the OOB area and serves as an inverse page table. After π writes, the physical block becomes full. The full physical block is added to a garbage collection queue called as GCQ. Additional writes that map to a full physical block are written to pages in the write queue (shown as dark gray in Figure 1). The write queue serves as a buffer for writes from the time a physical block becomes full until that physical block is garbage collected. A *write queue tail* serves as the index to the next available page in the write queue. There is only one write queue for the entire flash, thus, there exists a *write queue map* which maps the logical address (sector) to a $\langle block, page \rangle$ of the write queue. Algorithm 1 shows that the bounds on taken by write is T_{wrpg}.

4.2   GFTL Reads

A read to a given sector is first searched in the write queue map since it holds the most recent copy. In case of a write queue map miss, the block mapping table is used to determine the physical block corresponding to the sector. The

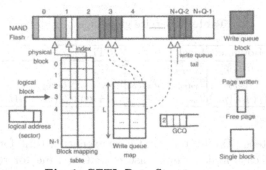

Fig. 1. GFTL Data Structures

Algorithm 1. GFTL write

```
 1: writesect(sector, buffer)
 2: Input: Function writesect, Sector sect, Buffer buf
 3: Output: return status
 4: vba ← sector/blocksize
 5: if (fsm.state = READ ∨ ERASE) ∧ fsm.blk = vba then
 6:    cached ← true
 7:    writebuffer(buffer); /* Write to RAM O(1) */
 8:    goto PARTIALGC
 9: end if
10: if ¬ cached then
11:    pba ← blockmap[vba].block /* RAM lookup O(1) */
12:    if pba = NULL then
13:       pba = find_free_blk() /* RAM lookup O(1) */
14:       nandwrite(pba, 0, buf) /* Write to flash O(Twrpg) */
15:       goto PARTIALGC
16:    end if
17:    if pba.status = BLOCK_FULL then
18:       pba ← writequeue.block
19:       page ← writequeue.tail
20:    else
21:       pba ← blockmap[vba].index
22:    end if
23:    nandwrite(pba, page, buf) /* Write to flash O(Twrpg) */
24: end if
25: PARTIALGC:
26: if GCQ.size > 0 then
27:    do_fsm() /* Invoke partial GC FSM to determine next state */
28: end if
29: return
```

OOB area of the physical block is searched backwards starting from the page pointed to by the index field of the block mapping table.

A read from the write queue will result in one OOB read and one page read. A read from block mapping table on the other hand will result in π OOB reads in the worst case followed by the actual page read. Therefore, the best case AMAT for reads is $T_{rdpg} + T_{rdoob}$ and the worst case is $\pi T_{rdoob} + T_{rdpg}$.

A write either goes to the next available location pointed to by the index field of block mapping table (Figure 1) or into the write queue in case of a full physical block. In either case the time taken is constant i.e., T_{wrpg}. Due to the 1 : 1 mapping between virtual and physical blocks, a physical block is guaranteed available for the very first write. Further, in case of a full block, the size of write queue is such that a page is guaranteed to be available.

4.3 GFTL Flash Management

The only flash management performed in GFTL is based on partial block cleaning which takes care of both garbage collection and wear leveling. The idea

---

Algorithm 2. GFTL read

1: *readsect*(`sector`, `buffer`)
2: *Input:* Function **readsect**, Sector **sect**, Buffer **buf**
3: *Output:* return status
4: **if** sector ∈ writequeue **then**
5:     pba ← writequeue[sector].block
6:     page ← writequeue[sector].page
7: **else**
8:     pba ← blockmap[vba].block /* *RAM lookup O(1)* */
9:     **for all** page ∈ pba **do**
10:        *nand_read_oob*(pba, page, oob) /* $O(\pi \times T_{rdoob})$ */
11:        **if** sector = oob.sec **then**
12:            *nand_read_page*(pba, page, buf) /* $O(T_{rdpg})$ */
13:        **end if**
14:     **end for**
15: **end if**
16: **if** GCQ.size > 0 **then**
17:     *do_fsm()* /* *Invoke partial GC FSM to determine next state* */
18: **end if**

---

behind partial block cleaning is to perform garbage collection on a single block at a time. Further, each such single block garbage collection is divided into "partial" steps such that the time taken to perform each step is *no longer* than the longest atomic flash operation i.e., T_{er}. The partial steps are interleaved between servicing read/write requests. The garbage collection of a single block, say B_i, amounts to the following phases:

1. *Block Read:* In this phase, the pages that belong to B_i are first read from the write queue followed by reading the remaining valid pages out of the block B_i. In a worst case, this step can result in reading $(\pi - 1)$ pages from the write queue followed by π OOB reads of B_i to search the remaining valid page. Thus, the worst case time is $(2\pi - 1)T_{rdoob} + \pi T_{rdpg}$.
2. *Block Erase:* Block B_i is erased in time T_{er}.
3. *Block Write:* The pages that were read in phase 1 are written to a free block, say B_{new}. In a worst case, π pages will be written resulting in a worst case time of πT_{wrpg}.

The idea behind partial block cleaning is to divide the block read and block write phases into partial steps, each of which is of a duration equal to T_{er} as shown in Figure 2(a). Let $\alpha = \lceil (2\pi - 1)T_{rdpg}/T_{er} \rceil$ denote the number of partial steps into which a read phase can be split as multiple of T_{er}. Similarly, $\beta = \lceil \pi T_{wrpg}/T_{er} \rceil$ denotes the number of partial steps that a block write can be broken into. Thus partial block cleaning divides the three block cleaning phases into $(\alpha + 1 + \beta)$ steps, each of a duration T_{er}.

The core of GFTL acts as a real-time executive that implements the finite state machine shown in Figure 2(b). As shown in Figure 2(a), GFTL first dispatches

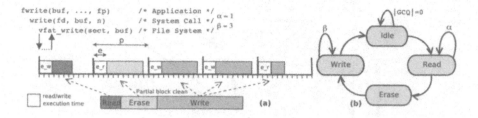

Fig. 2. Partial block cleaning and FSM

any read/write request followed by performing a step of partial block cleaning (if the GCQ is non-empty). This approach lets GFTL provide read/write service guarantees shown in Table 3 while accepting requests at a rate equal to $\mathcal{L}(p)$. The wear level is taken care of in GFTL due to a round robin approach to allocating free blocks.

4.4 Write Queue Limit

In order to determine the write queue limit (i.e., the limit on L), we consider a worst case write request arrival sequence. The following is a worst case write request arrival sequence: $N \times \pi$ write requests arrive such that each request is to a unique page. Thus, at the end of $N \times \pi$ write requests, we have a full flash. Now, each subsequent request will start filling the write queue. Note that if each request filling up a write queue belongs to a unique logical block, garbage collecting such write queue block cannot be started until each block whose page is written to the write queue block has been reclaimed. For example, if a write queue block Q_i has π pending writes that belong to unique logical blocks $\{B_1, B_2, ..., B_\pi\}$, the write queue block Q_i cannot be reclaimed (garbage collected) until each block in $\{B_1, B_2, ..., B_\pi\}$ has been reclaimed. Therefore, the worst case sequence of logical blocks to which writes arrive are $\{0, 1, 2, ..., N-1, 0, 1, 2, ..., N-1, ...\}$ (Figure 3 "Block Numbers Arrival Sequence"). This results in each write queue block being filled with π pending writes, each of which belongs to a unique logical block. Therefore, a write queue block cannot be reclaimed until π blocks are first garbage collected (i.e., worst case for a write queue block). Thus, the write request grows at a rate equal to $1/\mathcal{L}(p)$ (Figure 3 "Arrival Rate"). However, every $(\alpha + \beta + 1) \times \mathcal{L}(p)$ time units, a block is garbage collected (Figure 3 "Service Rate") resulting in a net growth of write queue (Figure 3 "Theoretical Write Queue Length"). In this case the arrival rate $1/\mathcal{L}(p)$ is greater than the service rate $1/(\alpha + \beta + 1)\mathcal{L}(p)$ (Figure 3) leading to an infinite queue length. However, in our worst case arrival model, after N writes, every incoming write request already has at least one other pending write in the write queue that belongs to the same logical block as the incoming write. Similarly, after $2N$ writes, every write request has 2 pending requests that belong to the same logical block. Thus, with time, the growth of the write queue length decreases every N requests reaching a steady state value (Figure 3 "Write Queue Length"). Specifically, the write

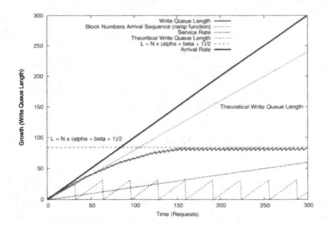

Fig. 3. Write Queue Length Growth

queue length reaches a maximum value of $L = [N \times (\alpha + \beta + 1)/2]$ after which the write queue attains a steady state. Figure 3 depicts the growth of write queue buffer with $\mathcal{L}(p) = 1$.

The following proof provides a limit on the upper bound of the write queue length. The proof is derived for the worst case arrival sequence mentioned above (i.e., the write queue pages fill up such that each page belongs to a different logical block and the distance between two pages in the write queue that belong to the same block is N).

In Figure 3, the ramp function denotes the growth of write queue in terms of the logical block numbers. The actual growth is denoted by the curve entitled "Write Queue Length". Assuming $\kappa = (\alpha + \beta + 1)$, the service rate is given by $y(x) = x/\kappa$.

Every κ interval, a physical block B_i is reclaimed. Since the block B_i is reclaimed, every page $p \mid p \in writequeue \wedge physical\_block(p) = B_i$ is also rendered obsolete. Every N^{th} interval, the number of such write queue pages $\mid p \mid$ (that are rendered obsolete) increases by 1 until κ times. This can be seen as the intersection of "Service Rate" and the ramp function in Figure 3. After κ times, the growth of the write queue reaches a steady state as the number of pages that are rendered obsolete i.e., $\mid p \mid$ equals κ. Therefore, the write queue length reaches a steady state where it grows by an amount κ and then decreases by the same amount every κ intervals due to multiple pages in the write queue being rendered obsolete.

Thus, the upper bound on the length of the write queue can be obtained by summing the growth of write queue (given the arrival rate) and the decrease in write queue due to partial garbage collection. The write queue increases monotonically in the worst case. The decrease due to block cleaning is given by intersection of the service rate with the ramp function. The first intersection is found at $y = x/\kappa$ for $x = N$. The second intersection is found at $y = 2x/\kappa$ for

$x = 2N$ and so on. The summation until the steady state gives the worst case bound on the write queue length L

End of 1st interval $L_1 = N - \lfloor N/\kappa \rfloor$
End of 2nd interval $L_2 = N - \lfloor 2N/\kappa \rfloor$

...

End of $\kappa - 1^{th}$ interval $L_{\kappa-1} = N - \lfloor (\kappa - 1)N/\kappa \rfloor$

Summing, $\Sigma_i^{\kappa-1} L_i = (N \times (\kappa - 1)) - (N \times (\kappa - 1)/2)$

$$\Sigma L = N \times (\kappa - 1)/2$$

To this summation, we add N additional entries to accommodate the floor function rounding off as a buffer. Thus, the upper bounds on write queue limit is

$$L = N \times (\kappa - 1)/2 + N$$
$$= N(\kappa + 1)/2$$

Note that though L is greater than N (total blocks), the actual write queue length in terms of the number of additional blocks is $[N(\kappa+1)/2]/\pi$ as each block can store π pending writes. Thus, for a given flash the write queue length (L), can be calculated at design time by looking at the flash specs and independent of workload or flash state.

5   Results

We used the following benchmarks representing a variety of workloads. The *Andrew* benchmark [8] consists of five phases involving creating files, copying files, searching files, reading every byte of a file and compiling source files. The *Postmark* benchmark measures performance of file systems running networked applications like e-mail, news server and e-commerce [9]. The *iozone* benchmark [10] is a well known synthetic benchmark. We ran iozone to do read, write, rewrite, reread, random read, random write, backward read, record rewrite and stride read. The file sizes ranged from 64KB to 32MB in strides of 2× (i.e., 64, 128, ...32768). Besides these standard benchmarks, we used our own benchmark called *consumer* which simulates flash activities used in consumer electronics devices such as image manipulation, data transfer, audio and video playback.

A set of benchmarks were run in sequence to generate a file system *trace*. The first trace, called the *synthetic* trace was generated by running the following sequence: format flash → andrew → postmark → iozone. Similarly, consumer trace was generated by formating a flash followed by running the consumer benchmark. In order to perform a rigorous evaluation of GFTL, each read/write in the trace was simulated with a periodicity of $\mathcal{L}(p)$ i.e., there is *no idle period*. Further, the synthetic trace consists of 4.3 million writes and 27,841 reads and

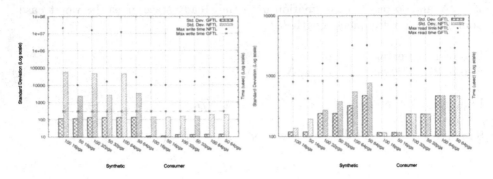

Fig. 4. NFTL vs. GFTL writes   **Fig. 5.** NFTL vs. GFTL reads

the consumer trace consists of 125, 596 writes and 76, 479 reads. The flash size at
100% utilization for synthetic trace is 136 and 260 MB for the consumer trace.

Figures 4 and 5 compares GFTL and NFTL in terms of read/write performance. The variation in write times is more than an order of magnitude less
for GFTL due to partial block cleaning. The maximum write time of GFTL is
constant as opposed to NFTL. The maximum read time is proportional to the
number of pages per block i.e., π. This is due to the fact that reads requires
a sequential read of the OOB area until a desired sector is found. The average
overhead calculated across the traces and across all page, block size combinations
is 16%.

6   Related Work

While there have been several block based FTLs, the real time aspect of
NAND flash was first investigated by [11]. The authors proposed an innovative approach towards using a garbage collector thread (instance) for each real
time task. The garbage collector thread has a execution time of
$(\pi - \alpha) \times (T_{rdpg} + T_{wrpg}) + T_{er}$+cpu_time). In [11] each garbage collector invocation is takes at least $(\pi - 1)(T_{rdpg} + T_{wrpg}) + T_{er}$ time (ignoring cpu time)
in the *best case*. In our approach, the overhead of partial GC is T_{er} in the *worst
case*. Moreover, with GFTL we do not associate an additional GC task thereby
avoiding overhead. [11] requires file system support for special *ioctl* calls. GFTL
can be run on top any unmodified file system. Results from [11] are based on
two tasks $T1 = (3, 20)$ and $T2 = (5, 20)$ resulting in creation of two GC tasks
$G1 = (22, 160)$ and $G2 = (22, 600)$ at 50% utilization. The execution time of
GC thread is comparable to 10 times T_{er}. GFTL on the other hand provides a
delay that is around T_{er}. Moreover, we provide a rigorous where each request is
considered a real-time task along with high utilization.

In [12], the authors address soft real-time issues by modifying the file system. The techniques in [12] focus on commonly used access patterns and not
strict guarantees. In [6], the authors survey a wide range of garbage collection

algorithms as part of their study. However, the garbage collectors are not aimed at real-time systems. An exhaustive research on flash memories for real time systems was done by [13]. The conclusions in [13], supports our motivation for the lack of real-time, deterministic guarantees for flash. The results on wear level and details on benchmark performance is in[14].

7   Conclusion

In this paper we provided the algorithms to implement an FTL called GFTL that guarantees $O(1)$ write time and a read time that takes π (pages per block) searches of the flash OOB in the worst case. Further, we provided a proof that determines the bounds on space overhead required by GFTL using partial block cleaning. Thus, for a given flash the write queue can be computed at design time independent of flash workload or state. Using the approach of partial block cleaning, real-time guarantees can be provided for NAND flash (that are close to an ideal case). The overhead of partial block cleaning is less than 20% across the benchmarks used in our experiments.

References

1. Lawton, G.: Improved flash memory grows in popularity. Computer 39(1), 16–18 (2006)
2. MemCon: MemCon. (July 2007), http://linuxdevices.com/news/NS6633183518.html
3. One Laptop Per Child Project, http://laptop.org
4. Canon: Vixia HD Camcoder (January 2008)
5. Ban, A.: Flash file system optimized for page-mode flash technologies. US Patent 5,937,425 (August 10, 1999)
6. Gal, E., Toledo, S.: Algorithms and data structures for flash memories. ACM Comp. Surv. 37(2), 138–163 (2005)
7. Chang, L.P., Kuo, T.W.: Efficient management for large-scale flash-memory storage systems with resource conservation. Trans. Storage 1(4), 381–418 (2005)
8. Howard, J.H., et al.: Scale and performance in a distributed file system. ACM Trans. Comput. Syst. 6(1), 51–81 (1988)
9. Katcher, J.: Postmark: A new file system benchmark. Technical report, Net App. Inc. (TR 3022) (1997)
10. Norcutt, W.: IOZONE benchmark, http://www.iozone.org
11. Chang, L.P., Kuo, T.W., Lo, S.W.: Real-time garbage collection for flash-memory storage systems of real-time embedded systems. TECS 3(4), 837–863 (2004)
12. New techniques for real-time fat file system in mobile multimedia devices. IEEE Transactions on Consumer Electronics 52, 1–9 (2006)
13. Parthey, D.: Analyzing real-time behavior of flash memories. Diploma Thesis, Chemnitz University of Technology (April 2007)
14. Choudhuri, S., Givargis, T.: Deterministic service guarantees for NAND flash using partial block cleaning. In: CODES+ISSS 2008. ACM, New York (to appear, 2008)

An Operating System for a Time-Predictable Computing Node

Guenter Khyo, Peter Puschner, and Martin Delvai

Vienna University of Technology
Institute of Computer Enginering
A1040 Vienna, Austria
peter@vmars.tuwien.ac.at,
http://ti.tuwien.ac.at

Abstract. The increasing complexity of speed-up mechanisms found in modern computer architectures makes it difficult to predict the timing of the software that runs on this hardware, especially when the software itself has many different execution paths. To fight this combined hardware-software complexity that makes an accurate timing analysis infeasible, we have conceived a very simple software structure for real-time tasks: We do not allow that decisions about the control flow are made at runtime, i.e., all decisions are resolved in an off-line analysis before runtime.

In this paper we show that simple control structures generated before runtime can as well be used within the operating system of an embedded real-time system. In this way we make not only task timing but also the timing of the operating system and thus the timing of the entire real-time computer system fully deterministic, thus time-predictable. We explain the principles and mechanisms we use to achieve this predictability and show the results of an experiment that demonstrates the feasibility of our concepts.

Keywords: Real-Time Operating Systems, Time-Triggered Architecture, Determinism, Temporal Predictability.

1 Introduction

Real-time systems need to provide timing guarantees in order to provide safe operation. In practice, the problem in achieving these guarantees is that hardware and software systems have become overly complex. It is therefore difficult to design time-predictable systems and provide evidence that a constructed system really meets the demanded timing properties. The reason for this complex behavior, which is hard to analyze, is mainly the fact that (a) dynamic decisions are taken at runtime, and that (b) the effects of a possibly long execution history have to be considered when argueing about the system state at a particular time instant.

The goal of our work is to develop an architecture that provides predictable and repeatable timing. The focus of this paper is on the operating system. We

U. Brinkschulte, T. Givargis, and S. Russo (Eds.): SEUS 2008, LNCS 5287, pp. 150–161, 2008.

describe the architecture and operation of an operating system that provides completely deterministic, reproducable timing and can thus be the basis for constructing entire applications with predictable timing.

The operating system shall serve as a basis for building real-time systems for which the timing of every operation can be predicted with an accuracy of a single CPU clock cycle. We will show how we can achieve this goal by using an adequate task-execution model – the single-path model – and a time-triggered, table driven control approach in the operating system, together with a realization of all kernel and operating-system routines in single-path code.

The interface of the proposed architecture is a time-triggered state message interface that blocks all asynchronous external control signals (Section 2). The propose software architecture builds on a simple task model and time-triggered, table-driven scheduling (Section 3.1) as well as on a deterministic code execution scheme (single-path code) in applications and in the operating-system code (Section 4). Within the paper we will focus on the description of the operating system that manages the resources of the system in a pre-planned manner. We will demonstrate that it is possible to get along with an OS implementation that uses a combination of single-path code and a static parameterization, i.e., the parameters of all calls to the operating system can be evaluated before runtime. This design yields a timing that can be fully predicted in a pre-runtime timing analysis (Section 5). The predictability will finally be demonstrated by a simple evaluation of a prototype implementation of the operating system (Section 6).

2 The Safety-Critical Subsystem Interface

In this section we describe the interface of the proposed architecture. As a prerequisite for building a time-predictable (sub)system, the interface of this system has to be predictable as well.

The following description uses the model and terminology of the DECOS integrated architecture [1]. This does, however, not mean that our work is only useful in the context of DECOS. On the contrary, the architecture can be adopted to any architecture that provides a time-triggered state message interface.

2.1 The Connector Unit

A DECOS component consists of two separated subsystems, the safety-critical subsystem for executing all safety-critical tasks and the non safety-critical subsystem for performing all other, non-critical services. Both types of subsystems are connected to the rest of the distributed computer system via so-called connector units. The connector units realize the architectural services of the distributed architecture, comprising the predictable transportation of messages, the fault-tolerant clock synchronization, fault isolation, and the consistent diagnosis of node failures [1].

Within this paper our focus is on the operating system of the safety-critical subsystem of a component (see Figure 1). This is where time predictability is

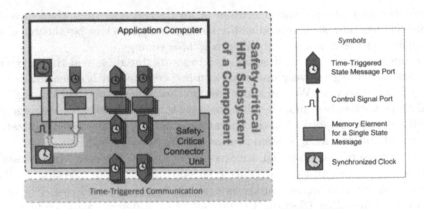

Fig. 1. Interfacing between the safety-critical hard real-time subsystem of a component and the time-triggered communication channel

needed. The application computer of this subsystem communicates with its environment solely via the safety-critical connector unit. The connector unit provides the following services in support of the time-predictable software architecture of the application computer.

- The connector unit implements a temporal firewall interface [2] for all data elements exchanged between the application computer and the communication subsystem. The read and write operations of the communication subsystem access the memory elements of the temporal firewalls only at predefined times, according to the a-priory known time-triggered communication schedule (in Figure 1 small rectangles represent the memory elements and the arrows marked with light clocks show the accesses of the communication subsystem to the firewalls).
- The time windows during which the communication system accesses the memory elements of the connector unit are known for each temporal firewall.
- The communication system provides a time-signal service to the application computer. A dedicated memory element in the connector unit can be written to set the timer (Figure 1, left). When the global system time reaches the timer value, the connector unit sends an interrupt signal over the signal port to the application processor.

3   A Time-Predictable Application Computer

The timing of the actions performed by a computer system depends on both, the software running on the computer and the properties of the hardware executing the software [3]. We therefore list the hardware and software features that in combination allow us to make an application computer time-predictable.

3.1 Hardware Architecture

A central idea of our approach is to obtain time predictability by constructing software that has an invariable control flow. By applying this restrictive software model we can allow for the use of hardware features that are otherwise considered as being "unpredictable" (e.g., instruction caches) and yet build systems whose timing is invariable. So the idea is to keep hardware restrictions and modifications within limits (e.g., we restrict caches to direct-mapped caches but do not demand special hardware modifications as, for example, needed for the SMART cache [4]). To support our execution model, the following hardware properties have to be fulfilled:

- The execution times of instructions do not depend on operand values.
- The CPU supports a conditional move instruction or a set of predicated instructions that have invariable execution times.
- Instruction caches are either direct mapped or set-associative with LRU replacement strategy.
- Memory access times for data are invariable for all data items. (This is the strongest limitation. We will try to relax it in future work).
- The CPU has a programmable instruction counter that can generate an interrupt when a given number of instructions has been completed.

3.2 The Software Architecture

To construct a time-predictable computer system we need to be very strict about the software structure. The proposed software architecture does not allow for any decisions in the control flow whose outcome has not already been determined before the start of the system. This property is true for both the application tasks and the operating system. Even task preemptions are implemented in a way that does not allow for any timing variation between different task invocations.

Task Model. The structure of all tasks follows the simple-task model (S-task model) found in [5]. Tasks never have to wait for the completion of an input/output operation and do never block. There are no statements for explicit input/output or synchronization within a task. It is assumed that the static schedule of application tasks and kernel routines ensures that all inputs for a task are available when the task starts and that outputs are ready in the output variables when the task completes. The actual data transfers for input and output are under control of the operating system and are scheduled before respectively after the task execution.

An important and unique property of our task model is that all tasks have only a single possible execution path. By translating the code of all real-time tasks into single-path code we ensure that all tasks follow the only possible, predetermined control flow during execution and have invariable timing. For more details about the single-path translation see Section 4.

Operating System Structure. If not properly designed, the activities of the operating system can create a lot of indeterminism in the timing of a computer system. We have therefore been very restrictive in the design of the operating system and its mechanisms (see Section 5).

Predictability in the code execution of the operating system is achieved by two mechanisms. First, single-path coding is used wherever possible. Second, all data that are relevant for run-time decisions of the operating system are computed at compile time. These data include the pre-determined times for I/O, task communication, task activation, and task switching. They are stored in static decision tables that the operating system interprets at runtime.

Task communcation and I/O is implemented by simple read and write operations to specific memory locations. As these memory accesses are pre-scheduled together with the application tasks, no synchronization and no waiting is necessary at run time.

The programmable time interrupt provided by the communication system is used to synchronize the operation of the application computer with the global time base. This way we ensure that the application computer performs all activities in synchrony with its environment, i.e., the rest of the system.

3.3 Tool Support

The software structure of our architecture is very specialized. Code generation for an application therefore needs to be supported by a number of tools:

- To generate single-path code, either a special compiler or a code conversion tool that converts branching code into single-path code is needed.
- A tool for worst-case execution-time analysis returns the execution times of the tasks and the operating system routines.
- An off-line scheduler generates the tables that control all operations of the application computer. The scheduler has to resolve all precedence and mutual exclusion constraints between task pairs as well as tasks and the communication system. It further has to plan all preemptions, thereby taking into account the effects of the preemptions on the system timing.

4 Deterministic Single-Path Task Execution

As all branches in the control flow of some code may cause variable timing, we translate the code of all tasks as well as the operating-system code into single-path code [6]. The code resulting from the single-path translation has only a single execution trace, hence the name single-path translation.

The strategy of the single-path translation is to remove input-data dependencies from the control flow. To achieve this, the translation replaces all input-data dependent branching operations by predicated code. It serializes the input-dependent alternatives of the code and uses predicates (instead of branches) and, if necessary, speculative execution to select the right code to be executed at runtime. All loops with an input-data dependent termination condition are transformed into loops with a constant number of iterations. The termination condition of the original loop is transformed into a condition that

occurs in the body of the new loop and makes the loop body execute conditionally, thus simulating the semantics of the original loop. More information about
the conversion can be found in [7].

5   The Time-Predictable Operating System

The operating system has to be carefully designed in order to achieve predictability at the instruction level of the CPU. There must be no jitter in the execution
times of the operating system routines.

5.1   Kernel Design

One of the key design decisions was to follow a microkernel-based design. From
the perspective of timing analysis, microkernels have two significant advantages:
First, microkernels are very small in code size and therefore, timing analysis gets
much easier. More importantly, however, most of the activities of the operating
system can be controlled at the task level, and thus, the static schedule and the
progress of time determine the actions of the OS.

All components of the OS, i.e., the microkernel and the system tasks, are
written in single-path code. The if-conversion is the most frequently applied rule
to the code, followed by the rule for loop conversions.

5.2   Communication

Communication is an integral part of every operating system. In our OS, we
use a simple model of interprocess communication which S-Tasks may use when
they need to communicate with other tasks or the real-time environment.

Interprocess Communication. Figure 2 illustrates our model of interprocess
communication. This model has been adopted from [8].

Every task has access to a local buffer in which messages are stored (1). These
messages will be copied by a privileged task (the IPC task) into a global buffer
called the message base upon its activation(2). All tasks have read access to
the message base. The IPC task further has access to the message schedule.
This schedule contains an entry for each message that has to be processed and
copied to the message base. Messages are always broadcast within a node and
written to a specific address in the message base. This address is determined
offline and listed in the message schedule. If specified in the schedule, a message
can also be sent to another node over the network. In this case, the IPC task
accesses the temporal firewall and writes the message into the message buffer
of the temporal firewall (see Section 2). The main advantage of this model is
temporal transparency, as the point in time when a message is being processed
is solely determined by the message schedule. This schedule is calculated offline.

System Calls. Most operating systems provide a set of system calls to enable tasks to communicate with the kernel. Because interprocess communication

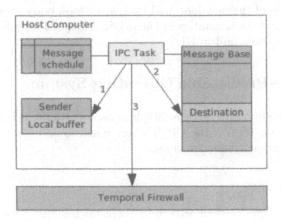

Fig. 2. Interprocess communication

depends on the corresponding IPC task (and thus, has to be scheduled), the scheduler makes use of system calls to communicate with the kernel. As explained in Section 5.3, the scheduler informs the dispatcher about the tasks that have to be executed according to the off-line calculated schedule. The scheduler also requests the reset of the global timer to an offline-calculated, specific value. All other tasks have to use the underlying IPC model and do not need to communicate with the kernel.

5.3   Scheduling and Mode Switches

In a time-triggered RTOS, the schedule is determined offline. The scheduler is invoked at each global clock tick. After invocation, the scheduler interpets the scheduling table and tells the dispatcher which tasks have to be executed. To avoid blocking, these tasks are not invoked immediatly, instead the dispatcher "waits" until the scheduler has finished its current execution before executing all other tasks.

Any task may request a *mode switch*. We define the term mode switch as the transition from the current schedule to the requested schedule. A mode-switch request is encoded as a special message and written to a special location in the message base. Upon invocation, the scheduler and the IPC task read from this location and switch to the requested tables. The point in time when a mode-switch can be carried out is determined offline and implicitly defined by the scheduling and message tables.

5.4   Implementation of S-Tasks and Task Preemption

For each task, the programmer has to define two procedures. One procedure defines the initialization semantics of the task. This procedure is not constrained to timing bounds; it may take an arbitrary, non-defined amount of time for the procedure to finish. Memory for all tasks is allocated during the initialization phase. When all tasks have been initialized, the operating system switches to real-time mode. In real-time mode, when a task is activated, its real-time procedure will be called. The real-time procedure must be written in single-path code, i.e., it must have constant timing. The operating system will detect a deviation of the specified timing of a task within an uncertainty of one clock cycle.

5.5 Temporal Characteristics

For the real-time application designer and the planning tool, knowledge of the execution times of the core components of the OS is essential. Table 1 lists the timing of the various components of the OS which are relevant to timing analysis.

Table 1. Timing of the OS

Functionality	Component	Timing in CPU cycles
Scheduling	Scheduler	$666+Max(Tasks)\times621$
Context switch	Dispatcher	253
Task execution	Kernel/Scheduler	1626
IPC	IPC task	$349+M_i \times 199 + 10 \times M_i \times Size(M_i)$

Most parts of the operating system have constant timing. However, components like the scheduler and IPC task use bounded counting loops. Therefore, the entire timing behaviour of the OS is dependend on three parameters: (a) The maximum number of tasks that can be scheduled per timeslot, $Max(Tasks)$, (b) (for the moment) the maximum size of a message, $Size(M_i)$, and the number of messages that have to be copied to the message base, M_i, where i refers to the corresponding index in the messaging table. All these parameters are determined offline and are stored in the scheduling and message tables.

6 Experiments

In order to show the feasibility of the presented approach we implemented a prototype operating system running on Spear2, a micro-controller developed at our department. In this section we first describe the hardware platform. Subsequently we explain two experiments performed on it. The first experiment shows that the timing of the OS is stable and free from execution-time jitter. The second experiment illustrates the impact of traditional code (i.e., branching code) on the timing of the OS.

6.1 Hardware Platform

Our platform consists of the soft processor core, Spear2 *(Scalable Processor for Embedded Applications in Real-time environments 2)* and associated tools. Spear2 constitutes a harvard architecture with separated data and instruction

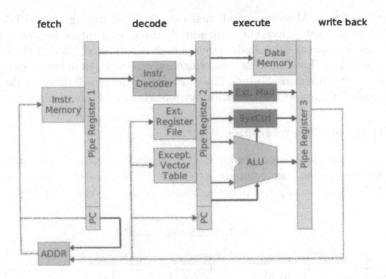

Fig. 3. Spear2 processor core

memories. While the instruction memory is always 16 bit wide, the data memory can be configured (16 or 32 bit). The register file comprises 16 registers, whereas two registers are reserved for storing the return addresses for subroutines (JSR and ISR). The instruction set consists of 119 instructions, most of them are predicated. All instructions are executed within one single clock cycle. Currently, there is no instruction caching.

However, tasks must not be preempted when they execute a jump instruction and trigger a pipeline flush because this could cause timing glitches.

Spear2 can be customized by mapping so called extension modules into the data memory. These modules can be accessed by ordinary load/store instructions. An extension module itself is an application specific hardware module which has a well defined interface: It consists of 32 eight-bit wide registers. The two first registers provide module status information while registers three and four are reserved for passing configuration parameters to the module. The remaining 28 registers can be used for data exchange. The position of the extension module register inside the data memory is defined by the so called *base address*. For instance, the instruction/clock cycle counter required to realize our operating system was implemented within an extension module.

A further interface – an AMBA interface – for the Spear2 processor core is under development. In this way Spear2 can be equipped with wide range of AMBA IP cores, among others a cache control. In the future, this will allow us to extend our investigations to more complex hardware structures.

Software is developed in C, using a C compiler based on gcc (*spear32-gcc*). The compiler creates either binaries for execution by SPEAR or a text file containing

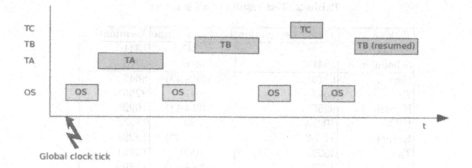

Fig. 4. Simple schedule of three S-Tasks

assembler code. The assembler code can be fed into a simulator that serves as debugging environment.

6.2   A Simple Application

Figure 1 depicts a simple schedule consisting of three S-tasks. This schedule is executed periodically, i.e., after task T_B finishes, task T_A will be executed again, then task T_B, and so on.

The following roles are assigned to the tasks: (a) T_A iteratively generates all permutations of a fixed-size array consisting of the numbers 1 to 5. The computed permutation is transferred to the message base by the IPC task. As task T_B sorts the array, it is interrupted by a high priority, dummy task T_C. After the completion of task T_C, T_B resumes and sorts the remaining part of the array.

6.3   Timing Measurements and Test Results

The goal of the experiments was to verify that for every execution cycle of the schedule, the timing behaviour is stable and identical to all other cycles. We used a logic analyzer to keep track of the program counter and the progress of time. We set the timing parameters as follows: $Size(M_i) = 8$ and $M_i=1$ for the IPC task and $Max(Tasks) = 8$ for the scheduler (for testing purposes we set the values of the parameters higher than necessary). For every task (T_A, T_C and T_B, Scheduler and Kernel) we measured the execution time in CPU cycles.

We took approximately 280 measurements using different input data sets and all samples showed exactly the same temporal behaviour. Table 2 lists the results we obtained with the logic analyzer.

For each task T, the time it takes the kernel to activate T is exactly 1626 CPU cycles. The only exception is the scheduler which is always activated after 1341 cycles. The activation times for all tasks are identical for every execution cycle. Note that after the (partial) execution of each task, 43 cycles have to be added. These 43 cycles are consumed by the kernel which checks the timing of the corresponding task.

Table 2. Test results of all samples

Task	Time of activation	Execution time	Termination
Kernel	0	1341	1341
Scheduler	1341	5634	6975
Kernel	6975	1626(+43)	8644
T_A	8644	611	9255
Kernel	9255	1626(+43)	10924
IPC	10924	628	11552
Kernel	11552	1626(+43)	13221
T_B	13221	1000	14221
Kernel	14221	1626(+43)	15890
T_C	15980	37	15927
Kernel	15927	1626(+43)	17596
$T_B(resumed)$	17596	1771	19369

Because the OS and the tasks are written in single-path code, we implicitly tested all possible execution scenarios (with the exception of those that involve the change of the timing parameters, i.e., the modification of loop bounds). Therefore, we can conclude that the timing is indeed stable and predictable.

The Impact of Traditional Code on the Timing Behaviour. An interesting question is how severe the implications of traditional code are on the timing behaviour of the OS. After all, in a time-triggered system, decision are taken offline. So one might hastily conclude that the execution-time jitter is neglectable. Therefore, we modified the kernel by transforming some parts of the interrupt service routine and the dispatcher back to the original (branching) code. By performing the same type of measurements again the kernel showed a variation of 52 clock cycles, which equals a jitter of 3.5%. Clearly, if we had modified more parts of the OS, the results would have been even more dramatic.

7   Summary and Conclusion

In this paper we showed that the realization of a time-deterministic operating system is feasible. The software of the operating system uses single-path code together with a parameterization of OS tasks that is based on a pre-runtime analysis to avoid that run-time decisions influence the run-time behavior of the operating system. The operating system synchronizes its time base with the environment by means with a programmable clock interrupt that the design system of an application guarantees to arrive at a time instant when no other system or task activity is in progress.

Experiments on a prototype implementation have demonstrated the feasibility of our approach: The task execution times and the execution times of the kernel routines and operating system tasks are invariable and can be predicted with the accuracy of a single CPU clock cycle.

Acknowledgments. The research leading to these results has received funding from the European Community's Seventh Framework Programme [FP7/2007-2013] under grant agreement no. 214373.

References

1. Obermaisser, R., Peti, P., Kopetz, H.: Virtual Networks in an Integrated Time-Triggered Architecture. In: Proc. 10th IEEE International Workshop on Object-Oriented Real-Time Dependable Systems, Feburary 2005, pp. 241–253 (2005)
2. Kopetz, H., Nossal, R.: Temporal Firewalls in Large Distributed Real-Time Systems. In: Proc. 6th IEEE Workshop on Future Trends of Distributed Computing Systems, October 1997, pp. 310–315 (1997)
3. Puschner, P., Burns, A.: A review of worst-case execution-time analysis. Journal of Real-Time Systems 18(2/3), 115–128 (2000)
4. Kirk, D.B.: Smart (strategic memory allocation for real-time) cache design. In: Proc. 10th Real-Time Systems Symposium, Santa Monica, CA, USA, December 1989, pp. 229–237 (1989)
5. Kopetz, H.: Real-Time Systems. Kluwer Academic Publishers, Dordrecht (1997)
6. Puschner, P., Burns, A.: Writing temporally predictable code. In: Proc. 7th IEEE International Workshop on Object-Oriented Real-Time Dependable Systems, January 2002, pp. 85–91 (2002)
7. Puschner, P.: Transforming execution-time boundable code into temporally predictable code. In: Kleinjohann, B., Kim, K.K., Kleinjohann, L., Rettberg, A. (eds.) Design and Analysis of Distributed Embedded Systems. IFIP 17th World Computer Congress - TC10 Stream on Distributed and Parallel Embedded Systems (DIPES 2002), pp. 163–172. Kluwer Academic Publishers, Dordrecht (2002)
8. Reisinger, J.: Konzeption und Analyse eines zeitgesteuerten Betriebssystems für Echtzeitanwendungen. Ph.D thesis, Technisch-Naturwissenschaftliche Fakultät, Technische Universität Wien, Wien, Österreich (July 1993)

Data Services in Distributed Real-Time Embedded Systems

Woochul Kang and Sang H. Son

University of Virginia, Charlottesville VA 22904, USA

Abstract. The computing systems are becoming deeply embedded into ordinary life and interact with physical processes and events. They monitor the physical world with sensors and provide appropriate reaction and control over it. This cyber-physical interaction, which occurs through ubiquitous embedded systems, has the potential to transform how humans interact with and control the physical world. Applications of such systems include infrastructure management and environmental monitoring. For these applications, the demand for real-time data services is increasing since they are inherently data-intensive. However, providing real-time data services in such large-scale and geographically distributed environment is a challenging task. In particular, both unpredictable communicational delays and computational workloads of large-scale distributed systems can lead to large number of deadline misses. In this paper, we propose a real-time data service architecture called DRACON (Decentralized data Replication And CONtrol), which is designed to support large-scale distributed real-time applications. DRACON uses cluster-based replica-sharing and a decentralized control structure to address communication and computational unpredictability.

1   Introduction

Recent years have seen the emergence of large-scale distributed real-time embedded (DRE) systems. They monitor the physical world with sensors and provide appropriate reaction and control over it. The scale of such cyber-physical interactions is very wide; embedded systems of such interactions range from resource-constrained stand-alone devices to global-scale networked embedded systems. This cyber-physical interaction, which occurs through ubiquitous embedded systems, has the potential to transform how humans interact with and control the physical world. Applications of such systems include advanced traffic control, global environment control, irrigation network control, and nation-wide electric power grid control. For many of these systems, providing real-time data services is essential since they need to handle large amounts of data in real-time to satisfy the timing constraints from physical processes and events. The issues involved in providing predictable real-time data services in centralized or small-scale distributed database systems have been studied and the results are promising [1][2][3].

U. Brinkschulte, T. Givargis, and S. Russo (Eds.): SEUS 2008, LNCS 5287, pp. 162–173, 2008.

In large-scale distributed environments, it is challenging to provide data services with QoS guarantees while still meeting temporal requirements of transactions. One main difficulty lies in long and highly variable remote data access delays. Unlike small-scale systems, which utilize highly deterministic local-area networks, large-scale DRE systems in wide geographical areas have to use a network that is shared by many participants for cost-effectiveness. A second challenge involves the complex interactions among a large number of nodes, which can incur unpredictable workloads for each node. For instance, a local node may experience a dramatic load increase during cascading disturbance in power grids. A third challenge is the data-dependent nature of transactions or tasks. End-to-end QoS can be achieved only when both timely access to remote data and timely computation are guaranteed. For example, QoS management schemes that do not consider the timely access to remote data [4][5] can not provide the eventual QoS guarantees in DRE systems, in which large number of nodes have complex remote data access patterns.

In this paper, we propose a distributed real-time database (DRTDB) architecture called *DRACON (Decentralized data Replication And CONtrol)*, which supports QoS in a scalable manner. In particular, DRACON features a scalable replica-sharing mechanism that enables not only bounded-delay remote data access, but also a decentralized, thus scalable, QoS control structure. DRACON is designed to support scalable real-time data services, by considering both communicational and computational unpredictability of large-scale DRE systems. Previous approaches either ignore the data-dependent nature of tasks/transactions in providing QoS guarantees [4][5], or are not scalable [3].

Data replication can help database systems meet the stringent temporal requirements of real-time applications [3][6]. A node can access local replicas, which are updated periodically for freshness, without long communication delays. However, naïve replication approaches such as full replication, which is commonly found in small-scale distributed database systems, can incur high computational and communicational overhead as the system size scales up, leading to a large number of deadline misses. In DRACON, nodes are partitioned into *clusters* for high scalability, in which replicas are shared by member nodes of the cluster, instead of having a local replica at each node. Each node of a cluster is responsible for maintaining a fair share of replicas. Further, the replica-sharing clusters are constructed such that the intra-cluster communication delay to access the shared replicas is bounded with high statistical guarantees. This clustering algorithm is implemented and tested on *PlanetLab* [7], a world-wide distributed Internet testbed. The result demonstrates that, despite the variability of wide-area networks, delay bounds can be guaranteed with a high probability.

Even though the *replica sharing* technique in DRACON should decrease the replication overhead significantly, replication still incurs non-negligible overhead, making the system sensitive to workload unpredictability. To deal with this problem, DRACON provides a decentralized and hierarchical control technique that guarantees tight deadline miss ratio under unpredictable workload. In particular, the workload control structure of DRACON is decentralized into replica-sharing clusters. Since all remote data access requests from a node are handled within the cluster, clusters have less interactions with each other and are decoupled. This decoupling enables highly scalable decentralized control structure in DRACON.

The rest of the paper is organized as follows. The design of DRACON is described in detail in Section 2. Related work is briefly discussed in Section 3. Section 4 concludes the paper and discusses further research issues.

2   Approach

In this section, we present the design of DRACON that provides data services with QoS guarantees for large-scale DRE systems.

2.1   DRACON Architecture

Figure 1 shows the architecture of one node of DRACON. The architecture has 3 layers, *remote data access layer*, *QoS enforcement layer*, and *real-time DBMS layer*.

The *remote data access layer* enables transparent access to remote data within a bounded communication time. Remote temporal data are replicated locally to provide timely access to them. However, to avoid the high cost of full replication in large-scale distributed systems, the system is partitioned into clusters, and member nodes of each cluster share replicas of the cluster, instead of having respective local replicas. A local replica of remote data is made only if a replica is not found in the cluster that the node belongs to. Each node of a cluster is responsible for maintaining a fair share amount of replicas of remote data. The fair share amount of replicas for each node is controlled by the QoS enforcement layer to guarantee the desired QoS.

In *QoS enforcement layer*, QoS is guaranteed by feedback control loops. The primary metrics of QoS are transaction deadline miss ratio and utilization. A key intuition that affects the architecture of the feedback control loops is that the dynamics of DRACON manifest two different time-scales. At each node, fast

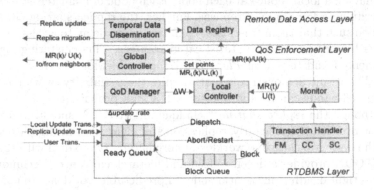

Fig. 1. The architecture of one DRACON node

dynamics are observed. These dynamics arise from changing data access patterns. At the global system level, slower dynamics are observed. They arise from changing global load distribution. Therefore, DRACON's feedback control architecture has two sets of control loops, local and global ones. In particular, since the cluster-based replica-sharing decouples clusters and decreases the interaction between clusters, DRACON's global control structure is decentralized into each cluster, making DRACON highly scalable. The global control information is exchanged only among member nodes of each cluster.

The *real-time database (RTDBMS) layer* does typical real-time transaction handling; the incoming transactions are dispatched and processed by the transaction handler. The transaction handler consists of a concurrency controller (CC), a freshness manager (FM), and a scheduler (SC). In the SC, update transactions are scheduled in the high priority queue while user transactions are scheduled in the low priority queue. Update transactions are either updates from local sensors to local data objects or updates from primary nodes to replicated temporal data objects. Within each queue, transactions are scheduled using Earliest Deadline First (EDF). The FM checks the freshness before accessing a data object using the corresponding *absolute validity interval* (avi). A sensor data object O_i is considered valid, or fresh, as long as $(current\ time - timestamp(O_i)) < avi(O_i)$ If the data object is not fresh, user transactions accessing the data object are blocked until the data object is updated.

2.2 Bounded-Delay Communication

In a distributed real-time system like the power grid, which interacts with physical processes and events, the latency of data propagation from one node to the other should be predictable and bounded in time to make a timely control decision. For example, the power grid monitoring and control in wide-area requires that status information from a control station should be delivered to the other control stations in a bounded time to prevent cascading disturbances. However, deterministic delay bound guarantees is virtually impossible to achieve in Internet-like networks. Instead, we try to achieve delay bounds with a high probability.

In DRACON, the temporal data is delivered indirectly from a source node to a destination node via a node that has a replica of the original data. Therefore, the total propagation delay of temporal data from a source node to a destination node in a different cluster is sum of inter- and intra-cluster communication delay as shown in Equation 1.

$$PropagationDelay(n_i, n_j) = Comm_{inter} + Comm_{intra}(n_j), \qquad (1)$$

where $Comm_{inter}$ is the inter-cluster communication delay and $Comm_{intra}$ (n_j) is the intra-cluster communication delay of the cluster that node n_j belongs to. Figure 2 shows inter- and intra communication delays with 2 replica-sharing clusters.

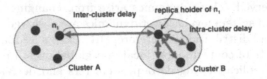

Fig. 2. Clusters and inter/intra delays

Since a temporal data of one node can be replicated by any node in the system, $Comm_{inter}$ is the communication delay between any arbitrary nodes of the system, and it is the global property of a given communication network; the bound on $Comm_{inter}$ is not affected by a cluster construction mechanism. However, the bound on $Comm_{intra}(\mathcal{N})$ of an arbitrary cluster $\mathcal{N}$ is determined by the member nodes of the cluster. $Comm_{intra}(\mathcal{N})$ is bounded by d with p probability:

$$p \leq Pr\left\{Comm_{intra}(\mathcal{N}) \leq d\right\}, \tag{2}$$

where

$$d = \max_{n_i, n_j \in \mathcal{N},} (p \text{ quantile of measured delays btw. } n_i \text{ and } n_j). \tag{3}$$

Therefore, clusters should be constructed to guarantee that the partitioned clusters satisfy the requirement of an application on its data propagation delay bound. Generally speaking, the bound on $Comm_{intra}$ of a cluster is inversely proportional to the size of the cluster. However, the computational and communicational overhead increases proportionally to the number of clusters as will be shown in the Evaluation section.

In power grids and other wide-area DRE systems, the requirement on the data propagation delay is highly related to the geographical distance between two nodes since the travel speed of physical disturbances is linearly proportional to the geographical distance. For example, disturbances travel at the speed of $500km/sec$ in power grids [8]. Therefore, the geographical distance should be considered in constructing clusters. The requirement can be stated as follows:

$$PropagationDelay(n_i, n_j) + \alpha \leq \frac{Dist(n_i, n_j)}{PSpeed}, \tag{4}$$

where $Dist(n_i, n_j)$ is the geographical distance between the two nodes, $PSpeed$ is the travel speed of the disturbance, and α is the additional overhead to process the data including actuation latency. Intuitively, this requirement tells that status data should be delivered and processed faster than the propagation of a physical disturbance.

Given this requirement, the system is partitioned into *clusters* using Algorithm-1 when the system is deployed. In Algorithm-1, clusters are recursively partitioned into smaller clusters until each cluster satisfies application's requirement. In the resulting replica-sharing structure, each cluster $\mathcal{N}$ has $Comm_{intra}(\mathcal{N})$ as its remote data access delay bounds. The temporal data

---

Algorithm 1. GeographicalPartitioning(cluster $\mathcal{N}$)

Input: Distance between nodes
Input: End-to-end delay bounds between nodes
foreach *node n_i in neighbor clusters* **do**
   foreach *node n_j in cluster $\mathcal{N}$* **do**
      if *PropagationDelay(n_i, n_j)* $+ \alpha \leq \frac{Dist(n_i, n_j)}{PSpeed}$ **then**
         continue;
      else
         partition $\mathcal{N}$ geographically into $\mathcal{N}_1$ and $\mathcal{N}_2$;
         GeographicalPartitioning($\mathcal{N}_1$);
         GeographicalPartitioning($\mathcal{N}_2$);
      end
   end
end

---

propagation delay bound from an arbitrary node to a node in the cluster $\mathcal{N}$ is given as $Comm_{inter} + Comm_{intra}(\mathcal{N})$. In wide-area networks, the delay bounds are statistical.

Algorithm-1 runs only when the system is first deployed since we assume that the network characteristic of future Internet-like networks for critical infrastructures will be less dynamic than the current Internet once they are deployed. In a network with highly time-varying characteristics, Algorithm-1 should be extended to include post-adjustment capability with dynamic network probing. We leave this as our future work.

Delay Bounds in Wide-Area Networks. We demonstrate the communication delay bounds that can be achieved in the current Internet with the proposed replica-sharing mechanism. This also shed light on the feasibility of the proposed approach in future Internet-like networks. Algorithm-1 is implemented and tested on *PlanetLab*, a world-wide distributed Internet testbed, with 64 nodes in eastern United States.

Before running Algorithm-1, the round-trip communication latencies were probed for 24 hours at every 30 second. Figure 3 shows the probability distribution of round-trip communication latencies between arbitrary two nodes. This graph shows that 99.999% of round-trip times between any arbitrary two nodes are less than $250ms$. The size of data packet has little impact on communication latency. The result indicates that the tight delay bounds for inter-cluster communication, $Comm_{inter}$, is $250ms$ with 99.999% statistical guarantees.

The measured delay bounds between arbitrary two nodes were provided as inputs to Algorithm-1. Instead of setting a specific requirement on the propagation delay, a cluster with the longest intra-cluster delay bound was partitioned recursively until we had 8 clusters.

The resulting replica-sharing clusters has $300km$ inter-cluster distance at a minimum. In power grid, this implies that it takes at least $600ms$ for the electric disturbance to propagate to neighbor clusters. The average intra-cluster delay bounds, $Comm_{intra}$, of the 8 clusters is $181ms$ with 99.99% probability.

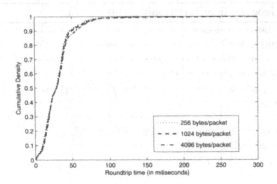

Fig. 3. Round trip time between arbitrary two nodes

Therefore, the propagation delay bounds of data from a node to the other in a different cluster is $431ms(= 250ms + 181ms)$ with 99.99% probability.

This result shows that the indirect access to temporal data through replica-sharing does not violate the requirement on the data propagation delay as long as an application requires data propagation delay no less than $431ms$. For example, it is feasible to take control action to avoid cascading electric disturbance between clusters as long as overhead for data processing and actuation takes less than about $169ms$ since it takes $600ms$ on average for a disturbance to propagate to a neighbor cluster in the stated geographical setting[1].

In practice, the requirement on the data propagation delay of most wide-area DRE systems, which were mentioned in Introduction, is much longer since the speed of physical process is much slow, e.g., the speed of road traffic, and tsunami.

2.3 Decentralized QoS Control

In this section, we design feedback control loops for DRACON. The goal of the feedback control loops is to maintain the desired deadline miss ratio and utilization both locally and globally.

Local QoS Control. At each node, there are a local miss ratio controller and a local utilization controller as shown in Figure 4. The local feedback controllers are responsible for tracking the QoS set points set by global controllers, MR_L and U_L, and ensuring that transactions have a minimum miss ratio and the node remains fully utilized.

Each node has a desired deadline miss ratio, MR_L, and a desired utilization, U_L, as its specification from the node's global miss ratio and utilization controllers. At each sampling instant, the local miss ratio controller takes the current miss ratio, compares them with the desired miss ratio, and computes

---

[1] In practice, electric disturbances typically take minutes before they become serious enough to cause widespread disruption [9].

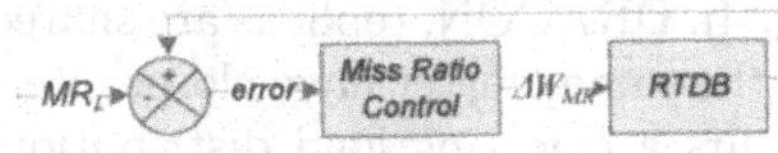

(a) Miss ratio controller 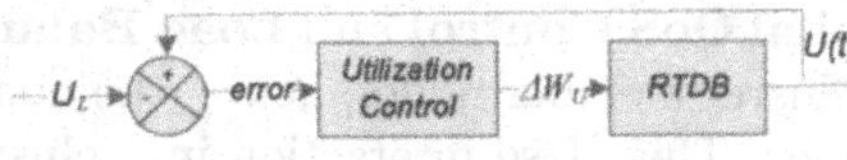   (b) Utilization controller

Fig. 4. Local controllers

the local workload control signal, ΔW_{MR}, which is used to adjust the utilization at the next sampling period. The local utilization control loop takes the similar control action as the local miss ratio controller. Employing a utilization control loop is to avoid a trivial solution, in which all the miss ratio requirements are trivially satisfied by under-utilizing the system. At each sampling instant, we set the current control signal $DeltaW = Minimum(\Delta W_{MR}, \Delta W_U)$ to support a smooth transition from one system state to another.

The target utilization from the local controller is achieved by switching between the on-demand update scheme and the immediate update scheme for selected temporal data objects. The candidate data objects of this *dynamic update-mode switch* are selected based on the communication delays between a primary node n_i and its replica holder node n_j of data object O_i. The $avi(O_i)$ should be large enough for O_i to be still fresh even when the data object is updated on-demand as shown in Equation 5.

$$Comm_{inter} + Comm_{intra}(n_j) + \beta < avi(O_i). \tag{5}$$

In the equation, $Comm_{inter} + Comm_{intra}(n_j)$ is the communication delay for on-demand update, and β is the expected processing time to retrieve O_i at the primary node. Since the communication delay bounds of any two arbitrary nodes are known with high statistical guarantees from the system partitioning procedure, we can get the set of candidate data objects, O_{cand}, which satisfy the above condition. When the estimated load adaptation from the update-mode switch of data object O_i is $U_c(O_i)$, the maximum adjustable load is $\sum_{O_i \in O_{cand}} U_c(O_i)$. After the candidate data objects for the update-mode switch are selected, the notion of *Access Update Ratio (AUR)* for a data object is applied O_i as follows to select target data objects:

$$AUR[i] = \frac{Access\ Frequency[i]}{Update\ Frequency[i]}. \tag{6}$$

AUR models the ratio of the benefit (*Access Frequency*) to the cost (*Update Frequency*) of O_i. It is clear that data objects with high AUR should be updated aggressively; if they are out-of-date when accessed, potentially multiple transactions may miss their deadlines waiting for the updates. Therefore, data objects are considered in the order of smaller AUR for update mode switch.

In the design of controllers, each local RTDB is modeled as an *first-order time-invariant linear model*, and *proportional integral* (PI) control law is used for controllers. The details of our local controller design procedure can be found in [2].

Global QoS Control and Load Balancing. In DRACON, replicas are shared by cluster member nodes; hence, the nodes in the same cluster have closer interactions. This close interaction in a cluster incurs a changing load distribution. Global controllers at each node balance this load distribution.

At each global sampling period, global controllers exchange utilization/miss ratio information with other member nodes in the same cluster to calculate the average miss ratio, MR_A, and utilization, U_A. The global control outputs of each node are determined from the following difference equations:

$$MR_L(k) = MR_L(k-1) + K_M(MR_A - MR(k-1)).\tag{7}$$

$$U_L(k) = U_L(k-1) + K_U(U_A - U(k-1)).\tag{8}$$

The global control outputs, $MR_L(k)$ and $U_L(k)$, are the set points for the local miss ratio controller and the local utilization controller, respectively. The controller gains, K_M and K_U, determine the characteristics of the controllers. Note that global control information is exchanged only among cluster members since cluster-based replica sharing decouples each cluster from the others. Furthermore, the control information delivery time is highly predictable since the communication delay in an arbitrary cluster c is bounded by $Comm_{intra}(c)$ with high statistical guarantees.

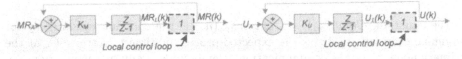

(a) Global Miss ratio control   (b) Global Utilization control

Fig. 5. Block diagram for the global system

The interaction between local and global controllers is modeled by simplifying a local feedback control loop into an identity transfer function. This simplification of the local feedback control loop is possible since a local feedback control loop has several orders of magnitude faster dynamics than a global control loop. When a system has multiple dynamics, the fast mode of the system can be discarded for model simplification [10][11]; this enables modeling of a complex system. With this technique, the global system can be modeled as shown in Figure 5. In the figure, the blocks with an identity transfer function are local feedback control loops. Intuitively, modeling a local feedback control loop into an identity transfer function means that a QoS set point (MR_L or U_L) from a global controller is achieved instantaneously by the local controller and the state is maintained until the next global sampling period.

In the above block diagrams, the poles of closed loops are $\frac{1}{K_m+1}$ and $\frac{1}{K_U+1}$, respectively. A discrete system is stable if and only if the poles of the closed loop are inside a unit circle [12]. Therefore, the closed loop for the global system in Figure 5 is stable if positive values for the controller gains, K_M and K_U, are selected. The final controller parameters are determined in consideration of other desired characteristics of the closed loop system such as a settling time and an overshoot.

Once target miss ratio and utilization are set for local controllers, they are tracked by local controllers at each node. However, the maximum achievable load adjustment from a local control loop can be limited by data freshness requirements; the update mode of a data object can be switched to on-demand update only if Equation 5 is satisfied. The remaining workload adaptation is achieved by migrating replicas between cluster member nodes. At each global sampling period k, the amount of load that a node i needs to transfer (or to receive), $\Delta TW_i(k)$, is the difference between the required load adaptation to achieve the new set points, $\Delta W_i(k)$, and the local controller's maximally achievable load adaption, $AW_i(k)$:

$$\Delta TW_i(k) = \Delta W_i(k) - AW_i(k). \tag{9}$$

If $\Delta TW_i(k)$ is positive, the node is overloaded and it can not be fully controlled by its local controller. Therefore, some replicas are migrated to neighbor nodes, which have a negative $\Delta TW(k)$, until $\Delta TW_i(k)$ becomes less than or equal to zero. Since local target set points, MR_L and U_L, are determined to track the average miss ratio and the utilization of cluster nodes, $\sum_i \Delta TW_i(k)$ approaches zero, making each cluster balanced.

3   Related Works

Distributed real-time databases (DRTDBs) have drawn research attention in recent years [13][14]. Wei et. al. proposed replication techniques for DRTDBs [3][6]. However, their approaches do not consider communication delay bounds in wide-area networks, and their workload control mechanism is not scalable in large-scale systems.

Feedback control has been applied to QoS management in real-time systems due to its robustness against unpredictable operating environments [15][1]. In particular, several distributed feedback control schemes have been proposed for distributed real-time systems [5][11][4]. However, those approaches target small-scale distributed systems and do not consider communication delays in wide-area networks.

4   Conclusions

DRACON has been designed to provide a highly scalable data service with QoS guarantees in large-scale distributed real-time systems. DRACON features a replica sharing mechanism that enables bounded-delay access to remote data in a highly scalable manner. Furthermore, the replica sharing resolves the complex interactions between nodes by decoupling clusters, allowing a decentralized, hence scalable, QoS control structure.

Currently we are evaluating the performance of DRACON in large-scale applications. The preliminary results show that DRACON is capable of achieving a significant performance improvement compared to baselines in providing the desired miss ratios while maintaining high utilization in wide-area networking environments. While these results are promising, there are several technical challenges that need further research. We plan to address the following questions:

1. *Variability of Network:* How does the variability of the network affect the replica-sharing scheme? Our preliminary work is based on the assumption that the communication network is stable in its delay characteristics. However, if a communication network's end-to-end delay characteristics change significantly in different time periods, e.g., days and nights, the clusters need to be post-adjusted at runtime. A dynamic scheme for network status monitoring and modeling is required to achieve that.

2. *Inter-Cluster Load Balancing:* How can the load-imbalance between clusters be resolved? In DRACON, each cluster is decoupled by cluster-level replica-sharing. However, it is still possible that there exist some interactions between clusters. In such situations, we may need higher level controllers/load balancers to resolve the inter-cluster load imbalance. What would be the constraints in designing such inter-cluster level controllers?

3. *Dependability:* DRACON considers real-time data replication to reduce data access time. However, replication is also effective in improving the dependability of the system. By having multiple replicas of sensor data, the system can guarantee that the critical information is accessible on time even when some nodes are unavailable, although it requires additional cost. We will investigate how to improve the dependability with minimal cost, using the idea of adaptive virtual replication we have developed for embedded sensor networks [16].

4. *Interaction with physical processes:* How does the timing constraints from physical processes affect the QoS management architecture? We will use real-world examples to investigate appropriate QoS models for networked embedded systems.

References

1. Kang, K.D., Son, S.H., Stankovic, J.A.: Managing deadline miss ratio and sensor data freshness in real-time databases. IEEE Transacctions on Knowledge and Data Engineering 16(10), 1200–1216 (2004)
2. Kang, W., Son, S.H., Stankovic, J.A., Amirijoo, M.: I/O-aware deadline miss ratio management in real-time embedded databases. In: The 28th IEEE Real-Time Systems Symposium (RTSS) (December 2007)
3. Wei, Y., Son, S.H., Stankovic, J.A., Kang, K.D.: Qos management in replicated real time databases. In: RTSS 2003: Proceedings of the 24th IEEE International Real-Time Systems Symposium (2003)

4. Wang, X., Jia, D., Lu, C., Koutsoukos, X.: DEUCON:Decentralized End-to-End Utilization Control for Distributed Real-Time Systems. IEEE Transactions on Parallel and Distributed Systems 18(7), 996–1009 (2007)
5. Stankovic, J.A., He, T., Abdelzaher, T., Marley, M., Tao, G., Son, S., Lu, C.: Feedback control scheduling in distributed real-time systems. In: RTSS 2001: Proceedings of the 22nd IEEE Real-Time Systems Symposium (RTSS 2001) (2001)
6. Wei, Y., Shlinger, A.A., Son, S.H., Stankovic, J.A.: ORDER: A Dynamic Replication Algorithm for Periodic Transactions in Distributed Real-Time Databases. In: RTCSA 2004, Gothenburg, Sweden (August 2004)
7. Anderson, T., Peterson, L., Shenker, S., Turner, J.: Overcoming the internet impasse through virtualization. IEEE Computers 38(4), 34–41 (2005)
8. Thorp, J.S., Seyler, C.E., Phadke, A.G.: Electromechanical wave propagation in large electric power systems. IEEE Transactions on Circuits and Systems 45(6), 614–622 (1998)
9. Birman, K.P., Chen, J., Hopkinson, E.M., Thomas, R.J., Thorp, J.S., Renesse, R.V., Vogels, W.: Overcoming communications challenges in software for monitoring and controlling power systems. In: Proceedings of the IEEE (2005)
10. Nils, R., Sandell, J., Varaiya, P., Athans, M., Safonov, M.G.: Survey of decentralized control methods for large scale systems. IEEE Transactions on Automatic Control 23(2), 108–128 (1978)
11. Lin, S., Manimaran, G.: Double-loop feedback-based scheduling approach for distributed real-time systems. In: Conference on High Performance Computing (HiPC) (2003)
12. Hellerstein, J.L., Diao, Y., Parekh, S., Tilbury, D.M.: Feedback Control of Computing Systems. Wiley, IEEE press (2004)
13. Peddi, P., DiPippo, L.C.: A replication strategy for distributed real-time object-oriented databases. In: Symposium on Object-Oriented Real-Time Distributed Computing, pp. 129–136 (2002)
14. Wei, Y., Prasad, V., Son, S.H., Stankovic, J.A.: Prediction-based qos management for real-time data streams. In: RTSS 2006, pp. 344–358 (2006)
15. Lu, C., Stankovic, J.A., Son, S.H., Tao, G.: Feedback control real-time scheduling: Framework, modeling, and algorithms. Real-Time Syst. 23(1-2), 85–126 (2002)
16. Mathiason, G., Andler, S., Son, S.H.: Virtual full replication for saclable and adaptive real-time communication in wireless sensor networks. In: Second International Conference on Sensor Technologies and Applications, Cap Esterel, France (August 2008)

QoS-Adaptive Router Based on Per-Flow Management over NGN[*]

Boyoung Rhee[1], Sungchol Cho[1], Sunyoung Han[1,**], Chun-hyon Chang[1], and Jung Guk Kim[2]

[1] Department of Computer Science and Engineering, Konkuk University
1 Hwayang-dong, Gwangjin-gu, Seoul 143-701, Korea
{boyoung,cschol,syhan,chchang}@konkuk.ac.kr
[2] Deptment of Computer Engineering, Hankuk University of Foreign Studies
San 89-1, Wangsan, Mohyun, YongIn City, Kyunggi-do, Korea
jgkim@hufs.ac.kr

Abstract. In the present paper, we designed a specific router which provides the required level of QoS over NGN(Next Generation Network) by controlling data flows. We called this router QoS-Adaptive router, which consists of two parts, a legacy routing part and a QoS guarantee routing part. In order to provide differentiated services, QoS-Adaptive router enables data taking broad bandwidth or data requiring high-level QoS to be processed immediately and not to be affected by other services. And, we used the definition of flow for per-flow management, and assigned new service types to the flow label field of IPv6 header so as to provide differentiated services according to the packet type. By doing this, we designed a distinguishing mechanism in order to adapt to NGN that concentrates upon QoS. We built not only a small network to test QoS-Adaptive router but also a simulation environment called OMNeT++, and we could verify the performance of QoS-Adaptive router supporting QoS based on subscriber and service levels.

Keywords: QoS, NGN(Next Generation Network), Resource Management, Data Flow, User Level, Service Level, Bandwidth.

1 Introduction

The requirements of quality of services using the Internet increase continuously. However, there is a limit to QoS because IP transport technology focuses on internet services based on 'best effort'. Therefore, the current network architecture is evolving to NGN(Next Generation Network), which supports guaranteed quality of broadband multimedia services that are integrated with communication, broadcast and the internet. According to the main concept of NGN, NGN architecture should support various services requiring high-level QoS such as a real-time service even though users use

---

[*] This research was supported by the MKE(Ministry of Knowledge and Economy), Korea, under the ITRC(Information Technology Research Center) support program supervised by the IITA(Institute for Information Technology Advancement) (IITA-2008-C1090-0804-0015).
[**] Corresponding Author.

U. Brinkschulte, T. Givargis, and S. Russo (Eds.): SEUS 2008, LNCS 5287, pp. 174–185, 2008.
© IFIP International Federation for Information Processing 2008

any kinds of communication networks and terminals. To provide integrated network services, NGN needs different network architecture from the existing network one, and the development of some equipment such as a router, should evolve so as to be suitable for NGN. Therefore, we added a few functions, such as classifying packets, adjusting bandwidth and keeping flows from others, to the existing router in order to support QoS. Furthermore, we extended the role of RACF(Resource and Admission Control Functions) in NGN QoS architecture to communicate with the proposed router.

2 Background

2.1 RACF in NGN QoS Architecture

NGN QoS architecture is made up of 'Service Stratum' in charge of application signaling and 'Transport Stratum' in charge of packet transmission as shown in Fig. 1 [1].

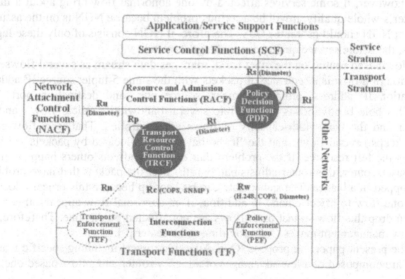

Fig. 1. RACF in NGN QoS Architecture

SCF(Service Control Functions), which implements signaling with terminals, transmits QoS requirements to real networks via RACF in order to provide network services. TCF(Transport Control Functions), which is made up of NACF and RACF, acts as an arbitrator for connecting two strata, Service Stratum and Transport Stratum. NACF (Network Attachment Control Functions) provides a registration function at the access level and an initialization function of end-user functions to access NGN services. These functions provide network-level identification/authentication, and also authenticate an access session. RACF(Resource and Admission Control Functions) provides QoS control functions including a resource reservation, admission control and gate control in order to get desired QoS for communication and permission to access certain resources. RACF is composed of PDF(Policy Decision Function) which exchanges signaling and resources information with SCF, and TRCF(Transport Resources Control Function) which analyzes network resources and status. TF (Transport Functions) is the set of functions that support the transmission of media information and control information [1].

The router in the present paper sets itself up with QoS policies, and communicates with TRCF in order to receive QoS policies and report the data flow status which this router collects and analyzes. TRCF, which received the status from this router, also communicates with PDF.

2.2 Legacy Router vs. Flow-Based Router

A legacy router accepts input data irrespective of its bandwidth, and this router is not responsible for the result such as packet loss, delay, and so forth. In NGN environment, however, if some services affected by one abnormal flow bring about a falloff in router's whole quality, it will be a serious problem because NGN is on the assumption that NGN should guarantee QoS. Therefore, if NGN consists of only these legacy routers, the whole service quality cannot be guaranteed.

A flow-based router, on the other hand, manages data stream as several flows. The definition of a flow is a sequence of packets with the same 5-tuple: source IP address, destination IP address, protocol number, source port, and destination port. This router's whole bandwidth is divided into several bandwidths called 'flow', and the number and the bandwidth capacity of flows are controlled. That is, a flow-based router keeps several flows, and the flows that are not allocated by packets are managed as the left resource. If the problem that one flow affects others happens in the flow-based router, this router adjusts bandwidth, after the packets that have problems are dropped in advance. The stable state can be kept up because this process does not allow one flow to affect others. In addition, if an abnormal flow appears, this router just can drop this flow so that other flows are not affected by this one. Therefore, this per-flow management makes QoS providing to be easier [2].

In the present paper, we propose 'QoS-Adaptive router' including specific features which are composed of a few advantages of a legacy router and a flow-based one.

3 Requirements and Design

3.1 RACF's Information Collection

CPE(Customer Premises Equipment) sends service request signaling to SCF(Service Control Functions), and then SCF informs PDF of QoS requirements from CPE. Once receiving a resource requirement, PDF collects information about the subscriber and available resources. In order to get the subscriber information, PDF communicates with NACF(Network Attachment Control Functions) which provides control functions about network attachments based on the information of subscriber's registration such as a subscriber level and security level, and of a terminal used by the subscriber. To obtain the network resources information, PDF gets a message from TRCF periodically. This

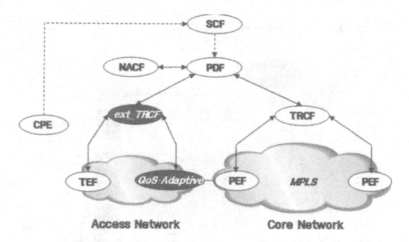

Fig. 2. Relationship between RACF's Parts and QoS-Adaptive router

message is the information that TRCF makes up of by receiving and analyzing messages from QoS-Adaptive router. In this way, PDF can get two kinds of reports; one is about subscriber's level from NACF, and the other is about network information from TRCF, actually QoS-Adaptive router. PDF makes a decision about whether this service can be accepted or not, and about QoS policies if it is accepted. Fig. 2 shows the relationship of RACF's parts and QoS-Adaptive router as stated above.

To support QoS for NGN, a core network is made up of MPLS(Multi Protocol Label Switching) and QoS-Adaptive router is located at each edge, a traffic ingress point [4]. We also designed TRCF including some extended roles such as to communicate with several parts in QoS-Adaptive router, to make up new messages, and to inform PDF of the network's status. We call this TRCF 'ext_TRCF'.

3.2 QoS-Adaptive Router Architecture

Two NGN objects for QoS are to provide differentiated quality services and to protect services from others. These will make most of subscribers be satisfied with the QoS over NGN. Therefore, QoS-Adaptive router, that can guarantee QoS and differentiated services, will be a meaningful component of NGN.

QoS-Adaptive router consists of a legacy part that acts as a legacy router and a flow part which supports QoS and controls bandwidth. As Fig. 3 depicts, QoS-Adaptive router needs Classifier to classify packets according to their own levels, Premium Processor to handle some high-level packets, and Legacy Processor to handle the others. In addition, to communicate with each other or ext_TRCF in RACF, a few communication passages are needed.

1) Classifier

Discriminative transport can be done according to the designated value of the flow label as a newly added field in IPv6, which can support real-time traffic controls or packets that require the same processing [3]. Classifier, as a module in a data input part, classifies packets into several types of packets referring to the flow label field in

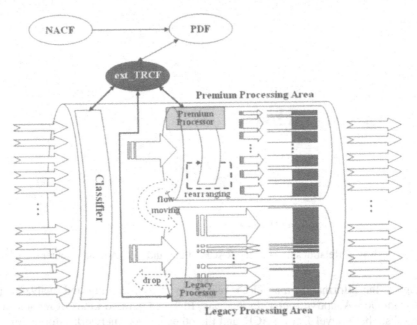

Fig. 3. QoS-Adaptive Router Architecture

IPv6 header. We used just low 9-bit of the flow label field. We assigned an urgent mark to 1 bit, types of service to 4 bits, and the rest 4 bits are for subscriber levels in our mechanism. - The detailed contents like using more bits can be adjusted according to the policy by service providers and administration or RACF manager.

Classifier communicates with ext_TRCF periodically in order to obtain a classification policy which is applied in classifying packets, and to report real information about the component ratio of packets. For example, A level's rate is 15%, B level's rate is 23%, and so on. There is the information on messages between Classifier and ext_TRCF in Table 1.

Bandwidth allocation in Legacy Processing Area is done by PDF, and PDF decides which level's packets move into Premium Processing Area. This information is sent to Classifier that classifies real packets. After applying a policy from PDF, Classifier observes packet streams that move into Premium Processing Area and into Legacy Processing Area for a while, and then reports a classified packets' ratio to PDF via ext_TRCF. This process is done periodically. PDF controls the whole bandwidth in QoS-Adaptive router based on this report continually.

2) Legacy Processor

General data move through Legacy Processing Area. Specific data, however, should move through Premium Processing Area by the flow label field in IPv6 header. There are a few cases that data streams move from Legacy Processing Area to Premium Processing Area.

Table 1. Information between Classifier and ext_TRCF

Information		Description
Message ID		Message Identification (Including a mark that this message is from Classifier, Premium Processor or Legacy Processor)
Sequence No.		Sequence Number
Total Stream		Total number of stream in each processor or Classifier
Information	Level	Level type (for instance, 'A')
	Rate	Component rate of this packets' stream
	Loss	Packet loss of this stream
	Level	Level type (for instance, 'B')
	Rate	Component rate of this packets' stream
	Loss	Packet loss of this stream
	...	...

(a) From Classifier to ext_TRCF

Information	Description
Message Type	General Processing / Emergency Processing
Stream Information (Level)	If processing for a general or warning message from Legacy Processor, the minimum level of stream moving into Premium Processing Area. If processing for an emergency message from Premium Processor, the level of stream that should move into Legacy Processing Area or dropped.
Bandwidth	Initial bandwidth value to move streams from Legacy Processing Area to Premium Processing Area If processing to an emergency message from Premium Processor, this information is not needed.

(b) From ext_TRCF to Classifier

Packet is urgent one or requiring high quality. Data, which are urgent or require high quality, should move from Legacy Processing Area into Premium Processing Area, since these kinds of data should be transmitted immediately even though the performance of QoS-Adaptive router may slow down. For this, we designed an urgent mark and level marks in IPv6 header, and Classifier makes these packets move into Flow Processing Area based on packets' flow label field.

There is little bandwidth in Legacy Processing Area. When almost all of the bandwidth in Legacy Processing Area is used, Legacy Processor should make a stream using the largest bandwidth move into Flow Processing Area. In this case, Legacy Processor sends a warning message to ext_TRCF. After getting this warning message, ext_TRCF sends this status to PDF. And then, PDF regulates the amount of bandwidth in Legacy Processing Area which should be left, and sends a reply with a new policy including the level bound, which should be moved into Premium Processing Area, to ext_TRCF which takes a role of communicating with Classifier in order to apply this new policy. This process is done in large-bandwidth order until the amount of bandwidth in Legacy Processing Area appointed by PDF is left. This mechanism not only allows the bandwidth used in Legacy Processing Area to lower, but also guarantees the QoS in this area. Table 2 tells us the information that Legacy Processor sends to ext_TRCF.

Table 2. Information from Legacy Processor to ext_TRCF

Information		Description
Message ID		Message identification (Including a mark that this message is from Classifier, Premium Processor or Legacy Processor)
Sequence No.		Sequence Number
Message Type		General message / Warning message
Level		The highest level among packets' levels which are through this area to find out level boundary.
Information	Stream ID and Level	Stream's identifier and its level (For instance, '0001' and 'A')
	Loss	Packet loss of this stream
	Bandwidth	Bandwidth size of this stream
	Stream ID and Level	Stream's identifier and its level (For instance, '0011' and 'B')
	Loss	Packet loss of this stream
	Bandwidth	Bandwidth size of this stream
	...	...

3) Premium Processor

Data which move through Premium Processing Area are managed as flows of a flow-based router. There are three cases where data move into Premium Processing Area. First, if a packet includes a high quality level mark in IPv6 header, this packet moves into Premium Processing Area. Soon after CPE sends service request signaling to SCF, this high level is decided by PDF based on the subscriber and service information. This means that the packet's level is assigned before this packet comes into QoS-Adaptive router. Second, if a packet is an urgent one, this packet moves into Premium Processing Area irrespective of its level. In our mechanism, this packet has priority over the packets in the first case, and this urgent sign also is marked in the flow label field of IPv6 header. Last, if there is little bandwidth which is left in Legacy Processing Area, a stream holding the largest bandwidth moves into Premium Processing Area. Since this stream is taking big bandwidth but the service level is not high, the bandwidth of this stream should be lowered in order not to affect other streams. To this management, this stream should move from Legacy Processing Area into Premium Processing Area. Premium Processor allocates some bandwidth to this stream based on the surplus bandwidth in Premium Processing Area and the level of this stream. In most cases, Premium Processor allocates lower the amount of bandwidth than the amount which this stream required.

In Premium Processing Area, following problems can happen, and Premium Processor should handle these cases.

Abnormal flow takes almost bandwidth. If the problem that one abnormal flow takes almost bandwidth in Premium Processing Area happens, once Premium Processor has to drop this flow in advance, and then rearrange its bandwidth based on the surplus bandwidth in this area. This is to protect normal flows from an abnormal flow. This status is reported to PDF via ext_TRCF.

There is little bandwidth in Premium Processing Area. In this case, Premium Processor sends an emergency message to ext_TRCF. ext_TRCF analyzes the status of Legacy Processing Area, and distributes some flows' bandwidth in Premium Processing Area into Legacy Processing Area in low-grade order if there is extra bandwidth in Legacy Processing Area. However, if there is no extra bandwidth, to protect high level services, Legacy Processor starts dropping the lowest level stream until there is the amount of bandwidth settled by PDF.

The information from Premium Processor to ext_TRCF is similar to Table 2. Just two different things are that there is emergency information in a message from Premium Processor instead of warning information, and this message is processed first. And the information of 'Level' is the lowest level among packets' levels which are through this area.

3.3 Procedure of QoS-Adaptive Router

Fig. 4 shows us the whole procedure of QoS-Adaptive router.

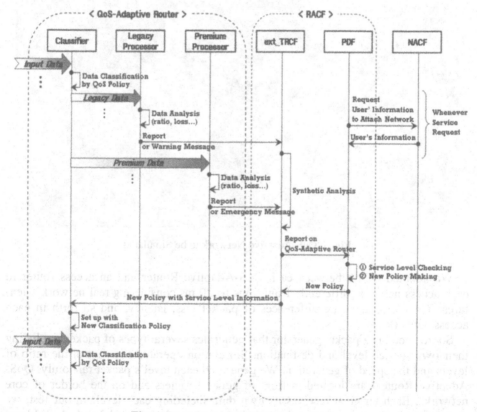

Fig. 4. Procedure of QoS-Adaptive router

This procedure is repeated periodically. As a matter of fact, general reports are sent to each destination by periodic, but a warning message from Legacy Processor or an emergency message from Premium Processor is reported to ext_TRCF immediately so as to be managed without delay.

4 Performance Evaluation

We implemented a simulation using a network simulator named OMNeT++ to evaluate the performance in a broader range [9]. For QoS-Adaptive router, we configured a network environment as shown in Fig. 5.

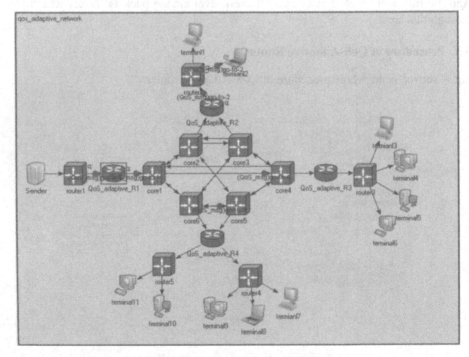

Fig. 5. QoS-Adaptive Network to be Simulated

We adopted delays between each QoS-Adaptive Router and an access router in each access network, differently from 5 ms to 20 ms considering real network's features. Therefore, there are differences of packet loss, latency, and so forth in each access network.

Source node is a packet generator that generates several types of packets including their own service level and destination. Simulation operator can control the ratio of levels and the speed of generation. We generated each level's packet randomly. QoS-Adaptive Routers are located in front of general routers and on the border of core networks. Each terminal receives its own data including each level. In our test, we sent 1st level data to terminal 2, 4 and 7, 2nd level data to terminal 3 and 11, 3rd level data to terminal 1, 6 and 8, and 4th level data to terminal 5, 9 and 10. And we made the level of data to terminal 5 be upgraded to the 2nd level in course of the test.

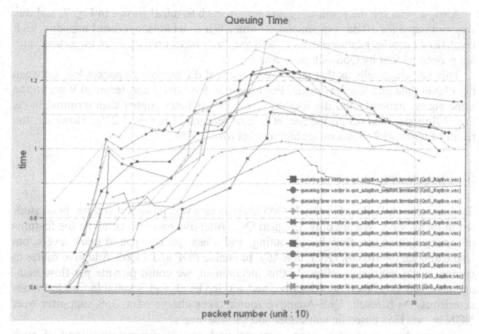

Fig. 6. Simulation Result (1) - Queuing Time

Fig. 6 illustrates the queuing time to arrive at each terminal as a result of our simulation. There were few data in the early stage of the test. As the number of data increases, however, the difference of queuing time to reach each terminal can be checked. The queuing time of the data including 1st level mark is short, whereas the one of the data including 4th level mark is rather long. Also, we can check that the queuing time of upgraded data diminished abruptly.

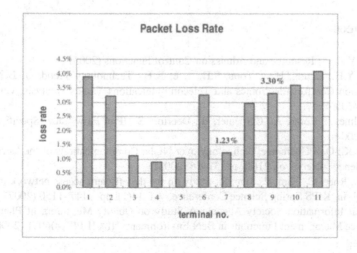

Fig. 7. Simulation Result (2) – Packet Loss

Also, we can see the result of packet loss in each terminal shown in Fig. 7, and this was simulated for 10 days in simulation time. When network overhead happens, high level flows can be guaranteed because these ones have priority over the others, and are processed first by QoS-Adaptive router.

This bar graph tells us that there are numerical differences of packet loss between high level data and low level data. For example, terminal 7 and terminal 9 are in the same access network, and the level of terminal 7 is much higher than terminal 9. As Fig. 7 illustrates the result, the packet loss of terminal 7 is low, 1.23%. However, the result of terminal 9 shows rather high packet loss, 3.30%.

5 Conclusion

To guarantee QoS, RACF in NGN QoS architecture was proposed and has been studied in many ways. We not only designed QoS-Adaptive router to combine the features of legacy routing and flow-based routing, and a new packet type to mark levels, but also extended the role of TRCF in RACF to enable PDF and a QoS-Adaptive router to communicate with each other. By this mechanism, we could provide per-flow management which is based on subscriber and service level, and is suitable for QoS characteristics. As a result, QoS-Adaptive router takes charge of a QoS supporter over NGN by working based on subscriber and service levels.

This mechanism could be used in any network services for guaranteeing QoS such as real-time services. In addition, one main aspect of NGN services is to grasp the receiver's situation and feeling of satisfaction about services in order to analyze and provide QoE(Quality of Experience). QoE means end-to-end QoS in subscriber's point of view, and makes subscribers be served with suited services for each one. Our mechanism will help this work. Also, Quality Management Center, which acts on behalf of specific service or content providers and NGN Managers, can obtain the service and network status from QoS-Adaptive routers, and this information will be used to regulate a NGN policy, fix the price of the service, create new services, and so on.

References

1. ITU-T Y.2111: Resource and Admission Control Functions (2005)
2. Jeong, Y.H., Chung, H.S., Yoon, S.H., Lee, K.H.: Technology Trends of BcN-Resource Admission Control: Electronics and Telecommunications Trends Analysis, vol. 21(6), pp. 20–31 (2006)
3. Rajahalme, J., Conta, A., Carpenter, B., Deering, S.: IPv6 Flow Label Specification: RFC 3697 (2004)
4. Choi, J.K.: QoS Guarantee Technology over NGN: Communications of the Korea information science society, vol. 21(8), pp. 51–66 (2003)
5. Cho, S., Rhee, C., Kim, E., Han, S.: Study on for the efficient access network management on BcN. In: KIPS Spring Science Conference, vol. 14(1), pp. 1147–1150 (2007)
6. National Information Society Agency: A Study on Quality Measurement Plans Based on Resource Management Functions in BcN Environment: NIA II-PER-06041 (2006)

7. Rhee, B.Y., Kim, C.C., Koh, K.M., Han, S.Y., Chang, C.H.: QoS-Aware Overlay Multicast Architecture over NGN. In: International Conference on Ubiquitous Information Technology and Application, pp. 474–482 (2007)
8. Song, J.T., Park, H.: NGN QoS Control Technology Trend Focusing on Resource and Admission. IPTV and BcN Convergence Feature Articles, 65–70 (2006)
9. OMNeT++ version 3.3, http://www.omnetpp.org

Analysis of User Perceived QoS in Ubiquitous UMTS Environments Subject to Faults

Andrea Bondavalli, Paolo Lollini, and Leonardo Montecchi

Università degli Studi di Firenze,
Dipartimento di Sistemi e Informatica,
viale Morgagni 65, I-50134, Firenze, Italy
http://rcl.dsi.unifi.it/
{bondavalli,lollini,lmontecchi}@unifi.it

Abstract. This paper provides a QoS analysis of a dynamic, ubiquitous UMTS network scenario in the automotive context identified in the on-going EC HIDENETS project. The scenario comprises different types of mobile users, applications, traffic conditions, and outage events reducing the available network resources. Adopting a compositional modeling approach based on Stochastic Activity Networks formalism, we analyze the Quality of Service (QoS) both from the users' perspective and from the mobile operator's one. The classical QoS analysis is enhanced by taking into account the congestion both caused by the outage events and by the varying traffic conditions.

Keywords: QoS analysis, UMTS networks, partial outages, compositional modeling, stochastic activity networks, simulation.

1 Introduction

Ubiquitous infrastructures are typically composed by a high number of mobile devices that move within some physical areas, while being connected to networks by means of wireless links. The supported mobile-based applications should be capable to provide the expected services in a dependable way, and maintaining the required Quality of Service (QoS) levels.

In this paper we adopt a compositional modeling approach based on Stochastic Activity Networks to assess the QoS provided over complex, ubiquitous and dynamic infrastructures, taking as motivating example a use-case scenario defined in the ongoing EC HIDENETS project [1]. The analyzed system is characterized by a UMTS communication network composed by several partially overlapping cells, and by a set of users (i.e., cars and emergency vehicles, equipped with UMTS network devices) moving through the network and requiring different UMTS-based applications (e.g., voice call and entertainment). The user perceived QoS level should always be higher than a minimum level, and this aspect becomes particularly critical when emergency situations are considered, for example in the case of an ambulance that is using a streaming application to transmit the ECG traces of an injured person while moving to the hospital. Since

U. Brinkschulte, T. Givargis, and S. Russo (Eds.): SEUS 2008, LNCS 5287, pp. 186–197, 2008.
© IFIP International Federation for Information Processing 2008

the user perceived QoS level depends on the availability of network resources, base stations' faults are also considered. More in detail we allow the presence of partial outages that may affect the availability of the UMTS resources.

The rest of this paper is organized as follows. Section 2 provides the description of the analyzed system and it outlines the corresponding QoS measures of interest. The main UMTS aspects influencing the QoS analysis are discussed in Section 3. The modeling approach is then sketched in Section 4, while Section 5 presents and discusses some of the obtained results. Finally, the conclusions are drawn in Section 6.

2   The System Context and the QoS Indicators

HIDENETS [1] is an ongoing EC project addressing the provision of available and resilient distributed applications and mobile services with critical requirements on highly dynamic and possibly unreliable open communication infrastructures. A set of representative use-case scenarios has been identified, each one composed by different applications (mostly selected from the field of car-to-car and car-to-infrastructure communications), different network domains (ad-hoc/wireless multi-hop domains, infrastructure network domains), different actors (end users, servers, routers, gateways), and characterized by different failure modes and challenges. In the following we give a brief description of the "car accident" scenario, which is analyzed in this paper and used as motivating example to describe the modeling process.

2.1   Definition of the "Car Accident" Use-Case Scenario

The "car accident" use-case scenario evolves around a scene with an accident on a road, involving cars. The use-case covers mainly what happens after the accident but also involves some issues directly before and during the accident. The analyzed network scenario is composed by a set of overlapping UMTS cells covering a high-way, and a set of mobile network devices (embedded or inside cars and emergency vehicles) moving in the high-way and requiring different UMTS class of services (e.g., conversational, interactive, and background).

Directly before the accident, several applications are used by the different mobile users, like entertainment and voice call. Right after the accident, many people may try to call the emergency services, call home, and send text and multimedia messages. Some time after the accident, an ambulance is approaching. Arriving at the place of the accident, and heading back to the hospital with the injured, there will be a need to transmit information on the positioning of the ambulance to communicate that it is approaching the hospital and at the same time maintain a multimedia connection with the medical expertise by use of voice, video and data transmission ("access to medical expertise" application).

The concrete UMTS scenario under analysis is depicted in Figure 1. Four base stations are considered: A, B, C and D. The base stations are subject to faults, which may reduce their available network resources. The users are moving in

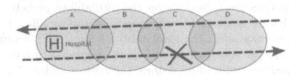

Fig. 1. The analyzed scenario

two different road lanes: part in the left to right lane (from A to D) and part in the right to left one (from D to A). We assume that the accident occurs in the C zone, in the left to right lane, forcing other users approaching that area to stop until the ambulance arrives, the crash site is cleaned and the normal traffic flow restored. The emergency vehicle heads back to the hospital towards the A zone where we suppose the hospital is located.

Concerning the available UMTS services, we suppose that a generic user can use three different services (Telephony, Web Browsing and File Transfer), while the ambulance uses the "access to medical expertise" application that consists of two simultaneously running services (Emergency Streaming to transmit the ECG traces, and Emergency Video-conference to fully interact with the hospital), having higher requirements in term of signal to interference ratio with respect to the non-emergency services. The services mainly differ for the activity factor, the uplink and downlink throughput and the required signal-to-interference ratio. Using well-known UMTS formulas (e.g., see [2]), these parameters are summarized into a single value that represents the workload increment they produce on the network (δ_{ul} and δ_{dl} parameters of Equation (1), Section 3).

2.2   QoS Indicators

The measures of interest concern the QoS levels both from the users' perspective and from a mobile operator's point of view. The QoS level perceived by users (both normal cars and emergency vehicles) depends on their capability to successfully use the network services when required and for the time required. The users involved in the traffic-jam should be capable to call home, while the ambulance should be capable to maintain the multimedia connections while moving towards the hospital. Typical user-oriented QoS indicators are: the following:

- The probability that a service request is successfully completed (P_{succ}),
- The probability that a service request is blocked (P_{block}) or dropped (P_{drop}).

The network workload is another system aspect that deserves special attention. Right after the accident, the behavior of the users involved in the consequent traffic-jam changes from normal to emergency, for example intensifying the service requests and trying to call the emergency services and call home, and this may cause congestion in the radio access network. In this context, typical mobile operator-oriented indicators are the following:

- The load factor, both in uplink (η_{ul}) and downlink (η_{dl}),
- The number of allocated traffic channels, which corresponds to the average number of served users.

3   Communication-Level Aspects Influencing the QoS Analysis

In this section we focus on the communication level aspects related to the "car accident" use-case, and in particular on three UMTS characteristics having important effects on the QoS: the *random-access procedure*, the *admission control* strategy and the *soft handover* mechanism. These characteristics mainly influence the so called "connection-level" QoS, which are the quality indicators related to the connectivity properties of the network, like the call blocking or dropping probability.

When a user needs a service from the UMTS network, its User Equipment (UE) sends a channel request to the network through the Physical Random Access CHannel (PRACH), a specific channel dedicated to the uplink transmission of channel request. The access method, based on a *random-access procedure* (RACH), may cause collisions among requests by different UEs, thus worsening the expected QoS (e.g., see [3] for more details on this aspect).

The *admission control* strategy is needed to decide whether a new service request can start based on the available network "capacity". Once the network receives the channel request, it performs the admission control procedure to decide if a traffic channel can be allocated to this new request. The goal is, in general, to ensure that the interference created after adding a new call does not exceed a pre-specified threshold, thus preventing the QoS to degrade below a certain level. There are several types of admission control algorithms studied in the literature, each one having different properties and aiming at optimizing different network parameters (e.g., [4]). Here we consider an admission control algorithm based on the workload of the UMTS cell: a new call is accepted if the workload level reached after adding the call does not exceed a pre-specified threshold, both in uplink and in downlink. Equivalently:

$$\eta_{ul} + \delta_{ul} \leq \eta_{ul\_threshold}, \qquad \eta_{dl} + \delta_{dl} \leq \eta_{dl\_threshold}, \qquad (1)$$

where η_{ul}, δ_{ul} and $\eta_{ul\_threshold}$ (or η_{dl}, δ_{dl} and $\eta_{dl\_threshold}$) are, respectively, the cell workload before the admission of the new call, the workload increment due to the admission of the new call and the pre-specified threshold level in uplink (or downlink).

Another key aspect to be addressed is *soft handover*, a feature of the 3rd generation mobile networks, where a User Equipment can have two or more simultaneous connections with different cells (or cell sectors) and receive from them the same information signal. The signal received from different sources is then combined using rake receivers and under certain conditions this results in a amplified signal and better link quality. Beside providing better link quality, soft handover is also a key point in maintaining an ongoing service call, since it provides seamless switching between base stations.

4   Modelling Process

In such ubiquitous landscape, system complexity comes out to be a paramount challenge to cope with from a number of different points of view, including dependability and QoS evaluation. In order to master complexity, a modelling methodology is needed so that only the relevant system aspects need to be detailed, allowing numerical results to be effectively computable. The complexity of models depends on the dependability measures to be evaluated, the modelling level of detail, and the stochastic dependencies among the components. Several works have been presented in the literature trying to cope with the complexity problem (see [5] for a nice survey), and some of them try to tackle the complexity problem building models in a modular way through a *composition* of its submodels (e.g., [6,7]), which are then solved as a whole. Most of the works belonging to this class define the rules to be used to construct and interconnect the sub-models, and they provide an easy way to describe the behavior of systems having a high degree of dependency between subcomponents.

In this paper we adopt a compositional modeling approach based on Stochastic Activity Networks (SAN) [8], that are stochastic extensions to Petri Nets. The composition operators available for SAN are the *join* and *replicate* operators [9]: the first is used to compose different system models possibly sharing some places, while the second is used to combine multiple identical copies of a submodel, which are called replicates. Another key point of the modeling approach is the "model parametrization". Following the object oriented philosophy, we develop some "template" SAN models describing the general behavior of the main system components. The overall model results from the composition of some "instances" of such classes, where an instance is a specification of a template model with a proper parameters' setting. Using this approach we avoid duplicating the code and the structure of similar models, which is a very time-consuming and error-prone process; as a consequence, the overall model is easier to be modified and it can be more easily adapted to represent different scenarios.

In Figure 2 we have depicted the main basic SAN models (called "atomic" models in the SAN language) with their dependency relations (the arrows). An arrow from model X to Y means that model X can influence the stochastic behavior of model Y or, equivalently, that the Y state can depend on the X state.

For the sake of brevity the actual implementation of the atomic models is not described here. An exhaustive and detailed description of such models can be found as a technical report in [10]. In the following we outline the main system aspects captured by the different models.

- **Phases** atomic model. It represents the sequence of periods (phases) composing the system lifetime, each one characterized by diverse applications running, diverse types of users's behavior (normal behavior, before the car accident, or emergency behavior, right after the car accident) and different dependability properties to be ensured.
- **User** atomic model. It describes the user's behavior mainly in terms of services requested, duration of the services and idle periods.

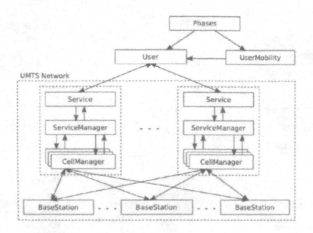

Fig. 2. Atomic models and their interactions

- **UserMobility** atomic model. It represents the user movement across the UMTS network scenario.
- The "UMTS Network" model consists of several instances of the **BaseStation** atomic model and a number of models representing the available services. A network service is represented using three kinds of atomic models: **Service**, **ServiceManager** and **CellManager**. The Service atomic model represents the upper network layers and it is directly connected with the User model. When the user requests a network service, the User model interacts with the respective Service model which serves as interface between the user and the network. The Service model then asks for the needed resources to the ServiceManager atomic model, which handles the soft handover mechanisms allowing user to be served by multiple base stations. This is achieved using several instances of the CellManager atomic model, which serve as interfaces between the ServiceManager atomic model and each BaseStation model. Finally the BaseStation model represent a UMTS base station, with failure and repair activities, and holds the current base station state, like its current workload and the number of allocated channels. In case of outage events this model also implements the congestion control algorithm, which drops (interrupt) a certain number of connections if the current workload exceeds the remaining available system resources.

Once such basic template models have been developed, several different scenarios can be easily obtained resembling different network topologies, users' behaviors, users' mobility patterns and available applications. Therefore, the modularity of the modeling framework improves both the readability and the maintenance of the models, as well as their reusability. In the following Section 4.1 we detail the overall model for the "car accident" use-case scenario defined in Section 2.1.

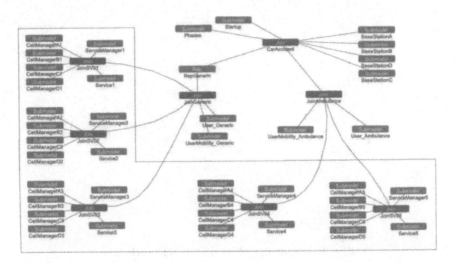

Fig. 3. The overall composed model corresponding to the analyzed use-case scenario

4.1 The Overall UMTS Network Model

As described in Section 2.1, the analyzed scenario consists of four partially over-lapping base stations and five services: services 1 (Telephony), 2 (Web Browsing) and 3 (File Transfer) are assumed to be services for the "normal" users, while 4 (Emergency Streaming) and 5 (Emergency Video-conference) are assumed to be services used by the emergency vehicle and will have higher requirements in term of signal to interference ratio.

Figure 3 depicts the corresponding composed model. The composition involves three join levels. Starting from the lower level (the boxed part of the figure), joins relative to different services are shown, each one formed by four CellManager models (one for each base station), a Service and a ServiceManager model, as sketched in Figure 2. In the second level the services are joined with the respective user models, so services 1-3 are composed with User_Generic and UserMobility_Generic (on left part of the figure), while services 4-5 are composed with User_Ambulance and UserMobility_Ambulance (on right part). The generic user is then replicated as needed and added to the top-level join, which also includes the ambulance join, the four BaseStation models, the Phases model and the Startup model (used to initialize the multiple instances of the other atomic models with the proper values).

The advantage of using model parametrization is evident considering the effort required for the model construction process. To build the composed model shown in Figure 3, 40 atomic models are needed (exactly 20xCellManager, 5xServiceManager, 5xService, 4xBaseStation, 1xStartup, 1xPhases, 1xUser_Generic, 1xUserMobility_Generic, 1xUser_Ambulance and 1xUserMobility_Ambulance). Using model parametrization we need to create the basic template atomic models only, one for each type. For this scenario only 10 atomic models have been built, and those depicted in Figure 3 are just instances of these basic 10 models. Once the basic template models have been defined, we can easily build and analyze different scenarios with a very small effort. For example, deleting the JoinAmbulance composed model in Figure 3 we can limit the analysis to normal (not emergency) services, while adding another base station (thus obtaining a different network topology) would simply consist in adding another CellManager atomic model to each JoinSV composed model, and another BaseStation atomic model (BaseStationE) to the CarAccident composed model.

5 Numerical Evaluations

In this section we sketch some of the results that we obtain through the solution of the models previously described. A transient analysis has been performed, using the simulator provided by the Möbius tool [11]. Each point of the graphs has been computed as a mean of at least 1000 simulation batches, converging within 95% probability in a 0.1 relative interval, and a AMD Athlon XP 2500+ PC (2Gb RAM) has been used for the computations.

Table 1. Workload increment per accepted service, in uplink (δ_{ul}) and downlink (δ_{dl}), with or without soft-handover

		Service1	Service2	Service3	Service4	Service5
Workload increment (no SHO)	Downlink (δ_{dl})	0.01357	0.08774	0.2125	0	0.09917
	Uplink (δ_{ul})	0.01632	0.06675	0.0620	0.11923	0.10814
Workload increment (with SHO)	Downlink (δ_{dl})	0.00995	0.03781	0.1275	0	0.07083
	Uplink (δ_{ul})	0.00984	0.03411	0.03781	0.08543	0.0620

The setting of the model's parameters has been mainly derived from [2] and adapted to the analyzed scenario. With reference to Equation (1), the values assigned to δ_{ul} and δ_{dl} are shown in Table 1, while the maximum load factor in uplink ($\eta_{ul\_threshold}$) and downlink ($\eta_{dl\_threshold}$) has been set, respectively, to 0.65 and 0.8. Each base-station has a coverage area of 2 Km, and 25% of the cell radius is overlapping with the adjacent cell. Whenever not differently specified, we consider a total of 50 cars moving in the scenario (and 1 ambulance), with an average speed of 90 Km/h (120 Km/h for the ambulance) when not involved in the traffic jam caused by the car accident. Moreover, we suppose that the car accident happens in the C cell at time t=10500 sec., and that the ambulance stays 600 sec. at the crash site before heading back to the hospital. The complete set of model's parameters and their setting can be found in [10], and it is not reported here for the sake of brevity.

5.1 Results

Figure 4 shows the load factor of the base station C, considering no outage events (i.e., 100% of the network resources are always available). The vertical line represents the instant of time when the accident occurs, while the horizontal ones represent the maximum allowed load factor in downlink ($\eta_{dl\_threshold}$) and

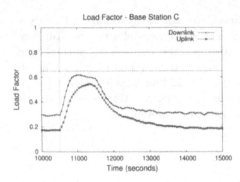
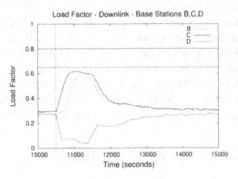

Fig. 4. Load Factor of the base station C   **Fig. 5.** Load Factor of different base stations (downlink)

in uplink ($\eta_{ul\_threshold}$). As shown in Figure 4, right after the accident the C cell becomes rapidly congested due to the users that are stopped in that area (due to the consequent traffic-jam). The congestion phenomenon is also exacerbated considering that the users' behavior changes during emergency conditions, in particular reducing the idle time between two consecutive service requests. After a while the load factor starts to decrease, because the normal traffic flow is restored after the ambulance heads back to the hospital, and because the users behavior becomes again normal. The load factors of base stations near the accident zone are summarized in Figures 5 (downlink) and 6 (uplink). After a certain delay a congestion is also produced on the base station B and this is due to the traffic-jam reaching its coverage area. On the contrary, the load factor of D rapidly decreases right after the accident, since the cars are blocked in the preceding cells. When the crash site is cleared and user (cars) are capable to move again all the load factors slowly return to the level they had before the car-accident.

Figure 7 shows the impact of an outage affecting the base station C at time t=11000 sec. on the "access to medical expertise" application used by the ambulance (plot '4+5 Combined'). The probability of service interruption rapidly increases considering higher percentage of resources unavailability, reaching its maximum for values greater than 60%. Analyzing the single services forming the application (plots 'Emergency Streaming' and 'Emergency Video-conference'), initially the probability is lower for 'Emergency Streaming', but when limited resources are available 'Emergency Video-conference' has a lower probability of interruption. This happens because we have assumed that 'Emergency Streaming' requires more uplink resources than 'Emergency Video-conference' (see Table 1), and after the outage the available uplink resources are lower than the downlink ones. For a better understanding, in Figure 8 we depict the uplink and downlink load factor of the base station C considering an outage equal to 70% (i.e., 70% of the cell resources becomes unavailable), at varying of time. The load factor (both in uplink and downlink) increases after the car accident (at time t=10500 sec.), and then rapidly decreases after the outage event

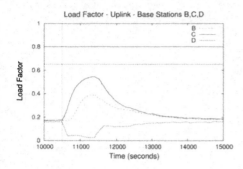

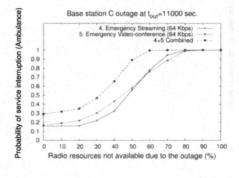

Fig. 6. Load Factor of different base stations (uplink)

Fig. 7. Probability of interruption of emergency services, with C cell outage

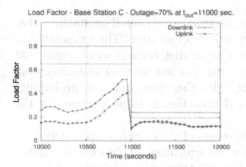

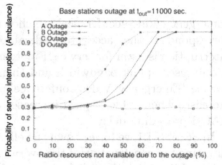

Fig. 8. Load Factor of the base station C, with outage=70%

Fig. 9. Probability of interruption of ambulance services (4+5 combined) when a single base station fails

at time t=11000 sec. (due to the dropped services). After the outage the uplink load factor is near to its maximum allowed value and then the services requiring higher uplink resources will be probably not satisfied (due to the selected admission control algorithm, see (1)).

Figure 9 shows the impact of the outage on the probability that the "access to medical expertise" application is interrupted, at varying of the outage severity (percentage of unavailable cell resources) and at varying of the base station affected by the outage. As expected, base station C is the most critical one, since it is the cell where the car accident occurs and the traffic is blocked, thus determining a high network congestion. Cell D does not influence the ambulance connection at all, since the ambulance doesn't even enter the D zone.

Figure 10 shows the probability that the multimedia connections between the ambulance and the hospital are interrupted while the ambulance is going back to the hospital, varying the vehicle's average speed (no outages considered). Individual probabilities for the emergency services 'Emergency Streaming' and

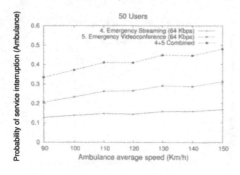
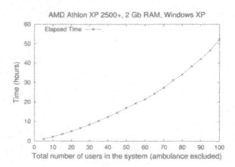

Fig. 10. "Access to medical expertise" interruption probability

Fig. 11. Average time to produce Figure 10, at varying of the total number of users in the system

'Emergency Video-conference' are shown, as well as the overall probability that corresponds to the "access to medical expertise" application. The probability of interruption is lower for service 'Emergency Streaming' because we assumed that it only uses uplink bandwidth and then it requires less network resources than service 'Emergency Video-conference'. Results also show that the probability increases when vehicle speed increases and this effect is in part caused by the RACH procedure delay.

In Section 4.1 we have shown the effectiveness of the modeling approach in facilitating the construction of the overall model, which can be obtained as composition of 40 models derived from a set of 10 basic template models only. Anyway, the modeling approach is really effective only if the computational cost required to solve the overall model is still manageable. In Figure 11 we present the average time (in hours) needed to produce Figure 10, at varying of the total number of users in the system. The values in Figure 10 have been obtained performing 7 simulations, one for each considered 'ambulance average speed' value. As we can see, the computational time increases almost linearly for a low number of users, and the rate of grow slightly increases considering more than 60 users. Nevertheless, in the worst case (i.e., for number of users equal to 100) the whole set of simulations completed in less than 56 hours (therefore, less then 8 hours for each simulation).

6   Conclusions

In this paper we have proposed a QoS analysis of a dynamic, ubiquitous UMTS network scenario identified in the ongoing EC HIDENETS project, including different types of mobile users, applications, traffic conditions, and outage events affecting the availability of the network resources. The final goal was to quantitatively evaluate some QoS measures regarding both the users (the probability that an ongoing service request is interrupted) and the mobile operators (the load factor of the UMTS cells). To do this, we have adopted a modular, hierarchical modeling approach based on composition, replication and parametrization, which facilitates the model construction process as well as the model reusability. The produced numerical results provides a useful insight in the relationships between the selected QoS measures, the users' behavior and the users' mobility. In addition, they show the effectiveness of the modeling approach considering the computational time required to solve the overall model by simulation.

Acknowledgment

This work has been partially supported by the EC IST Project HIDENETS [1].

References

1. European Project HIDENETS: contract n. 26979, http://www.hidenets.aau.dk
2. Laiho, J., Wacker, A., Novosad, T.: Radio Network Planning and Optimisation for UMTS, 2nd edn. Wiley, Chichester (2006)
3. Lollini, P., Bondavalli, A., Di Giandomenico, F.: QoS Analysis of a UMTS cell with different Service Classes. In: CSN-2005 The Fourth IASTED International Conference on Communication Systems and Networks, September 12-14 (2005)
4. Andersin, M., Rosberg, Z., Zander, J.: Soft and safe admission control in cellular networks. IEEE/ACM Transaction on Networking 5(2) (1997)
5. Nicol, D.M., Sanders, W.H., Trivedi, K.S.: Model-based evaluation: From dependability to security. IEEE Transactions on Dependable and Secure Computing 1(1), 48–65 (2004)
6. Rojas, I.: Compositional construction of SWN models. The Computer Journal 38(7), 612–621 (1995)
7. Bernardi, S., Donatelli, S.: Stochastic petri nets and inheritance for dependability modelling. In: Proceedings of the 10th IEEE Pacific Rim International Symposium on Dependable Computing (PRDC 2004), March 2004, pp. 363–372 (2004)
8. Sanders, W.H., Meyer, J.F.: Stochastic activity networks: formal definitions and concepts, pp. 315–343 (2002)
9. Sanders, W.H., Meyer, J.F.: Reduced base model construction methods for stochastic activity networks. IEEE Journal on Selected Areas in Communications 9(1), 25–36 (1991)
10. Lollini, P., Montecchi, L., Bondavalli, A.: On the evaluation of hidenets use-cases having phased behavior. Technical Report rcl071201, University of Florence, Dip. Sistemi Informatica, RCL group (December 2007), http://dcl.isti.cnr.it/Documentation/Papers/Techreports.html
11. Daly, D., Deavours, D.D., Doyle, J.M., Webster, P.G., Sanders, W.H.: Möbius: An extensible tool for performance and dependability modeling. In: Schaumnurg, I.L., Haverkort, B.R., Bohnenkamp, H.C., Smith, C.U. (eds.) TOOLS 2000. LNCS, vol. 1786, pp. 332–336. Springer, Heidelberg (2000)

Cost-Performance Tradeoff for Embedded Systems

Julie S. Fant and Robert G. Pettit

The Aerospace Corporation
Chantilly, Virginia USA
{julie.s.fant,robert.g.pettit}@aero.org

Abstract. Software engineering requires creativity, thorough design and analysis, and sound design decisions. Design decisions often have tradeoffs and implications associated with them. Therefore, it is important that design decisions are based on sound analysis. With respect to embedded systems, key drivers are often performance and cost. Thus the purpose of this paper is to describe an approach to aid in the design decision process on cost and performance tradeoffs for embedded systems. Specifically, it presents a model-driven approach to understand and communicate the performance-cost tradeoff.

Keywords: software performance, cost, UML, embedded systems, model-driven design, tradeoff.

1 Introduction

Software engineering, like other engineering disciplines, requires creativity, thorough design and analysis, and sound design decisions. Design decisions often have tradeoffs and implications associated with them. Thus these decisions should be examined with proper analysis to ensure the best overall decision is made.

Embedded systems are a special type of system where the computers and associated software are components embedded within a larger system such as mobile phones, household appliances, automotive controls, etc. In these types of systems, performance and cost are often key drivers. Many times the solution to achieving better performance is simply to purchase more expensive hardware. This, however, is not always a good solution since the additional cost of the high performance hardware may not result in an equivalent performance gain. For example, one may spend a large sum of money for the fastest central processor available but find that input/output (I/O) constraints limit the benefits from the high-performance CPU. Therefore it is critical to spend the time analyzing the different options to ensure the best decision is made between cost and performance.

The purpose of this paper is to describe an approach to aid in the design decision process by helping to understand and communicate the performance-cost tradeoff for embedded systems. Specifically, it presents a model-driven approach that combines software performance analysis techniques with techniques to analyze and compare the cost-performance aspects of potential hardware implementations.

This paper is structured as follows: Section 2 describes the related works. Section 3 presents the approach to cost-performance analysis and its benefits. Section 4 describes a case study using the proposed approach. Finally, Section 5 contains the major conclusions and future work.

U. Brinkschulte, T. Givargis, and S. Russo (Eds.): SEUS 2008, LNCS 5287, pp. 198–208, 2008.

2 Related Work

Many approaches to analyze the performance of embedded and real-time systems have been developed. For our purposes, these approaches can be broadly categorized as those exploring performance through analytical techniques [1-6] or through simulation [7-10]. The cost-performance analysis approach presented in this paper does not prescribe the use of a particular performance analysis method. Rather, it attempts to illustrate how cost-performance tradeoff decisions can be compartmentalized and input to analytical or simulation techniques that will assist the decision making process.

3 Analysis Approach and Benefits

The paper presents an approach to performing cost-performance tradeoff analysis for embedded systems. The purpose of this approach is to help communicate and understand the cost-performance tradeoffs associated with different hardware implementation options. It has five major steps, which are as follows: 1) Develop a platform independent model; 2) Select the hardware configurations to analyze; 3) Conduct performance analysis on each of the hardware configurations; 4) Perform cost-performance tradeoff analysis; and 5) Make and document the design decision. Each step is described below in more detail.

The first step in the proposed tradeoff approach is to build a platform independent model of the software system. The purpose of this step is to show how the software is meeting the functional requirements. Additionally the platform independent model will serve as the foundation for predicting software performance. It is recommended that the models be captured using the Unified Modeling Language (UML) since it is the de facto object oriented modeling language in industry.

The next step is to select the hardware implementation options for the software system. A good way to promote creativity and to enumerate the different potential options is to develop morphological box. A morphological box is an existing systems engineering technique that uses a two-dimensional table of components and physical architecture options, as depicted in Table 1.

Table 1. Morphological Box Generic Example

Component A	Component B	Component C
Physical Option A1	Physical Option B1	Physical Option C1
Physical Option A2	Physical Option B2	Physical Option C2
Physical Option A3	Physical Option B3	

Each column represents a component and each row in the column represents a physical instantiation option. Different system physical architectures can be analyzed by selecting one box from each column [11]. This same technique can be applied to software for determining and selecting hardware implementation options. The columns will represent hardware elements and the rows will represent different physical hardware options for the elements. For example, one column may be the microcontroller with possible options being an H8 or an ARM 7 microcontroller. Once the morphological box is created, the engineers can select the hardware implementations to analyze by selecting one row from each column. The morphological box will likely produce a large number of potential options. However, not all of these options need to be analyzed. Engineers should only select a subset that they are considering for the end system. Selections can be made with certain characteristics in mind such as lowest cost hardware or highest performance hardware.

Once the potential hardware implementations have been identified, the third step is to perform software performance analysis for each implementation. Any software performance analysis technique can be used in the proposed approach. For example, the UML platform independent model can be annotated with platform specific information using a UML profile and then subsequently analyzed. Alternatively, the UML platform independent model can be converted into a Petri-net model and subsequently analyzed for performance. The performance metrics produced in the software performance analysis should coincide with the software performance requirements. For example, if the system has a requirement for a maximum latency, then latency should be calculated in the performance analysis.

The fourth step in the proposed tradeoff approach is to compare the different hardware implementations against cost and performance. This should be done by developing tradeoff x-y scatter plots of performance and cost. The plots should again be based on the performance requirements. This will clearly show the tradeoff of different hardware configuration options on one graph. For example, if there is a performance requirement on the maximum latency, then the tradeoff x-y scatter plot should plot latency versus cost. Additionally, the performance requirements can also be added to the graph to show the system's threshold. To illustrate this point, consider Figure 1.

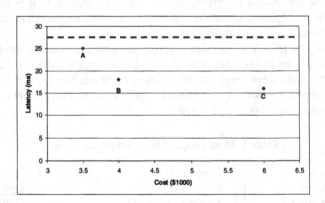

Fig. 1. Example Tradeoff Plot

This is an tradeoff x-y scatter plot of worst case latency versus cost for three hardware options and the performance requirement for maximum latency is denoted with a red-dotted line. In this example, all the options meet the performance requirement since they are below the maximum latency threshold. It can be clearly seen that there is a 28% increase in performance and a 14% cost increase between options A and B. Between options B and C there is an 11% performance increase, however the cost is

50% more. In this case, since option B provides the best balance between cost and performance, it is the best choice for the example system.

Finally, after the different options have been analyzed and a decision has been made, the design decision should be documented so that future maintainers of the system will understand why this decision was made.

The proposed tradeoff analysis approach has several benefits. First, the proposed tradeoff approach does not prescribe any particular performance analysis technique. This is good because it enables organizations to leverage their currently existing performance analysis techniques. Another benefit of the proposed tradeoff approach is that it provides an easy means to understand and communicate tradeoff decisions. The scatter plots present the data from all the potential hardware options on a single graph while illustrating the cost-performance impacts of each option. Finally, the proposed tradeoff approach helps directly link design decisions to performance requirements.

4 Case Study

In this section, we illustrate the cost-performance tradeoff approach using a robot controller case study. The robot controller is an autonomous robot with an infrared light sensor and two motors (actuators). The goal of the robot is to search an area for colored discs while staying within a course boundary and avoiding obstacles. In this case study, a light sensor is used as the sole input sensor, responsible for detecting boundaries, obstacles, and discs according to different color schemes. In order to avoid hitting obstacles and boundaries, the robot controller must process the light sensor inputs in a timely manner. For our purposes, the rover has a requirement to react to a light sensor event within a travel distance of 0.5 cm, which corresponds to 50ms in the configurations used for this study. The following subsections details each step in the proposed tradeoff approach.

4.1 Platform Independent Model

The first step in the tradeoff approach is to build a platform independent model of the robot controller to show how the system will meet its functional requirements. We designed the case study following the COMET method and stereotypes [5]. The system is divided into three active, concurrently executing objects (detect, rover, and nav), one passive object (map), and three external I/O objects for receiving light sensor input and for modeling output to the two motors. Figure 2 depicts a UML sequence diagram for how the different objects interact. The detect, rover, and nav objects all operate asynchronously and all messages between the active objects have synchronous, buffered communication.

4.2 Hardware Configuration Selection

The next step in the tradeoff approach is to develop the different hardware implementation options. In this example there are four hardware elements which are the two motors, the light sensor, and the microcontroller platform. In this configuration, the microcontroller platform performs all of the processing and the light sensor is the sole

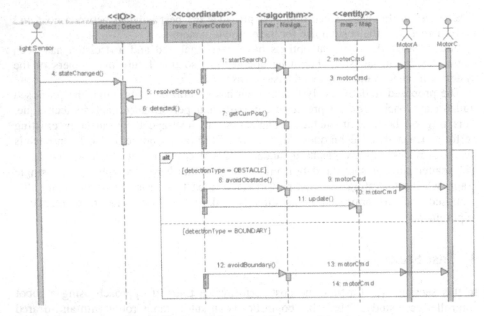

Fig. 2. Platform Independent Sequence Diagram

input for determining discs and obstacles. The microcontroller platform uses two motors which are used to maneuver the robot. Turning is achieved by rotating the left (Motor A) and right (Motor C) motors in opposite directions. These four elements become the columns in our morphological box and each element was given at least one hardware option.

The final morphological box for the robot controller is depicted in Table 2. In this example, we consider two types of motors, three different light detectors, and three different microcontrollers. These platform specific performance characteristics and costs were also listed in the morphological box. The performance characteristics were selected based on the notational embedded system framework described in [9]. This framework shows which platform characteristics need to be included in the design of concurrent software. We determined the platform specific characteristics and costs using online pricing, historical data, hardware specifications, and published benchmarks for the different systems [12-16].

After the morphological box is populated, it is time to select the hardware implementations that will be considered. In this example, we chose to analyze the cheapest option which is referred to as RP: two RCX interactive servo motors, the CDS photoresister, and the RCX Intelligent Brick. The second option we selected uses the highest performance hardware which is called JN: two NXT interactive servo motors, the NXT light sensor, and JOP. The third option we picked was the standard RCX configuration which is referred to as RR: two RCX interactive servo motors, the RCX light sensor, and the RCX Intelligent Brick. Finally, we also chose to analyze the new Mindstorms™ NXT system which is referred to as NN: two NXT servo motors, the NXT light sensor, and Mindstorms™ NXT processor.

Table 2. Morphological Box for the Robot Controller

Motor A	Motor C	Light Sensor	Platform
RCX Interactive Servo Motor Latency=1ms cost=$18	**RCX Interactive Servo Motor** Latency=1ms cost=$18	**Mindstorms™ Light Sensor** detectionLatency=10.3ms Cost=$17	**RCX Intelligent Brick - Hitachi H8 μ controller** IPS=18M clockspeed=16MHz csOverhead= < 1ms kbMemOverhead=17.5 RAM=28KB Cost=$45
NXT Servo Motor Latency=1ms cost=$18	**NXT Servo Motor** Latency=1ms cost=$18	**CDS Photoresister** detectionLatency=30ms Cost=$0.60	
		NXT Light Sensor detectionLatency=5ms Cost=$39	**JOP - Altera Cyclone EP1C6 FPGA Board** IPS=10406M clockspeed=20 MHz csOverhead= < 1ms kbMemOverhead=3KB RAM=92KBits Cost=$310.00
			Mindstorms™ NXT – ARM 7 μ controller IPS=80M clockspeed=40MHz csOverhead= <1 ms kbMemOverhead=20 RAM=64MB Cost=$135

4.3 Performance Analysis

The third step in the tradeoff analysis approach is to conduct the performance analysis. This is the step where the different hardware implementations are analyzed for performance. In this case study, to illustrate the flexibility of the cost-performance trade-off approach, we will show the performance analysis using both an analytical and a simulation approach. The follow subsections show the details for each approach.

4.3.1 Analytical Technique

For an analytical technique, we start with a UML model augmented with platform specific characteristics and then apply event sequence analysis for certain performance scenarios. Here, platform specific UML models are annotated using the UML Profile for Schedulability, Performance and Time (SPT) [17]. The UML SPT profile is scheduled to be replaced by the UML Profile for Modeling and Analysis of Real-time and Embedded Systems (MARTE) [18], however the SPT profile is still adequate for the purposes of this paper.

Using this approach, we created a platform specific UML model for each of the hardware configurations being analyzed. At a minimum, the platform specific UML model must capture the hardware configuration in a deployment diagram and the processing steps in interaction diagrams such as a sequence diagram. Figure 3 shows the platform specific sequence diagram for the RCX Intelligent Brick with CDS photoresistor (RP) configuration. We estimated demand times for each step by dividing the number of estimated instructions per step by the microcontroller's IPS rate.

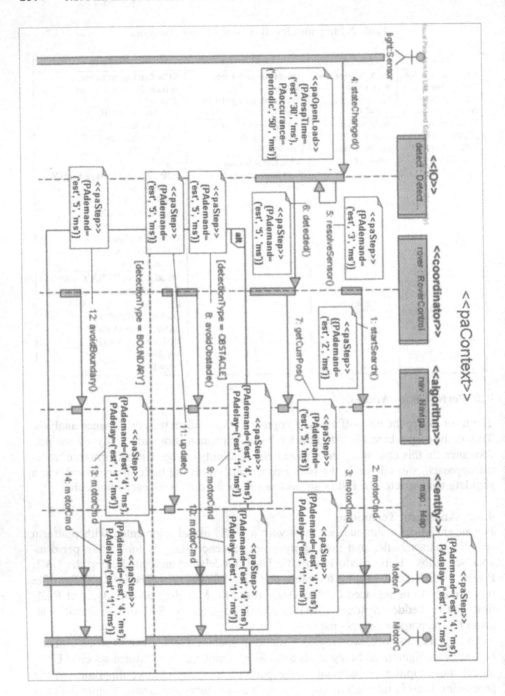

Fig. 3. Platform Specific UML Sequence Diagram for the RP configuration

After we created the platform specific UML models, we then performed event sequence analysis to determine the worst case latency through the system. Event sequence analysis is used to determine the tasks that need to be executed in order to service a given event. This is computed by calculating the time for the tasks in the event sequence plus any time used for context switching and message communication [5]. Table 3 provides a summary of the results for each of the configurations.

Table 3. Summary Performance Analysis Results

Short Name	Configuration	Worst Case Latency
JN	JOP w/NXT light sensor	6.1ms
RP	RCX Intelligent Brick w/photoresistor	50.7ms
RR	RCX Intelligent Brick w/RCX light sensor	31ms
NN	Mindstorms™ NXT w/NXT light sensor	10.5ms

4.3.2 Simulation
The simulation technique we used in this case study is simulation through coloured Petri nets(CPNs) by Pettit and Gomaa [7-9]. This method assigns behavioral patterns to the UML objects and constructs CPN templates for each behavioral pattern. Connecting the templates and populating with application and platform specific characteristics provides for an executable CPN model of the system that can be used to analyze such properties as throughput and concurrent behavior. Applying time-stamps to the tokens within the net also allows us to monitor the flow of events and messages over time and provides us with the capability to analyze response time (latency) from the receipt of an event to the output action associated with that event.

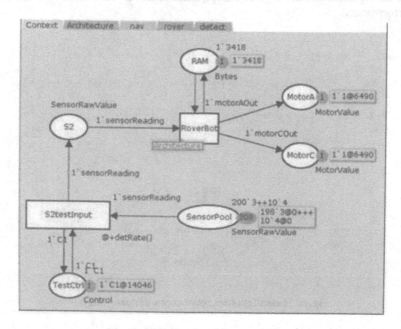

Fig. 4. CPN Simulated Response Time

Figure 4 shows the high-level results of simulating response times for the RR configuration. In this scenario, a light sensor event occurs at time 6459 (not shown on the figure) and a response to the motors is observed at time 6490 (simulation time in milliseconds). Thus, the reaction time for this case is 31ms. Further execution runs resulted in response times no greater than this value.

4.4 Cost-Performance Tradeoff Analysis

After we conducted performance analysis on the all the different hardware configurations, we created the cost-performance tradeoff plot. These plots can be derived from the analysis data, the simulation data, or both, depending on the availability of models and the desired confidence in the results. Figure 5 is the tradeoff plot of our performance analysis shows cost versus worst case latency. From this tradeoff plot we can see that the RP configuration does not meet the performance requirement; therefore it cannot be selected. We can also tell from the tradeoff plot that the lowest cost option that still meets the performance requirement is the RR configuration. The tradeoff plot also clearly shows that while the NN configuration does cost more (Δ$112), it does provide a significant performance increase (Δ20.5ms). We can also tell from this graph that the highest cost option, JN, does yield the fastest performance. However, this graph illustrates that the relative performance gain of Δ4.4ms between the NN and JN configuration probably does not outweigh the additional cost of Δ$175.

In summary, the tradeoff plot helps engineers in their design decision process. For this system, if the overall goal is to keep costs low, then the RR configuration is the best option since it is the lowest cost option that still meets the performance requirements. If the overall goal is to maximize performance while keeping costs down, then the NN configuration is the logical choice since it has a reasonable balance of cost and performance.

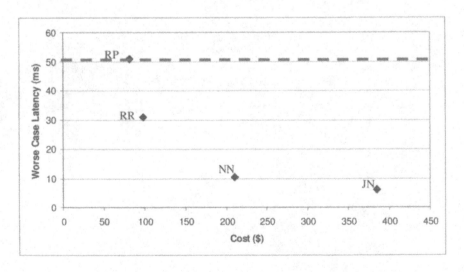

Fig. 5. Tradeoff plot for robot controller case study

5 Conclusions and Future Work

In conclusion, the proposed cost-performance tradeoff approach is intended to help in the design decision processes to ensure the best overall decision is made. Specifically, it helps to examine and illustrate the tradeoffs between cost and performance for embedded systems. This helps engineers ensure performance requirements are met and cost is considered in the processes. This helps avoid the unnecessary purchase of expensive hardware and helps keep the overall system cost low. The approach is also flexible enough to work with any software performance analysis technique which companies maybe using. This enables organizations to leverage the performance analysis technique already in existence. Finally, it provides an easy means to understand, communicate, and document tradeoff decisions. The tradeoff plots present the data from all the potential hardware options on a single graph which makes the data easy to communicate and understand.

A next logical extension of this approach would be to tradeoff decisions with other non-functional aspects of software such as security or reliability. For example, the approach can examine the performance impacts of including various security measures in a system. Tests should also be expanded to larger systems to prove scalability of the approach.

References

1. Wu, X., Woodside, M.: Performance modeling from software components. In: Proceedings of the 4th international workshop on Software and performance, Redwood Shores. ACM Press, California (2004)
2. Woodside, M., et al.: Performance by Unified Model Analysis (PUMA). In: Fifth International Workshop on Software and Performance (WOSP 2005), Palma, Illes Balears, Spain (2005)
3. Sabetta, A., et al.: Annotating UML Models with Non-Functional Properties for Quantitative Analysis. In: Bruel, J.-M. (ed.) MoDELS 2005. LNCS, vol. 3844, pp. 79–90. Springer, Heidelberg (2006)
4. Wu, X., McMullan, D., Woodside, M.: Component Based Performance Prediction. In: 6th ICSE Workshop on Component-Based Software Engineering: Automated Reasoning and Prediction, Portland, Oregon (2003)
5. Gomaa, H.: Designing Concurrent, Distributed, and Real-Time Applications with UML, 3rd edn. Addison-Wesley Object Technology Series, Boston (2000)
6. Street, J., Gomaa, H.: An Approach to Performance Modeling of Software Product Lines. In: 9th International Conference on Model Driven Engineering Languages and Systems Modeling and Analysis of Real-Time and Embedded Systems (MARTES) Workshop, Genova (2006)
7. Pettit, I.R.: Analyzing Dynamic Behavior of Concurrent Object-Oriented Software Design Ph.D Dissertation, in Department of Information and Software Engineering, George Mason University: Fairfax, VA (2003)
8. Pettit IV, R., Gomaa, H.: Modeling Behavioral Design Patterns of Concurrent Objects. In: Conference on Software Engineering (ICSE), Shanghai, China (2006)
9. Pettit IV, R., Gomaa, H.: Analyzing Behavior of Concurrent Software Designs for Embedded Systems. In: ISORC 2007. IEEE, Los Alamitos (2007)

10. Ober, I., Graf, S., Ober, I.: Validating timed UML models by simulation and verification. In: Workshop on SVERTS: Specification and Validation of UML models for Real Time and Embedded Systems, San Francisco, California, USA (2003)
11. Buede, D.: The Engineering Design of Systems Models and Methods. Wiley Series in Systems Engineering. Sage, Thousand Oaks (2000)
12. Performance of Various Java Processors (2006) [cited May 2008], http://www.jopdesign.com/perf.jsp
13. MINDSTORMS(R) - Legos Shop [cited May 2008], http://shop.lego.com/ByTheme/Leaf.aspx?cn=17&d=70
14. Macron Photoresistor Specification [cited May 2008], http://www.macron.com.hk/spec_photoersistor.htm
15. Radio Shack [cited May 2008], http://www.radioshack.com/sm-cds-photoresistorsassortment-of-5-pi-2062590_tb-techSpecs.html
16. Altera Online [cited May 2008], http://www.altera.com/
17. The UML Profile for Schedulability, Performance and Time (January 2005) cited, http://www.omg.org/technology/documents/formal/schedulability.htm
18. UML Profile for Modeling and Analysis of Real-time and Embedded Systems (MARTE) (2007) cited, http://www.omg.org/cgi-bin/doc?ptc/2007-08-04

Resolving Performance Anomaly
Using ARF-Aware TCP

Seehwan Yoo, Tae-Kyung Kim, and Chuck Yoo

Department of Computer Science and Engineering
Korea University

Abstract. In this study, we propose ARF-aware TCP that resolves the performance anomaly in 802.11 WLAN networks. Performance anomaly is a network symptom that fairness among the nodes is broken when multiple nodes in the same channel have different link rates. Recent studies on the performance anomaly focus on QoS mechanism at MAC layer. However, MAC layer approach has drawbacks such as framing overhead or side-effects at transport protocol. ARF-aware TCP successfully provides a fair-share of wireless links in an easier way. By adjusting the congestion window size during a RTT period, we can get high fairness and enhanced throughput. The fairness index in our cases increases from 0.63, 0.74 to 0.99, 0.99 respectively. In addition, it improves the performance of sessions up to 30% by resolving the performance anomaly.

1 Introduction

In WLAN network, it has been reported that performance anomaly occurs when nodes in the same channel have different operating rates[1]. If the nodes have different sending rates, then the channel utilization of each node becomes different. A slow node consumes the wireless channel longer than a faster node. Performance anomaly is a network problem that the fairness of channel utilization among the nodes is broken because of the link rate adaptation mechanism. When the performance anomaly happens, the performance of a faster node is seriously degraded by the neighbor nodes that operate at slower rate regardless of the current operating rate. In performance anomaly scenario, the higher rate node and the lower rate node have the same throughput in the end.

WLAN ARF (Automatic Rate Fallback) mechanism changes the network sending rate as the link status fluctuates[2]. Namely, ARF is not designed for the link fairness but designed to adapt to link status. It changes the channel coding scheme so that redundancy in channel coding hides the wireless channel error. However, ARF makes difficult to keep the fairness among the nodes in the channel. When a slower rate node grabs the channel, it takes longer to transmit the same-length frame than a higher rate node. Although a slower node is more resilient against the wireless channel error, it breaks the fairness. Because WLAN keeps the fairness only based on the medium access probability, a slower rate node consumes more channel time than the other nodes.

U. Brinkschulte, T. Givargis, and S. Russo (Eds.): SEUS 2008, LNCS 5287, pp. 209–220, 2008.
© IFIP International Federation for Information Processing 2008

The performance anomaly occurs because of this WLAN ARF function. Namely, channel time is unfairly distributed because the slower rate node grabs more channel time than the higher rate node. To resolve the performance anomaly, channel utilization among the nodes should be equally distributed. Recent studies[7,6,5,3,4] on performance anomaly focus on resolving the anomaly using QoS adaptation at MAC layer.

This paper proposes ARF-aware TCP that is an adaptation protocol for resolving the performance anomaly. Existing study on performance anomaly focuses on MAC layer approach because ARF is a MAC layer function and it can be resolved at MAC layer using framing modification or adjusting a parameter to achieve service differentiation. However, it also has drawbacks as follows: 1) MAC layer QoS adaptation would incur unexpected side-effect on end-to-end rate control protocols such as TCP-Vegas. When ARF is applied, transmission delay is changed, and it affects RTT of the session. When RTT is increased, transport protocol estimates that network is congested, and it starts congestion control algorithm. This results in performance degradation from unnecessary congestion control. 2) MAC layer QoS adaptation is hard to be implemented because it is normally implemented as a firmware. On the other hand, ARF-aware TCP resolves performance anomaly by just modifying a variable to adjust the sending window size.

ARF-aware TCP achieves high fairness among the sessions easily and enhances the performance without side-effects.

2   Related Work

The performance anomaly[1] was analyzed by Heusse. In the study, the performance anomaly happens when there are multiple nodes, on the same wireless channel, that are operating at different rates. The authors have shown that when the performance anomaly happens, throughputs of all the nodes are equalized regardless of own link rate. Namely, the higher rate node should get smaller link utilization and performance is degraded and the throughput drops as much as that of the lower rate node.

802.11e performance extension standard has a TXOP option[8]. Using TXOP option, higher rate node combines multiple frames into one, and sends it once when it grabs the wireless channel. To resolve the unfair network utilization, TXOP option intentionally gives more time to the higher rate node. It makes a fair-share of network resources in terms of link utilization.

Kim et al. presents a novel mechanism to resolve the performance anomaly[3]. Proposed scheme adjusts the parameter in the MAC layer, Contention Window (CW). The authors insist that service differentiation can be achieved by simply adjusting the CW parameter. Because CW decides the probability to access the wireless channel, it increases or decreases the CW as the operating link rate. The scheme resolves performance anomaly by service differentiation. Namely, the link utilization is differentiated and distributed as the link rate, and utilization is kept fairly.

Yoo et al. proposed a scheme to eliminate the performance anomaly[4]; the authors insist that performance anomaly can be eliminated by adjusting the frame size. In the study, they proved that the aggregated throughput becomes higher when it is resolved.

Sadeghi proposed an opportunistic media access mechanism for multi-rate WLAN[5]. In the paper, the authors proposed OAR(Opportunistic Auto Rate) protocol, which improves performance in multi-rate WLAN networks. In the protocol, the sender opportunistically transmits multiple back-to-back data packets whenever the channel is good. The authors insist that OAR achieves a significant throughput gain because the channel coherence times typically exceed multiple packet transmission times for both mobile and non-mobile users.

Godfrey revealed inefficiency in multi-rate WLAN network[6]. The authors proved that multi-rate WLAN DCF function can reach to undesirable Nash equilibrium that makes total network performance degraded. Their idea has proved in analytic method as well as simulation. In another paper[7], he presented that time-based fairness can improve the performance in multi-rate WLAN network. In the study, the authors focus on the impact of rate adaptation on AP based WLAN network. They proposed a new traffic regulator, TBR(Time-Based Regulator), which runs on the AP and works with MAC protocols. TBR presents a good performance in terms of fairness as well as total throughputs. In addition, the authors insist that TBR can cooperate with the existing MAC protocols.

3   ARF-Aware TCP: Resolving Performance Anomaly Using Transport Layer Control

The main idea of ARF-aware TCP is that transport protocol, which is responsible for end-to-end rate adaptation, controls the sending rate considering the fair link utilization. That is, ARF function at the MAC layer notifies the higher layer protocol, TCP, to adapt the available bandwidth estimation. If we reduce the congestion window size of a TCP session, then the packets in the network will be decreased, and channel utilization will also be reduced. Namely, TCP is aware of the ARF function at MAC layer, and controls the maximum sending rate to achieve fair network utilization.

If MAC layer adopts QoS mechanisms, higher layer protocols would experience unexpected performance degradation. For example, TXOP option of 802.11e can affect the RTT of the session. TXOP option aggregate multiple packets into one jumbo packet and send it at once. This affects the RTT experienced at transport layer because the transmission delay is affected by the link rate and frame size. Moreover, it affects the RTT variance because the packet error rate becomes large. Note that larger packets are more probable to have more bit errors and requires longer time to recover.

MAC layer QoS mechanisms perform fine-grained access control; however, they do not consider the long term behavior estimation such as available bandwidth estimation. On the other hand, rate adaptation at transport protocol is performed for the larger scale network adaptation. Transport protocol finds a proper sending rate based on bandwidth estimation, and it controls network congestion using distributed algorithm(AIMD). Because the transport protocol performs an end-to-end adaptation, it finds the bandwidth of the bottleneck link and adjust the sending rate to the link. Because ARF function can change the available bandwidth, the bandwidth estimation at transport layer should be modified. Otherwise, transport protocol would keep increasing the sending rate although the available bandwidth is reduced significantly.

Bandwidth estimation at transport layer is performed based on the bottleneck link. Consequently, the estimation mechanism should be modified properly when ARF is activated because it can change the bottleneck link. The transport protocol should find another bottleneck link with its available bandwidth, which requires an amount of time.

In addition, ARF-aware TCP is more flexible than the MAC layer QoS adaptation mechanisms because MAC layer protocols are difficult to be modified. In many cases, it is implemented in firmware, and software modification is limited. On the other hand, TCP can handle rate adaptation by simply modifying some variables. At the sender side, it works very simply. We adapt the congestion window size as the current link rate changes. For example, if the link rate is changed from 11Mbps to 1Mbps, then the congestion window size variable is scaled down to keep the bandwidth estimation history.

By controlling the congestion window size, we have the identical result with the adaptation at the MAC layer. If the transport layer does not transmit packets, then the link layer protocol should wait. If we increase the cwnd size, the TCP sender would transmit at higher speed, and will utilize more wireless channel. On the other hand, if we decrease the cwnd size, then the sender would decrease the sending rate, and the channel utilization will be decreased, in turn.

We introduce a ratio variable k, which is an indicator of ratio between the current link rate and the maximum link rate.

Detailed algorithm of ARF-aware TCP is as follows:

$$cwnd := CongestionWindow,$$
$$k := [maximumlinkrate/currentlinkrate].$$

When a WLAN link rate changes, arf_cwnd, which is a new congestion window in arf mode is calculated.

$$\text{arf\_cwnd} := \lfloor \tfrac{cwnd}{k} \rfloor, \quad \text{if } \lfloor \tfrac{cwnd}{k} \rfloor \geq 1,$$
$$\text{arf\_cwnd} := 1, \quad\quad\quad \text{otherwise.}$$

ARF-aware TCP enters the arf mode when link rate is changed from the highest speed $11Mbps$. When the ARF at MAC layer changes the link rate from the highest rate, it notifies ARF-aware TCP, and changes the mode from normal node to arf mode. TCP uses arf_cwnd when in the arf mode, and also saves cwnd.

At this time, new congestion window(arf_cwnd) is used to adjust outgoing traffic. When the link rate is recovered to the highest rate, then the saved cwnd value is used again. When the link rate is recovered to the highest rate, then ARF-aware TCP changes mode from the arf mode to the normal mode.

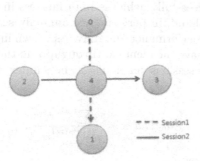

Fig. 1. Simulation Topology

ARF-aware TCP adjusts the sending rate from arf_cwnd. Our assumption is that the WLAN link became an bottleneck in the path. If the bottleneck was not the WLAN, congestion window does not need to be shrunken as much as the link rate changes. In the case, congestion window is smaller than a proper value. However, the AIMD algorithm finds an available bandwidth with increasing the congestion window size, and the TCP will adapts the sending rate in time.

Our mechanism is easy to be deployed because it does not require global information. That is, every node controls its sending rate in distributed manner. Because each node knows its own link rate, TCP sender can get notification from its own MAC layer. To notify the TCP, a little change at MAC layer is required.

In general, there are two options for implementing the ARF notification. 1) Device driver can directly notify the link rate change. Because ARF is implemented as a device driver optimization option, it does not require firm-ware level modification. On the other hand, standardized DCF algorithm is usually implemented in firmware and hard to be modified. 2) Link rate can be known at TCP indirectly using another protocols such as SNMP(Simple Network Management Protocol). In this case, no modification is required. However, it has an overhead to check the link rate periodically.

In this study, we assume that the link modification can be performed easily and efficiently in terms of modifying the WLAN device driver and having less overhead, respectively.

4   Simulation Result

To validate our study, we performed extensive simulation using NS-2. At first, we present whether ARF-aware TCP can resolve the performance anomaly problem. Figure 1 presents our simulation topology. Node0 and Node1 use FTP applications using TCP. Both nodes begin sessions at 1 second. Initial link rate is 11Mbps. At 20 second, Node0 changes link rate from 11Mbps to 1Mbps. In real network environment, link rate is gradually decreased as the operating mode, but we changed it for the sake of simplicity. Finally, TCP newReno is used for comparison with Delayed ACK option.

ARF-aware TCP successfully achieves high fairness in performance anomaly scenario. On the other hand, in performance anomaly scenario, TCP new-reno sessions suffer from the performance anomaly. As shown in performance anomaly study[1], both sessions have the identical throughput in the end. We can compare the fairness between the sessions via Jain's fairness index. Jain's fairness index[9] is defined as follow:

$$FairIndex = \frac{(\sum_n^{i=1} x_i)^2}{n \cdot \sum_n^{i=1} x_i{}^2}. \tag{1}$$

We can define x_i as follow:

$$x_i = \frac{R_i}{T_i}, \tag{2}$$

where R_i is a measured throughput of session i, and T_i is an optimal throughput for session i. In addition, we can define optimal throughput T_i as follow:

$$T_i = \sum_{L_r} \frac{L_r \cdot (\text{Time duration of operating rate at} L_r)}{(\text{Total simulation time})}, \tag{3}$$

where operating link rate $L_r \in \{\text{possible operating mode}\}$.

Fairness index ranges from zero to one. If all the nodes perfectly share the network fairly, then the fairness index becomes one. T_i defines the optimal throughput when there is only one session which uses ARF.

Table 1. Comparison of ARF-aware TCP and TCP newReno (simple topology)

	ARF-aware TCP	TCP newReno
Throughput of Session1 (11Mbps→ 1Mbps at 20 sec.)	486 kbps	616 kbps
Throughput of Session2 (11Mbps)	998 kbps	595 kbps
Fairness Index	0.926377	0.746335
Aggregated throughput	1484 kbps	1211 kbps

Because ARF-aware TCP resolves performance anomaly, ARF-aware TCP achieves much higher fairness value as presented in Table 1.

Besides the fairness index, aggregated throughput is also enhanced in ARF-aware TCP. The reason of aggregated throughput enhancement is that the higher rate node can utilize the channel more than the lower rate node.

The session throughput variation in performance anomaly scenario is presented in Figure 2. The graph shows transmitted number of packets per second. In ARF-aware TCP, throughput of Session1 drops at 20 second because the sender adjusts the congestion window as arf_cwnd. In this scenario, ratio k is 11, and the congestion window size is decreased to cwnd11. On the other hand, Session2 keeps sending rate as before, and utilizes the channel as before.

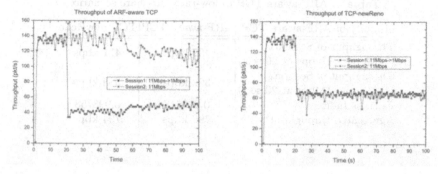

Fig. 2. Throughput(pkt/s) variations of ARF-aware TCP sessions and TCP newReno sessions

On the contrary to ARF-aware TCP, TCP newReno suffers from performance anomaly as presented in Figure 2. Both sessions utilize the channel time at equal proportion, and Session2 is also affected by the Session1 regardless of its own link rate.

Because performance anomaly is resolved, the aggregated throughput of sessions is increased. We can compare aggregated throughput through the table 1. ARF-aware TCP present slightly higher throughput than the Reno sessions. The performance gain from resolving performance anomaly is about 20% in this scenario.

To present that the original TCP newReno performs fairly, we measured throughput of two TCP newReno sessions without performance anomaly scenario. Namely, we did not change the link rate of Session1 in Fair-share scenario (remains 11Mbps). TCP newReno originally achieves high fairness as shown in Table 2. However, the fairness is broken when performance anomaly happens.

Table 2. Comparison of TCP newReno in the anomaly and fair-share scenario

Performance of TCP newReno	Fair-share scenario	Performance anomaly scenario
Throughput of Session1	1070 kbps	616 kbps
Throughput of Session2	1031 kbps	595 kbps
Fairness Index	0.999656	0.746335
Aggregated throughput	2101 kbps	1211 kbps

Because original TCP newReno keeps fairness, ARF-aware TCP also keeps fairness when both sessions reduce the link rate. We measured throughput result when both sessions reduce the link rate from 11Mbps to 1Mbps at 20 sec. ARF-aware TCP performs stably when both sessions reduce the link rate as presented in Table 3.

To confirm that ARF-aware TCP performs well in multi-session scenario, we increased the total number of sessions. In this case, we modified the network topology as shown in Figure 3. To simplify the simulation, we changed link rate

Table 3. ARF-aware TCP in low-rate fair-share scenario

Stability of ARF-aware TCP	ARF-aware TCP	TCP newReno
Throughput of Session1 (11Mbps→ 1Mbps at 20 sec.)	407 kbps	411 kbps
Throughput of Session2 (11Mbps→ 1Mbps at 20 sec.)	392 kbps	383 kbps
Fairness Index	0.999648	0.998758
Aggregated throughput	799 kbps	794 kbps

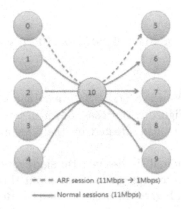

- - - ARF session (11Mbps → 1Mbps)
—— Normal sessions (11Mbps)

Fig. 3. Simulation topology of multi-session scenario

Table 4. Comparison of ARF-aware TCP and TCP newReno in multi-session scenario

	ARF-aware TCP	TCP newReno
Throughput of Session1 (11Mbps→ 1Mbps at 20 sec.)	127 kbps	341 kbps
Throughput of Session2(11Mbps)	444 kbps	320 kbps
Throughput of Session3(11Mbps)	430 kbps	305 kbps
Throughput of Session4(11Mbps)	485 kbps	298 kbps
Throughput of Session5(11Mbps)	512 kbps	286 kbps
Fairness Index	0.996125	0.626977
Aggregated throughput	1998 kbps	1550 kbps

from 11Mbps to 1Mbps directly. Yet, it does not lose generality because the operation mode can be set individually. In our best result, throughput gain is higher than traditional Reno sessions about 30%.

The result is presented in Table 4. ARF-aware TCP achieves much higher fairness index as well as aggregated throughput.

For more realistic case, we performed simulation for diverse rates. All the five nodes changes to different operation rates (1Mbps, 2Mbps, 5.5Mbps, 11Mbps). That is, Node0 changes from 11Mbps to 1Mbps, Node1 from 11Mbps to 2Mbps, Node2 from 11Mbps to 5.5Mbps, so forth. Note that the ratio variable k is rounded.

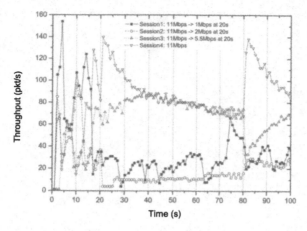

Fig. 4. Throughput of ARF-aware TCP in multi-session multi-rate scenario

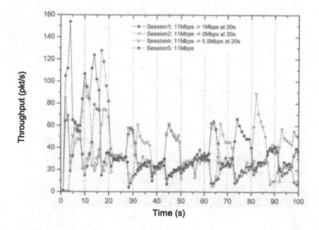

Fig. 5. Throughput of TCP-newReno in multi-session multi-rate scenario

Table 5. Multi-session, multi-rate scenario

	ARF-aware TCP	TCP newReno
Throughput of Session1 (11Mbps→ 1Mbps at 20 sec.)	127 kbps	290 kbps
Throughput of Session2 (11Mbps→ 2Mbps at 20 sec.)	163 kbps	262 kbps
Throughput of Session3 (11Mbps→ 5.5Mbps at 20 sec.)	277 kbps	256 kbps
Throughput of Session4 (11Mbps)	670 kbps	260 kbps
Fairness Index	0.94693	0.831825
Aggregated throughput	1237 kbps	1068 kbps

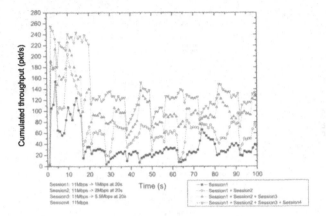

Fig. 6. Aggregated throughput of ARF-aware TCP in multi-session multi-rate scenario

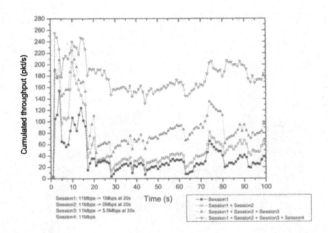

Fig. 7. Aggregated throughput of TCP newReno in multi-session multi-rate scenario

The throughput result confirms our study that ARF-aware TCP achieves high fairness as well as enhanced aggregated throughput as presented in Table 5.

We can observe the network utilization among the nodes by the throughput variation, presented in Figure 4.

ARF-aware TCP shares network bandwidth as the link rate as presented in Figure 4; however, the TCP newReno shares network bandwidth very inconsistently (Figure 5). Moreover, the cumulated throughput in Figure 6 and presents an interesting result that ARF-aware TCP keeps network utilization even in the performance anomaly scenario. On the other hand, the cumulated throughput drops very seriously in TCP newReno case as the Figure 7.

When the ARF-aware TCP recovers from the arf mode to normal mode, it boosts the sending rate and recovers the original rate very quickly. Consequently, it keeps fairness very stable when compared with the TCP newReno.

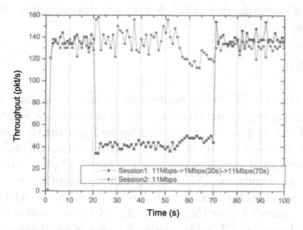

Fig. 8. Throughput(pkt/s) variation of ARF-aware TCP in recovery scenario

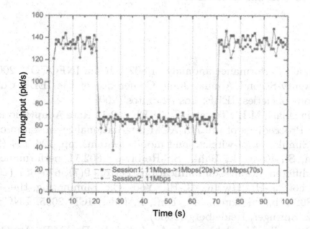

Fig. 9. Throughput(pkt/s) variation of TCP newReno in recovery scenario

The following simulation is based on the topology presented in Figure 1. Node0 changes link rate from 11Mbps to 1Mbps at 20 second, and recovers back to 11Mbps at 70 second.

We can observe the quick recovery from the performance anomaly through the throughput graph shown in Figure 8. Session2 keeps high sending rate in the anomaly period, and Session1 successfully recovers from the performance anomaly and shares the link with Session2.

TCP newReno presents performance anomaly during the anomaly period. However, it also successfully recovers from the anomaly as shown in Figure 9.

Proposing ARF-aware TCP resolves performance and achieves much higher fairness among sessions. It also naturally enhances aggregated throughput of sessions. In addition, it works stable because it keeps fairness in the case that both nodes are in arf mode. Finally, it presents much higher fairness and throughput in more practical scenarios that multiple nodes are operating at different rates at the same time.

5   Conclusion

We present ARF-aware TCP that resolves performance anomaly in the transport layer, which can largely enhance the fairness in multi-rate WLAN networks. ARF-aware TCP resolves performance anomaly by adjusting the congestion window size. It can be easily deployed because MAC layer modification is not required. ARF-aware TCP enhances not only the fairness but also the aggregated throughput. In our simulation, ARF-aware TCP presents a good performance in the performance anomaly scenarios. Fairness index among ARF-aware TCP sessions always achieves higher than 0.9, while TCP newReno achieves 0.74 or 0.62 in cases. ARF-aware TCP achieves high fairness in multi-session, and multi-session multi-rate scenario, also. In addition to fairness, aggregated throughput is enhanced by 30% in our best case.

References

1. Heusse, M., et al.: Performance anomaly of 802.11b. In: INFOCOM 2003, Proceedings of the twenty-Second Annual Joint Conference of the IEEE Computer and Communications Societies. IEEE, Los Alamitos (2003)
2. Lacage, M., Manshaei, M.H., Turletti, T.: IEEE 802.11 Rate Adaptation: A Practical Approach. In: Proceedings of the 7th ACM international Symposium on Modeling, Analysis and Simulation of wireless and mobile systems, pp. 126–134 (2004)
3. Kim, H., Yun, S., Kang, I., Bahk, S.: Resolving 802.11 performance anomalies through QoS differentiation. Communications Letters 9(7), 655–657 (2005)
4. Yoo, S.-h., Choi, J.-H., Hwang, J.-H., Yoo, C.: Eliminating the Performance Anomaly of 802.11b. In: Lorenz, P., Dini, P. (eds.) ICN 2005. LNCS, vol. 3421, pp. 1055–1062. Springer, Heidelberg (2005)
5. Sadeghi, B., Kanodia, V., Sabharwal, A., Knightly, E.: OAR: An Opportunistic Auto-Rate Media Access Protocol for Ad-Hoc Networks. Wireless Networks 11(1), 39–53 (2005)
6. Tan, G., Guttag, J.: The 802.11 MAC protocol leads to inefficient equilibria. In: proceedings of the INFOCOM 2005. 24th Annual Joint Conference of the IEEE Computer and Communications Societies, vol. 1, pp. 1–11 (2005)
7. Tan, G., Guttag, J.: Time-based fairness improves performance in multi-rate WLANs. In: Proceedings of the USENIX Annual Technical Conference 2004 on USENIX Annual Technical Conference, pp. 269–282 (2004)
8. IEEE 802.11e-2005, in Part 11: Wireless LAN Medium Access Control (MAC) and Physical Layer (PHY) specifications, Amendment 8: Medium Access Control (MAC) Quality of Service Enhancements, IEEE (2005)
9. Jain, R., Chiu, D.M., Hawe, W.: A Quantitative Measure of Fairness and Discrimination for Resource Allocation in Shared Systems, DEC Research Report TR-301 (1984)

Context-Aware Deployment of Services in Public Spaces

Ichiro Satoh

National Institute of Informatics
2-1-2 Hitotsubashi, Chiyoda-ku, Tokyo 101-8430, Japan
ichiro@nii.ac.jp

Abstract. This paper presents the context-aware deployment of user-assistant services in public spaces, e.g., museums. Using location-sensing systems, it detects the locations of users and deploys user-assistant services, e.g., visitor guides, at computers near to the their current locations. When users move between exhibits in a museum, it enables agents to follow users to annotate the exhibits in personalized form and navigate them to the next exhibits along their routes. To demonstrate the utility and effectiveness of the framework, we constructed and operated a location/user-aware visitor-guide service in a museum as case studies in the development of context-aware services in public spaces.

1 Introduction

The use of user/location-aware services in public spaces, including cities, stations, and museums, has attached much attention from researchers over the past few years. This paper addresses context-aware services to guide visitors in a museum as case studies for developing ubiquitous computing systems for city-wide public spaces. Few visitors in museums have sufficient knowledge about the exhibits. Therefore, they need annotations on these. However, their knowledge and experiences are varied so that they may become puzzled (or bored) if the annotations provided to them are beyond (or beneath) their knowledge or interest. To solve this problem, we construct a context-aware system for providing visitors with services to annotate exhibits in their personalized forms at nearby computers, even when they move between exhibits.

There have been several academic or commercial attempts to develop context-aware services for museums with the aim of enabling visitors to view or listen to information about exhibits at the right time and in the right place and to help them navigate between exhibits along recommended routes. However, most of existing attempts have been developed to the prototype stage and tested in small-scale laboratory-based experiments. They have been designed in an ad-hoc manner to provide specific single services in particular spaces, i.e., research laboratories and buildings. As a result, they are not suitable for public spaces or for applications that they were not initially designed to support. In addition, they implicitly or explicitly assume centralized management systems, so their scalability could be a serious problem.

We construct a framework for providing context-aware services in a real museum with real users. It provides each user with mobile agent-based software components to deploy application-specific services at computers independently of the underlying infrastructure and other services. It can also spatially bind a user to their agent/s using location-sensing systems. For example, when a user stands in front of an exhibit, his/her

U. Brinkschulte, T. Givargis, and S. Russo (Eds.): SEUS 2008, LNCS 5287, pp. 221–232, 2008.

agent is deployed at a computer close to his/her position and provides him/her with annotation services about the exhibit in a personalized form that has been adapted to the individual user.

2 Approach

Our final goal is to construct a general-purpose infrastructure for providing context-aware services in large public spaces, e.g., building-wide and city-wide spaces. It was inspired by real requirements of museums rather than our academic interests.

2.1 Background

There have been many academic and commercial attempts to provide context-aware services to visitors in public museums. A typical approach has been to provide visitors with audio annotations from portable audio players. These have required end-users to carry players and explicitly input numbers assigned to exhibits if they wanted to listen to audio annotations about the exhibits in front of them. Many academic projects have provided portable multimedia terminals or PDAs to visitors. These have enabled visitors to interactively look at and operate annotated information displayed on the screen of their players, e.g, the Electronic Guidebook [3] and Museum Project [2]. They assume that visitors car carrying portable terminals, e.g., PDAs and smart phones and they are required to explicitly input their positions, the identifiers of exhibits, and items of interest by using user interface devices, e.g., buttons, mice, or touch panels of terminals. However, such operations are difficult for visitors, particularly children, the elderly, and handicapped people, and often prevent them from viewing the exhibits.

To solve this problem, several projects have used sensing systems to detect the positions of visitors, e.g., the Hippie [6], the ImogI [5], and the Rememberer [3]. Portable smart devices, including PDAs, with location sensing systems may be popular in academic projects, but museums tend to avoid using such devices because they are too expensive to lend to visitors and also require regular maintenance, e.g., replacing or recharging the batteries every day. In fact, cost issues are one of the most serious problems in deploying context-aware services at public spaces, including museums. Therefore, several existing approaches, which assume to make use of expensive or delicate devices, will not always be used in real museums, even though they are interesting within academic research communities. In addition, one of the most serious problems associated with portable smart devices in museums is that they prevent visitors from focusing on the exhibits because they tend to become interested in the device rather than the exhibition itself and therefore concentrate on operating the PDA buttons or touch panel instead of looking at the exhibits.

2.2 Requirements

To solve these problems, we should support visitors from stationary sensors and computing devices. We discuss the requirements of visitor guides in museums.

- Visitor-guide services for exhibits should be selected and customized according to the behaviors of users, e.g., the exhibits they looked at, how long they stayed around specific exhibits, and their current locations in addition to knowledge and interest.

- User-assistant services, including visitor-guide services in public spaces, are likely to be accessed often by users. Such services should be executed at nearby computers to minimize communication delays between user-interface devices and server-side computers.
- Visitors move between exhibits in a museum. When he/she moves to another exhibit, his/her agent should be deployed at a computer close to his/her destination by using location-sensing systems.
- Visitor-guide services should be personalized, even when they are provided in public spaces. Services should be provided and interact with users in a personalized manner adapted to individual needs.
- Computers in ubiquitous computing environments often have only limited resources, such as restricted levels of CPU power and amount of memory. They cannot support all the services that may be needed. We therefore have to deploy software that defines services at computers only while those services are needed.
- Our final aim is widespread building-wide and city-wide deployment of ubiquitous computing systems. It is almost impossible to deploy and administer a system in a scalable way when all of the control and management functions are centralized. Our system consists of multiple servers, which are individually connected to other servers in a peer-to-peer manner. Each server only maintains up-to-date information on partial contextual information instead of on tags in the whole space.

2.3 Approach

To meet these requirements, our system uses mobile-agent technology.

- Each mobile agent is a self-contained autonomous programming entity. Our system itself is independent of application-specific services. Instead these services are defined and performed within mobile agents.
- Each agent is spatially bound to, at most, one user. When a user gets closer to an exhibit, our system detects the migration of the user by using location-sensing systems and then instructs the user's agents to migrate to a computer close to the exhibit.
- Each agent can migrate from computer to computer. When an agent moves to another computer, both the code and the state of the agent are transferred to the destination. After arriving at its destination, an agent can continue working, e.g., on a user-assistant task, without losing results, such as the content of instance variables in the agent's program, at the source computer.
- Each agent can maintain per-user preferences on a user and record the user's behavior, e.g., exhibits that they have looked at. The agent can also define user-personalized services adapted to the user and access location-dependent services provided at its current computer.

Mobile agents help to conserve limited resources, because each agent only needs to be present at the computer while the computer needs the services provided by that agent. Agents can be managed in a non-centralized manner. When an agent migrates to another computer, it does not have to interact with the source computer.

3   Deployable Context-Aware Agent Platform

Our context-aware system consists of three subsystems: (1) an agent host, (2) context-aware directory servers, called CDSs (Fig. 1), and (3) service-provider agents. The first can execute service-provider agents, where we assume that the computing devices are located at specified spots in public spaces. The second is an autonomous entity that defines application-specific services for visitors. The third is responsible for reflecting changes in the real world and the location of users when services are deployed at appropriate computers. User/location-aware visitor-guide services are encapsulated within the third subsystem so that the first and second subsystems are independent of any application specific services and other agents, which are simultaneously running to provide different services.

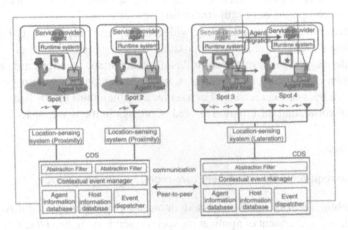

Fig. 1. Architecture of Context-aware Service Provider Agent System

3.1   Agent Host

Each agent host is a computer that can provide visitor-guide services through user-interface devices, e.g., display screens and loudspeakers. It provides a runtime system for executing and migrating agents to other hosts. Each runtime system is built on the Java virtual machine (Java VM), which conceals differences between the platform architectures of the source and destination hosts. It governs all the agents inside it and maintains the life-cycle state of each agent. When the life-cycle state of an agent changes, e.g., when it is created, terminates, or migrates to another host, the runtime system issues specific events to the agent. Some navigation or annotation content, e.g., audio-annotation, should be played without any interruptions. It can exchange agents with another runtime system on a different host through a TCP channel using mobile-agent technology. When an agent is transferred over the network, not only the code of the agent but also its state is transformed into a bitstream by using Java's object serialization package and then the bit stream is transferred to the destination. The host on the receiving side receives and unmarshals the bit stream. Agents may have to acquire various resources, e.g., video and sound, or release previously acquired resources.

3.2 Context-Aware Agent Deployment

Each CDS spatially binds an agent to a user. It maintains two databases. The first stores information about each of the agent hosts and the second stores each of the agents attached to users. It can exchange this information with other CDSs in a peer-to-peer manner.

Tracking systems can be classified into two types: proximity and lateration. The first approach detects the presence of objects within known spots or close to known points, and the second estimates the positions of objects from multiple measurements of the distance between known points. The current implementation assumes that museums provide visitors with tags. These tags are small RF transmitters that periodically broadcast beacons, including the identifiers of the tags, to receivers located in exhibition rooms. The receivers locate the presence or position of the tags. To abstract away differences between the underlying location-sensing systems, CDS maps geometric information measured by sensing systems to specified areas. We assume such areas contain exhibits and computing devices to play annotations. We call the areas *spots*.

When the underlying sensing system detects the presence (or absence) of a tag in a spot, it sends the arrival and departure message to a CDS. The CDS attempts to query the locations of the agent tied to the tag from its database. If the database does not contain any information about the identifier of the tag, it multicasts a query message that contains the identity of the new tag to other CDSs. It then waits for reply messages from other CDSs. Next, if the CDS knows the location of the agent tied to the newly visiting tag, it instructs the agent to migrate to a computing device.

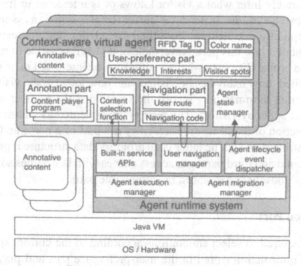

Fig. 2. Architecture of agent host

4 Context-Aware Service-Provider Agent

Each agent is attached to at most one visitor and maintains the preference information for its user and programs to provide annotation and navigation to its visitor. To enable agents to be easily developed and configured agents without any professional administrators, we divided each agent into three parts:

- **The user-preference part** maintains and records information about visitors, e.g., knowledge, interests, routes, their name, and durations spent at exhibits they visited.
- **The annotation part** defines a task for playing annotations about exhibits or interacting with visitors.
- **The navigation part** defines a task for navigating visitors to their destinations.

When an agent is deployed at another computer, the runtime system invokes a specified callback method defined in the annotation part and then one defined in the navigation part. Although these parts are implemented as Java objects, they are loosely connected with one another through data attributes by using Java's introspection mechanism so that they can be replaced without any compilations and linkages for their programs. The current implementation uses the standard JAR file format for archiving these parts because the format can support digital signatures, enabling authentication. Each agent keeps the identifier of the tag attached to its visitor. Each agent can specify a requirement that its destination hosts must satisfy in CC/PP form and the runtime system can select an appropriate destination among multiple destination candidates through a comparison between the capabilities required by agents and the capabilities of the candidates.

4.1 User-Preference Part

This is responsible for maintaining information about a visitor. In fact, it is almost impossible to accurately infer what a visitor knows or is interested in from data that are measured by sensing systems. Instead, the current implementation assumes that administrators will explicitly ask visitors about their knowledge and interests and manually input the information into this part. Nevertheless, it is still possible to make a qualified guess with some probability as to what a visitor may be interested in, if we know which spots he/she visited, how many he/she visited, and how long he/she visited. Each agent has a mechanism to automatically record the identifiers, the number of visits to, and length of stays at spots by visitors. This part is implemented as a hash-table for maintaining the collection of data entries. Each entry is a pair of a name and a value, where the former is a string data and the latter is an arbitrary data structure represented as Java objects. The second and third parts can access entries with key names so that these parts can be combined loosely and replaced by compatible parts.

4.2 Annotation Part

Each agent is required to select annotations according to the current spot and route in addition to the information stored in the user-preference part and play the content in its user's personalized form. This part defines a content selection function and a set of programs for playing the selected content. The function maps more than one argument, e.g., the current spot, the user's selected route, and the number of times a user has visited the spot into a URL referring to the annotative content. The content can be stored in the agent, the current agent host, or external http servers. That is, each agent can carry a set of its content, play the selected content at its destinations, directly play the content

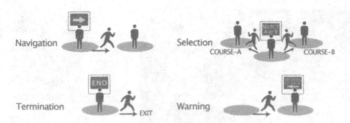

Fig. 3. User-navigation patterns

stored at its destinations, or download and play the content stored in web-servers on the Internet. Such content is provided in a variety of multimedia representations, e.g., text, image, video, and sound. The annotation part defines programs for playing this content. The current implementation supports (rich) text data, html, image data, e.g, JPEG and GIF, video data, e.g., animation GIF and MPEG, and sound data, e.g., wav and MP3. The format for content is specified in an MIME-based attribute description. Since the annotation part is defined as Java-based general-purpose programs, we can easily define interactions between visitors and agents. The current implementation can divide the part into three sub-parts: opening, annotation, and closing, which are played by turns.

4.3 Navigation Part

Our agents are required to navigate visitors to their destinations along routes recommended by museums or the visitors. After executing their annotation part, the navigation part is invoked by the runtime system to provide visual (or audio) information on the screens of displays (or from loudspeakers) of the current agent host. For example, the agents display the directions to exhibits that their visitors should next see. We also introduced visitor movements between exhibits as an implicit operation for selecting the routes that they wanted and evaluating what they had learned from the exhibits, because visitor movement is one of the most primitive and natural behaviors in museums. This part provides the four navigation patterns, outlined in Fig. 3.

- *Navigation* instructs users to move to at least one specified destination spot.
- *Selection* enables users to explicitly or implicitly select one spot or route from one or more spots or routes close to their current spots by moving to the selected spot or one spot along the selected route.
- *Termination* informs users that they have arrived at the final spot.
- *Warning* informs users that they had missed their destination exhibit or their routes.

The user's route is described as a sequences of primitives corresponding to the above free patterns with our language for specifying the itineraries of mobile agents for network management [11] and they are stored in the user-preference part. No agent knows the spatial directions to the destinations because the directions themselves depend on the spatial relationships between the locations of the current agent host and the locations of the destinations, as well as the direction to the current host's screen. The current implementation permits administrators to manually input the directions of possible

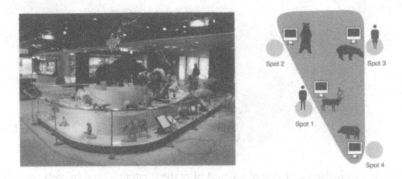

Fig. 4. Experiment at Museum of Nature and Human Activities in Hyogo

destinations and the direction to the screen. Agent hosts provide built-in APIs to their visiting agents. For example, if an agent has at least one destination, it invokes a specified API corresponding to the first pattern with the name of the destination; its current host returns the direction to the destination to it or displays the direction on the screen on its behalf.

5 Experience

To prove the utility of the propose system, we constructed and operated an experiment at the Museum of Nature and Human Activities in Hyogo, Japan, using the proposed system. Figure 4 has a sketch that maps the spots located in the museum. The experiment was carried out at four spots in front of specimens of stuffed animals, i.e., a bear, deer, racoon dog, and wild boar. Each spot could provide five different pieces of animation-based annotative content about animal, e.g., its ethology, footprints, feeding, habitat, and features, and had a display and Spider's active RFID reader with a coverage range that almost corresponded to the space, as shown in Fig. 5.

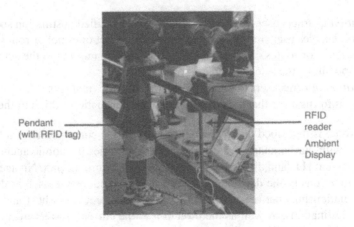

Fig. 5. Spot at Museum of Nature and Human Activities in Hyogo

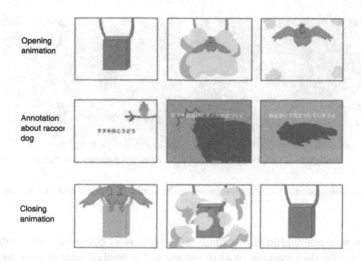

Fig. 6. Opening animation, annotation animation, and closing animation for orange pendant

When a visitor first participated in the experiment, an operator input the point of interest and the route for the new visitor and created his/her service-provider agent. As shown in Fig. 6, an agent tied to a pendant played the opening animation and then played the annotation. It next plays the closing animation.

We simultaneously provided two kinds of routes for visitors to evaluate the utility of our user-navigation supports. Both routes navigated visitors to destination spots along the way (Fig. 7). They made each visitor go around an exhibit booth consisting of four spots two or three times, as shown on the right of Fig. 4. That is, a visitor might visit the same spots two or three times depending on the navigation of their agents. In addition, the first route enabled visitors to explicitly select subjects they preferred by moving to one of the neighboring spots corresponding to the subjects selected in specified spots at specified times. The second route provided visitors with several quizzes to review what they had learnt about the animals by selecting neighboring spots corresponding to their answers in specified spots at specified timings. Both the experiments offered visitors animation-based annotative content about the animal in front of them so they could learn about the animal while observing the corresponding specimen.

The experimental system consisted of one CDS and four agent hosts. It enabled curators to configure annotation content through a GUI-based monitoring and configuration for agents (right of Fig. 8) and to operate the assignment of annotation to visitors by using a Web browser running on a portable terminal (Apple iPod Touch) equipped with a WiFi interface (left of Fig. 8).

When the CDS detected the presence of a tag bound to a visitor at a spot, it instructed the agent bound to the user to migrate an agent host contained in the spot. After arriving at the host, the runtime system invoked a specified callback method defined in the annotative part of the agent. The method first played the opening animation defined in the agent and then called a content-selection function with his/her route, the name of the current spot, and the number of times that he/she had visited the spot. The latency of migrating of an agent and starting its opening animation at the destination after visitors

Navigation to one destination   Selection from two destinations

Fig. 7. Navigation patterns for user navigation at Museum of Nature and Human Activities in Hyogo

arrived at a spot was within two seconds, so that visitors could view the opening animation soon after they stood in front of exhibits. The method next played the selected content and then played the closing animation. After that, the runtime system invoked a specified callback method defined in the navigation part. An agent bound to a user could recommend two or more destination spots by using the *Selection* pattern provided on its current agent host. When a visitor moved to one of the spots, his/her agent could record their selection. If the selection corresponded to a quiz choice, when a user moved to a spot corresponding to a correct or incorrect answer, their agent modified the visitor's profile, which was maintained within it. Furthermore, if a user left out his/her route, the navigation part invoked a method to play warning content to return him/her to his/her previous spot.

Portable administration   Terminal for monitoring the positions of
terminal (iPod touch)   visitors and customizing agents

Fig. 8. Portable management terminal (left figure) and GUI-based system for monitoring and configuring agents (right figure)

We operated the experiment over two weeks. Each day, more than 60 individuals or groups took part in the experiment. Most of the participants were groups of families or friends aged from 7 to 16. Most visitors answered questionnaires about their answers to the quizzes and their feedback on the system in addition to their genders and ages.

Almost all the participants (more than 95 percent) had positive feedback on the system. Their typical feedback were "We were very interested in or enjoyed the system.", "We could easily answer to the quizzes by our moving between the spots.", and "We gained detail knowledge about the animals with our watching them in front of our standing positions." As application-specific services could be defined and encapsulated within the agents, we were able to easily change the services provided by modifying the corresponding agents while the entire system was running and more than two different visitor-guide services could also be simultaneously supported for visitors. Even while visitors were participating, curators with no knowledge of context-aware systems were able to configure the annotative content by doing drag-and-drop manipulations using the GUI-based configuration system. Such dynamic configuration is useful, because museums need to provide and configure services with visitors without any stopping.

6 Related Work

As we discussed in Section 2, there have been many attempts to provide visitor-guide systems in museums, but most existing projects assume that visitors carry smart terminals. On the other hand, there have been several research attempts on smart spaces equipped with stationary sensors and terminals. Cambridge University's Sentient Computing project [4] provides a platform for location-aware applications using infrared-based or ultrasonic-based locating systems in a building. Using the VNC system [7], the platform can track the movement of a tagged entity, such as individuals and things, so that the graphical user interfaces of the user's applications follow him/her while he/she moves around. Although the platform provides similar functionality to that of our framework, its management is centralized and their services are executed in centralized servers. Microsoft's EasyLiving project [1] enabled services running on different computers to be combined dynamically according to contextural changes in the real world, but aimed at private spaces, e.g., living rooms. It could not deploy services at different computers.

We discuss differences between the framework presented in this paper and our previous frameworks. We previously presented an approach for deploying mobile agents spatially bound to physical places and objects at computers that moved in the places or were close to the objects [9]. However, it was not designed for user-navigation, unlike the framework proposed in this paper. We also constructed a location model for ubiquitous computing environments. The model represents spatial relationships between physical entities (and places) as containment relationships between their programmable counterpart objects and deploys counterpart objects at computers according to the positions of their target objects or places [12]. This was a general-purpose location-model for context-aware services, but was not an infrastructure for deploying and operating such services. We presented some basic evaluation on the usability of mobile agent-based services in public museums in our another paper [13].

7 Conclusion

We designed and implemented an agent-based system for building and operating context-aware visitor-guide services in public museums. When a visitor moves from exhibit to exhibit, his/her agent can be dynamically deployed at a computer close to the current exhibit to accompany him/her and play annotations about the exhibit according to his/her knowledge, interest, and the exhibits that he/she watched. His/her agent can also navigate him/her to exhibits along his/her route. To support large-scale context-aware systems, the system is managed in a non-centralized manner. Using the system, we constructed and operated location/user-aware visitor-guide services at a museum as case studies in our development of ambient computing services in public spaces.

References

1. Brumitt, B.L., Meyers, B., Krumm, J., Kern, A., Shafer, S.: EasyLiving: Technologies for Intelligent Environments. In: Proceedings of International Symposium on Handheld and Ubiquitous Computing, pp. 12–27 (2000)
2. Ciavarella, C., Paterno, F.: The Design of a Handheld, Location-aware Guide for Indoor Environments. Personal and Ubiquitous Computing 8(2), 82–91 (2004)
3. Fleck, M., Frid, M., Kindberg, T., Rajani, R., O'BrienStrain, E., Spasojevic, M.: From Informing to Remembering: Deploying a Ubiquitous System in an Interactive Science Museum. IEEE Pervasive Computing 1(2), 13–21 (2002)
4. Harter, A., Hopper, A., Steggeles, P., Ward, A., Webster, P.: The Anatomy of a Context-Aware Application. In: Proceedings of Conference on Mobile Computing and Networking (MOBICOM 1999), August 1999, pp. 59–68. ACM Press, New York (1999)
5. Luyten, K., Coninx, K.: ImogI: Take Control over a Context-Aware Electronic Mobile Guide for Museums. In: Workshop on HCI in Mobile Guides, in conjunction with 6th International Conference on Human Computer Interaction with Mobile Devices and Services (2004)
6. Oppermann, R., Specht, M.: A Context-Sensitive Nomadic Exhibition Guide. In: Thomas, P., Gellersen, H.-W. (eds.) HUC 2000. LNCS, vol. 1927, pp. 127–142. Springer, Heidelberg (2000)
7. Richardson, T., Stafford-Fraser, Q., Wood, K., Hopper, A.: Virtual Network Computing. IEEE Internet Computing 2(1), 33–38 (1999)
8. Rocchi, C., Stock, O., Zancanaro, M., Kruppa, M., Kruger, A.: The Museum Visit: Generating Seamless Personalized Presentations on Multiple Devices. In: Proceedings of 9th international conference on Intelligent User Interface, pp. 316–318. ACM Press, New York (2004)
9. Satoh, I.: SpatialAgents: Integrating User Mobility and Program Mobility in Ubiquitous Computing Environments. Wireless Communications and Mobile Computing 3(4), 411–423 (2003)
10. Satoh, I.: A Location Model for Pervasive Computing Environments. In: Proceedings of IEEE 3rd International Conference on Pervasive Computing and Communications (PerCom 2005), March 2005, pp. 215–224. IEEE Computer Society, Los Alamitos (2005)
11. Satoh, I.: Building and Selecting Mobile Agents for Network Management. Journal of Network and Systems Management, 14(1), 147–169 (2006)
12. Satoh, I.: A Location Model for Smart Environment. Pervasive and Mobile Computing 3(2), 158–179 (2007)
13. Satoh, I.: Context-aware Agents to Guide Visitors in Museums. In: Proceedings of 8th International Conference on Intelligent Virtual Agents (IVA 2008), September 2008. LNCS. Springer, Heidelberg (2008)

An Ontology Supported Meta-interface for the Development and Installation of Customized Web Based Telemedicine Systems

Jackei H.K. Wong[1], Wilfred W. K. Lin[1], Allan K.Y. Wong[1], and Tharam S. Dillon[2]

[1] Department of Computing, Hong Kong Polytechnic University, Hung Hom, Kowloon, H.K.S.A.R.
[2] Digital Ecosystems & Business Intelligence Institute, Curtin University of Technology, Australia
{cshkwong,cswklin,csalwong}@comp.polyu.edu.hk,
tharam.dillon@cbs.curtin.edu.au

Abstract. The novel and generic meta-interface (MI) paradigm proposed in this paper automates the generation of customized telemedicine software systems (CTSS), directly from the customized application interface (CAI) specifications given. The MI paradigm was tested and verified in the TCM (Traditional Chinese Medicine) telemedicine environment of Nong's Company Limited of the PuraPharm Group, a local Hong Kong TCM telemedicine developer that funded this research. The CAI specification is made by "gluing" together icons selected from the enterprise icon library (IL). The CTSS generation, in effect, extracts the corresponding portion of the subsumption hierarchy from the master ontology, an enterprise standard. Since CTSS prototypes were verified in the Nong's TCM telemedicine environment, they were built with the Nong's master TCM ontology core (onto-core) as the basis and reference. In this light, the ontological extraction for a CAI specification is turned into the local TCM onto-core for the CTSS prototype. The enterprise TCM onto-core, the local TCM onto-core, and the icons in IL all contain formal knowledge derived from the enterprise TCM vocabulary. In Nong's case the enterprise vocabulary is the standard of CTSS terminology, gathered from TCM classics, treatises, and case histories by domain experts with consensus certification. Using CAI as the single input to automate the whole CTSS generation process would eliminate MSPM (multi-site project management) problems. Since the Nong's MC (mobile clinics) based telemedicine system is web-based and pervasive, the CTSS is also referred to as the Nong's web-based telemedicine systems (WTS).

Keywords: Meta-interface paradigm, software development, CAI, CTSS, WTS, telemedicine system, ontology, enterprise vocabulary, automated.

1 Introduction

We propose in this paper the innovative meta-interface (MI) paradigm for developing remotely deployable ubiquitous web-based telemedicine systems (WTS). The goal is to customize each client's WTS from a single master ontological core (onto-core),

U. Brinkschulte, T. Givargis, and S. Russo (Eds.): SEUS 2008, LNCS 5287, pp. 233–244, 2008.
© IFIP International Federation for Information Processing 2008

which would then be maintained by the enterprise (i.e. enterprise/master onto-core). Nong's Company Ltd., of the PuraPharm Group in the Hong Kong SAR, is one such enterprise and a local leader in supplying TCM (Traditional Chinese Medicine) WTS to hospitals and clinics across the globe. The company had created its own enterprise TCM onto-core with consensus certification [1] to support MC (mobile clinics) based telemedicine systems. From this enterprise TCM onto-core, Nong's customizes WTS variants specified by the customers. After deployment each customized WTS is automatically linked over the mobile Internet to the PuraPharm/Nong's (PP/N) mobile-business (MB) core.The proposed MI paradigm now offers a solution to the PP/N management's long search for a way to effectively automate the WTS customization process. Their lengthy search is understandable because successful development of qualitative software systems and applications is no easy task. This development process needs to satisfactorily address different contemporary issues [2] that deal with problem domains, varied operational environments, and cultural differences (e.g. natural languages). These issues could be complicated when developing web-based applications that are distributed over diverse geographic locations and involve complex ICT (information communications technology) concerns and MSPM (multi-site project management) activities. Even with the same project requirements MSPM linguistic variations could cause ambiguity, resulting in incorrect implementation or non-interoperable software modules [3]. The lack of an enterprise vocabulary to coordinate and disambiguate software development activities means a high cost-effectiveness ratio, indicated by the following surveys:

a) *High cost*: In Australia and USA it is common for 50% or more of enterprise expenditures to be spent on software development and maintenance.
b) *Prone to failure*: Less than 50% of software development projects in the Western world were completed successfully.
c) *Same trend*: The trend of roughly 70% software project failures will continue into the future, remaining the same as it was three decades ago.

Although the software engineering discipline has been evolving fast [1], the generic waterfall model in Figure 1 can still abstract the system development cycle in four phases:

a) Phase 1 - Requirement specification and analysis. Its goal is to analyze and accurately extract the following elements from the narrated requirements: the necessary and sufficient number of functions for the target system; formal parameters for each of these functions; and the execution serializability (logical control flow) among the identified functions to ensure coherent and meaningful results. A function normally performs only one application-specific task of transforming the actual parameters into the expected result. For example, if $f(x_1, x_2)$ is a function, (x_1, x_2) are two formal parameters that would assume actual values/parameters before execution (i.e. the transformation process). The functions and their intertwined logical relationships form the *functional specification*; constraints specified for these relationships form the *constraints specification* to govern the ambit of system behavior/dynamics. The *functional* and *constraints* (F&C) *specifications* together form the domain of semantics for the system to know exactly *what to do*.

b) Phase 2 – Design specification. Details of *how the final system should work* are addressed by: i) organizing the system semantics into small manageable modules (modularization) by the principle of *information hiding*; ii) specifying how the modules should synchronize and associate; iii) proposing the subsumption hierarchy for the modules that can be separated into two basic groups by their nature: control-oriented (CO) and data-oriented (DO); higher-level CO does little computation but controls the timely invocation of other modules; the objective of the lower-level DO is to produce useful information from actual parameters for use by the higher-level modules; iv) proposing the system architecture to support the final system operation; and v) evaluating data structures and algorithms/protocols to support information retrieval and inter-modular synchronizations for coherent operations.

c) Phase 3 – Implementation. This phase aims to correctly translate the design specification into an intermediate form for: i) human understanding and manipulation, and ii) conversion into the machine-executable representation. The intermediate form is a program or software of a specific language (e.g. C++ or Visual Basic). To humans, the program syntactically represents the system semantics; the machine executes its compiled form (executable code).

d) Phase 4 – Testing and debugging. Test cases are created to validate and verify that the implemented system prototype indeed fulfils all the functions indicated in the requirement specification. Debugging a distributed application is more an art than science for we can rarely apply traditional approaches. From the literature the only recognized technique to debug distributed software effectively is program visualization (e.g. [4,5]).

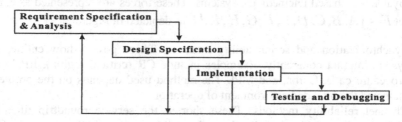

Fig. 1. Generic waterfall development life cycle

The feedback loops (Figure 1) show that if errors are found in the engineering process, changes have to be repeatedly made in the upper source(s). Too many loop-backs make the process expansive. Thus, the emphasis is on producing correct F&C specifications, and this can be achieved by using practical formal methods (e.g. Petri net). The errors in translating the F&C specifications into the design specification can be reduced by using semi-formal, semi-automatic tools such as the DBDesigner (DBD) by Microsoft. The DBD converts the semantic net in the form of a subsumption hierarchy (e.g. DOM (document object code) tree drawn in the DBD format) into logically matched XML-annotated code. The SQL system (also by Microsoft) then can convert the annotated code directly into a usable database. If the CO and DO modules are programmed in VB.net (Visual Basic for the Internet), they interact readily with the SQL database. DBD, SQL, VB.net together fulfill the *congruent automation principle* (CAP) to be explained later. If the activities in Figure 1 are supported by a management scheme that controls system migration, software changes, system versioning, and maintenance, a *configuration control* (CC) framework is formed [1].

2 Related Work

Successful software engineering in the 21st century needs to overcome a set of formidable challenges, including rapid and uncertain technological changes/emergence, cultural diversity leading to ambiguous understanding of the target system, and heterogeneity in hardware and software that prevents interoperability. The paper by Boehm [6] sums these formidable challenges nicely, and one of his guidelines is to avoid THWADI (*"that's how we've always done it"*). This applies well to developing remotely deployable ubiquitous web-based telemedicine systems, which is an emerging phenomenon of the 21st century. In reality, the THWADI guideline is unavoidable, for computing requirements evolve rapidly in different eras, governed by the Moore's Law [7]: i) Amdahl's era (early 1960s) – synchronizing sequential processes correctly was the focus; ii) Gustafson-Barsis era (mid-1980s) – parallel computing (i.e. High Performance Computing (HPC)) to yield speedup; iii) megacomputing era (mid-1990s) – distributed systems formed with an Internet basis; and iv) pervasive era (early 2000) – concern for the mobility of hardware and software entities supported by location-aware capability. Despite the rapid evolution driven by various contemporary forces, we still find that: i) the waterfall model is the foundation; ii) optimal placement of program tasks is a focal issue; and ii) coherent synchronization of these tasks is needed for correct results. From the literature we identified ten major forces that affect the success of developing remotely deployable web-based telemedicine systems. These forces are represented as entries in the set $F = \{A, B, C, D, E, F, G, H, I, J\}$ as depicted in Figure 2:

A. Synchronization and serializability methods: These govern how entities in the system interact coherently. Examples include CR (critical region), RPC (remote procedure call), Corba, and MPI. The method used depends on the problem domain and the intended environment of operation.
B. Channel reliability methods: These shorten the service roundtrip time in client/server interaction. Usually dynamic or adaptive methods are more effective than static methods [8].
C. User participation: This is a necessity for effective fast prototyping so that immediate user feedback improves the prototype. It is ideal if the user participates in all stages of the waterfall model.
D. Software engineering by parts: This is integration of software parts (modules/artifacts) built by other groups into the system being built. It can be physical code inclusions (into the system software) or logical remote invocation via predefined linkages. The parts can be in various programming languages but do not affect the final system performance [4].
E. Tools/methods for creating/managing data structures and databases: These represent the paradigm that data structures on the blueprint are realized automatically into physical databases; for example, converting a DBD drawing directly into a physical SQL database (i.e. Microsoft environment).

F. Testing and debugging tools: These support different testing and debugging situations. For example, program/system behavior visualization is suitable for monitoring distributed agent-based software in which agents are mobile in a real-time sense [4].

G. System security issues: The aim is allow a system run smoothly without unnecessary interruptions.

H. MSPM (multi-site project management): Usually teams based in different geographic locations are involved in the development of a successful enterprise software system. To eliminate ambiguity a vocabulary to bridge cultural and language differences among working groups needs to be created. The creation of such a vocabulary is regarded by many researchers as an ontological approach (i.e. the vocabulary is the "enterprise ontology") [9].

I. ICT (information communications technology): This discipline combines appropriate technologies to build an efficient web application.

J. Trend and era issues/laws: Inevitably, as the computing industry advances through various trend-setting eras and laws into today's mobility era with mobile hardware for location-aware networks and mobile software agents that migrate at will, some of the older methods and tools will be invalidated.

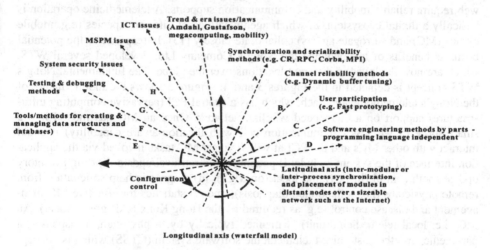

Fig. 2. Ten external forces that affect software system success

The longitudinal and latitudinal axes in Figure 2 form the backbone of the configuration control (CC) to balance these ten forces into equilibrium. Although the waterfall model is the basis for the CC, the two key issues of modular task placement into network nodes and ensuring correct task synchronization to achieve coherent results still need to be addressed. Unfortunately, no previous experience on devising an effective CC scheme for pervasive telemedicine system development has been found in the literature. The Nong's in-house experience, which used the traditional waterfall model as the basis to balance (by trial-and-error) some of the forces shown in Figure 2 is the only useful clue so far. Besides, very limited experience can be found in the literature about formulating telemedicine system architectures. The only useful example that we encountered was the UMLS (Unified Medical Language System) [10].

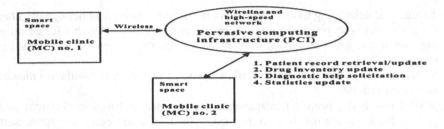

Fig. 3. A pervasive telemedicine system model

3 Nong's Telemedicine Framework Background

Telemedicine, a term that was consolidated around 1999 [12], aim is to electronically deliver healthcare (i.e. e-health) to every corner of the globe. Its realization over the mobile Internet, however, is an art for there is little experience published in the literature for this budding discipline. Since the mobile Internet supports both wireline and wireless communication technologies, interacting agents of a telemedicine system on the web require reliable mobility and communication supports. A telemedicine operation is basically a digital ecosystem, in which agents/entities of different species (e.g. mobile clinics (MC) and surrogate agents) collaborate closely [13]. In response to the potential business benefits of telemedicine the Nong's Company Ltd. developed several WTS, which are now deployed in different locations over the globe. The fundamental Nong's WTS concept is depicted in the Figures 3 and 4. Figure 3 shows the mobile nature of the Nong's telemedicine approach, which has a central PCI (pervasive computing infrastructure) support on a high-speed wireline network. Once an MC has moved into a smart space (a wireless communication cell with location-aware capability) it could interact with other MCs and the PCI at will. Typical MC tasks invoked via the application interface of the system include: i) patient record retrieval/update; ii) drug inventory update (both central (in PCI) and local (on MC)); iii) diagnostic help solicitation from remote physicians (i.e. collaborated diagnosis); and iv) statistics for effective MC management and disease control (e.g. as required by the Hong Kong SAR government). An MC (i.e. local telemedicine unit) is manned typically by: a physician, a dispenser, a paramedic, and the customized telemedicine software system (CTSS) which is conceptually depicted in Figure 4 as CAI. The CTSS is architecturally similar to the UMLS by having three distinctive layers (Figure 5) but functionally it differs by supporting real-time frontline clinical practice.

The CTSS (or WTS (web-based telemedicine system)) architecture has three layers:

a) Bottom layer (i.e. CTSS bottom-domain in Figure 5): This is the local TCM onto-core customized from the enterprise's time-honored total knowledge as logically indicated by [V] in Figure 5.
b) Middle layer (i.e. CTSS middle-domain in Figure 5): This is the semantic net (network) that fully and logically represents the local CTSS TCM onto-core in the machine process-able form. The parsing mechanism (parser) is the software that draws the logical conclusion for the query input from the top layer (e.g. $Q\{p_1, p_2, p_3\}$; $\{p_1, p_2, p_3\}$ are parameters to drive the parsing mechanism).

c) Top layer (i.e. CTSS top-domain): This is the customized application interface (CAI) specification for the target CTSS (i.e. F&C specifications together) to syntactically represent the local CTSS semantic net for human understanding. The CAI specification is made up of icons selected from IL; new icons can be created and added to IL anytime. The terms in an icon are standardized by [V]. The whole CTSS or WTS is realized from the given CAI specification by the MI paradigm, and the physical GUI of the target WTS has the same appearance as the given CAI specification.

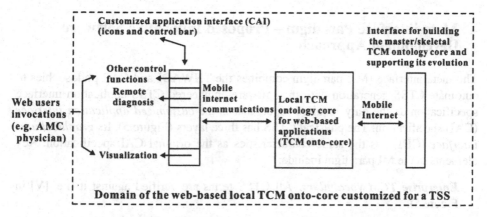

Fig. 4. Conceptualized CTSS (customized telemedicine software system)

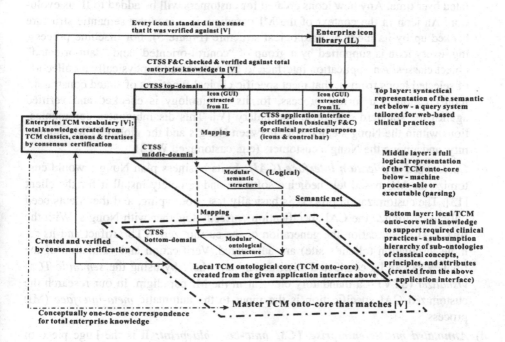

Fig. 5. The three-layer architecture of CTSS

The most engineered CTSS part is the top layer or the CAI specification because once it has been verified the whole system can be generated automatically. Working together, the three layers comprise a customized CTSS that effectively realizes the philosophical arguments of Gruber [14] in an integrated fashion. Gruber's ontology is a consensus-certified conceptualization, which is understandable to humans and meanwhile machine process-able. Guarino deepened this ontology concept by arguing that it should have a subsumption hierarchy of sub-ontologies with axiomatic associations to constrain interpretation [11].

4 Meta-interface Paradigm – Proposed Innovative Software Development Approach

The meta-interface (MI) paradigm combines the THWADI and CAP philosophies to automate CTSS generation with the software-engineered CTSS application interface specification as the only required input; that is the *customized application interface* (CAI) specification. The physical CTSS has three layers (Figure 5). Its *graphical user interface* (GUI) has the same characteristics as the original CAI specification. Key elements in the MI paradigm include:

a) *Enterprise TCM vocabulary:* All CTSS terms are verified against it (i.e. [V] in Figure 5).

b) *Unique icon library (IL):* This contains all the graphic icons that Nong's accumulated over time. Any new icons created for customers will be added to IL as evolution. An icon in the context of the MI paradigm is a modular semantic structure backed up by its modular ontological structure (Figure 5). For machine processing, every icon is supported by a group of "control-oriented" and "data-oriented" object classes. An application interface to be customized is physically a collection of selected icons from IL that meet specific clinical functions of stated constraints. Icon creation is a formal process, for its terminology is checked and verified against the standard enterprise vocabulary [V]. This disambiguates communications within the Nong's enterprise, between Nong's and the global TCM community, and among the Nong's customers (e.g. customized WTS).

c) *Customized application interface (CAI):* In its business plan Nong's would customize the MC based telemedicine software and remotely install it for the client [13]. The customization process is basically fast prototyping, and the clients need only to customize the CAI specification correctly together with Nong's. With the final CAI specification the generation of the customized WTS artifact and its remote installation (client's site) are automated. Verification and validation of the final WTS can be conducted anytime and anywhere by using the *semantic TCM visualizer* (STV) – a mandatory element in the MI paradigm. In our research the customized CAI specification is the input to the automatic *meta-interface* (MI) process.

d) *Annotated master/enterprise TCM onto-core blueprint:* It is the huge piece of annotated code (or blueprint) for the subsumption hierarchy of the entire enterprise

TCM onto-core to match the formal knowledge in the enterprise vocabulary [V]. The blueprint creation is semi-automatic to quicken rectification of errors by the group of TCM domain experts who perform consensus-certification. This semi-automatic process has two phases:

i. *Manual phase:* The DOM (document object model) tree for the master TCM onto-core has to be drawn manually. The drawing helps experts visualize and verify the necessary facts quickly against the canonical information in [V]. In fact, there are usable commercial tools in the field that can be support such drawing; the DBDesigner (DBD) by Microsoft is an example.

ii. *Automatic phase:* Firstly, the annotated blueprint is automatically generated from a drawn DOM tree. Annotation can be achieved by different metadata systems. For example XML, RDF, and OWL metadata systems are popular because the codes generated for them are interoperable [1]. In fact, the DBD system can generate the corresponding XML-annotated codes from its own drawings. Secondly, the GUI (graphical user interface) subsystem is automatically generated for the final WTS system for human interaction.

e) *Automatic CTSS/WTS database generation:* A physical CTSS/WTS is generated from the given CAI specification that indicates what portion of the enterprise TCM onto-core blueprint to be extracted automatically by the MI paradigm. The extraction, in the form of a piece of annotated code (blueprint), is then automatically instantiated into the respective local TCM onto-core.

f) *Appropriate programming language(s) for the logical object classes:* The executable forms of those functions in an icon in the IL are object classes. In the MI paradigm functions in an icon are instantiated as object classes selected from the main enterprise object library; the MI paradigm is object-based.

g) *Semantic TCM visualizer (STV):* This converts an XML-annotated code into the matching DOM tree and traces the parsing mechanism on line. In this way it verifies and validates any part of the physical CTSS anytime and anywhere.

h) *Remote CTSS installation:* The CTSS package contains: the GUI for human interaction; wireless communication capability for the MC; the CTSS database; object classes; and other auxiliary software tasks. It is sent via the web to remote sites for installation.

5   Experimental Results

Many experiments were carried out in the Nong's WTS (mobile clinics (MC) based) environment over the mobile Internet. The results verified that the novel MI paradigm proposed by this paper is indeed effective in customizing usable WTS. The set of results presented here include: i) the CAI specification customized for the physicians' diagnosis/prescription (D/P) procedure to treat patients; ii) the actual D/P GUI generated from a CAI specification by the MI paradigm; and iii) a partial DOM tree and its corresponding XML-annotated code or blueprint as visualized by using STV. The Chinese TCM terms in the results were translated into English by using the World Health Organization (WHO) standard [15].

Table 1. Traditional 4-step TCM diagnostic procedure and result examples

look ("望")	listen & smell ("聞")	question ("問")	pulse-diagnosis ("切")
e.g. pale face	e.g. cough, bad breath	e.g. headache? fever? loathe cold ambience? ("惡寒/怕冷")	e.g. taut and fast

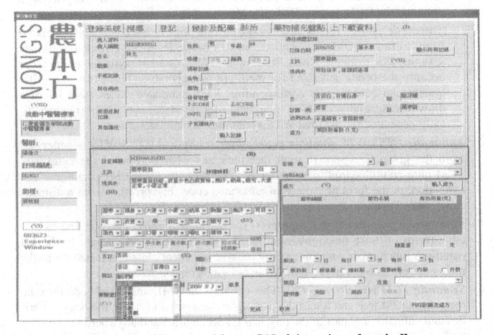

Fig. 6. The GUI generated from a CAI of chosen icons from the IL

5.1 The CAI Example

Figure 6 is a CAI specification (for generating the corresponding physical GUI) that includes: a) icon (I) – control bar; b) icon (II) – patient registration number (i.e. MX6060303001) and fields to be filled in the D/P process by the physician, including: patient's complaint ("主訴"), and diagnosis ("診斷") (e.g. illness/type (" 病"/"証") and treatment principle ("治則治法")); c) icon (III) – symptoms ("現病 史") obtained by a standard TCM diagnostic procedure; d) icon (IV) – pulse diagnosis ("脈診"); e) icon (V) – prescription(s) ("處方") to be dispensed with respect to the diagnosis; f) icon (VI) – experience window (record) entrance specific to the logon physician with medical practice registration (e.g. 003623); g) icon (IX) –diagnostic questions (e.g. Do you loathe cold ambience conditions ("惡寒/怕冷")?) and general physical inspections (e.g. complexion ("面色") – pale or red); h) icon (X) – tongue diagnosis ("舌診") (e.g. texture and coating color). Table 1 shows four steps in the traditional TCM diagnostic procedure: look ("望"), listen & smell ("聞"), question ("問"), and pulse-diagnosis ("切").

5.2 A Customized WTS Example

This example shows the operation of the physical WTS generated automatically from a given CAI (e.g. Figure 6) by the MI paradigm. The physical GUI for the operating WTS will appear the same as the parent/input CAI. In the GUI the set of symptoms, S\{ 怕冷重 (dislike cold ambience), 發熱輕 (light fever), 無汗 (no perspiration) \}, obtained from the patient were keyed-in and echoed in the symptoms window "現病史". Normally the parser will works automatically with the input query (e.g. Q\{ 怕冷重, 發熱輕, 無汗 \}). The parsing process can also be visualized by pressing the Parse button that invokes the STV (as shown in Figure 7). The parsed result for the symptoms (in the "現病史" window) includes: a) Diagnosed (診斷) illness (病): Flu (感冒) & type (証) is "wind cold" (風寒); b) Treatment principle (治則): heating & sweating (辛溫解表); and c) Prescription (處方): "荊防敗毒散".

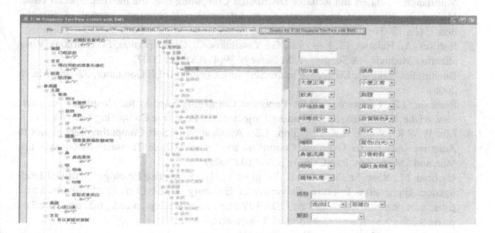

Fig. 7. Invoked STV to visualize a parsing operation

6 Conclusion

In this paper the meta-interface (MI) paradigm, which combines the THWADI and CAP philosophies, is proposed. It automates the generation of a client's CTSS directly from the given *customized application interface* (CAI) specification. This specification is constructed by "gluing" together icons selected from the enterprise icon library (IL) as part of a fast prototyping process. The automatic process extracts the portion of the subsumption hierarchy in the enterprise TCM onto-core that corresponds to the given CAI specification. The next step is to perfect the STV so that it visualizes and debugs more effectively.

Acknowledgement

The authors thank the Hong Kong Polytechnic University and the PuraPharm Group for funding the research, grants A-PA9H and ZW93.

References

1. Rifaieh, R., Benharkat, A.: From Ontology Phobia to Contextual Ontology Use in Enterprise Information System. In: Taniar, D., Rahayu, J. (eds.) Web Semantics & Ontology, Idea Group Inc. (2006)
2. Osterweil, L.J., Ghezzi, C., Kramer, J., Wolf, A.L.: Determining the Impact of Software Engineering Research on Practice, March 2008, pp. 39–49. IEEE Comp., Los Alamitos (2008)
3. Chan, C.: Ontological Methodologies, - From Open Standards Software Development to Open Standards Organizational Project Governance. Journal of Computer Science and Network Security 7(3) (March 2007)
4. Wong, A.K.Y., Lin, W.W.K., Dillon, T.S.: Local Compilation: A Novel Paradigm for Multilanguage-Based and Reliable Distributed Computing over the Internet. Special Issue: Mobile & Wireless Communications & Information Processing, Journal of Simulation 75(1), 18–31 (2000)
5. Katifori, A., Halatsis, C., Lepouras, G., Vassilakis, C., Giannopoulou, E.: Ontology Visualization Methods – A Survey. ACM Surveys 39(4) (October 2007)
6. Boehm, B.: Making a Difference in the Software Century. IEEE Computer, 32–38 (March 2008)
7. Bardram, J.E., Christensen, H.B.: Pervasive Computing Support for Hospitals: An overview of the Activity-Based Computing Project. IEEE Pervasive Computing 6(1), 44–51
8. Lin, W.W.K., Wong, A.K.Y., Dillon, T.S.: Application of Soft Computing Techniques to Adaptive User Buffer Overflow Control on the Internet. IEEE Transactions on Systems, Man and Cybernetics, Part C 36(3), 397–410 (2006)
9. Uschold, M., King, M., Moralee, S., Zorgios, Y.: The Enterprise Entology, Artificial Intelligence Applications Institute, University of Edinburg, UK, http://citesee.ist. psu.edu/cache/papers/cs/11430/ftp:zSzzSzftp.aiai.ed.ac.ukzSz pubzSzdocumentszSz1998zSz98-kerent-ontology.pdf/uschold95enterprise.pdf
10. UMLS, http://www.nlm.nih.gov/research/umls/
11. Taniar, D., Rahayu, J.W.: Web Semantics & Ontology. Idea Group Publishing (2006)
12. Kaar, J.F.: International Legal Issues Confronting Telehealth Care. Telemedicine Journal (March 1999)
13. Wong, J.H.K., Wong, A.K.Y., Lin, W.W.K., Dillon, T.S.: Dynamic Buffer Tuning: An Ambience-Intelligent Way for Digital Ecosystem. In: Proc. of the 2nd IEEE International Conference on Digital Ecosystems and Technologies (IEEE-DEST 2008), Phitsanulok, Thailand (February 2008)
14. Gruber, T.R.: A Translation Approach to Portable Ontology Specifications. Knowledge Acquisition 5(2), 199–220 (1993)
15. WHO International Standard terminologies on traditional medicine in the Western Pacific Region, ISBN 978 92 9061 248 7, World Health Organization (2007)

Cyber Biosphere for Future Embedded Systems

Franz J. Rammig

Heinz Nixdorf Institute
Universität Paderborn
Paderborn
Germany
franz@upb.de

Abstract. Future Embedded Systems are heading into a degree of complexity which is far beyond today`s level. As most technical artifacts will be interconnected in some sense ("*Internet of Things*") Embedded Systems of the future cannot be treated as isolated entities any longer. Two major tendencies to cope with this challenge can be observed. The first one takes its inspiration from the technical roots of Embedded Systems. They are looked at from their technical nature but the traditional boundaries of Embedded Systems, especially to consider them as isolated systems are overcome. This approach became well known under the name "*Cyber Physical Systems (CPS)*". The second approach observes the existence of highly successful and relatively stable systems in form of our *biosphere*. So it seems to be wise to take inspirations from the achievement of nature. This approach became rather popular under the term "*Biologically Inspired Systems*" or "*Organic Computing*"[1]. In this paper we will concentrate on the latter attempt to build the highly complex, highly sophisticated Embedded Systems of the future. Inspirations from ant colonies, from the hormone system, and from the immune system will shortly be discussed using specific examples. Some comparisons with the CPS approach will be made as well.

Keywords: Biologically Inspired Techniques, Ant Colony Algorithms, Artificial Hormone Systems, Artificial Immune Systems.

1 Introduction

Engineers are interested to build highly efficient, highly reliable, and highly deterministic systems; they are interested to keep their systems completely under control under all potential circumstances. For this purpose the embedded systems community, especially the real-time researchers have developed sophisticated solutions: deterministic real-time scheduling techniques, schedulability analysis, collision-free communication protocols, time-triggered architectures, formal proof techniques, just to mention some of them. Adapting inspirations from the biosphere, a world that seems to follow completely different approaches, appears to be strange idea at the first glance. On the other

---

[1] See http://www.organic-computing.de/ for the Organic Computing Initiative and http://www.aifb.uni-karlsruhe.de/Forschungsgruppen/EffAlg/projekte/oc/inhalte for the Organic Computing Priority Program funded by the German Science Foundation (DFG).

U. Brinkschulte, T. Givargis, and S. Russo (Eds.): SEUS 2008, LNCS 5287, pp. 245–255, 2008.
© IFIP International Federation for Information Processing 2008

hand engineers are impressed by the robustness of extremely complex biological systems. A human, made of billions of cells, interacting in a highly sophisticated manner, is continuously exposed to billions of enemies (antigens) which change their attacking strategies rapidly and in a non predictable manner. By simple MTBF calculations one would conclude that a human's lifetime should not exceed some hours. However such a complex system survives in a hostile environment for a very long time. The same can be said for any kind of complex bio-conglomerates. So, biological systems have proven to be extremely robust even in dynamically changing hostile environments. Of course engineers also are able to design highly complex systems. A today's SoC comprises a billion of transistors as well and it runs reliably for a long time. Giant SW systems like telephone switching systems are very reliable as well. What can be questioned, however, is the stability and robustness in case of changing environmental conditions or in case of unforeseen hostile circumstances. Of course biological systems can handle unforeseen situations also only to a certain amount. In cases beyond this level of flexibility the respective species disappears. However, it seems that this limit of biological flexibility is much broader than in conventional technical artifacts. From this observation it does not surprise that one of the most stable, most robust and most adaptive complex technical artifact is the internet. In fact the internet follows a couple of basic principles of biological systems like distributive design, postponing decisions and actions into the operational phase, self-organization, emerging redundancy, just to mention some of them.

Common to the highly complex systems of the future are the following key characteristics:

- complex volatile networks in which components cooperate as well as possibly compete,
- decentralized control and components acting autonomously,
- an unobservable global system state and thus components with only local knowledge,
- optimization of own benefits being the driving force of a component's cooperation,
- adapting to and learning from environmental changes as a universal ability of components,
- limited availability of resources combined with security and safety requirements.

In each of these settings, the global system state is neither observable nor would a knowledge of it (due to its complexity) be of any help. New properties emerge while the network's components adapt to and learn from other components. These fundamental characteristics raise a number of new research questions that need to be addressed in order to achieve any progress in this area. All the mentioned properties are present in biological systems as well. Therefore it seems to be attractive looking for inspirations in this domain. Biological systems seem to follow optimal strategies (or at least near-optimal ones) in the presence of partial or even unreliable information. Biological components are able to "decide" which information is relevant and which need not be considered. They follow "algorithms" reaching stable, robust, and desirable behavior in a distributed network. Biological entities find out about their right option of interaction with cooperating or even competing other components. Nature "invented" clever, adaptive, and efficient communication principles. All this is done under restricted resources and even in case of failing parts. Nature transformed most of the decisions and actions into the operational phase of biological artifacts which results in highly adaptable systems. These systems reflect on both their own and their environment's behavior and consequently change themselves. Nature provides techniques that can ensure the correctness of emergent volatile systems.

To sum up: Highly complex systems behave like global economy. By their tradition engineers tend to organize their artifacts in the way of planned economy. Nature is an economy driven by free enterprise of selfish agents. Such economies may be far away from optimality, they tend to locally show nondeterministic behavior at certain points of time. But they seem to be extremely robust on the long term. In this paper we would like to provide some hints why it could be wise for engineers to accept a certain amount of free economy as well.

2 Ant Colony Algorithms

The total biomass of ants on earth is more or less the same as the biomass of mankind. Ants can be seen as one of the most advanced examples of social bio-systems. Ant colonies can be interpreted as a specific kind of an organism, forming an interesting compromise between simple swarms of single cell life and highly organized multi-cell systems (e.g. mammals) where most cells are fixed at a specific location and play a specific role. Differently from these two extremes in an ant colony the individual constituent (an ant) is a multi-cell object, mobile, intelligent to a certain degree, but closely embedded into a global collaborative scheme. *Ant Colony Optimization* (ACO) is a cooperative meta-heuristic being successfully applied to various combinatorial optimization problems. Ants tend to find the shortest path from their nests to a food source in a relatively short time. For doing so, they communicate in an indirect manner, called *stigmergy*. Moving ants deposit traces of pheromone on their trail. On the other hand, ants have the tendency to follow trails which are marked by pheromone. This establishes a positive feedback which makes a marked trail even more attractive. Evaporation of pheromone establishes a negative feedback. When alternative trails are chosen randomly in the beginning, the pheromone level of a path is inverse proportional to the path's length with high probability. Dorigo et al. [5] were among the first to apply ACO to graph-related optimization problems like the Traveling Salesman Problem (TSP). A more general theory has been developed in his book [6], proceedings of dedicated conferences have been published as well [7, 8].

In their papers [3, 4] the authors describe the application of Dorigo's basic approach to the scheduling problem of MPEG streams via the 802.11e EDCA. For this purpose the precedence-constrained MPEG scheduling has to be mapped onto a directed graph, expressing the precedence relationships of MPEG *Groups of Pictures* (GoP). This results in a cyclic graph consisting of the various I, P, and B frames contained in the GoP being represented as nodes and the precedences as directed edges. A feasible solution represents a schedule of MPEG frames where each frame is expected to be transmitted within its (previously defined) delay bounds. On such a graph a colony of π ants is deployed. An ant of such a colony sitting on a "border" node of a partially feasible schedule selects an edge from this node to an attainable node according to a probabilistic function as in Dorigo's original work. A tour is said to be completed if all π ants of a colony have returned to the initial I-frame. Then the best selected path is evaluated by counting the number of timely scheduled frames. On each edge of this path the pheromone values are updated. The updated value is proportional to the ratio of the achieved solution and the optimal one (all frames of the GoP scheduled timely). As a result, near optimal solutions that entail higher concentration of pheromone will have a higher impact on the edge selection process in subsequent tours. In experiments this algorithm turned out to be nearly as efficient (concerning needed computation time) as a dedicated scheduling algorithm designed at our institute by the same author. However it showed a much more robust behavior with respect to rapidly changing load and transmission distortions.

Large ad hoc networks can be clustered following an approach based on division of labor in colonies of social insects like *Pheidole Rea*. The basic idea in this case is to treat each node of an ad hoc network either as a "major" ant or a "minor" one. A major represents a cluster head which means a higher workload while the minors are member nodes of clusters. The main power of the approach is originating from the built-in elasticity. Both types of species have a certain threshold to become major or minor. On the other hand they are stimulated by received signals. Whenever the strength of such signals is above a certain threshold the role of a major may change to a minor or vice versa. Typical stimuli signals are signal strengths of received messages, frequency of received messages, etc. Thresholds are established e.g. by the power reserve of a node. A cluster head with flattening power resources has a tendency to become a minor (member node), an "isolated" member node to become a cluster head; see [10] for more details. This approach again shows enormous robustness against rapidly changing situation.

In our fine-granular distributed RTOS *NanoOS*, services are distributed over the nodes of a cluster; the clusters being created as described above. The optimization goal here is to migrate services dynamically to such nodes that the global communication costs between services and application tasks requesting these services are minimized. Note that the requesting application tasks may reside on any nodes of a cluster. This problem again can be mapped onto an ACO problem. In our approach services are the equivalent of food sources, service locations are the equivalent of shortest paths, calls made by the requesters are the ants, and requesters are the nests. Wireless links form the paths which the ants can use for movement. While the requests are being routed to the destination service, they leave pheromone on the nodes. The pheromone, on the other hand, evaporates over time. This solution is further enhanced to also consider the specific workload on the destination nodes of potential migrations. In addition geographically related paths are handled in such a way that they bundle attracting force into their direction. Details can be found in [11].

3 Artificial Hormone Systems

All biological system can be seen just as a collection of individually operating cells which follow some collaborative principle of operation based on some communication means. Electrical signaling via the nerve system constitutes a means of directed communication in the sense of single-cast or multicast. Controlled and centrally coordinated actions like contraction of specific muscles to enable movement may serve as an example. In other situations when an extremely high number of potentially receiving cells have to be addressed and if those cells are widely spread across a body a multi-cast communication scheme is desirable. In bio-systems this is carried out by means of the hormone system which can be interpreted as a way of biological broadcasting. Specific chemicals are generated by the sending instance and cause reactions on the side of receiving cells. It is essential that the receiving cells can react in a specific manner. This specific reaction may depend on cell type or even on a specific cell instance and its current environmental setting. Even the set of hormones may be specific for the different cells. Hormones unknown to a certain receiver are just ignored. So the intended communication is established only between processing elements that share a joint reservoir of hormones. By this concept multi-cast can be implemented easily. This simple basic principle thus can be tailored in numerous ways to result in the desired behaviors.

In [1] the authors discuss an approach to apply concepts of artificial hormone systems to task allocation on heterogeneous processing elements. In their approach each of the processing elements and the tasks to be assigned may secret "hormones" or may react on receiving ones. This approach strictly follows a decentralized approach. Each processing element may have an individual rule set for the secretion of hormones or how to react on receiving certain ones. The only common rules are given by some agreement what hormones to be used. In their approach the authors implement a distributed feedback controller by means of two principle types of hormones, so called accelerators (positive feedback) and so called suppressors (negative feedback). The first ones are sent out to indicate the willingness of a processing element to attract additional tasks, the second one to indicate the inability to do so. The approach results in a couple of self-x properties: *self-configuration* as there is no central control, *self-optimization* as there may be included rules to re-open the assignment "market" periodically or stimulated by some events, *self-healing* as a failing task or processing element is no longer sending hormones and by this disturbs the equilibrium which causes some re-allocation. The authors have built a flexible simulation environment which allows them to experiment with a variety of parameter settings.

Stress response is a special version of a hormone system. The *"Fight-or-flight"*-theory by Walter Cannon [2] describes the reaction of humans and animals to threads. In such stress situations specific physiological actions are taking place by the sympathetic nervous system of the organism as an automatic regulation system without the intervention of conscious thought. For example, *epinephrine* a hormone is released which causes the organism to release energy to react on the threat (fight or flight). This concept is adopted to control the on-line reconfigurable real-time operating system DREAMS[2] (*Distributed Real-time Extensible Application Management System*) which has been developed by our group. This RTOS is able to manage system tasks and user tasks in the form of different "profiles" by means of a special resource manager [17]

---

[2] Recently a new version of DREAMS has been created, called **O**rganic **R**econfigurable **O**perating **S**ystem (ORCOS). It can be downloaded from https://orcos.cs.uni-paderborn.de

(*Flexible Resource Manager - FRM*). DREAMS is tailored to the special demands of self-optimizing applications. The manager tries to optimize the resource utilization at run-time. The optimization includes a safe over-allocation of resources, by putting resources that are held back for worst-case scenarios by tasks at other tasks' disposal. The interface to the FRM is called *Profile Framework*. By means of the Profile Framework the developer can define a set of profiles per application. Profiles describe different service levels of the application, including different quality and different resource requirements. All states belonging to one profile build the state space that can be reached when the profile is active. The different profiles can be assigned to specific emergency categories using a generic monitoring concept for self-optimizing systems. The intent is to protect tasks systematically against hazards or faults. These hazards or faults might result from their self-optimizing behavior themselves, but self-optimizing behavior can also support the re-allocation of resources to handle threats. The concept distinguishes four different emergency categories:

1) The system operates regularly and uses its self-optimization for the major system objectives.
2) A possible threat has been detected and the self-optimization is not only used to optimize the behavior but also to reach system states, which are considered to be safer than the current one.
3) A hazard has been detected that endangers the system. Fast and robust counter-measures, like a reflex, are performed to reach a safer state (1 or 2).
4) The system is no longer under control; the system must be immediately stopped or a minimal safe-operational mode must be warranted, to minimize damage.

The artificial hormone system is applied to ensure that the system can provide more resources to enable more efficient countermeasures whenever it experiences entering emergency category 2. The idea is, when a task of the system detects a threat for the system it releases virtual epinephrine. This distributed epinephrine forces non-critical tasks into a profile with lower resource consumption. By this, resources are freed and this permits the critical task to handle the threat more appropriately by switching into a specific emergency handling profile which usually is more resource-hungry. The virtual epinephrine carries the information how much additional re-sources the epinephrine secreting task requires to activate its threat-handling profile. It is assumed that all tasks are sorted according their safety critical nature. Like the cardiovascular system of an organism the resource manager broadcasts the epineph-rine to the tasks. Tasks with the lowest safety level have the shortest reaction time. When the epinephrine is injected into such a task it can react by switching into a spe-cial profile with lower resource requirements. The task then updates the information inside the epinephrine how much resources are still required. This updated epineph-rine then is secreted again, by this over-writing the hormone already received by tasks at higher safety levels which react more slowly. By this technique finally every task has information about the threat and can react accordingly. The complexity of this process is linear with respect to the number of tasks. The reaction of the tasks to the epinephrine ("consuming" it by update) is done in a short, constant time. Details can be found in [9].

4 Artificial Immune Systems

Immunocomputing intends to establish another kind of computing. The main idea is to copy the immune system's ability to identify abnormal objects ("*antigens*") with high separation precision and to attack such antigens using adapted means ("*antibodies*") in an extremely efficient manner. All this is done in a distributed but interlinked manner and is quickly adapted to varying situations (occurrence of previously unknown antigens) by a sophisticated learning ability. As biological immune systems are based on chemical reactions of proteins, immunocomputing is based on the "*Formal Protein*" as its basic element. A protein is an essential component of organisms and participates in every process within cells. Proteins constitute *epitopes* present in antigens and antigen presenting cells. Proteins constitute also *paratopes* present in antibodies. An epitope is the minimum molecular structure that is able to be recognized by the immune system. One epitope matches with a paratope in molecular recognition. An epitope or a paratope are made of around 10 amino-acids. An antigen presenting cell is a cell that has digested an antigen and presents in its surface an epitope. A protein is composed of amino-acids arranged in a linear chain. The 3D shape or tertiary structure of the epitope is recognized by a paratope. It means an epitope is a kind of surface protein. That is why proteins will be seen as the basic element in immunocomputing.

Cytokines are introduced as an additional concept into immunocomputing [18] to establish collaboration. In biological systems cytokines are groups of proteins secreted by many types of cells. Each cytokine binds to a specific cell's surface receptor signaling a specific action i.e. differentiation into plasma cells, antibody secretion or cell death. They bind also through own receptors constituted from proteins, too.

The basic entities in a biological immune system and therefore also in immunocomputing are so-called *B-cells*. B-cells in the immune system secrete antibodies, i.e. the actuators of immune reaction. On the other hand they also secrete cytokines in order to signal something to another cell. This introduces a positive feedback into the immune system. Then, a B-cell will be taken as a generic cell V_i with two components expressed by $V_i = (c_i, P_i)$ where $c_i \in N$ represents a cytokine (action to be carried out) and $P_i \in R^q = ((p_1)_i, ..., (p_q)_i)$ is a point in a q-dimensional space. P lies within a cube $max\{|(p_1)_i|, ..., |(p_q)_i|\} \leq 1$. It represents a protein transformed into the so-called FIN (*Formal Immune Network*) space. In biological terms it represents an antigen binding site (antigen detection) of an antibody or, simplifying, an antibody.

We applied cFIN (*cytokine FIN*) to build self-repairing FPGAs, following a *Built-in Self-Test (BIST)* approach. The circuit under test receives a test pattern and the response is evaluated by means of cFINs. In this case, an antibody represents the expected output, transformed into the FIN space. An antigen is the response of the circuit under test. A cytokine represents the action to be taken for fault recovery purposes. It is important that the system has to be trained beforehand using a training matrix $V(c,A)$. $A = A_1,...,A_n$ with $A_i = (Input_i, Output_i, Stimuli_i, State_i)$ is a matrix with information about expected responses under defined input patterns. Each expected or unexpected response then is linked to an action expressed by c with $c_i = (self_i, action_i)$. The first component indicates the differentiation between *self* and *not self*, the second one identifies the action to be taken. Using the cytokine communication system, on-line learning can take place during operation. Details can be found in [16]. For general readings on immunocomputing see [19, 20].

5 Discussion

The three approaches presented here are just examples of a broad potential when getting inspiration from nature. Of course these approaches include much more sophistication than the simple principles presented here just to initiate a discussion. In any case it is wise to collect more profound knowledge about biological systems before gaining real benefit out of them for engineering disciplines. Even the three sketches presented here, however, show some interesting similarities. The reason is that nature "invented" life by "inventing" cells. For billions of years life did exist solely in form of single cell entities. So whatever emerged as biological system remains a collection of individual cells, a collection of cells which may cooperate very closely, a collection of cells where the cells may be differentiated into highly specialized ones. However the cells never lost their property of autonomy. Biological systems are federated ones. Social insects may be seen as a copy of the same principle; now using more elaborate "macro cells". And this principle can be recursively extended. It may not be so surprising that the federation principle can be found using more and more complex "cells", a principle that reaches up to human societies. Federation seems to be a very useful principle to achieve robustness. Usually there is some dedication, some division of labor in federated systems. The degree of this division of labor increases by the complexity of the federal community. However it can be observed that in most cases there is more or less elasticity. Components of a community dedicated to specific tasks can take over other tasks whenever they receive stimulations beyond their present threshold. This observation certainly is a valuable inspiration for future embedded systems. Our own experiments in the areas of service migration, clustering, or real-time scheduling of media streams did show very robust and fault tolerant behavior when following this principle. Division of labor together with elasticity provides a good compromise between efficiency and avoidance of single points of failure.

Federated systems following the basic principle of delegation (distribute globally only what to do, let the individual components decide how to do) rely on an adequate communication scheme. It can be observed that nature created the entire bandwidth from unicast/multicast (nerve system) to multicast/broadcast (secreting hormones/cytokines or pheromones) and from dedicated "cabling" (nerve system) via *"powerline communication"* (hormones/cytokines) to wireless (pheromone). Common to all these communication approaches is the fact that they are tailored for federated systems. All biological systems are made as a collection of cells and each single cell is equipped with sensors and actuators. All higher order constructions make use of this basic principle. By the same reason similarities can be observed between the different communication concepts. Nerve threads are made by sequences of nerve cells communicating via their synapses making use of the ability of any cell to cause and sense electrical potentials. Other capabilities of cells for sensing and acting are given by the ability to expose specific proteins on their surface and to sense the surface of proteins (necessary in any case as part of a cell's digestion system). This principle is used within the hormone system, in immune-networks via cytokines, and also when using pheromone for communication. Common to these techniques is again the principle of delegation. It is up to a cell how to react on a sensed signal. This reaction may depend of the specific cell type or even cell instance (thus enabling multicast) or on actual environmental or state conditions of a cell. An interesting aspect is the reuse of energy flows (cardiovascular system) to transmit messages. This is a kind of biological powerline communication. Stigmergy can be seen as transforming hormones or cytokines to a more general environment. An important principle in any case is a decay mechanism for messages, evaporation of pheromones in case of ant colony communication via stigmergy. Of course, the communication demands in technical systems differ. However it is worth to consider biological communication techniques as inspiration as well. Large, complex systems need a certain degree of self-organization or, even less tight, self-coordination. Under such circumstances pre-planned communication systems seem to be no longer adequate. By the principle of delegation the amount of information to be communicated can be reduced dramatically. We discussed in this paper techniques to make efficient use of stigmergy as part of ACO solutions for service migration and soft real-time scheduling. Hormone-based communication has been discussed in applications for task allocation and stress management while cytokine-based communication plays an important role in our work on self-healing FPGAs based on artificial immune systems. All these communication techniques turned out to be sufficiently efficient and extremely robust.

More recently the discussion about Cyber Physical Systems (CPS) emerged. One of the major arguments within this community is that the traditional separation into functional and non functional properties of computation seems to be no longer adequate when building the deeply embedded but widely distributed systems of the future. Especially abstracting away time which in most areas of computing is a common principle turns out to be a dangerous assumption. The solutions proposed include the usage of a strict and very precise global time source and then abstracting this source to a "*sparse time*" model [14, 15]. Based on such a model adequate OO architectures can be built, e.g. using the TMO approach of UC Irvine [12, 13]. This approach seems to be completely different from the techniques of handling time in biological systems. They tend to follow an approach to approximate and correct afterwards if the approximation turns out to be wrong or not precise enough. It definitely makes no sense to look for inspirations from biology in an ideological manner. Technology opens potentials that were not available within evolution up to now and these potentials have to be used. Establishing a precise global time base was made possible by GPS and comparable systems and as it is available it should be used. Other aspects addressed in CPS research, however, match relatively well with inspirations we can get from biological systems. As already mentioned several times in this paper, all biological systems are build bottom-up using a strict cell-based approach. These cells are more comparable to components than to objects in the OO sense. Communication is done by signaling values; it then is up to the components how to react. This basic principle of delegation constitutes much of the success of biological systems and should be considered as a basic principle for CPSs as well. Biological systems do not distinct between functional and non functional properties. Nature always is aware of resources, is making use of what is available (considers the available "*platform*"), provides solutions how to handle lacking resources to a certain amount. This is another principle to be considered as inspiration when building CPSs. If such systems are built in a bottom-up manner by creating cells based on and closely adapted to available platforms, being sensitive for certain sets of rules, and being highly adaptive, capable of learning, then many of the

CPSs' challenges might be solvable. Building a generic framework, a *Cyber Biosphere (CBS)* may be an attempt worth to be worked on.

6 Conclusion

In this paper some arguments are presented for taking inspirations from biology when designing the complex technical artifacts of the future. Using some examples it has been shown, that such inspirations may be helpful especially when the systems have to behave in a robust manner in rapidly changing environments. However, one never should make the mistake just to copy nature into technical artifacts. Our artifacts have to work in a dependable manner for some years or decades. Nature "thinks" in terms of millions of years, short-term behavior is of minor interest. Nature optimizes the long-term global performance; the specific entity is of no interest. Engineers have to consider the single entity, they are liable for. So, taking inspiration from nature should always be an option but never more than an option among others.

References

1. von Renteln, A., Bringschulte, U., Weiss, M.: Examining Task Distribution by an Artificial Hormone System Based Middleware. In: Proc. 11th Symposium on Object-Oriented Real-Time Distributed Computing (ISORC 2008), pp. 119–123. IEEE, Los Alamitos (2008)
2. Cannon, W.B.: Bodily Changes in Pain, Hunger, Fear and Rage: An Account of Recent Research into the Function of Emotional Excitement. Appleton-Century-Crofts (1929)
3. Ditze, M.: Evaluation of an Ant Colony Optimization Based Scheduler for the Transmission of Multimedia Traffic in the 802.11e EDCA. In: Proc. of 3rd ACM Interntl. Worksh. on Wire-less Multimedia Networking and Performance Modeling (WMUNEP), Chania, Greece (2007)
4. Ditze, M., Becker, M.: An Improved Adaptive ACO Meta Heuristic for Scheduling Multimedia Traffic Across the 802.11e EDCA. In: Proc. of 15th Annual Multimedia Computing and Networking (MMCN 2008), San Jose, USA (2008)
5. Dorigo, M., Maniezzo, V., Clorni, A.: The Ant System: Optimization by a Colony of Co-operating Agents. IEEE Transactions on Systems, Man, and Cybernetics 26, 944–955 (1996)
6. Dorigo, M., Stützle, T.: AntColony Optimization. MIT Press, Cambridge (2004)
7. Dorigo, M., Birattari, M., Blum, C., Gambardella, L.M., Mondada, F., Stützle, T. (eds.): ANTS 2004. LNCS, vol. 3172. Springer, Heidelberg (2004)
8. Dorigo, M., Gambardella, L.M., Birattari, M., Martinoli, A., Poli, R., Stützle, T. (eds.): ANTS 2006. LNCS, vol. 4150, pp. 3–540. Springer, Heidelberg (2006)
9. Giese, H., Montealegre, N., Müller, T., Oberthür, S.: Acute stress response for self-optimizing mechatronic systems. In: IFIP Conference on Biologically Inspired Cooperative Computing (BICC 2006). Springer, Heidelberg (2006)
10. Heimfarth, T., Janacik, P., Rammig, F.J.: Self-Organizing Resource-Aware Clustering for Ad Hoc Networks. In: Obermaisser, R., Nah, Y., Puschner, P., Rammig, F.J. (eds.) SEUS 2007. LNCS, vol. 4761, pp. 319–328. Springer, Heidelberg (2007)

11. Heimfarth, T., Janacik, P.: Experiments with Biologically-InspiredMethods for Service Assignment in Wireless Sensor Networks. In: IFIP Conference on Biologically Inspired Cooperative Computing (BICC 2008). Springer, Heidelberg (2008)
12. Kim, K.H.: Object Structures for Real-Time Systems and Simulators. IEEE Computer 30(8), 325–333 (1997)
13. Kim, K.H., Li, Y., Rim, K.-W., Shokri, E.: A Hierarchical Resource Management Scheme Enabled by the TMO Programming Scheme. In: Proc. 11th Symposium on Object-Oriented Real-Time Distributed Computing (ISORC 2008), pp. 370–376. IEEE, Los Alamitos (2008)
14. Kopetz, H.: Embedded System Complexity. In: Self-optimizing Mechatronic Systems: Design the Future. 7th International Heinz Nixdorf Symposium, pp. 469–486. HNI-Verlagsschriftenreihe (2008)
15. Kopetz, H.: The Complexity Challenge in Embedded System Design. In: Proc. 11th Symp. on Object-Oriented Real-Time Distributed Computing (ISORC 2008), pp. 3–12. IEEE, Los Alamitos (2008)
16. Montealegre, N., Rammig, F.: Immuno-repairing of FPGA designs. In: IFIP Conference on Biologically Inspired Cooperative Computing (BICC 2008). Springer, Heidelberg (2008)
17. Oberthür, S., Böke, C.: Flexible resource management - a framework for self-optimizing real-time systems. In: Kleinjohann, B., Gao, G.R., Kopetz, H., Kleinjohann, L., Rettberg, A. (eds.) Proceedings of IFIP Working Conference on Distributed and Parallel Embedded Systems (DIPES 2004), pp. 177–186. Kluwer Academic Publishers, Dordrecht (2004)
18. Tarakanov, A.O., Kvachev, S.V., Sukhorukov, A.V.: A formal immune network and its implementation for on-line intrusion detection. In: Gorodetsky, V., Kotenko, I., Skormin, V.A. (eds.) MMM-ACNS 2005. LNCS, vol. 3685, pp. 394–405. Springer, Heidelberg (2005)
19. de Castro, L.N., Timmis, J.: Artificial Immune Systems: A New Computational Approach. Springer, London (2002)
20. Timmis, J., Bentley, P.J., Hart, E.: ICARIS 2003. LNCS, vol. 2787. Springer, Heidelberg (2003)

Leveraging GIS Technologies for Web-Based Smart Places Services

Cristiano di Flora and Christian Prehofer

Office of the CTO, Nokia, Finland
{cristiano.di-flora,christian.prehofer}@nokia.com
http://www.nokia.com

Abstract. This paper describes our experiences and lessons learnt in building a Geographic Information System (GIS) specifically designed for indoor location-based services within our smart places infrastructure. The proposed system was built by mashing-up commodity Open Source software and novel research prototypes realized within our labs. The overall approach relies on intense usage of standard web technologies and REpresentational State Transfer (REST) APIs as a way of enabling easy mashup of off-the-shelf and proprietary components. The key design and implementation aspects of our solution are described in detail, including a discussion on how we represented and augmented the concept of indoor location within our services. Further, we show how we integrated them with commodity GIS services originally designed for outdoor scenarios.

Keywords: Indoor, GIS, Smart Spaces.

1 Introduction

A smart space is a multi-user, multi-device, dynamic interaction environment that enhances a physical space by virtual services [3]. These services enable the participants to interact with each other as well as with other objects in the smart space. Indoor smart spaces are of particular interest in this context because people spend most of their time indoor rather than outdoor, which in turn makes the potential impact of indoor Location-Based Services (LBS) much bigger than that of outdoor LBS.

There has been considerable research and commercial success on outdoor GPS-based LBS, which motivated us to focus on services for indoor smart places. This paper describes our experiences and lessons learnt in building a Geographic Information System (GIS) specifically designed for indoor location-based services within our smart places infrastructure. While many research prototypes are built from scratch, our focus here is to understand how existing GIS technologies can be used for our mobile, indoor solution. In this way, we aim both to extend the scope of GIS systems and to use them as standards for indoor smart place applications. The proposed system was built by mashing-up commodity Open Source software and novel research prototypes realized within our labs. The overall approach relies on intense usage of standard web technologies and REpresentational

U. Brinkschulte, T. Givargis, and S. Russo (Eds.): SEUS 2008, LNCS 5287, pp. 256–267, 2008.

State Transfer (REST) APIs as a way of enabling easy mashup of off-the-shelf and proprietary components.

The paper is organized as follows. Section 2 discusses the rationale behind our work and related research. The key design and implementation aspects of our solution are described in detail in Sections 3 and 4, respectively, including a discussion on how we represented and augmented the concept of indoor location within our services, as well as on how we integrated them with commodity GIS services originally designed for outdoor scenarios. Section 5 concludes the paper by outlining the main lessons learnt and future research directions.

2 Motivation and Background

There is considerable research on ubiquitous and pervasive computing, also recently focusing more on internet of things or ambient computing. Many research projects have developed and trialed ubiquitous services. Also, several projects have developed software platforms and frameworks for this purpose. There is extensive literature on this, for instance [4] surveys 29 approaches up to 2004. This survey covers many systems for distributed mobile computing and most of them consider location information, even though positioning technology was not widely spread at this time. There is also more recent work on indoor positioning services, such as [5,13], and also on symbolic location models, going beyond plain coordinates [6].

GPS based LBS have been widely successful and have created an enormous ecosystem of applications using such services. It could even be argued that the easy access of web-based map tools has fueled the integration of applications by using the mashup approach. For instance, it is now very common for web-based services to show geo-tagged items on a map application. These interactive and integrated web-based applications have gained enormous momentum and are also labeled Web 2.0 technologies. Web 2.0 basically means that Web-sites are interactive, that users are actually creating content, and that the content and applications can be combined by application mashup and tagging of content.

This issue has been noted and research on user generated content for ubiquitous systems has been developed, e.g. in [7], focusing on annotating and user generated content. We think that there are a number of more essential research issues towards a wide spread eco-system of indoor positioning services. In our view, the key issues for the widespread usage of indoor positioning services are as follows:

- establishing common standards and practices for indoor positioning and map services which are interoperable and easily available;
- integrating indoor positioning services into existing web-based services;
- enabling mobile, context aware applications which are easy to deploy and use;
- ensuring privacy and security regarding personal data such as location information.

Regarding the first item, we see several missing pieces. First, indoor maps are currently not widely available in well-known standard formats, protocols, and positioning infrastructures. While GPS is nowadays widely available outdoors, there is no such established and deployed indoor positioning technology. Moreover, most of them need dedicated device-side or infrastructure-side hardware. Indoor positioning has been using very different technologies such as bluetooth, RFID or WLAN based. Even further, there are no established standards for handling maps and geo-spatial data, whereas such standards are available for outdoor LBS [12]. Our approach here is to build on WLAN based positioning, which we see as a widely available technology and further use such open standards for geospacial information systems for indoor settings.

Regarding the second issue above, integrating with existing services is a must, as such services not only provide considerable technology but also toolkits and substantial amount of already available geospatial data as, for example, in outdoor maps applications. This may also include personal data, such as private contacts or pictures. We also observe here that most of these application mashups use technologies which are simple and integrate easily into web applications, such as REpresentational State Transfer (REST) APIs and RSS feeds.

Another problem is that deploying mobile services is difficult, as there is a large variety of devices and different operating systems (in different version) on the market. Furthermore, these devices can be quite different in terms of resources like memory and connectivity. This problem has hampered the deployment of mobile services in general, and it is more severe in our case as we also want to integrate positioning information with other context data. We are focusing on web based applications as they are easy to access, to deploy, and to manage. However, they do not have access to local context data of the user. Different options can be chosen in this context, based on downloadable client software for context collection as well also using upcoming standards for browser-based access to context data such as the W3C Delivery Context Client Interface (DCCI) initiative [16].

We focus in this paper on the above challenges. In summary, we show how to use GIS solutions for indoor settings and show how the web can be used as a platform for these services. This covers connecting to services in other web based applications. We also discuss how to integrate context information into our service. A similar architecture for mobile devices is presented in [1], where the location context data is sent separately to a server, while the service is hosted from a web server which obtains the context data from this server. This paper focuses on visibility models and does not cover indoor positioning aspects as done here. Other works on applying mobile GIS solutions are for instance [8], which focuses on tour guide applications. [5] focuses on indoor GIS for mobile devices, but does not address application mashup and platform aspects nor interactive JavaScript frontends as we do here.

Another challenge, which is closely tied with the above ones, is to connect with (other) applications and enable application mashups while preserving privacy. The issue is that ubiquitous context information is typically privacy sensitive and existing application mashup techniques do not support this suffciently. We do not cover in full detail more secure ways for application mashup. Here, we see a few key ingredients emerging, such as OpenID and OpenAuth [19], which rely on novel and more flexible, decentralized approaches to authentication and authorization and thus can provide a mashup-friendly security infrastructure.

3   The Proposed Web-Based Indoor GIS

3.1   The Web as a Platform for Smart Places

Before discussing how we designed and implemented our indoor GIS, it is worth shedding some light on the architecture of the overall web based smart spaces platform that the GIS is part of. A detailed discussion of this architecture goes beyond the scope of this article. The interested reader may refer to [11] for further details about it. In this sub-section we will focus on the key design decisions underlying this architecture, and on their effects and implications on the proposed GIS solution. Compared to related work in this area, the decisions that characterize our approach are as follows:

HTTP-based communication: HTTP and web services are used as the primary means for integrating software across devices in the smart space, similarly to what currently happens on the Internet, where HTTP forms the cross platform glue that allows mashups across such an extremely heterogeneous network infrastructure like the Internet.

Reuse of existing web technology: a key problem with existing solutions in the ubiquitous and pervasive computing research community is that they are rarely reusable. By relying on existing web technology, the infrastructure opens up to a large number of devices already available in the current market.

Multiple runtimes for application execution: High end mobile devices are now offering a much wider range of runtimes for implementing and running applications and services, including traditional Java and C++ runtimes as well as support for Python and other scripting languages. In this way, platform developers can use several run times. This means that many existing components used on the web can be used in a smart space context as well. Moreover, having the basic location enablers available through HTTP based communication, makes it possible and easy to mashup local (both situated and on device) and remote location-based web services all together.

The system is organized in multiple layers, which are depicted in Figure 1 and briefly described in the following. It is worth noting that, as far as indoor GIS components are concerned, in this sub-section we will only describe their very high-level role within the overall Smart Places platform picture. Please refer to Section 4.2 for further details about how we designed the GIS components and what commodity components we included in them.

The **Base Platform & Communication** layer contains several commodity commercial and/or open source components that we see as necessary to realize a

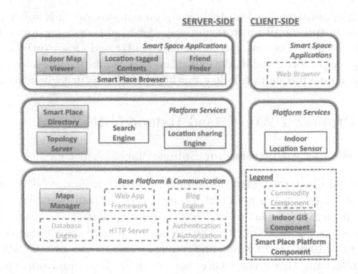

Fig. 1. Bird's eye view of our Smart Places platform, including server-side (left side) and client-side (right side) components. Greyed boxes represent Indoor GIS components. White boxes represent either commodity open source components (dashed border boxes) or smart places platform specific components (solid border boxes).

full web platform in the smart space. Using commodity web components allows us to bring many features to the smart space such as, for example, easy creation and deployment of services using well known authoring/distribution tools and framework for web applications, user management and security solutions, database and content management systems. As far as location-awareness support is concerned, the platform currently includes a **Maps Manager** component, which is in charge of providing Create Read Update Delete (CRUD) primitives for indoor maps data, i.e., raster layers representing building and floor plans, as well as several features (vector) layers representing floor topology elements (rooms, corridors, halls) and static Points-of-Interests (e.g., in an airport smart place, they could include restaurants, shops, check-in desks, terminals, gates, and other categories of interest to people visiting that space).

Platform Services can be created by using the technologies in the **Base Platform & Communication** layer. A few typical platform services are shown in Figure 1. They include two actual indoor GIS components, namely **Topology Server** and **Smart Place Directory**. The **Topology Server** is in charge of providing low-level information about the physical structure of the available smart places, such as for example details about how a given building is structured in floors, wings, and rooms. Places are modeled by using a hybrid hierarchical location model [6], and each physical location is assigned a URI that other services and applications can use as tags to associate items (e.g. media contents, blog posts, user location) to a certain physical location. The **Smart Place Directory** acts as a mediator between **Smart Space Applications** and the other indoor GIS components of the platform (i.e., components belonging to either the **Platform Services** or **Base Platform & Communication** layers). It provides a set of REST APIs that allow **Smart Space Applications** to access other **Platform Services** and **Base Platform & Communication** functionality through a consistent and common API. The API allows CRUD access to most of the location-dependent data available in the smart place, such as people location, location-specific contents, and POIs, in a web-application friendly way. In fact, it supports several widely adopted data-interchange formats, including XML-based formats like ATOM and RSS feeds, as well as more lightweight formats such as the JavaScript Object Notation (JSON). All the mentioned components so far are intended to be deployed on the server-side.

Smart Space Applications re-use and combine the **Platform Services** functionality with other on-device features in order to provide meaningful and helpful functionality to end-users. These may be web applications, which can be accessed using a browser and which can be hosted on the mobile web application server, or alternatively they can be implemented as stand alone applications written using any of the existing device specific development kits and that access the deployed **Platform Services** through http-based communication. In Figure 1 we show a few key examples of such applications, which are described in the following. The **Smart Place Browser** represents a very generic entry point to available applications, providing an AJAX API for **Smart Space Applications** developers to create new end-user applications. The API exposes and leverages the key abstractions implemented by **Platform Services** to a developer-friendly interface. New applications, such as the **Indoor Map Viewer**, **Location-tagged Contents**, or **Friend Finder**, can be easily implemented on top of this API, as we will show in Section 4.2.

It is worth noting that, as Figure 1 clearly shows, our approach is based on a very thin-client model, in which no particular **Base Platform & Communication** or **Smart Space Applications** components are assumed to be deployed and pre-installed on the client-side. In fact, in order to use the services, the client-side just needs to have a web browser capable of rendering rich web applications. Additional components, such as for example the **Indoor Location Sensor** in Figure 1, might be required in order to enable usage of some applications (like the **Friend Finder**) or to improve user experience with other applications (e.g., to automatically adapt or initialize the UI of the **Indoor Map Viewer** and **Location-tagged Contents** applications based on the actual indoor location of the end-user).

3.2   The Adopted Indoor-Positioning Technique

The proposed solution relies on an experimental WLAN indoor positioning technique under research and development at Nokia Research Center. The technique is based on WLAN scanning and on further processing of the scanning results, including measurement of the received signal strength from all reachable access points, from which the current location of the mobile device is calculated. All steps are performed on the terminal side, e.g. on end-users smart phone or PDA. In the rest of this sub-section we will just shed some light on the key aspects of this technique that are required in order to understand the herewith described indoor GIS solution. The interested reader can refer to [9] for further details on its design and implementation.

One interesting aspect of the adopted indoor positioning technique lies in its quick and easy deployment in out-of-the-lab real-world settings. In fact, the technique only requires a-priori knowledge of a list of known WLAN APs along with information about their physical location in the target building (which is typically a well-known piece of information for, but it does not require any off-line measurements of the received signal strength nevertheless. In other words, no radio maps of the target environment and related calibration of the algorithm are required, which in turn makes the proposed smart places infrastructure more easy to set-up than other state-of-the-art solutions [10].

The outcome of the proposed algorithm is a symbolic location information structured according to the location model mentioned in Section 3.1. It is worth noting that the concepts of building, floor, and section could be eventually replaced by other concepts and semantics if needed. In other words, different symbolic location models with different granularities could be adopted as far as the technique is accurate enough to support the required granularity. For example, in an environment with very large sections and rooms, such as a shopping mall or an airport, the model could also take into account the concept of rooms within a single section.

4   Implementation and Prototyping

4.1   Implementing the Indoor GIS Prototype

In Section 3.1 we introduced the main indoor GIS components at a very high-level of detail. Since we wanted to create a practical GIS solution for indoor smart spaces that could work also from mobile devices, we needed to combine the web-based smart space platform and the indoor positioning technique, described in Section 3.1 and 3.2, respectively, with additional components providing traditional GIS functionality, such as maps, navigation, and geo-spatial queries support to commercial mobile devices.

In compliance with our overall smart spaces approach described in Section 3, we decided to rely on open APIs and protocols suitable for integration with web-based applications and services. In the following we discuss a few key implementation decisions that we needed to take when prototyping the indoor GIS part of our smart places platform. In addition, we also provide further details about how indoor GIS components interact one with each other in order to fulfill their responsibilities. More specifically, we describe how we implemented and prototyped our first example of an indoor GIS system based on the design guidelines and concepts described in Section 3. The overall architecture of the implemented prototype is depicted in Figure 2.

When implementing the first prototype we had to satisfy the key requirement of providing simple REST APIs for other services to create composite functionality (mashups) out of the basic building boxes provided by our platform. To

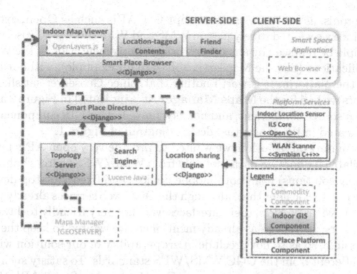

Fig. 2. The architecture of our indoor GIS implementation prototype. Greyed boxes represent Indoor GIS components. White boxes represent either commodity open source components (dashed border boxes) or smart places platform specific components (solid border boxes). Dashed lines, solid lines, and dash-dotted lines represent interaction related to Indoor Map Viewer, Location-tagged Contents, and Friend Finder case study applications, respectively.

this aim, we implemented the **Smart Place Directory** in the Python programming language by using the Django web application framework. Using the Django framework enabled us to quickly implement different facades for the same back-end data, in order to support CRUD interfaces to manage location-dependent smart place resources based on all the data interchange formats (JSON, ATOM, RSS) mentioned in Section 3.1. Similarly, most of the realized web services were implemented as Django applications. This gave us a lot of flexibility in designing the actual web service interfaces we wanted to use to expose the indoor location-dependent data stored in our back-end.

As far as the **Maps Manager** component is concerned, we wanted to rely as much as possible on established standards for representing indoor GIS data, such as maps, points-of-interests, and related meta-data: to this aim, we decided to adopt the Open Geospatial Consortium (OGC) Web Map Service (WMS) and Web Feature Service (WFS) [12] to represent maps and POIs in the **Maps Manager** component. This decision was motivated not only by technical requirements, but also by our higher level goal of evaluating how easy and feasible was the idea of using commodity GIS solutions to support indoor LBS. Several commodity implementations of WMS/WFS servers were available in both the commercial and open source community. After evaluating the different available options, we decided to adopt the open source Geoserver platform [14], which provided quite a complete implementation of WMS and WFS specifications. Geoserver was also very well integrated with other GIS tools (such as, for example, uDig [17] or GRASS GIS [18] standalone tools, as well as with JavaScript GIS APIs such as OpenLayers [15]). However, since we wanted to rely just on WMS and WFS services, Geoserver could be in principle be replaced by any other working implementation of the WMS and WFS specifications (like the Mapserver software for example), without affecting the rest of the platform. It is worth noting that, since Geoserver satisfied all the requirements we had for the **Maps Manager**, it is indicated in Figure 2 as a commodity open source component, and not as a novel indoor GIS component as previously indicated in the conceptual design diagram of Figure 1.

When designing our solution, we wanted to provide very open APIs for accessing the available Indoor GIS data (not only from WMS/WFS sources but also from other existing solutions) from both mobile devices and fixed/desktop devices. To this aim we had to consider that, although the OGC web services already provided a comprehensive set of APIs, their interfaces were not very friendly to JavaScript / Ajax developers. Moreover, as already mentioned, we wanted to keep the APIs as open as possible, so as to not preclude interoperability of our solution with other protocols different from the OGC WMS/WFS standards. To satisfy such requirements we decided to adopt the open source OpenLayers JavaScript API [15], which provided quite a comprehensive and developer-friendly set of JavaScript abstractions to deal with most common GIS functionality (e.g., dynamic creation of maps by mashing up map data coming from different sources, DOM interface to most of the supported GIS data representation formats) while solving already a lot of common cross-browser issues related to differences in the low-level JavaScript APIs of different browser engines.

4.2   Evaluating the Indoor GIS Prototype

In order to validate and to refine our JavaScript GIS interfaces, we implemented a case study application, namely **Indoor Map Viewer**, which combined our indoor GIS back-end services and accessed them through an OpenLayers interface. Similarly, in order to test the indoor location sensing feature, we implemented a **Friend Finder** application which allowed end-users to check their own friends' location, to see it on a map, and to evaluate the distance between themselves and their friends in the smart place. In order to show indoor maps, the **Friend Finder** application re-used most of the **Indoor Map Viewer** functionality. Similarly, in order to validate and refine the location-based search functionality, we implemented a **Location-tagged Contents** case study application, which allowed end-users to generate, search, and retrieve location-based contents, such as pictures, videos, text documents, and blog posts and comments.

The implemented applications allowed us to evaluate and refine the web-based approach to indoor LBS service provisioning to commercial mobile devices. The implemented applications confirmed the feasibility of using web technologies for fast and easy deployment of smart places services. Most of the time was spent to implement and refine the business logic of our indoor GIS components, and we were able to easily deploy and run the services on a heterogeneous device base. As for server-side components, we were able to deploy them on Linux, Windows, and Apple Mac Os X devices. The implemented case study examples, realized as Ajax applications, could be accessed from mobile devices, including Nokia S60 devices as well as Linux Internet Tablets (Nokia N800 and N810), and in general from any device running a web browser that included either the Mozilla or Safari web engines (including desktop / laptop clients).

As far as JavaScript clients for geospatial services are concerned, using Open-Layers raised a few performance issues for resource constrained devices like the Nokia S60 devices. These issues included at least the following problems. The first problem consisted in that dynamic memory footprint requirements of OpenLay-ers are still too large with respect to a not negligible set of commercial devices. OpenLayers maps initialization requires about 2.5 MB of RAM memory to be dy-namically allocated, and further usage of some special OpenLayers controls can easily increase the amount of dynamically allocated RAM up to 5 or 6 MB. The dynamic memory footprint analysis also showed that dynamic memory alloca-tion in OpenLayers components has not been optimized for memory constrained devices. A lot of RAM resources, allocated by OpenLayers code, were not re-leased, thus leading to frequent and not negligible memory leaks, which in turn caused also more recent and powerful devices to return memory full errors when trying to visualize some of the implemented applications. While these dynamic memory issues do not cause any problems in desktop or Internet Tablet devices, on certain low-end or less recent devices (e.g. Nokia N80 or E70) it was impos-sible to run the implemented applications, due to the limited amount of RAM memory available on those devices. We believe that this problem will be solved in future devices, since the amount of RAM memory available on such devices is rapidly increasing. However, the memory leaking problems can only be solved with a different and more efficient memory allocation / deallocation approach in OpenLayers implementation. We believe that similar problems may arise when trying to reuse other commodity libraries, initially designed for desktop clients, for mobile rich internet applications development.

Another problem we experienced is related to OpenLayers dependency on DOM 2.0 APIs. OpenLayers assumes a complete DOM 2.0 or 3.0 model to be supported by the browser engine. Unfortunately, browser engines even on very recent devices (like the Nokia N95) do not fully support these specifications. This created problems when parsing some of the XML documents returned by our smart places API through the DOM API. The problem was solved by re-coding the applications in such a way that they were relying on JSON-formatted interface rather than on ATOM/RSS formatted data. In this way we were able to guarantee that all applications could still work on all the mentioned types of devices. Such a modification had also the positive side-effect of improving the performance of the provided applications due to the more light-weight logic required for parsing and creating the data.

5   Lessons Learnt and Future Work

This paper discussed our experiences with building an indoor GIS based on commodity GIS standards and protocols and Web 2.0 application development principles. We showed that the combination of scripting languages with web application frameworks, such as Python and Django, gave us a lot of flexibility in designing the actual web service interfaces we wanted to use to expose indoor GIS data. We implemented a few case study applications on top of the proposed GIS solution, which confirmed the feasibility of using web technologies for fast and easy deployment of smart places services on a heterogeneous set of commercial off-the-shelf devices. As far as JavaScript GIS clients are concerned, we pointed it our that using commodity libraries, such as OpenLayers, can create a few performance issues for resource constrained devices. Moreover, commodity libraries might have not been designed by taking into account the limited RAM capacity of mobile devices. Frequent and not negligible memory leaks created problems also on more recent and powerful devices. Overall, we believe there is a clear need in research and industry to agree on standards for indoor LBS, with respect to both geospatial data representations and related APIs to re-use them in a Web 2.0 environment. Existing outdoor-related standards might lay the groundwork for such activities, even though they should be extended in order to support not only the concept of location as physical position but also symbolic location concepts. Our future work will concern refinement of the positioning technique and related location model, as well as work on more thin clients better suited for mobile usage in terms of memory consumption and UI paradigms.

Acknowledgments. The authors would like to acknowledge the contributions from the Smart Place project at Nokia Research, in particular Jilles van Gurp and Heikki Mattila.

References

1. Simon, R., Fröhlich, P.: A mobile application framework for the geospatial web. In: WWW 2007: Proceedings of the 16th international conference on World Wide Web, pp. 381–390. ACM, New York (2007)
2. Griswold, W.G., Shanahan, P., Brown, S.W., Boyer, R., Ratto, M., Shapiro, R.B., Truong, T.M.: Activecampus: Experiments in community-oriented ubiquitous computing. Computer 37(10), 73–81 (2004)
3. Wang, X., Dong, J.S., Chin, C.Y., Hettiarachchi, S.R., Zhang, D.: Semantic Space: an infrastructure for smart spaces. IEEE Pervasive Computing 3(3), 32–39 (2004)
4. Endres, C., Butz, A., MacWilliams, A.: A survey of software infrastructures and frameworks for ubiquitous computing. Mob. Inf. Syst. 1(1), 41–80 (2005)
5. Candy, J.: A Mobile Indoor Location-based GIS Application. In: 5th International Symposium on Mobile Mapping Technologies (MMT 2007), Padua, Italy (2007) (last checked on 6.5.2008),
   http://giswww1.bcit.ca/georanger/candy_jonathan.pdf
6. Becker, C., Durr, F.: On location models for ubiquitous computing. In: Personal and Ubiquitous Computing, vol. 9(1), pp. 20–31. Springer, Heidelberg (2005)
7. Lopez-de Ipina, D., Vazquez, J., Abaitua, J.: A context-aware mobile mashup platform for ubiquitous web. In: 3rd IET International Conference on Intelligent Environments, pp. 116–123 (2007)

8. Kim, J.W., Kim, C.S., Gautam, A., Lee, Y.: Location-Based Tour Guide System Using Mobile GIS and Web Crawling. In: Kwon, Y.-J., Bouju, A., Claramunt, C. (eds.) W2GIS 2004. LNCS, vol. 3428, pp. 51–63. Springer, Heidelberg (2005)
9. Hermersdorf, M.: Indoor Positioning with a WLAN Access Point List on a Mobile Device. In: International Workshop on World-Sensor Web (WSW 2006), Boulder, CO, USA, October 31 (2006) (last checked on 6.5.2008), http://www.sensorplanet.org/wsw2006/9_Hermersdorf_indoor_pos_WSW2006_final.pdf
10. Haeberlen, A., Flannery, E., Ladd, A.M., Rudys, A., Wallach, D.S., Kavraki, L.E.: Practical robust localization over large-scale 802.11 wireless networks. In: Proceedings of the 10th Annual international Conference on Mobile Computing and Networking (MOBICOM 2004), pp. 70–84. ACM, New York (2004)
11. Van Gurp, J., Prehofer, C., di Flora, C.: Experiences with Realizing Smart Space Web Service Applications. In: 1st IEEE International Peer-to-Peer for Handheld Devices Workshop at the CCNC 2008 conference in Las Vegas (2008)
12. OpenGIS standards specifications, http://www.opengeospatial.org/standards
13. Ekahau Inc., http://www.ekahau.com/
14. Geoserver web site, http://geoserver.org
15. OpenLayers web site, http://www.openlayers.org
16. Delivery Context Client Interfaces (DCCI) 1.0, W3C Candidate Recommendatio (December 2007), http://www.w3.org/TR/DPF/
17. uDig - User-friendly Desktop Internet GIS, http://udig.refractions.net/
18. GRASS - Geographic Resources Analysis Support System, http://grass.itc.it/
19. OAuth Core 1.0 Protocol (December 2007), http://oauth.net/core/1.0/

VeryIDX - A Digital Identity Management System for Pervasive Computing Environments

Federica Paci[1], Elisa Bertino[1], Sam Kerr[1], Aaron Lint[1], Anna Squicciarini[2], and Jungha Woo[1]

[1] CERIAS and Computer Science Department, Purdue University
[2] Information Sciences and Technology, The Pennsylvania State University

Abstract. The problem of identity theft, that is, the act of impersonating others identities by presenting stolen identifiers or proofs of identities, has been receiving increasing attention because of its high financial and social costs. In this paper we address such problem by proposing an approach to manage user identity attributes by assuring their privacy-preserving usage. The approach is based on the concept of privacy preserving multi-factor authentication achieved by a new cryptographic primitive which uses aggregate signatures on commitments that are then used for aggregate zero-knowledge proof of knowledge (ZKPK) protocols. We present the implementation of such approach on Nokia NFC cellular phones and report performance evaluation results.

1 Introduction

Today a global information infrastructure connects remote parties worldwide through the use of large scale networks, relying on application level protocols and services, such as recent web service technology. Execution of activities in various domains, such as shopping, entertainment, business and scientific collaboration, and at various levels within those contexts, is increasingly based on the use of remote resources and services. The interaction between different remotely-located parties should be based on little knowledge about each other. In such a scenario, digital identity management (DIM) technology is fundamental in customizing user experience, protecting privacy, underpinning accountability in business transactions, and in complying with regulatory controls. Digital identity can be defined as the digital representation of the information known about a specific individual or organization. As such, it encompasses not only login names, but many additional information, referred to as *identity attributes*. The management of identity attributes raises a number of challenges. On one hand, identity attributes need to be shared to speed up and facilitate authentication of users and access control in a variety of contexts, including mobile environments. Users should be able to manage their identity attributes when carrying transactions or other interactions from portable devices such as cellular phones. On the other hand, the identity attributes must be protected as they may convey sensitive information about an individual and can be target of attacks.

U. Brinkschulte, T. Givargis, and S. Russo (Eds.): SEUS 2008, LNCS 5287, pp. 268–279, 2008.

The management of identity attributes on portable devices is however challenging. First, it is not trivial to ensure the security and privacy of the identity attributes. By using technologies such as Bluetooth or RFIDs [13], a party, for example a service provider, could retrieve information from the user portable devices without user consent. A second issue is related to the storage and computational constraints of most portable devices which require efficient protocols for managing identity attributes. To date there are no comprehensive solutions for handling identity attributes on mobile devices and even solutions for conventional non-mobile environments are still at a preliminary stage.

In this paper we make some steps towards such a solution and present a multi-factor identity attribute verification approach for mobile devices. By multi-factor verification we mean that whenever an individual presents an identity attribute for carrying on a transaction with a party, such party may verify the right of this individual to use such identity attribute by asking him/her to present other identity attributes. The specification of which identity attributes have to be presented is stated by *verification policies*. Different parties in a distributed system may specify different policies. To assure that such an approach does not undermine privacy, we have developed a cryptographic protocol, referred to as *aggregate zero knowledge proof* [4]. Such a protocol allows a user to prove the knowledge of multiple secrets to a party without having to reveal them to this party. We have developed a version of such protocol for Near Field Communication (NFC) [13] enabled cellular phones. NFC is a standard-based, short-range ($\sim$ 15 centimeters) wireless connectivity technology supporting two-way interactions among electronic devices [13]. A NFC device embedded in the cellular phone is able to communicate not only with Internet via wireless connections but also with smart card readers. In addition, the cellular phone applications, referred to as MIDlets, can access the phone's tag for reading and writing data.

The rest of the paper is organized as follows. Section 2 provides an overview of VeryIDX, our system for managing identity attributes. Section 3 introduces the basic notions on which the multi-factor identity verification is based. Section 4 presents the protocols for securing, managing and using identity attributes on the cellular phone. Section 5 describes the implementation of the multi-factor identity verification protocol on Nokia NFC mobile phones. Section 6 presents experimental performance results. Section 7 discusses related work. Finally, Section 8 concludes the paper and outline some future work.

2   VeryIDX Overview

Our approach is based on an extended notion of federation. A federation is composed of the following entities: identity providers (IdPs), service providers (SPs), registrars and users. SPs provide services to users as in conventional e-commerce and other federated environments. IdPs issue certified identity attributes to users and control the sharing of such information. The *registrars* store and manage information related to *strong identity attributes*, that is, identity attributes uniquely identifying an individual, as opposed to *weak identity attributes* which do not have such property. The information recorded at the registrar is used to perform multi-factor identity attribute verification. Note that, unlike the IdPs, the information stored at the registrar does not iclude the values of the strong identity attributes in clear. Instead, such information only contains the cryptographic semantically secure *commitments* of the strong identity attributes which are then used by the clients, running on behalf of users, to construct zero knowledge proofs of knowledge (ZKPK) [10] of those attributes. The key elements of our solution can be summarized as follows:

1. Whenever a party P presents a strong identity attribute to a SP in the federation, the SP requires additional proofs of identity according to its local verification policies. The submission of additional proofs of identity by P and the corresponding verification by the SP is executed through the use of our aggregated ZKPK protocols. By using such protocol the party can prove knowledge of any strong identity attributes efficiently. Since the actual values of the identifiers are not revealed to the SP, this approach preserves the privacy of the parties.

2. Each strong identity attribute used by a party P in a federation, either for direct use or just for identity proof, must be registered with a registrar that, upon registration, provides P with a signature on the commitment of the identifier. The management of the registered strong identity attributes is based on a *identity record* (IdR) created for each registering party. The identity record collects the commitments corresponding to the strong identity attributes.

3. To prevent a malicious party from registering with a federation a strong identity attribute owned by another individual, a duplicate detection protocol is run upon registration to determine whether the same strong identity attribute has already been registered by a different party.

Example 1. Consider a user Bob who is part of the E-Mall federation, that offers a safe environment for online shopping. Bob enrolls at registrar Reg_1 and registers his strong identifiers: his credit card number (CCN) and his social security number (SSN). The commitments values of CCN and SSN signed by the registrar are maintained in Bob's IdR. Bob now can use his CCN and SSN to prove his identity. Suppose then that Bob wants to buy a book from $e - Follets$ SP. According to $e - Follets$'s policy, this store requires Bob's CCN along with a different form of identity verification for authentication. $e - Follets$ thus challenges Bob's SSN. As such, Bob, in order to prove the ownership of CNN, downloads his IdR from the registrar Reg_1 onto his NFC cellular phone. The device retrieves the identity tuples corresponding to CCN and SSN specified in the SP-'s $e - Follets$ policy and builds the aggregate proof of knowledge to be sent to $e - Follets$.

3   Preliminary Concepts

In this section we first introduce the cryptographic protocols that are used to implement our privacy preserving multi-factor identity verification approach. We first introduce the Pedersen commitments used to generate strong identity attributes secure commitments and the ZKPK protocol. Then, we briefly describe the Boneh's protocol [6] to generate aggregate signatures based on bilinear mappings.

Pedersen Commitment. Let g and h be generators of a group G of prime order q. A value m is committed by choosing r randomly from $\mathbb{Z}_q$ and giving commitment $C = g^m h^r$. Commitment C is opened (or revealed) by disclosing m and r, and the opening is verified by checking that C is indeed equal to $g^m h^r$. A prover can prove by using a zero-knowledge proof that it knows how to open such commitment without revealing either m or r.

Zero-knowledge proof of knowledge. In our approach we use the techniques by Camenisch and Stadler [7] for the various ZKPK of discrete logarithms and proofs of the validity of statements about discrete logarithms. We also conform to the same notation [7]. For instance to denote the ZKPK of values α and β such that $y = g^\alpha h^\beta$ holds, and $u \le \alpha \le v$, we use the following notation:

$$PK\{(\alpha,\beta) : y = g^\alpha h^\beta \wedge (u \le \alpha \le v)\}$$

Bilinear maps. For a security parameter k, let q be a prime of length k, and G_1, G_2, G_T be groups of order q. Let $g_1 \in G_1$, $g_2 \in G_2$ be generators. Function e: $G_1 \times G_2 \to G_T$ is a bilinear mapping if it satisfies the following properties:

1. For all $u \in G_1$, $v \in G_2$ and $a, b \in Z$, $e(u^a, v^b) = e(u,v)^{ab}$.
2. $e(g_1, g_2) \ne 1 \in G_T$.
3. There exists a computable isomorphism φ from G_2 to G_1, such that $\varphi(g_2) = g_1$.

Bilinear aggregate signatures. The aggregate signature concept has been proposed by Boneh et. al [6]. We refer to such signature scheme as BGLS. Informally, an aggregate signature scheme allows multiple signatures to be aggregated into one signature with respect to the public keys of the signers and the signed messages. The BGLS scheme consists of five algorithms: *KeyGen, Sign, Verify, Aggregate* and *AggVer*. Any principal P uses *KeyGen* to generate the private and public key pair (χ, v) such that $v = g_2^\chi$ where $g_2 \in G_2$, χ is the private key and v is the public key. The *Sign* algorithm computes the signature on input message m_i in G_1 by a full-domain hash function $h : \{0,1\}^* \to G_1$. The output $\sigma_i = h(m_i)^\chi \in G_1$ is the signature for m_i. The *Aggregate* algorithm aggregates the signatures $\sigma_1, \sigma_2, \ldots, \sigma_t$ for t different messages $m_1, m_2, \ldots, m_t$ into one signature $\sigma = \prod_{i=1}^t \sigma_i$. The *AggVer* algorithm verifies a signature and works like the *Aggregate* signature algorithm. For a set $m_1, m_2, \ldots, m_t$ of different messages, and public keys $v_1, v_2, \ldots, v_t$ and a signature σ, the verifier checks if $e(\sigma, g_2) = \prod_{i=1}^t e(h_i, v)$, where $h_i = h(m_i)$ and e is the bilinear mapping.

4   Protocols for the Multy-Factor Verification of Strong Identity Attributes

In this section, we present the protocols for multi-factor strong identity attribute verification. We first introduce the notion of identity records (IdRs) that provide a representation of user identity attributes. Then, we introduce the protocol for strong identity attributes enrollment that consists of creating secure commitments and in signing them with the private key of the registrar. Finally, we present the protocol to create and verify the aggregate ZKPK of strong identity attributes' committed values.

4.1   Identity Records

As we mentioned, each principal P in a federation has associated one or more IdRs, each recorded at some registrar in the federation. Each IdR in turn consists of several identity tuples, denoted as τ_i. Each identity tuple is associated with one strong identity attribute and records all information related to the verification of this identifier at the time of use. In particular, a strong identity attribute m is associated with a secure commitment denoted as M that is signed by the registrar upon enrollment. The signature on M, denoted by σ in the paper, is part of the identity tuple associated with m. M is computed as $g^m h^r$, where g and h are generators in group G of prime order q. G and q are public parameters of the registrar and r is chosen randomly from $\mathbb{Z}_q$. m is also tied to a set of *weak identity attributes*, denoted by $\{w_1, \ldots, w_k\}$. For example, assume 4040330043794877 to be a credit card number and Bob and Smith be the first and last name of an individual. Here, 4040330043794877 is the strong identity attribute value, while Bob and Smith are the associated weak identity attributes. All strong identity attributes' commitments and weak identity attributes are tagged with an attribute descriptor tag and two types of assurance, namely *validity assurance* and *ownership assurance*. Validity assurance corresponds to the confidence about the validity of the identity attribute based on the verification performed at the identity attributes original issuer. Ownership assurance corresponds to the confidence about the claim that the principal presenting a given identity attribute is its true owner. There are four levels of assurance: absolute assurance, tagged as A, corresponding to the absolute certainty about the claim; reasonable assurance, tagged as B, corresponding to case when one or more assertions from trusted parties exist regarding the certainty of the claim; unknown assurance, tagged as U, when there is no information to assert the certainty of the claim; and false assurance, tagged as F, denoting that the claim is incorrect. We assume that absolute validity of a given strong identity attribute can only be determined by authorities which have issued the strong identity attributes. This corresponds to value A of the validity-assure of the associated strong identity attribute. Instead, we mark as B the validity assurance of a strong identity attribute the validity of which has been asserted by a principal, whose identity record has a validity assurance set to A. If no entity other than the principal supports the validity of the strong identity attribute, this attribute is marked with unknown assurance U.

With reference to Example 1, Figure 1 shows an example of an IdR. Here the principal is known as Bob@Registrar1 and has enrolled two strong identity attributes, namely a CCN and SSN.

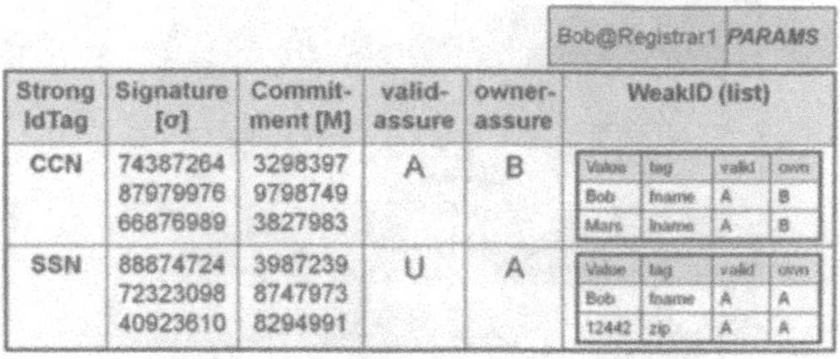

Bob@Registrar1 *PARAMS*									

Strong IdTag	Signature [σ]	Commit-ment [M]	valid-assure	owner-assure	WeakID (list)				
CCN	74387264 87979976 66876989	3298397 9798749 3827983	A	B	Value	tag	valid	own	
					Bob	fname	A	B	
					Mars	lname	A	B	
SSN	88874724 72323098 40923610	3987239 8747973 8294991	U	A	Value	tag	valid	own	
					Bob	fname	A	A	
					12442	zip	A	A	

Fig. 1. Simplified graphical representation of an IdR

4.2   Enrollment of Strong Identity Attributes

1. *Registrar parameters.* The registrar runs parameter generation algorithm *GenKey* that picks a prime q and three multiplicative groups G_1, G_2, G_T of prime order q. Also two generators g_1, h_1 in G_1 such that $log_{g_1} h_1$ and a G_2 group generator g_2 are returned by *GenKey*. Then, the registrar runs algorithm *KeyGen* to generate the secret key χ that is a random number from $\mathbb{Z}_q$ and the public key $v = g_2^\chi$. The resulting set of parameters is $(G_1, G_2, G_T, g_1, h_1, g_2, v)$.

2. *Commitment of a value $m \in \mathbb{Z}_q$.* The principal chooses a value $r \in \mathbb{Z}_q$, and computes $M = g_1^m h_1^r$.

3. *Zero-knowledge proof of the committed value.* The principal gives ZKPK of opening the commitment M to the registrar:

$$PK\{(m,r) : y = g_1^m h_1^r, m, r \in \mathbb{Z}_q)\}$$

4. *Signing of the committed value.* After performing the security checks on the committed value (namely the local consistency and federation duplicate detection), the registrar executes the *Sign* algorithm on the commitment M to output M^χ as the signature where χ is the secret key of the registrar.

4.3   Aggregate Zero-Knowledge Proof of Knowledge (AgZKPK)

Suppose that a principal P requests a service from a SP which requires P to first authenticate by proving that it knows how to open a specified set of commitments. To indicate this set of commitments a set of tags is given which is denoted by π_{SP}. The protocol that provides aggregate proof of knowledge of the commitments corresponding to π_{SP} is composed of the following steps:

1. *Principal's aggregation.* Let $\sigma_1, \ldots, \sigma_t$ be the signatures corresponding to the strong identity attributes in π_{SP}. The principal aggregates the signatures into $\sigma = \prod_{i=1}^t \sigma_i$, where σ_i is the signature of committed value $M_i = g_1^{m_i} h_1^{r_i}$. It also computes $M = \prod_{i=1}^t M_i = g_1^{m_1 + m_2 + \ldots + m_t} h_1^{r_1 + r_2 + \ldots + r_t}$. Finally, the principal sends $\sigma, M, M_i, 1 \le i \le t$, to the verifier.

2. *Zero-knowledge proof of aggregate commitment.* The principal and the verifier SP carry out the following ZKP protocol:

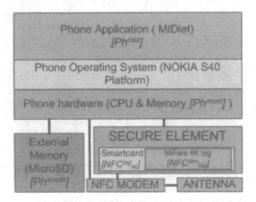

Fig. 2. Nokia NFC cellular phone components

$$PK\{(m,r) : y = g_1^m h_1^r, m, r \in \mathbb{Z}_q)\}$$

where $m = m_1 + m_2 + \ldots + m_t$ and $r = r_1 + r_2 + \ldots + r_t$.

3. *Verification of aggregate signature.* After the verifier accepts the zero-knowledge proof of the commitments, it checks if the following verifications succeed:
$M = \prod_{i=1}^{t} M_i$ and $e(\sigma, g_2) = e(M, v)$.

5 NFC implementation of the Multy-Factor Identity Attribute Verification Protocol

In this section we first describe the main components of the Nokia 6131 NFC cell phone and then we present some details about the implementation of the multi-factor identity attribute verification protocol.

5.1 NFC Cellular Phone Architecture

We have developed our portable multi-factor identity attribute verification protocol on the Nokia 6131 NFC cell phone (Ph^{NFC}) [13]. We assume that the SPs have a NFC reader (denoted as NFC_{reader}^{SP}) which transmits and receives messages from the NFC cellular phone. The phone is integrated with a NFC device and thus contains both reader and writer for the embedded smart card and tags that directly communicate with SP's reader. Ph^{NFC}'s components are shown in Figure 2.

The main software component for managing strong identity attributes is the MIDlet suite. The MIDlet suite consists of a Java Application Descriptor (JAD) and a MIDlet. A MIDlet (denoted by Ph^{mid}) is a Java program that runs on the Java Virtual Machine(JVM) enabled mobile device. The JAD controls possible permissions that the MIDlet can have. A Ph^{mid} is installed onto a phone and operates in a sandbox [16] so that different MIDlets are isolated from each other.

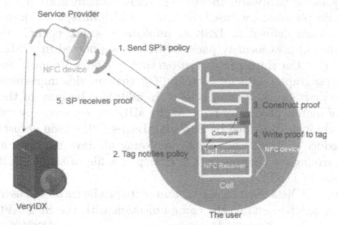

Fig. 3. Interactions between VeryIDX NFC module and SP card reader

The cellular phone has a secure element which can only be accessed by MIDlets signed by a trusted third party; these MIDlets should know the access key. The secure element consists of two main components, namely the Mifare tag (NFC_{tag}^{dev}) and Smartcard (NFC_{sc}^{dev}).

5.2 Implementation

In this section we describe how we have implemented the multi-factor identity attribute verification protocol on the Nokia 6131 NFC cell phone. We store the users' IdR in the external phone memory Ph^{xmem}, while the secret r used to compute the secure commitments is saved in NFC_{tag}^{dev}. We have implemented a MIDlet that creates the AgZKPK. The MIDlet execution is triggered when the user's cell phone tag NFC_{tag}^{dev} captures the verification policy sent by the SP's NFC_{reader}^{SP}[1] and the NFC_{tag}^{dev} transfers this policy to the cell phones main memory Ph^{mem}. The MIDlet retrieves from Ph^{xmem} the commitments corresponding to the strong identity attributes requested by the verification policy. Then, the MIDlet runs a new MIDlet which is executed in a protected domain with restricted permissions. This is necessary because the new MIDlet uses cryptographic secrets associated with the strong identity attributes to create the aggregate zero knowledge proof AgZKPK. Once the AgZKPK is computed, the MIDlet sends it to the main MIDlet. Upon receiving the AgZKPK, the main MIDlet transfers it to the NFC_{tag}^{dev} so that it can be read by the NFC_{reader}^{SP} (see Figure 3).

The MIDLets developed to generate the AgZKPK run on Java 2 Micro Edition (J2ME), a subset of Java 2 Standard Edition (J2SE), which provides environments and APIs for mobile and embedded devices. Since J2ME is aimed at hardware with limited resources, it contains a minimum set of class libraries

---

[1] The NFC reader is a device that can transmit as well as receive data using NFC technology.

for specific types of hardware. In our AgZKPK implementation on conventional non-mobile platforms, we used the java.math.BigInteger and java.security. SecureRandom class defined in J2SE to implement secure commitments, but both java.math and java.security package are not supported in J2ME. Therefore, we used the third-party cryptography provider BouncyCastle [1], a lightweight cryptography APIs for Java and C# that provide implementation of the BigInteger and SecureRandom classes. In addition, because of the limited memory size of mobile phone, we reduced the MIDlets' code size by using code obfuscation techniques provided by Sun's NetBeans IDE. Code obfuscation allows one to reduce a file size of 98% by replacing all Java packages and class names with meaningless characters. For example, a file of size 844KB can be reduced to a size of 17KB.

Moreover, the MIDlets must have read and write privileges on the user's phone tag NFC_{tag}^{dev} in order to enable the communication with the SP's NFC reader NFC_{reader}^{SP}. In fact, the SP's verification policy is saved in NFC_{tag}^{dev} and then passed to the MIDlet to create the proof. Then, the created AgZKPK is stored in NFC_{tag}^{dev} in order to be read by the SP NFC_{reader}^{SP}. In order to allow the MIDlets to access NFC_{tag}^{dev}, the MIDlets must be signed. To sign the MIDlets we used the Carbide.j tool [2] provided by Nokia that requires a code signing certificate released by a certification authority (CA) to generate the signature.

6   Experimental Results

In this section we present the results of the tests we have performed to evaluate the performance of the multi-factor identity attribute verification protocol implementation on the mobile phone. An aspect that might influence the performance of our protocols is the number of strong identity attributes that are aggregated and verified. Therefore, we have measured the time that the mobile client application takes to create the aggregate ZKPK and the time that SP's interface takes to perform the verification by varying the number of strong identity attributes that are verified from 1 to 50. We have compared the execution time to create the aggregate ZKPK on the mobile phone with the time to perform the same operation on the VeryIDX web-based implementation [3].

Figure 4 (a) reports the times required by the VeryIDX mobile phone implementation and by the web-based protocol implementation for generating the aggregate zero knowledge. In both cases, the AgZKPK protocol takes almost constant time for the ZKPK generation even if the number of identity attributes being proven increases. The reason is that the AgZKPK only requires a constant number of exponentiations [4]. Moreover, as expected, the time to create the proof on the mobile phone is higher than the time to perform the same operation on the web-based implementation due to the phone's limited computing power. The average time for the creation of an aggregate proof on the mobile phone is 2.257 seconds, while on the web-based application is around 0.02 seconds. Figure 4 (b) reports the time that the SP application takes to perform the strong identity attributes verification. Notice that the verification

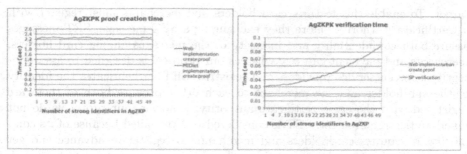

(a) AgZKPK Creation on Midlet versus (b) AgZKPK Verification versus Creation
Web-based implementation

Fig. 4. Experimental results

time linearly increases with the number of strong identity attributes to be verified. The reason is that during the verification the SP is required to multiply all
the commitments to verify the resulting aggregate signature.

7 Related Work

In this section we discuss related work on the use of cellular phones for e- and
m-commerce transactions involving identity attributes and other recent developments in mobile identity management initiatives.

With the advent of high-speed data networks and feature-rich mobile devices,
the concept of *mobile wallet* [12,5] has gained importance. A seminal work introduced the concept of wallets with observers [8] enabling off-line digital cash and
credentials to be used in commercial settings. A major difference of our approach
is that it does not require an observer, as the integrity of the strong identifiers
is based on the signature of the registrar on the strong identifiers. The addition
of the observer would, however, be beneficial if the usage of the strong identity
attributes were constrained for example by the number of times of use.

Other mobile identity management initiatives have gained importance with
the rapid adoption of second-generation mobile telecommunication systems, leading to the growth of m-commerce [14,11]. Two critical specific factors in this domain are usability and trust. Several approaches to enhance usability of mobile
devices have been proposed [9]. Trust on the device comprises of several security
and privacy properties such as confidentiality, integrity, user control and minimal
disclosure of the identity data stored on such devices. One approach to mobile
IdM is based on the GSM [14]. GSM based IdM uses the GSM infrastructure
and the Subscriber Identity Module (SIM) as the underlying platform.

The Secure Electronic Transaction (SET) [15] protocol was developed to allow
credit card holders to make transactions without revealing their credit card numbers to merchants and also to assure authenticity of the parties. SET deploys
dual signature for merchant and payment gateway. Each party can only read
a message designated for itself since each message is encrypted for a different

target. To enable this feature, card holders and merchants must register with a Certificate Authority before they exchanging a SET message. SET messages assure both confidentiality and integrity of the messages among card holders, merchants and payment gateway whereas our protocol is designed to assure integrity between service providers and registrar. SET authenticates the identity of the cardholder and the merchant to each other because both of them are registered with the same certificate authority. However, our protocols do not mandate this requirement. SET is considered to have failed because of its complexity. It requires cardholders and merchants to register in advance and get X.509 certificates to make transactions whereas the users need not to have such PKI certificate in our protocol[2].

8   Conclusion

This paper proposes protocols for managing identity attributes in cellular devices and supporting their secure and privacy preserving usage. The protocols are based on aggregate zero knowledge proof and aggregate signature on strong identity attributes' commitments. We have implemented the protocols on the Nokia NFC cellular phones and we have shown that the execution time to create the aggregate proof of knowledge is almost constant with respect to the number of strong identity attributes being aggregated. As future work we plan to extend our approach in several directions. A first direction is to adopt Shamir's secrete sharing scheme to protect the cryptographic secret r used to compute Pedersen commitments associated with strong identity attributes. A second direction is the support of more sophisticated verification policies.

Acknowledgements

This material is based in part upon work supported by the National Science Foundation under the ITR Grant No. 0428554 "The Design and Use of Digital Identities" and upon work supported by the U.S. Department of Homeland Security under Grant Award Number 2006-CS-001-000001, under the auspices of the Institute for Information Infrastructure Protection (I3P) research program. The I3P is managed by Dartmouth College. The views and conclusions contained in this document are those of the authors and should not be interpreted as necessarily representing the official policies, either expressed or implied, of the U.S. Department of Homeland Security, the I3P, or Dartmouth College.

References

1. Bouncy Castle Crypto APIs, http://www.bouncycastle.org/
2. Development tools, http://www.forum.nokia.com/main/resources/tools_and_sdks/carbide/index.html

---

[2] Only SPs and registrars must have certificates.

3. Bhargav-Spantzel, A., Woo, J., Bertino, E.: Receipt management- transaction history based trust establishment. In: Proceedings of the 2007 ACM workshop on Digital identity management, New York, NY, USA, pp. 82–91 (2007)
4. Bhargav-Spantzel, A., Squicciarini, A.C., Xue, R., Bertino, E.: Practical Identity Theft Prevention using Aggregated Proof of Knowledge, Technical report CERIAS TR 2006-26 (2006)
5. Boly, J., Bosselaers, A., Cramer, R., Michelsen, R., Mjolsnes, S., Muller, F., Pedersen, T.P., Pfitzmann, B., de Rooij, P., Schoenmakers, B., Schunter, M., Vallee, L., Waidner, M.: The ESPRIT Project CAFE - High Security Digital Payment Systems. In: Gollmann, D. (ed.) ESORICS 1994. LNCS, vol. 875, pp. 217–230. Springer, Heidelberg (1994)
6. Boneh, D., Gentry, C., Shacham, H., Lynn, B.: Aggregate and verifiably encrypted signatures from bilinear maps. In: Biham, E. (ed.) EUROCRYPT 2003. LNCS, vol. 2656. Springer, Heidelberg (2003)
7. Camenisch, J., Stadler, M.: Efficient Group Signature Schemes for Large Groups. In: Kaliski Jr., B.S. (ed.) CRYPTO 1997. LNCS, vol. 1294, pp. 410–424. Springer, Heidelberg (1997)
8. Chaum, D.: Security without identification: transaction systems to make big brother obsolete. Communications of the ACM 28(10), 1030–1044 (1985)
9. Dix, A., Rodden, T., Davies, N., Trevor, J., Friday, A., Palfreyman, K.: Exploiting space and location as a design framework for interactive mobile systems. ACM Transactions on Computer Human Interaction 7(3), 285–321, 200 (2000)
10. Fiege, U., Fiat, A., Shamir, A.: Zero knowledge proofs of identity. In: Proceedings of the nineteenth annual ACM conference on Theory of computing, New York, NY, USA, pp. 210–217 (1987)
11. Jendricke, U., Kreutzer, M., Zugenmaier, A.: Mobile Identity Management. In: UBICOMP 2002: Workshop on Security in Ubiquitous Computing (2002)
12. Mjolsnes, S.F., Rong, C.: Localized Credentials for Server Assisted Mobile Wallet. In: Proceedings of International Conference on Computer Networks and Mobile Computing, Los Alamitos, CA, USA (2001)
13. Near Field Communication Forum, http://www.nfc-forum.org
14. Rannenberg, K.: Identity management in mobile cellular networks and related applications, Information Security Technical Report, Johann Wolfgang Goethe University Frankfurt (January 2004)
15. SET Secure Electronic Transaction Specification Book 1: Business Description (1997)
16. Wolfe, A.: Toolkit: Java is Jumpin'. Queue 1(10), 16–19 (2004)

Delay-Aware Mobile Transactions*

Brahim Ayari, Abdelmajid Khelil, and Neeraj Suri

Technische Universität Darmstadt,
Dependable, Embedded Systems and Software Group,
Hochschulstr. 10, 64289 Darmstadt, Germany
Tel.: +49-6151-16-7066; Fax: +49-6151-16-4310
{brahim,khelil,suri}@informatik.tu-darmstadt.de

Abstract. In the expanding e-society, mobile embedded systems are increasingly used to support transactions such as for banking, stock or database applications. Such systems entail a range of heterogeneous entities - both the embedded devices and the networks connecting them. While these systems are exposed to frequent and varied perturbations, the support of atomic distributed transactions is still a fundamental requirement to achieve consistent decisions. Guaranteeing atomicity and high performance in traditional fixed wired networks is based on the assumption that faults like node and link failures occur rarely. This assumption is not supported in current and future mobile embedded systems where the heterogeneity and mobility often result in link and node failures as a dominant operational scenario. In order to continue guaranteeing strict atomicity while providing for high efficiency (low resource blocking time and message overhead) and acceptable commit rate, transactional fault-tolerance techniques need to be revisited perhaps at the cost of transaction execution time. In this paper, a comprehensive classification of perturbations and their impact on the design of mobile transactions is provided. In particular we argue for the delay-awareness of mobile transactions to allow for the fault-tolerance mechanisms to ensure resilience to the various and frequent perturbations.

Keywords: Transactions, mobile database systems, dependability.

1 Introduction

Future mobile embedded systems are increasingly characterized by frequent and varied perturbations. These are directly apparent to the delivery of services as constraints and failures. Mobile systems are also constrained by the scarcity of processing, storage and energy resources of mobile devices, and the continuously varying properties of wireless channels. Most of the failures which can occur in such systems are caused by node (given the mobility and size of these nodes) or communication failures. These failures can last from seconds, minutes or even hours e.g., network partitioning. Increasingly, the mobile environments are supporting applications that require strict atomicity like health-care home systems, coordination across autonomous networked vehicles,

---

* Research supported in part by EU NoE ReSIST, EU COMIFIN and DFG GRK 1362 (TUD GKMM).

U. Brinkschulte, T. Givargis, and S. Russo (Eds.): SEUS 2008, LNCS 5287, pp. 280–291, 2008.

m-commerce etc. Atomic commit protocols ensure strict atomicity of database transactions and play therefore a major role for the design of these applications. Most existing atomic protocols show a restricted perturbation-tolerance leading to either poor transaction commit rate or to high resource blocking time which consequently deceases the efficiency of the mobile system. In our previous work [1], we showed that sacrificing latency (time needed to decide about the outcome of the transaction) is necessary to cope with frequent and enduring perturbations without sacrificing performance in terms of efficiency and commit success rate.

In the literature computer transactions are usually delay-sensitive. A limited body of research exists for real-time transactions [2, 3]. However, to the best of our knowledge, delay-aware (i.e. also delay-tolerant) transactions have not yet been addressed. In this paper we argue for the necessity of delay-awareness of mobile transactions [4] in networked embedded systems. Our work in [1] investigated primarily infrastructure-based system models. We extend this base model here to cope with a more generalized mobile system that also involves ad-hoc communication scenarios.

The remainder of this paper is organized as follows. In Section 2, the system model is described along with a set of application scenarios and a classification of perturbations in mobile environments. The design requirements for mobile transaction protocols and systems are presented in Section 3. In Section 4, delay-aware mobile transactions are introduced along with a discussion of the main challenges of introducing delay-awareness in mobile systems. Section 5 concludes the paper and briefly outlines the future work.

2   System Model, Perturbations and Scenarios

2.1   System Model

In order to consider a broad class of mobile and networked embedded systems, we develop a generalized mobile distributed environment consisting of a set of mobile hosts (MH), a set of fixed hosts (FH) and a set of Wireless Sensor Networks (WSNs) composed of a number of sensor nodes (SN) and a sink. The sink collects data from SNs about a monitored area or goods etc. The architecture of the environment considered is illustrated in Fig. 1. The coverage of MSSs is much higher than the transmission area of ad-hoc communication technologies (e.g., if we compare GSM to bluetooth). The MHs intermittently connect to the wired network through *Mobile Support Stations (MSS)* via wireless channels (Fig. 1). The MHs can communicate directly with each other in an ad-hoc manner using Bluetooth or WLAN. Some MHs can also communicate with the sink(s) of involved WSNs. This generalized mobile distributed environment mainly consists of three basis system models which are usually tackled separately by commit protocol developers. In this work we will progressively tackle the complexity of the generalized system model by stepwise considering these sub-systems and finally combining them to our generalized system model:

1. *Infrastructure-based* scenarios involve only FHs, MSSs and a subset of MHs of the model of Fig. 1. This subset of MHs can only communicate with each other or with FHs using the services of MSSs.

2. *Ad-hoc scenarios* involve only a subset of MHs of the model of Fig. 1 and WSNs. These MHs can communicate with each other or with mobile sinks of WSNs only in ad-hoc manner.
3. *Hybrid scenarios* are a combination of both the infrastructure-based and the ad-hoc scenarios representing our generalized mobile distributed model.

We refer to a distributed transaction where at least one MH participates in its execution as a *Mobile Transaction (MT)*. Commit protocols are generally based on the existence of at least one *coordinator (CO)*, which is responsible for coordinating the execution of the corresponding transaction. For different transactions and mobile system models, different nodes may play the CO role. The CO is responsible for storing information concerning the state of the transaction execution. Based on the information collected from and about the participants of the transaction, the CO takes the decision to commit or abort the transaction and informs all participants about its decision.

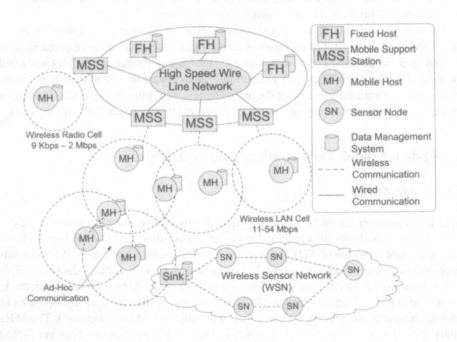

Fig. 1. Architecture of environment

2.2   Application Scenarios

In this section we classify the main applications scenarios for future embedded and ubiquitous systems, where strict atomic mobile transactions are required.

Bank/stock transactions: This type of application scenarios include mobile commerce (m-commerce) applications where users can buy or sell goods using their mobile devices and involving bank servers in fixed networks to accomplish their transactions. This is an example of application for infrastructure-based scenarios.

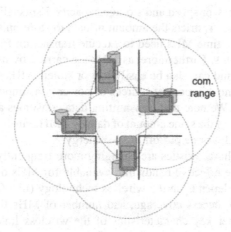

Fig. 2. Coordination between networked autonomous vehicles (livelock scenario)

Coordination between autonomous networked vehicles: In such an application scenario (which is a pure ad-hoc scenario) we present a potential future application where mobile transactions are needed for the purpose of coordination for safe navigation of unmanned autonomous networked vehicles. Like black boxes for airplanes, autonomous vehicles can be equipped with such black boxes which are basically mobile databases. Fig. 2 shows a scenario of four unmanned vehicles at a crossing. These vehicles need to agree on an order how they will pass the crossing. Prior to their actual passing this information needs to be agreed upon and recorded atomically to their corresponding black boxes. This information is needed e.g., afterwards by assurance companies in case an accident happens between these vehicles to determine which vehicle was responsible for the accident.

Health-care ubiquitous systems: For insurance purposes, in order to monitor old people living alone in their homes a set of WSNs should be deployed in these houses and transactions are needed to react to certain situations where some actuators e.g. need to be activated together either all of them or none and this data should also be written somewhere on MHs or on FHs belonging to hospitals or police etc. This application scenario is an example of the hybrid scenarios defined in the system model.

2.3 Classification of Perturbations

Within these networked embedded systems supporting such transactional applications, we now consider two main classes of perturbations: operational constraints (power, computing, connectivity etc.) and failures. We classify the environmental constraints relevant to mobile transactions into heterogeneity (of nodes and links), unstable storage and energy constraints. Failures of the mobile environment are classified into communication and node failures.

Constraints. The considered mobile environment is constrained mainly by the characteristics of *MHs* and *wireless links*. MHs intuitively possess less computational resources than FHs, such as processor speed and storage capacity. Especially some MHs possess limited disk space which restricts the amount of data to store on them. These resource constraints increase the time MHs need to execute transaction fragments or may even lead to execution failures. Furthermore, as MHs are carried by users, they incur operational wear and tear and can also be easily lost or stolen. MHs are often powered by batteries. Two of the most important sources of power consumption are transmissions and disk accesses [5]. We note that transmitting data consumes around three times as much energy as receiving the same amount of data by a MH. Furthermore, MHs may run in different energy modes or be put-off to save energy.

Wireless network characteristics are changing more frequently than those of wired links. For example, the effective bandwidth available for MHs over a wireless link is highly dynamic. This depends on the wireless technology (like GSM, GPRS, UMTS, WLAN, Satellite, . . .), access coverage, and number of MHs that have to share the wireless medium. Other key characteristics of the wireless links are higher latency and communication charges. These characteristics lead to considerably varied reliability/availability and connectivity of MHs.

Mobile nodes are considered to have *unstable storage* due to high vulnerability of these entities to catastrophic failures, e.g., loss, theft or physical damage and the immature replication strategies used in the mobile environment to replicate data like in [6]. Due to these issues the disk storage on a MH can not be considered as a stable storage.

The limitations and characteristics listed above outline the variation of constraints for the mobile environment being different from those in fixed networks. These constraints also complicate the design of appropriate mobile transaction protocols. For example, to abort a MT because of one slow participant is not a suitable design choice in mobile environments.

Failures. We now outline the common failure modes which we classify into primary classes of communication and node failures.

Communication Failures: These constitute the majority of failures in the mobile environment. We distinguish between two types of communication failures:

Message loss: Especially, messages exchanged between MHs themselves or between MHs and MSSs are highly vulnerable to loss due to the high bit error rate of wireless links and to network congestion and collisions. Message loss is much more probable to occur in mobile environments than fixed ones and need to be explicitly taken into consideration in the design of mobile systems.

Network partitioning: While moving, the MH can enter a geographical area out of coverage of any MSS or any other MH (to communicate in ad-hoc manner) so that it loses its connection to the network. While partitioned from the network, the MH is not able to send or receive messages. As network partitioning is not exceptional but rather part of the normal mode of operation, it needs to be explicitly considered in the system design.

Node Failures: We distinguish between MH, FH and CO failures. For MHs, we identify two main failures classes, i.e., *transient* and *permanent* failures. The CO can theoretically be either implemented on a MH or FH, and correspondingly exhibits either MH or FH failure modes. However, we separate CO failures from MH and FH failures given the central role the CO plays in commit protocols. In Section 4, we will fix the entity implementing the CO role and subsequently discuss the CO failures in detail. We do not consider deliberate failures such as Byzantine faults or intrusions, but in future work we want to extend the fault model incorporating deliberate faults.

Transient MH failures: These occur mainly due to either software or hardware faults and usually disappear if the MH reboots. A further common cause of transient failures is the lack of battery power to sustain operation of the mobile device. Transient failures are the most probable failures of MHs in the mobile environment. Opposite to network partitioning, in the case of a transient MH failure the content of the volatile storage of the MH and consequently the state of its recent computations is lost. in this work we concentrate only on network partitioning.

Permanent MH failures: These are irreparable failures such as loss, theft or physical damage of the MH itself or its non-volatile storage, where the data and logs are stored (media failure). Consequently, all the data stored in the MH is lost.

FH failures: We assume a crash-recovery model, i.e., if the FH crashes it stops receiving, sending and processing messages until it recovers after a finite amount of time. Volatile storage of the FH is checkpointed periodically to stable storage and the FH logs its computations and received/sent messages between two checkpoints. Once a backup is done the log is deleted and a fresh logging process is initiated. The FH corresponding DBMS takes care about the recovery from transaction and media failures. The recovery includes also all logging operations which need to be done when the FH is executing a transaction.

3   Design Requirements for Mobile Transactions Protocols

We now present the design requirements of transactions in the considered generalized mobile environment. A basic issue is on the need for new design requirements for mobile transactions in mobile environments? Is it not sufficient to abort a mobile transaction when a perturbation or anomaly appears and then restart it later? The problem with this methodology is that perturbations in mobile environments are increasingly the normal case than an exceptional situation. Another important argument is the fact that restarting the transaction involves other costs in term of energy consumption and charges for using the wireless links, which are not always tolerable in mobile environments. For this reasons we need to clearly define the boundaries in terms of design requirements. We identify the following main requirements and design issues:

Efficiency: The efficiency of mobile transaction protocols is measured in terms of messages and blocking time. The classical approach to improve the efficiency of such protocols is to reduce the communication overhead (message number and size) and to minimize the blocking time. The reason behind minimizing blocking time is that transactions, especially executing on FHs, often lock expensive resources. These resources can not be accessed by other transactions as long as they are locked by an uncommitted one. This transaction is isolated from the rest of the transactions by locking all relevant data needed by it. As long as the locks are held, no other transaction can access the same data. This data or resources are *blocked*. The more transactions per second an application can process, the better its scalability and throughput are. If resources are blocked, transactions using them are delayed waiting for the resources to be unlocked. The throughput of the system then suffers. For this reason blocking time, especially of FH resources (because they are frequently much more loaded than MHs), should be minimized.

Scalability: Transaction protocols are said to be scalable if they support growing number of participants without sacrificing efficiency. The resource blocking time as well as the capabilities of the CO are the main factors that determine the scalability of commit protocols.

Resilience to perturbations: (Fault-tolerance and recovery) To build resilient mobile transaction protocols, defining a comprehensive set of perturbations (constraints and failures) and a set of techniques to cope with constraints and recover from failures is mandatory. The categorization of perturbations assists the protocol designer in identifying the main concerns and developing appropriate solutions. The overall objective for fault-tolerance is to maximize the number of committed mobile transactions. A naive approach to provide for fault-tolerance is to abort the MT each time a failure occurs and to restart it (e.g., after a back-off time or after the failure disappears). However, this simplistic approach introduces a large overhead for the successful participants (due to frequent re-execution of the fragments) and requires some external intelligence (either from the user or from the ability of the system to detect failures). Therefore, we introduce the delay-tolerance design requirement for MT.

Delay-tolerance and -awareness: Masking latent faults such as long disconnections imposes that the MT execution time can be delayed till local Commit/Abort decisions can be collected. This implies that MT can last for minutes or even hours. We are dealing then with transactions that we refer to as *delay-tolerant transactions*. We believe that users can sacrifice latency for atomicity. In this paper, we expect that the application/user is able to specify an appropriate (tolerable) *lifetime* for each initiated MT. The delay-tolerance design requirement is orthogonal to the efficiency requirement and implies a real challenge for our framework.

4   Delay-Aware Mobile Transactions: Overview of the Basic Approach

In the considered generalized mobile environment, network partitioning (due to either node or link failures) is the most important and frequent failure that needs to be taken particularly into consideration. We investigate the impact of this failure on mobile transactions especially with respect to their delay-awareness and the challenges of the design of commit protocols resilience to such type of failures. We proceed progressively in this section. First we consider the existence of powerful fixed participants besides mobile participants (Infrastructure-based scenario). Then we consider only mobile participants that use ad-hoc wireless communication to communicate multi-hop with each other (Ad-hoc scenario). Finally, we consider a generalized MT, where both mobile and fixed participants are involved and some Mobile participants can communicate in ad-hoc manner with each other while being partitioned from the rest of the network (Hybrid scenario).

4.1 Infrastructure-Based Scenarios

For infrastructure-based scenarios, we investigated the problem of network partitioning and heterogeneity in nodes and links in [1] and developed a set of efficient and generic techniques to provide MT's resilience to these fundamental perturbations. In the following we briefly summarize these techniques. First we start with *decoupling* the commit of MHs from that of FHs. The execution of the transaction is then split into two phases: *(1)* a mobile data gathering phase called pre-commit phase where the votes (either to Commit or Abort the MT) and the logs of the MHs (containing all operations done by the MH during the execution of its part of the MT) are collected to provide progress, and *(2)* a core Two-Phase-Commit [7] (2PC) phase, which involves only FHs for the commit action as we represent MHs by agents (which are proxy entities) in the fixed part of the network. As shown in Fig. 3, these agents representing MHs in the fixed network store messages sent the MHs participating in the MT and forward them to their corresponding MHs when they reconnect to the network. Decoupling prohibits network partitioning of MHs to affect FHs especially their resource blocking times.

As network partitioning in this class of scenarios usually leads to the isolation of some MHs from the rest of the participants, the CO is chosen to run on one FH in the fixed part of the network. This is not the only reason why the CO is chosen to run on a FH, stable storage and energy overhead are also further reasons which consolidate this choice. So the CO is always able to take a decision about the outcome of the MT and inform all participants which are connected to the network. The CO usually waits for a specified time (TO_{CO}) to receive the vote from each MH participating in the MT. Obviously this time depends on the slowest mobile participant. In oder to have a good estimation of TO_{CO}, everyone of these participants is requested to send an estimation of the time it needs to execute its part of the MT and send its vote and its logs to the CO. This estimation can also be updated when needed. This strategy allows the CO to easily cope with both heterogeneity of participants and their network partitioning by waiting for the maximum of received timeouts.

The timeout concept described above introduces delay-awareness to mobile transactions. This awareness is driven by the heterogeneity of the MT participants and their connectivity. Some applications may impose a certain maximum execution time of the initiated MT. This models the time the user can sacrifice to receive the MT result. The initiator of the MT then estimates a lifetime for the MT and hand it to the CO. The CO aborts the MT when the lifetime expired. The optimal lifetime value should account for how long disconnections of the participants can last (see Fig. 3). This value is not trivial for a generalized system model, however easier for certain systems such as closed systems. The optimal lifetime value depends on the heterogeneity of participants and the duration of their disconnections. Since the user can only decide about his desired waiting time, recommendations may support the user deciding for an appropriate lifetime value. In order to allow for recommendations, the system should keep a history of system properties such as the average disconnection time of mobile participants. The application can also be given the possibility to extent this lifetime if needed.

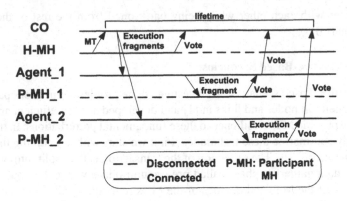

Fig. 3. Infrastructure-based scenario

4.2 Ad-Hoc Scenarios

For ad-hoc scenarios only MHs are participants in the MT and can only communicate in ad-hoc manner building a mobile ad-hoc network (MANET). Since the MHs are not connected to the fixed part of the network, the CO of the MT can not be chosen to be a FH. A MH is also not assumed to have a stable storage and therefore can not play the CO role alone. Failures of the CO in this case will also lead to the blocking of all participants. As shown in [8], there exists no non-blocking atomic commit protocol if network partitioning may occur. [9] proposes to use a *cluster of coordinators* preferably in single-hop distance from each other to avoid blocking of mobile participants in case one CO fails. The cluster of CO is represented by one member called *main coordinator*. The cluster of COs use 3PC protocol [10] to agree on a single decision either to commit or abort the MT. If the cluster of COs is partitioned or the main CO fails the authors use a termination protocol based on the Paxos Consensus protocol [11]. Two extreme cases that need to be considered are whether only one CO can be defined in these ad-hoc scenarios e.g. introducing a more powerful MH (with additional assumptions on it like stable storage) or the other extreme is whether it is possible to consider every single participant in the MT as a CO. In the following we illustrate the challenges network partitioning introduces in the case of ad-hoc scenarios.

Fig. 4 shows that estimating the lifetime of a MT in ad-hoc scenarios mainly depends on network connectivity, which in turn depends on different parameters like speed of the MHs, their communication range and obstacles in their vicinity. This makes estimating lifetime in ad-hoc scenarios a real challenge taking into consideration all these parameters. Another challenge for ad-hoc scenarios is the dissemination of parts of the MT to their corresponding MHs. For this partition-aware broadcast/multicast protocols can be used such as Hypergossiping [12].

Assuming that every MH in a partition knows all the members of the partition it is belonging to like in [13], then the members of every partition can exchange their votes (either to commit or abort the MT) and take a pre-decision on the outcome of the MT (Fig. 5 (a)). The pre-decision can be different from the final decision and is only a temporary decision inside one partition which is communicated to every

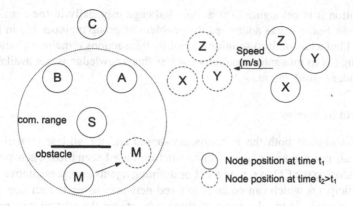

Fig. 4. Parameters for estimating lifetime in ad-hoc scenarios

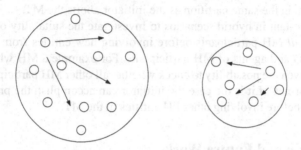

(a) Take a decision inside each partition

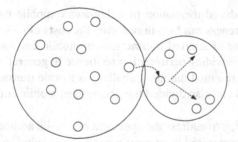

(b) Exchange decisions when partitions join

Fig. 5. Network partitioning in ad-hoc scenarios

member of the partition. If the pre-decision is to abort the MT, then every MH participant can safely abort the MT. If the pre-decision is to commit the MT, every member should wait until all participants are in the same partition. Alternatively, when two partitions merge or join (Fig. 5 (b)) then the pre-decisions are exchanged and if no further partition exists the outcome of the MT can be safely decided and all the MH participants can be informed about this outcome which is challenging as partition-aware protocols are required. The assumption that every MH in a partition knows all the members of the partition it is belonging to is a real challenge especially in the considered ad-hoc scenarios. Some works addressed the problem of group membership in MANETs like [14, 15],but a customized solution to mobile transactions remains a challenge. The real challenge is to guarantee atomicity even if this knowledge is not available in the scenario under consideration.

4.3 Hybrid Scenarios

As a combination of both the infrastructure-based and the ad-hoc scenarios, hybrid scenarios can use the advantage of infrastructure-based scenarios when possible for example choosing the CO to run on a FH or defining agents as representatives for some of MH participants which can connect to fixed networks using the services of MSSs. When it is impossible to take some of these advantages the system will behave like in ad-hoc scenarios. Mobile initiators that are partitioned can also exploit multi-hop communication in order to reach a pre-decision. This is particulary helpful if one (or more) participant in the same partition as the initiator aborts the MT.

It is also important in hybrid scenarios to investigate the suitability of ad-hoc solutions involving *all* MH participants before involving new entities from the fixed network like the CO and agents of MH participants. For example a MH which initiates a MT should be given the possibility to check whether all other MH participants are in the same partition or not. If it is the case the initiator can accomplish the pre-phase of [1] in ad-hoc mode before involving other FH entities in the MT.

5 Conclusion and Future Work

In this work we have introduced the notion of delay-aware mobile transactions. We have shown how delay-awareness can help in reducing the costs of mobile transactions and in deceasing the number of aborted transactions in mobile environments. Delay-awareness can also help in providing perturbation resilience in generalized mobile embedded systems. We have presented the main challenges atomic transaction protocols face in such mobile systems and also divided the generalized mobile embedded system into sub-classes.

In our future work, we plan to address the spectrum of mobile ad-hoc scenarios and find solutions that can be aggregated to present a generalized solution for the mobile embedded environment introduced in this work.

References

1. Ayari, B., Khelil, A., Suri, N.: FT-PPTC: An efficient and fault-tolerant commit protocol for mobile environments. In: SRDS 2006, pp. 96–105 (2006)
2. Liu, Y.S., Liao, G., Li, G., Xia, J.: Relaxed atomic commit for real-time transactions in mobile computing environment. In: Meng, X., Su, J., Wang, Y. (eds.) WAIM 2002. LNCS, vol. 2419, pp. 397–408. Springer, Heidelberg (2002)
3. Haritsa, J.R., Ramamritham, K., Gupta, R.: The prompt real-time commit protocol. IEEE Trans. Parallel Distrib. Syst. 11(2), 160–181 (2000)

4. Serrano-Alvarado, P., Roncancio, C., Adiba, M.: A survey of mobile transactions. Distrib. Parallel Databases 16(2), 193–230 (2004)
5. Forman, G.H., Zahorjan, J.: The challenges of mobile computing. IEEE Computer 27(4), 38–47 (1994)
6. Pradhan, D., Krishna, P., Vaidya, N.: Recovery in mobile wireless environment: Design and trade-off analysis. In: Proc. of the 26th International Symposium on Fault-Tolerant Computing, pp. 16–25 (1996)
7. Gray, J.: Notes on data base operating systems. In: Operating Systems, An Advanced Course, pp. 393–481 (1978)
8. Skeen, D.: Nonblocking commit protocols. In: SIGMOD 1981: Proceedings of the 1981 ACM SIGMOD international conference on Management of data, pp. 133–142 (1981)
9. Bose, J.H., Bottcher, S., Gruenwald, L., Obermeier, S., Schweppe, H., Steenweg, T.: An integrated commit protocol for mobile network databases. In: IDEAS 2005: Proceedings of the 9th International Database Engineering & Application Symposium, pp. 244–250 (2005)
10. Skeen, D., Stonebraker, M.: A formal model of crash recovery in a distributed system. IEEE Transactions on Software Engineering 9(3), 219–228 (1983)
11. Lamport, L.: The part-time parliament. ACM Trans. Comput. Syst. 16(2), 133–169 (1998)
12. Khelil, A., Marrón, P.J., Becker, C., Rothermel, K.: Hypergossiping: A generalized broadcast strategy for mobile ad hoc networks. Ad Hoc Netw. 5(5), 531–546 (2007)
13. Xie, W.: Supporting Distributed Transaction Processing Over Mobile and Heterogeneous Platforms. Dissertation. Georgia Institute of Technology (2005)
14. Roman, G.C., Huang, Q., Hazemi, A.: Consistent group membership in ad hoc networks. In: ICSE 2001: Proceedings of the 23rd International Conference on Software Engineering, pp. 381–388 (2001)
15. Briesemeister, L., Hommel, G.: Localized group membership service for ad hoc networks. In: IWAHN 2002: Proceedings of the 1st International Workshop on Ad Hoc Networking, pp. 94–100 (2002)

An Operating System Architecture
for Future Information Appliances

Tatsuo Nakajima, Hiroo Ishikawa, Yuki Kinebuchi, Midori Sugaya, Sun Lei,
Alexandre Courbot, Andrej van der Zee, Aleksi Aalto, and Kwon Ki Duk

Department of Computer Science and Engineering
Waseda University
3-4-1 Okubo Shinjuku Tokyo 169-8555, Japan
tatsuo@dcl.info.waseda.ac.jp

Abstract. A software platform for developing future information appliances requires to satisfy various diverse requirements. The operating system architecture presented in this paper enhances the flexibility and dependability through virtualization techniques. The architecture allows a system to use multiple operating systems simultaneously, and to use multi-core processors in a flexible way. Also, dependability mechanisms in our architecture will avoid crashing or hanging a system as much as possible in order to improve the user experience when defects in the software are exposed. We present a brief overview of each component in the operating system architecture and some sample scenarios that illustrate the effectiveness of the architecture.

1 Introduction

Information appliances become more and more complex for supporting a large number of new functionalities. For example, current Japanese mobile phones contain about ten million lines of source code and support a variety of functionalities such as an electronic wallet, a media player, an Internet browser/e-mail, and a photo camera. Other information appliances like televisions and car navigation systems contain almost the same size of software. Moreover, information appliances will need to satisfy diverse requirements for supporting various future services. Also, different types of information appliances will need to take into account diverse hardware platforms. In the near future, multi-core processors will become common although current operating systems for information appliances still have many issues to support the processors.

This paper proposes an operating system architecture to satisfy the diverse requirements for building attractive future information appliances. The uniqueness of the architecture is as follows:

- The architecture accommodates multiple operating systems on a multi-core processor simultaneously. This enables us to reuse a large amount of software on existing operating systems. Also, the number of CPU cores to execute an operating system will be changed dynamically due to energy consumption requirements.

U. Brinkschulte, T. Givargis, and S. Russo (Eds.): SEUS 2008, LNCS 5287, pp. 292–303, 2008.

- The architecture virtualizes crashing or hanging of an operating system as much as possible. The information appliance that adopts the architecture tries to postpone the crash until the user does not interact with the appliance anymore. Thus, the user is not aware of crashing or hanging of the appliance, and the user experience will be improved significantly.

In Section 2, we present some examples of future information appliances, and the requirements for the operating system architecture for building the appliances. In Section 3, we show the structure and components of the architecture. Section 4 shows some example scenarios that illustrate the effectiveness of our architecture. Section 5 concludes the paper.

2   Future Information Appliances and Their Requirements

In the near future, a variety of daily objects near us will become information appliances. These artifacts are connected to the Internet and enhance our daily activities. In our research group, we have enhanced various daily objects such as chairs [1], tables [3], toothbrushes [6], and mirrors [2]. These future information appliances will spontaneously collaborate with each other to compose more complex services from existing services [5] [6]. A variety of middleware infrastructures is necessary to develop various application services rapidly [4].

There are two characteristics to develop future information appliances. The first is to offer a huge amount of functionalities that need to satisfy diverse requirements to offer various attractive services. These diverse requirements cannot be implemented on any one operating system. Current information appliances adopt various types of operating systems to satisfy different requirements. For example, appliances controlling a variety of devices have used small operating systems that include only a real-time thread scheduler and some device drivers. The operating systems usually do not support memory protection domains, but are suitable for highly responsive services with tight timing constraints. The future operating systems architecture should support multiple operating systems running on a multi-core processor simultaneously, without violating real-time requirements of application services.

The second characteristic is diverse hardware platforms. Especially, future information appliances will need to use a multi-core processor dynamically to save energy consumption. As described in the previous paragraph, multiple operating systems should be executed on a multi-core processor. Each operating system allocates a suitable number of CPU cores according to the current workload. Let us assume a mobile phone that uses a multi-core processor. While a user does not use the mobile phone, only one CPU core is used to execute several background application services on multiple operating systems simultaneously. In this case, there are a few activities on these operating systems, and it is easy to satisfy all real-time requirements of these activities on a single CPU core. However, when a user starts watching a TV program, multiple CPU cores become active and most of them are used to process the TV program.

Dependability is one of the most important requirements in future information appliances. Crashing or hanging of a service on an appliance will degrade user experience significantly. For example, if the service is hung, a user needs to find a reset switch and push the switch to restart the appliance. Usually, a user interacts with information appliances for a short time. Although some errors inside a kernel may damage the kernel, usually the appliance can be avoided to crash while a user is interacting with it by repairing the damaged kernel data structure. The kernel will be restarted for a complete repair after a user finishes to use the application service.

3   Operating System Architecture

This section presents an operating system architecture for future information appliances. We describe the structure of the proposed architecture and show why the architecture satisfies the requirements described in the previous section.

3.1   Overview of Architecture

Figure 1 shows the structure of our operating system architecture. The architecture consists of six components. The first component is the SPUMONE hardware abstraction layer. The second is the L4 micro-kernel [10]. The third is the ArcOS dependable real-time operating system. The fourth is the monitoring service, and the fifth one is the anomaly detection service. The last one is the Linux kernel.

The SPUMONE hardware abstraction layer runs on a multi-core processor, and it is an infrastructure to satisfy the diverse requirements described in the previous section. SPUMONE takes into account the diversity of application services and hardware platforms.

The L4 micro-kernel is a small real-time kernel. The kernel offers only basic functionalities such as process and memory management. Most of operating system services such as a file service and device drivers are implemented in independently schedulable protection domains. Also, L4 offers a powerful IPC mechanism that makes it is easy to develop application services decomposed into multiple protection domains.

The ArcOS dependable real-time operating system runs on the L4 micro-kernel. Its purpose is to increase the dependability of control processing services running on ArcOS. The most important concept in ArcOS is self-healing. The integrity of a system is maintained without help of a system administrator, and is recovered automatically when the inconsistency inside the application service is exposed.

The monitoring service is running on ArcOS. It maintains the integrity of the Linux kernel to enhance its dependability, and recovers the integrity automatically by observing critical data structures inside the Linux kernel. The monitoring service is isolated from the Linux kernel to avoid the effect of the inconsistency in the Linux kernel.

The anomaly detection service is implemented in the Linux kernel. It enhances the dependability of the Linux application services. The service uses the

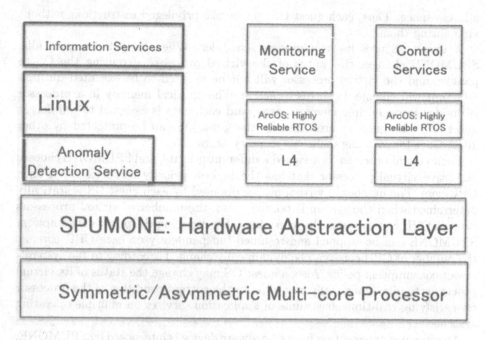

Fig. 1. An Overview of Our Operating System Architecture

monitoring and tracing facilities offered by the Linux kernel to detect anomalies in application services.

The architecture also improves user experience when an anomaly in a system occurs. ArcOS increases the robustness of the monitoring service, and the monitoring service repairs the anomaly in the Linux kernel. When SPUMONE detects crashing or hanging in Linux, it converts them to recoverable errors that can be handled in applications services. However, we do not assume that the monitoring service repairs the damage of the kernel completely. Thus, the monitoring service will restart the Linux kernel while a user does not interact with an appliance. The anomaly detection service detects the anomaly in application services on Linux, and restarts the abnormal services to maintain the integrity of the services.

3.2 SPUMONE: Hardware Abstraction Layer

SPUMONE offers the abstraction called virtual processors to satisfy the diverse requirements by using multiple operating systems as described in the previous section. One or multiple virtual processors are assigned to each guest OS. If a guest OS is configured as an SMP operating system, multiple virtual processors may be multiplexed on a single CPU core or be executed on different CPU cores. An instance of SPUMONE is created on each CPU core and may schedule multiple virtual processors. For reducing the overhead of switching virtual processors, both guest operating systems and SPUMONE are located in the same privileged address space. Thus, each guest OS can invoke privileged instructions without virtualizing them.

A guest OS uses its own process scheduler. When the OS becomes idle, SPUMONE changes the status of the virtual processor executing the OS to passive, and the virtual processor will not be selected to be executed until an interrupt will change its status to active. The physical memory in a processor is divided into multiple memory areas, and each area is assigned to a different guest OS. The memory area used by the guest OS can be protected by other guest OSes for avoiding malicious memory access.

Each virtual processor is assigned a different priority, and SPUMONE chooses an active virtual processor that has the highest priority to be executed on a CPU core. The number of virtual processors used by each guest OS is statically determined when the system is booted. Also, the number of virtual processors on each CPU core is statically determined. For reducing the power consumption, SPUMONE can be stopped and resumed independently on each CPU core, so the number of CPU cores can be dynamically changed according to the system's power consumption policy. Also, a guest OS may change the status of its virtual processor to idle dynamically according to the current condition of the processor for satisfying real-time constraints of application services on multiple operating systems.

An interrupt or exception from a hardware device is interposed by SPUMONE. The mapping between interrupt sources and virtual processors is statically specified in SPUMONE. In traditional OSes, an interrupt processing is scheduled before the execution of all processes. However, in SPUMONE, low priority interrupt processing can be delayed while executing a virtual processor with a high priority. This means that the priority of interrupt processing is integrated with the priorities of virtual processors. Thus, an interrupt with a low priority does not affect the execution of a virtual processor with a high priority.

SPUMONE has three mechanisms to increase its flexibility. The first mechanism is the priority integrity mechanism. To guarantee different guest OS's timing constraint requirements, each guest OS changes the priority of its virtual processor dynamically according to the priority of the executing process. When a CPU core multiplexes several virtual processors, the priority of the executing process is mapped to its virtual processor. Thus, the virtual processor on which a guest OS runs to schedule a process with highest priority is selected to be executed on a CPU core. The second mechanism is a CPU accounting mechanism to limit the CPU capacity used by each virtual processor. This is useful to protect the capacity of a CPU core from the monopolization by a specific guest OS. The third mechanism is a mechanism to virtualize errors occurring on each CPU core. When SPUMONE detects hanging or crashing on the CPU core, it changes the current program counter and stack pointer to the initially specified value to convert the errors to easily recoverable errors. For example, when hanging or crashing is detected during the execution of a system call, the system call raises an exception to an application process, and the process will recover from the exception by re-executing the system call or executing an alternative system call.

Currently SPUMONE runs on a single core SH4A architecture processor. Linux, L4 and TOPPERS are running on SPUMONE and can be run concurrently on a single CPU core. We are working on supporting a multi-core processor that contains four SH4A CPU cores.

3.3   ArcOS: Dependable Real-Time OS

ArcOS is an operating system that has an ability of automatic self-healing. In ArcOS, each software component is implemented in an isolated protection domain that can be independently restarted when hanging or crashing occurs in these components. ArcOS is a multi-server operating system built on top of the L4 micro-kernel. System components such as a file system and device drivers run in independently isolated protection domains, and are also restarted in case these system components violate their integrity and the violation is exposed by some errors.

The most fundamental functionalities of ArcOS are involved in the root servers that we assume to be highly reliable. P3, which is one of the root servers, is a dedicated memory manager of each software component. An error detector and a persistent storage mechanism described below are implemented in P3, so that each component can use the mechanism as an infrastructure service.

A component implemented on ArcOS tries to recover an error caused by the anomaly through various exception handling strategies. Also, ArcOS tries to virtualize the error to convert the unrecoverable error to the recoverable error if possible. Since the aggressive recovery strategies used in ArcOS may not resolve the inconsistency in the component, the inconsistency should be completely removed by scheduling the restart of the component when the effect of the restart becomes minimal. In case the exposed error cannot be recovered with any aggressive recovering strategies, ArcOS will restart the component immediately.

Since each service is decomposed into multiple software components in ArcOS, the integrity of a system is maintained by restarting respective components using the micro-rebooting technique [8]. The most important issue when using the micro-rebooting technique is to quickly restart a software component to reconstruct internal data structures. Candea et. al.[8] have proposed crash-only software to make is easy to build highly reliable Internet services. However, for building information appliances, it takes a long time to reconstruct data structures in a restarted component if it is implemented as crash-only software. ArcOS assumes that each component stores some critical data in a persistent storage. Also, the component defines a recovery procedure, which is invoked when the component is restarted. The procedure reconstructs internal data structures quickly by retrieving data from the persistent storage. The persistent storage stores critical data structures that may take a long time to recover. Also, session data maintained by system services are stored in persistent storage. For example, a file service keeps data about currently opened files for reconstructing the data when it is restarted. Some errors caused by the anomaly in a component may make the data in the persistent storage inconsistent. Since transactional updates are not suitable to implementing various services on information appliances, ArcOS virtualizes the errors to prevent data in the persistent storage from becoming inconsistent. A component continues to execute even when errors are exposed after the completion to access data structures and the consistency is maintained.

ArcOS offers three mechanisms to maintain the system's integrity. The first mechanism is to invoke a recovery procedure before a software component is restarted. As described in the previous paragraph, the mechanism enables the component to be recovered very quickly. The second mechanism is a persistent storage that is used to store critical data for supporting quick restarting. The last mechanism is a failure detection service that detects a crash or hang in a component and restarts it. ArcOS also offers a programming framework that hides details to use the persistent storage to develop self-healing application services in an easy way.

In the current implementation, we have developed a couple of device drivers on ArcOS to show the effectiveness. The device driver is a source of the fragileness of the current operating systems. As described in previous research [11], it is not easy to develop self-healing device drivers even when using micro-kernel-based operating systems. ArcOS enables various device drivers to be recovered quickly and makes it possible to use the micro-rebooting technique in information appliances.

3.4 Monitoring Service

The motivation for our monitoring service is driven by handling system anomaly and security attacks. When information appliances will become more complicated, they may behave in a strange or unexpected way due to undisclosed bugs or faults that are not handled correctly, which is known as system anomaly. Currently once the anomaly of information appliances occurs, it is difficult to perform either anomaly analysis or further recovery. In a similar way, information appliances suffer from security attacks. Virus programs might inject malicious codes into the target host OS through the Internet and then compromise it. Because most of the end users lack enough technical knowledge, they usually cannot solve such security problems themselves and even cannot notice that the system has been compromised. The monitoring service is designed for satisfying the above requirements by providing both the inconsistency detection inside the OS kernel and the automatic recovery mechanism.

Conventional solutions usually suffer from the high memory overhead. In prior researches, the backward-recovery technique takes snapshots at checkpoints to perform a recovery from some fatal errors. On every checkpoint, the system will make a memory snapshot of some specific processes, which introduces the overhead of memory resources. In signature-based intrusion detection systems, a large mount of persistent memory has been used to track suspicious activities. Moreover, there will be more overhead when the monitored object behaves more complicated and nondeterministically, e.g. in the Linux kernel. Current information appliances are still limited by system resources to reduce its costs. Obviously, the above solutions are neither suitable for developing information appliances, nor for the detection and recovery of the anomaly in the Linux kernel. Moreover, our monitoring service is more light-weight.

The monitoring service observes the integrity in the Linux kernel by monitoring the consistency of its critical data structures. When the service detects an inconsistency, a repair function is invoked. A similar technique described in [7] is used for repairing consistent data structures. In the repair function, we do not assume that the consistency is completely recovered. There is always the possibility that inconsistencies like memory-leakage remains. The consistency will be recovered completely after the entire Linux kernel is restarted while a user does not interact with an appliance.

Since the monitoring service is implemented as quickly restart-able components by using the ArcOS framework, each component of the service can be efficiently restarted automatically when a component crashes or hangs. The monitoring service is developed as several Linux kernel modules and a single independent inconsistency detection module running on the L4 micro-kernel and ArcOS. The kernel modules are in charge of the kernel data structure repair. The inconsistency detection module can access the memory of the Linux kernel at runtime through shared memory between the Linux kernel and the inconsistency detection module. The Linux kernel's internal critical data structures are periodically checked for consistency against the built-in anomaly detection database. Once inconsistency in some data structures has been detected, the corresponding repair functions will be invoked. Since the inconsistency detection module runs outside the Linux kernel, and it is completely isolated and hidden from Linux, the faults or bugs inside the Linux kernel does not affect the detection process running on ArcOS.

Currently, several case studies have been carried out to show the effectiveness of the monitoring service, such as the kernel-level hidden process detection and memory leak recovery.

3.5 Anomaly Detection Service

The role of the anomaly detection service is to detect anomalies in a Linux application service before the inconsistency caused by the anomaly is exposed. The user level application services implemented on the Linux kernel becomes more and more complex in future information appliances. These application services may misbehave temporally or can be attacked by malicious programs. For making the behavior of the services more stable, detecting the anomaly of the services is very important.

The service records the fine-grained CPU resource usage of each process and a variety of detailed events traced inside the Linux kernel such as invoking system calls or occurring interrupts and exceptions. The information allows the anomaly detection service to analyze the behavior of applications services without modifying them. For example, the communication patters among user processes can be extracted by analyzing the kernel events traced in the network protocol module transparently. The approach is similar to Magpie [13], but our approach also uses the fine-grained resource usage to make it easy to reduce the overhead to analyze a large amount of kernel events.

The anomaly detection service can be used to detect abnormal behavior in application services, and increase the dependability of a system significantly by restarting abnormal services before the violation of the integrity becomes serious. It learns the normal pattern of the behavior of a target application service by using a variety of machine learning techniques. When it detects the abnormal pattern, the target service is restarted to recover its integrity. For example, the fine-grained CPU resource usage of each process may be used to detect intrusion inside an information appliance. Also, by using a similar approach described in [12], the service detects the anomaly caused by software bugs in application services. The approach may enable us to detect unknown anomaly by classifying abnormal behavior from normal behavior.

The anomaly detection service consists of four modules. The first module is a kernel tracing module that traces a variety of events inside the Linux kernel. Currently, LLTng [14] is used as the kernel event tracing module. The second module is an accounting system that calculates the fine-grained CPU resource usage for each process [15]. Of course, the information can be extracted from the information generated by the kernel event tracing module, but our approach can reduce the overhead caused by analyzing a large amount of kernel events, and it is more suitable for developing information appliances. The third module is a logging module that records the information generated in the first and second modules. The fourth module is an analysis module that is a set of user processes retrieving a model from the logs stored in the logging module. A different process is implemented to retrieve a different model from the logs. When the analysis module detects abnormal behavior, the causing process will be restarted to recover the integrity of an information appliance.

4   Sample Scenarios

The section presents several sample scenarios showing the effectiveness of the proposed operating system architecture.

Robust Control Processing Service: ArcOS enables us to develop robust control processing services. The services can be decomposed into multiple components and each component can be restarted independently. By using the framework offered by ArcOS, a service recovers its integrity by restarting it when an inconsistency is detected.

The execution of Linux is isolated from the execution of a control processing service by SPUMONE. SPUMONE configures the execution in Linux to be postponed when the execution of control processing services is active. The approach makes it possible that the temporal effect of Linux does not affect the execution of control processing services. Also, restarting Linux does not affect the execution of the control processing services. For example, the execution of a continuous media processing service on ArcOS does not violate its timing constraints even when Linux is restarted.

Virtual Dependability: If a user is not aware of the restart of an appliance, the appliance becomes virtually dependent on the user. The monitoring service and

SPUMONE repair the Linux kernel's internal integrity to continue the execution even when a crash or hang in the Linux kernel occurs. However, since our repair takes an optimistic approach, the inconsistency that does not affect the execution of the kernel for a short time will remain in the kernel. The inconsistency can be removed completely by restarting the kernel. SPUMONE schedules the reboot of the kernel when a user does not interact with an appliance.

SMP Emulation on SPUMONE: Interrupt processing time can be very long in the current Linux kernel when burst network traffic is received while a single CPU core is used. This violates the timing constraints of real-time applications. Our approach to solve the problem is that SPUMONE creates two virtual processors on a single CPU core, and switches the contexts of the virtual processors in a fine-grained way.

In this approach, one virtual processor executes all interrupt processing, and another virtual processor executes all other activities. Thus, when a virtual processor starts to execute a long processing interrupt in a high priority, the processing is blocked when the interrupt processing time exceeds the specific threshold. The CPU accounting mechanism in SPUMONE makes the configuration easy.

Using a Multi-core Processor: SPUMONE enables each CPU core to be turned on or off dynamically according to the current workload in Linux and the policy of the power management. For example, when the workload of an appliance is very low, one CPU core is active to execute both Linux and L4. On the other hand, if the workload is high, all CPU cores will be used to process the workload.

When several application services on multiple operating systems need to ensure their timing constraints, the integrity of priorities should be maintained. SPUMONE supports two approaches to maintain the priority integrity. The first approach is to coordinate all priorities in multiple operating systems by mapping them in global priorities. The approach requires taking into account all real-time activities on the multiple operating systems to ensure their timing constraints. The second approach uses different CPU cores for executing multiple operating systems. When Linux starts a real-time application, Linux and L4 use different CPU cores to schedule their applications independently. In this case, since different operating systems use different CPU cores, each operating system can schedule real-time activities without considering the real-time activities in other operating systems.

5   Conclusion and Future Directions

This paper presents an operating system architecture for future information appliances. Currently, we are implementing the operating system architecture on several hardware platforms that use Hitachi SH4 processors. One of them contains a multi-core processor with four SH4 processors.

There are a couple of future directions in our research. Of course, one of the most important directions is to build an actual information appliance using the proposed architecture. We are planning to build a simple audio player on ArcOS in such a way that Linux can be rebooted anytime without disturbing the execution of the audio player.

The second future direction is to use the monitoring service to monitor the hardware devices. This is very useful to detect various abnormal conditions of the appliance. For example, if the source of the anomaly is correctly localized, it may be possible to replace the damaged hardware easily. This makes the model-based diagnosis[9] possible. Also, if the damage is serious and has the potential to cause serious a accident in the near future, the appliance disables to avoid the risk of an accident. This is very useful to preserve sustain-ability.

The last future direction is to implement ArcOS on Linux. It makes it easy to decompose an application service into multiple processes. When the anomaly detection service detects abnormal processes, the processes are restarted to recover the integrity of the service. However, current Linux does not support sufficient functionalities to implement ArcOS. Thus, we will add some system calls for solving the problem.

References

1. Yamabe, T., Fujinami, K., Nakajima, T.: Experiences with Building Sentient Materials Using Various Sensors. In: Proceedings of 24th International Conference on Distributed Computing Systems Workshops (IWSAWC 2004) (2004)
2. Fujinami, K., Kawsar, F., Nakajima, T.: AwareMirror: A Personalized Display Using a Mirror. In: Proceedings of International Conference on Pervasive Computing (Pervasive 2005) (2005)
3. Iwasaki, S., Hirakawa, Y., Mase, H., Tokunaga, E., Nakajima, T.: Towards computer-supported face-to-face knowledge sharing. In: Extended Abstracts Proceedings of the 2006 Conference on Human Factors in Computing Systems (2006)
4. Nakajima, T., Fujinami, K., Tokunaga, E., Ishikawa, H.: Middleware design issues for ubiquitous computing. In: Proceedings of the 3rd International Conference on Mobile and Ubiquitous Multimedia (MUM 2004) (2004)
5. Nakajima, T., Satoh, I.: A software infrastructure for supporting spontaneous and personalized interaction in home computing environments. Personal and Ubiquitous Computing 10(6), 379–391 (2006)
6. Nakajima, T., Lehdonvirta, V., Tokunaga, E., Kimura, H.: Reflecting Human Behavior to Motivate Desirable Lifestyle. In: Proceedings of The 6th ACM Conference on Designing Interactive Systems (DIS 2008) (2008)
7. Demsky, B., Rinard, M.C.: Goal-Directed Reasoning for Specification-Based Data Structure Repair. IEEE Transactions on Software Engineering 32(12) (2006)
8. Candea, G., Kawamoto, S., Fujiki, Y., Friedman, G., Fox, A.: Microreboot - A Technique for Cheap Recovery. In: Proceedings of the 6th Symposium on Operating Systems Design and Implementation (OSDI 2004) (2004)
9. Peti, P., Obermaisser, R., Ademaj, A., Kopetz, H.: A Maintenance-Oriented Fault Model for the DECOS Integrated Diagnostic Architecture. In: Proceedings of 19th IEEE International Parallel and Distributed Processing Symposium (IPDPS 2005) (2005)
10. L4 eXperimental Kernel Reference Manual, Version X.2, Revision 6, System Architecture Group, Department of Computer Science, Universität Karlsruhe (2006)

11. Herder, J.N., Bos, H., Gras, B., Homburg, P., Tanenbaum, A.S.: Failure Resilience for Device Drivers. In: Proceedings of the 37th Annual IEEE/IFIP International Conference on Dependable Systems and Networks (DSN 2007) (2007)
12. Chen, M.Y., Accardi, A., Kiciman, E., Patterson, D., Fox, A., Brewer, E.: Path-based failure and evolution management. In: Proceedings of the 1st, USENIX/ACM Symposium on Networked Systems Design and Implementation (NSDI 2004) (2004)
13. Barham, P., Donnelly, A., Isaacs, R., Mortier, R.: Using Magpie for Request Extraction and Workload Modelling. In: Proceedings of the International Symposium on Operating Systems Design and Implementation (OSDI 2004) (2004)
14. Desnoyers, M., Dagenais, M.R.: The LTTng tracer: A low impact performance and behavior monitor for GNU/Linux. In: Proceedings of the Ottawa Linux Symposium (2006)
15. Sugaya, M., Oikawa, S., Nakajima, T.: Accounting System: A Fine-Grained CPU Resource Protection Mechanism for Embedded System. In: Proceedings of the 9th IEEE International Symposium on Object and Component-oriented Real-Time Distributed Computing (ISORC 2006) (2006)

M-Geocast: Robust and Energy-Efficient Geometric Routing for Mobile Sensor Networks*

Lynn Choi[1], Jae Kyun Jung[1], Byong-Ha Cho[1], and Hyohyun Choi[2]

[1] Korea University, Anam-Dong, Sungbuk-Ku, Seoul, Korea
{lchoi,kernel,sntblue}@korea.ac.kr
Tel.: +82-2-3290-3249; Fax: +82-2-921-0544
[2] u-Convergence Laboratory, Samsung Electronics Co., Ltd
hyohyun.choi@samsung.com

Abstract. In this paper we investigate a practical routing solution for a new class of wireless sensor networks where any node can be mobile anytime. Assuming GPS-enabled sensor nodes we propose a new geometric routing protocol called M-Geocast that is designed to efficiently support node mobility as well as location service for such mobile sensor networks. Unlike existing geometric routing schemes, M-Geocast can also discover a non-geometric path to the destination by exploiting the path history of location updates. Thus, the routing void can be minimized by alternating the two. In addition, M-Geocast employs two location-based optimizations to further reduce the overhead of on-demand route discovery on inevitable routing voids. Through detailed NS-2 simulations we demonstrate that M-Geocast can not only increase network performance but can also reduce energy consumption compared to the existing protocols based on on-demand route discovery or a plain geometric routing.

Keywords: mobility, sensor networks, geometric routing, MANET, void.

1 Introduction

Sensors are now sufficiently small and cheap so that people can carry them around. Coupling these sensors with a nearly billion mobile wireless devices will create a new network of mobile sensors in the future. Yet, most of existing studies on wireless sensor networks assume only stationary sensor nodes [1]. Recently several studies investigate the use of mobile sinks to improve coverage, localization accuracy, or energy efficiency [2, 4, 9, 11]. However, none of these studies have investigated the case of fully mobile sensor network (MSN) environment where any node can move anytime. In this paper we investigate a practical routing solution for this new class of wireless sensor networks where both sensor nodes and sinks can be mobile anytime.

Node mobility brings several challenges to large-scale sensor networking. First, the preconstruction of message delivery network may not be useful since the topology may change too frequently due to node movement. Second, the frequent location updates

---

* This work was supported by the Korea Science and Engineering Foundation (KOSEF) grant funded by the Korea government (MOST) (No. R01-2007-000-20958-0). This work was also supported by a Korea University Grant.

U. Brinkschulte, T. Givargis, and S. Russo (Eds.): SEUS 2008, LNCS 5287, pp. 304–316, 2008.

from a mobile node can lead to an excessive drain of sensors' limited battery power and increased collisions in wireless transmissions. Third, the situation can get worse when the number of mobile nodes grows. While MANET protocols [3, 8] may provide a reasonable performance for MSN but they would incur too much overhead in terms of traffic and energy consumption since they usually assume peer-to-peer randomized traffic rather than many-to-one traffic from sources to sinks assumed in MSN. One possible solution is employing a geometric routing scheme [5, 6, 7] rather than a topology-based routing protocol. Assuming location-aware sensor nodes the geometric routing is scalable, fast, and energy efficient since it does neither require global routing table maintenance nor the on-demand path discovery used in MANET protocols.

In this paper, we propose a new geometric routing protocol called M-Geocast to efficiently support routing for mobile sensor networks. In the presence of multiple sinks M-Geocast designates one of the sinks as the master sink. The *master sink* acts as a location service provider and also as a data collection and dissemination server. Only the master sink needs to flood its location information. Thus, all the nodes including sinks can send messages to the master sink using a simple geographic forwarding. As in all the geometric schemes, M-Geocast may encounter geographic holes [5, 6, 7]. To recover from such a routing void, M-Geocast uses the following novel approach. First, M-Geocast can discover a second path to the destination by using the path history of the location updates. This is called *path history forwarding*. Second, if both the geometric routing and path history forwarding fail either due to a routing hole or due to a broken link, M-Geocast can discover a new path to the destination on demand by flooding RREQ messages. Thus, M-Geocast can completely eliminate the routing void. To avoid excessive flooding caused by such on-demand path discovery, M-Geocast employs two location-based optimization techniques called *path history projection* and *geographic void prediction*. Together, M-Geocast can substantially outperform existing routing solutions in terms of both energy efficiency and network performance as demonstrated in Section IV.

The rest of this paper is organized as follows. Section II surveys the related work. Section III introduces M-Geocast's routing, location service, and detour methods. Section IV discusses the simulation results. Finally, Section VI concludes the paper.

2 Related Works

Numerous geometric routing schemes [5, 6, 7] have been proposed for ad hoc networks. In terms of forwarding strategy, existing greedy routing schemes can be classified as *Greedy* (minimize the distance to the destination) *MFR* (most forward progress within radius r), *NFP* (nearest with forward progress), *Compass routing* (select a neighbor closest to the straight line between the source and the destination), and *Random* selection depending on which neighbor node to forward to [7]. M-Geocast can be classified as Greedy, which selects a neighbor node that is closest to the destination as the next forwarding node.

In geometric routing a location service is necessary to learn the current position of a potential destination. Mobile nodes should register their current position with the location service provider. GLS [6] partitions the network field as a hierarchy of squares called quadtree. By issuing position queries up in the hierarchy, GLS ensures the position query to reach the correct location server. Another strategy called Home-zone [10] uses a hash function to locate the server. Both GLS and Homezone can be classified as an all-for-some service [7] since all nodes need to store the location information for some other nodes. In terms of location service, M-Geocast can be classified as some-for-some approach [7], since only a single location server maintains the position information of mobile sinks.

In geometric greedy forwarding any node may fail to find the next node when it arrives at a local maximum where none of its neighbors is closer to the destination than itself. To counter this problem, numerous schemes have been proposed [5, 7]. One intuitive strategy is selecting the node with the least backward progress if no nodes can be found in the forward direction. However, this leads to a looping problem [7]. The face-2 algorithm [7] and the perimeter routing strategy of GPSR [5] uses a simple planar graph traversal to find a path to the destination. However, this approach may fail to find a path when the network field has an open void [7]. In contrast, M-Geocast uses path history and other hints to recover from the routing holes and can guarantee the recovery by using the on-demand route discovery if necessary.

The idea of master sink is similar to the virtual sink concept used in VSR [2] which can support sink mobility assuming stationary sensor nodes. However, M-Geocast is different from VSR in the following aspects. First, M-Geocast does neither maintain routing table nor routing tree as in VSR. Second, VSR assumes only stationary sensor nodes. To support MSN, VSR needs to rebuild its routing tree continuously whenever there is a topology change, which might be too expensive to be used in MSN. Third, only a sink can perform the role of the master sink in M-Geocast, while a normal stationary sensor node is designated as a virtual sink in VSR. In summary, M-Geocast is a position-based routing protocol for mobile sensor networks while VSR is a topology-based routing protocol for static sensor networks with mobile sinks.

3 M-Geocast

3.1 M-Geocast and Master Sink

As in all geographical routing, M-Geocast marks each packet with the location information of its destination. A forwarding node can make a locally optimal, greedy choice by selecting one of its neighbors that is closest to the destination. This assumes that each node has the location information of all of its neighbors through neighbor discovery process as explained in Section III.2. In the presence of multiple mobile sinks M-Geocast designates one of the sinks as the master sink. The *master sink* acts as a data collection and dissemination server for all the nodes in the field. To accomplish this task, the master sink needs to periodically flood its location information throughout the sensor field. Thus, all the nodes in the field can send messages to the master sink using the geographic greedy forwarding. Figure 1 shows the routing path of M-Geocast when there are three sources and two destinations. Each source directs its messages to the master sink using the greedy forwarding. The master sink collects all the messages from the sources and forwards them to other sinks. To accomplish this, the master sink needs to track the location of other sinks.

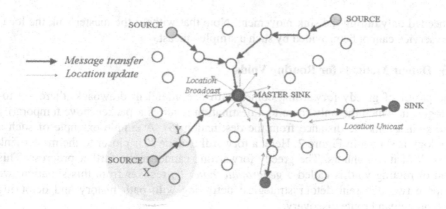

Fig. 1. Routing through a master sink in M-Geocast

3.2 Location Service and Neighbor Discovery

Adaptive Beaconing: For the geographic forwarding, each node in M-Geocast should maintain the location information of its neighbors. For this purpose, each node periodically broadcasts its location information to its neighbors. A simple beaconing provides all nodes with their neighbors' positions. Periodically, each node transmits a beacon using a MAC-level broadcast including only its own identifier (e.g., IP address) and position. However, in random waypoint model each node spends a significant portion of its time without movement. In stationary state, the periodic broadcast may generate too much unnecessary traffic. To avoid this, M-Geocast requires each node to broadcast its location only during movement. However, this creates another problem. Assume that a new node X moves in the area of node Y and node Y is in stationary state. Since node Y does not broadcast its location, the new node X cannot recognize the node X even though it does exist. To solve this problem, we propose a new neighbor discovery scheme called *adaptive beaconing*. First, a stationary node usually does not broadcast its beacon. However, whenever it hears the beacon of a new incoming node, it generates its beacon just once to inform its location to this newcomer. This allows each node to keep track of their neighbors' locations even during movement while suppressing the unnecessary beacon transmissions.

Location Broadcast from Master Sink: While the location information of a sensor node needs to be broadcast among its own neighbors, the location information of a master sink needs to be propagated throughout the sensor field because all the nodes assume the location information of the master sink. This is accomplished by a simple periodic flooding by the master sink. As in adaptive beaconing, the master sink needs to flood its location information only during its movement.

Location Unicast from Sink: To forward all the messages collected from sensor nodes, the location information of other sinks must be tracked by the master sink. This is accomplished by a simple unicast from each sink to the master sink by using the geometric greedy forwarding. Like in other location updates, this location update is needed only during the sink movement. Note that without the master sink the location service cannot be provided by such a simple unicast.

3.3 Detour Methods for Routing Voids

The power of greedy forwarding comes with one attendant drawback: there are topologies in which the only route to a destination requires a packet move temporarily *farther* in geometric distance from the destination [5]. A simple example of such a topology is shown in Figure 2. Here, a forwarding node X is closer to the master sink than all of its neighbors. The greedy forwarding cannot make further progress. This kind of routing void is called a *geographic hole*. To recover from this situation, we propose two different detour strategies: detouring with path history and detouring with on-demand route discovery.

Detour with Path History: The idea of this detour method is to use the path history of location updates. Note that the path from a source to a sink follows a reverse path of location updates from the sink to the source via the master sink. Figure 2 illustrates routing holes and a detour path from the source to the real sinks. It takes advantage of the fact that every node receives the location update from the master sink. If each node marks the neighbor node from which it has received the last location update, then it can follow the reverse path of the location update to find a path to the master sink as well as a path to the other sinks. In fact, M-Geocast can use two different routing strategies: one based on geometric greedy forwarding and the other based on the path history. We will investigate the performance impact of combining two different routing strategies in Section IV.

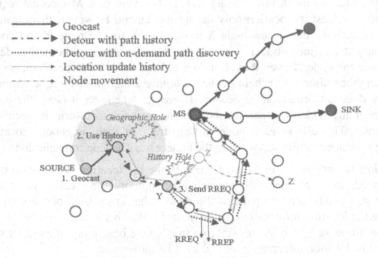

Fig. 2. Detour mechanisms of M-Geocast

Detour with On-Demand Route Discovery: The path history remains valid as long as the all the nodes in the path remain stationary. However, as time goes by, it is likely that a link in the path is broken due to node movement. The probability of the path failure increases as the distance between the source and the destination increases. We call this type of routing void as a *history hole*. For example, node Y in Figure 2 has a broken link to node Z due to Z's movement. If both the geometric routing and the path history routing lead to a routing void, we must resort to another detour method. Although several detour methods have been proposed [5, 7], theoretically it is possible to come up with a topology that can invalidate any sophisticated detour method based on a non-exhaustive search. To completely eliminate the routing holes, we use on-demand path discovery used in reactive MANET routing protocols [3, 8].

On a routing void, the forwarding node broadcasts RREQ (Route Request) which includes the address of itself, the destination address, and message type (RREQ). The destination node that receives RREQ replies with RREP (Route Reply) unicast including its location information. However, unlike AODV [8], M-Geocast does neither use source sequence numbers nor it does set up reverse route entries since it assumes unidirectional traffic from sources to sinks. The RREQ/RREP method is a robust detour method as it always finds a path to the destination as long as it does exist. However, the frequent use of RREQ/RREP may result in increased latency and energy consumption due to its flooding nature. To minimize the use of RREQ/RREP, we employ the following two location-based optimization techniques.

3.4 M-Geocast Optimizations

Geographic Void Prediction: To minimize the use of RREQ/RREP, we should avoid encountering a geographic hole whenever possible. From our simulation studies we found that if the direction pointed by the geometric routing is the opposite direction of the recent path history, there is a high chance of a geographic hole since the location updates from the master sink usually takes the shortest path. If such condition is met, M-Geocast predicts that the geometric routing may lead to a geographic hole and uses the path history instead. This is implemented by computing cosine θ between the direction of greedy forwarding and the direction pointed by the path history. If the value of cosine θ is greater than 0, M-Geocast adopts the path history. Otherwise, M-Geocast uses the greedy forwarding. To prevent a loop in the routing path, M-Geocast does not use greedy forwarding once path history is selected. As shown in Section IV, this can effectively reduce the number of geographic holes.

Path History Projection: The second option in minimizing the use of RREQ/RREP is to avoid a history hole. However, it is physically impossible to avoid a link failure if the next hop has disappeared due to node movement. Yet, we can still approximate the path history on a link failure. By using the location information of its neighbors, the forwarding node can send messages to a neighbor node which is located in the same direction as pointed by the previous path history. This is also implemented by selecting a neighbor node among its neighboring nodes that has the maximum cosine θ from the direction pointed by the path history. To prevent a routing loop, node S must be removed from the new path history. Note that both of these optimizations are possible due to location information of neighbor nodes, which are available only in geometric routing schemes.

4 Simulation

4.1 Simulation Methodology

We have implemented all the routing functions of M-Geocast in the ns-2 simulator [12]. We generate 200-node sensor field by randomly placing the nodes in a 1500 × 1500 m^2. Each node has a radio range of 250m. Unless otherwise mentioned, all sources are randomly selected from the sensor field following the random sources model [1] while sinks are uniformly scattered across the field. Each source generates one event per second and each event is modeled as a 64-byte packet. All the events are reported to all the sinks in the field. We use the random waypoint model [3] as a mobility model. The maximum pause time is 30 seconds. Each simulation run lasts for 100 seconds.

We use three metrics: average message latency, average dissipated energy, and delivery success ratio. *Average message latency* measures the average one-way communication latency between a source and a sink. *Average dissipated energy* measures the ratio of total dissipated energy per node to the number of distinct events seen by sinks. *Delivery success ratio* is the ratio of the number of distinct events successfully received to the total number of events originally reported. Similar metrics were used in early works [2, 5, 8]. For each metric, we vary the number of sources, the number of sinks, node speed, and node density.

All the metrics of M-Geocast are compared against a baseline geographic greedy forwarding (Geocast) and Active On-demand Distance Vector routing (AODV) [8]. Geocast is used to evaluate the impact of master sink in M-Geocast and AODV is one of the most popular and effective MANET routing protocol. We use the same energy model and MAC protocol as adopted in their ns-2 simulators. We use 1.6Mbps 802.11 DCF as the underlying MAC protocol. The idle-time power dissipation is 35mW, reception power dissipation is 395mW, and transmission power dissipation is 660mW.

4.2 Simulation Results

Varying the number of sinks: Figure 3 shows the results by varying the number of sinks from 1 to 16. Five sources were used for the simulations. Figure 3(a) shows the average message latency. AODV's latency is substantially higher than those of geometric schemes when the number of sinks is greater than 4. This is because RREQ flooding required by AODV generates significant traffic, and the additional contention induced by such traffic increases delay significantly. In Geocast the situation is less severe but its average message delay start to increase as the number of sinks grows since each sink generates location updates every 3 seconds during its movement. However, the delay remains constant in M-Geocast for all the cases simulated, which is noticeably faster than that of Geocast. Figure 3(b) shows the average dissipated energy. As the number of sinks grows, the gap between M-Geocast and other schemes start to grow substantially. For the 16 sink case, M-Geocast consumes only 41% of AODV's and 51% of Geocast's average energy consumption respectively. M-Geocast's energy savings are due to the fact that it requires location update from a single master sink while AODV and Geocast incur substantial overhead due to RREQ flooding and location broadcasts from multiple sinks respectively. Finally, Figure 3(c) shows the delivery success ratio. For all the cases simulated M-Geocast successfully delivers more than 99 % of all the events. Although Geocast shows comparable delivery ratios but its ratio drops to 94% with 16 sinks. In contrast, the delivery success ratio of AODV suddenly drops to 12% as the number of sinks increases from 4 to 8. This is because AODV incurs RREQ path setup for each sink.

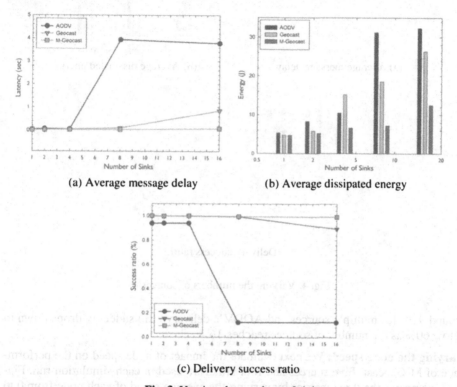

(a) Average message delay   (b) Average dissipated energy

(c) Delivery success ratio

Fig. 3. Varying the numbers of sinks

Varying the number of sources: Our second set of simulations evaluates the performance of M-Geocast by varying the number of sources from 1 to 16, which is shown in Figure 4. Two sinks are assumed for the simulations. As shown in the figure the latency of AODV increases substantially as we increase the number of sources because AODV requires RREQ flooding for each source. The numbers of both Geocast and M-Geocast are comparable and substantially smaller than that of AODV. In addition, the average dissipated energy of M-Geocast is smaller than Geocast and AODV especially when there are a large number of sources. This is because the protocol overhead incurred by AODV and Geocast steadily increases as the number of sources grows compared to M-Geocast. With 16 sources, M-Geocast's energy consumption is less than 33% of AODV and 66% of Geocast. Finally, M-Geocast successfully delivers almost all the events to the sinks while Geocast's delivery ratio is

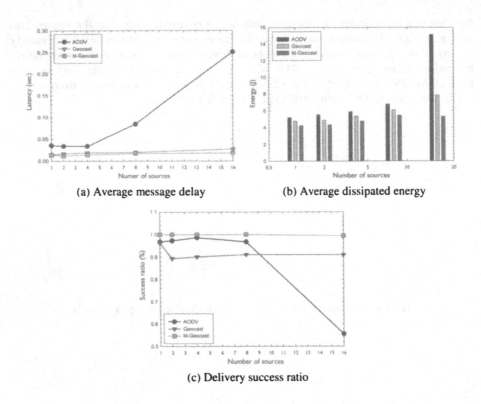

(a) Average message delay   (b) Average dissipated energy

(c) Delivery success ratio

Fig. 4. Varying the numbers of sources

around 91% for multiple sources and AODV's delivery ratio suddenly drops down to below 60% as the number of sources reaches 16.

Varying the node speed: We next evaluate the impact of node speed on the performance of M-Geocast. Five sources and four sinks are used in each simulation run. Figure 5 compares the three metrics by varying the average speed of each node from 0 to 20 m/s. As the node speed increases, both the delay of both Geocast and M-Geocast remains stable. This is because geometric routing does not incur additional overhead regardless of its speed as long as the location information of the destination remains valid. Surprisingly, Geocast's latency actually decreases as the node speed increases. This is due to the fact that Geocast cannot deliver some of its messages for medium to high speed movement as illustrated in Figure 5(c). Compared to the geometric schemes, the average message latency of AODV substantially increases as the node speed increases. As the node speed increases, the existing route entries cached by AODV become no longer valid. This requires AODV to flood RREQ for each message generated. As a result, the average message delay of AODV linearly increases. The latency of M-Geocast remains below 38ms while the latency of Geocast varies for different node speed due to its unstable message delivery. For all the cases simulated M-Geocast's average dissipated energy remains relatively constant, around 6.5J while the energy consumption of AODV steadily increases. As we expect from the

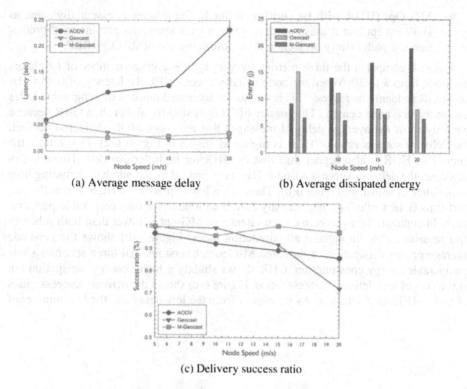

(a) Average message delay   (b) Average dissipated energy

(c) Delivery success ratio

Fig. 5. Varying the node speed

low delay and the low energy consumption of M-Geocast, M-Geocast consistently delivers more than 96% of all the events for all the cases, whereas Geocast's success ratio drops down to 72% for nodes with high speed, which is even lower than that of AODV. Yet, AODV's success ratio steadily decreases to 86% when the sink speed reaches 20m/s.

4.3 Detailed Evaluation of M-Geocast Under Routing Holes

In this section, we evaluate the impact of routing holes on the performance of M-Geocast by varying the node density in the sensor field. 16 sources and a single sink are used in each simulation run. Three versions of M-Geocast are tested as follows.

- **GHR (Geocast → History → RREQ/RREP):** In this scheme, a source node first uses geographic greedy forwarding. On a geographic hole, it rediscovers a second path using path history. If both fail, the scheme employs on-demand route discovery using RREQ/RREP.
- **HGR (History → Geocast → RREQ/RREP):** In this scheme, a source node first uses path history to find a path to the destination. If this leads to a broken link, the scheme tries geographic greedy forwarding. If both fail, the scheme uses on-demand route discovery.

- **MG-Opt (HGR with two optimizations):** The scheme is essentially same as HGR except that it uses two optimization techniques, geographic void prediction and path history projection to minimize the use of RREQ/RREP.

Figure 6 compares the three metrics by varying the average number of neighbors per node from 8 to 30. When the node density is below 10, the latency of both GHR and HGR suddenly increases. This is due to the increased number of geographic holes due to the low node density. The latency of HGR is slightly higher than GHR because we only show the average delay of messages that are successfully delivered. In fact, the delivery success ratio of HGR is higher as shown in Figure 6(c). In addition, the latency of HGR is also higher than that of GHR for high density case. However, in this case, the delivery success ratio of GHR is improved as the number of routing hole diminishes as shown in Figure 6(d). Thus, for a low density case HGR generally outperforms GHR while for a high density case both schemes show comparable performance. In contrast, the average message latency of MG-opt is lower than both schemes and remains stable throughout all simulation cases. Figure 6(b) shows the per-node average energy dissipation of the three M-Geocast versions. All three schemes show comparable energy consumption. GHR shows slightly a lower energy dissipation but at the cost of low delivery success ratios. Figure 6(c) shows the delivery success ratios of three M-Geocast schemes. As we expect from the low delay and the low number of

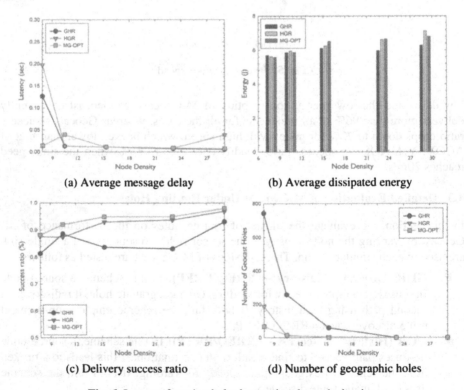

(a) Average message delay   (b) Average dissipated energy

(c) Delivery success ratio   (d) Number of geographic holes

Fig. 6. Impact of routing holes by varying the node density

routing holes, MG-opt consistently delivers more than 89% of all the events for all the cases, which is higher than HGR and GHR. In fact, GHR's success ratio drops down to 81% for low to medium density. This suggests that the two optimizations can effectively improve the performance of M-Geocast in terms of both average message delay and delivery success ratio. Figure 6(d) shows the number of geographic holes encountered during simulations by varying the node density. As shown in the figure, HGR can effectively reduce the number of geographic routing holes compared to GHR by trying history path first and MG-opt can further reduce the number by using the geographic void prediction and path history projection.

5 Conclusion

This paper proposes a new geometric routing protocol called M-Geocast that is specifically designed to support mobile sensor networks. M-Geocast provides scalable and energy efficient routing and location service that targets many-to-one traffic pattern of wireless sensor network and achieves significant performance and energy improvement over existing MANET routing protocols. Our detailed experimentation results on the ns-2 platform confirm that M-Geocast can significantly save energy while it can also reduce both the message delay and the message delivery failures compared to AODV and a plain geometric routing scheme. We also address the issue of routing holes, which has been the key focus of existing geometric routing schemes. By using the path history of location updates and also taking simple yet effective location-based optimization techniques, we can substantially reduce the number of geographic holes. As a result M-Geocast can effectively reduce both the energy consumption and average message delay compared to existing geometric schemes. This suggests that M-Geocast can be a scalable yet robust routing solution for mobile sensor networks when implemented with GPS-enabled mobile sensor nodes.

References

1. Al-Karaki, J.N., Kamal, A.E.: Routing Techniques in Wireless Sensor Networks: A Survey. Wireless Communications 11(6), 6–28 (2004)
2. Choi, L., Choi, K., Kim, J., Park, B.J.: Virtual Sink Rotation: Low-Energy Scalable Routing Protocol for Ubiquitous Sensor Networks. In: Proceedings of the 1st International Workshop on RFID and Ubiquitous Sensor Networks (USN 2005), Japan (December 2005)
3. Johnson, D.B., Maltz, D.A.: Dynamic Source Routing in Ad Hoc Wireless Networks. Mobile Computing, 153–181 (1996)
4. Juang, P., Oki, H., Wang, Y., Martonosi, M., Peh, L.S., Rubenstein, D.: Energy-efficient computing for wildlife tracking: design tradeoffs and early experiences with zebranet. In: Proceedings of the ACM 10th international conference on architectural support for programming languages and operating systems (ASPLOS-X), pp. 96–107 (2002)
5. Karp, B., Kung, H.T.: GPSR: Greedy Perimeter Stateless Routing for Wireless Networks. In: Proceedings of Mobicom 2000 (2000)
6. Li, J., et al.: A Scalable Location Service for Geographic Ad Hoc Routing. In: Proceedings of Mobicom 2000, pp. 120–130 (2000)

7. Mauve, M., Widmer, J.: A Survey on Position-Based Routing in Mobile Ad Hoc Networks. IEEE Network (November/December 2001)
8. Perkins, C., Royer, E.: Ad-hoc On-Demand Distance Vector Routing. In: Proceedings of the 2nd IEEE Workshop on Mobile Computing Systems and Applications (1999)
9. Poduri, S., Sukhatme, G.S.: Constrained Coverage for Mobile Sensor Networks. In: Proceedings of IEEE International Conference on Robotics and Automation (May 2004)
10. Stojmenovic, I.: Home Agent Based Location Update and Destination Search Schemes in Ad Hoc Wireless Networks. Technical Report TR-99-10, University of Ottawa (September 1999)
11. Tilak, S., Kolar, V., Abu-Ghazaleh, N.B., Kang, K.D.: Dynamic Localization Control for Mobile Sensor Networks. In: IEEE International Workshop on Strategies for Energy Efficiency in Ad Hoc and Sensor Networks (April 2005)
12. USC Information Science Institute, The Network Simulator ns-2 Documentation (2002), http://www.isi.edu/nsnam/ns/

Toward Integrated Virtual Execution Platform for Large-Scale Distributed Embedded Systems

Yukikazu Nakamoto[1], Issei Abe[1], Tatsunori Osaki[1], Hiroyuki Terada[1],
and Yu Moriyama[2]

[1] Graduate School of Applied Informatics, University of Hyogo
1-3-3, Higashi-Kawasaki-cho, Chuou-ku, Kobe 650-0044, Japan
[2] FUJITSU TEN Limited
2-28, Gosho-dori, 1-chome,Hyogo-ku, Kobe 652-8510, Japan
nakamoto@ai.u-hyogo.ac.jp

Abstract. The size and complexity of large-scale distributed embedded systems such as automotive and process control have increased recently. Sophisticated systems that are safe and environment friendly in the distributed systems require numerous types of sensor data, which are collected from various devices and sent to computers through networks. In order to develop the large-scale distributed embedded systems with high productivity and quality, a virtual execution environment platform is required. This platform integrates numerous CPU simulators and various device simulators through the network and provides network-wide simulation functionalities in the distributed system. In this paper, we present the requirements and initial system designs of a virtual execution environments platform for the development of the large-scale distributed embedded system software.

1 Introduction

The size and complexity of large-scale distributed embedded systems such as automotive and avionics systems have increased recently. The large-scale distributed embedded systems consist of numerous CPUs and devices which are controlled and accessed by the CPUs. We call CPUs and devices networked components. Such device includes physical objects and various hardware. We explain the situation with the automotive system. Approximately one hundred electronic control units (ECU), which are controllers for sensing data and actuating vehicle components, are used shown in Fig 1. The total program size of these systems is said to be more than seven million lines. Sophisticated automotive systems that are safe and environment friendly, such as radar cruise control with an all-speed tracking function and a pre-crash safety system, requires numerous types of sensor data, which are collected from various vehicle components and sent to computers through vehicle networks. For example, an adaptive cruise control system (ACC) requires several dozens of input parameters such as brake pressures and throttle angle (Eg. [5]). Further, information system such as navigation systems and vehicle control functionalities will be integrated in the next-generation automotive system (Eg. [4]).

U. Brinkschulte, T. Givargis, and S. Russo (Eds.): SEUS 2008, LNCS 5287, pp. 317–322, 2008.
© IFIP International Federation for Information Processing 2008

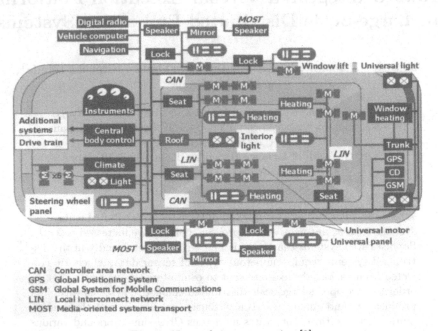

CAN   Controller area network
GPS   Global Positioning System
GSM   Global System for Mobile Communications
LIN   Local interconnect network
MOST   Media-oriented systems transport

Fig. 1. Network in automotive [9]

Meanwhile, the market pressure reduces the development period of large-scale distributed embedded systems as automotives is typical. As a consequence of the shorter development period, various types of simulators have been used to validate embedded systems. Simulators for the automotive system development are not only ECU (CPU) simulators but also vehicle component simulators that are controlled by ECUs, such as engines and brakes. To test ECU programs in the absence of actual vehicle components, a hardware-in-the-loop simulation (HILS) is used. The HILS is a real-time simulator and its inputs and outputs are performed at the same rate as those of actual vehicle components [6].

In order to develop the large-scale distributed embedded systems such as the next-generation automotive system with high productivity and quality, a virtual execution environment platform (VEEP) is required. The VEEP aims at validating of the large-scale distributed embedded system software.

In this paper, we address the requirements and initial system designs based on the requirements for a virtual execution environment for the large-scale distributed systems.

2   Requirements

We propose a VEEP for the large-scale distributed embedded systems on the basis of the software trends in the systems, as mentioned above. In order to perform the validating of CPU programs in the distributed embedded system networks,

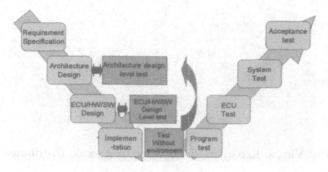

Fig. 2. Design level test using virtual environments

various simulators such as CPU simulators and device simulators should be integrated into the network and provides network-wide simulation functionalities in the large-scale distributed embedded systems. A device simulator is one that gives data detected by sensors to CPU and is controlled by the CPU based on the data. The VEEP implements the integration with the communication middleware, and the CPU simulators and device simulators are connected to the communication middleware.

Next, we summarize the requirements for the VEEP. We identify them from a viewpoint of validating networked components through the whole of the large-scale distributed systems such as automotive and avionics systems.

R1: Open standardized interface

Various simulators such as CPU simulators and device simulator are connected to the communication middleware. For the connection to be established to the communication middleware easily, the interface of the communication middleware should be open and standardized.

R2: Faster CPU simulation speed

The simulation speed of a cycle-accurate simulator, which is used in hardware-software co-design, is slow for debugging and testing programs in a CPU. The execution speed of simulators is expected to be faster and more flexible. For example, when testing for error injection, a slower simulation speed is desirable. Meanwhile, it is expected to be as fast as in an actual hardware in order to implement a man-machine functionalities or the hybrid simulator, as given below.

Meanwhile, the time model in the simulators will be quite simple. CPU and device simulators are synchronized with fine-grain time intervals needed for the validation in our application areas.

R3: Enabling design level validation

In the test phase, a bug in the design phase is detected and fixing this bug is expensive. To avoid such situation and to reduce the test time, validating the system design and software design at a higher level is very effective when using the device simulators in the VEEP, as shown in Fig 2. In the design

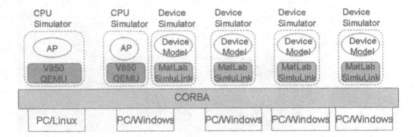

Fig. 3. Integrated Virtual Execution Platform for Large-scale Distributed Embedded Systems

level, dynamic properties of the programs are evaluated such as controllability, stability, and their timeliness.

At the design level of the automotive system, AutoSar[1] has proposed an automotive software architecture and development process to increase the software productivity. In AutoSar architecture, automotive software is designed as a software component independent of the automotive infrastructure such as ECUs and networks, and the software is delivered from component vendors to component users. In order to make the software independent of the infrastructure, AutoSar defines a virtual function bus (VFB) [1]. If we use AutoSar software components on the top of the VFB along with the device simulators in the VEEP, it becomes very effective for validating the ECU software design.

R4: Enabling hybrid simulation

If an actual device such as an ECU or a hardware simulator of a device is used, it connects to the communication middleware of the VEEP instead of the corresponding software simulator. Thereby the embedded software can be validated in the execution environment that is closer to the actual execution environment.

3   Initial System Designs of VEEP

The proposed architecture of the VEEP is shown in Fig. 3. The VEEP consists of a communication middleware, CPU simulators, and device simulators. We present the initial system designs of each subsystem of VEEP.

Communication middleware: We select Common Object Request Broker Architecture (CORBA) as the communication middleware as it provides solutions for **R1**. CPU and device simulators are executed as CORBA objects and communicate using the CORBA communication mechanism. We evaluated ACE/TAO[2] and MICO[3], and select MICO for the present evaluation. Since periodical communication with small-size data are done within hundreds μs in the large-scale

---

[1] http://www.autosar.org

[2] http://www.cs.wustl.edu/ schmidt/TAO.html

[3] http://www.mico.org/

distributed embedded systems, functionalities of MICO are considered to be sufficient for the purpose.

As an alternative, a framework to integrate an ECU simulator and mechanical simulators is proposed in [7]. In the framework, the mechanical simulator is implemented by MATLAB/Simulink [4] and a named pipe is currently used for commutation between the ECU simulator and the mechanical simulator. However, the named pipe is not scalable to integrate a huge number of the CPU and device simulators. Further the framework does not provide the synchronization methods by utilizing the clock services that are present in its own simulator [13].

We must consider the synchronization between CPU simulators and device simulators. We have two solutions: a centralized control and a decentralized control. In the central control, a certain time service software provides the synchronization information. For example, [11] defines the standardized time service interfaces present in CORBA. [3] describes yet another time service architecture in CORBA. In this architecture, the Synchronization Scheduler distributes a clock event to Synchronized Clerk, which exists in a node and delivers a clock event to a CORBA object in the node. The jitter time in the CORBA object side is limited to 100 μs and its average value is approximately 50 μs. This is implemented by the COBRA Event Service [12]. In the decentralized control, each node on the CORBA manages the time and delivers the synchronization information to the objects in the node. The TMO object provides an implementation method for that [8]. We think to develop a light-weight communication middleware which is optimized for minimum required CORBA APIs.

CPU simulator: We utilize QEMU [2] for developing CPU simulators. The QEMU itself is a virtual execution environment generator. The virtual execution environment, which is generated by QEMU, translates the target machine codes to host machine codes, and executes them. The translation is in two steps: firstly, a target machine code is translated to a number of intermediate codes and the intermediate code is compiled to host machine codes. The benefits of using QEMU in a CPU simulator in an embedded system support a variety of CPUs and QEMU provides many libraries for peripheral simulation of the target machine. A QEMU user can easily implement the functionalities when the target programs read or write with the byte access and word access.

We have developed the NEC V850 simulator that modifies the QEMU [10], which is used for various type of embedded systems. The total program size of the modified and appended C source is approximately 3,000 lines, while the total size of the QEMU is 233,000 lines. Moreover, we have modified the QEMU so that translated codes can communicate with the CORBA's communication middleware.

Device simulator: In order to implement a wide variety of device simulators, we use MATLAB/Simulink to simulate a physical object since they are widely used for modeling control systems and simulating models. A user develops a model

---

[4] MATLAB/Simulink are registered trademark of MathWotks, Inc.

the behavior of devices. MATLAB/Simulink with a device model is connected to the CORBA as a CORBA object.

4   Conclusions

In this paper, we present the requirements and initial system designs of a virtual execution environments platform for the development of next-generation large-scale distributed embedded systems. At present, we are in a nascent stage of the development. In the future, we intend developing the VEEP, especially to solve issues related to synchronization.

References

1. AUTOSAR. Technical Overview (June 2006)
2. Bellard, Y.: QEMU, a Fast and Portable Dynamic Translator. In: Proc. USENIX 2005 Annual Technical Conference, April 2005, pp. 41–46 (2005)
3. Calvo, I., Almeida, L., Noguero, A.: A Novel Synchronous Scheduling Service for CORBA-RT Applications. In: Proc. 10th IEEE International Symposium on Object and Component-Oriented Real-Time Distributed Computing, May 2007, pp. 181–188 (2007)
4. N. U. Center for Embedded Computing System. Operating System for in-vehicle multimedia systems,
   http://www.nces.is.nagoya-u.ac.jp/project/e-index.html
5. Han, D., Yi, K., Yi, S.: Evaluation of Integrated ACC (Adaptive Cruise Control)/CA(Collision Avoidance) on a Virtual Test Track. In: Proc. 2006 SICE-ICASE International Joint Conference, October 2006, pp. 2127–2132 (2006)
6. Isermann, R., Schaffnita, J., Sinsel, S.: Hardware-in-the-loop simulation for the design and testing of engine control systems. Control Engineering Practice 7(5), 643–653 (1999)
7. Ishikawa, M., McCune, D., Saikalis, G., Oho, S.: CPU Model-Based Hardware/Software Co-design, Co-simulation and Analysis Technology for Real-Time Embedded Control Systems. In: Proc. 13th IEEE Real Time and Embedded Technology and Applications Symposium, April 2007, pp. 3–11 (2007)
8. Kim, K.H., Liu, J.Q., Miyazaki, H., Shokri, E.H.: TMOES: A CORBA Service Middleware Enabling High-Level Real-Time Object Programming. In: Proc. 5th International Symposium on Autonomous Decentralized Systems, March 2001, pp. 327–335 (2001)
9. Leen, G., Heffernan, D.: Expanding automotive electronic systems. IEEE Computer 35(1), 88–93 (2002)
10. NEC. V850 FAMILY 32-bit Single-Chip Microcontroller Architecure User Manual (1994)
11. OMG. Time Service Specification, Version 1.1 (2002)
12. OMG. Event Service Specification, Version 1.2 (2004)
13. OMG. Real-time CORBA Specification, version 1.2 (2005)

A Novel Approach for Security and Robustness in Wireless Embedded Systems

Mohammad Iftekhar Husain, Shambhu Upadhyaya,
and Madhusudhanan Chandrasekaran

Department of Computer Science and Engineering
University at Buffalo, Buffalo, NY USA 14260
{imhusain,shambhu,mc79}@cse.buffalo.edu

Abstract. Security and robustness are paramount in wireless embedded systems due to the vulnerability of the underlying communication medium. To institute security and reliability, most of the existing schemes perform periodic re-establishment of authentication credentials and share secrets among various participating nodes. However, such measures result in overheads in an energy-constrained wireless environment. To alleviate this problem, we propose a software approach that exploits the features of the underlying communication protocol and uses the concept of steganography and covert channels. The highlight of our approach is that it does not require any changes to the protocol and relies only on the modification of frame contents without degrading the protocol performance. We argue that our covert-channel based communication scheme provides security and robustness at low cost and it neither requires centralized authority nor does it disrupt the overall network operation. We evaluate the security benefits of our proposed method in terms of the difficulty of detecting the covert channel by the adversary and compare our technique with other existing schemes. Performance evaluation is done by determining the bandwidth efficiency of the channel, backward compatibility with the standard MAC as well as the ease of implementation.

Keywords: Covert channel, Embedded systems, Media Access Control (MAC), RTS/CTS, Security, Wireless networks.

1 Introduction

Covert channels [1] are communication channels that are neither designed nor intended to transfer information. Covert channels usually exploit the legitimate use of shared resources and operations of a system to leak sensitive information to someone who is not authorized to access it. In the literature, two types of covert channels exist: storage and timing channels. A storage channel involves direct or indirect writing of a storage location by one process (sender) and direct or indirect reading of the storage location by another process (receiver) [2]. A timing channel involves a sender process that signals information to another by modulating its own use of system resources (e.g., CPU time) in such a way that this manipulation affects the real response time

U. Brinkschulte, T. Givargis, and S. Russo (Eds.): SEUS 2008, LNCS 5287, pp. 323–335, 2008.
© IFIP International Federation for Information Processing 2008

observed by the second process [2]. Also, there are hybrid channels where time and storage information are used together. Unlike traditional communication channels, a covert channel does not need to have a high capacity or transmission rate to be useful. In contrast, the difficulty of detection and resilience are much more important issues for covert channels. From an adversary's point of view, it should be hard for a monitor to discover the existence of the covert channel. Network covert channels leak information across the network through unused fields of network packets (storage channel) as well as the timing of sending and receiving packets (timing channel).

Steganography, on the other hand, refers to concealing the existence of a message when secret information is hidden in an innocuous cover object. From a security analyst's point of view, covert channels can therefore also make use of network packets as the cover object and thus can be used for secure communication. There are several research works in the literature [4], [5] that have studied data hiding techniques in the TCP/IP protocol suite.

As wireless embedded systems like sensors are gaining ground these days in mission critical applications, so does the need for effective security mechanisms for their operation. Because wireless networks comprising of embedded nodes might not have any infrastructure and/or operate in hostile and unattended environments, it is imperative that these security concerns be addressed for robust and dependable operation. However, due to inherent resource and computing constraints, security in wireless networks poses different challenges than traditional wired network security. A desirable feature in wireless embedded systems is that the security solutions be lightweight.

Cryptographic techniques in wireless networks such as WEP [17], [18] and its successors use lightweight methods based on sharing cryptographic credentials among the participating nodes or stations. If this information is compromised or revealed to an adversary, the older secrets must be revoked, followed by the reestablishment of the credentials. Even when the credential is not compromised, sometimes the nodes might need to update or verify the credentials periodically to maintain the security association. In a wired network, it is comparatively easier to update, verify or rebuild the credentials in a secure way. But in the wireless domain with bandwidth and energy constraints and due to the infrastructure-less open mode, re-establishing the security association is a difficult task. So, an important security problem in wireless domain is how to effectively and efficiently enable a node to communicate with its peer securely to update, verify or re-distribute security credentials without using the standard security mechanisms or cryptographic primitives. More precisely, the focus is to ensure the confidentiality and integrity of sensitive data that the node sends to its peer with minimum or no overhead.

To address this security issue, we propose a covert channel based communication mechanism using the concept of steganography. In other words, we use the technique of data hiding using normal network packets in the wireless domain. The reason for hiding data will become apparent shortly. The idea of the protocol is to share a predeployed secret and verify the secret using covert channels in an innocuous way. We refer to our protocol as Opportunistic Secure Communication (OpSeCom). This will allow us to detect and isolate compromised nodes in a wireless network. The protocol uses the technique of Bit Commitment [22] as a means to implement challenge-response (handshake). The characteristic of Bit Commitment is that it shares a pointer to the data first and reveals the actual data later, making it a good choice in our protocol for secret sharing. As IEEE 802.11 MAC is widely used in the wireless domain, we choose the two control packets, viz. RTS (request to send) and CTS (clear to send) to covertly (to defeat the adversary) communicate and verify the shared secret. As RTS and CTS are optional control packets in IEEE 802.11 MAC, appearance of these packets in the network is a normal phenomenon. Though, we are using bit commitment to share secret and RTS/CTS for covert communication to demonstrate the protocol in this paper, these are open for the user to choose. In other words, our proposed idea is generic and does not dependent on the choice of the algorithm for secret share or network packet for covert communication.

So, we design a storage based network covert channel for opportunistic secure communication in wireless domain for updating, verifying or re-establishing security credentials without using standard security mechanisms. Our proposal is neither dependent on a centralized authority nor it re-initializes the whole network to achieve the goal which makes it unique from other security mechanisms. We will demonstrate the security of our technique through the analysis of the covert channel and performance in terms of bandwidth efficiency, co-existence with standard MAC and the ease of deployment.

The rest of the paper is organized as follows: In the next section we will formulate the problem. Section 3 discusses our proposed solution: Opportunistic Secure Communication (OpSeCom). Sections 4, 5 and 6 deal with the security analysis, the robustness of the covert channel, and the performance analysis and comparison with related work, respectively. Section 7 concludes the paper.

2 Problem Definition and Related Work

2.1 Assumption

In this paper we assume wireless embedded systems network as a collection of decentralized embedded devices that use IEEE 802.11 MAC for shared medium access and RTS/CTS for virtual career sensing [17]. The stations (embedded devices) are subject to energy and computational constraints. They are pre-configured for wireless communication prior to deployment in the infrastructure-less mode.

We now discuss several application scenarios and available solutions to highlight the problem domain and to put our research in perspective.

2.2 Scenario 1: Verification of Existence of Malicious Nodes

Detecting malicious nodes like phantom nodes [8] and false beacon nodes [9] is important in wireless sensor networks because it hinders the normal operation of the network. There are several approaches [16] in the literature addressing detection of malicious nodes. These techniques can raise alerts against a suspicious node but they cannot exactly pinpoint the malicious nodes in a decentralized environment. They also produce false positives. There is still lack of effective techniques to accurately verify malicious nodes after an alert is raised so that such nodes can be excluded from the normal network operation once and for all.

2.3 Scenario 2: Re-establishing Security Credentials

Usually, in a wireless domain, a network-wide shared key is used for cryptographic operations in the network. Although, this makes the deployment and key management easier, a big disadvantage of this technique is, if the shared key is revealed, the whole network security is compromised. To restore network security, distribution of some sort of secret information is needed among the nodes. Several key management proposals [18], [19], [20] address this issue in an ad hoc manner by proposing to re-initialize the whole network operation with new keys or security credentials. But, this is not a viable idea in wireless domain because of the existence of energy and computational constraints as well as lack of infrastructure in most cases.

2.4 Scenario 3: Updating Trust and Security Credentials

Again, when a network-wide shared key is used, it is important to update the keys periodically for enhanced security. Though, the periodicity of update depends on the type of network, in wireless domain, a feasible solution will be something which is efficient in computation and communication as well as one that does not allow the malicious nodes to know that the credentials are being updated. Proposals addressing these issues [14], [15] use central authority based complex cryptographic operations which are computation-intensive. In addition, they involve exchange of multiple messages among the nodes to successfully update the credentials which incurs significant communication overhead. So, these ideas are not feasible for resource constrained wireless embedded systems communication.

2.5 Summary of Problem Domain

All the above mentioned scenarios in wireless embedded networks demand for careful communication and data transfer. Such communication should be lightweight, easy to implement and efficient. To address these issues we propose to exploit opportunities that may exist in the form of storage based network covert channel (example: RTS/CTS) as well as the idea of secret sharing (example: Bit Commitment). The next section presents the details of our protocol as well as the basics of RTS/CTS and the bit commitment protocol for a better understanding of the solution.

3 Proposed Method (OpSeCom)

3.1 Basics of RTS/CTS [17]

RTS/CTS (Request to send / Clear to send) is primarily a channel reservation mechanism used by the IEEE 802.11 MAC protocol to reduce frame collisions introduced by the hidden terminal problem and exposed node problem [17].

RTS Packet Format:

Frame Control (2)	Duration (2)	Transmitter Address (TA) (6)	Receiver Address (RA) (6)	FCS(4)

Fig. 1. RTS Packet (20 Bytes) Format

The RA field of the RTS frame is the address of the intended immediate recipient of the data. The TA field is the address of the node transmitting the RTS frame. The duration value is the time, in microseconds, required to transmit the pending data or management frame, plus one CTS frame, plus one ACK frame, plus three SIFS (Short Inter Frame Space) intervals. If the calculated duration includes a fractional microsecond, that value is rounded up to the next higher integer.

CTS Packet Format:

Frame Control (2)	Duration(2)	Receiver Address (RA) (6)	FCS(4)

Fig. 2. CTS Packet (14 Bytes) Format

The RA field of the CTS frame is copied from the TA field of the immediately previous RTS frame to which the CTS is a response. The duration value is the value obtained from the Duration field of the immediately previous RTS frame, minus the time, in microseconds, required to transmit the CTS frame and its SIFS interval. If the calculated duration includes a fractional microsecond, that value is rounded up to the next higher integer.

3.2 Bit Commitment Protocol

Bit commitment is a simple and straightforward cryptographic primitive to enable secret sharing between two mistrusting agents, say, Alice and Bob. This is how the protocol works. Alice puts her secret in a locked box and gives it to Bob. So, neither Alice nor Bob can change the secret as Alice does not have the box and Bob does not have the key. To reveal the secret, Alice simply sends the key later. This ensures secret sharing with cheat prevention. This protocol can be used in our scenarios to implement a challenge and response between peer nodes. Details of Bit Commitment protocol can be found in [22].

3.3 OpSeCom in Action

In order to illustrate our security protocol, we consider two wireless embedded devices Alice and Bob. Alice is the node under suspicion of a compromise and Bob is the verifying node. We assume that, there are some alarm mechanisms at Alice which will be triggered when Alice is under attack. For example, if Alice is a wireless sensor node, she can use photo sensors or motion sensors to detect an attack and trigger an alarm. Also, we assume that Alice can use some software mechanisms such as anomaly detectors to trigger an alarm if sensitive files are accessed or altered at the application layer. When an alarm is triggered, the system will automatically set the corresponding bit string in the CTS packet at the MAC layer. These changes at the MAC layer occur momentarily and the adversary at the application layer will be oblivious of such changes as it takes place as a triggered system task.

The problem here is to verify that Alice is indeed compromised. The protocol works in three phases as illustrated in Figure 3. Phase 1 and Phase 3 are mandatory whereas Phase 2 is optional since verification may be needed even when there is no attack. In the figure, horizontal arrows represent a communication while vertical arrows indicate progression in time.

1. **Secure Parameter Agreement Phase:** When the network is established, Alice sends two code words m and n to Bob, committing to the bit strings corresponding to normal situation and under-attack situation respectively. They will also agree upon the challenge sequence that Bob will send to verify the node condition. By default, Alice will have a special CTS packet set at the MAC layer containing the bit strings corresponding to normal situation as the covert data. This is illustrated in Fig. 3(a). There are several bit commitment protocols [22] in the literature and the implementer is free to choose one.

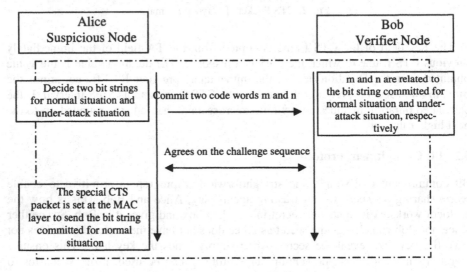

Fig. 3(a). Secure Parameter Agreement Phase

2. **Node under Attack Phase:** When Alice is under attack, she will trigger an alarm which will alter the bit string in the CTS packet at the MAC layer and set it to the bit string committed for under-attack situation as described earlier. At the same time, Bob can also sense some abnormality in Alice's behavior, for example too much deviation in data, activity/inactivity, excessive dropping packets, etc. This is illustrated in Fig. 3(b).

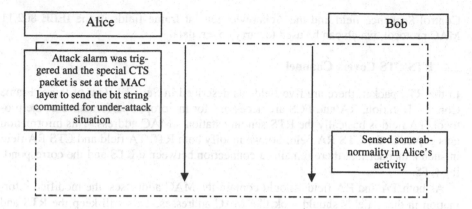

Fig. 3(b). Node under Attack Phase

3. **Covert Verification Phase:** When Bob suspects that Alice is under attack or when Bob desires to verify his security association with Alice, he will send an RTS packet containing the challenge sequence as the covert data. Upon receiving the special RTS packet, Alice will respond with special CTS packet already set at the MAC layer. This response is generated at the MAC layer and is beyond the notice of application layer. So, it is expected that, even if Alice is compromised or captured, the special CTS packet will contain correct bit string corresponding to the situation. So, Bob will verify the bit string and decide whether Alice is in normal operation mode or under-attack as shown in Fig. 3(c).

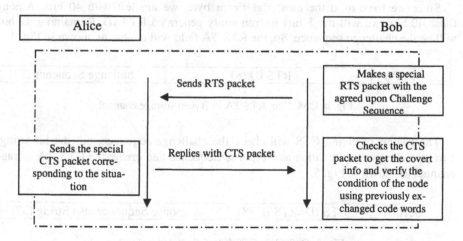

Fig. 3(c). Covert Verification Phase

The covert operation of RTS and CTS packets is described below. In this particular example we use TA and RA fields to hide data in a manner that is similar to [21]. However, the implementer can choose other network packets and fields to use as network covert channel. For example, there are lots of unused bits in the Frame

Control Sequence field and the Acknowledgement frame fields in the IEEE 802.11 MAC protocol, which can be used to carry covert data.

3.4 RTS/CTS Covert Channel

In the RTS packet, there are five fields as described in Sec. 3.1. Out of these, Frame Control, Duration, RA and FCS are necessary for the proper performance of the protocol. TA field is basically the RTS-sending station's MAC address. This information gets copied in the CTS RA field. So, we modify both RTS TA field and CTS RA field in such a manner that there remains a connection between a RTS and the corresponding CTS.

As both TA and RA fields should contain the MAC addresses, the modified information in those fields should look like MAC addresses. This will keep the RTS and CTS packets out of suspicion from non-OpSeCom nodes. This part is crucial because if non-OpSeCom nodes suspect and start brute force analysis of the packet, they can bring down the protocol within polynomial time. According to IEEE standard, universally administered and locally administered MAC addresses are distinguished by setting the second least significant bit of the most significant byte of the address. If the bit is 0, the address is universally administered. If it is 1, the address is locally administered. Again, if the least significant bit of the most significant byte is set to 0, the packet is meant to reach only one recipient (unicast). If the least significant bit of the most significant byte is set to a 1, the packet is meant to be sent only once but still reaches several stations (multicast). In our design, we will put it as a unicast locally administered MAC address. So, the first two least significant bits of the most significant byte will be set to 01 in our design.

Since we have used the most significant byte, we are left with 40 bits. Among these 40 bits, we will use 8 bits for randomly generated RTS ID. Remaining 32 bits will be the challenge sequence. So, the RTS TA field will appear as shown in Fig. 4.

02H(8)	RTS ID (8)	Challenge Sequence (32)

Fig. 4. OpSeCom RTS TA (6 Bytes) storage channel

The station receiving CTS will check the challenge sequence, put the bit strings corresponding to the situation as Response Sequence and create the CTS RA storage channel as shown in Fig. 5.

02H(8)	CTS ID=RTS ID (8)	Response Sequence=Bit String (32)

Fig. 5. OpSeCom CTS RA (6 Bytes) storage channel

As OpSeCom is a two way handshake, we need to modify the duration field of RTS/CTS also. The duration field of RTS will be the time, in microseconds, required to transmit one CTS frame, plus one SIFS interval. CTS duration value will be zero.

4 Security Analysis

Here we briefly discuss how OpSeCom can address the various security concerns described in the scenarios of Section 2.

4.1 Verifying Existence of Malicious Nodes

In order to verify whether a device is malicious or not, a verifier device can just generate and send an OpSeCom RTS packet to it. By malicious, here we refer to non-OpSeCom nodes or captured/compromised OpSeCom nodes. The verifier can then check whether the suspicious device can reply back with a proper OpSeCom CTS packet containing the committed bit string. If it is a non-OpSeCom node, the CTS-RA field will simply contain the copy the RTS-TA field. However, OpSeCom doesn't address malicious insider attack.

4.2 Re-establishing or Updating Credentials

For re-establishing or updating the credential, nodes can covertly exchange the credential after loosely authenticating the nodes to each other using OpSeCom (repeat phase 3). The capability of generating an OpSeCom RTS packet and responding back with an OpSeCom CTS packet itself provides a means of authenticating the nodes to each other. The data being hidden in network packets can be treated as confidential.

4.3 General Discussion

The core security of our protocol lies in the fact that the covert operation is done at the MAC layer and it is independent of the control of application layer. When an OpSeCom node gets a special RTS packet, it replies back to it with corresponding bit strings in the CTS packet without consulting the upper layer which ensures the integrity of the bit string.

In the secure parameter agreement phase of OpSeCom, the nodes exchange bit commitment code words and the challenge sequence. Though, we assume that this phase is secure, it is possible that this phase could come under attack. For example, a malicious outsider could sniff these packets. However, having these packets will not be of much use. Because of the property of bit commitment, even if the malicious outsider has the bit commitment code words, they won't give it any information about the bit strings committed. Again, knowing only the challenge sequence is of no use if the attacker does not know where the covert channel exists. As we have described earlier, selection of shared secret algorithm and covert channel is open to the implementer. So, the covert verification phase is also secure as the existence of the covert channel is obscured to the outsider.

5 Covert Channel Analysis

We analyze the OpSeCom Storage Covert Channel according to the framework proposed by [11].

5.1 Generation of the Covert Channel

The widespread use of RTS/CTS protocol in wireless embedded systems communication lends itself to use for covert channels. In our particular example, the unique existence of RTS/CTS and its capability to reuse RA/TA makes it a good choice as a covert channel. Strictly speaking, the legal definition of the protocol is broken as it is no longer guaranteed that all RTS packets can be uniquely distinguished based on the RTS ID field. However, in practice the probability of a collision is low. When we are using 8 bits for randomly generating the RTS ID field, the probability that two simultaneously generated RTS have different ID is $(1-1/2^8)$ which is very high.

Setting up the OpSeCom channel is simple and straightforward. A modified version of MAC with the desired properties is all what is needed to be implemented on the embedded devices. The node can then decide when to trigger the channel according to the scenarios described in Section 2.

5.2 Detection of the Covert Channel

As the OpSeCom storage covert channel is a noisy channel, it will be very difficult to detect. Specially, we are using some usual values in RA/TA field when replacing our own data with the MAC address. The uniqueness of our scheme is that the communicating devices just need to know the challenge sequence and the method of generating response sequence (bit strings).

6 Performance Analysis

6.1 Recognizing OpSeCom Devices

The receiver device identifies OpSeCom senders by inspecting RTS TA field. If the sender implements OpSeCom, the most significant byte will be 02H and the lower 32-bits will contain the challenge sequence.

As explained earlier, a receiver implementing OpSeCom extension will copy the 16 most significant bits from RTS TA to its CTS RA, and set the remaining 4 bytes of CTS RA to the corresponding bit string. In contrast, an IEEE standard implementation will respond with CTS RA exactly the same as RTS TA. When the sender receives a CTS packet, it inspects the CTS RA field. If the lower order 32 bits are still set to the challenge sequence, the sender can determine that the receiver station does not implement OpSeCom, and act accordingly.

6.2 Bandwidth

The RA/TA field is 48 bits long. We are using 32 bits of it to carry cover data. A bandwidth of 32 bits per packet can therefore be achieved. RTS and CTS packet size is 20 bytes and 14 bytes respectively. So, In the case of RTS this approximates to one fifth of the bandwidth of the MAC layer packet flow. For CTS, this is about one fourth of the flow.

6.3 Backward Compatibility with Standard IEEE 802.11 MAC

The modification to the RTS/CTS frame that we have proposed is compatible with the IEEE 802.11 MAC standard. The standard specifies the content of the CTS RA header to be the MAC address of the receiver. However, only the intended recipient of the frame needs to recognize that the packet is intended for it. Other stations use only the duration field of RTS/CTS frames to refrain from initiating communication. It follows that nodes implementing OpSeCom can coexist with standard IEEE 802.11 MAC terminals without any problem.

6.4 Effect on Overall Network Performance

Existence of OpSeCom devices does not impact the normal network operation for two reasons. First, this method works at the MAC layer. Non-OpSeCom nodes will either discard the special RTS packet or reply with an invalid CTS packet. Either way, it is limited to one hop neighbors only. Second, the necessary information is being exchanged covertly in network control packets. So, there won't be much communication overhead to hinder normal network functionality.

6.5 Comparison with Standard Cryptographic Solution

We now address the practicality of our protocol by comparing the performance of OpSeCom with public key cryptographic methods [23] that are enhanced for embedded systems. We use energy consumption as the evaluation metric. Existing cryptographic methods such as RSA and ECC incur both computation and communication overhead. However, OpSeCom has a very negligible computation overhead because it uses bit commitment realized through simple exclusive OR operation which is a single CPU cycle instruction. This computation overhead is trivially small compared to modular exponentiation or point multiplication used by RSA and ECC respectively. Therefore, we will calculate energy consumption due to communication.

For public key systems like RSA and ECC, one of the necessary operations is the public key transmission. Similarly, in OpSeCom, we need to have RTS/CTS transmission. For comparison purposes, we consider Imote2 sensor [24] clocked at 13 MHz as our target embedded system and calculate the energy consumption for these transmissions. Further, we assume its radio device (Chipcon's CC2420) to be operated with 0dB. At a supply voltage of 4.5V, the Imote2 draws a current of 31mA when the CPU is operating. From [24] we see that the current drawn for both sending and receiving is 44mA. Again, the 802.15.4 radio has an effective data rate of 250kb/s. So, the energy consumption E_{rs} for sending or receiving is: $E_{rs} = (44mA \times 4.5V) / 250kb/s = 792\mu J/b$. The size of RTS and CTS packets together is 34 bytes. Therefore the energy consumption for transmitting (i.e., sending and receiving) RTS/CTS is 0.4J. For RSA with 1024 bit key, the energy consumption will be 1.6J. Similarly, 160 bit ECC transmission will cost 0.25J. However, as we mentioned earlier, apart from the communication overhead, RSA and ECC also have high computation cost. For example, in case of Imote2, energy consumption for t sec CPU operation is: $E_{cpu}(t) = 31mA \times 4.5V \times t = 139.5t$ mJ which will be quite significant.

7 Conclusion and Future Work

In this paper, we proposed a method of opportunistic secure communication in wireless embedded systems using shared secret and storage based network covert channels. We have compared the energy consumption of our protocol with existing cryptographic solutions using the Imote2 platform. Our proposed method enables neighboring nodes to achieve security goals without the help of a centralized authority or impacting the overall network operation. These characteristics make OpSeCom a good choice to enhance security in wireless embedded networks. Also, this method has flexibilities to choose the secret sharing algorithm and the network packets to be used as the cover object. In the future, we plan to implement it on different types of wireless networks and do more rigorous performance analysis such as interoperability with the standard MAC protocol, quantification of OpSeCom nodes' impact on network performance, and so on. We also have plans to do test bed experiments to determine the efficacy of the new protocol on a real system.

Acknowledgments. This research is supported in part by U.S. Department of Defense Grant No. H98230-07-1-0243.

References

1. Gligor, V.D.: A Guide to Understanding Covert Channel Analysis of Trusted Systems. Technical Report NCSC-TG-030, National Computer Security Center, Maryland (1993)
2. U.S. Department of Defense: TCSEC. DoD 5200.28-STD Washington (1985)
3. Gray, J.W.: Countermeasures and Tradeoffs for a Class of Covert Timing Channel. Technical Report, HKUST (1994)
4. Ahsan, K.: Covert Channel Analysis and Data Hiding in TCP/IP. Master's Thesis, University of Toronto (2000)
5. Ahsan, K., Kundur, D.: Practical Data Hiding in TCP/IP. In: Proc. Workshop on Multimedia Security at ACM Multimedia, Juan-les-Pins on the French Riviera (2000)
6. Virendra, M., Jadliwala, M., Chandrasekaran, M., Upadhyaya, S.: Quantifying Trust in Mobile Ad-Hoc Networks. In: Proc. Int. Conf. Integration of Knowledge Intensive Multi-Agent Systems (KIMAS), Waltham (2005)
7. Zhang, Q., Yu, T., Ning, P.: A Framework for Identifying Compromised Nodes in Sensor Networks. In: Securecomm. and Workshops, Baltimore (2006)
8. Hwang, J., He, T., Kim, Y.: Detecting Phantom Nodes in Wireless Sensor Networks. In: 26th IEEE International Conference on Computer Communications, pp. 2391–2395. IEEE Press, Anchorage (2007)
9. Liu, D., Ning, P., Du, W.: Detecting Malicious Beacon Nodes for Secure Location Discovery in Wireless Sensor Networks. In: 25th International Conference on Distributed Computing Systems, Ohio, pp. 609–619 (2005)
10. Wang, Z., Deng, J., Lee, R.B.: Mutual Anonymous Communications: A New Covert Channel Based on Splitting Tree MAC. In: 26th IEEE International Conference on Computer Communications, pp. 2531–2535. IEEE Press, Anchorage (2007)
11. Llamas, D., Miller, A., Allison, C.: An Evaluation Framework for the Analysis of Covert Channels in the TCP/IP Protocol Suite. White Paper, ZDNet (2003)

12. Marti, S., Giuli, T.J., Lai, K., Baker, M.: Mitigating Routing Misbehavior in Mobile Ad Hoc Networks. In: Proc. of International Conference on Mobile Computing and Networking, Boston, pp. 255–265 (2000)
13. Yi, S., Naldurg, P., Kravets, R.: A Security-Aware Routing Protocol for Wireless Ad Hoc Networks. In: Proc. of the 2nd ACM International Symposium on Mobile Ad Hoc Networking & Computing, Long Beach, pp. 299–302 (2002)
14. Dini, G., Savino, I.M.: An Efficient Key Revocation Protocol for Wireless Sensor Networks. In: Proc. of the 2006 International Symposium on World of Wireless, Mobile and Multimedia Networks, Buffalo, pp. 450–452 (2006)
15. Hoeper, K., Gong, G.: Key Revocation for Identity-Based Schemes in Mobile Ad Hoc Networks. In: Kunz, T., Ravi, S.S. (eds.) ADHOC-NOW 2006. LNCS, vol. 4104, pp. 224–237. Springer, Heidelberg (2006)
16. Zhang, Y., Lee, W., Huang, Y.: Intrusion Detection Techniques for Mobile Wireless Networks. Wireless Networks, vol. 9, pp. 545–556. Kluwer Academic Publishers, Hingham (2006)
17. ANSI/IEEE Std 802.11, http://ieeexplore.ieee.org/xpl/standardstoc.jsp?isnumber=30234
18. Serge, V.: On Bluetooth Repairing: Key Agreement based on Symmetric-Key Cryptography. In: Feng, D., Lin, D., Yung, M. (eds.) CISC 2005. LNCS, vol. 3822, pp. 1–9. Springer, Heidelberg (2005)
19. Hegland, A.M., Winjum, E., Kure, Ø., Mjølsnes, S.F., Spilling, P.: Key Management in Ad Hoc Networks, Survey and Evaluation, UniK report, Oslo (2005)
20. Damodaran, D., Singh, R., Phu, D.L.: Group Key Management in Wireless Networks Using Session Keys. In: Proceedings of the Third International Conference on Information Technology: New Generations, Las Vegas, pp. 402–407 (2006)
21. Eriksson, J., Krishnamurthy, S.V., Faloutsos, M.: TrueLink: A Practical Countermeasure to the Wormhole Attack in Wireless Networks. In: Proc. of the 2006 IEEE International Conference on Network Protocols, Santa Barbara, pp. 75–84 (2006)
22. Schneier, B.: Bit Commitment, 2nd edn. Applied Cryptography, pp. 133–217. John Wiley and Sons, Inc., Chichester (1996)
23. Gura, N., Patel, A., Wander, A., Eberle, H., Shantz, S.: Comparing Elliptic Curve Cryptography and RSA on 8-bit CPUs. In: Proc. of Workshop on Cryptographic Hardware and Embedded Systems, Boston, pp. 119–132 (2004)
24. Imote2 Datasheet, http://www.xbow.com/Products/Product_pdf_files/Wireless_pdf/Imote2_Datasheet.pdf

The Role of Field Data for Analyzing the Dependability of Short Range Wireless Technologies

G. Carrozza and M. Cinque

Dipartimento di Informatica e Sistemistica, Università di Napoli Federico II
Via Claudio 21, 80125 - Napoli, Italy
{ga.carrozza,macinque}@unina.it

Abstract. The migration from mobile to ubiquitous Internet is at hand, due to the intense growth of short range wireless technologies. Users accessing the Internet through wireless devices are increasing, if compared to "wired" ones, and they expect the same dependability level they already experience on wired networks, that is high quality "always on" wireless networks. But how can we analyze the dependability level of a wireless network? Direct analysis of failures from the field of application is an effective practice to understand the actual dependability behavior of an operational system. However, despite its wide use over the last four decades on a large variety of systems, field data analysis has rarely been applied to wireless networks. Through the experience gained from extensive failure analysis of Bluetooth networks, the article shows how field failure data can play a key role to fill the gap on understanding the dependability behavior of wireless networks.

1 Introduction

Long time has passed since Meyer proposed of the idea of "Ubiquitous Computing", the paradigm which aims at *enhancing computer use by making many computers available throughout the physical environment*, and at making computers *effectively invisible to the user* [12]. Since then, embedded systems engineering and wireless communications have progressed fast, thus making the visionary idea of *Ubiquitous Computing* a reality. The intense device miniaturization and the increasing power of microprocessors, along with the availability of cheap wireless networks and connectivity, allows computers to increasingly pervade everyday human life and activities.

Longer time has even passed since the Internet was anchored to telephone wires and coaxial cables. Since 2005, cell phones have outnumbered PCs and, in the last few years, people access the Internet more from a wireless device than from a wired one, thus enabling mobile Internet access. According to ITU reports[1], mobiles dominate both in quantity and in quality. Small embedded devices have become a daily portable necessity, which is always no more than

---

[1] International Telecommunication Union, www.itu.int/osg/spu/presentations.

U. Brinkschulte, T. Givargis, and S. Russo (Eds.): SEUS 2008, LNCS 5287, pp. 336–347, 2008.

one meter away from users. PDAs, laptops, cellphones, MP3 players, webcams, and even fridges and microwave ovens, have embedded Internet connectivity, and allow to access the global network from everywhere. The power of mobile has cut off geographic boundaries, hence networks, people and devices are seamlessly connected both on a local scale and over the world: the transition from the Internet to the Ubiquitous Internet is at hand.

Short Range Wireless (SRW) technologies are at the core of such a revolution, as well as the key to ubiquitous networking. They are primarily meant for indoor use and over short ranges, in which they are able to connect portable devices with high connection speed and low power consumption. They are often used at the edges of the wired network, e.g., as wire replacement, to provide mobile users with the last hop to the Internet, from anywhere and at anytime.

Nevertheless, higher mobility means lower speed, as well as worst connection quality in terms of transmission capacity and reliability. Hence, many technical challenges have to be faced in order to serve today customers' demand, who expect the same level of quality they already experience on wired networks. In addition, the wide range of business critical applications in which SRW technologies are protagonists (e.g., mobile banking, mobile commerce, etc), along with their usage in mission critical scenarios (e.g., remote control of robots, rescue of catastrophe survivors, etc.) make it crucial to answer a simple question: *can we rely on these technologies?*

This simple question has not a simple answer. Research efforts in the field of dependability, wireless networks and ubiquitous systems, have to be merged to give a satisfactory response. Indeed, a non-negligible knowledge of the dependability behavior of SRW technologies is required in terms of what are the failure modes, how can we describe/model them, what are the dependability pitfalls and consequences to applications, and how can we face them.

Field Failure Data Analysis (FFDA) is an effective mean to gain the required knowledge. It consists in observing spontaneous occurrences of failures of an operational system, without forcing or inducing artificial failures in the system. The collected failure data provide accurate information which can characterize the dependability of the system under study.

FFDA has been successfully applied in the last four decades. Several studies have been conducted on a large variety of systems, including operating systems and the Internet. As for the former, hangs and the well known "blue screens", found on Windows NT 4 to be mostly due to application failures, were significantly reduced in the successive generation of the OS, Windows 2000, providing the kernel with greater isolation from errant applications [9]. As for the latter, [10] analyzes the causes of failures and the potential effectiveness of various techniques for preventing and mitigating failures in large-scale Internet services.

Despite the large use in both the academy and the industry, FFDA has rarely been used to characterize the dependability of wireless access networks. In this article we aim to show how field failure data can play a key role to gain the needed knowledge to model the failure behavior and to uncover dependability pitfalls of wireless access networks. The resulting understanding is essential for the effective design of any new solution for dependable wireless networking.

We focus on the Bluetooth technology, which has lots of potential applicability in the "last meter" for personal area networks (PANs). It has been estimated that in 2005 Bluetooth was a built-in feature for more than 600 million products, manufactured by several companies. CSR (Cambridge Silicon Radio), in its 2007 financial report, said it expects the proportion of new cars that include Bluetooth to increase from 5 up to 30 percent in the medium term. Car-kits use GPS high performance solutions embedded into a Bluetooth chip, thus bringing GPS into a wide range of new low-cost devices. Furthermore, portable devices are being more and more equipped with both Bluetooth and IEEE 802.11 (Wi-Fi), hence Bluetooth represents a cost-effective way to improve the connection availability in the case Wi-Fi networks are not available; as the number of Access Points to the Internet increases, Bluetooth demonstrated to scale better than Wi-Fi in terms of bandwidth, delay, fairness and energy efficiency [5].

This article provides an answer to the fundamental question posed above in the context of Bluetooth networks, by exploiting over four years authors' research experience on FFDA of mobile/wireless environments [3,2,8]. Conducted experiments allowed to define and to statistically model the failure modes of Bluetooth according to the layer they occur, i.e., application, system (Bluetooth stack and operating system), or wireless channel layer, according to both a *user-centric* and a *channel-centric* approach (see Section 2). Some of the key findings are summarized in the following. First, severe failures, such as connection failures and packet losses, may manifest to applications every eight minutes, on average. This is partially due to the bursty nature of observed channel failures, which are more likely to elude integrity checks performed by Bluetooth, hence propagating to the operating system and applications. Second, failures revealed in the absence of Wi-Fi interferences are rarer, but more severe and harder to recover than when Wi-Fi is present. Third, Bluetooth transport layers assume underlying data-link layers to be completely reliable, hence they do not perform error and integrity checks. However, presented results show that these layers are not able to tolerate low level failures.

These findings provide valuable insights that have to be considered when designing Bluetooth-based access networks with demanding dependability and ubiquity requirements.

2   A Combined Perspective to Gain from Field Data

FFDA studies usually account three consecutive steps: i) data logging and collection, where data are gathered from the operational system, usually exploiting system log files or failure reports, ii) data filtering and manipulation, concerning the extraction of the information which is useful for the analysis, and iii) data analysis, i.e., the derivation of the intended results from the manipulated data.

The operational system can be observed according to both a *top-down* and a *bottom-up* approach. The former is a well known practice in the field of

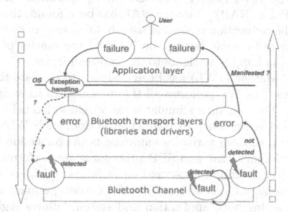

Fig. 1. User- and Channel-centric perspectives

dependability evaluation and measurement [10,4,3] that allows to infer the failure causes starting from the effects on application and Operating System (OS) layers, according to users' point of view (*user-centric* perspective). The latter, instead, is based on the novel idea of tracing how faults propagate to upper layers by directly observing low level causes [2]. With respect to wireless systems, this is a *channel-centric* perspective, in that data communication channel is the starting point for system observation.

Figure 1 emphasizes the differences between the two approaches, with reference to the Bluetooth stack. It is important to precise that, according to the terminology introduced in [1], channel failures can be seen as errors for system failures and as faults for application failures, as well as system failures can be seen as errors for application failures. The user-centric approach allows to analyze failure propagation traces only down to the OS level (Bluetooth drivers failures are logged on system log files). Conversely, by adopting a channel-centric approach, it is possible to monitor failures occurring at the Bluetooth data-link layer, namely Baseband, and to evaluate its *coverage* (i.e., Baseband's ability of self repairing corrupted frames).

In this work we show how combining both the perspectives provides a detailed characterization of SRW technologies dependability. In particular, by following this approach we are able to classify Bluetooth failure modes according to the layer they manifest, and to gain insights into failure propagation traces.

2.1 Testbed and Workload

Field data have been collected by running experiments on a real-world Bluetooth piconet (i.e. a network made up of 1 to 8 Bluetooth nodes, only one of them acting as the *master* or coordinator). Bluetooth piconets can be easily exploited to access the Internet, by means of the Bluetooth Personal Area Network (PAN) profile. A user willing to surf the web with his Bluetooth-enabled mobile phone, starts an inquiry/scan operation to discover other devices in the neighborhood, then - through a Service Discovery Protocol (SDP) operation - he looks for the Network Access Point (NAP). Once the NAP has been found, the user connects to it (note that the connection operation usually takes care of switching the role of the mobile device to slave, letting the NAP be the master of the piconet). Finally, the user can happily navigate to his web-mail inbox.

An application workload (WL) has been designed to emulate the behavior of a typical PAN user. The WL performs all the steps needed to setup the PAN, as mentioned above. The WL then stimulates the wireless channel by transferring data on it. To add uncertainty to piconet evolution, each WL cycle is characterized by several random variables modeling both connection establishment (e.g. whether the inquiry/scan and SDP procedures are performed or not) and channel usage (e.g. according to the random variables which are used to model actual Internet traffic, such as Web surfing, file transfer, e-mail, etc.). Running the WL, and collecting both application and system failures registered on OS log files is useful to achieve the user-centric perspective. During packets transmission, channel level data have been captured by using a Bluetooth air sniffer, in order to achieve the *channel-centric* perspective. The sniffer provided us with all the needed information, from failure reports at the Baseband layer to frame status as they are delivered up to L2CAP (Logical Link Control and Access Protocol, i.e., the Bluetooth transport) and BNEP (Bluetooth Network Encapsulation Protocol, which is used to emulate Ethernet links over Bluetooth).

The produced failure data come from multiple sources (WL log files, system log files, and sniffer traces). Combining these data with temporal coalescence algorithms permits to infer propagation traces from channel up to the application layer. Data have been properly filtered to discard useless information.

Several experiments have been conducted on the piconet, during a time span of almost two years, collecting more than 140 millions failure data items. In order to investigate the impact of Wi-Fi on Bluetooth failure modes, they have been performed both in presence and in absence of Wi-Fi disturbances.

3   Bluetooth Failure Modes

Field failure data demonstrate to be an effective mean to identify the failure modes of SRW technologies.

In our case, we were able to observe several failure modes and to classify them according to the level in which their occurrence is registered. Observed Failure modes are summarized in Fig.2. Applications exhibit a variety of failures according to the utilization phase where they occur, i.e., inquiry/scan and discovery phases, PAN connection, and data transferring. Failures during the connection can occur either while the connection is set up or while the role of the device is switched from master to slave. Unexpectedly, failures during data transfer, such as packet loss and mismatches in the received data, are experienced, despite error control mechanisms performed by Baseband, such as Cyclic Redundancy Codes (CRCs), Forward Error Correction (FEC), and Header Error Correction (HEC) schemes. However, as discussed in [6], the weakness of integrity checks is the

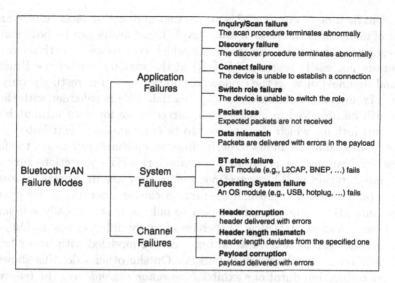

Fig. 2. Bluetooth Failure Modes as they are observed on the field

assumption of having memoryless channels with uncorrelated errors from bit to bit. In the case of Bluetooth, correlated errors (e.g. bursts) can occur due to the nature of the wireless media, affected by multi-path fading and electromagnetic interferences. The failure of the integrity checks is further investigated in the next section.

System level failures are grouped with respect to their location, i.e., Bluetooth software stack and Operating System. Failure types could be further refined according to the component which signals the failure, e.g., L2CAP and BNEP.

Finally, three channel level failures classes have been identified: (i) header corruption at the Baseband level, (ii) length mismatch, i.e., a mismatch in the packet length reported into the Baseband header and the actual one, and (iii) payload corruption (PC in the following) at the Baseband level. The last class deserves more attention, since these failures are the only ones that may propagate to system and application layers, in our settings. Failures belonging to the other two classes are instead successfully detected and masked by the Baseband's FEC, HEC and CRC schemes.

Failure data also allow to model failure dynamics as stochastic processes. The statistical distribution type then permits to better understand the failure phenomenology. In our case, we attempted to fit the time to failure (TTF) for application failures with three different statistical distributions: the Exponential, the Lognormal, and the Weibull distributions. The fitting has been conducted by means of a statistical software suite, using maximum likelihood estimators and goodness of fit tests. It results that almost all application level failures are distributed as Lognormal. The Lognormal distribution is used extensively in reliability applications to model failure times. A random variable can be modeled as Lognormal if it can be thought of as the multiplicative product of many small independent factors. In our case, this means that application level failures are the product of many small faults at a lower level. These faults can be both software faults, e.g., heisenbugs (i.e., design faults which conditions of activation occur rarely or are not easily reproducible [11]) at the various level of the Bluetooth stack, and channel faults, as the payload corruption case. Interestingly, only data mismatch failures are distributed as Exponential. This is coherent with the fact that, as will be observed in next section, direct cause for data mismatches are payload corruptions, which also resulted to be exponentially distributed.

More detailed analysis allows to derive interesting characteristics of the failure behavior. For instance, we attempted to characterize BT connections survivability, i.e., the duration of BT connections before they are unexpectedly lost due to failure (and not due to normal connection closing operation). We observed that the connection duration with respect to failures is statistically *self-similar*, i.e., it shows the same statistical properties at many different scales. On a side, this implies that connection duration times can be modeled with heavy tailored distributions (e.g., the Pareto distribution). On the other side, this shows evidence that connection durations exhibit *long range dependence*: the failure of a connection at a given time is typically correlated with connection failures at all future instants.

4   Bluetooth Uncovered Dependability Pitfalls

4.1   Impairments Due to Payload Corruptions Propagation

As stated in section 3, there exists a class of channel level failures, namely PC, that is able to elude Baseband error control mechanisms, and to propagate to upper layers with a non zero probability. When dealing with digital wireless communication, the causes of such failures lie into shadowing and electromagnetic noise, which may cause the bits to be flipped when transfered between two end points. Moreover, as previously mentioned, the presence of multi-path fading and electromagnetic interferences can cause correlated faults (i.e. bursts) to occur.

Thanks to field experiments, and to a thorough inspection of packets content, we were able both to observe the occurrence of PC on monitored Bluetooth channel, and even to pinpoint the flipped bits.

A snapshot of a corrupted payload is shown in Fig. 3. Note that we were able to uncover this corruption since we forced the WL to transfer a known character sequence with a fixed length, e.g. "CCCC". The highlighted burst is 136 bits long. This is the reason why it is able to elude Baseband error control mechanisms. Baseband adopts a 16-bit CRC-CCITT polynomial code which is able to detect 18 bits or longer bursts with 0.99998 probability (i.e. minor than one). We experienced that the length of the burst is a random variable, L, with an expected value equals to 512 bits and a standard deviation equals to 646 bits, hence they are longer on average than 18 bits.

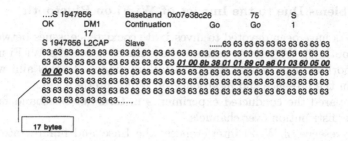

....S 1947856   Baseband 0x07e38c26   75   S
OK   DM1   Continuation   Go   Go   1
          17
S 1947856 L2CAP   Slave   1   ......63 63 63 63 63 63 63 63 63 63
63 63 63 63 63 63 63 63 63 63 63 63 63 63 63 63 63 63 63 63 63 63 63 63 63 63
63 63 63 63 63 63 63 63 63 63 63 63 *01 00 8b 38 01 01 89 c0 a8 01 03 60 05 00*
00 00 63 63 63 63 63 63 63 63 63 63 63 63 63 63 63 63 63 63 63 63 63 63 63 63
63 63 63 63 63 63 63 63 63 63 63 63 63 63 63 63 63 63 63 63 63 63 63 63 63 63
63 63 63 63 63 63 63 63 63 63 63 63 63 63 63 63 63 63 63 63 63 63 63 63 63 63
63 63 63 63 63 63......

17 bytes

Fig. 3. Example of corrupted payload

Graph in Fig. 4 shows how a PC can propagate. On the leftmost side of the graph, it is shown that 99.59 % of PC are detected by Baseband, hence they do not reach upper layers. With respect to the undetected failures, values on the graph links represent the conditional probability of failures given that a PC occurred and eluded Baseband control. Several consequences can then occur, according to the probabilities reported on the graph. In fact, PC can either remain latent (i.e. isolated) at the system level, or propagate to the user level in the form of *application failures*. In the former case, they are *confined* at system level even if no further error controls are performed (in fact, both L2CAP and BNEP assume underlying levels to be completely reliable). The actual induced

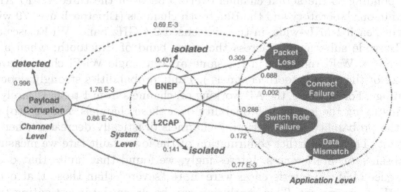

Fig. 4. Propagation phenomenology

failure depends on the location of the burst within the transmitted packet. For instance, if the corruption affects the L2CAP header, the packet can not be properly decoded. As a consequence, it will not be delivered to upper layers, thus causing a packet loss, i.e. an omission failure, at the user level. In the same way, if the burst is located in the L2CAP payload, the erroneous content can be directly delivered to the application, which may then exhibit a value failure, i.e. a data mismatch in the Figure.

4.2   Problems Due to the Impact of Wi-Fi on Bluetooth

Many efforts have been devoted to investigate coexistence issues between Wi-Fi and Bluetooth [7]. We tried to estimate how the presence of a Wi-Fi network in the neighborhood can impact Buetooth failure modes. To this aim we let WL run both in the presence and in absence of Wi-Fi interferences.

We compared the conducted experiments in terms of Baseband failure rate and failure distribution over channels.

In the presence of Wi-Fi interferences, the Baseband failure rate has been measured as 6.822 faults per second. Since the average number of transmitted frames per second is 596, this results into a frame error rate of about 0.012 (i.e., about 1 frame out of 100). However, the most of these errors are promptly detected and masked by Baseband's correction mechanisms, in that its coverage, with respect to all channel failures, has been measured as 0.9996. Undetected failures can be modeled as an exponential random variable with a 458716 ms mean. This means that about every eight minutes a Baseband error is not detected, and a wrong frame propagates to upper layers. As one could expect, a lower failure rate (equals to 0.516 faults per second) has been experienced when Wi-Fi Access Points (APs) in the neighborhood are turned off.

As for failure distribution across wireless channels, results are shown in Fig. 5. In particular, Fig. 5(a) shows failure probability for all failures (even detected ones) over channels when WiFi is present whereas results in Fig. 5(b) refer to the experiment conducted without WiFi disturbances. In the first case, error probability is highly concentrated over the channels evidenced by dotted lines corresponding to the actual channel overlap between the three Wi-Fi APs deployed in our laboratory and the Bluetooth channels (Bluetooth uses 79 wireless channels, each 1-MHz-wide, in the unlicensed 2.4 GHz band; Wi-Fi uses eleven 22-MHz-wide sub-channels across the same band of Bluetooth; when a Bluetooth and a WiFi radio are in the same area, a single Wi-Fi channel overlaps with 22 of the 79 Bluetooth channels.). Fault probabilities strongly depend on APs usage. For instance, the AP working on channels from 1 to 23 is rarely used, thus justifying the low fault probability over these channels. Figure 5(b) shows that the probability over interfering channels drastically decreases when WiFi is absent. This is a further confirmation of the lower fault rate we measured in the absence of interferences. Interestingly, we found that faults that occurred in absence of Wi-Fi interferences were more "severe" than those that occurred when Wi-Fi is present. This conclusion can be drawn by investigating time to failure statistics for all failures (detected and undetected). In both cases, they fit a Lognormal distribution, but with different values of distribution parameters (e.g. distribution shape). This leads us to observe that in absence of Wi-Fi short inter-arrival times of failures are more probable. In other terms, the absence of disturbances causes the faults to be more clustered in time. The reason for this is to be found into the frequency hopping scheme adopted by Bluetooth. In the presence of Wi-Fi, faults are mainly due to interferences which tend to be

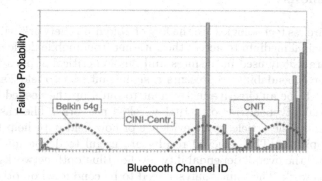

(a) WiFi present (overlapping zones for each AP are shown)

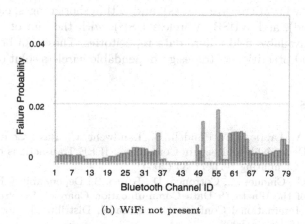

(b) WiFi not present

Fig. 5. Histogram of failure probability across Bluetooth channels

polarized on the overlapped channels. After the occurrence of a failure due to collision, the frame is retransmitted over a different channel. However, the channel might either be free or still occupied by the Wi-Fi interference. This variability causes both short- and medium-length inter-failure times. When Wi-Fi is not present, there are no polarized interferences, or, in other terms, the fault phenomena is spread (e.g., lost of synchronization among nodes or wide-band disturbances). Hence, it is more likely that a retransmission will fail.

In order to corroborate this intuition, we also investigate Mean Time To Recover (MTTR) in both circumstances. Consistently with above results, MTTR increases when Wi-Fi is not present (from $7.51ms$ to $9.52ms$) , i.e. more retransmissions are needed when the fault phenomenon is not polarized. Finally, the Baseband level exhibited a lower capability of detecting failures due to spread phenomena in that its coverage decreases by one order of magnitude (it passes from 0.9996 to 0.9968). This means that failures due to spread phenomena are more prone to elude Baseband's CRC integrity check.

5   Conclusions

Short range wireless technologies are the key of ubiquitous networking. They represent the principal medium to access the Internet from mobile devices. As these technologies are widely used in business and mission critical applications, characterizing their dependability represents a significant issue. Field Failure Data Analysis shows to be an effective instrument to build up the needed knowledge on the dependability behavior of actual wireless networks. The case of Bluetooth, analyzed in the article, gives evidence of how field data help to uncover dependability pitfalls. The achieved results are useful to define mitigation actions to improve the overall dependability level of Bluetooth networks, as shown in our previous work. The same analysis need to be conducted on other wireless networks enabling ubiquity both over long distances, e.g., WiMAX, (Worldwide Interoperability for Microwave Access), and within short ranges, e.g., UWB (Ultra Wide Band), and WUSB (Wireless USB), with the aim of building large and publicly available field failure data repositories. These can be exploited by researchers and practitioners to design dependable wireless solutions.

References

1. Avizienis, A., Laprie, J.C., Randell, B., Landwehr, C.: Basic Concepts and Taxonomy of Dependable and Secure Computing. IEEE Transactions on Dependable and Secure Computing 1(1), 11–33 (2004)
2. Carrozza, G., Cinque, M., Cotroneo, D., Russo, S.: Dependability Evaluation and Modeling of the Bluetooth Data Communication Channel. In: Proc. of the 16th Euromicro International Conference on Parallel, Distributed and network-based Processing (February 2008)
3. Cinque, M., Cotroneo, D., Russo, S.: Collecting and Analyzing Failure Data of Bluetooth Personal Area Networks. In: Proc. of the 36th IEEE International Conference on Dependable Systems and Networks (DSN 2006) (June 2006)
4. Iyer, R.K., Kalbarczyk, Z., Kalyanakrishnam, M.: Measurement-Based Analysis of Networked System Availability. In: Reiser, M., Haring, G., Lindemann, C. (eds.) Dagstuhl Seminar 1997. LNCS, vol. 1769. Springer, Heidelberg (2000)
5. Johansson, P., Kapoor, R., Kazantzidis, M., Gerla, M.: Personal Area Networks: Bluetooth or IEEE 802.11? International Journal of Wireless Information Networks Special Issue on Mobile Ad Hoc Networks (April 2002)
6. Koopman, P., Chakravarty, T.: Cyclic Redundancy Code (CRC) Polynomial Selection For Embedded Networks. In: Proc. of the 34th IEEE International Conference on Dependable Systems and Networks (DSN 2004) (June 2004)
7. Lansford, J., Stephens, A., Nevo, R.: Wi-Fi (802.11b) and Bluetooth: Enabling coexistence. IEEE Network, 20–27 (September/October 2001)
8. Kalbarczyk, Z., Iyer, R.K., Cinque, M., Cotroneo, D.: How do mobile phones fail? a failure data analysis of symbian os smart phones. In: Proc. of the 37th IEEE/IFIP International Conference on Dependable Systems and Networks (DSN 2007), Edinburgh, pp. 585–594 (2007)
9. Murphy, B., Levidow, B.: Windows 2000 Dependability. MSR-TR-2000-56, Microsoft Research, Microsoft Corporation, Redmond, WA (June 2000)

10. Oppenheimer, D., Ganapathi, A., Patterson, D.A.: Why do Internet services fail, and what can be done about it? In: Proc. of the 4th USENIX Symposium on Internet Technologies and Systems (USITS 2003) (March 2003)
11. Vaidyanathan, K., Trivedi, K.S.: A Comprehensive Model of Software Rejuvenation. IEEE Transactions on Dependable and Secure Computing 2(2), 124–137 (2005)
12. Weiser, M.: Ubiquitous computing. IEEE Computer 26(10) (October 1993)

RG-EDF: An I/O Scheduling Policy for Flash Equipped Sensor Devices

Adam Ji Dou and Vana Kalogeraki

Dept. of Computer Science and Engineering
University of California, Riverside, CA 92521
{jdou,vana}@cs.ucr.edu

Abstract. Flash equipped sensor devices are becoming increasingly complex and are now capable of supporting real-time multiple applications on a single sensor, rich sensing of visual and audio data, and storage of large amounts of data. With this increase in complexity, it is no longer sufficient to provide first in first out (FIFO) type capture of data into more persistent memories. In this paper we propose RG-EDF, a new scheduling policy for flash equipped sensor devices. RG-EDF aims at providing QoS support to multimedia tasks by considering the unique characteristics of flash-based devices. We have implemented our scheme on a CC1010 sensor node with a SD flash card attached and compared our technique to other popular scheduling policies. Our experimental results show the working and benefit of our system.

1 Introduction

Wireless Sensor Networks (WSNs), composed of small, low cost and low power sensor devices, have found popular applications in many situations including environmental monitoring, military surveillance, inventory tracking and seismic control. Typical sensor devices feature a low-frequency, low-power processor ($\approx$4-58MHz), limited memory (4-10KB), a wireless radio for communication, on-chip sensors, and an energy source such as a set of AA batteries or solar panels.

The introduction of flash equipped sensors (RISE [4], PRESTO [11]) has significantly enhanced the storage capacity of sensors; it allows storing large amounts of data locally. Since the power consumed by transmitting data is a magnitude higher [17] than storing it locally, the sensors can now store and process data, sending only relevant information to the sink in response to pre-set conditions or queries. Such in-network data storage provides a significant reduction in energy usage and a corresponding increase in the lifetime of the WSN.

As flash-based devices become increasingly popular, they are required to perform real-time tasks, such as storage and retrieval of multimedia data. Today, visual (Cyclops [15], CMUcam [2]) and audio (EnviroMic [13]) sensors enable the sensing of high bandwidth, rich data; providing much more information than simple scalar measurements of temperature, humidity, etc [10]. This rich data can supplement the simple measurements with more complete context information.

U. Brinkschulte, T. Givargis, and S. Russo (Eds.): SEUS 2008, LNCS 5287, pp. 348–359, 2008.

Multimedia data are different from traditional file systems, as they require large storage capacity and must support intensive real-time I/O traffic. It is common for data generated by the tasks to be sequentially positioned on the flash, while data generated concurrently by different tasks is multiplexed. However, such sequential storage can lead to significant latencies (as we show in the paper), thus limiting the ability to meet satisfy the real-time requirements of the tasks.

Although there have been proposed several quality of service (QoS) methods for traditional hard drives (HDD) in the literature [6,9,12], they do not readily lend themselves for implementation on sensors or for flash memories. Most of the traditional HDD based schedulers exploit the physical characteristics of hard drives to provide improved performance: access time affected by the positioning of the data access arm. This particular limitation is not applicable for flash memories, but flash memories do have other constraints and characteristics which must be considered. File systems specific for flash memories (ELF [8], JFFS [16], YAFFS [3]) work around the constraints of flash memories using log based structures, but these are more concerned with providing structures for storing files and efficient garbage collection for freeing space than QoS and I/O efficiency, which is the focus of our work.

In this paper we propose Reordering Grouped Earliest Deadline First (RG-EDF), a scheduling policy for flash-based sensor devices. Our policy aims at by combining multiple requests from the same task and selectively reordering the requests so that several requests can be written on the flash together. Our method provides much better performance than current method of data storage by taking advantage of the unique characteristics of flash memories. This is the first work, that we know of, which focuses on providing quality of service for storage in flash memories on sensor devices. We have implemented our scheme on a CC1010 sensor node with a SD flash card attached. We have experimentally compared our scheduler with FIFO and regular EDF schedulers. Our experimental results show the working and benefits of our proposed system.

2   Background

Traditional schedulers designed for improved efficiency in hard drive based systems ([14] [12] [7]) try to optimize the storage I/O by rearranging the order of operation in such a way to minimize drive arm movement. Although flash memories do not have the physical limitations of a drive arm, we are also trying to organize our data in a way to take advantage of I/O characteristics.

Anticipatory scheduling [9] is a proposed solution to combat prevents deceptive idleness by waiting for a while after requests for new requests from the process which has just been serviced. While we do not have the problem of deceptive idleness, we are inspired by the concept of waiting for additional requests in order to increase the overall throughput for flash storage.

Bisson et al , in [6] and [5], reduce the energy consumption and increase the efficiency of hard drive spin down algorithms through the addition of a flash memory cache. Although they do make use of flash memories, it is used as a

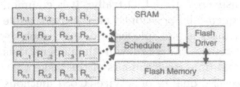

(a) The sensor system: each process generates a series of requests, which are placed into the scheduler residing in *SRAM*. The scheduler then interacts with the flash driver to complete the requests.

(b) The structure of a flash memory with *S* sectors, each containing *B* blocks. Blocks are labeled as Block$_{sector,block}$

Fig. 1. System and Flash Structure

temporary cache for increased hard disk performance and they are not concerned with the actual write efficiency to the flash memory itself.

Flash memories differ from traditional hard drive scheduling optimizations in several critical ways, the ones we are concerned about are the I/O characteristics. There is no disk arm on a flash device and the physical location of data on a flash device does not affect its access or read time, however, I/O operations in flash memory are performed in block sized units. If we wish to write or read less than a block of data, we incur the same time and energy penalties as if we were operating on an entire block.

Recently techniques have been proposed for data storage and indexing in sensor networks. A few flash-based file systems have been proposed, including RISE [4] and PRESTO [11]. File systems specific for flash memories (ELF [8], JFFS [16], YAFFS [3]) implement log-like file structure designed for wear-leveling. These are more concerned with providing structures for storing files and efficient garbage collection for freeing space. In contrast, our work focuses on scheduling for improving QoS and I/O efficiency, targeting real-time multimedia tasks.

3   System Design

In this section, we first present our system settings, assumptions, and highlight the design principles. We then present an overview of the core components of the system and how they interact with each other, we then detail the design of the our scheduler.

3.1   System Settings

To control the order of execution and improve the quality of service, we insert a scheduler which intercepts requests and reorders them (see Figure 1).

We focus on the I/O processes on a single sensor device. We assume that a sensor runs n processes $P_1...P_n$, each process P_i produces a series of requests $R_{i,1}, R_{i,2}, Rs_{i,3}, ...$ (refer to Figure 1(a)). Each request $R_{i,k}$ can be represented by a tuple $< t_{i,k}, d_{i,k}, size_{i,k} >$ where $t_{i,k}$ is the time the request is issued, $d_{i,k}$ is a deadline (time that the request must complete), and $size_{i,k}$ is the size of the request. We assume that requests arrive sequentially. A request $R_{i,k}$ is considered to be written successfully if it is stored to nonvolatile memory (flash memory, in this case) before time $t_{i,k} + d_{i,k}$, otherwise, it is considered to be a miss.

The flash memory is divided into S sectors with each sector containing B blocks of size B_{size} (this is shown visually in Figure 1(b). As mentioned earlier, due to the constraints of flash memory: Each write to flash memory takes $write_{time}$, must be exactly B_{size} and must occupy an entire block. Similarly, each read from flash Memory takes $read_{time}$, can read at most B_{size} and cannot cross block boundaries. When a block $b_{i,k}$ in sector s_i is deleted or modified, all other blocks $b_{i,l}$ in s_i must also be deleted (and possibly re-written).

3.2   Design Principle

Our work is based on the main observation of the read and write property of flash memories: all native operations are performed at a block level. When data is written or read from flash memory, requests for data smaller than a block still takes the same amount of time and energy as if an entire block is read or written. Consequently, we want our scheduler to avoid wasted capacity and maximize utility by trying to read and write only full blocks of data.

We exploit this property in our scheduler by grouping requests and completing them together instead of separately. Grouping requests together improves performance in two ways: by combining multiple requests together, we increase I/O utilization and are essential writing the extra requests for "free". Additionally, by writing multiple requests, we clear out the scheduler faster and reduce the number of drops due to scheduler saturation. In situations where request injection is bursty, grouping allows many of the requests from the bursts to be together, making it especially effective in these cases when compared to the simpler, non-grouping schedulers.

3.3   Requests

When a request is generated, space is allocated for data in the $SRAM$, and the request object is sent to the scheduler. The request object contains: process id, sequence number, the deadline of the request, its data size and a pointer to its actual data. We chose to use a pointer to the data rather than the storing the data in the request object because we wish to maintain a constant sized scheduler in memory even when requests differ in size.

When the I/O component becomes idle and the application is ready to perform the next I/O operation, it will retrieve a request object from the scheduler. Then, a check will be made to determine if the deadline of the request can be met and the operation is performed depending on the system's policies (e.g. drop request on miss).

3.4   Reordering Grouped EDF Scheduler

We introduce a new scheme, called Reordering Grouped-EDF (RG-EDF). RG-EDF attempts to avoid performing partial block requests by grouping consecutive tasks together each time the request with the smallest deadline will be served. Performance is further improved by allowing for additional flexibility in scheduling the order of writes.

We initially consider a Grouped EDF (G-EDF) scheduler. G-EDF (and RG-EDF) uses the same heap structure as the regular EDF scheduler. When a request needs to be retrieved, instead of just returning the top item in the heap, the G-EDF scheduler will search through the heap and try to find sequential requests from the same process to combine.

The request $R_{i,k}$, is at the top of the heap. The scheduler will scan the heap searching for requests $R_{i,k+1}, R_{i,k+2}, \dots$ and combine the requests until

$$\sum_{j=0}^{n} size_{i,k+j} > B_{size}$$

or all the items have been searched. The scheduler will then combine and return the requests $R_{i,k}...R_{i,k+n-1}$.

The RG-EDF scheduler improves upon the base G-EDF scheduler by selectively reordering the requests and waiting for new requests before returning a set of grouped requests. RG-EDF checks if better I/O utilization can be achieved by allowing another request with a later deadline proceed before the current earliest deadline request in cases where the deadline of the requests permit us.

Suppose $R_{i,k}$ is the earliest deadline request, we can allow a request $R_{j,l}$ to proceed ahead if we can accurately predict how long $R_{j,l}$ will take to service:

$$t_{i,k} > current_{time} + write_{time} + buffer_{time}$$

$$\sum_{a=0}^{n} size_{i,k+a} < \sum_{b=0}^{m} size_{j,l+b}$$

where

$$\sum_{a=0}^{n} size_{i,k+a} \le B_{size} and \sum_{b=0}^{m} size_{j,l+b} \le B_{size}$$

This allows for the group of requests $R_{j,l}...R_{j,l+m}$ which occupies a large portion of a block to proceed before $R_{i,k}...R_{i,k+n}$. This also provides the opportunity for more requests from process i to arrive while the I/O operation for process j is underway.

4   Implementation

We implemented the system on a CC1010 sensor with a SD flash card attached through the Serial Peripheral Interface (SPI) bus. This section discusses the main components of the CC1010 sensor, the interface and characteristics of the SD flash card and gives implementation details on our different schedulers. An implementation system diagram is shown in Figure 2.

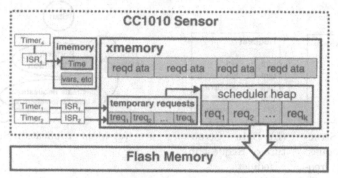

Fig. 2. Implementation structure of the schedulers

4.1 CC1010 Sensor

We are using is a Chipcon CC1010 sensor with an 8051 Enhanced Microcontroller [1]. The main features we are concerned about in the CC1010 are its memory model and its interrupt timers.

The memory is divided into two main sections: an internal memory (imemory) of 128 bytes and an external memory (xmemory) of 2024 bytes. Since the imemory is faster than the xmemory, we place frequently used and time sensitive data items (such as loops and the time counter) in imemory. We use xmemory for data structures which require large amounts of memory such as the queue and scheduler heap.

4.2 SD Flash Card

We used a 128 MiB Sandisk card with 512 byte blocks arranged in 256 block sectors. There are two basic operations supported by the flash SD card: reading a block and writing a block. Any erasing and recopying of information in a sector are handled internally by hardware on the flash card itself. Our custom flash driver implements the two basic read and write operations.

We connect to the flash card using a SPI bus. While this does limit the speed of reading and writing to the card, it also greatly simplify the hardware interface. Both of the basic operations mentioned above must be completed in blocks of exactly 512 bytes. To perform an operation, we first place the command followed by the address of the block onto the SPI bus. We then poll the serial interface to either read or write data to and from the card. In addition, after a write completes on the sensor, we must wait for an additional time while the card finalizes the operation.

Write time for a block to flash requires 9 ms, but reading from xmemory and writing the data typically takes up to 13 ms for a full block of 512 bytes. For the first write into a new sector, an extended write time ranging from 60 to 140 ms is required, this is a characteristic of the internal hardware of the SD flash card. This extra time is used to reorganize the data internally and speeds up

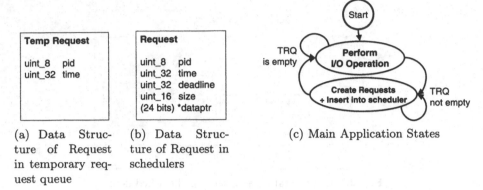

(a) Data Struc-
ture of Request
in temporary req-
uest queue

(b) Data Struc-
ture of Request in
schedulers

(c) Main Application States

Fig. 3. Data structures and application states

subsequent writes. Reading a block takes slightly more time than writing ranging
from 11 ms to 15 ms.

4.3 Timing and Request Injection

The CC1010 sensor provides 4 interrupt timers ($timer_1$ - $timer_4$), 3 of which we
can use. We set $timer_4$ as the highest priority interrupt for keeping a counter to
measure elapsed time in 1 ms increments. We simulate multiple processes issuing
requests by using the ISRs associated with $timer_1$ and $timer_3$.

To keep the interrupt handlers as compact as possible; a full request object
is not created at the time of an interrupt. Instead, a temporary request (treq)
object is placed into the temporary request queue (TRQ), and a request object
is created between I/O operations. The treq structure is shown in Figure 3(a)
and contains the timestamp at the time the request is injected. Between I/O
requests, complete request objects (shown in Figure 3(b)) are created for any
treqs in the TRQ and are inserted into the scheduler.

Request injection is handled by the ISRs invoked by $timer_1$ and $timer_3$. The
period that each timer fires its interrupt can be adjusted and this is what we
use to vary the request injection frequency. When a ISR is invoked, a treq is
created for each process and placed into the TRQ. $timer_1$ is always used to
control process 1 and $timer_3$ is used to control processes 2...n where there are
n total processes. We can then adjust $timer_1$ independently of $timer_3$ when we
wish to perform experiments where the frequency of only one process changes.

Bursty request injection is modeled by having the ISR inject multiple requests
instead of a single request. For example, on every 10th run of the ISR for $timer_1$,
5 requests are injected for process 1 instead of a single request.

4.4 Scheduler Implementation

The application has two main states (shown in Figure 3(c)): one state where
I/O operations are being performed and another when requests are generated

and insert into the scheduler from the TRQ. Two classes of schedulers are implemented: a FIFO queue and a EDF scheduler. Our RG-EDF scheduler is built on top of the EDF scheduler base. Our schedulers also have the ability to drop requests which are determined to miss their deadlines.

FIFO Queue. We simply used the TRQ as a FIFO queue. The TRQ is implemented as a circular queue in an array of treq objects. When this queue becomes full, no further requests are accepted and these requests are counted as dropped requests. In the I/O phase, we simply retrieve the first treq object from the queue, generate a full request object and perform the I/O operation.

EDF Schedulers. The base EDF scheduler is a priority queue implemented as a binary heap. The data structure of each request in the heap can be seen in figure 3(b). We only keep track of the time a request is generated for statistical purposes and can be optimized out.

By keeping the size of each request object constant, we are able to use a simple array-based heap structure. The top item in the heap will always be at index 0 and the child nodes for an item at index i would be at $i*2+1$ and $i*2+2$. In addition to being able to remove items from the top of the heap, we can also specify which heap index we wish to remove an item from.

Building on top of this base EDF scheduler heap, functions are introduced to group and reorder requests. When a request is made, a list of indices from the heap is returned containing requests which can be grouped together. Once the application receives the list of indices, it then proceeds to retrieve, and remove from the heap, each request, starting with the last index (this ensures that the remaining heap indices remain valid). After retrieving all the requests in the group, a single I/O operation can be performed.

Knowing the typical time required to write a request to flash, the scheduler can allow requests which have later deadlines proceed ahead of requests which have an earlier deadlines, if the earlier deadline is not violated. The scheduler compares the grouped size of the top request with the grouped size of the next request from a different process. If the second group of requests has a larger total size, the second group of will be allowed to proceed first. This improves the I/O utilization and also allows more requests from the first process to enter the scheduler while the I/O operation is underway.

5 Experimental Evaluation

5.1 Experiment Setup

We compare the performance of our systems: RG-EDF, with the traditional FIFO approach and an EDF implementation. We run the experiments with three data flows. Each data flow (i) is defined by the period of the request injections, the request sizes ($size_{i,k}$) and the deadline delay ($d_{i,k}$) for each request.

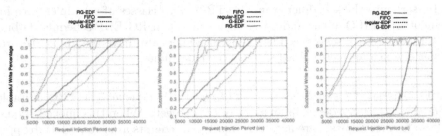

(a) Bursty requests with (b) Non Bursty requests (c) Bursty requests with-
dropping misses   with dropping misses   out dropping misses

Fig. 4. Varying period of request injection for all 3 processes with default deadline
delay ($d_{i,k} = 70$ ms) and request size ($size_{i,k} = 64$ bytes)

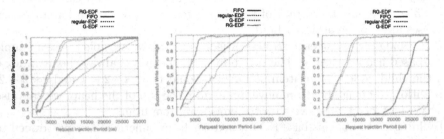

(a) Bursty requests with (b) Non Bursty requests (c) Bursty requests with-
dropping misses   with dropping misses   out dropping misses

Fig. 5. Varying period of request injection for 1 of 3 processes with default deadline
delay ($d_{i,k} = 70$ ms) and request size ($size_{i,k} = 64$ bytes)

We evaluate the schedulers by varying single parameters over a range of values.
We also choose some conservative default values such that each of the schedulers
perform well at these values:

- injection period: 40 ms
- request size: 64 bytes
- deadline delay: 70 ms

In addition to varying a parameter, we examined the effects of allowing the
schedulers to drop requests when it is determined that their deadlines cannot be
met. We also look at the performance in the presence of **bursty** traffic: instead
of a single request, 5 requests are injected for process 1 every 10 injection cycles.

For each experiment, 10 sets of 10 second runs were completed and the results
averaged. The results are also aggregated across all three processes running.

5.2   Varying Frequency

We vary the frequency for all three process at the same time. Since the deadlines
for all the request are the same and the periodic requests are injected at the same

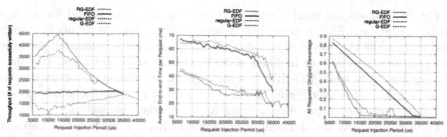

(a) Throughput in number of requests successfully written

(b) End-to-end time each request spends in the system

(c) Total # of dropped requests due to full scheduler and dropping misses

Fig. 6. Varying period of request injection for all 3 processes with default deadline delay ($d_{i,k} = 70$ ms) and request size ($size_{i,k} = 64$ bytes)

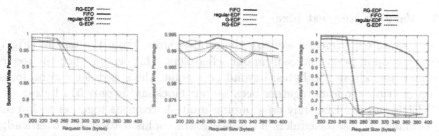

(a) Bursty requests with dropping misses

(b) Non Bursty requests with dropping misses

(c) Bursty requests without dropping misses

Fig. 7. Varying request size for all 3 processes with default injection period 40 ms and deadline delay ($d_{i,k} = 70$ ms)

time, the EDF scheduler is acting exactly like the FIFO scheduler, except the EDF scheduler has the additional overhead associated with the scheduler. The G-EDF and RG-EDF schedulers share the same overhead as the EDF scheduler but is able to compensate by grouping requests together, leading to much better performance. Figure 4 shows that G-EDF performs better than RG-EDF because there are not many opportunities for reordering and the extra overhead of reordering logic is demonstrated.

Figure 4 (a) and (b) show the difference in performance between bursty and non bursty traffic, all schedulers perform better when the traffic is non bursty, due to there being less requests overall, but G-EDF and RG-EDF handle bursty traffic better due to their ability to group these requests together.

When we disallow dropping misses (compare Figure 4 (a) and (c)), by allowing requests to complete even when they are going to miss their deadlines, we see that FIFO and EDF performance drop off rapidly due to missed deadlines causing more misses. When drops are enabled, FIFO and EDF perform much better since they are available to only perform on-time requests. Further, figure 6(c) shows that the majority of the drops for G-EDF and RG-EDF are due to scheduler saturation rather than being dropped due to misses.

Figure 5 shows the results when only varying injection period for a single process. FIFO and EDF perform better because there are less results in total to deal with: while the injection period of the single process is increased, the other two processes are injecting in 40 ms periods. G-EDF shows a modest amount of performance gain while RG-EDF has many more reordering opportunities and shows improvement over Figure 4. As the injection rate for the single process increases, more reordering opportunities are presenting themselves.

Figure 6(a) shows the throughput of each scheduler as the injection rates are increase. The FIFO scheduler has a constant throughput; it can write a constant number of request independent of how many are injected. EDF suffers from the scheduler over head is unable to keep up. G-EDF and RG-EDF both perform well and peak when scheduler saturation causes drops. Figure 6(b) shows that requests spend much less time in the G-EDF and RG-EDF schedulers.

5.3   Varying Request Size

In this set of experiments, we vary the request sizes. From the results (Fig 7), we see a drop in performance from our schedulers. This occurs when the request size increases above 256 bytes; beyond this point, the scheduler can no longer group multiple requests together because our block size is only 512 bytes.

G-EDF and RG-EDF rely on grouping multiple requests together to improve performance. These schedulers introduce extra sophistication and overhead; if requests are large and grouping not possible, they act like the EDF scheduler and the extra overhead will cause the grouping schedulers to perform poorly.

6   Conclusion

Sensor applications are become increasingly complex: requiring multiple streams of data storage and taking rich measurements such as visual and audio data which are frequently bursty. In this paper we have proposed the RG-EDF scheduling policy, which shows excellent performance in many cases where simple schedulers are insufficient. RG-EDF achieves that by taking into consideration the unique characteristics of flash-based devices when storing real-time multimedia data. RG-EDF is easy to implement, and thus makes it suitable for resource-constrained sensor nodes.

References

1. Chipcon cc1010, http://www.keil.com/dd/chip/3506.htm
2. Cmucam, http://cmucam.org/
3. Yaffs (yet another flash file system), http://www.yaffs.net/
4. Banerjee, A., Mitra, A., Najjar, W., Zeinalipour-Yazti, D., Kalogeraki, V., Gunopulos, D.: Rise- co-s: high performance sensor storage and co-processing architecture. In: IEEE Sensor and Ad Hoc Communications and Networks, Santa Clara, CA (September 2005)

5. Bisson, T., Brandt, S.: Reducing energy consumption with a non-volatile storage cache. In: Proc. of International Workshop on Software Support for Portable Storage (IWSSPS), held with RTAS 2005, San Fransisco, CA (March 2005)
6. Bisson, T., Brandt, S.A., Long, D.D.E.: Nvcache: Increasing the effectiveness of disk spin-down algorithms with caching. In: MASCOTS, Monterey, CA, September 2006, pp. 422–432 (2006)
7. Carrera, E., Bianchini, R.: Improving disk throughput in data-intensive servers. In: HPCA 2004, Madrid, Spain (February 2004)
8. Dai, H., Neufeld, M., Han, R.: Elf: an efficient log-structured flash file system for micro sensor nodes. In: SenSys 2004, Baltimore, MD, USA, pp. 176–187 (2004)
9. Iyer, S., Druschel, P.: Anticipatory scheduling: A disk scheduling framework to overcome deceptive idleness in synchronous I/O. In: 18th ACM Symposium on Operating Systems Principles, Chateau Lake Louise, Banff, Canada (October 2001)
10. Kulkarni, P., Ganesan, D., Shenoy, P.: The case for multi–tier camera sensor networks. In: NOSSDAV 2005, Stevenson, Washington, USA, pp. 141–146 (2005)
11. Li, M., Ganesan, D., Shenoy, P.: Presto: feedback-driven data management in sensor networks. In: NSDI 2006, San Jose, CA, p. 23 (2006)
12. Lumb, C., Schindler, J., Ganger, G.R., Riedel, E., Nagle, D.F.: Towards higher disk head utilization: Extracting "free" bandwidth from busy disk drives. In: OSDI 2000, San Diego, CA, pp. 87–102 (2000)
13. Luo, L., Cao, Q., Huang, C., Abdelzaher, T., Stankovic, J.A., Ward, M.: Enviromic: Towards cooperative storage and retrieval in audio sensor networks. In: ICDCS 2007, Washington, DC, USA, p. 34. IEEE Computer Society, Los Alamitos (2007)
14. Mumolo, E.: Prediction of disk arm movements in anticipation of future requests. In: MASCOTS 1999, College Park, Maryland (October 1999)
15. Rahimi, M., Baer, R., Iroezi, O.I., Garcia, J.C., Warrior, J., Estrin, D., Srivastava, M.: Cyclops: in situ image sensing and interpretation in wireless sensor networks. In: SenSys 2005, San Diego, California, USA, pp. 192–204 (2005)
16. Woodhouse, D.: Jffs: The journalling flash file system. In: Proc. Ottawa Linux Symp. (2001), http://sourceware.org/jffs2/
17. Zeinalipour-Yazti, D., Lin, S., Kalogeraki, V., Gunopulos, D., Najjar, W.A.: Microhash: An efficient index structure for flash-based sensor devices. In: FAST 2005, San Fransisco, CA (December 2005)

Methods for Increasing Coverage in Wireless Sensor Networks

Sunggu Lee and Younggyu Yang

Division of Electrical and Computer Engineering, Pohang University of Science and
Technology, San 31 Hyoja Dong, Pohang, South Korea
{slee,zhaoyue}@postech.ac.kr

Abstract. In a Wireless Sensor Network, it is important to be able to
maintain a sufficient level of *coverage* for a given target area. This paper
addresses the problem of determining *how many* and *where* to place additional sensor nodes in order to increase the coverage from k to $k + 1$.
Several possible candidate solution methods for this problem are proposed and evaluated using theoretical and simulation-based analysis.

Keywords: Wireless Sensor Network (WSN), Coverage, Algorithm.

1 Introduction

One of the most basic problems that must be addressed when working with
Wireless Sensor Networks (WSNs) is the issue of the level of *coverage* provided
by a set of WSN nodes. Since a WSN is most often used for "sensing" events
of interest in a target area, *coverage* normally refers to *sensing coverage*. Given
a target area being monitored by a set of WSN nodes, the area is said to be
covered if any location within that area is within the sensing range of at least
one WSN node.

More generally, a target area can be defined as being *k-covered* if any location
within that area is within the sensing range of at least k WSN nodes. Depending
on the WSN application, it may be necessary for an area to be k-covered with
$k > 1$. For example, triangulation-based localization techniques require an object
to be sensed by at least three WSN nodes. If localization is required within a
3-dimensional space, then four distance measurements are necessary (implying
a coverage level of $k = 4$). Fault-tolerance requirements may dictate the use of a
coverage level higher than the minimum for a particular application. Also, since
energy conservation is critical for many WSN applications, it may be necessary
for a region to be k-covered with $k \geq 2$ in order to be able to periodically place
sets of nodes in suspended mode.

There are several ways in which WSN nodes could be positioned within a target area such that it is k-covered with a prespecified k value. If WSN nodes can
be exactly positioned, then specific optimal layout patterns exist for several different types of areas and sensing coverage fields. For instance, if a 2-dimensional
rectangular area and circular sensing coverage fields with identical radii are assumed, then a hexagonal beehive-type layout (such as that used for cell phone

U. Brinkschulte, T. Givargis, and S. Russo (Eds.): SEUS 2008, LNCS 5287, pp. 360–368, 2008.

networks) is clearly optimal. In many applications, however, WSN nodes cannot be exactly positioned. This could be the case with WSN nodes spread out over rugged terrain or extremely large numbers of WSN nodes deployed over a short time interval. However, given such a set of haphazardly-placed WSN nodes, it may still be possible to *add* WSN nodes at specific locations such that the target area becomes k-covered. Following discussion of related work in Section 2, this problem will be formalized, and several candidate solutions proposed and analyzed, in Section 3. Then, to further assess these candidate solutions, simulation results will be presented and analyzed in Section 4. Finally, conclusions will be drawn in Section 5.

2   Previous Related Work

There are several approaches related to obtaining a *desired* level of coverage for a sensing field. In [1], three general models are used to define the coverage problem. The first model is the *binary model*, where each sensor's coverage region is modeled by a disk. The second is the *probabilistic model*. An event that occurs within the coverage range of a sensor is either detected or not detected by the sensor depending on a probability distribution. The last model considers the coverage problem by considering the movement of targets through the sensing field.

To determine either a given region is k-covered or not, the coverage of each region must be computed. An approximate solution for evaluating the coverage of each region involves dividing the entire sensing field into 1m x 1m *patches*. The coverage of a given region is approximated by measuring the number of active sensors that cover the patches within that region. Although this method is simple, managing the coverage values for all patches is a computationally heavy requirement. In [2], an alternative solution is proposed. Rather than determining the coverage of each patch, their solutions are based on checking the *perimeter* of each sensor's sensing range. An advantage of this solution is that it can be easily translated to a distributed protocol.

There are several methods used to obtain a desired level of coverage for a sensing field. [3] proposes a mechanism for step-by-step sequential deployment given a random initial deployment of sensors within the region to be monitored. The strategy consists of deploying a limited number of sensors at a time until the desired minimum exposure level is achieved. Several criteria are used for the efficient deployment of these sensors; however, the level of coverage achieved is not considered. [4] presents protocols that can be used to dynamically configure a network to achieve a guaranteed level of coverage and connectivity assuming that sufficient numbers of sensors have been deployed.

The main difference between this paper and the prior research work discussed above is that this work focuses on determining *how many* and *where* to place additional sensor nodes in order to *increase* the coverage level from k to $k + 1$. According to our survey of the public literature, this work is the first of its kind to address this particular problem.

3 Problem Definition and Candidate Solutions

Let us assume a set of WSN nodes $G = \{w_1, w_2, ..., w_n\}$. The sensing range of a node $w_i \in G$ is modeled by a circular disk with radius r_i. For simplicity, let us also assume that $r_i = r_j$ for all $w_i, w_j \in G$ (uniform circular sensing ranges). However, note that, as described in [2], coverage computation for nonuniform and irregularly-shaped sensing ranges can be achieved using simple extensions to the techniques used for uniform circular sensing ranges. In a like manner, the techniques presented in this paper can be extended to other sensing range models.

Given a uniform circular sensing range model, a set of haphazardly-placed nodes results in a set of regions formed by the intersection of the sensing range circles of nodes $w_i \in G$. Each such region can be labeled with a "coverage" value corresponding to the number of nodes that can detect events within that region. Fig. 1 shows an example of a set of haphazardly-placed nodes and the resulting coverage values.

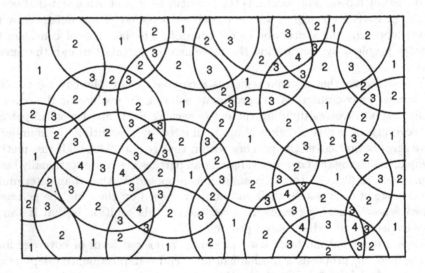

Fig. 1. A set of haphazardly-placed nodes and the resulting coverage values

Definition 1. *A coverage region CR_l is a contiguous area formed by the intersections of sensing range circles and the boundary of the target area A.*

Definition 2. *A coverage value CV_l is a nonnegative integer corresponding to the number of nodes that can detect events that occur within coverage region CR_l.*

Definition 3. *A node $w_i \in G$ covers a coverage region CR_l if w_i can sense any event that may occur within CR_l.*

Definition 4. *The* coverage level CL *of a set of nodes* G *is the minimum of the coverage values within the target area* A *covered by the nodes in* G.

Definition 5. *The* intersection point set IP_l *of a coverage region* CR_l *is the set of points at the boundaries of* CR_l *where two or more sensing range circles or the boundary of the target area* A *intersect.*

Given the above definitions, let us define the problem to be solved. Let us assume that there are a set of initially-placed WSN nodes G used to sense events of interest within a target area A. There are no limitations on the manner in which these nodes are placed. Thus, in general, we can assume that these nodes are initially deployed in a semi-random haphazard manner. Methods such as those introduced in [2] can be used to compute coverage regions, coverage values, and the overall coverage level given the set of nodes G and the target area A. If the coverage level is sufficient for a particular application, then there is nothing more to be done. However, if the coverage level needs to be increased, then how should additional nodes be deployed in order to reach the desired coverage level? This problem can be stated more formally as follows.

Problem INCC (INCreasing Coverage)

Input: A target area A, a set of initially-placed nodes G, a set of coverage regions (with coverage values), the coverage level CL and the desired coverage level CL^*, with $CL^* > CL$.
Output: A set of additional nodes G^* and their locations within A. $G+G^*$ should have a coverage level of CL^*.

Can the INCC problem be solved in an optimal manner in polynomial time? As discussed in the introduction, if a regular target area is used, the coverage ranges of all nodes are identical and regular and the nodes in G are deployed in a specific layout pattern, then optimal solutions can found in many cases by using predefined optimal layout patterns. However, in the general case, this is clearly a very difficult problem. More formally, it can be shown that the INCC problem is NP-hard. The proof of this statement follows from the fact that the Knapsack Problem, which is a well-known NP-hard problem [5], can be reduced (in polynomial time) to a restricted form of the INCC problem.

Several different heuristic solutions can be proposed for the INCC problem. One simple candidate solution is the the random method, in which additional nodes are placed randomly in the target area A until the desired coverage level is reached. However, as will be shown in our simulation results, the random method is close to the worst solution method that can be used. Better solutions should result if coverage regions and coverage values are taken into account. As shown in [6], intersection point sets (Defn. 5) can be useful in determining the WSN node sleep cycles to be used for energy conservation. Thus, taking a hint from their method, let us also consider the use of intersection point sets in determining the placement of additional nodes used to solve the INCC problem.

With these considerations, the following candidate solutions are proposed for the INCC problem.

Algorithm Random:

0: Let $G^* = \emptyset$.
1: Choose a location at random within the target area A.
2: Place a new node w_m at that location ($G^* = G^* + w_m$) and recompute CL.
3: If $CL \geq CL^*$, then stop. Otherwise, go back to Step 1.

Algorithm LowCoverage:

0: Assume $CL > 0$. Let $G^* = \emptyset$, $T = \{CR_l | CV_l = CL\}$.
1: Let CR_i = first element of T, $T = T - CR_i$.
2: Choose any node $w_i \in G \cup G^* | w_i$ covers CR_i.
3: Create a new node w_m and place it at the same location as w_i. Let $G^* = G^* + w_m$.
4: If $|T| > 0$, go back to Step 1.
5: Recompute the coverage level CL with $G + G^*$. If $CL \geq CL^*$, stop. Otherwise, let $T = \{CR_l | CV_l = CL\}$ and go back to Step 1.

Algorithm MaxIP:

0: Let $G^* = \emptyset$, $T = \{CR_l | CV_l = CL\}$.
1: Let CR_i = an element of T with the maximum number of intersection points, $T = T - CR_i$.
2: Create a new node w_m and place it at the "center of mass" of the intersection points in CR_i ($G^* = G^* + w_m$).
3: If $|T| > 0$, go back to Step 1.
4: Recompute the coverage level CL with $G + G^*$. If $CL \geq CL^*$, stop. Otherwise, let $T = \{CR_l | CV_l = CL\}$ and go back to Step 1.

Algorithm MaxIPinc:

0: Let $G^* = \emptyset$, $T = \{CR_l | CV_l = CL\}$.
1: Let CR_i = an element of T with the maximum number of intersection points.
2: Create a new node w_m and place it at the "center of mass" of the intersection points in CR_i ($G^* = G^* + w_m$).
3: Recompute the coverage level CL with $G + G^*$. If $CL \geq CL^*$, stop. Otherwise, let $T = \{CR_l | CV_l = CL\}$ and go back to Step 1.

Algorithm MaxCV:

0: Let $G^* = \emptyset$, $maxCV$ = maximum CV_l value, $T = \{CR_l | CV_l = maxCV\}$.
1: Let CR_i = an element of T with the maximum number of intersection points.

2: Create a new node w_m and place it at the "center of mass" of the intersection points in CR_i $(G^* = G^* + w_m)$.

3: Recompute the coverage level CL with $G + G^*$. If $CL \geq CL^*$, stop. Otherwise, let $T = \{CR_l | CV_l = CL\}$ and go back to Step 1.

The motivation behind the above algorithms is as follows. The Random algorithm is the simplest to implement since it uses random new node deployment. The LowCoverage algorithm is a simple method for ensuring that the coverage level is increased in a systematic manner. It has the following property.

Theorem 1. *Suppose $CL = 1$ and $CL^* = 2$. Then Step 5 of the LowCoverage algorithm will be executed only once. In addition, the minimum coverage value will not increase until the last iteration (inner loop) of the LowCoverage algorithm.*

Proof. In Step 1, T is defined as the set of coverage regions CR_l with the same coverage value as CL. By placing one new node at the same location as an existing node that covers a CR_l in T, CV_l will increase by one. This new node will not cover any other coverage region in T since the initial minimum coverage value (which is the same as the initial CL) is 1. Thus, with each inner-loop iteration of the LowCoverage algorithm, exactly one element of T will have its coverage value increased by one. When Step 5 is reached, all elements of T will have been traversed. Thus, the coverage level will increase at this point and the algorithm should terminate since $CL^* = CL + 1$. Finally, as long as elements remain in T, those elements will have their old coverage values. This proves the second part of the theorem.

The MaxIP algorithm places a new node at the "center of mass"[1] [7] of the intersection points of a coverage region with the minimum coverage value. This is done for all coverage regions with the minimum coverage value. However, even after all such regions have been covered, it is still possible for new smaller regions to be formed that still have the old minimum coverage value. Thus, this process needs to be repeated until the coverage level increases to the desired value. MaxIPinc is an "incremental" form of the MaxIP algorithm that recomputes the coverage level after each new node has been added.

Finally, in the MaxCV algorithm, we consider the possibility of placing new nodes within the coverage regions with the largest coverage values. The reasoning behind this strategy is that new nodes placed at such locations should have the "biggest" potential impact since they will impact the largest number of other coverage regions. However, simulations with this algorithm revealed that this impact was "negative" in most cases. Thus, the MaxCV algorithm could be considered as a "worst-possible" solution (useful for comparison purposes) for the INCC problem.

---

[1] The "center of mass" of a system of particles is a specific point at which, for many purposes, the system's mass behaves as if it were concentrated.

4 Simulation Analysis

Computer simulations were used to compare the proposed solutions for the INCC problem. A square target area (X meters on a side) was assumed. An initial set of WSN nodes were generated randomly within this area until a specific initial coverage level CL was achieved. However, in order to avoid extreme clustering of WSN nodes (we would also want to avoid such clustering in most practical application scenarios), if a newly generated random node was found to fall within the sensing region of an existing node (or E existing nodes in the more general case), then that newly generated node was discarded and another node generated randomly. The sensing range of all WSN nodes were assumed to be identical and in the shape of a circular disk with radius R. Simulation experiments were conducted with all of the proposed algorithms and various values for the X, CL and R parameters.

Fig. 2 shows the simulation results for all five proposed algorithms given $X = 40m$ (40m × 40m target area) and $R = 5m$ (sensing radius). This figure shows the trends in performance (number of additional nodes required to increase the coverage level by one) of the various algorithms as the initial coverage level CL is increased. The MaxCV algorithm was found to perform so poorly that it was not able to complete in a reasonable amount of time given $CL > 2$. The MaxCV and Random algorithms were found to perform significantly worse than

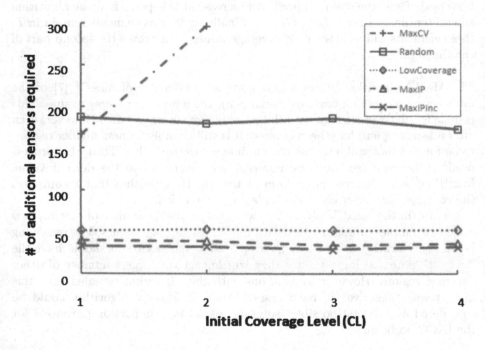

Fig. 2. Number of additional nodes required to increase CL to $CL + 1$ given a 40m × 40m target area and WSN nodes with 5m sensing radii

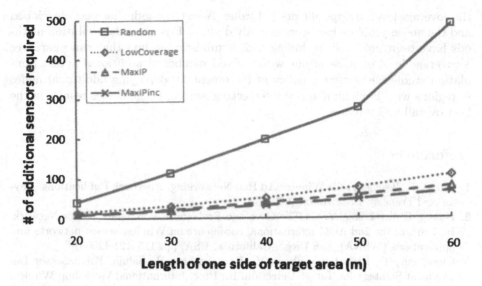

Fig. 3. Number of additional nodes required to increase $CL = 1$ to $CL^* = 2$ (given sensing radius $R = 5$m) versus X (assuming an $X \times X$ target area)

the LowCoverage, MaxIP and MaxIPinc algorithms. The MaxIPinc algorithm was found to perform the best.

In order to investigate the trends in performance as the size of the target area was increased, simulations were conducted with fixed CL and R and varying X parameter values. Fig. 3 shows these results for the Random, LowCoverage, MaxIP and MaxIPinc algorithms. The MaxCV algorithm was not simulated as its performance was found to be significantly poorer than all other algorithms (except the Random algorithm in certain situations), as demonstrated in the plot of Fig. 2. The results of Fig. 3 showed a linear increase in the number of additional nodes required to increase the coverage level by one (versus X, the length of one side of the target area) for the LowCoverage, MaxIP and MaxIPinc algorithms. The relative performance of all algorithms was the same as in Fig. 2.

5   Concluding Remarks

This paper investigated the problem of increasing the minimum sensing coverage value in a target area populated with wireless sensor network (WSN) nodes. By ensuring a minimum sensing coverage value, referred to as the *coverage level CL*, any event that occurs anywhere within the target area can be monitored by at least CL nodes. Alternatively, given $CL > 1$, subsets of the nodes can be placed in sleep mode in order to conserve energy and thereby extend the lifetime of the WSN.

The coverage level issue has been approached by investigating the problem of determining how many and where to deploy additional nodes in order to increase the coverage level to a specific desired value. A system model has been developed and the above problem has been formally defined. Five candidate solution methods have been proposed, including a deterministic method that can guarantee a coverage level increase of one with a fixed number of additional nodes. Simulation studies show that a policy of incrementally deploying additional nodes in regions with large numbers of intersecting sensing range circles results in the best overall performance.

References

1. Wu, S.-L., Tseng, Y.-C.: Wireless Ad Hoc Networking. Auerbach Publications (Taylor and Francis), Boca Raton (2007)
2. Huang, C.-F., Tseng, Y.-C.: The Coverage Problem in a Wireless Sensor Network. In: Proc. of the 2nd ACM international conference on Wireless sensor networks and applications (WSNA), San Diego, California, USA, pp. 115–121 (2003)
3. Clouqueur, T., Phipatanasuphom, V., Ramanathan, P., Saluja, K.K.: Sensor Deployment Strategy for Target Detection. In: Proc. International Workshop Wireless Sensor Networks and Application, pp. 42–48 (2002)
4. Wang, X., Xing, G., Lu, C., Pless, R., Gill, C.: Integrated Coverage and Connectivity Configuration in Wireless Sensor Networks. In: Proc. the 1st international conference on Embedded networked sensor systems (SenSys), Los Angeles, California, USA, pp. 28–39 (2003)
5. Garey, M.R., Johnson, D.S.: Computers and Intractability: A Guide to the Theory of NP-Completeness. Freeman and Co., New York (1979)
6. Huang, C.-F., Lo, L.-C., Tseng, Y.-C., Chen, W.-T.: Decentralized Energy-Conserving and Coverage-Preserving Protocols for Wireless Sensor Networks. In: Proc. IEEE International Symposium on Circuits and Systems (ISCAS), vol. 1, pp. 640–643 (2005)
7. Wikipedia, http://en.wikipedia.org/

Locks Considered Harmful:
A Look at Non-traditional Synchronization*

Michel Raynal

IRISA, Campus de Beaulieu, 35042 Rennes Cedex, France
raynal@irisa.fr

Abstract. This paper considers the implementation of concurrent objects in systems prone to asynchrony and process failures. It first shows that lock-based solutions have drawbacks that can make them redhibitory for systems deployed in very demanding environments, such as embedded systems. Then, considering the adaptive renaming problem as a paradigm of coordination and synchronization problems, the paper investigates wait-free implementations of an adaptive renaming object (wait-free means that these implementations do not rest on locks or waiting loops). This problem consists in assigning new distinct names (to the subset of processes that want to acquire a new name) in such a way that the new name space be as small as possible.

The best that can be done in asynchronous systems prone to process crashes, and where the processes communicate only through read/write atomic registers, is a new naming space of size $M = 2p - 1$, where p is the number of processes that want to acquire a new name (whatever the number of processes in the system). An algorithm providing such an optimal renaming space is described. Then, it is shown how the use of "additional power" such as appropriate failure detectors, or synchronization primitives stronger than read/write operations, allows to bypass the $2p - 1$ lower bound.

Keywords: Adaptive renaming, Asynchronous system, Atomic register, Concurrency, Failure detector, Fault-tolerance, Lock-free synchronization, Process crash, Shared memory system, Synchronization primitive, Wait-free computation.

1 Introduction

From mastering sequential algorithms to mastering concurrency The study of algorithms lies at the core of informatics, and participate in establishing it as a *science* with strong results on what can be computed (decidability) and what can be efficiently computed (complexity). It is consequently unanimously accepted by the community that any curriculum for undergraduate students has to include lectures on sequential algorithms. This allows the students not only to better master the basic concepts, mechanisms, techniques, difficulties and subtleties that underlie the design of algorithms, but also understand the deep nature of computer science and computer engineering.

Up to now, the implementation of concurrent objects (objects that can be concurrently accessed by several processes -or threads-) is mainly based on the use of locks.

---

* This work was supported by the European Network of Excellence ReSIST.

U. Brinkschulte, T. Givargis, and S. Russo (Eds.): SEUS 2008, LNCS 5287, pp. 369–380, 2008.

More precisely, a lock is associated with each concurrent object O, and each operation accessing the internal representation of O (e.g., a $push()$ operation on a shared stack) is required to first lock the object O (thereby preventing the internal representation from being concurrently accessed) and finally to release the corresponding lock when it terminates.

Albeit (at first glance) the use of locks is relatively simple, it has several drawbacks. When locks are used only at a large grain level they can severely reduce parallelism, while using them at a fine grain level is error-prone. Moreover, whatever the grain level, lock-based solutions are deadlock prone. A more severe drawback lies in the fact that, in asynchronous systems, locks cannot cope with process crashes. This is because, when the only means processes have to communicate is read/write atomic registers, a slow process (whose slowness can be due to interrupts, swapping, etc.) cannot be distinguished from a process that has crashed. These drawbacks can make locks harmful or even irrelevant for some applications, and become redhibitory for some classes of embedded applications. A new look at synchronization concepts and techniques is hardly needed. So, the algorithmics of synchronization has to be revisited.

Adaptive renaming as a paradigm for non-traditional synchronization. This paper considers the renaming problem to illustrate non-traditional synchronization concepts and mechanisms that need to be understood and mastered when one wants to implement concurrent objects while preventing the previously cited drawbacks related to the use of locks.

Let us consider a set of processes, each process having an initial name (taken from a large name space). The *adaptive renaming* problem consists in designing an algorithm that, despite asynchrony and process failures, allows processes to acquire new (distinct) names. Moreover, the new name space has to be as small as possible (in the following M denotes the size of the new name space). This means that M has to depend only on the number of processes that want to acquire a new name, and not on their total number of processes (that can be arbitrary).

The adaptive renaming problem is a paradigm of resource allocation problems: the new names are the resources acquired by the processes. The fact that no two processes can acquire the same new name gives it a mutual exclusion flavor. This problem has a simple lock-based solution: namely, a shared register that contains an integer, increased by one each time it is accessed, and protected by a lock, can be used to generate new names. Interestingly, this implementation is adaptive (the value of M depends only on the number of processes that compete to acquire a new name). Moreover, this size is optimal: if p processes want to acquire a new name, M is as small as possible, i.e., we have $M = p$. Unfortunately, as indicated before, as it is lock-based, this solution cannot cope with the net effect of asynchrony and process crashes.

Wait-free adaptive renaming. A *wait-free* algorithm is an algorithm that allows each process that does not crash to terminate in a finite number of computation steps, whatever the behavior of the other processes (i.e., despite the fact they are extremely rapid or slow, or even have crashed) [13]. So, a wait-free implementation of an object means absence of starvation despite asynchrony and process crashes. Trivially, a wait-free implementation cannot be lock-based.

Let p be the number of processes that require a new name. It has been shown [14] that in a system where the processes can communicate through atomic registers only, the size of the smallest new name space that can be obtained by a wait-free algorithm is $M = 2p - 1$. This shows that, due to asynchrony and failures, there is an inherent price that has to be paid in asynchronous read/write shared memory systems, namely, the size of the new name space is $M = p + (p - 1)$, i.e., p (the smallest size that can never be bypassed) plus $(p - 1)$. The quantity $(p - 1)$ is consequently the smallest price to be paid to master the inherent uncertainty created by the combination of asynchrony and failures in systems where processes communicate through atomic registers only.

It is important to see that adaptivity means the following. If "today" p' processes want to acquire a new name, their new names belong to the interval $[1..2p' - 1]$. If "tomorrow", p'' additional processes want to acquire a new name, their new names will be distinct from the previous ones and will belong to the interval $[1..2p - 1]$ where $p = p' + p''$.

Content of the paper. In order to investigate and illustrate non-traditional synchronization (i.e., synchronization that is not based on locks) the paper considers several wait-free implementations of an *adaptive renaming object*. The paper is made up of 7 sections. Section 2 first presents the system model, and Section 3 presents the adaptive renaming problem. Then, Section 4 presents a simple basic adaptive renaming [6] that provides an optimal new name space (i.e., $M = 2p - 1$ where p is the number of processes that participate in the renaming).

In the previous algorithm, processes communicate only through atomic registers. On another side, we know that we can obtain $M = p$ when the processes can additionally use locks. So, an important question is the following: How to enrich the system in order to provide a new renaming space whose size is smaller than $2p - 1$ while ensuring that the implementation remains wait-free? The paper presents two such approaches.

- Section 5 considers that the processes are provided with an appropriate failure detector and presents a corresponding adaptive renaming algorithm such that $M = p + k - 1$, where k is parameter that capture the power of the underlying failure detector.
- Differently, Section 6 considers that the system provides the processes with synchronization primitives more powerful than the basic atomic read/write operations. It shows that, in that case, the size of the new name space directly depends on the "power" of the synchronization primitive. The paper considers three such synchronization primitives, namely, test&set, k-set agreement and compare&swap.

Finally, Section 7 concludes the paper. It is important to notice that that paper can be considered from two complementary point of views. On one side, it presents a non-traditional view for synchronization in embedded systems, and new algorithms. On another side, it has a survey flavor that tries to capture the main issues of a new emerging research topic.

2   Base System Model

Process model. The system consists of n processes that we denote $p_1, \ldots, p_n$. The integer i is the index of p_i. Each process p_i has an initial name id_i. A process does not know the initial names of the other processes, it only knows that no two processes have the same initial name. (The initial name is a particular value defined in p_i's initial context.) The processes are asynchronous. This means that there is no bound on the time it takes for a process to execute a computation step. A process may crash (halt prematurely). After it has crashed a process executes no step. A process executes correctly its algorithm until it possibly crashes. A process that does not crash in a run is *correct* in that run; otherwise, it is *faulty* in that run.

Communication model. The processes cooperate by accessing atomic read/write registers. *Atomic* means that each read or write operation appears as if it has been executed instantaneously at some time between its begin and end events [15,16]. Each atomic register is a one-writer/multi-readers (1WnR) register. This means that a single process (statically determined) can write it. Atomic registers are denoted with uppercase letters. The atomic registers are structured into arrays. $X[1..n]$ being such an array, $X[i]$ denotes the register of that array that p_i only is allowed to write. A process can have local registers. Such registers are denoted with lowercase letters with the process index appearing as a subscript (e.g., $prop_i$ is a local register of p_i). The notation $\bot$ is used to denote a default value.

The shared memory provides the processes with an atomic operation that is denoted X.snapshot(), where $X[1..n]$ is an array of atomic registers [1]. That operation allows a process p_i to atomically read the whole array $X[1..n]$ (as if it was a single atomic register). This means that the execution of X.snapshot() operation appears as if it has been executed instantaneously at some point in time between its begin and end events. Such an operation can be built from 1WnR atomic registers [1]. To our knowledge the best snapshot() implementation proposed so far requires $O(n \log(n))$ read/write operations on base atomic registers [5].

3   Adaptive M-Renaming

The renaming problem has been introduced in [3]. Each process p_i has an initial name id_i such that no two processes have the same initial name. These initial names are taken from a set $\{1, \ldots, N\}$ such that $n \ll N$. Let new_name() be the (only) operation provided by an adaptive M-renaming object, i.e., an object that allows processes to obtain new distinct names belonging to the interval $[1..M]$ ([1]). The behavior of this object (i.e., the the adaptive renaming problem) is defined by the following properties. Let p denote the number of processes that invoke new_name() (the set of participating processes).

- Termination. If a correct process invokes new_name() it obtains a new name.
- Agreement. No two processes obtain the same new name.
- Adaptivity. A new name belong to $[1..M]$ where M is a function of p.
- Index independence. The behavior of a process is independent of its index.

The last property states that, if, in a run, a process whose index is i obtains the new name v, that process would have obtained the very same new name if its index was j.

---

[1] Trivially, whatever the operations the processes can use, there is no M-renaming object with $M < p$.

```
operation new_name(id_i):
(1)   prop_i ← 1;
(2)   while true do
(3)      STATE[i] ←< id_i, prop_i >;
(4)      view_i ← STATE.snapshot();
(5)      if (∀ j ≠ i : view_i[j].prop ≠ prop_i)
(6)         then return (prop_i)
(7)         else let X  = {view_i[j].prop | (view_i[j].prop ≠ ⊥) ∧ (1 ≤ j ≤ n)};
(8)              let free = the increasing sequence 1, 2, ..., 2p − 1 from
                          which the integers in X have been suppressed;
(9)              let Y  = {view_i[j].old | (view_i[j].old ≠ ⊥) ∧ (1 ≤ j ≤ n)};
(10)             let r  = rank of id_i in Y;
(11)             prop_i  ← the rth integer in the increasing sequence free
(12)     end if
(13)  end while.
```

Fig. 1. Read/write (optimal) wait-free adaptive $(2p - 1)$-renaming [6]

This means that, from an operational point of view, the indexes define an underlying communication infrastructure, namely, an addressing mechanism that can only be used to access entries of shared arrays. Indexes cannot be used to *compute* new names.

4   A Read/Write Adaptive $(2p − 1)$-Renaming Algorithm

This section presents a simple adaptive M-renaming algorithm that provides the participating processes with an optimal new name space, i.e., $M = 2p − 1$, when the processes can cooperate through atomic registers only. This algorithm (due to Attiya and Welch [6]) is an adaptation to asynchronous read/write shared memory systems of a message-passing algorithm described in [3].

The communication medium: shared memory The shared memory is made up an array of 1WnR atomic registers denoted $STATE[1..n]$. Each register $STATE[i]$ is a pair made up of two fields: $STATE[i].old$ will contain the initial name of p_i, while $STATE[i].prop$ will contain the last proposal of p_i to acquire a new name. $STATE[i]$ can be written only by p_i, and is initialized to $< ⊥, ⊥ >$.

The algorithm: underlying principle and description The algorithm is described in Figure 1 (code for the process p_i). The local register $prop_i$ contains p_i's current proposal for a new name. When p_i invokes new_name(id_i), it sets $prop_i$ to 1 (line 1), and enters a **while** loop (lines 2-12). It exits that loop when it has obtained a new name (statement return($prop_i$) issued at line 6).

The principle of the algorithm is as follows. A new name can be considered as a slot, and the processes compete to acquire a free slot in the interval of slots $[1..2p − 1]$. After entering the loop, a process p_i first updates $STATE[i]$ (line 3) in order to announce to all the processes its current proposal for a new name (let us notice that it also implicitly announces it is competing for a new name).

Then, thanks to the snapshot operation on the shared memory (line 4), p_i obtains a consistent view of the system global state. This view is locally kept in the array $view_i$. The behavior of p_i then depends on the the consistent global state of the shared memory it has obtained, more precisely on the value of the predicate $\forall \, j \neq i : \; view_i[j].prop \neq prop_i$. We consider both cases.

- Case 1: the predicate is true. This means that no process p_j is competing with p_i for the new name $prop_i$. In that case, p_i considers the current value of $prop_i$ as its new name (line 6).
- Case 2: the predicate is false. This means that several processes are competing to obtain the same new name $prop_i$. So, p_i construct a new proposal for a new name and enters again the loop. This proposal is built from the consistent global state of the system that p_i has obtained in $view_i$.

  The set $X \; = \; \{view_i[j].prop \; | \; (view_i[j].prop \neq \perp) \wedge (1 \leq j \leq n)\}$ (line 7) contains the proposals (as seen by p_i) for a new name, while the set $Y = \{view_i[j].old \; | \; (view_i[j].old \neq \perp) \wedge (1 \leq j \leq n)\}$ (line 9) contains the initial names of the processes that p_i sees as competing for obtaining a new name.

  The determination of a new proposal by p_i is based on these two sets. First, p_i considers the sequence (denoted $free$) of the integers that are "free" and can consequently be used to define a new name proposal (the sequence $free$ contains at least p empty slots). This sequence is the sequence of positive integers from which the proposals in X have been suppressed (line 8). Then, p_i computes its rank r among the processes that (from its point of view) want to acquire a new name (line 9). Finally, given the sequence $free$ and r, p_i defines its new proposal as its rank in this sequence (this rank is r, i.e., its rank in the set of processes it sees as competing processes).

A proof of this algorithm can be found in [6]. The proof that no two new names are the same does not depend on the way the new names are chosen, it depends only on the fact that all the $STATE$.snapshot() operations appear as if they were executed one after the other. The fact that the new names belong to the interval $[1..2p-1]$ depends on the way the new names are chosen (lines 9-11).

5   Enriching the System with a Failure Detector

Considering a system where the processes can communicate through 1WnR atomic registers (as before), this section shows that it is possible to bypass the $(2p-1)$ lower bound when the processes are additionally provided with a failure detector of an appropriate class. The main point is that the implementation remains wait-free. A failure detector is a device that provides the processes with information on failures [8]. That information can be more or less accurate according to the class (type) of the failure detector.

To that end, a new class of failure detectors (denoted Ω_*^k) is first introduced. The parameter k can be seen as measuring the strength of the failure detector. Then, a wait-free adaptive renaming algorithm (introduced in [19]) that provides the processes with a name space whose size is $M = \min(2p - 1, p + k - 1)$ is presented. Interestingly, this algorithm can be seen as generalization of the algorithm presented in the previous section.

5.1 The Class Ω_*^k of Failure Detectors

The class Ω_*^k of failure detectors has been introduced in [20]. A failure detector of that class provides the processes with a primitive denoted leader(). When a process invokes that primitive, it provides a set X of processes as input parameter and obtains a non-empty set of at least one and at most k processes. Let Π be the set of all the processes, and $Correct$ the set of processes that are correct in the considered run. The class Ω_*^k is made up of all the failure detectors that satisfy the following property for each set X such that $X \cap Correct \neq \emptyset$:

- Eventual multi-leadership for each set X. There is a time after which all the invocations leader(X) issued by correct processes return the same set L_X and this set is such that $X \cap Correct \cap L_X \neq \emptyset$.

The intuition that underlies this definition is the following. The set X passed as input parameter by the invoking process p_i is the set of all the processes that p_i considers as being currently *participating* in the computation. Given a set X of participating processes that invoke leader(X), the eventual multi-leadership property states that there is a time after which these processes obtain the same set L_X of at most k leaders, and at least one of them is a correct process of X. Let us observe that the (at most $k - 1$) other processes of L_X can be any subset of processes (correct or not, participating or not).[2]

5.2 An Ω_*^k-Based Adaptive M-Renaming Algorithm with $M = \min(2p - 1, p + k - 1)$

Shared memory. As before (algorithm described in Figure 1), the shared memory is made up of an array $STATE[1..n]$. The only difference is that now each atomic register $STATE[i]$ is made up of three fields, $STATE[i].old$ and $STATE[i].prop$ (whose content and meaning are as before), plus a boolean $STATE[i].done$. That field, initialized to *false*, is set to true by p_i when it obtains its new name.

Process behavior. The algorithm executed by a process p_i is described in Figure 2. A process starts the renaming algorithm by setting a local flag denoted $done_i$ to *false*, and its current proposal for a new name to $\perp$ (line 1). Then, it enters a **repeat** loop and leaves it only when it has acquired a new name (lines 6, 16 and 17).

In the loop body, a process p_i first writes its current state in $STATE[i]$ to inform the other processes about its current progress, and then atomically reads $STATE$ (using the snapshot() operation) to obtain a consistent view of the global state. If p_i has already

---

[2] If all invocations are such that $X = \Pi$ and $k = 1$, Ω_*^k boils down to the classical leader failure detector (denoted Ω) that is the weakest failure detector that allows solving the consensus problem [9]. Algorithms implementing leader failure detector in shared memory systems are described in [10].

operation new_name(id_i):
(1) $prop_i \leftarrow \perp$; $done_i \leftarrow false$;
(2)   **repeat**
(3) $STATE[i] \leftarrow < id_i, prop_i, done_i >$;
(4) $view_i \leftarrow STATE.\text{snapshot}()$;
(5)   **if** $(prop_i \neq \perp) \wedge (\forall j \neq i : view_i[j].prop \neq prop_i)$
(6)   **then** $done_i \leftarrow true$; $STATE[i] \leftarrow < id_i, prop_i, done_i >$
(7)   **else** $contending_i \leftarrow$
                   $\{view_i[j].old \mid (view_i[j].old \neq \perp) \wedge \neg(view_i[j].done)\}$;
(8) $leaders_i \leftarrow \text{leader}(contending_i)$;
(9)   **if** $id_i \in leaders_i$ **then**
(10)   **let** $X = \{view_i[j].prop \mid (view_i[j].prop \neq \perp) \wedge (1 \leq j \leq n)\}$;
(11)   **let** $free =$ the increasing sequence $1, 2, \ldots, 2p - 1$ from
                      which the integers in X have been suppressed;
(12)   **let** $r =$ rank of id_i in $leaders_i$;
(13) $prop_i \leftarrow$ the rth integer in the increasing sequence $free$
(14)   **end if**
(15)   **end if**
(16) **until** $done_i$ **end repeat**;
(17) return($prop_i$).

Fig. 2. An Ω_*^k-based adaptive M-renaming with $M = \min(2p - 1, p + k - 1)$ [19]

determined a new name proposal and no other process p_j has chosen the same new name proposal (the predicate of line 5 is then satisfied), p_i commits this last proposal that becomes its new name by announcing it to the other processes (write of $STATE[i]$ at line 6), and returns that proposal as its new name (line 16).

In the other case (the predicate of line 5 is not satisfied), p_i enters the lines 7-14 to determine another new name proposal. To that end, p_i first determines the processes that are competing to have a new name. Those are the processes p_j that, from p_i's point of view, are participating in the renaming (namely, the processes p_j such that $my\_view_i[j]$ $.old \neq \perp$) and have not yet obtained a new name (i.e., such that $\neg(view_i[j].done)$). Before starting the next execution of the loop body, processes have to change their new name proposal (otherwise, it could be possible that they loop forever). So, p_i does the following.

- After it has determined the set of processes it perceives as currently competing with it, p_i invokes leader($contending_i$) to obtain a set of leaders (lines 7-8) associated with this set $contending_i$ of competing processes.
- If it does not appear in the current set of leaders, p_i starts directly another execution of the loop body. Let us notice that, in that case, p_i's new name proposal is not modified.
- Differently, if it appears in the set of leaders (line 9), p_i determines a new name proposal before starting another execution of the loop body. This determination (done similarly to the previous algorithm, Figure 1) consists for p_i in first computing its rank within the leader set, and then taking as new name proposal the first integer that, from its point of view, is not used by the other processes (lines 12-13).

Size of the new name space. The most interesting part of the proof is the part showing that the size of the new name space is $\min(2p - 1, p + k - 1)$, where p is the number of participating processes. Let p_i be a process that returns a new name (line 17). The new name obtained by p_i is the last name it has proposed (at line 13 during the previous iteration). When p_i defined its last new name proposal, at most $p - 1$ other processes have previously defined a name proposal, i.e., $|\{j \ : \ (j \neq i) \wedge (view_i[j].prop \neq \perp)\}| \leq p - 1$ (O1). Moreover, due to the definition of Ω_*^k, when it defines its last new name proposal, the rank of p_i in $leaders_i$ is at most $\min(p, k)$ (O2). It follows from the observations (O1) and (O2) that the last new name proposal computed by p_i is upper bounded by $(p - 1) + \min(p, k)$, i.e., $M = \min(2p - 1, p - 1 + k)$.

The proof of the termination and agreement properties are similar to the ones of the previous algorithm. They can be found in [19].

6 Enriching the System with a Synchronization Primitive

This section considers the case where the asynchronous shared memory system is enriched with synchronization objects. This means that, in addition to read/write atomic registers, the shared memory provides the processes with registers that can be accessed by synchronization operations "stronger" than the base atomic read and write operations. Three types of synchronization objects are considered in the following, namely, k-test&set objects, k-set agreement objects, and compare&swap objects.

6.1 Shared Memory Enriched with k-Test and Set Objects

One-shot k-test&set objects A k-test&set object provides the processes with a single operation denoted $\mathsf{TS\_compete}_k()$. "One shot" means that, given such an object, a process can invoke that operation at most once (there is no reset operation). The invocations of $\mathsf{TS\_compete}_k()$ issued by the processes on such an object satisfy the following properties:

- Termination. An invocation of $\mathsf{TS\_compete}_k()$ by a correct process terminates.
- Validity. The value returned by an invocation of $\mathsf{TS\_compete}_k()$ is 1 (winner) or 0 (loser).
- Agreement. At least one and at most k processes obtain the value 1.

The instance $k = 1$ does correspond to the usual test&set object proposed by some processors. This object allows to elect exactly process from a set of processes. In our context, as processes can crash, it is possible that some (or even all the) winner processes are faulty.

The power of k-test&set objects when solving renaming. A wait-free adaptive algorithm, based on read/write atomic registers and k-test&set objects, that provides a renaming space of size $M = 2p - \lceil \frac{p}{k} \rceil$ is described in [18]. This algorithm results from an incremental construction (k-test&set objects are used to build intermediate k-participating set objects, that are in turn used to build the renaming algorithm). Due to space limitations, this construction is not described here.

It is shown in [12] that $M = 2p - \lceil \frac{p}{k} \rceil$ is the smallest new name space size that can be obtained when one can use atomic registers and k-test&set objects only. It follows that the algorithm described in [18] is optimal as far as the size of the renaming space is concerned.

6.2 Shared Memory Enriched with k-Set Agreement Objects

k-set agreement objects. A k-set agreement object allows processes to propose values and decide values. To that end such an object provides the processes with an operation denoted $SA\_propose_k()$. A process invokes that operation at most once on an object. When it invokes $SA\_propose_k()$, the invoking process supplies the value v it proposes (input parameter). That operation returns a value w (called the value "decided by the invoking process"; we also say that the process "decides w"). The invocations on such an object satisfies the following properties:

- Termination. An invocation of $SA\_propose_k()$ by a correct process terminates.
- Validity. A decided value is a proposed value.
- Agreement. At most k distinct values are decided.

The power of kset agreement objects when solving renaming. A renaming algorithm, based on atomic registers and k-set agreement objects is described in [11]. The size of the new name space is $M = p + k - 1$ which has been shown to be optimal in [11,12].

It has been shown that the synchronization power of a k-set agreement object is stronger than the one of a k-test&set object [12]. This difference in the synchronization power translates directly in the size of the new name space[3].

6.3 Shared Memory Enriched with Compare&Swap Objects

Compare&swap objects. In a precise sense (based on the consensus number theory [13]), a compare&swap object belongs to class of the strongest synchronization objects. Such an object CS is initialized to some value (say $\perp$) and can be accessed only through an atomic operation denoted Compare&Swap() that takes two inputs parameters and returns a value. Its effect can be described by the following specification:

operation Compare&Swap(old, new):
    $prev \leftarrow CS$; **if** ($CS = old$) **then** $CS \leftarrow new$ **end if**; return($prev$).

Optimal renaming space from compare&swap objects. It is possible to design a very simple renaming algorithm whose renaming space is $M = p$ (i.e., M is the smallest renaming space that can be obtained whatever the synchronization power we are provided with), as soon as the processes can communicate through atomic read/write registers and compare&swap objects.

---

[3] It is easy to see that (1) for $k = 1$ we have $p + k - 1 = 2p - \lceil \frac{p}{k} \rceil$, and (2) $\forall k : 1 < k < n - 1$, $\forall p : 1 \leq p \leq n$ we have $p + k - 1 \leq 2p - \lceil \frac{p}{k} \rceil$, and there are values of p such that $p + k - 1 < 2p - \lceil \frac{p}{k} \rceil$.

```
operation new_name(id_i):
(1)  for x from 1 to n do
(2)      r ← CS[x].Compare&Swap(⊥, id_i);
(3)      if (r = ⊥) then return(x) end if
(4)  end for.
```

Fig. 3. A (optimal) compare&swap-based adaptive p-renaming algorithm

Such a (very simple) wait-free adaptive renaming algorithm is described in Figure 3. It uses an array $CS[1..n]$ of underlying compare&swap objects, each initialized to $\bot$, and consists of a simple loop. During the xth iteration, the process p_i invokes $CS[x]$.Compare&Swap$(\bot, id_i)$. If it succeeds in switching $CS[x]$ from its initial value $\bot$ to its old name id_i, the process p_i adopts x as its new name and stops looping (line 3). Otherwise, the process p_i proceeds to the next iteration step and then invokes $CS[x+1]$.Compare&Swap$(\bot, id_i)$.

It is easy to see that, at each iteration step, exactly one process "wins" by writing its initial name in the compare&swap object associated with that iteration step. It follows that if p processes want to acquire a new name, at most p iterations of the loop will be executed, hence $M = p$. Let us finally notice that replacing n in the **for** loop by $+\infty$ (line 1), and assuming as many compare&swap base objects as participating processes, gives an adaptive renaming algorithm that works for any number of processes.

7 Conclusion

The aim of this paper was to show that lock-based solutions have inherent drawbacks that make them irrelevant for some applications where live synchronization in presence of asynchrony and process crashes is crucial. To cope with this problem, the wait-free approach has been presented and illustrated with a problem that is paradigm of synchronization in presence of failures and asynchrony, namely, the adaptive renaming problem. A simple solution based on read/write atomic registers has been presented. This solution provides a new name space whose size is $M = 2p - 1$ where p is the number of participating processes. The paper has then shown how this "read/write" lower bound can be circumvented when, in addition to atomic registers, one can benefit from an appropriate failure detector, or from synchronization primitives such as k-test&set, k-set agreement or compare&swap.

The renaming problem has given rise to a large literature. In addition to the papers previously cited in this text, the interested reader can have a look at the following (non-exhaustive) list of articles [2,4,7,17] that shed additional light on the problem.

References

1. Afek, Y., Attiya, H., Dolev, D., Gafni, E., Merritt, M., Shavit, N.: Atomic Snapshots of Shared Memory. Journal of the ACM 40(4), 873–890 (1993)
2. Afek, Y., Merritt, M.: Fast, Wait-Free $(2k - 1)$-Renaming. In: Proc. 18th ACM Symposium on Principles of Distributed Computing (PODC 1999), pp. 105–112. ACM Press, New York (1999)

380   M. Raynal

3. Attiya, H., Bar-Noy, A., Dolev, D., Peleg, D., Reischuk, R.: Renaming in an Asynchronous Environment. Journal of the ACM 37(3), 524–548 (1990)
4. Attiya, H., Fouren, A.: Adaptive and Efficient Algorithms for Lattice Agreement and Renaming. SIAM Journal of Computing 31(2), 642–664 (2001)
5. Attiya, H., Rachman, O.: Atomic Snapshots in $O(n \log n)$ Operations. SIAM Journal on Computing 27(2), 319–340 (1998)
6. Attiya, H., Welch, J.: Distributed Computing: Fundamentals, Simulations and Advanced Topics, 2nd edn., 414 pages. Wiley-Interscience, Chichester (2004)
7. Borowsky, E., Gafni, E.: Immediate Atomic Snapshots and Fast Renaming. In: Proc. 12th ACM Symposium on Principles of Distributed Computing (PODC 1993), pp. 41–51 (1993)
8. Chandra, T., Toueg, S.: Unreliable Failure Detectors for Reliable Distributed Systems. Journal of the ACM 43(2), 225–267 (1996)
9. Chandra, T., Hadzilacos, V., Toueg, S.: The Weakest Failure Detector for Solving Consensus. Journal of the ACM 43(4), 685–722 (1996)
10. Fernandez Anta, A., Jimenez, E., Raynal, M., Travers, C.: A Timing Assumption and two t-Resilient Protocols for Implementing an Eventual Leader Service in Asynchronous Shared Memory Systems. Algorithmica (to appear, 2008)
11. Gafni, E.: Renaming with k-set Consensus: an Optimal Algorithm in $n + k - 1$ Slots. In: Shvartsman, M.M.A.A. (ed.) OPODIS 2006. LNCS, vol. 4305, pp. 36–44. Springer, Heidelberg (2006)
12. Gafni, E., Raynal, M., Travers, C.: Test&set, Adaptive Renaming and Set Agreement: a Guided Visit to Asynchronous Computability. In: 26th IEEE Symposium on Reliable Distributed Systems (SRDS 2007), pp. 93–102. IEEE Press, Los Alamitos (2007)
13. Herlihy, M.P.: Wait-Free Synchronization. ACM Transactions on Programming Languages and Systems 13(1), 124–149 (1991)
14. Herlihy, M.P., Shavit, N.: The Topological Structure of Asynchronous Computability. Journal of the ACM 46(6), 858–923 (1999)
15. Herlihy, M.P., Wing, J.M.: Linearizability: a Correctness Condition for Concurrent Objects. ACM TOPLAS 12(3), 463–492 (1990)
16. Lamport, L.: On Interprocess Communication, Part II: Algorithms. Distributed Computing 1(2), 86–101 (1986)
17. Moir, M.: Fast, Long-Lived Renaming Improved and Simplified. Science of Computer Programming 30, 287–308 (1998)
18. Mostéfaoui, A., Raynal, M., Travers, C.: Exploring Gafni's Reduction Land: from Ω^k to Wait-free Adaptive $(2p - \lceil \frac{p}{k} \rceil)$-Renaming via k-Set Agreement. In: Dolev, S. (ed.) DISC 2006. LNCS, vol. 4167, pp. 1–15. Springer, Heidelberg (2006)
19. Mostéfaoui, A., Raynal, M., Travers, C.: From Renaming to k-Set Agreement. In: Prencipe, G., Zaks, S. (eds.) SIROCCO 2007. LNCS, vol. 4474, pp. 66–80. Springer, Heidelberg (2007)
20. Raynal, M., Travers, C.: In Search of the Holy Grail: Looking for the Weakest Failure Detector for Wait-free Set Agreement (Invited talk). In: Shvartsman, M.M.A.A. (ed.) OPODIS 2006. LNCS, vol. 4305, pp. 3–19. Springer, Heidelberg (2006)

From Model Driven Engineering to Verification Driven Engineering

Fabrice Kordon[1], Jérôme Hugues[2], and Xavier Renault[1]

[1] Université Pierre & Marie Curie, Laboratoire d'Informatique de Paris 6/MoVe
4, place Jussieu, F-75252 Paris CEDEX 05, France
xavier.renault@lip6.fr, fabrice.kordon@lip6.fr
[2] GET-Télécom Paris – LTCI-UMR 5141 CNRS
46, rue Barrault, F-75634 Paris CEDEX 13, France
jerome.hugues@enst.fr

Abstract. The definition and construction of complex computer-based systems require not just software engineering knowledge, but also many other domain-specific techniques to ensure many system's functional and non-functional properties. Hence, there is a trend to move away from programming languages to models on which one can reason: model-driven engineering. Yet, this remains a complex task: one need to master many techniques. In this paper, we claim that MDE is incomplete: it is "just" an implementation framework to support advanced model-based techniques, verification of systems non-functional properties, code generation, etc. There is a conceptual gap to fill to know "what" to do with models. We propose to switch from MDE to VDE: Verification-Driven Engineering, so that the user knows how to model a system to analyze it. We sum up existing techniques and their relevant application domains.

1 Introduction

Industry-critical applications are facing multiple dimensions challenges: increasing interaction patterns from traditional one-to-one to large scale peer-to-peer interaction; support for multiple level of assurance like security, reliability, timeliness. A synthesis of these challenges is faced by ubiquitous-like systems, which increase complexity due to their massively parallel execution and the variety of participants (infrastructure, service provider, user peers, etc). The notion of quality is therefore hard to define and must reflect both the notion of service provided, and corresponding level of support to meet user expectations in terms of cost and criticality such as mission or life-critical.

There is a trend to extend classical development methods to reduce such complexity. Model Driven Engineering (MDE) proposes a first step to reach that goal by using models (specifications) at every stage of the software life cycle [54]. This approach is also called MDD for Model Driven Development [55]. Development becomes "model centric". Eventhough this idea seems appealing, some issues are raised.

In a MDE setting, the engineer first models a system, implements and validates it. Testing distributed programs cannot be done easily due to the interleaving of several instruction flows. Some more adequate abstraction is needed to perform reasoning on the system and deduce undesired behavior or situations. As such, exploitation of models

U. Brinkschulte, T. Givargis, and S. Russo (Eds.): SEUS 2008, LNCS 5287, pp. 381–393, 2008.

in a MDE approach means nothing if the underlying techniques to process the model are not efficient enough, or even non-existent.

It is now well accepted that traditional simulation approaches are not satisfactory when applied to models: it is impossible to *compute* properties or *systematically* detect unexpected situations. There is a need for formal methods to reason on specifications.

However, using formal methods is more difficult that one could expect [29], even if maturity in that domain grows (industrial tools are now available such as Atelier-B [5] or SCADE [26]). There is still a methodological issue for engineers who are not specialists of formal methods but want to use them to validate some aspects of their system. The key challenge is to know how to select techniques, to determine when these techniques are relevant and what benefits we can expect from the existing tools.

Hence, we propose to move from MDE (Model Driven Engineering) to VDE (Verification Driven Engineering). In this context, we claim that one need to consider Model-Driven Engineering as a generic framework in which verification plays a specific role at several points in the development, from early validation phase up to in-depth analysis, with benefits to quality of system to certification.

One key guideline is to provide verification facilities to system designers. Since there is no "silver bullet", we must also provide enough information to help picking up the correct technique and tools. Hence, the formal method community must provide a classification of verification techniques, and a methodological framework so that designer can select the appropriate techniques to verify model. Finally, one must find a way to ease the use of these appropriate notations (e.g. automata, lemmas, etc.), probably by using some dedicated language(s).

The objective of this paper is first to sum up existing formal verification techniques, discuss their trade-off and see how and when they can meet engineering needs. Section 2 presents existing elements in MDE to be considered for VDE and section 3 proposes our vision of VDE.

2   Building Blocks from MDE

In this section, we list existing methods and processes one can apply to build complex systems. Through MDE, one may process its model and analyze it, generate code on testbed or final hardware. Still, the question of building a processable model remains.

2.1   From Models to Model Driven Engineering

The use of models is a typical step in many engineering domains, e.g. civilian engineering use models for building bridges. Surprisingly, it expanded through the software domain only recently through OMG's UML. It becomes of particular benefits for complex software because it helps to understand a complete problem and its potential solutions through different levels of abstraction.

As authors in [55] advocate: *Model-driven development methods were devised to take advantage of this opportunity, and the accompanying technologies have matured to the point where they are generally useful. A key characteristic of these methods is their fundamental reliance on automation and the benefits that it brings. However, as with all new technologies, MDD's success relies on carefully introducing it into the existing technological and social mix.*

The base concept of MDE is the model itself, built upon a meta-model which defines guidelines and constraints on valid models: allowed components, composition of components and related semantics checks. This view expands from the compiler-vision of programs based on a Backus-Naur formalism.

A model is nothing but a set of well-formed entities. To process the model and perform verification, one need to extract information required to perform a specific analysis. MDE, as a process, provides methods and tools to automate this analysis. It relies on implementation artifact (MOF and QVT frameworks, XML representation) to ease interoperability between tools, and to support easy construction of tools in a uniform framework like Eclipse. Yet, MDE is an implementation framework for model-based tools: one need to reflect on concepts conveyed by models to build analysis tools on top of this framework.

2.2 Formal Methods and Other Analysis Techniques

Mathematical analysis are interesting as they allow one to reason on a model based on formal grounds. Through different theories (sets, automata, stochastic, ...), engineers have access to a large panel of methods. In this section, we list some of them.

Algebraic Approaches. such as Z [1] or B [3] allow to describe a system using axioms and then, prove properties of this specification as a theorem to be demonstrated from these axioms. These methods allow one to check for the consistency of interfaces through a complete type checking mechanism, or even to go further and prove theorems (lemmas, invariants) on a set of interface.

These are of particular interest because the proof is parametric and abstract ; for instance a property can hold for a number of entities taken in the natural range. However, theorem provers that help elaborating the proof are difficult to use and still require highly skilled and experienced engineers.

Model Checking. [14] is the exhaustive investigation of a system's state space. A designer express a property to be tested on a model, using a logic formula expressing a possible behavior of the system. This formula is compared with all the paths in the system's state space. If there is a path that does not satisfy the property, then the property does not hold and the returned path exhibits a counter-example to the property.

The main advantage of this technique is that it is now fully automated. Yet, results are obtained for a particular set of resources (e.g. N threads), and can be generalized. Besides, it is theoretically limited by the combinatorial explosion and can mainly address finite systems. However, recent techniques based on so called symbolic techniques[1] allow to scale up to more complex systems. More recent studies also investigate model checking of infinite-state systems [45]. Other extensions contemplate the verification of time-related or probabilistic properties on a model.

---

[1] The word *symbolic* is associated with two different techniques. The first one is based on state space encoding by means of decision diagrams and was introduced in [10]. The second one relies on set-based representations of states having similar structures and was introduced in [12].

Analytical Techniques. defines a set of formulae that can be applied on a well-formed model. Typical example is the Rate Monotonic Analysis [43] that provides such techniques. These techniques are defined by a set of preconditions that a model must match for being amenable to analysis, and a set of computation steps to compute a metric on a model and conclude. Yet, these frameworks are limited to computable results. In this context, in-depth scheduling analysis shows complexity issues that cannot be solved.

Simulation-Based Techniques. proposes methods to compute an estimation of some properties of a system, like the Monte-Carlo method. This technique is required when no analytical techniques can easily be derived from a system because of the many interfering factors, e.g. peers in an ad hoc wireless network under the influence of electromagnetic perturbation. In this setting, only simulation can help gaining an estimate on the achievable bandwidth. Yet, simulation-based, just like model checking suffers from the combinatorial explosion problem. Furthermore, the parameters required for the simulation might be complex. The designer need a simple way to express these parameters in a way close to the mathematical model of the underlying phenomenon.

So, if formal verification techniques are getting more mature, there is no silver bullet since no technique can be used easily on any type of problems [40]. One technique can be useful at one step of the software life cycle and irrelevant at the next . It is necessary to use the right approach at the right stage of software design and development.

2.3   Related Difficulties

The use of models is delicate. Engineers must consider models quality (appropriateness) [55], language limitations [54] or methodological aspects [38]. Appropriateness of models is crucial if engineers want to reason on them. Languages involved in the design and development process must be able to capture basics required for such reasoning. Basics range from static considerations (such as the composition of interfaces, the compatibility of Quality of Service policies), to dynamic one (ensure liveness of a model up to safety properties). This is difficult to achieve in a unified way (in the meaning of UML) because the language becomes too complex to use and generalization is usually against precision that is required in industrial critical applications.

Methodological aspects are also often underestimated. The way models and associated languages are used is very important to ensure that an analysis can be performed. Concepts and details must be considered in an appropriate way. This is even more important when formal methods are involved since a detail may ruins all the effort and make the proof or the verification false because some hypothesis on the configuration have been forgotten. Furthermore, the application of formal methods may face implementation limits through the so-called "state-explosion" problem, or the inability to compute some metrics (reliability, schedulability).

It is important to clearly state what can be achieved by each family of formal methods and to know when to use them. Then, one can states that they can provide an appropriate answer to expected properties.

2.4   Towards a Better Use of Formal Methods

MDE defines a methodological framework to elaborate models, whereas formal methods exploit some information and derive some statements for a system. The key challenge is to orchestrate requirements for an easy modeling framework dedicated to the designer, and the capability to apply formal methods in an efficient and consistent way. Therefore, we propose the following requirements as a baseline to define a consistent VDE framework that integrate MDE and verification.

$R1$ A modeling notation that allows the designer to capture the multiple dimension of his system: interfaces, functionnal, non-functionnal and behavioral properties. This requires a notation that is non-ambiguous. Standards like AADL or UML and its profiles like MARTE define such framework.

$R2$ A mapping between some models elements and a mathematical framework. This requires the modeling notation to have enough semantics, properties or expression power to derive such mapping. For instance, core UML does not support scheduling entities, whereas MARTE does.

$R3$ Eventhough semantics is present, one need to focus on the expression of complex interaction patterns to be analyzed, like ad hoc networks, consensus, . . .

$R2$ and $R3$ requires the intervention of the formal method community in order to guide the engineer in its modeling work. This can be a set of guidelines, wizards or specific front-end to indicate what are the relevant information to be provided.

$R4$ If multiple analyzes are required, it is important to make sure the different modeling artifacts are consistent and reflect the same model.

$R5$ An automated process should occur, to derive the engineer's model onto a model suitable for the analysis technique. Such process can be defined through the notion of "model-bus" to exchange models.

We point out that most of these requirements where already present when the UML-SPT profile was designed. Yet, the integration of tools is inefficient and support a limited set of analysis, mostly performance analysis.

3   Verification Driven Engineering

Sections 2 listed requirements for integrated verification in a MDE framework. This section defines our vision of an extended use of MDE that puts emphasis on the exploitation of models to verify and validate properties. We call it *VDE* for *"Verification Driven Engineering"*.

If modeling the system is important, engineers often forget that a model has properties that must be defined as soon as possible. The testing research field states that tests must be elaborated jointly with specifications. This is the same for modeling as it is suggested in the B approach with so called "proof obligation" [3,23].

However, there are several types of property that should be elaborated at various levels of the software life cycle. We here propose a classification of such properties.

3.1 Classification of Properties

There are three types of useful properties when designing a system: *1) Structural properties, 2) Qualitative properties* and *3) Quantitative properties.*

Structural properties are the ones related to the structure of the system :

- connection and consistency between interfaces of system's components,
- invariants to be maintained in the system,
- fault-tree analysis (dependencies between system's components when one fails).

Most of these properties should be established at an early stage in the design process and at a coarse grained level. They can be refined later or enriched with some smaller coarse grained, when design is being detailed.

Qualitative properties deal with the behavior of the system e.g. schedulability, liveness, causality and deadlock detection.

To ensure such properties, the behavior of the system must be defined. They are usually described later in the software process, when information are known about components behavior. If specifications moves to programming early (e.g from UML class diagram directly to implementation), these properties are not set up since it is more difficult to elaborate them on programming language.

However, some recent work try to propose solutions to behavioral analysis of programs from their source code [33]. Some tools are already operational: Feaver [31] and then Modex [34]. They are able to analyze C-ansi code and perform model checking using SPIN [32]. QUASAR [27] is able to generate a communication model using Petri Nets from an Ada Program to check for communication problems (e.g. deadlocks).

Quantitative Properties are used to evaluate performances of the system or to evaluate its behavior considering characteristics such as probability of actions to occur when non-determinism occurs, or the time execution time.

To set up such properties, even ore information is required such as an estimation of execution time (for time analysis).

3.2 Relations between Properties, Techniques and Tools

Table 1 links properties to verification techniques and list well-known related tools.

We selected a set of well known verification techniques. *Simulation* is not formal but remains widely used, at least as a first approach to analyze a new system. *Semantic Analysis* is analyzing source code to make sure it does not violate some elementary semantic checks (e.g. arithmetic on integers) or more advanced one (concurrent access on variables like in the Esterel synchronous language). Different *type checking* techniques rely on calculi and are now embedded in typical programming languages like Ada, Eiffel or CAML. Other techniques like theorem proving and model checking have already been presented in section 2.2.

There are several categories of model checking that are differentiated by their combinatorial explosion: there now exist efficient techniques like symbolic representation

Table 1. Relations between verification needs, techniques suitable to address these needs, and some related available tools

Frameworks	Interface consistency	System invariants	Fault-Tree Analysis	Schedulability	Liveness	Causality/deadlocks	Performance analysis	Available tools
Simulation				×				Cheddar [56], CPNTOOLS [19], Rhapsody [58], Renew [20], SCADE [26], Simulink [46]
Semantic Analysis	×			×		×		Cheddar [56], MAST [21], SPARK [51], TRAIAN [62]
Type checking	×							EiffelStudio [25], FuZZ [44], Z/EVES [48]
Theorem proving	×	×	×		×	×		Atelier B [5], Coq [16], Z/EVES [48], PVS [57]
Model Checking...	×	×		×	×	×		CHARON [59], CPN-AMI [42], FAST [41], SMV [47], SPIN [32], SCADE [26], SPOT [24]
...timed							×	CADP [61], Kronos [22], TINA [8], UPPAAL [60]
...stochastic							×	GreatSPN [30], PRISM [52], QPME [50]

of states based on the computation of symmetries in the system [13] or symbolic encoding of states by means of decision diagrams [10,17,18] that allow to cope with state space explosion. The use of symmetries can still be applied with some success for stochastic systems (like in GreatSPN) as well as some decision diagram encoding (like in PRISM). However, none of these techniques can be applied to timed analysis for which analysis limitations are reached faster.

Table 1 illustrates that some properties may be evaluated using more than one technique. It is up to engineers to select the most appropriate one. It is important to point out that all the referenced tools may rely on different notations. For instance, the tools we refer in Table 1 for model checking with time relies on timed automata (CADP, Kronos, UPPAAL) or times Petri nets (TINA). The choice may be delicate since techniques and tools may have week and strong parts that are not the same.

3.3 Formal Methods, Drawbacks

There are numerous success stories in the use of formal methods in various domains. This concerns numerous formal verification approaches like general Model Checking [15], Model Checking from programs [11], Petri Net based techniques applied to telecommunication systems [9] or algebraic methods (B) applied on the MÉTEOR subway line [6]. However, the underlying techniques are not easy to operate.

First, as Table 1 illustrates, a given type of property can be verified using several techniques, and multiple tools. Each technique or tool has its advantages and drawbacks. To be efficient, engineers must select the appropriate technique and tool for his problem. It remains an open problem since the skills needed to address this problem require experience. This is why formal verification is costly.

Second, there is a consistency problem between: *(1)* the specification, *(2)* its mapping to formal specifications (required for verification) and *(3)* its implementation. Hence, one must ensure that what is verified is what is implemented. Usually, *(1)* is a high-level (standardized) specification that is easier to handle than a formal notation. So far, there are several approaches to tackle this problem:

- Using transformation engines from MDE to perform in a rigorous way the transformation from *(1)* to *(2)* and code generation from *(1)* to *(3)*. One need to prove that the transformations are correct. See [37] for preliminary works in the context of CCM.
- Perform "extreme-programming like approach" and consider that *(1)*, *(2)* and *(3)* are the programming language [33].
- Use the formal notation as *(1)* and perform code generation from this notation [6].
- Use a pivot notation associated to *(1)* that provides a concrete semantics and translations from this pivot notation to *(2)* and *(3)* like in the MORSE project [28].

In all cases, there is an entry point notation that acts as a pivot notation which relates several types of specifications (e.g. semi-formal, formal, implementation).

Third, when does a given property should be verified during software development ? We sketch a proposal in section 3.4, based on our experience to link the verification of a given property to a step in the software life cycle.

3.4   The VDE Design Process

In this section, we explicit the way VDE can be applied in a software development process. We propose an helicoidal life cycle inspired from the prototyping based approach presented in [39]. This life-cycle is illustrated in figure 1. Each loop corresponds to one refinement of the system as follows:

1. Developers must first build (or refine) a model.

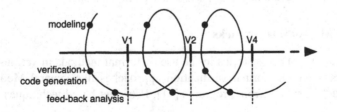

Fig. 1. The VDE helicoidal life cycle

2. Then, they perform some verification operations using some of the techniques and tools mentioned in table 1. To enable formal techniques, the model should be transformed into a formal specification. Otherwise, informal approaches such as simulation are also acceptable if the model remains executable.
3. If verification results are satisfactory, then the system can be generated and additional analysis can be performed (tests in the execution environment of the implemented properties). To reduce implementation costs, code generators are required.
4. Finally, analysis of collected date (from verification and execution) is stored for feed back. From this feed back, issues for the next refinement (loop) are deduced.

Towards Application with AADL. In [36], we evaluate potential impacts of VDE on the development of High-Integrity systems.

We contemplated the use of AADL as a mean to describe a systems on which analysis techniques can be applied. In fact, AADL is rich enough to express multiple aspects of a real-time system in a concise way.

Numerous efforts are currently done to help full analysis with some of the tools we listed: schedulability analysis with Cheddar [56]; model checking of behavioral properties with Petri Nets and CPN-AMI [42], or CHARON [59]; dimensioning analysis with OSATE [2], etc. We think this demonstrates VDE is a feasible concept.

3.5 Open Issues

Of course, current practice and tools do not yet allow the full picture depicted in section 3.4. Several problems remain to have VDE fully operational. So far, there mainly are two open issues.

First, it is important to have a consistent set of information in the input specification, from which one can derive formal specifications, in a mathematical meaning.

UML is a typical example: numerous works propose to derive formal specifications from specific diagrams such as state-charts like [7] or sequence-charts like [4] but none proposes simultaneous analysis from several UML diagrams. This is because connection between diagram is not formally defined. Additional interpretation must be performed (possibly by means of UML profiling like in UML-MARTE [49]). Compared to UML, AADL [53] is better to derive formal specification because all features are expressed in one single language: interface and non-functional properties are better defined and thus more exploitable for verification purpose. For instance, connections with SCADE have been improved [35]. So, we think the elaboration of a pivot notation with links to verification and code generation is mandatory.

Second, verification techniques and their related implementation are difficult to select. One tool may complete analysis on given model and be enable to cope with another one. So far, deep knowledge of the involved techniques are required. This problem is more difficult to solve, but analysis and design frameworks are still studied in the context of large projects like IST-ASSERT[2] or AVSI[3].

---

[2] http://www.assert-project.net
[3] https://avsi-tees.tamu.edu/

4 Conclusion

Bringing verification techniques to engineer is now recommended to ensure more confidence in safety critical systems. Model-Driven Engineering emerged as an efficient way to reason about systems. However, MDE usually focus on the "how-to-model" rather than the "what-to-model". It is therefore difficult to know whether a system is suitable for analysis. A model that cannot be processed is useless for engineers, except for documentation purposes.

This paper proposes to reflect on concepts conveyed by models, and on existing formal methods and analysis techniques to draw a landscape of available tools. Therefore, one may move from MDE to VDE: verification driven engineering. In this context, the user would know exactly what are the facets of this system relevant for a family of analysis (e.g. schedulability), and what are the tools available to perform it.

We proposed a list of techniques and associated tools, based on a comprehensive state of art. So far, there is no silver-bullet: one need to combine multiple analysis; but also for a given analysis technique, one may need to pick the appropriate tools for interoperability, performance or its supported features.

From this complex landscape, we note there is a trend towards the integration of all these techniques around modeling notations like AADL or MARTE. We note these two notations provide strong support for the embedded systems domain.

Besides, one need to reflect on the exact goal of software engineering. Efficient application of verification techniques must be set up in a methodological approach. To do so, we propose an helicoidal cycle and advocate for its iterative nature.

From these considerations, one may provide advanced modeling tools, in which a "wizard" would guide the engineers to build its system and validate it. Defining such a process, and associated tools remain a key challenge for both the academic and industrial communities.

References

1. ISO/IEC 13568. Z formal specification notation — syntax, type system and semantics (2002)
2. SEI AADL. Osate: An extensible source aadl tool environment. Technical report, SEI (2004)
3. Abrial, J.-R.: The B book - Assigning Programs to meanings. Cambridge Univ. Press, Cambridge (1996)
4. Alur, R., Holzmann, G., Peled, D.: An analyser for mesage sequence charts. In: Margaria, T., Steffen, B. (eds.) TACAS 1996. LNCS, vol. 1055, pp. 35–48. Springer, Heidelberg (1996)
5. Atelier, B.: Atelier B, the industrial tool to efficiently deploy the B Method (2008), http://www.atelierb.eu/index_en.html
6. Behm, P., Benoit, P., Faivre, A., Meynadier, J.M.: Météor: A successful application of b in a large project. In: Wing, J.M., Woodcock, J.C.P., Davies, J. (eds.) FM 1999. LNCS, vol. 1708, pp. 369–387. Springer, Heidelberg (1999)
7. Bernardi, S., Donatelli, S., Merseguer, J.: From UML sequence diagrams and statecharts to analysable petrinet models. In: Workshop on Software and Performance, pp. 35–45 (2002)
8. Berthomieu, B., Vernadat, F.: The TINA home page (2008), http://www.laas.fr/tina/
9. Billington, J., Díaz, M., Rozenberg, G. (eds.): Application of Petri Nets to Communication Networks, Advances in Petri Nets. LNCS, vol. 1605. Springer, Heidelberg (1999)

10. Burch, J.R., Clarke, E.M., McMillan, K.L.: Symbolic model checking: 10^{20} states and beyond. Information and Computation (Special issue from LICS90) 98(2), 153–181 (1992)
11. Chandra, S., Godefroid, P., Palm, C.: Software model checking in practice: an industrial case study. In: Proceedings of the 22nd International Conference on Software Engineering (ICSE 2002), pp. 431–441 (May 2002)
12. Chiola, G., Dutheillet, C., Franceschinis, G., Haddad, S.: On well-formed coloured nets and their symbolic reachability graph. In: Jensen, K., Rozenberg, G. (eds.) Procedings of the 11th International Conference on Application and Theory of Petri Nets (ICATPN 1990). Reprinted in High-Level Petri Nets, Theory and Application. Springer, Heidelberg (1991)
13. Chiola, G., Dutheillet, C., Franceschinis, G., Haddad, S.: A symbolic reachability graph for coloured Petri nets. Theoretical Computer Science 176(1–2), 39–65 (1997)
14. Clarke, E., Grumberg, O., Peled, D.: Model Checking. MIT Press, Cambridge (2000)
15. Clarke, E., Wing, J.: Tools and partial analysis. ACM Comput. Surv. 28(4es), 116 (1996)
16. CoQ Project at INRIA. The Coq proof assistant,
http://coq.inria.fr/coq-eng.html
17. Couvreur, J.-M., Encrenaz, E., Paviot-Adet, E., Poitrenaud, D., Wacrenier, P.-A.: Data decision diagrams for Petri net analysis. In: Esparza, J., Lakos, C.A. (eds.) ICATPN 2002. LNCS, vol. 2360, pp. 101–120. Springer, Heidelberg (2002)
18. Couvreur, J.-M., Thierry-Mieg, Y.: Hierarchical Decision Diagrams to Exploit Model Structure. In: Wang, F. (ed.) FORTE 2005. LNCS, vol. 3731, pp. 443–457. Springer, Heidelberg (2005)
19. CPN group, Univ. Aarhus. cpntools - Computer Tool for Coloured Petri Nets (2008),
http://wiki.daimi.au.dk/cpntools
20. CS dept. Univ. Hambourg. Renew (2006), http://www.renew.de
21. CTR team. Modeling and Analysis Suite for Real-Time Applications,
http://mast.unican.es/
22. Daws, C., Olivero, A., Tripakis, S., Yovine, S.: The tool Kronos (2002),
http://www-verimag.imag.fr/TEMPORISE/kronos/
23. Ducass, M., Roz, L.: Proof obligations of the b formal method: Local proofs ensure global consistency. In: Bossi, A. (ed.) LOPSTR 1999. LNCS, vol. 1817, pp. 10–29. Springer, Heidelberg (2000)
24. Duret-Lutz, A., Poitrenaud, D.: SPOT, Spot Produces Our Traces,
http://spot.lip6.fr/wiki/
25. Eiffel software. EiffelStudio - A Complete Integrated Development Environment (2008),
http://www.eiffel.com
26. Esterel-technologies. SCADE Suite (2008), http://www.esterel-technologies.com/
27. Evangelista, S., Kaiser, C., Pajault, C., Pradat-Peyre, J.-F., Rousseau, P.: Dynamic tasks verification with quasar. In: Vardanega, T., Wellings, A.J. (eds.) Ada-Europe 2005. LNCS, vol. 3555, pp. 91–104. Springer, Heidelberg (2005)
28. Gilliers, F., Kordon, F., Velu, J.-P.: Generation of distributed programs in their target execution environment. In: Proceedings of the 15th International Workshop on Rapid System Prototyping, Geneva, Switzerland, pp. 127–134. IEEE Computer Society, Los Alamitos (2004)
29. Gogen, J., Luqi.: Formal methods: Promises and problems. IEEE Software 14(1), 75–85 (1997)
30. GreatSPN group. GreatSPN home page, http://www.di.unito.it/~greatspn
31. Holzmann, G.: Logic Verification of ANSI-C Code with SPIN. In: Havelund, K., Penix, J., Visser, W. (eds.) SPIN 2000. LNCS, vol. 1885, pp. 131–147. Springer, Heidelberg (2000)
32. Holzmann, G.: On-the-fly, LTL Model Checking with SPIN (2007),
http://spinroot.com/spin
33. Holzmann, G., Joshi, R.: Model-driven software verification. In: Graf, S., Mounier, L. (eds.) SPIN 2004. LNCS, vol. 2989, pp. 76–91. Springer, Heidelberg (2004)

34. Holzmann, G., Smith, M.: An Automated Verification Method for Distributed Systems Software Based on Model Extraction. IEEE Trans. Software Eng. 28(4), 364–377 (2002)
35. Hugues, J., Pautet, L., Zalila, B., Dissaux, P., Perrotin, M.: Using AADL to build critical real-time systems: Experiments in the IST-ASSERT project. In: 4th European Congress ERTS, Toulouse, Paris (January 2008)
36. Hugues, J., Zalila, B., Pautet, L., Kordon, F.: From the Prototype to the Final Embedded System Using the Ocarina AADL Tool Suite. ACM Transactions in Embedded Computing Systems (TECS) (October 2008)
37. Kavimandan, A., Narayanan, A., Gokhale, A.S., Karsai, G.: Evaluating the Correctness and Effectiveness of a Middleware QoS Configuration Process in Distributed Real-Time and Embedded Systems. In: 11th International Symposium on Object-oriented Real-time distributed Computing (ISORC 2008), pp. 100–107. IEEE Computer Society, Los Alamitos (2008)
38. Kordon, F.: Design methodologies for embedded systems: Where is the super-glue? In: 11th International Symposium on Object-oriented Real-time distributed Computing (ISORC 2008), Orlando, USA (page to be published, May 2008)
39. Kordon, F., Luqi.: An Introduction to Rapid System Prototyping. IEEE Transactions on Software Engineering 70(3), 817–821 (2002)
40. Kordon, F., Petrucci, L.: Toward Formal-Methods Oecumenism? IEEE Distributed Systems Online 7(7) (July 2006)
41. Labri. FAST - Fast Acceleration of Symbolic Transition systems (2006),
    http://www.lsv.ens-cachan.fr/fast
42. LIP6/MoVe. The CPN-AMI home page, http://www.lip6.fr/cpn-ami/
43. Liu, C.L., Layland, J.W.: Scheduling algorithms for multi-programming in hard-real-time environment. Journal of the ACM (January 1973)
44. Spivey, M.: The fuzz type-checker for Z,
    http://spivey.oriel.ox.ac.uk/mike/fuzz/
45. Madhusudan, P. (ed.): Proceedings of the 9th International Workshop on Verification of Infinite-State Systems (INFINITY 2007), Lisboa, Portugal, September 2007. Electronic Notes in Theoretical Computer Science. Elsevier Science Publishers, Amsterdam (2007)
46. Mathwork. Simulink - Simulation and Model-Based Design (2008),
    http://www.mathworks.com/products/simulink/
47. McMillan, K.L.: The SMV System,
    http://www.cs.cmu.edu/~modelcheck/smv.html
48. Meisels, I., Saaltink, M.: The z/eves reference manual (for version 1.5)
49. OMG. A UML profile for MARTE, Beta 1. Technical Report ptc/07-08-04, OMG (2007)
50. OPERA Group, Univ. Cambridge. QPME Homepage (2007),
    http://www.dvs.tu-darmstadt.de/staff/skounev/QPME/
51. Praxis Hight Integrity Systems. SPARKAda (2008),
    http://www.praxis-his.com/sparkada/
52. PRISM Team. PRISM - Probabilistic Symbolic Model Checker (2008),
    http://www.prismmodelchecker.org/
53. SAE. Architecture Analysis & Design Language (AS5506). SAE (September 2004),
    http://www.sae.org
54. Schmidt, D.: Guest editor's introduction: Model-driven engineering. IEEE Computer 39(2), 25–31 (2006)
55. Selic, B.: The pragmatics of model-driven development. IEEE Software 20(5), 19–25 (2003)
56. Singhoff, F.: The Cheddar project: a free real time scheduling analyzer (2007),
    http://beru.univ-brest.fr/~singhoff/cheddar/
57. SRI/CSL. PVS Specification and Verification System (2008),
    http://pvs.csl.sri.com/index.shtml

58. Telelogic. Rhapsody (2008), http://www.telelogic.com/products/rhapsody/
59. Upenn, Dept of Computer Science. CHARON, http://rtg.cis.upenn.edu/mobies/charon/
60. UPPAAL Group. UPPAAL, http://www.uppaal.com/
61. VASY Project - INRIA. Construction and Analysis of Distributed Processes (2005), http://www.inrialpes.fr/vasy/cadp.html
62. VASY Project - INRIA. TRAIAN: A Compiler for E-LOTOS/LOTOS NT Specifications (2008), http://www.inrialpes.fr/vasy/pub/traian

On Scalable Synchronization for Distributed Embedded Real-Time Systems

Sherif F. Fahmy[1], Binoy Ravindran[1], and E. Douglas Jensen[2]

[1] ECE Dept., Virginia Tech, Blacksburg, VA 24061, USA
fahmy@vt.edu, binoy@vt.edu
[2] The MITRE Corporation, Bedford, MA 01730, USA
jensen@mitre.org

Abstract. We consider the problem of programming distributed embedded real-time systems with distributed dependencies. We show that the de facto standard of using locks and condition variables in conjunction with threads can have significant overhead and semantic difficulty and suggest alternative programming abstractions to alleviate these problems. We also discuss several alternatives for implementing these programming abstractions and discuss the algorithms and protocols needed.

1   Introduction

As Moore's law appears to be reaching its limits, manufacturers of computing machinery are turning (again) to parallelism as the next frontier in the quest for faster computers. Today, most machines produced are multi-core and the use of distributed systems is on the increase. Coinciding with this new direction of using concurrency to increase application throughput, is the discovery of a rich set of applications that are a natural fit for parallel and distributed architectures. From distributed databases to emerging distributed real-time systems [1], such emerging applications are only meaningful in a distributed system with multiple computing cores cooperating to execute the semantics of the application.

This parallelism offers a great opportunity for improving performance by increasing application concurrency. Unfortunately, this concurrency comes at a cost: programmers now need to design programs, using existing operating system and programming language features, to deal with shared access to serially reusable resources and program synchronization. The de facto standard for programming such systems is using threads, locks, and condition variables. Using these abstractions, programmers have been trying to write correct concurrent code ever since multitasking operating systems made such programs possible.

Unfortunately, the human brain does not seem to be well suited for reasoning about concurrency [2]. The history of the software industry contains numerous cases where the difficulty inherent in reasoning about concurrent code has resulted in costly software errors that are very difficult to reproduce and hence debug and fix. Among the more common errors encountered in lock-based software systems are deadlocks, livelocks, lock convoying, and, in systems where priority is

U. Brinkschulte, T. Givargis, and S. Russo (Eds.): SEUS 2008, LNCS 5287, pp. 394–405, 2008.

important (e.g, embedded real-time systems), priority inversion. Such errors stem from the difficulty in reasoning about concurrent code.

Transactions have proven themselves to be a successful abstraction for handling concurrency in database systems. Due to this success, researchers have attempted to take advantage of their features for non-database systems. In particular, there has been significant recent efforts to apply the concepts of transactions to shared memory. Such an attempt originated as a purely hardware solution [3, 4] and was later extended to deal with systems where transactional support was migrated from the hardware domain to the software domain [5]. Software transactional memory (or STM) has, until recently, been an academic curiosity because of its high over-head. However, as the state-of-the-art improved and more efficient algorithms were devised, a number of commercial and non-commercial STM systems have been developed (see implementations section of [6]). In this position paper, we discuss the issues involved in implementing software transactional memory in distributed embedded real-time systems.

2 Motivation

Currently, the industry standard abstractions for programming distributed embedded systems include OMG/Real-Time CORBA's client/server paradigm and distributable threads [7] and OMG/DDS's publish/subscribe abstraction [8]. The client/server and distributable threads abstractions directly facilitate the programming of causally-dependent, multi-node application logic. In contrast, the publish/subscribe abstraction is a data distribution service for logically-single hop communications (i.e., from one publisher to one subscriber), and therefore, higher-level abstractions must be constructed – on an application-specific basis – to express causally-dependent, multi-node application logic (e.g., publication of topic A depends on subscription of topic B; B's publication, in turn, depends on subscription of topic C, and so on). All of these abstractions rely on lock-based mechanisms for concurrency control, and thus suffer from their previously mentioned inherent limitations.

In particular, lock-based concurrency control can easily result in local and distributed deadlocks, due to programming errors that occur as a result of the conceptual difficulty of the (lock-based) programming model. Detecting and resolving deadlocks, especially distributed deadlocks, that can potentially arise due to distributed dependencies is complex and expensive. Note that deadlocks can only be detected and resolved, as opposed to being avoided or prevented, in those distributed embedded systems where it is difficult to obtain a-priori knowledge of which activities need which resources and in what order. When a deadlock is detected in such systems, the usual method of resolving it is to break the cycle of the waiting processes by terminating one of them. Unfortunately, the choice of which process to terminate is not a simple one in real-time systems. By terminating one of the processes that are waiting in a cycle, we produce a chain of waiting processes. Depending on how, i.e., where, we break this cycle, it may or may not be feasible to meet the timing requirements of the remaining processes. Thus, we need to consider the structure of the dependency chain, after terminating a process to end the deadlock, in order to break the cycle in a way that optimizes end-to-end timeliness objectives. Furthermore, a process's dependencies must be taken into account when making the choice about which process to terminate. For example, if a significant number of processes depend on the result of a process, terminating it to resolve a deadlock may not be in the best interest of the application. In addition, the cost of deadlock detection/resolution is exacerbated by the extra work necessary to restore the system to an acceptable state when failure occurs. Thus, deadlock resolution is a complex process.

The problem of distributed deadlock detection and resolution has been exhaustively studied, e.g., [9,10,11,12,13,14,15]. A number of these algorithms turned out to be incorrect by either detecting phantom deadlocks (false positives) or not detecting deadlocks when they do exist, e.g., [16,11]. These errors occur because of the inherent difficulty of reasoning about distributed programs. This led to attempts at providing a formal method for analyzing such protocols to ensure correct behavior (e.g., [13]). Despite the difficulty of reasoning about distributed deadlock, solutions for this problem on synchronous distributed systems have been developed. Unfortunately, for asynchronous systems, errors in the deadlock detection process become inevitable. For real-time systems, these issues become more severe [9]. The semantic difficulty of thread and lock based concurrency control and the high overhead associated with detecting and resolving distributed deadlock, as indicated above, are the driving motivations for finding different programming abstractions for distributed embedded real-time systems.

3   Previous Work

3.1   Alternatives to Lock-Based Programming

Academia, and certain parts of industry, have realized the limitations of lock-based software, thus a number of proposed alternatives to lock-based software exist. The design of lock-free, wait-free or obstruction-free data structures is one such approach. The main problem with this approach is that it is limited to a small set of basic data structures, e.g., [17, 18, 19]. For example, to the best of our knowledge, there is no lock-free implementation of a red-black tree that does not use STM. Most of the literature on lock-free data structures concentrates on basics such as queues, stacks, and other simple data structures. It should be noted that lock-freedom, wait-freedom and obstruction-freedom are concepts and as such can encompass non lock-based solutions like STM. However, we use these terms in this context to refer to hand crafted code that allows concurrent access to a data structure without suffering from race conditions.

The discrete event model presented in [20,21] provides an interesting alternative to thread based programming. While interesting and novel, it still remains to be seen whether programmers find the semantics of the model easier than the semantics of thread-based computing. In addition, the requirement of static analysis to determine a partial order on the events makes the system inapplicable to dynamic systems where little or no information is available a priori.

Transactional processing, the semantic ancestor of STM, has been around for a significant period of time and has proven its mettle as a method of providing concurrency control in numerous commercial database products, in addition, it does not place any restriction on the dynamism of the system on which it is deployed. Unfortunately, the use of a distributed commit protocol, such as the two-phase commit protocol, increases the execution time of a transaction and can lead to deadline misses [22]. STM is a lighter-weight version of transactional processing, with no distributed commit protocol required in most cases. As such, it allows us to gain the benefits of transactional processing (i.e., fault tolerance and semantic simplicity), without incurring all its associated overhead.

We believe that STM is an attractive alternative to thread and lock-based distributed programming, since it eliminates many of the conceptual difficulties of lock-based concurrency control at the expense of a justifiable overhead that becomes less significant as the number of processors in the system scales.

3.2 Software Transactional Memory

Since the seminal papers about hardware and software transactional memory were published, renewed interest in the field has resulted in a large body of literature on the topic (e.g, see [23, 24, 25]). This body of work encompasses both purely software transactional memory systems and hybrid systems where software and hardware support for transactional memory are used in conjuncture to improve performance. Despite this large body of work, to the best of our knowledge, only three papers investigate STM for distributed systems [26, 27, 28].

We believe that distributed embedded systems stand to benefit significantly from STM. Such systems are most distinguished by their need to: 1)' react to external events asynchronously and concurrently; 2) react to external events in a timely manner (i.e., real-time); and 3) cope with failures (e.g., processors, networks) – one of the raison d'être for building distributed systems. Thus, concurrency that is fundamentally intrinsic to distributed embedded systems naturally motivates the usage of STM. Their need to (concurrently) react timely to external events in the presence of failures is also a compelling reason – such behaviors are very complex to program, reason about, and obtain timing assurances using lock-based concurrency control mechanisms.

There has also been a dearth of work on real-time STM systems. Notable work on transactional memory and lock-free data structures in real-time systems include [29, 30, 18, 31, 32]. However, most of these works only consider uni-processor systems (with [32] being a notable exception). In this position paper, we propose to study the issues involved in implementing STM in distributed embedded real-time systems. Past work has shown that STM has lower throughput for systems with a small number of processors compared to fine-grain lock-based solutions but that this difference in performance is quickly reversed as the number of processors scales [33]. This, coupled with easier programming semantics of STM, makes it an attractive concurrency control mechanism for next generation embedded real-time systems with multi-core architectures and high distribution.

With STM, deadlocks are entirely or almost entirely precluded. This will immediately result in significant reductions in the cost of scheduling and resource management algorithms, as distributed dependencies are avoided and no expensive deadlock detection/resolution mechanisms are needed. Implementing higher level programming constructs, like, for example, Hoare's conditional critical regions (or CCR) [34], on top of STM [33], allows programmers to take advantage of the deadlock freedom and simple semantics of STM in their programs.

4   STM for Distributed Embedded Systems

There are a number of competing abstractions for implementing STM in distributed embedded real-time systems. An interesting abstraction is the notion of real-time distributed transactional objects, where code is immobile and objects migrate between nodes to provide a transactional memory abstraction. Another alternative is to allow remote invocations to occur within a transaction, spawning sub-transactions on each node (where they are executed using STM), and using a distributed commit protocol to ensure atomicity. A third alternative is to provide a hybrid model, where both data and code are mobile and the decision of which is moved is heuristically decided either dynamically or statically. Several key issues need to be studied in order to use STM in distributed embedded systems, these are:

- Choosing an appropriate abstraction for including STMs in distributed embedded systems,
- Designing the necessary protocols and algorithms to support these abstractions,
- Implementing these abstractions in a programming language by making necessary changes to its syntax and in the run-time environment, and
- Designing scheduling algorithms to provide end-to-end timeliness using these new programming abstractions.

4.1   Choosing an Appropriate Abstraction

STM is a technology for multiprocessor systems, to use it in a multicomputer environment, we need to develop appropriate abstractions. We are currently considering three competing programming abstractions into which to incorporate STM:

- A model where cross-node transactions are permitted using remote invocations and atomicity is enforced using an atomic commit protocol;
- A model where a distributed cache coherence protocol is used to implement an abstraction of shared memory on top of which we can build STM; and
- A hybrid model where code or data is migrated depending on a number of heuristics such as size and locality.

In the first approach, we manage concurrency control on each node using STM, but allow remote invocations to occur within a transaction. Thus we allow a transaction to span multiple nodes. At the conclusion of the transaction, the last node on which transactional code is executed acts as a coordinator in a distributed commit protocol to ensure an atomic commitment decision. Our preliminary research, which we intend to elaborate upon, indicates that such an approach may be prone to "retry thrashing" especially when the STM implemented on each node is lock-free.

Since lock-free STM is an optimistic concurrency control mechanism, extending the duration of a transaction by allowing it to sequentially extend across nodes results in a significantly higher probability of conflicts among transactions. Such conflicts lead to aborted transactions that are later retried. Retrying is antagonistic to real-time systems since it degrades one of the most important features of real-time systems: predictability. Lock-based STM tends to reduce some of this "thrashing" behavior since it eliminates part of the "optimism" of the approach. However, long transactions are still more susceptible to retries and introducing locks into the STM implementation necessitates a deadlock detection and resolution solution. Fortunately such a solution does not need to be distributed since it only needs to resolve local deadlocks.

Implementing STM on top of a distributed cache coherence protocol has been investigated in [26, 27]. In this approach, code is immobile, but data objects move among nodes as required. The approach uses a distributed cache coherence protocol to find and move objects. We intend to design real-time cache coherence protocols, where timeliness is an integral part of the algorithm. We plan to design STM on top of these protocols and compare their performance to the flow control abstraction. An important advantage of this approach is that it eliminates the need for a distributed commit protocol. Since distributed commit protocols are a major source of inefficiency in real-time systems [22], such an approach is expected to yield better performance.

The last approach we intend to study is touched upon in [28]. This is a hybrid approach where either data objects or code can migrate while still retaining the semantics of STM. By allowing either code or data to migrate, we can choose a migration scenario that results in the least amount of communication overhead. For example, suppose we have a simple transactional program that increments the value of a shared variable X and stores the new value in the transactional store. Assume further that X is remote, using a data flow abstraction would necessitate two communication delays; one to fetch X from its remote location and the other to send it back once it has been incremented. Using a control flow abstraction in this case may be more efficient since it will only involve a single communication delay.

On the other hand, assume that several processes need access to a small data structure and that these processes are in roughly the same location and are far away from the data they need. Since communication delay depends on distances, it may make sense to migrate the data to the processes in this case rather than incur several long communication delays by moving the code to the data. In short, the choice of whether to migrate code or data can have a significant effect on performance. In [28], this is accomplished under programmer control by allowing an *on* construct which a programmer can use to demarcate code that should be migrated. We intend to elaborate on this by coming up with solutions that would use static analysis at compile-time (or dynamically at run-time) to make decisions about which part of the application to move using a number of heuristics such as, for example, size of code/data and locality considerations.

4.2   Designing Suitable Protocols and Algorithms

The algorithms and protocols that need to be designed depend on the programming abstraction we choose to implement. Some of the necessary abstractions have been touched upon in Section 4.1, here we elaborate on these points.

For the model where code migrates, creating cross-node transactions, and data is immobile, the main abstraction that needs to be designed is a real-time distributed commit protocol. Since cross-node transactions are permitted, with each node involved hosting part of the transaction, a distributed commit protocol is necessary to ensure atomicity. A number of distributed commit protocols have been studied in the literature, with the two phase commit protocol being the most commercially successful protocol. Unfortunately, the blocking semantics of the two phase commit protocol may not be very suitable for real-time systems. Therefore alternatives like the three phase commit protocol (despite its larger overhead) may be more appropriate due to its non-blocking semantics. Other alternatives that involve the relaxation of certain properties of distributed commit protocols in order to improve efficiency are discussed in [22]. We intend to design distributed commit protocols whose timeliness behavior can be quantified theoretically and/or empirically, in order to allow the system to provide guarantees on end-to-end timeliness.

For the approach where code is immobile and data migrates, the most important protocol that needs to be designed is a distributed real-time cache coherence protocol. This protocol needs to be location aware in order to reduce communication latency and should be designed to reduce network congestion. The cache coherence problem for multiprocessors has been extensively studied in the literature [35]. There are also some solutions for the distributed cache coherence problem (see [36,37,38,39] for a, not necessarily representative, sample of research on this issue). Distributed cache coherence bears some similarity to distributed hash table (or DHT) protocols which have been an active topic of research recently due to the popularity of peer-to-peer applications. Examples of DHT algorithms that are of interest are [40,41,42].

We envision a cache coherence algorithm based on hierarchical clustering to reduce network traffic and path reversal to synchronize concurrent requests, an approach used in [26]. Other approaches for implementing distributed cache coherence will also be considered. An important part of our research in this area will be to design cache coherence protocols that can provide timeliness guarantees that we can verify theoretically and empirically.

For the hybrid abstraction, where both code and data can move, several issues need to be determined. Among the issues that need to be resolved are the different methods of distributing transactional meta-data in order to ensure efficient execution of the STM system, providing a mechanism to support atomic commitment when code is allowed to migrate thus resulting in multi-node transactions, aggregating communication in order to reduce the effect of the extra communication necessary to manage the STM system (possibly by piggybacking this information over normal network traffic) and optimizing network communication to reduce latency. It is also necessary to design appropriate mechanisms for choosing whether data or code migration is going to occur. Currently, the choice of which part of the program to migrate is performed under programmer control [28]. We intend to design automated methods for deciding which part of the program moves through either compile-time analysis or at run-time.

4.3 Programming Language Implementation

We need to incorporate the programming abstraction chosen and the protocols and algorithms necessary to support them into a suitable programming language. Issues that need to be addressed are extending the programming language syntax to include support for higher level abstractions built upon STM. We introduce a number of syntactic modifications to support the new constructs we propose to implement. The most basic syntactic extension required is a method for demarcating atomic blocks (i.e. blocks of code that will be executed within the context of STM), additions such as programmer controlled retry and providing alternative transactional execution can also be considered.

In addition to these syntactic extensions, modifications to the run-time environment are also required. Our top candidate for implementing these abstractions is the emerging DRTSJ RI. We choose this language for a number of reasons. First, the language is still under development with a substantial part of the implementation details coming out of our research group. Second, the RI will be evaluated by the standard's expert community (e.g., Sun's JSR-50 experts group in the case of DRTSJ) as part of the standard's approval process, resulting in immediate and invaluable user feedback. Third, using a garbage collected language alleviates some of the issues involved in memory management associated with STM (by, for example, eliminating the problem of having transactions free allocated memory explicitly while other transactions are still working on it). Of course this necessitates augmenting the garbage collector with information about STM in order to prevent harmful interference with STM's meta-data.

Naturally, the actual modifications made to the programming language will depend on the programming abstraction chosen. Regardless of the choice made about the abstraction used to incorporate STM in distributed embedded systems, modifications to the run-time environment are necessary to support STM. The actual modifications made are dependent on the particular design we choose for our implementation of STM and so will not be elaborated upon in this position paper. However, some of the design issues involved are choosing appropriate meta-data to represent STM objects, providing appropriate mechanisms to atomically commit transactions (for example by using atomic hardware instructions such as compare-and-swap, or CAS, on suitably indirected meta-data), providing implementations for the different design choices of STM (e.g., visible reads versus invisible reads and weak versus strong atomicity).

4.4   Scheduling Algorithms and Analysis

Finally, we will design scheduling algorithms that allow systems programmed using STM to meet end-to-end timeliness requirements. This is a challenge due to the fact that the retry behavior of STM is antagonistic to predictability. There have been several attempts at providing timing assurances when STM is used in real-time systems or when lock-free data structures are used in real-time systems [29, 30, 18, 31]. These approaches only consider uni-processor systems and use the periodic task arrival model to bound retries.

Some of the approaches are fairly sophisticated and use, for example, linear programming [30] to derive schedulability criteria for lock-free code. The basic idea of these approaches is that, on a uni-processor system, the number of retries is bounded by the number of task preemptions that occur. This bound exists because a uni-processor can only execute one process at a time. Since it is not possible for a process to perform conflicting operations on shared memory, and hence cause the retry of another process, unless it is running, the number of preemptions naturally bounds the number of retries on uni-processors. Given this premise, the analysis performed in [29, 30, 18, 31] bounds the number of retries by bounding the number of times a process can be preempted under different scheduling algorithms. This analysis allows the authors to derive schedulability criteria for different scheduling algorithms based on information about process execution times, execution times of the retried code sections, process periods, etc.

More recently, attempts have been made at providing timeliness guarantees for lock-free data structures built on multiprocessor systems [32]. The approach used in [32] is suitable for Pfair-scheduled systems and other multiprocessor systems where quantum-based scheduling is employed. The most restrictive assumption made in this approach is that access to a shared lock-free object takes at most two quanta of processor time. Using this assumption, the authors go on to bound the number of retries by determining the worst-case number of accesses that can occur to a shared object during the quanta in which it is being accessed. For an M processor system, the worst-case number of processes that can interfere with access to a particular shared object is $M - 1$. Given an upper bound on the number of times a process can access a shared object within a quanta, it is possible to derive an upper bound on the number of retries in such a system. The authors also go on to describe how it is possible to use the concept of a "supertask", basically a single unit that is composed of several tasks that are to be scheduled as one unit, to reduce the worst-case number of retries and hence improve system performance.

The particular method used to bound the number of retries in the system(s) we develop will depend on the model we target. There are two possible alternatives. The first approach is to target uni-processor distributed systems. In such systems, each node has only one processor. In order to provide scheduling criteria for such systems, we would use the approaches developed for uni-processor systems to derive the number of retries that can occur on each node, and then combine these bounds to determine the number of retries that can occur to cross-node transactions, thus deriving schedulability criteria for STM implementations.

The second approach is to consider multiprocessor distributed systems. In such systems, each node is a multiprocessor or multi-core machine. Schedulability analysis and scheduling algorithms for such systems are considerably more difficult due to the difficulty in deriving bounds on the number of retries in the system. A first possible approach is to consider the Pfair-scheduling algorithm considered in [32] for obtaining bounds on the number of retries on each node and then combining these bounds to obtain bounds for cross-node transactions. Other approaches will also be considered in order to reduce the number of assumptions made on the system model. We will design scheduling algorithms that can ensure that timeliness requirements are not violated by the retry behavior of STM on distributed systems, and provide analytical expressions for the schedulability criteria of these scheduling algorithms.

5   Conclusions

Programming distributed systems using lock-based concurrency control is semantically difficult and computationally expensive. In order to alleviate some of these problems, we propose the use of STM for concurrency control. In order to achieve this goal, a number of issues need to be addressed. This position paper outlines these issues and proposes a method for solving them.

Three different abstractions for incorporating STM into distributed embedded real-time systems are mentioned, and the algorithms and protocols necessary for implementing these abstractions are briefly outlined. We also briefly indicate the type of schedulability analysis that will be required to provide timeliness guarantees for systems programmed using these abstractions.

References

1. Cares, J.R.: Distributed Networked Operations: The Foundations of Network Centric Warfare. iUniverse, Inc. (2006)
2. Lee, E.A.: The problem with threads. Computer 39(5), 33–42 (2006)
3. Herlihy, M., Moss, J.E.B.: Transactional memory: Architectural support for lock-free data structures. In: Proceedings of the Twentieth Annual International Symposium on Computer Architecture (1993)
4. Knight, T.F.: An architecture for mostly functional languages. In: Proceedings of ACM Lisp and Functional Programming Conference, August 1986, pp. 500–519 (1986)
5. Shavit, N., Touitou, D.: Software transactional memory. In: PODC, pp. 204–213 (1995)
6. Wikipedia: Software transactional memory — wikipedia, the free encyclopedia (2008) (accessed May 24, 2008), http://en.wikipedia.org/w/index.php?title=Software_transactional_memory&oldid=213906392
7. OMG: Real-time corba 2.0: Dynamic scheduling specification. Technical report, Object Management Group (September 2001)
8. Pardo-Castellote, G.: Omg data-distribution service: Architectural overview. ICD-CSW 00, 200 (2003)

404   S.F. Fahmy, B. Ravindran, and E.D. Jensen

9. Shih, C., Stankovic, J.A.: Survey of deadlock detection in distributed concurrent programming environments and its application to real-time systems. Technical report, Amherst, MA, USA (1990)
10. Roesler, M., Burkhard, W.A.: Resolution of deadlocks in object-oriented distributed systems. IEEE Trans. Comput. 38(8), 1212–1224 (1989)
11. de Mendívil, J.R.G., Federico Fari, N., Garitagoitia, J.R., Alastruey, C.F., Bernabeu-Auban, J.M.: A distributed deadlock resolution algorithm for the and model. IEEE Trans. Parallel Distrib. Syst. 10(5), 433–447 (1999)
12. Kshemkalyani, A.D., Singhal, M.: A one-phase algorithm to detect distributed deadlocks in replicated databases. IEEE Trans. on Knowl. and Data Eng. 11(6), 880–895 (1999)
13. de Mendivil, J.R.G., Demaille, A., Auban, J.B., Garitagoitia, J.R.: Correctness of a distributed deadlock resolution algorithm for the single request model. In: PDP 1995: Proceedings of the 3rd Euromicro Workshop on Parallel and Distributed Processing, Washington, DC, USA, p. 254. IEEE Computer Society, Los Alamitos (1995)
14. Elmagarmid, A.K.: A survey of distributed deadlock detection algorithms. SIGMOD Rec. 15(3), 37–45 (1986)
15. Mitchell, D.P., Merritt, M.J.: A distributed algorithm for deadlock detection and resolution. In: PODC 1984: Proceedings of the third annual ACM symposium on Principles of distributed computing, pp. 282–284. ACM, New York (1984)
16. Choudhary, A.N., Kohler, W.H., Stankovic, J.A., Towsley, D.: A modified priority based probe algorithm for distributed deadlock detection and resolution. IEEE Trans. Softw. Eng. 15(1), 10–17 (1989)
17. Cho, H., Ravindran, B., Jensen, E.D.: Space-optimal, wait-free real-time synchronization. IEEE Transactions on Computers 56(3), 373–384 (2007)
18. Anderson, J., Ramamurthy, S., Moir, M., Jeffay, K.: Lock-free transactions for real-time systems. In: Real-Time Databases: Issues and Applications. Kluwer Academic Publishers, Amsterdam (1997)
19. Herlihy, M., Luchangco, V., Moir, M.: Obstruction-free synchronization: Double-ended queues as an example. icdcs 00, 522 (2003)
20. Zhao, Y., Lee, E.A., Liu, J.: Programming temporally integrated distributed embedded systems. Technical Report UCB/EECS-2006-82, EECS Department, University of California, Berkeley (May 2006)
21. Zhao, Y., Liu, J., Lee, E.A.: A programming model for time-synchronized distributed real-time systems. In: RTAS 2007: Proceedings of the 13th IEEE Real Time and Embedded Technology and Applications Symposium, Washington, DC, USA, pp. 259–268. IEEE Computer Society, Los Alamitos (2007)
22. Gupta, R., Haritsa, J., Ramamritham, K., Seshadri, S.: Commit processing in distributed real-time database systems. In: 17th IEEE Real-Time Systems Symposium, December 4-6, 1996, pp. 220–229 (1996)
23. Marathe, V.J., Scott, M.L.: A qualitative survey of modern software transactional memory systems. Technical Report TR 839, University of Rochester Computer Science Dept (June 2004)
24. Bobba, J., Rajwar, R., Hill, M.: Transactional memory biblography, http://www.cs.wisc.edu/trans-memory/biblio/swtm.html
25. Korenfeld, B., Medina, M.: Transactional memory. Technical Report MIT/LCS/TM-475, University of Tel-Aviv Computer Engineering Dept. (June 2006)
26. Herlihy, M., Sun, Y.: Distributed transactional memory for metric-space networks. Distributed Computing 20(3), 195–208 (2007)

27. Manassiev, K., Mihailescu, M., Amza, C.: Exploiting distributed version concurrency in a transactional memory cluster. In: PPoPP 2006, March 2006, pp. 198–208. ACM Press, New York (2006)
28. Bocchino, R.L., Adve, V.S., Chamberlain, B.L.: Software transactional memory for large scale clusters. In: PPoPP 2008, pp. 247–258. ACM, New York (2008)
29. Manson, J., Baker, J., Cunei, A., Jagannathan, S., Prochazka, M., Xin, B., Vitek, J.: Preemptible atomic regions for real-time java. RTSS 0, 62–71 (2005)
30. Anderson, J., Ramamurthy, S.: A framework for implementing objects and scheduling tasks in lock-free real-time systems. In: Proceedings of IEEE RTSS, December 1996, pp. 92–105. IEEE, Los Alamitos (1996)
31. Anderson, J., Ramamurthy, S., Jeffay, K.: Real-time computing with lock-free shared objects. In: Proceedings of IEEE RTSS, December 1995, pp. 28–37. IEEE Computer Society Press, Los Alamitos (1995)
32. Holman, P., Anderson, J.H.: Supporting lock-free synchronization in pfair-scheduled real-time systems. J. Parallel Distrib. Comput. 66(1), 47–67 (2006)
33. Harris, T., Fraser, K.: Language support for lightweight transactions. In: Object-Oriented Programming, Systems, Languages, and Applications, October 2003, pp. 388–402 (2003)
34. Hoare, C.: Towards a theory of parallel programming. In: Hoare, C., Perrott, R. (eds.) Operating System Techniques, Academic Press, pp. 61–71. Academic Press, London (1972)
35. Stenström, P.: A survey of cache coherence schemes for multiprocessors. Computer 23(6), 12–24 (1990)
36. Chang, Y., Bhuyan, L.N.: An efficient tree cache coherence protocol for distributed shared memory multiprocessors. IEEE Transactions on Computers 48(3), 352–360 (1999)
37. Tamir, Y., Janakiraman, G.: Hierarchical coherency management for shared virtual memory multicomputers. Journal of Parallel and Distributed Computing 15(4), 408–419 (1992)
38. Aguilar, J., Leiss, E.L.: A general adaptive cache coherency-replacement scheme for distributed systems. In: Böhme, T., Unger, H. (eds.) IICS 2001. LNCS, vol. 2060, pp. 116–125. Springer, Heidelberg (2001)
39. Kent, C.A.: Cache coherence in distributed systems. WRL Technical Report 87/4 (1987)
40. Hildrum, K., Krauthgamer, R., Kubiatowicz, J.: Object location in realistic networks. In: SPAA 2004: Proceedings of the sixteenth annual ACM symposium on Parallelism in algorithms and architectures, pp. 25–35. ACM, New York (2004)
41. Plaxton, C.G., Rajaraman, R., Richa, A.W.: Accessing nearby copies of replicated objects in a distributed environment. In: SPAA 1997: Proceedings of the ninth annual ACM symposium on Parallel algorithms and architectures, pp. 311–320. ACM, New York (1997)
42. Rowstron, A.I.T., Druschel, P.: Pastry: Scalable, decentralized object location, and routing for large-scale peer-to-peer systems. In: Guerraoui, R. (ed.) Middleware 2001. LNCS, vol. 2218, pp. 329–350. Springer, Heidelberg (2001)
43. Jensen, D., Wells, D.: A framework for integrating the real-time specification for java and java's remote method invocation. In: ISORC 2002: Proceedings of the Fifth IEEE International Symposium on Object-Oriented Real-Time Distributed Computing, Washington, DC, USA, p. 13. IEEE Computer Society, Los Alamitos (2002)

Implementation of an Obfuscation Tool for C/C++ Source Code Protection on the XScale Architecture[*]

Seongje Cho[1], Hyeyoung Chang[1], and Yookun Cho[2]

[1] Dept. of Computer Science & Engineering, Dankook University, Gyeonggi-do, Korea
[2] School of Computer Science and Engineering, Seoul National University, Seoul, Korea
{sjcho,hychang}@dankook.ac.kr, cho@os.snu.ac.kr

Abstract. Obfuscation is one of the most effective methods to protect software against malicious reverse engineering intentionally making the code more complex and confusing. In this paper, we implement and evaluate an obfuscation tool, or *obfuscator* for protecting the intellectual property of C/C++ source code. That is, this paper presents an implementation of a code obfuscator, a tool which transforms a C/C++ source program into an equivalent one that is much harder to understand. We have used the ANTRL parser generator for parsing C/C++ programs, and applied some obfuscation algorithms. Performance analysis is conducted by executing two obfuscated programs on the XScale architecture to establish the relationship between the complexity and the performance of each program. When the obfuscated source code has been compared with the original source code, it has enough effectiveness in terms of potency and resilience though it incurs some run-time overhead.

Keywords: Obfuscation, Source Code Protection, Reverse Engineering.

1 Introduction

The major types of attack against software protection mechanisms can be classified as software piracy, malicious reverse engineering, and tampering. *Software piracy* is the illegal distribution and/or reproduction of software applications for business or personal use. Global PC software piracy alone accounted for nearly $40 billion annual loss [1] to the software industry in 2006. Many software developers therefore try to protect their programs against illegal copying. They also worry about their applications being *reverse engineered* [2,3,4,5]. Certain classes of automated reverse engineering tools can successfully attack compiled software to expose underlying code. In some cases, a valuable piece of code may be extracted from an application and incorporated into a competitor's code. Another related threat is *software tampering* [2,5,6]. Any illicit modification of program file or attack against program integrity should make the software unusable.

As the use of a client code like 'mobile agent' programs downloaded or installed on a host becomes more general, the client software is more frequently threatened by

---

[*] This work was supported by the Korea Research Foundation Grant funded by the Korean Government (MOEHRD, Basic Research Promotion Fund)(KRF-2008-314-D00340).

U. Brinkschulte, T. Givargis, and S. Russo (Eds.): SEUS 2008, LNCS 5287, pp. 406–416, 2008.

the host. This results from the power of the adversary model in digital rights management (DRM) systems, which is significantly more vulnerable than in the traditional security scenarios. The adversary can even gain complete control of the client node–supervisory privileges along with the full physical as well as architectural object observational capabilities. Unfortunately, the traditional security techniques to protect software from malicious client may not be applicable to protect a client code against a host attack [2, 3]. As a result, software protection has recently attracted tremendous commercial interest, from major software vendors to mobile DRM venders.

While it is generally believed that complete protection of software is an unattainable goal, recent results have shown that some degree of protection can be achieved. Software watermarking, obfuscation, and tamper-proofing have emerged as feasible methods for the intellectual property (IP) protection of software [2-11]. Watermarking, a defense against software piracy, is a process that makes it possible to determine the origin of software. Obfuscation, a defense against reverse engineering, is a process that renders software unintelligible but still functional. Tamper-proofing, a defense against tampering, is a process so that unauthorized modifications to software (for example, to remove a watermark) will result in nonfunctional code.

In this paper, we focus only on obfuscation techniques useful for protecting software from reverse engineering. The paper describes the implementation and evaluation of an obfuscation tool which converts a C/C++ source codes into an equivalent one that is much harder to understand. We implement some obfuscation algorithms on the XScale architecture and evaluate the performance and effectiveness of the obfuscation tool in terms of potency, resilience, and cost.

The rests of the section in this paper is organized as follows. Section 2 explains obfuscation, its related work, and the evaluation metrics of obfuscation. It is then followed by the description of the proposed method in section 3. Section 4 describes the implementation of obfuscation algorithms. We present the performance results of our implementation in section 5. Finally, section 6 concludes the paper.

2 Obfuscation

Software obfuscation can be defined as a semantics-preserving code transformation of a program in an attempt to make the code as complex and confusing as possible. Obfuscation protects the intellectual property (IP) of software from reverse-engineering attacks. The IP can be the software design, algorithms, or data contained in the software. Obfuscating transformations are primarily classified depending on the kind of information they target. Some simple transformations target the lexical structure (the layout) of the program while others target the data structures used by the program or its flow of control [2,4,7,8,11].

Layout obfuscations are aimed at making the code unreadable by introducing 'formatting change', 'remove comments', 'remove debug information', and 'scramble identifiers' methods. Most commercial obfuscators fall in this category. Crema, one of the oldest Java obfuscators, uses layout obfuscation. Data obfuscations are aimed at obscuring data and data structures used in the program. These data transformations can be classified into the following methods: 'split variables', 'array transformation including splitting and folding', and 'modifying inheritance including class split and class insertion'.

Control obfuscations are aimed at obfuscating the flow of execution by applying 'opaque construct', 'redundant code introducing opaque predicates and multiple obfuscated loops', 'inline removing procedural abstraction', and 'outline creating bogus procedural abstraction' algorithms [2,7,8]. Several control obfuscations rely on the existence of *opaque variables* and *opaque predicates*. A variable V is opaque if it has some property q which is known a priori to the obfuscator, however is difficult for de-obfuscator to deduce. Similarly, a predicate P (a Boolean expression) is opaque if its outcome is known at obfuscation time, but is difficult for the de-obfuscator to deduce. We write P^T (P^F) if P always evaluates to TRUE (FALSE), and $P^?$ if P may sometimes evaluates to TRUE and sometimes to FALSE.

In general, three criteria are considered in evaluating the quality of an obfuscation method; including potency, resilience, and cost [2-9]. The potency refers to what degree the transformed code is more obscure than the original. Software complexity metrics define various complexity measures for software, such as number of predicates it contains, depth of its inheritance tree, nesting levels, etc. While the goal of good software design is to minimize complexity based on these parameters, the goal of obfuscation is to maximize it.

The resilience of the software is a measure of how well the transformed code can resist attacks from either the programmer or an automatic de-obfuscator. It is a combination of the programmer effort to create a de-obfuscator and the time and space required by the de-obfuscator. The highest degree of resilience is a *one-way* transformation that cannot be undone by a de-obfuscator. An example is when the obfuscation removes information such as source code formatting. The difference between potency and resilience is that a transformation is potent if it can confuse a human reader, whereas it is resilient if a de-obfuscator tool cannot undo the transformation.

The cost of a transformation defines to how much computational overhead is added to the obfuscated program. Examples of the cost are the extra execution time and space penalty incurred by the obfuscation.

There are many software protection tools such as Cloakware, DashO, Dotfuscator, Kava (Konfused Java), JHide, and Semantic Designs' source code obfuscator [2,4,5,9,10,11]. Cloakware is capable of providing significant control and dataflow obfuscations of C source code. DashO and Dotfuscator can construct layout transformations including dead code removal and identifier renaming for Java and Microsoft Intermediate Language (MSIL), respectively. Semantic Designs' source code obfuscators provide a software developer with identifier renaming and optional whitespace removal for several high-level languages. A tool called Sandmark measures the effectiveness of software-based methods for protecting software against piracy, reverse engineering, and tampering [4]. MacBride et. al. [9] presented a qualitative measurement of the capability of two commercial obfuscators, DashO-Pro and KlassMaster. The measurement showed the two obfuscators both could cause variations in the performance of the algorithms used for testing.

3   The Structure of C/C++ Source Code Obfuscator

The approach we are going to consider is source code obfuscation to protect intellectual property embedded in C/C++ source programs. The source code obfuscator accepts a source file, and generates another functionally equivalent source file which

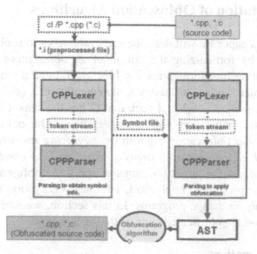

Fig. 1. Structure of high-level obfuscator

is much harder to understand or reverse-engineer. This is useful for technical protection of intellectual property in the following cases[1]. First, the source code must be delivered for public execution purposes. Second, commercial software components must be delivered in source form for direct integration by a customer into her end product (portable applications in C or PHP etc., code libraries or hardware components coded in Verilog or VHDL). Third, we have to send test cases derived from proprietary code to vendors. Fourth, an object code still contains many clues such as class public methods used only inside an application, as with java class files.

Figure 1 shows the overall structure of our source code obfuscator. We use a parser generator called ANTRL, *ANother Tool for Language Recognition* [12], to obfuscate the C/C++ source programs. The parser generated by the ANTRL takes C/C++ programs as input and analyzes a sequence of tokens to determine grammatical structure with respect to a given formal grammar. It captures the implied hierarchy of the input text and transforms it into abstract syntax tree (AST), or just syntax tree. The parser can use a separate lexical analyzer (*lexer*) to create tokens from the sequence of input characters. The AST is a finite, labeled, and directed tree, where each interior node represents a programming language construct and the children of that node represent meaningful components of the construct. It is used in the parser as an intermediate between a parse tree and a data structure. Based on the information contained in the AST, we implement the obfuscation algorithms by inserting, modifying, and restructuring a proper node after locating the node to apply the algorithms.

The obfuscation tool consists of two parts; one part shown in left side of Figure 1 obtains symbol information and the other part shown in right side constructs obfuscation algorithms utilizing the derived symbol information. The symbol information includes the attributes of identifiers such as the name, type, and size of all the variables. We can finally transform an original source program into an obfuscated source program by both using the symbol information and reconstructing the AST.

---

[1] http://www.semdesigns.com/Products/Obfuscators

4   The Implementation of Obfuscation Algorithms

In the remainder of this paper we will describe and evaluate various obfuscating transformations. We start by formalizing the notion of an *obfuscating transformation*. Given a set of obfuscating transformations $T = \{T_1, ..., T_n\}$ and a program C consisting of source code objects (classes, methods, statements, etc.) $\{S_1, ..., S_k\}$, find a new program $C' = \{ ..., S'_j = T_i(S_j), ... \}$ such that C' has the same observable behavior as C, i.e., the transformations are *semantics-preserving*. Our obfuscator have currently implemented some obfuscation algorithms: *modifying an original program's layout, splitting variables, restructuring arrays, extending loop conditions*, and *adding redundant operand*. As the target programs to apply the obfuscation algorithms, we have selected three programs, bubblesort, advanced encryption standard (AES), and Diffie-Hellman key exchange programs. In this section, we mainly consider the original source code and the obfuscated code of the AES program.

4.1   Layout Transformations

We first introduce layout obfuscation altering the formatting of the source file. This involves removing source code comments, and changing the names of elements such as the class, member variables, and the local variable. Source code comment removal and formatting removal are free transformations, since there is no increase in space and time from the original application. The potency is low because there is very little semantic content in formatting. It is a one-way transformation because the formatting, once removed, cannot be recovered. Scrambling of variable names is also a one-way and free transformation, but it has much higher potency than formatting removal.

4.2   Split Variable

Integer variables and other variables of restricted range can be split into two or more variables. Figure 2 shows an example where the splitting principle is applied to integer variables. Here, the elements of i are distributed over two short variables, _888 and _15871. The algorithm can sometimes substitute a target variable with a function which returns the same value as the variable. The potency, resilience, and cost of this method all increase with the number of variables into which the original variable is split.

4.3   Restructure Arrays: Array Folding

A number of transformations can be devised for obscuring operations performed on arrays: we are trying for a programmer to be able to split an array into several subarrays, merge two or more arrays into one array, fold an array (increasing the number of dimensions), or flatten an array (decreasing the number of dimensions). Figure 3 demonstrates how a one-dimensional array sbox can be folded into a two-dimensional array sbox. Array folding increases the data structure complexity of the potency metrics.

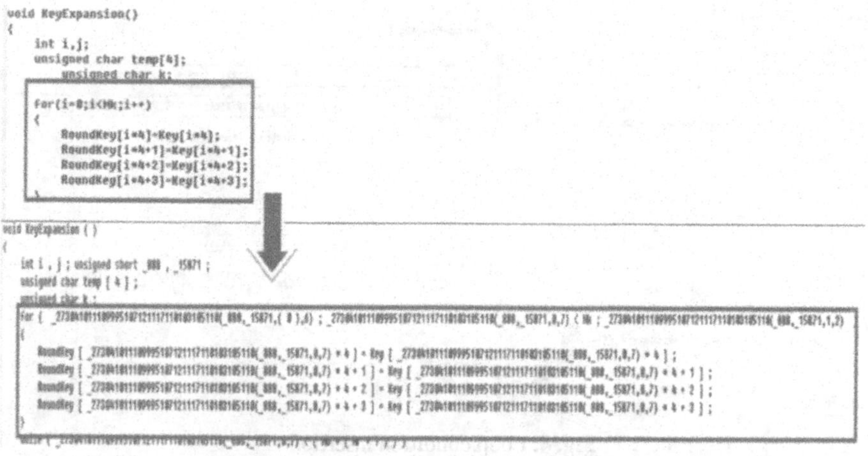

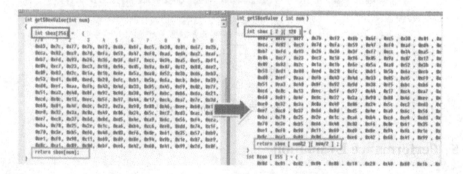

Fig. 2. A data transformation that splits variables

Fig. 3. Array restructuring: Array folding

4.4 Extend Loop Conditions

Figure 4 shows how we can obfuscate a loop by making the termination condition more complex. The basic idea is to extend the loop condition with a P^T or P^F predicate which will not affect the number of times the loop will execute. In Figure 4, our obfuscator has added to the termination condition of the loop the '&&' operator followed by the predicate P^T which will always evaluate to TRUE, and the '||' operator followed by the predicate P^F which will always evaluate to FALSE.

4.5 Add Redundant Operand

By constructing some opaque variables, we can use algebraic laws to add redundant operands to arithmetic expressions. This will increase the program length metric of the potency metrics. Obviously, this method works best with integer expressions where numerical accuracy is not an issue. In the obfuscated statement in Figure 5, we construct an *opaque sub-expression* (int) (856* 0.0001)*4 whose value is 4.

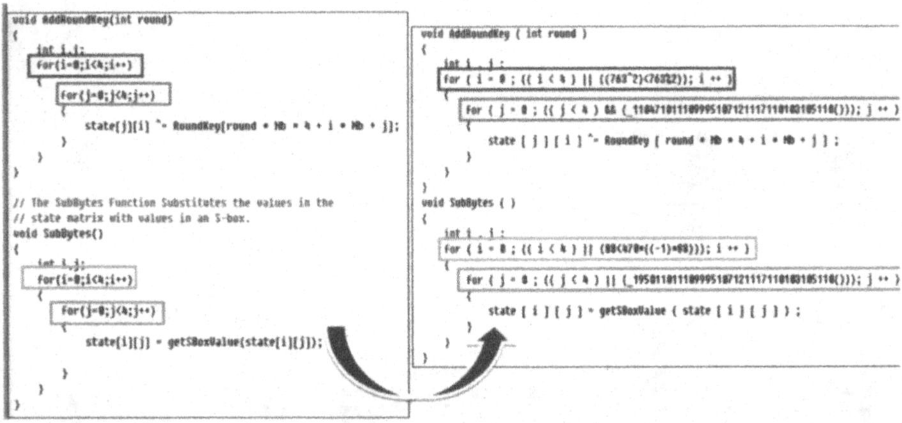

Fig. 4. Loop condition insertion

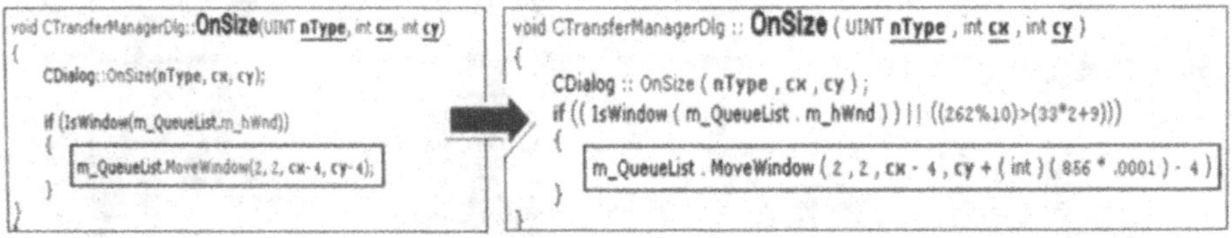

Fig. 5. Add redundant operand

5   Performance Evaluation

The transformation constructing the obfuscation algorithms may increase execution time, program complexity, and cost. We think there will always be a trade-off between the level of obfuscation and the performance overhead incurred. In this section, we have analyzed the quality of the obfuscation algorithms on an embedded board equipped with the Intel XScale PXA255 400MHz CPU, 128 megabyte SDRAM, and 32 megabyte Flash ROM. Embedded Linux kernel 2.4.19, g++ compiler, and the AES and Diffie-Hellman programs have been used for performing the experiments. The potency, resilience, and cost are considered in evaluating the quality of obfuscation methods: 'layout transformations', 'split variable', 'array folding', 'extend loop conditions', and 'add redundant operand'.

5.1   Measures of Potency

Even though there are many complexity metrics to evaluate the degree of the potency [8], we consider only some of the complexity measures listed in Table 1. The goal of an obfuscating method is to maximize these measures. The *potency* is measured by the summation of the series for the five complexity values in Table 1. An obfuscation method is a *potent obfuscating transformation* if the following equation, its *relative potency ratio* with respect to a program, is satisfied.

$$\{Potency(\text{obfuscated program}) / Potency(\text{original program})\} - 1 > 0 \qquad (1)$$

Table 1. Overview of some software complexity measures

Metric	Metric name and Its meaning
μ_1	**Program Length** Complexity of a program increases with the number of operators and operands in a program
μ_2	**Cyclomatic Complexity** Complexity of a function or method increases with the number of predicates in a function or method
μ_3	**Nesting Complexity** Complexity of a function or method increases with the nesting level of conditionals
μ_4	**Data Flow Complexity** Complexity of a function or method increases with the number of inter-basic block variable references
μ_5	**Fan-in/out Complexity** Complexity of a function or method increases with the number of formal parameters to the function or method, and with the number of global data structures read or updated by the function or method.

Table 2 shows the complexity values and relative potency ratio obtained by measuring the five metric values of the AES and Diffie-Hellman programs. In Table 2, we can see that the obfuscator has increased the relative potency ratio by 0.675 for the AES program and 0.848 for the Diffie-Hellman program, respectively when both data and control transformations were applied.

Table 2. Complexity and potency ratio of each code before and after applying obfuscation

	AES				Diffie-Hellman			
	Original	Data	Control	Data+Control	Original	Data	Control	Data+Control
μ_1	10356	15605	13264	17311	3299	5001	4519	6094
μ_2	17	23	38	32	22	30	31	41
μ_3	21	25	43	37	21	25	30	37
μ_4	29	50	64	71	18	34	35	50
μ_5	12	21	27	32	26	33	31	36
Potency ratio		0.507	0.288	0.675		0.513	0.372	0.848

5.2 Measures of Resilience

It is not easy to quantitatively measure resilience of the obfuscated codes. As shown in Figure 6, we measure it on a scale from trivial to one-way according to the criteria proposed by Collberg et. al. in [8]. One-way transformations are the highest resilience

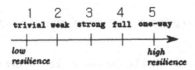

Fig. 6. Resilience of an obfuscating method

Table 3. Resilience of the implemented algorithms

Target	Transformation Algorithm	Resilience	Value
Layout	Remove Comments	One-way	5
Control flow	Extend Loop Condition	Weak ~ Strong	2~3
	Add Redundant Operands	Weak ~ Strong	2~3
Data	Split Variable	Weak	2
	Fold Array	Weak	2

in the sense that they can never be undone. Other transformations add unnecessary information to the program that do not change its functional behavior, however which make it difficult to construct an automatic tool to undo the transformations or executing such a tool will be extremely time-consuming. Table 3 shows the resilience of the obfuscated algorithms implemented in Section 4.

5.3 Measures of Cost

We measured the file size and execution time of the target programs before and after applying obfuscation methods. The experimental results are shown in Table 4. Each execution time of the AES encryption and Diffie-Hellman key distribution programs present the average time consumed to encrypt a plaintext file of 262144 bytes and to generate a secret key of 128 bits, respectively. We can see from the table that the obfuscator increases the file size and execution time of the obfuscated programs.

Table 4. File size (in *bytes*) and execution time (in *seconds*) before and after applying obfuscation

	AES				Diffie-Hellman			
	Original	Data	Control	Data+ Control	Original	Data	Control	Data+ Control
Source file size	9658	15605	13352	17332	3299	5001	4519	6094
Object file size	9180	13228	13200	15416	2904	3748	3896	4660
Execution time	6.610s	7.666s	6.677s	7.711s	0.176s	0.210s	0.225s	0.250s

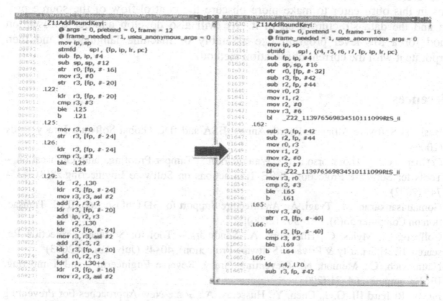

Fig. 7. Comparison of assembly codes before and after applying obfuscation

5.4 Comparison of Assembly Codes

Finally, we have compared the ARM assembly language of an original program with that of its obfuscated one to check if the transformation algorithms are effective in the machine-level code. Figure 7 shows the assembly codes corresponding to some part of the function *AddRoundKey()* in the AES program. The right side part of the figure shows the assembly code after applying two obfuscation algorithms, *'split variable'* and *'extend loop condition'*. The assembly code of the obfuscated function is quite different from that of the original one. As a result, our C/C++ obfuscator for the XScale architecture is effective even though it incurs some space and time overhead.

6 Conclusion and Future Work

This paper presents the implementation of an obfuscation tool, or *obfuscator* on the XScale architecture that protects C/C++ source code against malicious reverse engineering by making the code as complex and confusing as possible, but still functional. To render software unintelligible, the obfuscator uses layout transformations, data transformations including *'split variable'* and *'fold array'*, and control transformations such as *'extend loop conditions'* and *'add redundant operand'*. We have also evaluated the quality of obfuscation methods using three criteria: potency, resilience, and cost. Experimental results have shown that our obfuscator can enhance the potency and resilience of the obfuscated code, but incur some space penalty and the extra execution time.

The future work for this research is to continue to introduce other obfuscation algorithms in this obfuscator to make more obscure the control-flow of the source program and the data structure used in it. We will also develop another obfuscation method for a low-level program like assembly or machine languages, and then incorporate it with the current obfuscation method.

References

1. Business Software Alliance, Fourth Annual BSA and IDC Global Software Piracy Study (2006)
2. Collberg, C.S., Thomborson, C.: Watermarking, Tamper-Proofing, and Obfuscation – Tools for Software Protection. IEEE Transactions on Software Engineering 28(8), 735–746 (2002)
3. Gomathisankaran, M., Tyagi, A.: Architecture Support for 3D Obfuscation. IEEE Transaction on Computer 55(5), 497–507 (2006)
4. Collberg, C., Myles, G., Huntwork, A.: Sandmark – Tool for Software Protection Research. IEEE Security & Privacy (Software Protection), 40–49 (July/August 2003)
5. Naumovicb, G., Memon, N.: Preventing Piracy, Reverse Engineering, and Tampering. IEEE Computer, 64–71 (2003)
6. Fu, B., Richard III, G.G., Chen, Y., Husseiny, A.: Some New Approaches For Preventing Software Tampering. In: Proc. of the 44th ACM Southeast Regional Conference (ACM SE 2006), pp. 655–660 (2006)
7. van Oorschot, P.C.: Revisiting Software Protection. In: Boyd, C., Mao, W. (eds.) ISC 2003. LNCS, vol. 2851, pp. 1–13. Springer, Heidelberg (2003)
8. Collberg, C., Thomborson, C., Low, D.: A Taxonomy of Obfuscating Transformations. Technical report 148, Dept. of Computer Science, University of Auckland, New Zealand (1997)
9. MacBride, J., Mascioli, C., Marks, S., Tang, G., Head, L.M.: A Comparative Study of Java Obfuscators. In: IASTED International Conference on Software Engineering and Applications, Phoenix, Arizona, November 14 –16, 2005, pp. 82–86 (2005)
10. Ertaul, L., Venkatesh, S.: JHide – a tool kit for code obfuscation. In: Proc. of the 8th IASTED International Conference Software Engineering and Applications (2004)
11. Kruegel, C., Robertson, W., Valeur, F., Vigna, G.: Static Disassembly of Obfuscated Binaries. In: Proc. of the 13th USENIX Security Symposium, pp. 255–270 (2004)
12. ANTLR, http://www.antlr.org

Automated Maintainability of TTCN-3 Test Suites Based on Guideline Checking

George Din[1], Diana Vega[2], and Ina Schieferdecker[2]

[1] FOKUS Fraunhofer Institut, Kaiserin Augusta-Allee 31, Berlin, Germany
george.din@fokus.fraunhofer.de
[2] Technical University of Berlin, Franklinstr. 28-29
Berlin, Germany

Abstract. Similar to software development, the test development must be accompanied with a set of rules specifying how to write tests. They are grouped together into a document called guideline. Guidelines are especially necessary for large test specifications involving many developers and have the goal to reduce the effort of the overall development. So far, no universal guidelines for the TTCN-3 language [1] have been defined. Instead, each company or team defines and follows own development rules for test structuring and development. This paper deals with the problem of how to automate the validation whether a TTCN-3 test specification complies or not with an established guideline, i.e. guideline checking. The results of the validation process are a list of non-consistencies. A follow up step is the refactoring which automatically proposes and applies changes to improve the test suite compliance level, and thus its quality.

1 Introduction

In software engineering, guidelines may be defined for various aspects: models, programming, code documentation, users guides, developers guides, user interfaces, etc. They are useful for many reasons. First of all they help to establish a common understanding within the developing team. Next, they allow for easier development, changes or extensions. Any team member is able to understand the contributions of the rest of the team, and may even be able to extend parts contributed by other team members. Furthermore, new developers can integrate into the team by understanding much easier a complex system and being able to easily recognize its structure.

In this paper we consider the guidelines for test specifications written in the standardized Testing and Test Control Notation (TTCN-3) language [2]. We selected this language due to its popularity in the nowadays test developments. Its popularity grown over the last decade when many test suites have been specified in this language. Lots of resources have been invested by the industry and research groups in order to make out of TTCN-3 a general and standard testing framework. However, an important contribution to the spreading of TTCN-3 had the European Telecommunication Standardization Institute (ETSI)[3] which standardized various TTCN-3 test suites for telecommunication protocols.

Two obvious questions occur with respect to TTCN-3 based test specifications: on one hand, how well the tests are designed and, on the other hand, how to evaluate

U. Brinkschulte, T. Givargis, and S. Russo (Eds.): SEUS 2008, LNCS 5287, pp. 417–430, 2008.

that they are well written in a consistent manner. Both questions can be answered by analyzing guidelines for TTCN-3 test development.

In testing area, the guidelines have the same importance as for software engineering. More specific we look into the problem of how to *automate* the guideline checking of test specifications and how to recognize potential non-consistencies with the specified guideline. To achieve that, we analyze several existent guidelines used for TTCN-3 test specifications. Then, we define a method to specify guidelines in such form that they can be used by an automated tool for guideline checking.

From a test quality perspective, the use of guidelines is an essential requirement. According to the quality model for test specifications proposed in [4], the guidelines compliance contributes the the overall quality of the test with respect to the selected quality criteria. In that model, the quality is seen as a set of characteristics; each characteristic being composed of further sub-characteristics. Several of these sub-characteristics may be evaluated in relation with guidelines:

- *understandability*: documentation and description of the overall purpose of the test specification are key factors in understanding a test suite.
- *learnability*: to be able to extend or modify a test suite, the test developer must understand how it is structured. Proper documentation or style guides have positive influence on learnability.
- *analyzability*: concerns the degree to which deficiencies in a test specification can be localized. For example, test specifications should be well structured to allow code reviews.
- *changeability*: describes the capability of the test specification to enable necessary modifications to be implemented. E.g. badly structured code or a test architecture that is not expandable may have negative impact on this.

One important question is how to check whether a guideline is fulfilled or not. As long as the nowadays software systems are very large and complex, the guideline checking should be automated as much as possible. Moreover, the guideline checking should not only determine whether an entity (e.g. documentation, program) is compliant with the guideline but also deliver a list of inconsistencies with precise localization information where the issues appear.

The information delivered by the guideline checker should then be used to fix the non-consistencies. The inconsistencies are of different types as for instance: a) *naming convention related*, e.g. a function does not start with f_ , b) *logical*, e.g. a piece of functionality is placed in a wrong file, c) *structural*, e.g. a file is placed in a wrong package, etc. Also in this respect, we see the need for automation. This can be realized only on top of a taxonomy of types of inconsistencies which may appear. The automated approach should be such programmed that any type of inconsistency can be solved automatically or with very little human intervention.

The automation of guideline checking and inconsistencies solving should offer a tremendous help for rapid test specification improvement. An obvious result of automated approach is the better maintainability and reusability. This way the test specification can be specified in a consistent manner and changes can be easier propagated, etc. In addition, the same guideline can be used for different specifications belonging to the same application domain. Furthermore, the pieces of functionality (e.g. libraries) specified according to a guideline are easier to be reused for another test specification that follows the same guideline.

This paper is structured as follows. The next section gives a short introduction of the TTCN-3 language. Section 3 looks in more detail into the structure of a guideline while Section 4 presents our method to define guideline checking rules and presents a classification of the refactoring possibilities. The guidelines of the IPv6 testsuite[5], written in TTCN-3, are provided as example and discussed in Section 5. The paper finishes with the overview on related work and the conclusion sections.

2   A Short TTCN-3 Overview

The TTCN-3 language is a text-based language and has the form of a modern programming language, which is obviously ease to learn and to use. Specially designed for testing, it inherits the most important typical programming language artifacts, but additionally it includes important features required for test specification.

A TTCN-3 based test specification is called Abstract Test Specification (ATS) and it usually consists of many files grouped into folders and subfolders. Each file contains one or more **modules**. The **module** is the top level element of the TTCN-3 language which is used to structure the *test definitions* of:

- test data: **types** of messages, instances of types called **templates**,
- test configurations: **ports** and **components** to define the active entities of a test,
- test behaviours: **functions**, **altsteps**, **testcases** which implement the interactions between the **components** and the SUT and which make use of the test data,
- control: a global behavior to control the flow of **testcases** execution

Each afore mentioned definition type (except control which does not need an identifier)) has an identifier and can be placed in any module. TTCN-3 also offers the possibility of grouping elements into **groups**. The test developer is free to choose how to name the identifiers, how to group the definitions and in which modules to place them. However, the **group** element does not impose a new scope for the grouped elements, but only at the logical and visual level.

As long as the test specifications contain thousands of definitions, it is extremely important to be consistent in writing TTCN-3 test definitions and in maintaining a clear test suite structure and file structure. The language is similar to a programming language such as Java or C++, therefore lots of structuring possibilities, naming conventions etc. are allowed.

Currently, all ETSI test specifications are written in the TTCN-3 language [6]. Along the last decade, the ETSI test specifications adopted different guidelines for structuring, naming conventions etc. We are interested in this evolution in the testsuite design and try to derive a general view on guideline rules design.

We analyzed a number of test specifications (SIP[7], IPv6[5], M3UA[8]) standardized by ETSI in order to learn which guidelines have been used and check how consistent are they along the whole test specification. A classification of these rules is realized in Section 3 while in Section 4 we present a method of how to describe guideline rules such that an automated guideline checker is capable of checking the test specification consistency with respect to those rules.

3 Guideline Rules Classification

A comprehensive guideline should take into account various aspects. We propose a method to classify these aspects for TTCN-3 into three levels: *physical level*, *language level* and *architectural level*. Guideline rules are defined at each level and, consequently, they contribute with requirements to the global guideline. Fig. 1 illustrates these levels.

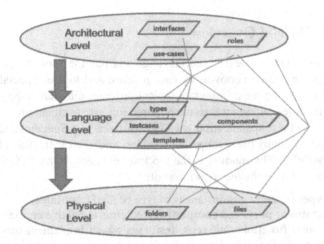

Fig. 1. Guideline Levels

The architectural level refers to information related to System Under Test (SUT) (interfaces, use-cases, roles etc.), the language level refers to the definition of test constructs in the TTCN-3 language (types, components, testcases, etc.), while the physical level deals with file system information such as files and folders. In this classification, the information from one level may propagate only to the levels below (top-done) and never to the above ones. We analyze these levels in greater detail.

3.1 Architectural Level

The architectural level includes guideline rules derived directly from the SUT architecture.

- *SUT interfaces*: the interaction between the Test System (TS) and SUT is realized over at least one interface. To increase the readability, a common guideline rule is to group together the definitions related to one interface.
- *roles*: the test behavior can be designed for different roles, e.g. client, server, proxy. The test definitions defined for one role should be grouped together.
- *use cases*: a test behavior corresponds to a type of interaction, i.e. use case, with the SUT. Multiple use cases can be treated within the same test specification. To avoid mixing the test behaviours from different use cases, a common practice is to group together the definitions related to a use case.

– *version*: a test specification may refer to multiple versions of the tested SUT' specification. A common practice is to avoid that test definitions for different SUT versions are mixed.

The information from the architectural level is used to structure the test specification and, consequently, imposes guideline rules to the two levels below. At the language level, the architectural information is used to group related test definitions into TTCN-3 modules and groups. Additionally, naming conventions can also be used in order to embed architectural information into the TTCN-3 identifiers.

We give as example an SUT which has two interfaces: Interface1 and Interface2. An architecture level guideline rule should say that the test definitions related to each interface should be placed in the same group. At the logical level we have several options to propagate the architectural rule. We may either define two TTCN-3 modules or two groups. In either case the definitions will be grouped together:
Interface1_Definitions_Module (or Group) and
Interface2_Definitions_Module (or Group). A further option is to use also naming conventions for the involved TTCN-3 types, templates or testcases such as tc_interface1_Test1, tc_interface1_Test2, where the prefix tc_ stands for testcase abbreviation. However, the three posibilities can be combined. For instance, the tc_interface1_Test1 can be added to a group of testcases for Interface1 Interface1_Testcases_Group which is defined in a module named Interface1_Definitions_Module as illustrated in Listing 1.1.

Listing 1.1. Test Structuring Example

```
1    module Interface1_Definitions_Module {
2        group Interface1_Testcases_Group {
3            testcase tc_interface1_Test1
4                runs on C system S {
5                    . . .
6            }
7            testcase tc_interface1_Test2
8                runs on C system S {
9                    . . .
10            }
11        }
12    }
```

At the physical level, the architectural information is used to store the test definitions into files and folders. Also in this case, naming convention rules can be used to name the files and folders. Following the example provided above, we can store all definitions related to each interface into separate folders such as: types/interface1/File1.ttcn3, components/interface1/File2.ttcn3, etc. When more than one architectural guideline rules apply, they can be combined in an arbitrary order.

3.2 Language Level

The language level contains guideline rules for writing the TTCN-3 code. They can be classified into:

- *formatting rules* related to indentation, braces, white spaces, blank lines, new lines, control statements, line wrapping and comments
- *naming conventions* related to the names of the identifiers of the TTCN-3 constructs (types, templates, testcase, components, etc.)
- *structural rules* related to grouping the test definitions into groups and modules.

The naming conventions concern prefixing (and sometimes postfixing) rules and apply to all TTCN-3 elements which require an identifier: types, templates, functions, altsteps, testcases, groups, modules, variables, etc. For easier localization, the TTCN-3 identifiers can be prefixed with a string indicating a group of definitions of the same category. For example, the message types can be prefixed by strings such as `Type`, `type`, `type_`, `T_` etc. Multiple prefixes can occur. For example, type definitions can be grouped into types of messages to be sent to SUT, e.g. `Send_Msg`, and types of messages to be received, e.g. `Received_Msg`. If multiple prefixes are used, they can simply be concatenated or separated by the "_" character.

The structural rules concern the grouping of the definitions into groups and modules. This can be realized in many ways:

- *grouping by categories*: the definitions of the same category can be grouped together (e.g., types in a group of types, templates in a group of templates).
- *grouping by libraries*: the reusable definitions which are at the same time also general enough to apply to different test suites should be grouped into libraries.

3.3 Physical Level

The physical level offers further structuring possibilities of TTCN-3 definitions:

- files: store particular groups of definitions in separate files
- folders: files can be further grouped into folders and subfolders.

Also at the physical level the naming conventions should appear. They are usually propagated from the upper levels and impose prefixes for the names (or even impose the name itself) of files or folders. For example, a file located as `/types/interface1/usecase1/sending.ttcn3` combines information from the architectural level i.e. `interface1` and `usecase1` with information from the language level i.e. `types` and `sending`. This file name means that it contains all types of messages to be sent to SUT defined for `usecase1` and for `interface1`.

4 Test Analyzability and Refactoring

To ensure that a guideline is followed consistently along the whole test specification, a *guideline checker* is needed. *Test analyzability* is the characteristic of a test to be validated against a guideline and it includes the mechanisms to define and check guideline rules. *Refactoring* is the mechanism which enables to fix inconsistencies detected during the analyzability phase.

4.1   Guideline Checker Types

Guideline checking implies that all guideline rules are verified on top of a test specification. Our realization approach is illustrated in Fig. 2. The guideline rules are all managed by a common repository and are loaded by the guideline checker. Another input of the checker is the test specification itself. The guideline checker consists of rule checkers which are of different types. Moreover, each checker type can be instantiated for an arbitrary number of times (one instance per guideline rule). The checker reports for each rule how many identifiers matched that rule and how many of them did comply with it.

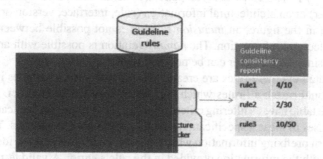

Fig. 2. Guideline Rules Checkers

We identify two types of checkers: *naming conventions checkers* and *structural checkers*. A guideline rule is instantiated in one of these checker types and it is applied to all identifiers of a test specification. The naming convention checkers evaluate the name of the identifier and determines if it is composed correctly. The structural checkers verify whether the test definition whose identifier is evaluated is placed in the correct structure (group, subgroup, module, file and folders).

4.2   Checking Rules Specification

A guideline rule consists of three parts: a *filtering criterion* which indicates which identifiers should follow the rule, a *relation* and an *entity*. The relation and the entity define *what* the test definition selected by the filtering criterion *should comply with*.

Table 1. Rules examples

Rule1	*(testcase)(naming:prefix)(tc_)*
Rule2	*(testcase)(inclusion:module)("Testcases")*
Rule3	*(testcase)(naming:prefix)(arch_info:interface)*
Rule4	*(testcase)(inclusion:group)(arch_info:use-case)*

Fig. 3 depicts the structure of a rule. There are two types of relations: *naming relations*, which define how the identifiers should be created, and *inclusion relations*, which describe where to place a test definition into a structural element (group, module or file).

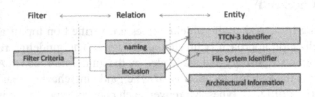

Fig. 3. Rule Specification

The *entity* can be a TTCN-3 identifier of a structural construct (group or module), a non-structural TTCN-3 construct (component, testcase, etc.), a file system identifier (of a file or folder) or an architectural information (role, interface, version or use case).

As shown in the figure, an *inclusion* relation is not possible between an identifier and an architectural information. The *naming* relation is possible with an architectural information since an identifier can be prefixed with such information.

To illustrate how these rules are created we provide a few examples in Table 1. An identifier should match all rules which apply to it in a top-down order. All four rules defined in the table have as filtering criterion the TTCN-3 construct "testcase" and means that all testcases in the test specification should comply with these rules. The Rule1 and Rule3 concern prefixing information which means that a valid testcase identifier should be prefixed with the information provided in the rule's *entity*. A valid testcase identifier is `tc_Interface1_test1` since it is prefixed first with `tc_` according to Rule1 and with `interface1` according with Rule3. The `tc_test2` is not correct since it does not comply with the Rule3. The second rule says that all testcases should be defined within the module with the name "Testcases" given as a string. The forth rule requires that the testcases are grouped into groups which have names derived from use-cases names.

4.3 Refactoring

Refactoring has been discussed in detail in [9]. For testing, refactoring is defined similar to software engineering refactoring, as the manual or automated improvement of the structure of a test specification. There are many types of refactorings we can encounter in a test specification. We highlight here the most used ones:

- *formatting*: implies indentation and changes of the locations of test definitions in a file in terms of lines and columns.
- *renaming of identifiers*:gives the possibility to rename an identifier (TTCN-3 language element, file name, etc). Some parts of the identifier (e.g. if the identifier should be prefixed by the module name but it is not) can be changed in an automated way. The refactoring task should also change all references to that identifier in the associated visibility scope. This type of refactoring is used for situations when an identifier does not follow a naming convention rule, as for instance: a component type should be prefixed by `CT_` or should start with capital letter but it does not.
- *moving a definition into another group*: we distinguish between moving an identifier into a group in the same module or into a different module or file. The latest two cases fit into the next refactoring schemas since they affect the module

importing and file inclusion settings. If an identifier is moved to a group within the same module, the refactoring mechanism has to take care whether the identifier name should be prefixed by the group name. This type of refactoring is needed to handle inconsistencies such as, for instance, a component type definition is not placed in the group which should contain component definitions.

- *moving a definition into another module*: in this case, the moved test definition has to be imported in the modules where it is referred by using the **import** construct. Also in this case, the refactoring has to be consistent with the naming conventions regarding identifier prefixing.
- *moving a definition into another file*: has the same constraints as the case of moving an identifier to another module (moving a test definition to another file implies moving to another module as well) but also impacts the file inclusion settings for the whole project with respect to compilation.

Sometimes, for a given non-consistency, more than one refactoring possibilities may apply. In these situations the manual intervention is required.

Many refactoring rules can be derived from software engineering [9] and applied to TTCN-3 as presented in [10]. However, our aim was not to identify all of them but rather to develop a method to classify the guideline rules on various levels (architectural, language and physical) and understand how they propagate from one level to another. The refactoring schemes are only example of how non-consistencies can be handled in an automated manner.

5   An Example - The IPv6 Test Suite

We selected for our analysis the standardized TTCN-3 test suite IPv6 [5] published and free to download from ETSI web site [3]. Test specifications for IPv6 protocols are foreseen to cover both conformance testing and interoperability testing for IPv6 core protocols (such as IPv6 specification, neighbor discovery and stateless address auto-configuration) and extended protocols (such as security, mobility, and transition).

5.1   Test Specification Analysis

Architectural and Physical Level Guidelines Analysis. Fig. 4 shows a view of how the ATS has been structured at the physical level. Three important guideline rules have been applied at this level:

- *folder structuring guideline*: First, the TTCN-3 files which belong to a common logical functionality are grouped together. This structure combines an architectural level rule with the physical level and it is reflected in the existence of two types of folders: a) with common functionality, i.e. library folders such as libCommon, Libcore, etc. and b) with specialized functionality, e.g. AtsCommon, AtsCore.
- *folder/file/module naming convention guideline*: Two guideline rules have been applied in top-down order. The first rule regards the association between a file and a folder. It is reflected by the naming convention which requires that the file name has to start with the name of the folder that contains that module,

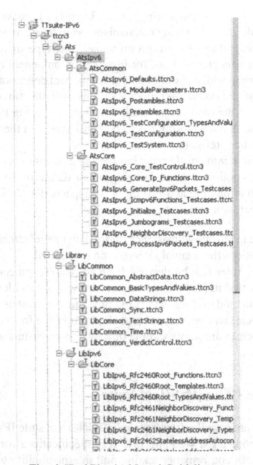

Fig. 4. IPv6 Physical Level Guidelines

e.g. `LibCommon_AbstractData.ttcn3` is placed in the folder `LibCommon`. The second rule specifies that the file name has to encapsulate the description of the predominant type of TTCN-3 elements enclosed in the analyzed module.

- *structuring based on architecture information*: The testcases have been grouped in files caring the names of the use cases such as initialization, neighbor discovery: `AtsIpv6_Initialize_Testcases`, `AtsIpv6_NeighborDiscovery_Testcases`, etc.

With respect to guideline checking, the validation of the first guideline is difficult to automate since it is not possible to decide which functionality should belong to a library. However, the second and the third guidelines can be checked in an automated manner since they only verify the established naming or inclusion convention.

Language Level Guideline Compliance. There are many naming conventions used in this specification. We provide, as example, the naming convention for the behavioral names. These are based on the rule:

```
<protocol>_<main functionality>_<role>
_<functionality>_<type>_<nnn>
```

The <protocol> is the IPv6 specification (IP6). <main functionality> separates definitions by protocol header type into Header (HDR) and Extension header (EHR). The roles are also used for classification. <role> is one of following: Host (HST), Router (RTR), Node (NOD), Source Host (SOH) and Destination Host (DEH). The <functionality> is used to classify test definitions by use case into General (GEN), hop-by-hop options header (HBH), destination options header (DSH), routing header (ROH), fragmentation header (FRH) and IPsec headers (SEC). <type> further classifies test definitions into Valid Behavior, Invalid Behavior, Inopportune Behavior and Timers (TI). The <nnn> is a simple sequential number between (001 999) to distinguish different tests of the same category.

Many naming conventions rules regarding other TTCN-3 constructs are presented in Fig. 5 together with their statistics.

5.2 Implementation

For the automation process of guideline checking we provide an implementation based on the TTworkbench [11] tool, an Eclipse-based IDE that offers an environment for specifying and executing TTCN-3 tests. The main reason for selecting this tool, is that it provides a metamodel for the TTCN-3 language which is technically realized on top of Eclipse EMF [12]. EMF is a Java framework and code generation facility which helps turning models rapidly into efficient, correct, and easily customizable Java code.

Language Element	Naming Convention	Prefix	Example	Statistics
Module	Use upper-case initial letter	none	IPv6Templates	0 / 47
Group within a module	Use lower-case initial letter	none	messageGroup	262 / 343
Data type	Use upper-case initial letter	none	SetupContents	0 / 264
Message template	Use lower-case initial letter	m_	m_setupInit	0 / 0
Message template with ...	Use lower-case initial letter	mw_	mw_anyUserReply	0 / 39
Signature template	Use lower-case initial letter	s_	s_callSignature	0 / 0
Port instance	Use lower-case initial letter	none	signallingPort	0 / 18
Test component instance	Use lower-case initial letter	none	userTerminal	0 / 0
Constant	Use lower-case initial letter	c_	c_maxRetransmission	0 / 362
External constant	Use lower-case initial letter	cx_	cx_macId	0 / 0
Function	Use lower-case initial letter	f_	f_authentication()	0 / 562
External Function	Use lower-case initial letter	fx_	fx_calculateLength()	0 / 4
Altstep	Use lower-case initial letter	a_	a_receiveSetup()	0 / 6
Test case	Use ETSI numbering	TC_	TC_COR_0009_47_ND	0 / 268
Variable (local)	Use lower-case initial letter	v_	v_macId	5 / 78
Variable (defined within...	Use lower-case initial letter	vc_	vc_systemName	3 / 4
Timer (local)	Use lower-case initial letter	t_	t_wait	0 / 0
Timer (defined within a ...	Use lower-case initial letter	tc_	tc_authMin	0 / 15
Module parameters	Use all upper case letters	none	PX_MAC_ID	0 / 99
Formal parameters	Use lower-case initial letter	p_	p_macId	0 / 97
Enumerated Values	Use lower-case initial letter	e_	e_syncOk	0 / 12

Fig. 5. Guidelines Rules Compliance View

Our work on the automated guideline checker follows up an earlier work [13] where TTCN-3 test quality indicators are derived from a static analysis of a TTCN-3 test suite, i.e. only the test sources are need. This is different from a dynamic analysis where the investigations regard the test execution as well. The implementation is designed as a plug-in whose invocation triggers the following actions:

- access the EMF metamodel instance of the TTCN-3 test specification
- traverse and correlate the elements of interest
- validate the guidelines and store the results
- refactor the whole test specification according to guideline rules.

We implemented and applied the set of ETSI TTCN-3 naming conventions [14] on the Ipv6 test specification. An intuitive guideline compliance statistic is always welcome by test developers and has the advantage of a rapid identification of the issues in the test specification. Therefore, we choose the tabular presentation format encapsulated in a new Eclipse View. Fig. 5 presents the applied naming convention and what level of compliance has been achieved, i.e. in a statistical manner:

$$ComplianceLevel = \frac{No\ of\ non\ respectig\ elements}{No\ of\ elements}$$

Each line in the table corresponds to a rule and consists of a) the expression-pattern that the name has to follow, b) an example, and c) the obtained statistic. The list of non-consistencies can be visualized in a separate window presenting the identifiers of non-conforming entities. Each identifier can be replaced with a new one; the refactoring process behind will refactor the new name along the whole test suite.

Looking into the results, we notice that the ETSI IPv6 test suite respects integrally the naming conventions except the ones related to the *group* and variable names. As the Fig. 5 indicates, 262 out of 343 groups do not respect the convention of lower-case initial letter.

With respect to refactoring, the user has then the possibility to select one of the rules which are not entirely fulfilled, e.g., the rule selected in Fig.5 is not satisfied by 5 identifiers out of 78. Next, the GUI provides the list of inconsistencies for that rule. For each inconsistency the user is asked to introduce a new identifier. By applying the new modifications, the old identifier is replaced with the new introduced one within the whole test suite.

6   Related Work

The guidelines are designed to help the developer in writing better code. They are available for almost any programming language and have impact on different levels such as: coding level, for instance for C++ in [15], design level, for instance for Java in [16], formatting level, comments level, etc.

On the testing side, the existing work focuses more on the guidelines regarding the effectivity of various types of tests: unit tests, integration tests, system tests etc. The work in [17] highlights a set of 27 guideline rules for writing jUnit tests.

With respect to TTCN-3, reusability has been explored in [18]. This work concentrate in great detail on guidelines for writing reusable TTCN-3 code. Maintainability aspects, and in particular refactoring, have been concerned in [19] where catalog of 20 refactoring rules derived from Java [9] have been proposed and implemented. Refactoring is seen as a technique to systematically restructure code to improve its quality and maintainability while preserving the semantics.

7 Conclusion

In this paper we introduced, analyzed and classified TTCN-3 test specification guidelines. In order to investigate and identify the compliance to guidelines, a reverse engineering mechanism is needed. The automation of this process is essential as long as the nowadays test specifications consists of thousands of test definitions.

The introduced concepts ensure a structured and rule oriented thinking of guidelines. The novelty of this approach relies on identifying the levels of guideline rules for TTCN-3 test specifications. Additionally, we take into account the rule propagation from one level to another.

We foresee several possible extensions. The guideline rules can be extended to further rules such as: ontology based naming conventions, code documentation, etc. Another idea to be explored in future work is the combination of guideline rules obtained from the architectural information with test definition generation. This will make possible the systematic generation of test specification skeletons from a minimal information about the SUT (interfaces, use cases, roles, versions).

References

1. ETSI: Etsi standard es 201 873-1 v3.1.1 (2005-06): The testing and test control notation version 3; part 1: Ttcn-3 core language. European Telecommunications Standards Institute (ETSI), Sophia-Antipolis, France (2005)
2. Willcock, C., Dei, T., Tobies, S., Keil, S., Engler, F., Schulz, S.: An Introduction to TTCN-3. John Wiley & Sons, Ltd, Nokia Research Center, Nokia, Germany, Nokia, Finland (April 2005)
3. ETSI: European Telecommunication Standards Institute - ETSI
4. Zeiß, B., Vega, D., Schieferdecker, I., Neukirchen, H., Grabowski, J.: Applying the ISO 9126 Quality Model to Test Specifications Exemplified for TTCN-3 Test Specifications. In: Software Engineering 2007 (SE 2007), March 2007. Lecture Notes in Informatics (LNI), Copyright Gesellschaft für Informatik, Köllen Verlag, Bonn (2007)
5. European Telecommunication Institute - ETSI: Internet Protocol version 6 (IPv6) Conformance Test Specification (2006)
6. Wiles, A.: ETSI testing activities and the use of TTCN-3 (2001)
7. European Telecommunication Institute - ETSI: Session Initiation Protocol (SIP) Conformance Test Specification (2006)
8. European Telecommunication Institute - ETSI: MTP Level 3 User Adaptation Layer (2002)
9. Fowler, M.: Refactoring: Improving the Design of Existing Code. Addison-Wesley, Boston (1999)
10. Zeiß, B.: A Refactoring Tool for TTCN-3. Master's thesis, Masterarbeit im Studiengang Angewandte Informatik am Institut für Informatik, ZFI-BM-2006-05, ISSN 1612-6793 (Tippfehlerbereinigte Version), Zentrum für Informatik, Georg-August-Universität Göttingen (March 2006)

11. TestingTechnologies: TTworkbench: an Eclipse based TTCN-3 IDE,
    http://www.testingtech.de/products/ttwb_intro.php
12. Eclipse: Eclipse Modeling Framework (EMF) (2008)
13. Vega, D.E., Schieferdecker, I.: Towards quality of TTCN-3 tests. In: Gotzhein, R., Reed, R. (eds.) SAM 2006. LNCS, vol. 4320. Springer, Heidelberg (2006)
14. ETSI: ETSI Naming Conventions (2007)
15. Stroustrup, B.: The C++ Programming Language. Addison-Wesley, Reading (1986)
16. Sun Microsystems, I., Javasoft: Java Look & Feel Design Guidelines. Addison-Wesley Longman Publishing Co., Inc., Boston (1999)
17. Services, G.S.: Unit testing guidelines (2007)
18. Mäki-Asiala, P.: Reuse of ttcn-3 code. Master's thesis, VTT Electronics Helsinki (2005)
19. Zeiß, B., Neukirchen, H., Grabowski, J., Evans, D., Baker, P.: Refactoring and Metrics for TTCN-3 Test Suites. In: Gotzhein, R., Reed, R. (eds.) SAM 2006. LNCS, vol. 4320, pp. 148–165. Springer, Heidelberg (2006)

Author Index